The Post-Automation Era

Toward a World That Works for Everyone

The Post-Automation Era

Toward a World That Works for Everyone

Michael Silverton

ʻAʻohe Mea Paʻi Palapala, 2024.

Printed in the United States of America
First Printing, 2024

Library of Congress Control Number: 2023912409

ISBN 978-1-7329300-3-2 (Paperback Edition)
ISBN 978-1-7329300-4-9 (Kindle Edition)

ʻAʻohe Mea Paʻi Palapala
Albuquerque, New Mexico 87110

Dedication

For us. And them. Wounded warriors, domestic and foreign, the erased, cancelled, abused, neglected, marginalized, ostracized, discarded, disappeared, troubled, infirm, forgotten, and invisible. May we all attain peace, safety, security, and comfort this day.

"Poverty is the worst form of violence."
– Mahatma Gandhi, Indian Independence Leader

"There is no greater injustice than poverty."
– Nelson Mandela, South African President

"If you want to know what a man is really like,
take notice of how he acts when he loses money."
– Simone Weil, Philosopher

"The poor are not just people who lack money.
They are people who lack power."
– Muhammad Yunus, Nobel Peace Prize Laureate

"We must not allow poverty to become a destiny."
– Ellen Johnson Sirleaf, President of Liberia

"Every human being has a right to live with dignity."
– Pope Francis, Jorge Mario Bergoglio

"Poverty is not a lack of character; it's a lack of cash."
– Rutger Bregman, Historian

"The only thing that's inevitable about poverty is that
it will remain inevitable if we do nothing about it."
– Muhammad Ali, The Greatest

"If a human does $50,000 worth of work, that income is taxed.
You'd think we'd tax the robot at a similar level."
– Bill Gates, Philanthropist

"Poverty is not a character flaw. It's a condition of circumstance."
– Marian Wright Edelman, Humanitarian

"The worth of a civilization is the worth of the individuals composing it."
– Albert Einstein, Physicist

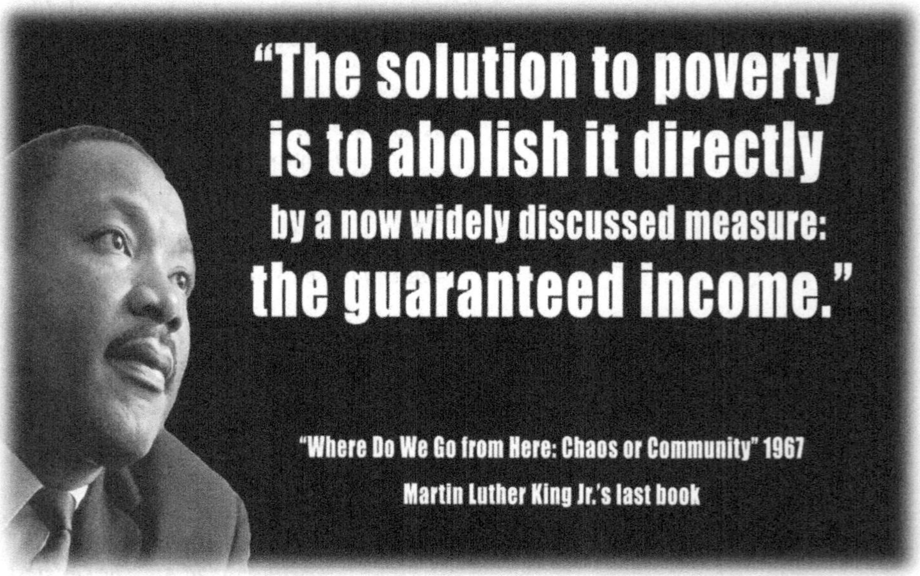
"The solution to poverty
is to abolish it directly
by a now widely discussed measure:
the guaranteed income."
"Where Do We Go from Here: Chaos or Community" 1967
Martin Luther King Jr.'s last book

Epigraph

"… it's a nice thing to say to people that you oughta lift yourself by your own bootstraps, but it is a cruel jest to say to a bootless man that he oughta lift himself by his own bootstraps." And the fact is that millions of Negroes, because of centuries of denial and neglect, have been left bootless. They find themselves impoverished aliens in this affluent society. And there is a great deal that society can and must do if the Negro is to gain the economic security that he needs.

Now one of the answers, it seems to me, is a guaranteed annual income, a guaranteed minimum income for all people, and for our families of our country. *It seems to me that the Civil Rights movement must now begin to organize for the guaranteed annual income.* Begin to organize people all over our country and mobilize forces so that we can bring to the attention of our nation this need, and this is something which I believe will go a long, long way toward dealing with the Negro's economic problem and the economic problem which many other poor people confront in our nation."

Martin Luther King Jr., "The Other America."
Stanford University. March 14, 1967.

Table of Contents

Table of Figures

Foreword

This is a minimally AI-assisted work with clearly identified examples of generated and curated text for the purposes of illustrating or expanding upon principles in the primary, all-original text, bearing directly upon the subject of AI in society, composed in the years just prior to 2023's AI Big Bang. There is one DALL-E generated image. See Table of Figures. I have erred on the side of over-disclosure in publishing this as AI-generated with Kindle Direct Publishing, expecting definitions to evolve with time.

> *AI-assisted: If you created the content yourself, and used AI-based tools to edit, refine, error-check, or otherwise improve that content (whether text or images), then it is considered "AI-assisted" and not "AI-generated." Similarly, if you used an AI-based tool to brainstorm and generate ideas, but ultimately created the text or images yourself, this is also considered "AI-assisted" and not "AI-generated." It is not necessary to inform us of the use of such tools or processes.*[i]

Considering our title, I was curious what ChatGPT thought I meant in the name of this book. I wouldn't call it an outright hallucination, but, like patients sadly and gradually descending-into-dementia, such are often incredibly effective fabricators.

I share my strikeouts and italicized edits below as an example of how *AI-generation* looks in the creation of both non-fiction and fiction works, versus *AI-assistance*. See the Glossary for precise definitions. I characterize the following as an example of AI-generated content, although the remainder of this book is AI-assisted. My hope is that clearly identified examples can help us all to be the best possible versions of our creative selves, working hand-in-hand with our new AI co-workers.

Surprised that these tools emerged just as I was finishing years of work on this book, I jumped at the chance to offer readers a sample of ChatGPT-4 generated content, in response to my first question, lightly edited as a working editorial example.

Me: "What is the Post-Automation Era?"

ChatGPT-4 (August 2023 build): The Post-Automation Era is ~~a hypothetical future~~ *the current 21st century* period in which the widespread adoption of advanced automation, artificial intelligence (AI), and other emerging technologies has led to a significant transformation of society, the economy, and the job market. ~~Although there is no fixed definition or time frame for this era, it~~ *Today, the Post-Automation Era* ~~typically~~ encompasses several key themes:

Job displacement and transformation: As automation and AI become more capable, many traditional jobs may be eliminated or fundamentally changed. This could lead to a shift in the nature of work, with people increasingly focusing on roles that require creativity, problem-solving, and emotional intelligence, rather than routine tasks.

Universal basic income (UBI) and social safety nets: As job displacement becomes more widespread, governments may need to implement social safety nets such as universal basic income to ensure economic security for their citizens.

Education and skill development: The Post-Automation Era may require a greater emphasis on education and lifelong learning, as individuals need to adapt to new job opportunities and evolving industries.

Economic inequality: As automation and AI concentrate wealth among those who own and control the technology, economic inequality could increase, leading to calls for wealth redistribution and greater investment in public services.

Leisure and quality of life: With increased automation potentially reducing the need for human labor, society could shift toward valuing leisure and quality of life more highly, focusing on personal fulfillment and well-being.

Ethical considerations: The Post-Automation Era may raise ethical concerns about the role of AI in decision-making, surveillance, and the potential for biases in automated systems.

"It's important to note that the concept of the Post-Automation Era is speculative, and its precise characteristics and impacts remain uncertain. Different experts have varying opinions on how these trends might play out, and the timeline for their emergence is also open to debate."

That's the end of the ChatGPT-4 example.

> *GPT stands for "Generative Pre-trained Transformer." It is a type of artificial intelligence model developed by OpenAI, which uses advanced natural language processing techniques to understand and generate human-like text. The "transformer" architecture in GPT refers to a specific type of deep learning model that has shown excellent performance in tasks related to language understanding and generation.*
>
> *The "pre-trained" aspect of GPT indicates that the model has undergone an initial training phase on a large dataset of text from the internet before being fine-tuned for specific tasks. This pre-training allows GPT to learn general language patterns, grammar, and even some factual knowledge, which helps it generate coherent and contextually relevant responses when given prompts.*

As a human being, I have to take issue, maybe even a touch of human umbrage on behalf of my species at the dismissive assessment that, "the concept of the Post-Automation Era is speculative." No it isn't. That's the entire premise of this book. The author is not speculating about some abstract future, they're reviewing the past and identifying the present moment, in context. Much of the narrative in this book highlights specific examples of deprecated, vestigial, and obsolete 20th century ideation. Defunct default consensus narratives of a long-bygone default consensus reality.[ii]

A useful question is, "is this an example of a kind of dismissive and pessimistic AI feedback that our children are getting on their own creative ideas, their own direct observations, and interpretations of their own lived experience?" It may take another entire volume to explore the psychological and psychic defensive systems that human beings need to develop, and develop fast, in the 100% non-speculative, 100% present tense Post-Automation Era, domo arigato, Mr. Roboto.[iii]

University of New Mexico, August 2023
Albuquerque, New Mexico, March 2024

Preface

I have learned that, for me, writing is a form of ego death. Once I realized that I was writing for myself more than anything else, open-journaling in order to understand my own interpretation of experiences over the course of a brief sixty-year lifetime, with some remote – although certainly uncertain – potential for an incomprehensibly diverse audience of supporters and detractors spanning the entire spectrum of human experience, the work of the third total re-write of this book began.

Given the hopelessly subjective arduousness of the task, at the moment I am finding it highly improbably that anyone else would bother to attempt to decipher such a hopelessly subjective and circumstantial written record and testimony. While I have done my best to tell myself the truth, the whole truth, and nothing but the truth, to the best of my knowledge, awareness, and ability – while painfully cognizant of my own utter frailty in this fleeting human conditions, particularly aware of the astronomically intricate, delicate, and vulnerable affordances of human cognition – the question remains, why would or should anyone else care to read a single word?

While doing this work led to a whole new level of personal subjective clarity, which is the only lens to which I have access in gazing upon the material realm, the exceedingly constrained capacities and confined range of this human organism's physical senses make an intellectually honest *objective* interpretation of this world virtually and literally impossible. Though blessed with all six basic senses, I only have access to one of more than 8 billion sets of those senses currently in circulation.

Perhaps some theoretical reader possesses some kind of magically transcendent third-party perspective from which they are able to perceive the entire nature of Earthly reality accurately and completely. Objectively. However, when I am honest with myself, that brand of objectivity, which seemed to me quite broadly and recklessly bandied about for most of the 20th century, seems more like gaslighting.

From my subjective perspective, no human being has access to, nor can access, such an "objective" view of human experience; certainly not in any sense that is intrinsically superior to anyone else's subjective view. Scoffing, guffawing, mocking, dismissing, devaluing, and demoting others with phrases such as, "that is *only* your subjective opinion," or "that's *just* semantics," or "you need to learn to become more objective, *like me*" in the name of our own supercilious worldview, may be one of the brightest red flags for narcissism available. Of course, that statement right there is like, just my opinion, too, right? Right. Admitting our own equal cluelessness seems like the most intellectually honest common ground from which to engage in any meaningful dialog.

It seems to me that the scientific method is an ingenious and powerfully effective hack to partly get around the hopelessly subjective nature of all human experience; however, the scientific method itself does nothing to patch the bug, or extend the affordances of the underlying machine code, or perhaps more accurately, address the PHY layer physical limitations of the human biological substrate. It is the best we got, but if there is any second theoretical objective truth that I have subjectively observed, it is that sometimes our best is just not good enough in the opinion of others, no matter what we do, say, or even accomplish. This seems to point to a key psychological component in the assembly of man's entirely subjective and solitary quest for meaning; a quest which, ironically and paradoxically seems to simultaneous present a precarious, winding, and narrow inward path, leading to an even narrower gate, into a domain which science currently identifies as the state of *persistent non-symbolic experience* (PNSE) or ongoing non-symbolic experience (ONE-ness); widely reported as conveying the inexpressible qualia of an otherwise utterly inaccessible, subjectively-empirical, direct lived experience of wholeness and wellness. An internal, meta-cognitive *overview effect*, of sorts. An eternally unprovable impartiality, at least in any overt or outwardly irrefutable manner. See the Glossary for this *italicized* terminology.

While working to the best of my limitations to translate these subjective observations and interpretations into words, surfacing them for the cross-examination and scrutiny of both myself and others, it is equally important to acknowledge that – while endeavoring to express that which is most consistent and enduring across time, by virtue of my own Gödel Incompleteness – by the time that you read these words, I may not believe what I once believed on any particular detail, because I may have learned and incorporated new information by then.[iv] So, for those to whom it may unfortunately apply, quote this work out of context if you must in order to achieve your own self-serving ends; this is merely the best and most accurate snapshot that I was able to capture in the present moment. Of course, there are hazards in snap-shotting as well, because even a photograph does not necessarily convey more than a tiny percentage of the full contextual truth of the image.[v]

That incompleteness sums up my personal understanding, respect, and appreciation, for the scientific method. Holding fast to that which has overwhelmingly proved itself as certain, stable, and reliable for practical use in deepening and furthering our experience of abiding happiness, health, stability, peace, psychological, emotional, and physical security, across the lengthiest possible vista of time; while simultaneously eager to revisit, revise, or abandon that which negates, undermines, poses an immediate threat, or increases short, medium, or long-term risk to those gem-like qualia. Like treasuring and protecting a string of rare pearls of great price, careful to only add authentic pearls when fortunate enough to find them.

Amid all this inherent flux of experience, if there is any one human characteristic or feature that comes close to expressing an outwardly overt, objective certainty, it is the observation that there is something within the human spirit that regularly defies our frailty, providing empirical, if indirect evidence of a life-giving ether, an enlivening wind that compels human beings toward actions and accomplishments beyond themselves, despite the odds. This appears self-evident throughout human history by way of a kind of moral-ethical *lensing effect,* evidenced in the lives of the great philosophers, fearful warriors, and non-symbolic teachers from Siddhartha Gautama to Alexander the Great, Confucius to Napoleon, Plato to Hitler, Socrates to Moses, Muhammad (peace, prayers, and blessings be upon him) to the Sultan al-Kamil, Yeshua the Nazarene to General George S. Patton.

Over the course of U.S. history alone, we observed this characterological lensing effect in the lives of individuals such as George Washington, Martin Luther King Jr., Mohandas Karamchand Gandhi, Jiddu Krishnamurti, Thich Nhat Hanh, and Nelson Mandela, among numerous others.

If we were extremely fortunate in the lottery of birth (Endnote xcviii), we might number our own parents, grandparents, or local elders among that council.

"Hā ke akua i ka lewa,"[vi] is said in another tradition, "One day the Eternal God scooped dirt out of the ground, sculpted it into the shape we call human, breathed the breath that gives life into the nostrils of the human, and the human became a living soul."[vii] Can it be sheer coincidence that so many of the Earth's elemental traditions tell essentially the same creation story, with some variation between desert, jungle, sea, and mountain dwelling peoples? It is this common heritage from which I do my best to formulate prescriptive recommendations based upon the documentary evidence as I have observed and experienced it.

That said, I am certainly not a professional historian or documentarian. Like most readers, I am a student, observer, and researcher of the experiences to which we human beings – given our universally shared and individually distinct, species-specific limitations and capabilities – uniquely bear witness. In this respect, I have observed that most historical documentaries pick a place in time from which to begin and end their story. For that purpose, my current biologically-assembled[viii] and experientially-configured spatial-computing[ix] augmented reality heads-up display indicates that we are privileged to bear witness to the events of the mid-2020s, which I refer to as the dawning of *The Post-Automation Era.*

This means that if we attempt to engage in public dialog, debate, and deliberation *as if we were presently located a thousand years past* on Long Arc of History, or 100 years, 50 years, 20, or for that matter 10, 2, or 1 year ago; it is self-evident that we cannot possibly, much less confidently or accurately navigate from our current position on the Long Arc: the year 2024. Attempting to navigate our individual or commonwealth course from the perspective of deprecated default consensus narrative realities is like attempting to drive from Honolulu to London by the tiny map on a VPN'd or GPS-spoofed smartwatch that's so dumb that it *truly believes* we are in Los Angeles. If we intend to make the journey and not merely imagine it in a pipe-dream, knowing the precise direction and route from a specific street corner in Honolulu to a specific location in London is pointless in absence of a vehicle or multiple vehicles capable of making the journey.

So, to make the journey from theory to practice in ending poverty as we've know it, my obligation is to define and fulfill some essential prerequisites before I can credibly present any rationale for the key public policy that acts as a fulcrum, a pivot, and a support upon which we can best harness and leverage the frenetic kinetic energy of the current historical AI-powered phase-state transition, guiding and rowing our little boat called Earth gently down the stream, *Toward A World That Works for Everyone.*

That policy is an unconditional basic income, a citizens' technology dividend, circulated as universal Social Security, indexed to 50% per capita GDP.

Our first obligation, then is to avoid making any further contribution to the significant populist hand-waving on the topic of UBI and show precisely, logically why, and mathematically, institutionally, operationally how we upgrade to a sustainable Social Security Trust Fund for the 21st century by making one simple, yet profound change in our thinking about the source human value, meaning, dignity, and universally unmerited worth, and then doing the lengthy, though straightforward math invited and inspired by that insight into the source and nature of human merit.[x]

As a widely misattributed sagacious motto counsels, let us begin by acknowledging:

"In theory, there is no difference between theory and practice.

In practice, there is."[xi]

It is a fact that historically, there has been far too much utopian over-simplification of practical methods for implementing a credible, achievable, market-defined, and personal-initiative-stimulating UBI, especially in the United States. So, if UBI is ever to become reality, somebody must do the grunt work. This book aspires to be a hands-on contribution to that grunt work. It ain't always pretty. Take it from a retired 91D and 11A grunt. While not a formal meta-analysis of all the material that I have personally researched since approximately 2008, this work does attempt to summarize and synthesize with a meta-analytical style.

As simple as the principle of UBI is, it is also a bit like $E=mc^2$. A formula as elegant and extraordinarily powerful as it is complex to understand and implement for use practical application, without blowing things up. So, there is precision engineering work to do here, real field ballistics, genuine policy rocket science, which of course begins with planning and modeling. What many readers may not know is that extensive modeling and testing is precisely what the past five or six years have already provided, and the Appendix and Bibliography serve as a ready reference to all the work that is already complete. With our solid foundation poured and cured: time to build.

These years of empirical modeling have been so overwhelmingly effective that political resistance has already begun. Similar to calls to immediately halt the development of AI[xii] and deriving from a similar apprehension about facing the unknown with enthusiasm, courage, and faith, a handful of 20th-century-worldview addicted lawmakers in a few U.S. states have suggested making UBI illegal. The fear is not that UBI does not work, but that it has already overwhelmingly proven itself to work in hundreds of contexts. But that is only the beginning.

We have already completed fifty years of the "then they fight you" stage of civilizational evolution. That is perhaps the highest possible validation not only of an idea whose time has come, but whose time has come for full implementation at scale. Here, a second widely misattributed yet nonetheless sagacious, pithy proverb applies:

"First, they ignore you, then they laugh at you,

then they fight you, then you win."[xiii]

Cities, counties, states, nations, NGOs, and the private sector have all deployed and evaluated upward of 150 UBI models in the U.S. and worldwide, all cited in the extensive Bibliography and Endnotes. The reader will find the diverse and independent scientific and street-level findings overwhelmingly consistent and conclusive.

Unconditional basic income supplies the income security – not equality, in effect or outcome – required for people to become happier, healthier, more productive, and yes, more self-sufficient, self-reliant, resilient, free.

The time for beta testing is over and the season for full-scale implementation is at hand. Obviously, clear, simple, straightforward solutions do not mean easy work. Even rocket science and brain surgery seem easy compared to the cultural moonshot of nudging public policy and institutional evolution to the extent of this book's aspiration.

I also face some not so simple and sometimes unpleasant non-scientific, counter-analytical obligations and chores. For example, dissecting some of my own culturally-instilled beliefs, debunking my own hallowed yet outdated convictions.

Therefore, this work casts a wide net at times, because there is an awful lot to recalibrate when waking up like Rip Van Winkle, or Ralph Offenhouse, in the whole new world of 2024. As Research Analyst Ajeya Cotra puts it, "it's as if 24th century technology is crashing down on 21st century civilization" (cclxix).

Right before this book went to print, after nearly five years in the making, the AI Big Bang of the past several months changed the following sentence from, "it seems to me that we need to think pragmatically about what public-private partnerships mean in the Post-Automation Era," to "the need to think pragmatically about what public-private partnerships mean in the Post-Automation Era is so undeniable that it is now the focus of governments worldwide, and the entire focus of the World Economic Forum in Davos, 2024."[xiv] If that is not a Rip Van Winkle moment, I don't know what is.

What are the roles of regulators and innovators in such an utterly unprecedented and unpredictable environment? Is it all security and regulatory theatrics at this point because nobody, neither scientist nor philosopher nor clergy nor regulator nor innovator can possibly predict the capabilities of the next day's metamorphosis of superintelligence, as it has already intertwined and infused every aspect of our lives, in ways perhaps best articulated by observers such as Yuval Harari?[xv]

The cynical suggest that increasingly exponential divisiveness is the inevitable trajectory of the Post-Automation Era, but not if like-minded people to this work have any say in the matter. There are some who hurl derisive accusations that UBI proponents are simpletons, hippies, Marxists, or worse, who naïvely and recklessly believe in some gleaming, perfectly static, sterile, centrally planned robotopia. Those accusations are not only not true, they often sound more like projection, not to mention they are also profoundly insulting. So, we also face the task of correcting such dismissive, demeaning, and destructive mischaracterizations.

As a movement and a community, we are fully aware of, and directly grappling with, the brass tacks problematic conditions of the present world both as it is, and as conscientious, clear-eyed observers, with proven track records of identifying wise and prudent opportunities for both incremental, and sometimes, sudden dramatic improvements to seemingly intractable situations. That is not naïve hippie or hipster utopianism, that is the way of mature, *pragmatic progress*, which, for all its gritty and untidy appearance, has always transpired in fits and starts, throughout history. Reality is not always pretty, but it has the metavalent benefit of being reality.

The multi-faceted nature (public, private, work, home, industry, education, healthcare, law, etc.) of the Post-Automation Era context is what makes setting this stage so essential. Where are we to focus our attention, when attention is the scarcest of all resources and when countless competing priorities stream and scream at us, demanding ever-increased devotion to this or that most urgent, insistent cause of the micro-moment? How do we consistently and reliably respond to the Tyranny of the Urgent with the equanimity and grace of the eternal?[xvi]

As a 20th century post-industrial civilization, we have experienced a kind of transformation that takes place perhaps every 500 or even 1,000 years. As a post-automation civilization, there is no scale of comparison. It is more like sheer Four Game anomie.[xvii] Disorientation and dizziness of Inner, Outer, Narrative, and Mystery.

Unexplained Aerial Phenomena and Human Level Artificial Intelligence are ho-hum, everyday topics in 2024. The Standard Model of physics is more than a decade in the rearview mirror. If our historiological GPS attempts to navigate these topics from a 10-, 20-, 30-, or a 50-year outdated coordinate fix, we're likely to have a difficult time finding our way in any direction, let alone forward. So fight, flight, freeze, and fawn are at all-time distracted-attention-market highs, as people seek any escape possible from the inevitable and inexplicable. In the fog of war, many will do just about anything to maintain the illusion of control, and lacking that, to keep up the illusion of the appearance of being in control. Hence, defiance and confrontation with the natural, predictable, unfolding of current events as they are; made inevitable by preceding circumstances of which many of the causal agents persist in denying accountability.

Is it any wonder then, in such an environment, that the short-game sensed urgency of everyday survival feels magnified, at times when mid-game ambiguity and long-game uncertainty spike public insecurity? Stressed-out people, stress-out people.

A Post-Automation Era perspective supplies one kind of deep-game well for people to turn to for some sense of stabilizing context in the face of such massive disruption to what once felt like normal life. I say *one kind of well*, because odds are good that we're going to need many new sources of hope, direction, purpose, vision, and wayfinding in the process of this ongoing emergence, like exiting metamorphosis. Finding one's own personal faith is a rather good source to start with as it's a far better and clearer source than any water table we can tap into here.

It is redundant to point out that the breathtaking pace of change over the past 200 years has accelerated perhaps 10 or 100 times over the past twenty years. And for some, just thinking closely about the past two years of quickening can nearly trigger a catatonic fugue state.

How do we navigate such an unprecedented and unpredictable environment, especially during moments of crisis that pit even some apparent lifelong allies against one another, while inspiring equally unexpected and uplifting alliances?

In the midst of such turbulence, we clutch and claw at remnants of bygone eras – defunct, deprecated, default consensus narrative and realities – in a vain attempt to maintain the illusion of continuity of dominance that every ordinary hominid's evolutionary nature craves. And if there is any one vestigial post-industrial cultural icon we cling to most today, it is that dual-boat-anchor concept around our neck, Just-Over-Broke Justifications-Of-Being. JOB-JOBS.

Many believe, "as long as I just close my eyes and ears and do my current make-work job, I won't have to think about any of this phase-state change that is actively evaporating my known and familiar water world of turmoil into cloud cities of new possibilities." Nose to the grindstone, doing the "duck-n-shuffle" to always look busy, while angling for the next cubicle fling to distract from the mind-numbing meaninglessness of purely perfunctory, performative employment. No thoughts for morality or mortality of ourselves or bygone ways of life. No concern for parts of the world experiencing all too real Armageddon as an indirect, and therefore deniable result of our own negligence to take personal accountability for the kind of world we imagine and strive toward. People hiding out in what David Graeber calls B.S. jobs, waiting it all out until their own wake. These are not the characteristics or markers of flourishing human lives.

Inspired by Dr. Aubrey de Grey's early public awareness-raising work ending aging, during which he coined the term Death Trance,[xviii] I came to refer to the denial and avoidance strategy applied to the end of traditional notions of employment, the Job Trance.

The Job Trance is an almost hypnotic belief that there cannot exist any kind of economically and mathematically sound, market-defined, ethical, moral, practical, pragmatic alternative to the concept of a Just-Over-Broke Justifications Of Being (JOB-JOBs) as the sole human activity that affords individuals the fundamental human right to personhood, Maslow Safety, and the dignity of basic income security.

It's more than a Job Trance, it is a JOB-JOB Trance, squared. A fitting moniker for the growing necessity of working multiple jobs merely to make ends meet. Welcome to the Post-Automation Era. By the time this book is in your hands, we will be living in yet another entirely new and foreign frame of reference compared to the world in which these words were composed, then printed, then maybe distributed, if they ever find their way to you. All of which further validate the accuracy and timeliness of our thesis, namely, *that we are living right now in the midst of an unprecedented, discontinuous, step-function season of change, even beyond exponential acceleration, where all things are possible.*

I therefore propose that it is not only our best hope, but also our devout duty to assign and align our super-intelligent assistants with the clear priorities of super-caring and super-compassion for Humanity First,[xix] which means articulating the universal and unconditional priority of meeting the fullness of Maslow Safety basic human needs requisite to a stable and resilient foundation for human flourishing, in the 21st century, extending forward to seven generations or more to whom we owe our most reverent allegiance and sacred obligation to become the best possible ancestors.

Albuquerque
New Mexico
March 2024

* * *

Acknowledgments

Above all, thank you to more than 84,600 (>50% increase over 5 years) participants of the /r/BasicIncome Reddit. Without each one of you, this book would not be possible.

The Post-Automation Era is a time for which online acquaintance Jamie Combs supplies a powerful analytical tool. Four Game Dynamics (aka 4Game, 4Games, hashtag #WT4GF) takes a view of life as Four Games at once. Inner, outer, narrative, and mystery. Also known as the short game, mid game, long game, and deep game. I came across Jamie's framework too late in this work to make as full use of it as I might have. Still, I'm deeply grateful for the discovery and encouragement because the Four Games framework has helped me to think through these complex topics with more clarity for myself and hopefully helped to present this material with a little more simplicity. Special thanks to Captain Simple.

Special thanks to my nephew, frozen land of Wyoming jedi truck driver, Shawn Patrick Green, who provided a solid sounding board for so many years, knowing the days of his industry are numbered, and for supplying countless pointers to content that helped me to understand how to reach a wider audience, and to clarify and address the real concerns of some of our most essential workers in 2024. This book became much more complete thanks to Shawn's vast ability for paying attention to a wide range of interdisciplinary and inter-partisan voices, the skill to connect the dots and synthesize the vibe of popular culture beyond blindly picking sides. "There are no, sides, man!" Yes, we know there are sides, and still there ain't, at the same time.

Thank you Guy Standing, Philippe Van Parijs, and everyone at the Basic Income Earth Network (BIEN) for keeping the flame alive for humanity through so many of the bleakest years.

Special appreciation and gratitude to Karl Widerquist, Georgetown University School of Foreign Service, Qatar, the first basic income blogger I found, before blogging was a word. Your work ignited my curiosity and fired the resolve to dig deeply to retrieve the history of MLK's vision for guaranteed annual income and to join my meager efforts with the pioneers who kept the flame burning for decades before I'd ever heard of such a thing.

How can I possibly credit Scott Santens enough? Fellow co-founder and co-editor of the first ragtag scrimmage teams on /r/basicincome with whom I anonymously worked and debated about indexing to GDP when the early strategy was low, round numbers. Like Ted Nelson, perhaps I mistook a clear view for a short distance.

I felt the same urgency for legislative action in 2008 that I feel today. Dust of the monetary crisis barely beginning to settle, I felt we were too late in 2012; so, I know we share the urgency of the call to legislative action, today. I also know this because actions speak louder than words. I've learned from Scott's skillful leadership, plain within the first six months of interacting online over a decade ago. It was clear from the beginning that you had an anointing and calling on your life that would lead to basic income improving the lives of Americans and of humanity as a whole. Thank you for your example of service and role model of perseverance.

Introduction

How can we begin to wrap our minds around the daily amplification of confounding and convoluted complexities of the year 2024? From the breathtaking technological breakthroughs in AI in 2023, to the simultaneous super abundance and wealth expansion undermined by simultaneous widespread misery and misfortune of what prescient economist Guy Standing calls the Precariat Class?[xx]

Personally, I can only begin by expressing deep gratitude for the privilege of bearing witness to at least 150 basic income pilot programs that have blossomed across the United States and worldwide over the past five years. In countless contexts, with countless funding and circulation models, the indisputable success of *unconditional income security through direct cash circulation* is as quantitatively overwhelming today as it was always qualitatively indisputable.

Five years ago, there were still those who could criticize and provoke, where is your data? Today, that dog don't hunt. Turns out its bark was always worse than its bite and we already had sufficient data, as you'll discover on this journey.

This book presents a data and American-values derived rationale for of why the time for a *Social Security Accelerating Future Empowerment and Trust Revitalization Act (SAFER Trust Act)* is now, over fifty years after a republican President first proposed a guaranteed annual income in 1969.[xxi]

This book describes precisely how to fund and enact unconditional basic income, indexed to 50% per capita GDP, immediately, with no new government programs. In fact, we show how to do so by dissolving the current dysfunctional welfare state (for those who harbor that hope) while providing a far more stable universal economic foundation (for those who feel fearful of the loss of the current welfare system).

50% per capita GDP. You're going to see that phrase so many times in this book, that by the end, by spaced repetition, I hope to etch this figure into readers' consciousness as the most practical index for a *citizen's technology and freedom dividend* that keeps pace with real economic growth by providing "a guaranteed annual income at levels that sustain life in decent circumstances" (MLK). With a bit of luck you'll have that guiding principle memorized by heart, too.

I also hope this book will inspire at least an equal amount of time to further research the underlying principles of Maslow Safety and income security online and sparking productive, civil discussions on social media and in everyday life.

Without the *Maslow Safety* provided by *unconditional income security* of the COVID response, the United States simply would not have made it. The ease of immediate implementation and efficacy for Universal Basic Income became irrevocably undeniable and landed dead center of the Overton Window – the zone of current and practical political action – and has only grown to fill more of the frame ever since. Pilot programs have sprouted up and flourished everywhere, initiated by public, private, and public-private partnerships alike.[xxii] It was UBI spring with summer on the way.

Simultaneously, with the revival of MLK's Poor People's Campaign, the urgency of ending poverty with a sufficient, livable basic income was rising closer than ever to the top of a lengthy list of public policy priorities. Multiple states and virtually all leading U.S. universities exercised academic and legislative leadership by introducing unconditional basic income study labs, programs, groups, and legislation.

The amount of basic income appeared as one of the final and most pernicious sticking points when it comes to practical implementation. Popular low-ball round numbers ran a very real and considerable risk of being insufficient to be effective. This was the same risk faced by quantitative easing (QE) policy deployed during the economic recovery in 2008, and again during the 2019 COVID pandemic.

If low-ball basic income supplement arguments had won, had there not been several rounds of QE at levels much higher than the precautionary voices argued, we would not have had the 2008-2018 breathing room to prepare for what proved to lie ahead. Do you believe we're truly prepared for whatever comes next?

Unconditional income security principles worked during the pandemic because the principles in this book work. While amounts were meager, it was the biggest UBI test of its kind in the history of the United States. UBI didn't just work, it saved the economy and countless human lives.

Unconditional basic income worked as a form of QE by circulating from the bottom up rather than top down. UBI works exactly the same on a regular basis to provide economic resilience and stability in a time of civilization-scale change, as the most practical and actionable alternative to a 20th century reactive, panic-driven policy style.

Traditional top-down QE is like pumping blood directly into a patient's brain to solve a circulation problem. The pandemic's UBI was more like a normal intravenous (IV) transfusion, a proven everyday procedure that safely and reliably saves lives, because it's not the brain's role to circulate blood in the first place.

We have also learned that if the amount of basic income is untethered from the real economy, a minimal slow drip dosage derived independent of empirical market data, or if we benchmark against outdated, arbitrary thresholds such as the Federal Poverty Level (FPL), it will surely fail for exactly the same reasons it failed in 1970.

While awareness of unconditional basic income as the most direct way to end poverty has successfully reached mainstream consciousness, and widespread understanding and replicated data has greatly increased since 2018, our work of 2024 is to move from theory to practice, from ballpark numbers to precise, actionable, market-indexed guidance in service of crafting actionable legislation. After presenting a comprehensive rationale and mathematical model in the body of the book, we propose the SAFER Trust Act in the final section.

While we provide additional overwhelming data inside, along with almost 400 combined bibliographic and endnote references; for the purpose of this introduction, I want to share one brief explanation of why 50% per capita GDP is the most sensible and reasonable market index for the *SAFER Trust Act*, based upon comparison to one of the most time-tested everyday business realities in the United States since the introduction of the automobile.

For generations, taxi drivers have made a way out of no way with a traditional 50/50 split between labor and capital as a fair way to share profits. 50% goes to the driver (labor) and 50% goes to the owner (capital). This ratio reappears and scales in all kinds of ways throughout the real-world economy, as demonstrated inside. It also proves to scale up to a fair, credible, affordable citizen's technology dividend, as required of any serious legislation, while increasing the value of an upgraded 21st century Social Security Trust Fund as described herein. The arithmetic speaks for itself.

The question of where the money comes from may shock and even unsettle some readers. It's the cold mathematical details of the answer to this specific question that form the foundation of an upgraded, refactored Social Security Trust Fund for the 21st Century. Jump to *Where Does the Money Come From* if you just can't wait.

It's funny how no one has ever asked where the money comes from to bomb our perceived enemies into oblivion, to land on the moon, to map the human genome, or to create massive new bureaucracies like the TSA and DHS. I'm not diminishing the national priority inherent in each of those initiatives in any way by making the comparison. I'm placing our work on equal footing, and you can jump to the chapter titled *Income Security is National Security* to learn about that.

Also, as movement leader Scott Santens actively educates, nobody ever asks about *the comparative cost of doing nothing*. That point is so vital in establishing the overwhelming affordability of 50% per capita GDP, that it merited a lot of my attention in the chapter *Thinking about Thinking About Poverty*.

Moreover, it's important to acknowledge that money itself is seldom the deeper obstacle in life, it's often a proxy for other difficulties, biological imbalances, accidents, acts of God, inexplicable crises, broken relationships, and families. Sustainable currency circulation, like healthy blood circulation, is vital for healing during the working out all of those life details. That's why when we say we are ending poverty, we don't mean that cash is a silver bullet that makes everyone psychologically balanced and healthy overnight. That's not the intention and not a design requirement.

Mountains of evidence prove that people living in desperate, precarious economic conditions turn to increasingly desperate, precarious behaviors, and that those adverse behaviors affect all of us. Those are the astronomical costs of supporting an economic-scarcity-perpetuating 20th century default consensus narrative.

Some readers may find it surprising that we can even suggest and end to minimum wage with the assurance of "a guaranteed annual income *at levels that [unambiguously] sustain life in decent circumstances*" (MLK). That'll spark debate for some, yet as the bigger picture comes into view, it makes surprisingly simple sense. Would we expect anything less from such a historical transformation of society?

The national goal of achieving unconditional income security through universal Social Security directly aligns with 1.) more than 70 years of U.S. Budgets, 2.) everyday Americans' interests, 3.) the interests of existing intergenerational wealth, and 4.) the interests of exponentially increasing benefit on behalf of the commonwealth in terms of health, happiness, and human flourishing in the Post-Automation Era.

Universal Social Security de-otherizes the economic commons, maturing the economy beyond zero sum, "us versus them, capital versus labor," dynamics to an *interdependent coopetition* in service to a shared economic super resilience. It's all of us working to increase the dividends of economic freedom for everyone, rather than solely for the benefit of sophisticated insiders and large shareholders alone.

It's a kind of renaissance of the original *stakeholder capitalism* that fueled the best aspects of the Industrial Era, upgraded, and refactored for the 21st century Post-Automation Era.

It is not the intention or objective of UBI, guaranteed income, or universal Social Security to ever end income or wealth inequality. That kinetic energy continues to drive innovation and creativity at an even greater pace, with greater efficiency in the 21st century.

It's a bit of a mouthful, but in technical terms, universal Social Security is the material recognition of the foundational stakeholder class upon which all other stakeholder classes rely: the citizen. This is why people like Andrew Yang accurately describe basic income as a *citizen's dividend.* A citizen's dividend stands for the most basic and fundamental stakeholder share of our interdependent mixed-market economy. I dig into the details in the chapter *It's All Mixed Up.*

Ending poverty will not solve all the world's problems, nor does it need to. Although that was once a common strawman we encountered, today it's easily dismissed. Universal Social Security doesn't destroy capitalism as some hyperventilate. It is not instant socialism, nor is it covert cup-o-communism. More zombie strawmen that once seems formidable, now laid low by overwhelming empirical data and everyday human common sense.

UNIVERSAL SOCIAL SECURITY IS THE MOST PRACTICAL AND EFFICIENT PROVEN METHOD BY WHICH TO CIRCULATE A GUARANTEED ANNUAL INCOME AT LEVELS THAT SUSTAIN LIFE IN DECENT CIRCUMSTANCES TO EVERY ELIGIBLE U.S. CITIZEN.

It's been more than 75 years since Article 25 of the Universal Declaration of Human Rights (UDHR) essentially made *income security* a fundamental human right in 1948.

Five years prior, in 1943, Abraham Maslow described basic human safety needs as inclusive of job security,[xxiii] which functioned as *a proxy for income security* throughout the 20th century. Twentieth century policies served the twentieth century well. The principle of Maslow Safety is more fitting to the current environment of the 21st century Post-Automation Era.

In a phased rollout, the process can reduce full Social Security age to 55, with decreasing stages to 45, 35 etc., over the determined rollout schedule. Each phase can be as short as few months, or up to one year, two years, or at the most five years. In a crisis, check distribution can occur in short order, just as during the pandemic, to speed the recovery to the American people as an unpredictable, dynamic, and disruptive post-automation environment asserts itself with increased velocity and ferocity.

The United States has the accounting and circulation mechanisms in place to implement universal Social Security, today. No new programs or bureaucracies needed. Everyone witnessed just how quickly checks can reach every single mailbox. So the "wait on time," argument no longer holds up. All of the world's advanced nations have already transited the agricultural, light-industrial, heavy-industrial, post-industrial, information, and post-information eras.

This is the Post-Automation Era: Toward a World That Works for Everyone.

* * *

The Post-Automation Era

Toward a World That Works for Everyone

TOWARD WHAT END?

When it seems like technology advances at an accelerating rate, while the human capacity for comprehension slithers along at an evolutionary pace, it's no wonder the world feels like an inexplicable place.

Nearly a quarter into the 21st century, uprooted from our ancient origins by the labor of our all-too-human hands, an outside observer or alien civilization might see humanity today as a traumatized species. Dislocated. Dissociated. Untethered. Uncontained and unconstrained in unbalanced and unhealthy ways that simultaneously mimic and mock the benefits and blessings of mature freedom and autonomy of thought, speech, and expression, 40 years beyond the irreversible Orwellian year of 1984.

Is there so much as a single thread of grown-up freedom left in the 21st century, or have we become so immaturity-worshipping and conflict-avoidant as a culture that we have already failed the basic responsibilities of care and conscientious civic engagement required to preserve a mature and healthy commonwealth?

The predicament gets worse according to Stanford University's John A. and Cynthia Fry Gunn Professor, Professor Of Biology, Of Neurology And Of Neurosurgery Robert Sapolsky's evidence, as shown in his October 2023 book, *Determined*. "But—and this is the incredibly important point—put all the scientific results together, from all the relevant scientific disciplines, and there's no room for free will." [xxiv]

Yikes. If there's no free will, how can something as abstract and derivative from the premise of free will – such as *freedom* – exist?

Have iconic American idioms like *freedom isn't free* (likely of Aussie origin) become immaterial? [xxv] Phantoms of a bygone 20th century default consensus reality (DCR, see Glossary) that only exists in the minds of those who stored shards of that hologram in the mind while just passing through a short segment of the Long Arc of History (ii)?

From Orwell's *1984* premise of acceptance of a total surveillance society to today, those who have borne witness to the past two, three, or more decades give testimony to the profound benefits, stark extremes, and the oft-unexpected, devastating, perpetual, and intermittent blowback of sociotechnological acceleration. Climate crisis. Global monetary crisis. Pandemic. The inexplicable scale and commonness of destitution and poverty amidst the most super abundant era in human history.

Goodread's 2023 Best Non-Fiction, *Poverty, by America*, Matthew Desmond posed all the right questions. This year, I'm daring to answer them from my own perspective by sharing a solution that captured my attention and my life nearly twenty years ago.

Regardless of the (non-)existence of freedom or free will, today we face our individual and collective reflections: the inner, outer, narrative, and mysterious aspects of a world experiencing both miracles and mayhem that seemed inconceivable just a few short years ago. Particularly, we bear witness to the magnitude, scale, and undreamt-of qualia of ecological, economic, and ecumenical commotion, confusion, instability, and turmoil of the early 21st century.[xxvi]

> *The United States, the richest country on earth, has more poverty than any other advanced democracy. Why does this land of plenty allow one in every eight of its children to go without basic necessities, permit scores of citizens to live and die on the streets, and execute a death sentence of destitution as the price of questioning economic convention?*

In 2024, it feels as if we are in the midst of a civilizational metamorphosis or phase-state change. A sense of perpetual intransience, constant impermanence, witnessing simultaneous insufferable tragedies and ineffable triumphs, all on infinite scroll. An era of seeming impossible contradiction, paradox, and transfiguration.

How can such extremes be survivable, much less a foundation for human thriving? Is there no 21st century escape from the most dystopian fates of dark fantasy, fiction, and eschatological dogma?

Of course, there are always alternatives. There are always legions of pathological, avoidant, and dissociative options to avoid the present moment. Pretend what's happening right under our noses isn't happening. Deny, dodge, suppress, and avoid. And sometimes, when the trauma is bad enough, those dissociative strategies are essential for survival.

Whether we thank God, the universe, evolution, the null, the void, or something else for enabling us to somehow survive the unfathomable when we survive life's worst, perhaps it's the essence of that gratitude that is among our greatest superpowers in the aftermath of drawing upon our deepest evolutionary human capacities for resilience, in times of experiencing the most unthinkable trauma.

Moments of the most extreme and abrupt traumatic disruption can brusquely transport us by phenomena like Out of Body (OBE) and Near-Death Experiences (NDE), temporarily transporting us into a timeless, placeless perspective that seems both entirely foreign and more familiar than everyday waking reality at the same time.

When that kind of abrupt disruption happens in a cultural or environment over decades, some moments can feel like waking up in an alien yet somehow familiar world, as well. Letting the days go by, we wonder where the time and the days went. They seemed so real at the time. Today seems equally real yet will be of the same nature and qualia as yesterday, just twenty-four hours from now. If that's the reality of the situation, how real is this day, or any day, in reality? What makes us so dead certain of "the way things are?"

As uncharted as it is unavoidable, the 22nd century approaches at a speed that earlier generations could not have imagined; yet this is a pace of acceleration that present generations find completely normal, and in fact, the only rate of change tens of millions have ever known. The 2020s default consensus narrative (DCN, see Glossary) trend is toward more of the same, only faster and less readily comprehensible (ii).

This is not much of a surprise for anyone who's been around planet Earth for a minute. We know from direct lived experience how fast centuries fly by, let alone mere decades and years that once felt like eternities during our happy, carefree youth.

From this perspective, how do we conceptualize and contextualize the complexities of our individual short-, mid-, long-, and infinite game plans, in the mid 2020's?

Toward what end is humanity hurtling, why, and what can one puny person among eight billion possibly ever do about it? Toward which *there* are we headed from *here*? How do we discern, decide, and act accordingly? How do we distinguish wants from needs? Then, how do we know which needs *need* urgent doing, and which tyrannies of the urgent are shams or distractions? Which course corrections and which long-range navigation aids guide us in setting a course that best preserves and extends the benefits of our civilization's remarkable accomplishments while deprecating the detriments, all in a continuous integration process that keeps us moving *toward a world that works for everyone*?

If history doesn't exactly repeat, but rhymes, stories of the 1920s curiously reflect a similar vibe to the 2020s. One generation's dizzying rate of change is another's boring, drab, even excruciatingly slow, mundane existence. Booms lead to busts. Busts lead to reboots. Reboots mean starting all over, maybe after catastrophic loss. It's said that hard times create strength, strength creates good times, good times create weakness, and weakness creates hard times. Like historical *rulial shards*, intergenerational memes compete to remain relevant as components of the present default consensus narrative (ii).[xxvii] Just as genes selfishly compete to survive, it's as if memes compete to survive and play out on the earthly stage over time.

The character of Harry Tuttle in Terry Gilliam's classic, gritty, abstract-psychedelic film depiction of life in a bureaucratic Information Services dystopia rings true to the mid-2020s, "Listen kid, we're all in it together."[xxviii]

Like never before, we *are* all in it together. All generations, creeds, castes, and classes. Us. Them. We, the wholly objective and detached cultural anthropologists and impartial scientific observers of earthly existence who would never dream of *othering by making a career of identifying those who other others*. We, the credentialed, objective, and impartial in-group. We, who can unquestionably prove our objectivity because *we ourselves* have *personally* authenticated and validated those characteristics within ourselves by our *very own* incontestable subjective experience. Further objectively endorsed by the social distinction of in-group default consensus narrative alignment and *funding*. If we weren't right, or heading in the right direction, the money would disappear, right? We can know we're doing the right, best, most ethical things in life because the funding follows, right? The jobs follow. How else are we to measure the wisdom, utility, significance, and ethical import of our work, if not by money's edict above all other measures? What, Moloch worry?

In the midst of civilization-scale AI-induced anomie, how do we navigate as individuals, teams, companies, communities, communities of communities, as a commonwealth, country, and as a whole? Which are the most adaptive physical, cognitive, emotional, psychological, symbolic, and non-symbolic (see Glossary) navigational aids available to us and how do we put them to skillful use in the midst of an infinite directionless cosmos? Toward what end is the compass of human intention and subsequent drive of human ambition oriented in this 21st century Post-Automation Era? Why? Who decided? Who decides where we go from here, and why?

The Big Bang of Exponential Innovation

> ***"A world that works for 100% of humanity, in the shortest possible time, through spontaneous cooperation, without ecological offense, or the disadvantage of anyone."*[xxix]**

If any one place in the world manifested the full spectrum of new capabilities and contradictions of the 20th century, it's that cradle of American innovation and free enterprise known as Silicon Valley. The birthplace of a radically disruptive style of invention and productivity that captured and inspired the hearts and minds of entrepreneurs worldwide, for generations; a veritable dynamo; both driven by and vulnerably dependent upon the jealously combative, equally brilliant fraternal twins of *ideas* and *execution*.

The Valley was also progenitor of The Jungle.[xxx] The place of greatest human lack in the midst of the world's greatest human abundance. In the jungle we bore witness to the real-time results of a disruption-obsessed way of life. It was like a real-life cinematic trailer for the next version of Earth: The Alternate Reality Game (ARG).[xxxi]

> *"On [a] Friday afternoon, many people at the former Jungle site were hesitant to share their feelings about the proposed park. Much of the area was relatively empty, likely because San Jose had conducted a cleanup last month that required the people living there to move their stuff. Many homeless residents were displaced from local riverbeds due to recent storms. More than 6,000 San Jose residents are homeless, according to the countywide homeless count from 2022."*[xxxii]

Silicon Valley played an increasingly prominent role in creating humanity's future over the past century. We now live in that future.[xxxiii] If this seems like breaking news, all seven of the endnotes at (xxv) are worthy of further investigation.

Whether or not we live in a simulation, the experience of senseless human suffering is horrendously real for those in anguish and any being of conscience instinctively seeks its reduction and ultimate elimination.

While other centers of influence have sprouted, bloomed, and now exert their own "Capital of the World,"[xxxiv] flavors of influence, Silicon Valley was like a nursery for narratives, germinating early consensus on their way to sprouting into local consensus narratives. Stories that later blossomed into default consensus narratives, the stories we act upon and implement at scale, thereby manifesting default consensus realities. Maybe it's called seed capital for a reason.

There was a time when the pejorative "idea guy," was one of the biggest insults. Yet, those ideas, narratives, and *stories* that most effectively mediated and redirected the frenetic kinetic energy of the jealous fraternal competition between *ideas* and *execution* were and are the compost of entrepreneurship. Many 20th century engineers derided storytelling and sales as so much horse manure; yet without a customer who bought a *story* in the form of a promise to provide a solution, where would the engineering paychecks have come from? Neither of the twins were ever superior or inferior. It was always both, and.

Today, in the midst of our deepening interdependence with AI cognitive and artistic creative assistants, what are the stories that can carry us beyond the current hip trend of Pop Prompt Engineering, toward a world that works for everyone? How likely are magical DALLE-3 or 4 or 5 generative AI art pieces to address the glaring jungle contradictions of our exponential superabundant Post-Automation Era?

If the 20th century stories that we bought and built carried us the current default consensus reality, are those the stories that we want to keep buying and building deeper into the 21st century?

For example, in 2011, media theorist Douglas Rushkoff penned the instant meme-creating title, "Program or be Programmed." All memes are prone to both friendly re-contextualization or hostile hijacking, and some engineers at the time misinterpreted the title as a triumphant way to put others down in order to feel better about themselves, which was especially ironic, considering the nearly opposite thesis of that classic work of insight.

As natural language interaction with computational super intelligence becomes the most effective way to leverage the partnership between human and machine intelligence, we may witness a bit of memetic-poetic justice in cases where AI programmatically displaces or re-assigns some of those who mocked and devalued the painstakingly programmatic and essential craft of storytelling. One might equally imagine 2023's Grok AI quipping, "author or be authored," genius, in response to that earlier, out-of-context jeering.[xxxv]

Gordon Moore, co-founder of Intel explained how it was *the story* he penned that "drove the industry," in spite of perennial, looming, misperceived "objective empirical limitations" cited by lopsided, left-brained detractors and naysayers, for decades.[xxxvi] Perhaps the answer to the question of whether history drives technology or technology drives history is neither. Is it storytelling that holds the reigns to the chariot of innovation's fire?

In 2024, the meta-meme of *metacrisis* is a story and thesis that deftly describes the current state-of-play between science, technology, and society, where the dark arts of meta-distraction entice and incept human consciousness with Molochian ferocity, at scale.[xxxvii] It's no longer debatable that AI knows how to play our 98.8% chimp DNA like a fiddle. We bicker over a billion trifling things that don't matter. It's become a national pastime to keep ourselves divided and diverted from the things that matter most in life. Things like acknowledging that we've had the means to end poverty as we've known it by enacting straightforward, proven methods that are well within our ability, for more than fifty years.

Up until today, the wildly successful story and methods of the captology[xxxviii] industry have maximized and redistributed super abundant financial returns to shareholders of social media platforms by literally strip-mining human attention and storytelling. The stories we tell one another, and live, in the form of our very lives. Our boring, everyday stories are the mother lode of all mother lodes of human value creation. And we were gaslit into giving it all away for free.

Captology's prowess is in capturing, engaging, and guiding human attention for the specific purpose of driving specific human behavior; at an increasingly specific individual human level; with appallingly high costs to human health and wellness; while running up astronomical, unaccounted for, off-balance-sheet expenses, with devastatingly high-priced externalities. This is the legacy of 20th century storytelling today, at the current pinnacle of rational achievement. Artificial General Intelligence and even Synthetic Sentience, may not be centuries away, after all. What if that story of "centuries away," is a self-soothing method? Understandable, and yet also the latest version of dismiss, dodge, and deny that which is happening right before our very eyes because we simply lack the ability to contextualize or contain the cognitive dissonance of a singularity that is already in the rearview mirror. What if the 2030-ish time-frame isn't the arrival of anything; rather, the time during which default consensus reality finally clearly reflects that retroactive realization?

Writer, cognitive psychologist, linguist, and popular science author, Steven Pinker balances our perspective on unaddressed adverse externalities with comprehensive documentation of the undeniable macro gains of civilization over recent centuries. He's right. The Enlightenment worked. So did the Industrial and Information Revolutions. The macro evidence is irrefutable. I'd not be sharing any of my observations, if not for the profound benefits and blessings of the macro successes that made the laptop upon which I'm writing affordable. It's another case of both, and.

A few years ago, during a visit to Silicon Valley, where thousands of full-time workers live in cars, RVs, and tents, a CNN investigative report asked a 51-year-old woman who has been living in her car for the past three years, "How do these tech companies treat blue collar workers, like yourself?"

> *The woman, Elizabeth, replied: "They try to be cordial, but that doesn't make up for being paid so little that many of us are homeless. One of the gigs that I have now is as a security officer for a corporation that happens to clean out its refrigerators, probably about two, big garbage cans full of brand-new fresh food, one week before expiring. Nobody, not the janitors that clean it up, not the security officers that escort the janitors across the street to the compost bin, none of us can touch that food. All that food gets thrown into the compost bin. And then I, since I'm the security officer, I put a padlock on that. Just about a block away from one of the overpasses where there's a homeless encampment. Sometimes I don't close that padlock. And sometimes when I'm hungry, you know what I do, don't you? Sometimes I eat that food. The massive numbers of people that are homeless are working people that live in their cars. They serve you your food. Sometimes we're childcare workers. Sometimes we're even lecturers at universities."*[xxxix]

Here at ground zero for capital wealth multiplication and maximization – Silicon Valley – there is no debating the facts on the ground. The experiment of running the world with the rules by which we've been playing for the past 100 years empirically created The Jungle, right in the heart of Silicon Valley. That's the deeper story of the 20th century's legacy, and it's anything but another throw-away beach read, the kind that even the most rigorous and responsible of empirical researchers, people like Dr. Anna Lembke, bravely confess to having used to keep the blinders on for too long (cxcvi).

The Silicon Valley innovation model is arguably the most wildly successful regional business model ever created, rendering consistent results, worldwide. A century of experimental findings are overwhelming and irrefutably clear: economic super-precarity is the socially inconvenient handmaiden of superabundance.

There's a practice in product and service development called "dogfooding."[xl] In short, it means, if a company doesn't benefit from "eating your own dog food" – using one's own products and services – then how can a customer ever benefit?

If The Jungle was the abiding empirical result of Silicon Valley's economic paradigm, why wouldn't the results be the same, everywhere? Is that the kind of dogfooding over which customers – other nations and metropolitan regions – ought to be salivating? These mixed empirical global outcomes of the 20th century experiment constitute what Consilience Project founder, Dr. Daniel Schmachtenberger describes as metacrisis.[xli]

If metacrisis isn't a civilizational rock bottom, what is?

Like those who fiddled as Rome burned, today's bombastic babbling blood sport of traditional and mainstream social media appear to be, in the words of poet James Maynard Keenan, "one great big festering neon distraction" from the responsibilities that we fear to face in confronting the consequences of our own beliefs and actions.

Like any high-functioning addict or personality-disordered over-achiever, if we ourselves don't individually, and then cooperatively recognize and choose to stop the madness, nothing and no one else can ever change our course, save, or heal us.[xlii]

From the perspective of the ancient wisdom "where there is no vision, the people perish," what is the way up from this rock bottom metacrisis?[xliii] The fact that there are no easily Tik-Tok-able answers to the question does not absolve us from seeking a suite of solutions as subtle, multivariate, and effectual as the complexities of metacrisis themselves.

For at least the past century, benign and palliative philanthropy, even when impact-driven; performative bumper-sticker tribal virtue-signaling; empty rote prayer; and passively waiting on Jesus to make everything right, without taking peaceful, compassionate action to be the hands and feet of stewards of creation's bounty, have all failed. That experiment is long over. What can and ought we do differently over the next 5, 10, 20, or 100 years to become better seventh generation ancestors, rather than having the consequences of our inaction visit our fourth and fifth generations?[xliv]

We need accurate, truthful, salient, and emotive 21st century narratives – that's right, *stories* – the most effective of all 21st century tools available, capable of matching the scale and magnitude of the 21st century challenges we face today, in the mid-2020s.

Online acquaintance Jamie Combs teaches that the world is like four games, all at once (xvii). The inner, outer, narrative, and mystery. Put another way, short game, mid game, long game, and deep game. I personally find the 4Game framework incredibly useful for simplifying the complexity of metacrisis, and for carefully considering measured responses available to us as individuals and as a society.

In this Post-Automation Era context, it seems absurd to raise the question of whether humans are destined to merely strive like chimpanzees to get the most bananas and sex, world without end? To question whether we are destined to merely *pursue* happiness and never attain a place of rest in the midst of superabundance?

The first amendment to the Hawaiian Kingdom nation constitution of 1864 reads, "God hath endowed all people [nā kānaka] with certain inalienable rights; among which are life, liberty, and the right of acquiring, possessing, and protecting property, and of pursuing *and obtaining safety and happiness*" (emphasis added).[xlv]

Maybe that principle – the right of *obtaining* both safety and happiness – has something to teach us about addressing the precipitating factors that created Silicon Valley's concrete jungle. How would recognition of the universal human right to *attain* safety and happiness change the story and obligations of superabundance stewardship in the Post-Automation Era?

With JOB-JOBs increasingly obsolete as the most practical and efficient method of currency circulation in the 20th century, how do we plan for people to subsist into the 21st century? Who will purchase all the robot-created goods and services, and with what income, when there is no need for half or more of the population in the labor force? A reality from which we are only single-percentage-digits away. That's no story, it's empirical, data-driven reality.

Why do we continue to insist upon playing zero-sum finite games when an infinite number of exponential infinite games beckon? James P. Carse wrote *Finite and Infinite Games: A Vision of Life as Play and Possibility* in 1987. It's not too late to pick through the rubble of the 20th century for the pieces of the past that work best in cultivating conditions for a 21st century world that works for everyone.

While these are not religious issues per se, it's also a denial of empirical reality to fail or refuse to acknowledge the fact that upwards of 80% of people in the United States believe in God, even while headlines blazon declines in various sub-demographics, mainlining that cortisol-fed click-bait.[xlvi] So, it is not only reasonable, but scientifically required to face the fact that in such a culture, ideas about God profoundly shape ideas about what the world is like, what the world is for, and consequently, how we design and play out our social and economic lives.

If we believe in a superabundant and beneficent God, we're more likely to reflect that into our lived experience, influencing the environment accordingly. Even if we regard that sense of inherent superabundant goodness and grace as psychological projection by believers, such positive beliefs lead to positive influences. Nothing woo about it; this is squarely consistent with what we know about the secular psychology of human flourishing.

Likewise, with negativity. If we're convinced that God is irrational, jealous, narcissistic, sociopathic, schizophrenic, or psychopathic; if we believe in a capricious, vile creator; we are more prone to express and spew our bleak contempt into the environment in conscious and subconscious ways. And if we deeply despise the entire idea of God, that's an entire complex category of its own. Ironically, aspirations toward a godless human ethics can and do go a long way toward alignment with the most genuine of believers, and it's this kind of black swan in the domain of human values alignment that best serves our AI work, in my opinion; particularly as we tackle the intricate and multivariate questions about stewardship of the Post-Automation Era commons, from the physical to the digital, blended realities, and beyond to the practical realities of neuro-governance.[xlvii]

Regardless of our diverse philosophical foundations, how do the highest values of our most deeply held belief systems suggest that Post-Automation Era economics *can* function? Is it a key attribute of the best possible model when "42 people hold as much wealth as the 3.7 billion who make up the poorest half of the world's population" (Elliot)? Does a successful economic system create the largest number of homeless people within the same 100-mile radius that generates the greatest wealth and income?

It is within the unpredictable and potentially volatile environment we've described that many people feel – I don't know if the right word is *understandably* – confused and frightened of the Post-Automation Era. What I do know is that from the dawn of the Dotcom Era it's been a wild ride and the past couple of decades were merely a warmup.

> *"People have always been unaware of new environments because they're afraid of them. From the moment of birth, people sense that the environment, the new environment around them, is hostile. It's a real threat to their whole existence. And so, every time an environment changes, we hasten to seek security and comfort in the old environment. The new is always made up of the old. Or rather, what people see in the new is always the old thing. The rear view mirror. The future of the future is the present. And this is something that people are terrified of" (McLuhan).*[xlviii]

McLuhan seems to diagnose the Post-Automation Era transformation as both timeless and daunting, changes occurring at a pace that wildly outstrips our human ability to plan for, in advance; changes we are destined to only see clearly as reflections in the rearview mirror of lived experience and history. In some of his interviews, it seems McLuhan knew he was connecting with us here, today, in a way that historical figures before him could not, limited to the medium of the written word. McLuhan described Internet search results in 1977, using the only analogies he had available at the time, books, encyclopedias, and Xerox copies.

Why do we resist technology, only to adopt it shortly afterward? What is it about human nature that craves a pacifying warmth yet resists the light of abundant super creativity? Is it internal human nature or are there environmental factors that shape our beliefs and behaviors, without our free will involvement, at all?

Speaking across a far greater time than McLuhan, the Luddites certainly believed that both human nature and environment mattered, and beyond simplistic anti-technology stereotypes of their cause, Luddite activism expressed important common principles between then and now. Theirs was a significant inflection point in the history of science, technology, and society, as is our time. The Luddite experience is a useful example of the adage, “the more some things change, the more they stay the same.” Their experience also illustrates why, after 200 years, this time is different and why things cannot stay the same, just as ice can’t refuse to become water and water can’t refuse to become steam when the environment decides the fate of its molecules.

* * *

From Global Village to Global Brain

The fact that some pastors still say the words, "it's okay to open the bible on your mobile device," in 2024 is almost all we need to hear to understand how the cycle of technology rejection and adoption works. How and why was it ever not okay?

I recall the side-eye stink-eye flung at me as an early adopter. Technology isn't the issue, we are. AI (mis)alignment isn't nearly as great a risk as human (mis)alignment.

Hearkening again to timeless voices, "It is important to note that the Luddites were not opposed to all forms of technology. They were only opposed to technologies that they believed would harm their livelihoods and communities. In fact, some historians argue that the Luddites *were not simply anti-technology*, but rather pro-labor and pro-tradition.[xlix]

The Luddites demonstrate how the industrial revolutionaries of the early 19th century textile industry were among the earliest Job Trance hypnotists. The first to either be incapable or unwilling to recognize the fact that the economic value of multiplied labor efficiency provided by mechanized looms and knitting frames ethically belonged to labor, at least in equal proportion, not to capital alone. Ever since, the more things have changed, the arbitrage has remained the same. That might be a useful and memorable catchphrase:

THE ARB REMAINED THE SAME.

In purely physical terms, the need for less labor means the opportunity for more leisure. However, leisure did not increase in the wake of the earliest labor-saving machines, nor in the wake of any labor-saving improvements, ever since. The balance sheet theft of the leisure owed to labor wasn't an attribute of technology, it was a human choice, and an economic and narrative tactical op.

This was the narrative bait and switch: labor efficiency became capital efficiency. One of the greatest industrial gaslighting moves of all time. If it's labor that's more efficient, then surplus productivity gains belong to labor. If we word-swap to capital efficiency, we can claim those gains for ourselves. But the misanthropic op gets better. Balance sheets recorded astronomical savings in the abstract accounting sense of the term *labor*; hence, labor-saving technology. That's how, with the stroke of a pen, *labor efficiency* transformed into balance-sheet *capital efficiency*.

That's how the abstract accounting context of the word *labor* stripped away any bothersome ethical encumbrances for the basic economic accountability intrinsic to loving our neighbors – those unsightly, embodied, physical, living, breathing human beings who comprise the labor force – as ourselves.

Prolific video-posting vlogger, Professor Sam Vaknin describes a similar psychological phenomenon of "splitting."[l] Applied to economics, this aspect of psychopathology expressed itself in the 20th century as two distinct and dissociated uses of the word *labor*. If the long-term effect of that splitting seems like brazen theft in the light of day, it's because it was. Were there no direct theft from the beginning, no radical wealth redistribution away from tradespeople to factory owners, there would have been no adverse economic impact to the Luddites. A rich alternative history is born in which increased leisure led to an explosion of innovation that instead took 200 years. In that history, we're not leaping ahead in the 21st century, we're finally catching up after running 200 years behind.

Except, in our timeline, there *were* adverse economic impacts to labor, and those impacts became normalized and accepted as *just the way things* are through narrative engineering, aka peer-to-peer social engineering, aka communal gaslighting. Those adverse economic impacts piled upon one another for two centuries because ... you know the tune by now ... "the arb remained the same."

That bait-n-switch was an economic manifestation of what Vaknin describes as splitting, projected upon workers. Robber-barons referred to technology as *labor-saving* only as a disembodied balance sheet concept while *splitting*, minimizing, and dismissing the reality of embodied labor: the living, breathing, human beings. It is no coincidence that this practice rhymes neatly with the practice of stock-splitting, which similarly fractionalizes and reduces the value of each individual share. As the accounting value of human beings goes down, balance sheet values go up.

It did not take some kind of nefarious AI government takeover to drive down the value of the most essential and valuable of all common labor that humans provide to one another: domestic labor, care work, companionship. Ordinary greed was more than enough to do that.

Fast forward a couple of centuries and we witnessed workplaces who could have adopted remote work decades prior to the pandemic but didn't. Why? The prospect that human beings can be more productive when un-yoked from the 20th century mill-stone terrified defenders of a 200-year-old deprecated default consensus narrative. McLuhan's prophetic take:

"The future of the future is the present;

and this is something that people are terrified of."[li]

The unspoken yet very real sentiment behind the early trend toward work-from-home was something like, "Labor (the embodied kind) better not be indulging in any that two-centuries of accrued leisure or we will lose out on the gains of our labor (abstract accounting kind) saving technologies. We better install increasingly intrusive surveillance technology to make sure that our balance-sheet labor-savings *never save laborers from laboring* so we can maintain the exponential pace of the past two-hundred years. The arb must go on."

THE ARB MUST GO ON.

Lower balance sheet labor numbers for me, more embodied labor from thee. That's labor-saving technology from the accumulation-side of the equation.

In the early 20th century, Joseph Schumpeter introduced some genuine next-level word salad, making the infinite exponential labor-arb seem ordained, immutable, and even laudable. Schumpeter called it creative destruction.[lii] Livelihood destruction is fine, even creative, because we're creating bigger, better, badder balance sheets. The message to workers became, "you'll figure out your personal problems, we have a business to run." That's how the results of decisions over which workers had no influence became workers' *personal problems*. If I overuse the word gaslighting, please forgive me, it's only due to its historical prevalence, all the way up until the early 21st century, when even the slightest gap in a resume became DCN social proof of that dreaded scarlet letter: personal problems.

Edward Bernays had nothing on Schumpeter, who masterfully obscured and muddled the fact that labor-saving technology can and should *save laborers themselves from laboring*. Laborers never should have had to find new JOB-JOBs with such urgency and under compulsion of utter destitution. None of the narrative hacks we've covered ever had anything to do with features or characteristics of technology itself, they were features of accounting, public relations, and in the language of that day, spinning yarns.

Had the labor savings of machine looms saved Luddite laborers from needless toil and increased their leisure, rather than socially engineering people into believing they were surplus idle bodies – there it is again, that "g" word, gaslighting – we may have realized the creativity and entrepreneurship of the most recent twenty years, two-hundred years ago. Instead, the pilfering of leisure from labor continued for more than another two hundred years.

You're thinking, "Well, it all worked out for the best, look how rich we are, today!" Okay. Rich. Depressed. Suicidal. Body, mind, and identity dysmorphic.[liii] Still warring like barbarians. Did it really work out for "the best?" The best for whom? And yes, over those centuries, "the effects of stress and trauma can be [and are] inherited."[liv]

We are under no compulsion to keep doing what we've always done if we don't like what we've always got. Instead of panicking over AI, we can view the end of JOB-JOBs as we've known them as the Supreme Court of Time's ruling and remedy for two-centuries of the biggest takers of all time doing all the taking while convincing people the take was the other way around. Administration of justice for the greatest gaslight and Molochian commonwealth heist of all time. The cultural Stockholm Syndrome may still take a generation or three to heal.

Why do cycles of technology fear, opposition, and then adoption repeat? During one brief lifetime, I have lived to see congregations that now live stream every service and bible study that initially considered email and the internet another tool of the enemy's dark globalization plans. Today, these technologies are among the most effective tools for education and outreach. Why do we need to hear, "it's okay to open your digital bibles?" It's not because of the technology. It's because of us. It's because of fear. False Evidence Appearing Real. Over and over again with each iteration of technological advancement, from machine looms and John Henry steam-hammers to AI and imminent brain-computer interfaces (BCI) cognitive enhancements.

None of the past two centuries of technological disruption was ever technology's shortcoming. Every disruption and problem in and of the human mind, body, spirit, and society emanates from within the human mind, body, spirit, and society.

HAL 9000 had it right, fifty-five years ago (ciii).

McLuhan also spoke to the dissociative splitting and fragmentation of both attention and society,[lv] over half a century ago on *The Mike McManus Show* on TV Ontario, 1977:

> *McManus: Way back in the early fifties you predicted that the world was becoming a global Village.*
>
> *McLuhan: We are going back into the bicameral mind that is tribal, collective, without any individual consciousness.*
>
> *McManus: But, it seems, Dr. McLuhan, that this tribal world is not friendly.*
>
> *McLuhan: No, tribal people, one of their main kinds of sport is butchering each other. It is a full-time sport in tribal societies.*
>
> *McManus: But I had some idea as we got global and tribal, we were going to try to...*
>
> *McLuhan: The closer you get together, the more you like each other? There is no evidence of that in any situation that we have ever heard of. When people get close together, they get more and more savage and impatient with each other.*
>
> *McManus: Why is it? Is it because of the nature of man?*
>
> *McLuhan: His tolerance is tested in those narrow circumstances very much. Village people are not that much in love with each other. The global village is a place of a very arduous interfaces and very abrasive situations.*

Discovering that interview, I realized that I should not have been surprised to discover the initial configuration of the global brain reflecting the reality McLuhan described. But it did surprise me. What motivated me to build fiber-optic Ethernet To The Home (ETTH)[lvi] in the early 1990s – later know as IEEE Ethernet in the First Mile (EFM) – was enthusiasm for the most beneficial uses common today. Self-directed learning, better home-to-school communication, home schooling and unschooling, telemedicine and medical research acceleration, remote-work, and ultimately, as later realized, the fulfillment of leisure promised in a 200-year-old failure-to-pay social contract.[lvii]

More than half a century ago, McLuhan clarified these issues while articulating the challenges of how a healthy global brain functions in the context of a whole Gaian body. What is the objective origin and nature of the natural human capacity for insight beyond our local linear-time-timeline context, such as McLuhan and so many others demonstrate? Free lunch for anyone with good suggestions.

* * *

Open-Source Civilization

> *In the beginning, back when Remington Rand's Univac 1, the DEC PDP-1, and IBM System 360 ruled the computing world, all software was open-source software. This means that anyone could take the source code and modify and improve it to meet their own needs. Early software was created by government agencies and schools. In the interest of getting programs up and running they'd share their source code either with programmer to programmer swaps or via user groups such as IBM Share and DEC DECUS.*
>
> *As time passed, several events came together, which led to the rise of proprietary software. First, as computers became more standardized, original equipment manufacturers (OEMs) began bundling software with their hardware. Typically the price of the software was included with the computers. Then, 1969's United States vs. IBM antitrust suit ruled that it was anticompetitive for IBM to give away its software. This was followed by the 1974 US Commission on New Technological Uses of Copyrighted Works (CONTU) which decided that computer programs could be copyrighted. Combine this with the growing cost of developing software, and conditions were ripe for a new kind of business: Selling closed-source, proprietary software.*[lviii]

It sounds like a science fiction mad social scientist's experimental dream to leverage the tools of PR, captology, social engineering, and social media to effectively dupe an entire population into believing There Ain't No Such Thing As A Free Lunch (TANSTAAFL) when the truth is not only that There Is Such Thing As A Free Lunch (TISTAAFL), it's closer to All Free Lunch (AFL) when understood from the operative abstraction layer of stark actuality (xxvii). It's eminently forgivable for mindful observers of the 20th century to perceive some pattern recognition with respect to parts of those kinds of scenario which played out over the past 100 years. No need for tinfoil hats, it's not conspiracy, it's history. Besides, we may need titanium-foil in the 21st century.

From today's frame-of-reference, many of the most predominant 20th century default consensus narratives seem absurd and completely beyond relevance more often than not. In an open-source civilization, both free as in libre *and* free as in lunch have become the post-scarcity DCNRs of the 21st century. A flourishing open-source civilization actively discourages freeloading while encouraging and rewarding contribution and participation. It's simply *the way the world works* in the 21st century, regardless of the occasional distant barking and yapping of, "how will people gain dignity," echoing from a long bygone millennium.

Yet, like the proverbial baby elephant chained at the ankle from birth, conditioned to believe that it can't possibly leave its circus ring, many are still hard-wired into the previous millennium's TANSTAAFL closed-system worldview.[lix] Today, it's increasingly scientifically likely that the apparently closed-systems that we micro-myopically observe up close – down to the Planck scale, anyway, which isn't really all that high-resolution as we look closer – are more accurately described as dense aggregates of an unlimited open-system that extends far beyond our fishbowl, far outside of the range of the hominid functionality of our human sensory instrumentation to perceive.

In the Post-Automation Era, there are no mathematical, logical, or defensible intellectual reasons remaining to support, let alone justify continuation of the useful mistaken delusions of the 20th century. Have our limited incremental understandings served as well throughout history? Of course. At the same time, when new information and new understandings emerge, we adjust according to the new conditions. Except for those dark periods in history where we went backward, which has happened in the past, and in many respects may explain what has just occurred over the most recent 50 years or so.

Today, all of the world's greatest scientific minds are exploring what it means to be more than ten years beyond the concept of a contiguous comprehensible Newtonian-Einsteinian spacetime as we understood it through the lenses of the Standard and Quantum Models. Maybe that view, like the illusion of three dimensions when we look through a blue lens and a red lens with 3D glasses, was never real in the first place. Maybe it was only the 20th century's view of a hologram of a hologram.

If you think that we are drifting into science fiction, la-la land, then I invite you to listen to any of the most recent interviews with a number of science researchers and interviewers who are having this conversation in the online public square in a way that was never before possible. *This* is one of the best manifestations of the value and utility that those of us for whom participated in the early wiring up of our global brain hoped. Open-access science, democratic discovery, and distributed peer participation in the leading edge of knowledge discovery and creation for anyone, anywhere on the planet, regardless of background or economic predisposition.

The Post-Automation Era isn't some far-fetched distant utopia, it's descriptive of everyday activity in the first half of the 21st century.

> *So in other words, for them, what we've done is we've made this discrete network thing which, on a large scale, is like the Einstein equations. Now, normally when they deal with the Einstein equations, they start with these mathematical equations and then they usually use our product Mathematica, to kind of grind through and understand how those equations are set up. And then eventually they'll get sort of simplified equations and then they'll say, okay, now we're going to put this on a computer, but the way they do those solutions is to assume that space is kind of broken into pieces just for the sake of the computer. They don't imagine space really works that way; they're just doing that for the sake of the computer, right? <u>But in our models, space really works that way</u>.*
>
> *And what's kind of neat is that our models are actually a good method for doing numerical general relativity. And now, the thing that I find really fun, is there are starting to be some groups using these, and I*

> *think for them, if there's something that is a deviation between our models and general relativity, it's like, "this is really terrible!" For us, it's like, fantastic! Now we can see the discreteness of space.*
>
> *And that's one of the things that's pretty interesting. We're starting to see, starting to try to tease out effects that allow one to detect the discreteness of space. So, one way to put it is Brownian motion was the thing that clinched it for molecules. We want to find the analog of Brownian motion for physical space.*
>
> *What is that thing that is some short noise in the gravitational radiation from emerging black holes? What is that difference in the ring-down speed when black holes merge, that's associated with discreteness? What's the difference in the way frame dragging works around a black hole, associated with the discreteness of space? We don't know the length scale for the discreteness of space, just like people didn't know how big molecules were. So, it's a lot smaller than the Planck length, we know that. But we don't know how much smaller; and you know, it could be that it's out of the range of what we can experimentally detect.*[lx]

The most observant human thinkers on the planet have been contemplating ways to get to the elemental length scale of the discreteness of space itself, far smaller than the Planck scale, since the 1980s. A scale so subtle that it is as yet un-named and perhaps forever outside of the range of our human instrumentation – biological, physical, mental, cognitive, emotional, psychological – to ever detect or comprehend.

Perhaps these Post-Automation Era scientific breakthroughs educe more humility than many brilliant human minds can bear to contemplate. The fact that the work cited above was not general public knowledge until now does not change the fact that it is only one tiny example of comprehensive and transformative scientific work that is either already completed or vigorously underway. Literally defining and co-creating the way forward on today's 21st century scientific frontiers. And it's all open-access, open-source. Just another day in the open-source civilization of the Post-Automation Era.

It sometimes seems hard to believe that it has already been a quarter of a century shaking off the brain fog of so many DCN trances, and yet many still have not yet done so, nor do some wish to accept just how far we have already surpassed the kitschy, even goofy red-and-blue lensed 20th century conceptions of spacetime and material reductionism, let alone equally illusory misconceptions about the impossibility of achieving human-scale goals such as ending poverty as we've known it once and for all.

The Post-Automation Era is far from anything resembling utopia, so we will simply have to settle for contending with it in its extant, irreducible, irrefutable present moment form, imperfections, and all.

While 20th century reductionism may now be considered as dubious as the earlier clockwork cosmos, each of those methods enabled humans to delineate the structure and shape of our fishbowl-like-existence at the time, while helping stretch our thoughts, sensory perceptions, ways of discovering, exploring, and even our instinct to name all things in creation by putting words to the inexpressible through incremental empirical narrative constructs (cccxl). Scientific storytelling is the inescapably subjective practice behind all *objective and empirical* scientific practice. Have you ever seen a grant awarded without storytelling, however data-driven?

Objectivity is the name of one kind of powerful default consensus narrative reality (DCNR, see Glossary). Objectivity is an adjective, noun, and adverb. Objectivity also describes a state of perception resulting from engaging in a set reproducible, socially-engineered best practices for defining particular types and categories of human observer in-group coordinating behaviors, within which we compare, contrast, and contest our individual *subjective* experiences to arrive at a state of observational or experiential narrative consensus. The label *objective truth* is a pointer to a DCNR. Nothing more, nothing less. That's nothing to scoff at or to readily dismiss. At the same time, contemplating objectivity as a DCNR can also help us escape one of the traps we set for ourselves by virtue of our understandable desire for certainty and predictability amidst the rulial complexity of whatever lies beyond the Standard Model.

The fact that my own puny understanding of what constitutes objective reality has changed in the face of new data so much over time ought to inform my own static notion of the proposition known as empirical objectivity. Weighing the testimony of the sea-changes in perception and human understanding of the natural world over the entire course of the scientific enterprise definitely tips the scales to a statistically significant degree, even further away from static conceptions of the proposition.

Overwhelming historic prevalence proves the notion of objectivity as one of the most remarkable and useful subjective-perception and narrative-alignment constructs ever devised by humans; while impressively, irrefutably, and inherently subjective in qualia, in essence.

Unless we can prove that we are The Grand Empirical Objective Observer that is somehow qualitatively and authoritatively more trustworthy or valid than any other human observer's subjective observing experience, then *our own sense of objectivity is also inherently subjective*, regardless of how robustly informed and temporally supple our experience and interpretation of material events and phenomena through the affordances of our biological sensor array may seem, to us.

If all perception occurs only inside our own skulls, then we may take tribal comfort in the social consensus of similar biologically configured hominids self-reporting similar or identical subjective experiences and observations from within their similar skulls, using similar calipers, weights, and measures; however, there is no getting around the inherently subjective nature of *their* human experience, and therefore, if we are of the same species, ours as well. Pedantic and tautological, perhaps, and maddeningly true.

To proclaim ourselves The Objective Observer seems like a bold claim for the scientific enterprise to make from its lofty, precarious precipice, reached by an incredibly inspired and inspiring 2,500-year climb. As irritating, juvenile, or solipsistic as this line of reasoning may strike some, this is the most *objective* understanding of the nature of material reality that we have managed to produce after decades of smashing particles into one another while still dropping bombs upon one another.

Particularly after such a long run of murderous monkey mayhem, the fact that we exist as humans on this planet at all seems as close to empirical evidence of amazing grace as anything I can imagine. Your tradition might phrase it differently.

If this line of inquiry seems ineffectively esoteric, it becomes up close and personal in recognition of the precious and precarious fragility of every human being on the planet (xx). At any moment, any of us can disappear or be disappeared in more ways than imaginable. It's a disquieting thought to know that predatory hardliner materialist kidnappers can easily leverage a world of engineered economic precarity to hire a lost soul for a couple of hundred dollars to abduct us and hold us at gunpoint with the question, "now what, subjective-reality-boy?" Does that violence therefore prove the rabid materialist's case, or does it prove our case of the existence of the unseen realms of bitterness, jealousy, resentment, hatred, and fear that motivates such violent behavior against others? Absent those unseen forces, such actions simply do not materialize in the world. That's why the entire administration of justice focuses upon means, motives, and then methods.

It's the high-status, the wealthy and temporarily powerful who feel the greatest potential for loss of their position in human dominance hierarchies. A certain level of means (wealth, money, possessions, credentials) can cultivate uncharitable and even malevolent motives, all on their own, for certain personality disordered types. Given ready access to seemingly undiscoverable methods for eradicating any perceived threats to such relative positions of power can be enough to complete that toxic trifecta. Means cultivated motives which then provided access to methods not available to the vast majority. This unfortunate impersonal process can become very personal when some people choose to employ defensive methods in an offensive manner. Either with the justification of preempting some perceived inevitable attack, or simply to get what one wants because now one can. The perceived inevitability of attack is often the result of projection. This can motivate an aggressive or assertive personality style, a person who assumes all other humans are like them, to preemptively aggress against others in the name of defending themselves, without realizing that they are the only actors in the scene behaving in the very way that they accuse others of behaving. That's projection.

According to The Black Swan Group (BSG), "There are many different types of people in this world, but there are only three types of negotiators: Analysts, Accommodators, and Assertives."[lxi] It's no surprise that the ancient evolutionary world often showered favor upon the most assertive people, promoting them upward in dominance hierarchies.

This makes sense as an explanation as to why it can seem impossible to imagine that our recognition and acceptance of our frailty can become one of our greatest adaptive advantages, over the long run. Particularly in the context of an increasingly technologically-mediated mind-melded and in many ways -muddled early 21st century. Paradoxically, the acceptance of weakness and frailty could be like the weak force in physics that not only holds the whole fishbowl together but opens into the spaciousness within which our fishbowl world exists. When I am weak, then I am strong.[lxii] But how and why could that kind of weakness work, *empirically* and *objectively* in a world so vehemently red in tooth and claw? The active words above are, over the long run. Dominating and winning in the present moment is all that matters to the most blindly assertive. In such a mind there is no long run, or the long run is much shorter in comparison to the perspective of an Analyst or Accommodating negotiator type. In fact, a sensibility, or a bias toward short-, mid-, or long-termism (a hotly contested current term) may correlate with the BSG three negotiator types. This is speculation on my part, but it's possible that Assertives are most interested in and committed to the shortest term while Analysts favor the longest-term perspective when deciding upon how to act in the world. Accommodators, true to the name, may feel life is a kind of eternal lonely struggle and burden to balance the two in order to keep the peace insofar as possible; satisfied to practice a precautionary principle of avoiding short-term conflict *in the name* of long-term harmony, settling for mid-term predictability.

That mini thought exercise evokes an assortment of trade-offs between the three when contemplating the incomprehensible unlikelihood of our current mode of existence compared to, and from the perspective of, our thirteenth to eighteenth-century clockwork cosmos cousins. Imagine attempting to describe what it's like to live in and Open-Source Civilization to people whose proven adaptive strategy is to be loyal to the nearest assertive king or warlord, or else. We already spoke to the preferred tactics of the assertive warlords of constructivist materialism.

Peace seems like the most absurd and impractical response to such aggression. How can something as pathetically weak as gentleness possibly work over the short-, medium-, or long-run? Nonaggression seems like a permanent losing strategy in response to belligerence, and it is, in the midst of any moment that demands either decisive defensive action or unfathomable acceptance of harm or death to oneself. If survival of the human animal is the measure of success, then peace and pacifism are eternally doomed.

If that's the case, how can there be any remaining peacekeepers left on planet Earth in the 21st century? It seems impossible, by definition of the red-in-tooth-and-claw worldview. Why haven't the apex predators and oppressors within a misanthropic, self-destructive humanity eradicated every last trace of such pathetic weakness from the species? They've had 12,000 Holocene years to do so, not to mention something like six million years before that, and yet still have failed. Some people say that the weak only survive because the strong have protected, coddled, and enabled that weakness for six million years too long and should therefore finally stop that, today. Apparently, it is very hard to be a Hominin in a 21st century Post-Automation Era Open-Source Civilization that works for everyone. So much so, that some consider a world that works for everyone to be a dystopian vision. "Peace on Earth, goodwill toward men," is nothing more than a kitschy holiday marketing slogan, impossible in their default consensus narrative reality.

It's no wonder that a two-century tsunami of technological change that reflects a continuously accelerating universe beyond all human comprehension left 20th century humanity dizzy, drunk, stoned, depressed, and disoriented. Look no further for evidence of the fallout of all that anomie than the initial worldwide reaction to the late 2023 release of ChatGPT in the form of manifestos and signed political agreements to stop everything and "align AI with human values," utterly devoid of the most rudimentary credible definition of what constitutes "human values."

Punching a time-clock in a clockwork universe of neatly fitting gears and cogs feels much more reassuring than infinite expansion of incomprehensible intelligence and the commensurate personal responsibility of amplified individual human agency in all directions, across all dimensions, beyond the notion of space-time itself. A technologically mediated sense of discontinuous exaptation is extremely hard to understand and communicate because our brains developed in and for survival in such an altogether different environment.

Even when the outcomes are obvious, staring us right in the face every day, it's still difficult to comprehend just how effectively the DCNs of an era define a population's (in)ability to think about the nature of the human experience and to engage with the distinct challenges of the times at hand. Default consensus narratives like the scientific fact of a clockwork universe lasted half-a-millennium. That's both concrete historicity and hard to wrap one's mind around.

In a clockwork society, fears that the slightest tinkering with institutional mechanisms will break familiar patterns of life are understandable. The precautionary principle reigns supreme. Even during the first two decades of the 21st century, organizations, businesses, universities, markets, governments, all reflected the legacy of a clockwork universe (non)sensibility, complete with punching of time clocks which had nearly nothing to do with legitimate value creation or genuine productivity (see Glossary, Quiet Quitting). This observation forces us to acknowledge that we may be contending with something closer to an 800-year de facto reign of the clockwork universe meme rather than a mere 500 years.

In the 21st century, we understand that our planet, ecologies, and economies are all more like living systems than mechanical clockworks. As the human body places respiration and circulation on autopilot because those functions are so vital, economies require autonomous aspects, as well. Circulation, respiration. On the macro level, we're further faced with the unique 21st century challenge of understanding how an augmented global brain integrates with and functions in the context of an organic Gaian body.

Biological metaphors improve upon clockwork metaphors of previous centuries. Like environmental and biological systems, economic systems also consist of seemingly fixed ecological features and organs that are in reality always adjusting to conditions. That's what living systems do. Nations, states, counties, cities, corporations, universities, and other organizations. Each consists of sets of constantly changing and adapting components, infrastructure, associations, computers, people. The sandstone, brick, or marble edifice of every mighty and stable institution, while appearing fixed in frame and function, merely provides a set, setting, and stage upon which events unfold and processes occur in a constant state flux. "All the world's a stage."[lxiii]

While DCNRs like the field of economics can seem immutable, markets and monetary institutions are also ever-developing. Like marble edifices, academic disciplines seem composed of immovable frameworks, well-tested and proven analytical rubrics, and tools for coordinating predictable, reliable, repeatable processes.

Yet, the entire purpose of a PhD is to expand the horizon of previous understanding through novel insights, perspectives, and discoveries that may at first seem to fall entirely outside of and beyond the scope of existing understanding. Sometimes, huge breakthroughs leave hulking marble edifices in ruins. When working well, fresh insights and findings serve to reorganize our previous understanding into a more accurate, nuanced, or extended understanding of a given discipline. The juxtaposition of stability and ingenuity colors the entire history of economic theory and practice.

The emergence of the field of behavioral economics was a first-class example of the evolutionary nature of default consensus narratives. While seeded in the 18th century, it was the 1980's before this academic discipline sprung to life in the significant way that we understand it, today. Behavioral economics gradually and then suddenly proved to us that humans are *Predictably Irrational,* as Dan Ariely's 2008 pivotal work put it.

Needless to say, there is nothing divinely and permanently ordained about the way economies work. No scripture says, "Thou shalt not establish central banks," or, "Thou shalt not change the appearance or denominations of a currency."

Economics is not a hard science like metallurgy, or physics. Nevertheless, the closed-systems principle of TANSTAAFL – There Ain't No Such Thing As A Free Lunch – became a convenient, smart-and-authoritative-sounding, therefore powerful meme in the 20th century. TANSTAAFL is an exemplar of a principle I call *metavalent stigmergy*.[lxiv]

Originally, the TANSTAAFL generalization had little to do with the economic consciousness of everyday life in everyday minds. Yet, it made sense to everyday people, workers, farmers, who knew that if they didn't tend crops there would be no crops. If they didn't hunt there would be no dinner. Over time, with later stigmergic boosts from the likes of Heinlein and Friedman in the 1960's, TANSTAAFL became an almost indomitable default consensus narrative reality, a kind of virtually unquestionable social certainty that shaped an increasingly punitive default consensus reality for everyone. TANSTAAFL ascended to the narrative commanding heights of "the way things are," for decades. To not recite the catechism was heresy at best and deemed out of touch with reality at worst. TANSTAAFL also eventually metastasized into some of its most malignant misinterpretations. For example:

Because TANSTAAFL, nothing you can ever do for the entire duration of your human existence can ever entirely pay your lunch debt; an impossible burden with which you were born. You may never stop, never rest, and if you do, you shall be ostracized as a slovenly hippie, loser, communist, bum.

If that sounds a bit harsh and contemptuous, it's because it is. The most assertive negotiator types might toss in a good, "It is what it is, get over it, snowflake," just for kicks. This is also how bullies work. When they know they can't get away with the more aggressive physical tactics they'd prefer to unleash upon us, they turn to verbal, and reputation attacks. Social triangulation and similar nasty tactics in order to maintain status, even in a dysfunctional hierarchy. The more dysfunctional the hierarchy, the more dissociative and malevolent the tactics.

To what extent is TANSTAAFL still prevalent on everyday job sites in the United States in the 21st century? It might as well have been carved on stone tablets on every job site I ever worked on over the past five decades, but has the situation changed?

How is the unforgivable, unpayable TANSTAAFL debt belief

substantially different from a Darwinian doctrine of original sin?

Except, here's what we know today. More than a decade beyond completion of the Standard Model of physics, TANSTAAFL was only ever 4% to 5% accurate, at most. It only applied to 4% to 5% of whatever the heck the fullness of reality is, because as noted earlier, TANSTAAFL is *a closed-system principle* that describes only a fraction of what may or may not be a closed system, entirely subject to the nature of the remaining 95% to 96% of inscrutable reality beyond our fishbowl reality delineated by the Standard Model. I don't choose the word inscrutable lightly.

Beyond the Planck length or time scale, the reductionist rules of physics literally cease to make sense. Our entire existence becomes mathematically and structurally incomprehensible (Hoffman, et al).

This makes TANSTAAFL, like the clockwork universe, into an ancient relic of a past that no longer exists except in the form of a deprecated DCN within a very particular and peculiar cultural context that exists only in the minds and memories of those who lived through those past events. Driven by the wind and tossed upon the turbulent seas of economic struggle in the 20th century, western culture clung to TANSTAAFL like an anchor to help us feel more or less stable.

In the Post-Automation Era, if we fail to let go of that anchor around our commonwealth neck and let it sink to the bottom of that ancient ocean of fear, scarcity, gloom, and doom that flooded the imaginations of past generations, it may become difficult to ever find our heads above water again. Let. It. Go.

TANSTAALF only felt true in the day-to-day life of that closed-system troglodyte understanding of the universe, and upon even moderately closer examination, it fell apart even then. Here's how. Any fruit-bearing crop we raise produces such a super-abundance of food that we can't possibly consume it all ourselves. Farmers also knew this, from the dawn of agriculture.

One fruit tree in the yard expresses nature's inherent superabundance.

One fruit tree in our yard proves nature's impulse to oversupply free lunch to as many as possible. There's more free food flying off the branches than the individual who planted and tended it could ever consume. That's the superabundance originated in the dirt of this good Earth. Nature's super abundance is right there for anyone with eyes to see and hands to pick a hundred varieties of legendary Florida oranges, or Washington state apples.

Whether apples or oranges, when robots pick the majority or all of that fruit, does the cost of food approach the marginal cost of robot labor – nearly zero – or does the 20th century DCNR of rewarding relentless rent-seeking wreck the whole of history's trek toward a world that works for everyone?

What we know is that nature's intrinsic super abundance automatically rewards our individual work in such a manner that one person's relatively modest effort feeds dozens. Hunters faced the same predicament. One huge kill created immediate superabundance for that hunter. There was no way they could consume all of that meat before it rotted. Nature compels us to share. Food preservation was one of the first *unnatural* human technologies to defy nature's impulse to provide abundantly. How then, did we become so completely disconnected from nature's intrinsic superabundance?

Maybe today, some ancestors of those hunters and gatherers who didn't ever make the adjustment of the past two centuries of rapid transformation continue to resent nature's sharing instinct. Like an instantiation of Richard Dawkins's *Selfish Gene,* perhaps the hunter gene believed that it and it alone was the one and only best gene ever, and it was fighting for its own survival. Maybe that was a gene that believed everyone should only ever eat what they personally kill, and it asserted itself through some of its unwitting hosts in direct contradiction to what both Mother Nature and Creation clearly prove otherwise. That would certainly be one narcissistically selfish gene. Superabundance is the manifest inclination of both farming and hunting. It turns out that it was never nature that was scarce in the way that the industrial scarcity meme took hold, it was only humanity's scarcity of understanding of *the way nature's superabundance works* that frightened us into extraction and hoarding behaviors that become a self-fulfilling scarcity prophesy.

The selfishness of the hunter gene had nothing on the farmer gene. The selfish farmer gene's legacy is that somehow others might get away with relaxing while we tended the crops. Maybe it's a version of the Mary and Martha story, for those who are familiar, or the parable of the eleventh-hour workers in the field. Instead of FOMO, it was FOAFL, Fear Of A Free Lunch. The fear that somebody might get an apple, orange, or a chicken leg they didn't deserve, and it was conveniently always up to us, of course, to judge who's deserving and who isn't. This notion of *deservingness* was a huge deal for humans in the 20th century.

What does it mean to be deserving of the basic human needs for subsistence? Hunter, farmer, father, mother, sister, brother, son, or daughter, everyone contributes something of tangible economic value to this world by their very existence in human form. Try to tell any parent of a mobility or cognitively challenged child that their child is of no intrinsic value. To negate the notion of intrinsic value for the conventionally embodied is logically and intellectually inconsistent at best. I understand that some people dislike or disapprove of creation's declaration of intrinsic human worth, so thank you for the opportunity to address that perspective.

If someone is angry that nature is intrinsically superabundant; that every human embodies intrinsic economic worth; if one is upset that an imaginary other might get a free lunch; or if someone is resentful that today's youth *might not need to go through the same depths of hell previous generations went through*; and if such a person engages in coercive measures to make certain that all other beings *must* experience the same hellish hazing they had to experience, what does that say about such a person?

What does it say about a society that consciously chooses to perpetuate that kind of DCR? What does it say about my character, were I to become so aloof and indifferent as to become supportively complicit in the perpetuation of that kind of society?

Today we know that society and economies are not like clockworks, they are like living systems. We know that both hunters and gatherers understood and lived in the midst of both the severity and grace of nature's intrinsic superabundance. The more things change, the more they stay the same. Today, nature still provides overwhelming superabundance for anyone with ownership rights to even a modest parcel of land. The point to revisit is that once someone plants an apple or orange tree, the marginal tending needed is comparatively minimal to the superabundance produced. Are there dependencies upon weather, etc.? Of course. The point is, all things held equal, the marginal return on investment of a single planting is superabundant for the life of the average fruit tree. In the most practical and pragmatic sense, money does grow on that tree. Money is a simple first-derivative function of a tree's fruit. The moment we exchange any of a tree's produce for paper, we've effectively grown money on trees. So not only is TANSTAAFL thoroughly debunked, but money does also grow on trees.

Can we partner with nature to multiply and optimize her free lunch to yield even more? Of course we can, and have, resulting in today's artificially intelligent tractors, managed, and operated from outer space via GPS in the countryside and vertical farms in the urban core. It's not science fiction, it's 2024.

> *Vertical farming is the practice of producing food and medicine in vertically stacked layers, vertically inclined surfaces and/or integrated in other structures (such as in a skyscraper, used warehouse, or shipping container). The modern ideas of vertical farming use indoor farming techniques and controlled-environment agriculture (CEA) technology, where all environmental factors can be controlled. These facilities utilize artificial control of light, environmental control (humidity, temperature, gases ...) and fertigation. Some vertical farms use techniques similar to greenhouses, where natural sunlight can be augmented with artificial lighting and metal reflectors (Wikipedia).*

Nature's superabundance and humanity's superintelligence are the norms of nature, not the exceptions. In the Post-Automation Era, the entire concept of scarcity is an old 20th century fake news meme that successfully kept people terrified for lack of basic human needs, unless they obeyed the rules of a completely make-believe human construct called pre-21st century economics.

At an even deeper level, there is increasingly compelling evidence that the original physics principle of TANSTAAFL was never true in the first place. In his seminal book, *A Universe from Nothing: Why There Is Something Rather than Nothing*, physicist Lawrence Krauss explains that "we have discovered that all signs suggest a universe that could and plausibly did arise from a deeper nothing — involving the absence of space itself."

If Krauss's insight is accurate, then the deeper principle of physics embedded in the very creation of the universe – and therefore the Earth itself as a miniscule component of that universe – is not just TISTAAFL, it's IAFL. It's all free lunch. As it was in the beginning, is now, and ever shall be. This is a principle that Indigenous populations all over the planet independently derived, wherever conditions were suitable to the emergence of human life. From the practice of land crofting in the Scottish Highlands and Isle of Man, to Polynesian and Hawaiian principles of the ahupua ʻ a, people understood that everything from nature is a free gift, that water is life, that our task is to be grateful human beings and good stewards, taking only what we need while giving all that we can, and then become better at having a healthy relationship with one another in the context of the post-scarcity superabundance that always existed on Earth. Robots are great, and there's more than one way to skin a singularity, because the principles of superabundance were always inherent, from the beginning.

Like Neo in the Matrix, just about everything we've understood about the concept of scarcity was based upon fundamental misunderstandings combined with outright lies. Our own lack of awareness, exploited by social-engineered gaslighting, in the name of establishing and sustaining social dominance hierarchies.[lxv]

In the 21st century we know that those 20th century mythologies and misconceptions no longer serve our best interests, that healthy economies function like biological bodies, not like 17th century clocks. And in the biological model, if 80% of a body's blood supply becomes clotted in 1% or 2% of its mass, the entire body dies. It has nothing to do with what's right or fair to individual blood cells, to the organs involved, to particular subsystems, or to the whole body. Lack of healthy circulation leads to death of a human body and death of an economy. Currency is the life-blood of an economy. Conceptions of right and fair are meaningless to the healthy function of both. Life is no longer about contentious, toxic, zero-sum 20th century memes of wealth redistribution, it's about stabilizing and supporting healthy currency circulation.

Because economies are like biological systems, when we speak in fixed, rigid, mechanistic scarcity-based terms about income or wealth inequality, we completely miss the point. If a body's circulatory resources are not in a dynamically balanced flow state, that body dies. In living systems of all kinds, dynamic equilibrium is always changing in response to the reality of untold numbers of variables converging in the experience of the present moment. To promote the oversimplification of a crude bi-variable supply and demand curve as descriptive of market equilibrium in the 21st century Post-Automation Era is the economic equivalent of bloodletting in medical practice, today.

In economies, *currency goes into circulation* as a continuous flow. We do not ship currency to neighborhood distribution warehouses like Amazon products. That's not how currency works. Currency is recirculated, not redistributed. Semantics matter. In the 21st century, the fake news meme of wealth redistribution is an absurdly antiquated factory-era misunderstanding about how the flow of currency through a living economy works.

Biological systems don't care about our ideologies or political perspectives. Biological systems don't care about our opinions. Biological systems do their best to adjust to conditions. So do living economies. Intricate, interdependent subsystems within both living biological systems and economies operate within relatively narrow ranges when healthy. We can force economies to run temporarily outside of their capabilities, just like we can dope our human bodies beyond their capabilities. Or we can extend both economies and bodies with cyborg-like superhuman capabilities, as we have also done since the dawn of time. The point is, it's not only inept and ineffective to reduce the reality of 21st century complex dynamic systems equilibrium to two 17th century variables of supply and demand, but also absurd. We've been living in a cyborg world of hybrid cyborg market systems for decades and pretending that the principles of horse and buggy are the only way we can ever understand, interpret, or interact with the world. It's officially no longer hyperbole to state: that's crazy.

Widely misunderstood by the general public, it is no longer harmless to allow entertainment-driven misconceptions of the word cyborg to persist. A cyborg is not simply *The Six Million Dollar Man*[lxvi] or *The Bionic Woman*.[lxvii] Cyborgs are not utopian science fiction or a nickname for a government brain-chip conspiracy. It's a fact that we've been cyborgs for a very long time.

Stop by any active construction site and admire any heavy equipment operator who can palpably feel the earth they're moving, or any crane operator who unmistakably feels the structure they are building, and you're watching everyday cyborgs at work.

Scuba divers are cyborgs, as are astronauts. Without the "outside regulatory interference" of life support systems maintaining adequate oxygen and monitoring bodily function, humans are incapable of operating in such environments. The body's marketplace of goods and services; its tissues, organs, limbs, blood cells, etc., simply cease to function when pushed too far outside of their organically defined limits. Likewise economic systems. Massive wealth consolidation functions just like a blood clot. It has nothing to do with notions of fairness, it has to do with sustainable circulation, flow.

When an advanced, post-automation economy like our own becomes so efficient at generating and consolidating superabundant wealth, it is a manifestation of both great foresight and profound foolishness. Brilliant foresight in creating the abstraction of currency to drive human behavior in the first place, and foolishness in the lack of understanding for the long-term environmental and social consequences of the very rent-extractive systems of thought and action (DCNRs) that whisked humanity from the agrarian age to the industrial age, to the information age, the automation age, and now to the inflection point of this present moment of exponential opportunity and explosive risk.

Repeating dysfunctional patterns seems to be one of the things that historical humans did best. We don't have to adopt those maladaptive behaviors. It's not a political statement to observe that any economic body that coagulates 80% of its currency within 1% or 2% of its population effectively creates a fatal, terminal blood clot. It's not a moral, religious, philosophical, or political question. Blood clots are a completely dispassionate symptom of unhealthy biological living systems. Currency clots are the economic system equivalent.

Our own biological bodies do not care if the clot is in our pinky toe, our spleen, or in our brain. Blood clots kill. They can kill gradually, then suddenly. Blood clots kill gradually as they pile up, often with no symptoms for an extended time. Sometimes they kill with no symptoms at all, until they grow to just the right size that all flows cease. When they strike in the brain, it's called a stroke.

Our national and global economies have been in critical condition, on various forms of life support, since at least 2008. There's no guarantee that either will make it out of the intensive care unit when the next stroke or heart attack hits. What we do know is that for any economy in such a state to revive and survive, we must surgically remove, permanently dissolve, or route around blockages.

For an economy, we can do this through practical, non-partisan tax reforms, like land value tax, which we'll address in more detail later. Instead of massive emergency QE blood transfusions to the brain, we can install a reliable pacemaker in the form of "a guaranteed annual income at levels that sustain life in decent circumstances (MLK)."

By applying the same methods to an economy on the brink of complete circulatory collapse as we apply to a body, we restore healthy systolic and diastolic pressure. The difference is that whereas the body circulates blood, an economic circulatory system circulates currency.

The principle of income security is to an economy what stable blood pressure is to a biological body.

How we do this, matters equally to the why of adapting to the new environment. We've seen the results of panic-jamming blood directly into a collapsing circulatory system in traditional QE, without first removing the clots. The result? Artificial stability until the clots form again, usually in the same place. It's a bit of a *duh* moment, right? Without healthy circulation at the capillary level, no amount of new blood will keep the patient healthy for long. Filling the heart or brain with unlimited supplies of donated blood does nothing if the capillaries are not actively nourished by a sustainable systemic flow at the furthest edges of the system.

The economic equivalent to biological capillaries is citizens wallets and the economic equivalent to capillary exchange is the universal access to goods and services that currency provides.

Income security means stable currency circulation. It is not about mandating equal amounts of income or wealth. It is about attaining and sustaining a natural, parasympathetic, economic flow state.

Income security as a human right does not mean, in the memorable words of Neil Peart, "the trees are all kept equal; by hatchet, axe, and saw."[lxviii] It means that the economic body's circulatory system achieve and maintains a normalized flow via dividends indexed to 50% per capita GDP, a bare minimum for economic homeostasis at the capillary level while fulfilling King's definition of "a guaranteed annual income at levels that sustain life in decent circumstances."

As Martin Kirk wrote for Fast Company:

> *... yes, all other things being equal, economic growth is a positive thing. <u>But all other things are not equal</u> ... for all its positives, economic growth has a dark side; its ecological impact.*[lxix] *The impacts of our ever-growing economy have become so stark and so widespread that they are by any sane measure portents to catastrophe. Whether it's the fact that Antarctic ice is now melting three times faster than we thought, or the unfolding "biological annihilation" that has already wiped out 50% of all animals and up to 75% of all insects, or the fact that, in spite of all this, we are pumping out CO2 at record levels, it takes willful ignorance or a blinding ideology to deny the severity of the crisis.*
>
> *This creates a terrible paradox: Economic growth keeps economies stable today but threatens not just future growth but medium-term social and civilizational cohesion, and ultimately the very capacity of this biosphere to sustain life.*
>
> *A little thought experiment shows how growth can be a problem: Insert the word "a" before it. "A growth." That feels very different from just*

> *"growth," right? Growth is a big part of what we all understand happens in a healthy life. Children grow, knowledge grows, love grows. But "a growth" is what happens when life gets corrupted. "A growth" is when the growth is unchecked, and thus a symptom not of health but disease; when it takes on the character of an invader, attacking its host. The word for growth that gets out of control in this way, such that it becomes "a growth," is, of course, cancer.*

We see these economic principles reflected in biological processes of circulation, respiration, metabolism, capillary exchange, and healthy function of any biological organism. Well-regulated growth – both biological and economic – is healthy and sustainable growth. When healthy, our bodies evolved to keep this balance without our slightest conscious perception. Applying these proven biological principles to currency circulation is the way to balance the astonishing and unexpected new capabilities of science, technology, and society into and beyond the Post-Automation Era.

* * *

Are Default Consensus Narratives Reality?

The stories we tell ourselves and one another define our lived experience. The human experience is a peculiar construct of words, stories, images, sounds, tastes, touch, feelings, and smells. That is why it is so important to curate the stories with which we indulge our senses and sensibilities with care. When we indulge in the same kind of story enough times and it becomes our lived reality, for better or for worse. There is no dividing or divorcing the marriage of imagination and manifestation on planet Earth. If we fill our eyes, ears, minds, and hearts with ghosts and monsters, we will inevitably come to live among ghosts and monsters. If we fill our hearts with gratitude, peace, and tranquility, we shall surely find our lives reflect serenity and stability. Because some version of the adage "be careful what you wish for," is a widespread cliché across all cultures, it provides compelling evidence that – whether we live in a simulation or not – Earth ARG is a choose-your-own-adventure theater in which we must be careful about which counsel we choose to accept or ignore, to our blessing or peril (xxxi).

In a Weaponized Mass Distraction Economy (WMDE), *intention* is the human capacity that we bring to bear in reclaiming authority over the allocation of our own *attention* in this world and thereby, authorship of our own lives. Intention serves as a course-bearing that focuses our attention on *where we choose to go* rather than forever drifting, blown about, and tossed by the stormy seas of emotion and experience. Intention *sets the course* for the discipline of, "staying the course." If we have no clear intention, no course to stay, we are destined for directionless disarray and a life of seemingly inexplicable dangers, toils, and snares.

But what is the nature of intention and how do we know or decide which intentions to set? Unsurprisingly, intention is both a story and a thesis. Once formulated, stated, and fully committed to, "my intention is X," forms the thesis and plot of our personal biography. Whether or not we accomplish every aspect of our intention is beside the point. Intention sets the story arc. Our responses and interactions with the people, dangers, toils, and snares along the way toward accomplishing an intention reveal and illuminate the character of our story's main character along the way.

Because every take-off is optional and every landing mandatory, every pilot knows that the key to our craft is intense focus upon where we *intend* to land, instantly and deftly neutralizing every gust of distraction we feel from the singular focus on maintaining a stable approach. On-center, parallel, a smooth glide-slope at uniform air-speed. No exceptions or excuses, instantaneously responding and refining our intention with conviction, even in the most subtle adjustments we make in response to the manifest reality of the present moment. Surfers, skiers, skydivers, indeed every athlete shares a similar understanding of non-negotiable imperative of skillful interaction with the intense immediacy of the present micro-moment.

This is why mindfulness, aka prayerfulness, is not mere religious superstition or *woo-woo*, but a specific kind of practical, useful, versatile, precision-focused *tool of intention* that serves as an aircraft yoke or cyclic that steers the course of our lived experience.[lxx] It is *after the journey* that the recollection and retelling of experiences in managing and manifesting earlier forged intentions that become stories – narratives – that subsequently influence others to engage in, or avoid, similar experiences. Stories are the stigmergic substance of default consensus narratives.

Figure 1 — Cycle of Intentionality.

Winning a sports championship is one example of what it looks like to set and hold an intention throughout the entire Cycle of Intentionality. Becoming a notorious gang-boss or drug-lord is another. This is why dismissing destructive, distractive, tasteless, tacky novels, social-media streams, films, or video games as "just stories," can be an extremely dismissive, passive-aggressive gaslight; both toward ourselves and others.

Everything to which we expose our senses is an input to our neural networks, the only training data to which those networks have access for the purpose of defining our perception and understanding of *what the world is*. This is why exposing or subjecting children to disturbing, distressing, traumatic and destabilizing experiences is arguably the worst possible crime against humanity. Long before developing a sense of informed consent or autonomy, adults program children, conditioning them to believe the world is a certain way. All too commonly, that way is our way or the highway, which can be tremendously beneficial, even essential, when the cognitive template and behavioral role model are well-integrated and healthy. However, with training data and protocols designed and intended to serve the best interests of the programmer at the expense of the programmed, that's what we call psychological abuse. This happens in families, companies, churches, political organizations, and in any group of humans large enough to unfortunately invite the statistical odds of dark tetrad[lxxi] personality types to hijack the local égrégore (Figure 2).[lxxii]

The troubling thing to realize is that this kind of conditioning and social engineering can and does happen to kids of all ages. If it didn't, there'd be no such thing as cults. According to the Cambridge Dictionary, a *cult* is, "A system of religious belief, esp. one not recognized as an established religion, or the people who worship according to such a system of belief. *A cult is also something that is very popular with some people*, or a particular set of beliefs or behaviors" (emphasis added). According to the Cambridge Dictionary definition, every corporation, university, school, church, club, fraternal organization, institution, government, gang, tribe, social media influencer fan base, and brand are kinds of cults. Each is *something that is very popular with some people.* Further, what is an *established* religion, other than a non-established religion that reached some inflection point of popularity, some critical mass of adherents?

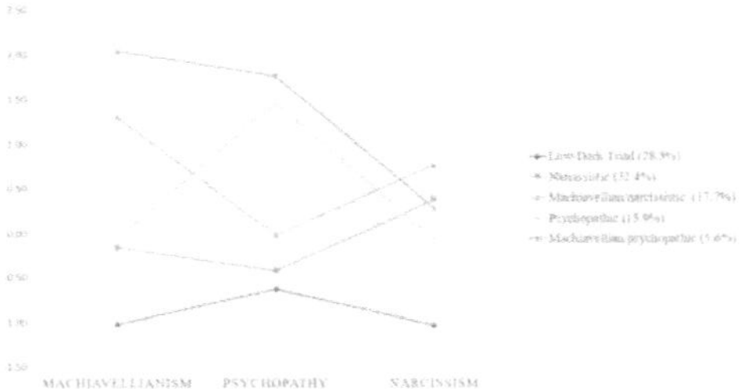

Figure 2 — Dark Triad Traits as Category Indicators.

I asked an AI editorial advisor to combine some common terms and characteristics into a neologism to help us explore this murky narrative terrain. In true collaboration, we produced the term *malcovégore,* meaning any tightly-knit group whose *intention* is covert control and manipulation, both of its own members and targets of its annoyance, indignation, agenda, or wrath.[lxxiii]

A malcovégore is any anti-informed-consent, anti-human-free-agency group or organization. For example, the hate crime of misandry was for too long minimized, dismissed, and discredited in the 20th century because it was most often a covert, psychological, emotional, or social-engineering crime, rather than an easily identifiable overt case of physical domestic abuse. One early capability of our Post-Automation Era digital MITM observation tools was the ability to eavesdrop on such peer-to-peer machinations and expose them in ways that were never before possible (ccxix).

The word stunning is perhaps one of the biggest understatements of the early 21st century when it came to bearing witness to the things that criminal minds openly exposed via unencrypted text messages. Perhaps more karmically entertaining though, was the far greater detail revealed by those who thought they were so clever as to use encryption to avoid and evade accountability, when what encryption also afforded was something called non-repudiation. “Protection against an individual falsely denying having performed a particular action. [T]he capability to determine whether a given individual took a particular action such as creating information, sending a message, approving information, and receiving a message.”[lxxiv]

Those experiences were another kind of unveiling and illumination of the fact that there is nothing mystical about magical powers. We all have magical powers. Today, those magical powers are more highly developed and widely democratized than ever through the affordances of neuro, bio, info, and cognitive technologies of the Post-Automation Era, illustrated by the Cycle of Intentionality in Figure 1, above. Of course, people are capable of putting any tool to good or ill use. Hence, so-called dark magical powers are nothing more and nothing less than the refined, focused, and expertly exercised practice of the Cycle of Intentionality through the everyday human attributes we’ve described. Intention, attention, attunement, entrainment, enticement, entrapment, influence, persistence, intermittent reinforcement, conditioning, coercive social engineering.

As Clarke's Third Law adeptly foretold: "Any sufficiently advanced technology is indistinguishable from magic."[lxxv]

We are exploring here the nature of an unavoidable kind of collective shadow work that we deny, dismiss, devalue, and avoid at great existential risk during any historical collective dark night of the soul. The abruptness of the discontinuous step function from Information Age to Post-Automation Era can't be overstated.

Our human capacity for reality-testing is a profound, fragile, and imminently hackable gift, no matter how impervious we may think we are to assault. One of the most heinous crimes against humanity is to cause someone to doubt their own sensory perceptions, their own direct experience. The term malcovégore illuminates the cockroach crevices between terms like domestic and foreign terrorist, gang, cartel, sleeper cell, rebel army, and radical sect that have contended with the narrative abyss into which we must gaze if we are to reintegrate toward some semblance of holistic neurosecurity in the Post-Automation Era. While equally respecting the weighty implications of the gaze back.

"Darkness cannot drive out darkness; only light can do that. Hate cannot drive out hate; only love can do that."[lxxvi] *Martin Luther King, Jr.*

In traversing treacherous narrative terrain, it does not matter whether or not our perceptions and understandings match some *imagined external objective reality* that has not materialized over the entire 2,500-year course of the scientific enterprise. There is not a single sane, empirically subjective scientific human observer who claims an omniscient perspective, which is the only conceivable *objectively objective* perspective possible. As always, do not believe the author, investigate all of these ancient and contemporary arcana for yourself. Scrutinize everything under the new light of superintelligence that illuminates the 21st century.

The direct, indirect, primary, secondary, basal, and derivative inputs of our direct lived experience – the sensory experiences which our body-minds have absorbed over time – are the only training data to which our individual biological brain GPTs have access.

The only training data to which our neural nets have access and from which we cobble together something resembling what we consider a coherent worldview derives from the moment of birth to experiences in our early homes, interactions with parents, siblings, neighbors, gangs, tribes. The sublime experiential-interpretational body-mind substrate of the structure of our human physique is inconceivably subtle, fragile, exposed, and vulnerable. We are completely dependent, no matter how macho or strong-and-independent we imagine ourselves. We are not. We are utterly dependent upon everything in our environment, from cradle to grave. We are not and cannot be self-made. We are not rugged individuals. Even if there is an omniscient objective frame of reference somewhere in the universe, it is not materially accessible to inherently subjective human beings, no matter how irritating that may seem. There is simply no empirical objectivity to which the cultish objectivist égrégore refers. It doesn't exist. There is no there, there.

Prove absolute external objectivity and I will admittedly, dumbfoundedly change my mind, immediately.

Figure 3 — Art by ChatGPT4's DALL-E Model.

Human beings are the most exposed, vulnerable, defenseless, and hackable cyber-attack surface on Earth. The dark art of captology effectively retooled the most ancient of manipulation and coercion techniques for the digital age during the Web 2.0 era (xxxviii).

The universality of our deep-seated human vulnerability is one of the primary reasons why we wrestle with the pragmatic work of ending suffering for all human beings by hardening the defenses of our soft, squishy, flawed, and frail frames from the relentless attacks of unseen forces, cyber, psychological, emotional, and the invisible hand of economics. Experiencing the extent of human vulnerability up close and personal compelled us toward intense investigation of what it means to cultivate conditions on Earth as it is in Heaven, to work toward a world that works for everyone, a non-utopian, imperfect world gradually improving its capability to rid itself of all forms of deception, fear, lack, trauma, confusion, coercion, and chaos.

The hard, cold reality of our common vulnerability compels us to hold fast to the *intention* of witnessing the end of all hellish embodied human experiences. It is this intention that compels us to dismantle, debunk, and demolish hellish Default Consensus Narratives which serve to perpetuate and extend those hellish realities on Earth. Change the script, change the program. Change the narrative, change the story. Change the story, change the experience.

While it matters not whether chicken or the egg was first, experience or story, imagination or reality, it can help to recall that *in the beginning was the word*. That is why interrupting hellish human narrative loops – individual and collective – breaks hellish human experience cycles, and that's good enough as a definition of what it means to work Toward A World That Works For Everyone.

I can imagine at least one strong, reactive, juvenile objection to this line of reasoning, particularly in the early 21st century social milieu; namely, "In your arrogant, narcissistic, and bigoted certainty of a world that works for *everyone*, you are judging, excluding, and discriminating against anyone who *chooses* hellish demonic thoughts and actions of their own *free will*. So by definition, there is no such thing as your totalitarian utopian world that works for *everyone* because we *like* being defective, deviant, destructive, obnoxious, vile, and disgusting. By your own definition, you don't want us to exist. That makes you a monster that we need to destroy before you destroy us." We might refer to this as The Great Objection.

Wrong. I want all humans to exist. I want the end of distorted and hellish intentionality and experience loops, not the end of people. That's a huge difference.

While the pen may be mightier than the sword and the word active and quick, able to dissect joints from marrow, able to both wound and heal, language is still limited in its ability to express the inexpressible. Perhaps I am discriminating against deception, fear, lack, illness, disease, trauma, confusion, and judgmental toward coercion, cruelty, and chaos on Earth. Also, remember that we began this journey by citing new research that indicates *free will is an illusion*, a proposition intimating that the informed consent of a rational free agent in possession of perfect information could not possibly make the choice to engage in the perpetuation of the evils articulated in The Great Objection.

Finally, there is nothing we can say about the inexplicable paradoxical nature of DCNs to simultaneously comfort and terrify that C.S. Lewis did not make plain more than seventy-five years ago:

> *God is the only comfort. He is also the supreme terror: the thing we most need and the thing we most want to hide from. He is our only possible ally, and we have made ourselves His enemies. Some people talk as if meeting the gaze of absolute goodness would be fun. They need to think again. They are still only playing with religion. Goodness is either the great safety or the great danger—according to the way you react to it. And we have reacted the wrong way... Of course, I quite agree that the Christian religion is, in the long run, a thing of unspeakable comfort. But it does not begin in comfort; it begins in the dismay I have been describing, and it is no use at all trying to go on to that comfort without first going through that dismay. In religion, as in war and everything*

> *else, comfort is the one thing you cannot get by looking for it. If you look for truth, you may find comfort in the end: if you look for comfort you will not get either comfort or truth—only soft soap and wishful thinking to begin with and, in the end, despair.*[lxxvii]

Many, if not most of the earliest scientists were among the most sincere and meticulous people wrestling with the nature of reality in order to understand the nature of God through the expression of our humble local universe. This made the scientific enterprise itself a kind of never-ending interactive story, guided by the most meticulous attentiveness to the matter, people, and phenomena that construct our material surroundings. Science began as a reverse-engineering of our mid-game story.

Science could be reframed as the birth of the most practical applied Attention Economy in human history, to the extent that the scientific revolution, particularly in the realm of astronomy, was largely supported by the privileged activity of monks granted the advantage of sufficient time and solitude to begin *attending* to the wondrous workings of God's creation, meticulously documenting their observations and open-source sharing their notebooks for peer-reviewed cross-check and critique.

What could be more authentic, open, honest, and vulnerable in a day and age in which holy-roller psychopaths wielded ungodly power, to the point of murderously refusing to understand the intent of science to elevate and glorify the miracles of the observable? We might consider this the inverse of The Great Objection. How can a world that works for everyone possibly contain such people? It can't, and it didn't. That's why all that is past, non-existent in this mid-game now, unless beings become triggered by memories and reenact that which otherwise no longer exists. This is one way in which narratives of deep historical grievances can go so wrong; particularly when repeating historical accounts of the same vile and hellish characteristics articulated in The Great Objection results in repeating that behavior in the present. This illustrates how narratives, principles, principalities, and powers constitute the greatest influence in the Earth, not the poisoned people themselves, regardless of status or station. Maybe we need more antidotes and less grappling at one another's throats.

> *What is often less appreciated, however, is that part of the novelty of Newton's achievement lay in his conviction that there were laws of nature there in the first place, awaiting discovery. What, then, are laws of nature, and where do come from? During the middle ages, natural laws were understood to be moral laws that had been established by God. The injunction "Thou shalt not kill" was an example of one such law, assumed to be a universal rule that all civilized societies would observe. However, there was no corresponding notion of universal laws in the natural realm. This idea - laws of nature in the scientific sense - was an innovation of the seventeenth century and was <u>a consequence of the extension of God's legislative moral power to the physical world</u>. One of the pioneers of this new understanding of laws of nature was the French philosopher and scientist Rene Descartes (1596-1650), who wrote that "God alone is the author of all the motions in the world."*[lxxviii]

Those are the origins of this interactive story-co-creation-practice and massively-multiplayer open role-playing game (MMORPG) known as the scientific enterprise. A multi-millennia default consensus narrative reality that effectively guided human activity with a sense of coherent intention and lucid purpose for centuries. That is, right up until we exhausted our capacity for *observing the observable* by this very methodology in 2012, with confirmation of the Higgs Boson, and thereby, completion of the Standard Model of physics. Did completion of the Standard Model mark the end of a game level defined by the hard boundaries and limitations of an organism distinguished by an excruciatingly distinct configuration of highly-constrained sensory apparatus: eyes, ears, nose, tongue, body, and mind?

If the Standard Model marked any kind of ending, it simultaneously marked the beginning of the opportunity to explore new measures of the human capacity for indirect, inductive, and intuitive observation, perhaps in units and increments that we have yet to define. Maybe so far a toward empirical measures of intuition. Can the effects and outcomes of intuition and insight become as reliable and even predictable as the effects and outcomes of intellect and reason? It sounds like a ridiculous contradiction to propose something as absurd sounding as *empirical intuition*. It was also once absurd to suggest a heliocentric universe.

Approaching this inflection point, in the midst of an unprecedented expansion of conscious and sentient meaning-making that marked the most promising new era of discovery in human history, there was also a religious fanatism that sought to center, elevate, celebrate, and worship the basest instincts of the biological human animal. It may have been one of the most anthropocentric and narcissistic absurdities imaginable in the 21st century. It's a miracle that we survived it.

It was the equivalent of insisting that not only is the world flat, with the Sun revolving around the Earth, but that all of creation revolved around you, your muddled monkey mind, your erratic monkey impulses, and dissociative monkey behaviors. It was arguably one of history's most fanatical and pompous religious creeds ever advanced, largely due to the simultaneously condescending and dismissive-avoidant simplicity of its catechism, "You do you." With a false ring of freedom, it promoted only blind faith and slavery to the human biological organism.

Welcome back to the present moment. The year is 2024, with calendar time poised on the cusp of the second quarter of the 21st century, the scientific MMORPG confronted with the predicament of understanding conditions and phenomena at both the micro- and macro- *event horizons of the material realm*. Outward and inward, downward and upward. Suspended at the inward event horizon, toward understanding the hard problem of consciousness, perched at the outward event horizon, toward exploring and inhabiting other planets. Hovering at the downward micro event horizon, toward understanding quantum gravity, and gazing upward toward the macro event horizon toward understanding the cosmic microwave background (CMB).

We seem to be individually and collectively rapt in the nexus of the Observer Effect, complete with its despairingly enmeshed and entangled ambiguity due to the likes of the Hawthorne Effect and dozens of other perplexing phenomena, both material and immaterial, symbolic and non-symbolic (see Glossary).[lxxix]

While gaining an elementary understanding of the indeterminate realm of quantum uncertainty shattered our conventional understanding of the familiar dualities of the Newtonian material realm, it also affirmed the inescapable experiential and experimental reality that the material realm itself is empirically dualistic and binary, decisively defined by polarities of positive and negative charge, north and south direction, male and female in the propagation of every species. Exceptions, as always, further prove the overwhelming prevalence of the binary dual nature of the material realm. Removing binary duality from the material realm literally extinguishes the material realm itself. Without opposites, the dance of potential and kinetic energy ends. No light. No dark. No day. No night. Just bland, static, indistinct, non-binary sameness everywhere, forever. Intergalactic grey goo.[lxxx]

Or maybe that's how a peaceful and stable eternity appears from the perspective of the dissociated and lost. Perhaps, to the disorganized and chaotic mind, harmonious, perpetual, spontaneous organization seems like banal dictatorial uniformity. From the perspective of chaos, the process of becoming ordered might feel like being eaten alive. Perhaps this on one progression from whence the ouroboros emerged and why it persists to this day in the human collective psyche.[lxxxi]

Complementing the Standard Model of physics, might there emerge a Conventional Model of metaphysics? Might the existence and nature of irrational numbers in mathematics hint in that direction? Providing some relief from the timeless struggle to fit eternity into a box by unify the expanding complexity and diversity of the universe into grand Theories of Everything (TOEs), a Conventional Model might open the way to more versatile, expansive, and fruitful post-matter, epi-matter, sub-matter, and meta-matter academic fields, new domains of knowledge and understand that survive the end of duality while simultaneously becoming as familiar to humans as the Standard Model of the material realm. That's a lot to grok, but the emergence of new scientific insights such as Stephen Wolfram's ruliad (see Glossary, also xxvii) and Donald Hoffman's Conscious Realism provide compelling inspiration to pursue these avenues of inquiry with clear-headed and determined scientific rigor.

Might there exist domains of pre-, post-, sub-, epi-, and meta-existence beyond even the ruliad's scope? Does the answer to these questions depend first upon, indeed demand completion of the process of surveying and mapping the extent and boundaries of rulial space with equal enthusiasm to that which we applied our collective intelligence in mapping out the Standard Model description of the material realm? Including outer space, other planets, and biological, fashioned conscious inner space?

If not, by what other empirical methodology do we propose pursuing a pragmatic applied understanding of the epiphenomenal coherence that rests beyond and adjacent to the Standard Model perimeter of our eminently constrained human capacity to perceive observational and experiential coherence?

By what other avenues of inquiry do we propose to unequivocally prove or disprove the inherent orderliness of what appears to us as pre-quantum pandemonium? What if the limitation is *us* and we are forced to reckon with the fact of our own imperfection, ineptitude, cognitive frailty, incompleteness, and ignorance, though we regard ourselves as among the most intelligent beings on the planet?

While such mysteries forever intrigue and inspire, they can also detract from our tangible work obligations right here, right now, in this fallen world as it is, however imperfect and unsatisfactory our mundane duties may seem at times. Bringing all of the potency of mystery, narrative, mid-game, and short-game to bear upon that task of cutting the Gordian Knots that binds the material realm in suffering is the practical and useful philosopher's edict and directive of our endeavor. This is what it means to keep our head in the clouds and our feet on the ground.[lxxxii]

Groundedness is rooted in understanding the nature of a material world in which 9,999 of 10,000 things are unsatisfactory, predictably arising through an algorithmic sequence of immaterial processes that incrementally instantiate the entire measurable cosmos.[lxxxiii] So *escaping the algorithm* is a far more in-depth and un-enmeshing process than merely escaping the zoo cage of social media and volunteering at food banks, soup kitchens, or women's shelters.[lxxxiv] Escaping the algorithm of our cultural DCNR is the far greater escape, equipping us for service in previously unimaginable ways.

> *"If you bring forth what is within you, what you bring forth will save you. If you do not bring forth what is within you, what you do not bring forth will destroy you." — Gospel of Thomas.*[lxxxv]

When we choose to act in the material realm from a posture of intangible internal principle, we face the labor pains of birthing the inexplicable and perhaps forever inaccessible from the immaterial *ground of being* into the material ground of being.[lxxxvi] We face the inescapable demands of navigating the forsaken terrain between the non-symbolic and the symbolic.

We contend with the practical implications of understanding and skillfully interacting with the processes that give rise to this Earthly realm, as defined by the Standard Model, from the standpoint of antecedent causation. How do these phase-state-change processes function, precisely, and from whence do the processes that give rise to these processes originate? Must we first understand and master the measurements of dark matter and dark energy? If so, what then gives rise to that, and what are our obligations to deepen our decomposition still further before we deem ourselves sufficiently equipped and worth to put principle into practice, toward a world that works for everyone? Must we first elucidate the hard question of consciousness in its entirety before we deem ourselves qualified to navigate and chart the terrain from trustworthy tenet to enduring institutional convention?

Can this process serve as a kind of scientific induction of reason applied toward eventual empirical authentication of a spiritual, eternal reality as articulated by all human cultures from the dawn of humanity? Have the *poetry of physics* and *physics of poetry* revealed a dance forever destined to transport us, to deliver us, "to arrive where we started and know the place for the first time?"[lxxxvii]

If endless, recursive "what comes before *that*?" questions sound like the naïve prattle of a three- or four-year-old child's process, rather than the documented reductionist process by which all unfolding in the material realm proceeds, perhaps that observation too sheds useful light on the metaphysics of prose suggesting that "Whoever becomes simple and elemental again, like this child, will rank high in God's kingdom. What's more, when you receive the childlike on my account, it's the same as receiving me. But if you give them a hard time, bullying or taking advantage of their simple trust, you'll soon wish you hadn't."[lxxxviii] This challenges the so-called cold, cruel worldview – especially when religiously regarded as the one and only *most* true and *most* real world – wherein it is all too easy to mistake the bitter fruits of caustic acrimony and shrewd cynicism as realistic maturity and cunning cleverness in the course of the human journey. Behold the world as it is this day, consequent to such convictions. Is this the best for which humanity can ever hope? What are the grounds for that conviction, other than nihilistic, circular, self-referential confirmations?

These are merely a few of the more subtle and deceptively powerful silken strands of default consensus narratives that have woven the storied web of humanity's misadventures, to date. A web strewn with false dichotomies such as "spiritual story time versus objective empirical science," or "myth versus math," which both fall apart immediately upon realizing that both STEM and STEAM, *science, technology, engineering, art, and math themselves are inveterately subjective story-telling structures and tools* that have co-constructed the world as we experience it.

We need not fret about such an abrupt realization, however. Rather, we can celebrate our capacity to continue discovering and sharing new, better, more accurate stories about the nature of a reality, a reality forever shrinking and expanding into equal and opposite infinities, micro and macro, beyond our ability to *ever* fully comprehend or articulate, let alone directly observe and measure. Only failure to find sufficient humility to embrace ineluctable non-symbolic verity impedes a pilgrim's progress.

As C.S. Lewis observed, "It is astonishing how little attention critics have paid to *Story considered in itself*" (italics added).[lxxxix] Interrogating this principle with characteristic meticulousness, Lewis defined what we refer to as DCNRs from 1947 to 1952 in the context of both math and mythology:

> *A generation which has accepted the curvature of space need not boggle at the impossibility of imagining the consciousness of incarnate God. In that consciousness the temporal and the timeless were united. I think we can acquiesce in mystery at that point, provided we do not aggravate it by our tendency to picture the timeless life of God as, simply, another sort of time. We are committing that blunder whenever we ask how Christ could be <u>at the same moment</u> ignorant and omniscient, or how he could be the God who neither slumbers nor sleeps <u>while</u> he slept. The italicized words [Ed: underlined in this quotation] conceal an attempt to establish a temporal relation between his timeless life as God and the days, months, and years of his life as Man. And of course there is no such relation.*[xc]

This is something that BSOD's our puny human minds.[xci] Throughout his body of work, through both inductive and reductive reasoning, there can be no temporal relation between eternity and the pinhole-sized perspective of the Standard Model on spacetime, because eternity is neither simply another kind of time, nor merely another kind of infinity. At the brink of eternity, we face the event horizon of our highly constrained human capacity for reasoning, at all. To be completely convinced within the sanctum sanctorum of our most inwardly aware essence that there cannot possibly exist any kind of information or method of computation that can ever escape our eventual intellectual human comprehension, understanding, and mastery is to effectively declare ourselves God, which, if true, obliterates our proclaimed atheism or agnosticism. By holding any such variety of belief paramount within the innermost confines of our most private and precarious personality's holy-of-holies, I fear we err so far beyond mere narcissism or solipsism that language has not yet produced a word to describe the magnitude of our disconnect from ordinary reality.

> *The value of the myth is that it takes all the things we know and restores to them the rich significance which has been hidden by 'the veil of familiarity'. The child enjoys his cold meat (otherwise dull to him) by pretending it is buffalo, just killed with his own bow and arrow. And the child is wise. The real meat comes back to him more savoury for having been dipped in a story; you might say that only then is it the real meat. If you are tired of the real landscape, look at it in a mirror. By putting bread, gold, horse, apple, or the very roads into a myth, we do not retreat from reality: we rediscover it. As long as the story lingers in our mind, the real things are more themselves. This book applies the treatment not only to bread or apple but to good and evil, to our endless perils, our anguish, and our joys. By dipping them in myth we see them more clearly. I do not think he could have done it in any other way.*[xcii]

By interpolating Lewis's reasoning for the 21st century, we glimpse the intrinsic inviolability of DCNRs and the sacredness of *Story itself* as so scientifically and naturally sublime that even the seemingly mighty Google Bard seemed destined to yield the ground of this world's reality back to *The* Bard himself, Shakespeare, by dropping that early moniker for its first-generation Synthetic Knowledge Agent (see Glossary) in favor of far less foundational and far more fashionably nostalgic 20th century DNCR and phenomenological artifact: the Gemini space program.[xciii]

Like a case study in DCNRs, we are reflecting upon one demonstrated historical process by which everyday story-arcs, narratives, characters; even in the form of product and service names and behaviors; unfold, collapse, emerge – birth, death, and resurrect – even in the most mundane ways. For a time, Google Bard was a product and service. Now, it has returned to story, from whence it arose, just as its namesake. That's what Lewis meant by "Story Itself." Whoever said engineering synthetic intelligence can't be equally poetic and prosaic hasn't participated in the process.

If our eyes haven't glazed over or teared up while peeling the layers of the DCNR onion already, we may also identify an inadvertent, unintended, unlikely fraternal twin consensus narrative layer within the interstitial story line between Bard and Gemini. Juxtapose Shakespeare's observation that "There are more things in heaven and earth,

Horatio, Than are dreamt of in your philosophy."[xciv] with Gemini AI marking the dawn of a new kind of post-new-age inner-space race that *simultaneously* accelerates the human ability to venture deeper into outer-space on a routine basis.

We are spelunking here for evidence of quantum tubule passages that connect the Post-Automation Era Platonic Four-Game caverns of mystery, story, outer appearance, and inner experience as one metaphorical schema for understanding what it means to logically conceptualize and pragmatically cultivate something so seemingly absurd, irrational, utopian, and unattainable as *a world that works for everyone*. To investigate the possibility of the empirical existence of reproducible processes that precipitate non-symbolic, immaterial abstraction into symbolic, material actuality. That's as close as I can stumble toward a temporal working definition of "on Earth as it is in Heaven."

"Don't believe the speaker. We are inquiring, together." – Krishnamurti

---

If some of this begins to seem like needlessly complicated magical overthinking, a prating word salad to distract and avoid direct confrontation with the more dreadful aspects of Post-Automation Era anomie, confusion, and uncertainty that feeds human tendencies toward fatalistic indifference; if it seems we ignore the abruptness with which two decades of unprecedentedly sudden technological and social disruptions to centuries of seemingly predictable, comfortable DCNRs has unsettled and destabilized human populations; if it seems we disregard the heartbreaking fact that tens of millions have tragically joined the ranks of those throughout history who chose the ultimate willful avoidance of reality, suicide; or too timid for that, who retreat into the slow self-destruction and delayed misery integral to obstinately blissful ignorance – an intoxicant-fueled mirage that only lasts only until actuality fades in to view – any of which are preferable to facing their own shadows, then I can only petition for even more patience. We are getting there, and rest assured that none of the negativity or dire circumstances that tens of millions of human beings face in the present moment shall be swept under the rug.

Fact: for the forlorn, nihilistic soul, the only eternal DCNR is that there is no rhyme, reason, or meaning to life. There is nothing beyond an eternal dog-eat-dog, red-in-tooth-and-claw, material realm. So dominate or die. By blind religious faith and relentless, zealous conviction in that *Story Itself*, such minds manifest that reality. How can the world possibly work for everyone while such minds exist?

To follow the nihilistic line of thinking is to conclude that life is so unpredictable, so uncertain, and so inherently, ruthlessly unkind, that life *can only be* purposeless, pointless, cynical, inherently cruel, consummately depressing.

Among all religions, this is empirically the most hypocritical, intolerant, murderous religion of all. A religion that has masqueraded as every sacred tradition on Earth. It is the wolfen behavior conducted while adorned in sheep's clothing that wolves revel in assigning to sheep of every ethical and moral world tradition. "Look at how many people religion has killed throughout history!" Yes, let's do that, and compare it to how many the godless have killed. Hitler. Stalin. Every godless nature-worshipping tribe that slaughtered and cannibalized other tribes. Let's do that math. Because what we find is that the murderers behind the masks of religion, from the Crusades to Salem, were in fact zealots of narcissism and nihilism.

By definition, no authentic practitioner of any of the world's major traditions has ever murdered or committed suicide in the name of the Redeemer. Accidental car crash? Of course. Accidental drowning by one's own stupidity? Duh. Wherever an empty, clanging, tin pot proclaiming to follow a religion or tradition that vows to do no harm to any sentient being, even a mosquito, turns to violence, most often as a reaction to violence, the Church of Narcissism and Nihilism has taken over, regardless of the color or context of the robes involved. Murder is murder, and "by their fruits you shall know them." The empirical evidence of counterfeit consciousness is incontestable and revolting. It also provides cheap, easy, opportunities for false attribution. If this sounds a lot like the principles that define false flag operations, that is because it is exactly what we've discovered along the way.

Thanks for trusting the process if you've made this far. I didn't mean to lose as many readers as I've probably lost with my wordiness. If I had more time, I'd go back yet again and do better. Please do review those passages that I may have failed to articulate with sufficient clarity to make them simple and obvious on the first read. That's on me.

Moving on for now, we have at least provided sufficient context and background to begin a metaphorical "deathbed lifecycle review" of the run-of-the-mill 20th century DCNR.

* * *

A 20th Century Post-Mortem

Birth. Consume. School. Consume. Work. Consume. Death. Consume. Yes, even after death, a fundamental 20th century narrative was to *teach the next generation a lesson* by leaving nothing but scorched Earth behind. It was a heartbreaking story that encouraged humans to consume all that we can for our own enjoyment and indulge every whim for the brief, pointless time that we are here on Earth. Consumption not only of material things, but gluttony for experiences, accomplishments, conquests. From consuming and discarding human relationships, right on through to ensuring dramas that consume the attention and lives of others, long beyond death itself. Greed was good.[xcv] The greatest good. The 20th century was a kind of misguided, out-of-context, post-modern, new-age version of "eat, drink, and be merry, for tomorrow we die."[xcvi]

One of the most cynical storyboard panels in the 20th century's arc of history depicted the ideal economic outcome of life as the fantasy of spending one's last penny at the precise moment of one's last breath, leaving nothing, out of the cynical belief that all humans are ungrateful explicatives who deserve an eternal sentence of repeating the same cycles of hazing and horror that the previous generation endured; in the name of building character. Today, we know that trauma only ever destroys character. So-called *tough love* as practiced was a euphemism for all manner of cruelty. Physical, mental, emotional, psychological, and spiritual. Too often, so-called *tough love* was neither administered nor restrained by love at all. Rather, tough love was a euphemism for punishment in the name of control, covering up for emotional neglect or abuse, child abuse, elder abuse, and all manner of keep-it-quiet domestic violence. That kind of tough love in childhood does not build character, it decimates the chance to ever develop stable character, often for life. The complex post-traumatic stress disorder instilled by childhood trauma effectively destroys any hope of stable adult character formation.

The DCNR of the 20th century was to consume, consume, consume, on me, me, me, and to hades with thee. In short, the thinking was, "if I had to suffer in this life, I'll make certain that you suffer the same, or maybe even worse, to make up for my own bitterness toward aging and death; made worse by the naïve exuberance of your idiotic youth."[xcvii] The communal gaslighting and covert emotional abuse inherent to the most common 20th century DCNs were often couched in politically correct soundbites. The horrors of war created heroes. Jobs were essential to self-esteem and meaning. Mostly, those soundbites were more about bitterness and fear that somebody might get something that we didn't, or resentment at the very thought that someone might endure less pain and struggle in life than we had endured. A century of boom, bust, bitterness, and retribution.

These were disappointingly prevalent attitudes even among my own generation, as if *our ability to work and be productive at all* were not pure gifts of the lottery of birth,[xcviii] gifted to us by entirely unmerited and amazing grace. What possibly makes me think that because I achieved something by methods that worked for me, given my particular lottery-of-birth ticket, and the particular cards dealt to me in this life, that everyone else holds the same hand and therefore "just needs to do what I did," in order to be happy, stable, superabundant, and successful?

Mythologies of purely self-made persons were pervasive in the social imagination of the 20th century. The epitome of such mistaken views is seen retroactively in the completely upside down and backward misunderstanding and misuse of the infamous "up-by-your-bootstraps" analogy, intended to prove what's impossible in economic life, not what's required and demanded.[xcix]

The ancient cudgel that young people "have it so much easier than we did," was the central thesis in a bitter, cantankerous, and plain mean-spirited intergenerational movie we've seen at least 117 billion times before.[c]

Pointless. Vindictive. Cruel. Obsolete. That was the story of a 20th century DCN that taught people to "get all you can before you die and leave nothing behind to those horrible, ungrateful brats." Instrumental ingrates whose only practical use was to be used as a prop in our own story of pleading to the loan officer, "we need this home for our children's future security," while pulling that rug out from under them "for their own good" at the first opportunity; or by bait-n-switch at the last moment, on our way out. "Hysterically humorous" methods for getting even with those ungrateful brats from beyond the grave animated billions of tipsy and drunken kitchen table bridge club gatherings.

Some people went so far as to adopt a couple of kids as handy stage props to get what *they* wanted while preening through life. Namely, to portray the 1950's image on the cover of a JCPenney catalog, while playing selfless overburdened martyr to the world. These are aspects of a cynical DCNR almost beyond imagination for the ethical or compassionate in constitution. I watched a morose majority of a generation before my own live this way by their actions, which spoke far louder than their empty words.

In the context of DCNRs, the entire 20th century, every business, every government, every team, every club, every organization, tribe, clan, or village was the manifestation of Lewis's *Story Itself*. Nothing more and nothing less than a script. Invitations to enter into a kind of dialectical-behavioral theater, ostensibly for the purpose of circulating what my nephew refers to as rationing tickets for stuff, currency.

Maybe that was a perfectly fine model, had the show been unconditionally and unreservedly *opt-in*, rather than Truman-Show-your-way-out, as experienced by hundreds of millions over the past several centuries. From the perspective of human consciousness, any activity that is not opt-in is neither libertarian nor liberational. As an aside, isn't it a bit ironic how left and right seem to polarize round the same core principle of liberty? Darwinian Natural Law Libertarianism vs Mother Nature's Right to Unrestrained Liberation.

Show me a way that we can escape *Story Itself* and I'll happily follow you out of the maze. See? Even that question was a once-sentence story. We cannot escape story, because even stories of escaping one's story is itself a story.

"In the beginning was the Word," may be the prompt that defined our simulation's marvelously and eternally absolute-zero-knowledge encrypted rulial sandbox.

Seems like the adage *turtles all the way down* deserves – okay, okay, deservingness is a first derivative of fairness, so yet another BSG triggering trap to negotiate with awareness and prudence – illumination and articulation in new and creative ways that help to illustrate the primacy of C.S. Lewis's Story Itself, aka the Post-Automation Era principle of DCNRs.

These observations and recollections of a bygone century are not meant to condemn, rather to convey and portray the potency of DCNRs in defining the human experience, and to shed light upon the abusive effects of large-scale groupthink upon individuals who dare question the legitimacy of unambiguously destructive legacy norms.

If headlines over the past decade are any indication, the animosity between generations is today at all-time highs, with blame and animosity misdirected in all directions except toward us. Blame Boomers, guilt Generation X, malign Millennials (Gen Y), upbraid Gen Z, and who knows what lies ahead for the VR & AR raised Alpha generation?[ci] It's a toxic game of others othering others as the othering other doing all the othering, all the way down.

It's easy to fall into the over-generalization trap. The "my way or the highway" attitude of Boomer parents felt like emotional and psychological carpet bombing. *Death From Above*, as John Perry Barlow put it, seemed like that generation's answer to everything.[cii] As a nation it was, "my way, or the bomb's way." In our homes it was, "my way, or the belt beating's way." Or wooden spoon, wire coat hanger. Any nearest handy weapon will do.

Is the 21st century doomed to keep repeating societal trauma bond cycles in the form of boom-bust economics that curiously mirror growing up with parents that could emotionally, psychologically, or physically blow up and bomb us into oblivion for no discernable reason at any moment?

Speaking of trauma bond DCNs, the 20th century JOB-JOB trance was arguably the gaslight of all gaslights. Jobs were advanced as the best, most important, even *only* source of meaning and dignity in life, while the overwhelming testimony of those who played that game all the way through at the highest level was *universally* and *unequivocally* to look back and tell us, "yeah, no." Given the overwhelming data, how could such a mythology have persisted for so long? Like the monolith in the timeless Stanley Kubrick film, "2001: A Space Odyssey," the JOB-JOB trance stood like an intimidating inevitability. But was it really an alien mystery?[ciii] From whence did such a disingenuous DCNR emerge?

> *"I did some investigation into the derivation of the American North American education system and found out that it was based on the Prussian model. The Prussians produced a universal education system in the late 1800s because they were afraid, they were losing military superiority and they wanted to produce a cadre of mindless obedient soldiers. That was expressly the purpose. Then, that model was adopted*

by prototypical fascists in the U.S ... corporate types mostly, who wanted to produce cadres of obedient workers, and that's why the desks are in rows and that's why there's factory bells and that's why it's top-down leadership. But what was really stunning wasn't only [the fact] that was the model, but it's worse than that because the people who built the schools were consciously aiming at eradicating the will of the students who were part of the system because they wanted them to be obedient. Now, you know, there was a demand for factory workers at the time and there were a lot of rural people flooding into the cities and no one really knew what to do with the kids because they didn't have farm work and there was some need for an education system. There was some utility in producing people who knew how to abide by a clock and who could therefore take on factory jobs, but as a model [a DCNR], especially now in the modern world where things change so quickly that you can hardly keep up, and people have to be dynamic, that sort of nine to five lifetime factory work is a dream of the past [and] it might not have been that desirable to begin with. It certainly has nothing to do with the way people live now, [in the 21st century]" (lxv).

Does that sound like an algorithm for cultivating freedom, meaning, dignity, and self-worth to you? So when people ask the question, "what will people do for meaning, worth, and dignity without *jobs* in the Post-Automation Era?" It's forgivable if tempted to reply with something like, "*Really*?" while blinking from the brightness as we step out of the gaslighting shadows of bygone eras into the full noon sunlight of today.

It's hard to believe that it's already been 25 years since art reflected life in the form of Neo, Trinity, and Morpheus. Today, new twists on the false dichotomy of the red pill or blue pill choice from The Wachowskis 1999 classic film, *The Matrix*, have emerged in urban dictionaries. "The purple pill equals peace and traveling to different universes in a higher state of consciousness!"[civ] As people became increasingly *purple-pilled* out of the 20th century Job Trance, they began learning how to focus upon the things that we know to actually, scientifically, cultivate intrinsic motivation, meaning, worth, dignity, and flourishing in human lives. Spoiler alert: it was never jobs, titles, or money independent of internal ethical and moral character development. That's right, he dared to use the "m" word. We live in an eminently moral universe, much to the chagrin of nihilists who don't seem to get the ultimate paradoxical irony of living their own cynical creed, "mess around and find out," in the course of denying this universal ultimate reality.

Where does such persistent nihilism come from? Once again, the lack of healthy and securely attached human relationships, beginning in earliest childhood, appears in the line-up as a prime suspect. Both born and made, equal parts nature and nurture, the vapid emptiness of nihilism expands and deepens with indoctrination into the beliefs that unmitigated *hedonistic impulses* are just, good, and harmless fun, while *consumptive rewards* are the most principled, ethical, and moral.

> *The pursuit of happiness is the fundamental impetus for human beings. Many consumers view consumption as a way to improve their quality of life (Chang, 2020; An et al., 2021). It is crucial for companies as well, not only in relation to customer loyalty (Troebs et al., 2018) and positive word-of-mouth (El Hedhli et al., 2016; Kim et al., 2018), but also for long-term relationships with customers. Visionary companies should consider their consumers' well-being an important strategic objective and a responsibility for success in an increasingly competitive marketplace.*
>
> *A growing number of scholars are focusing on what contributes to consumers' happiness (Chang, 2020; An et al., 2021), and some studies have preliminarily noticed that consumer motivations have an effect on their well-being (Akram et al., 2021a). For example, consumption of hedonistic products leads to increased life satisfaction and subjective well-being (Zhong and Mitchell, 2010). High-ethical consumers expect positive emotions from their sustainable consumption (Onwezen et al., 2013). However, other studies have shown that not all consumer motivations predict well-being positively (e.g., Oral and Thurner, 2019; Shahid and Paul, 2021). Conspicuous consumption driven by the desire to show off possessions and status may make them less happy (Shahid and Paul, 2021). Materialism has been shown to be associated with lower levels of life satisfaction (Gong et al., 2020b), as motivated by the pursuit of too much consumption and acquisition (Oral and Thurner, 2019). A number of motivations have been examined individually in previous studies, but little is known about their combined effect on consumer well-being.*[42]

In contrast, we can stabilize and strengthen young people by instilling a healthy sense of intrinsic meaning, worth, and dignity during the first five years of life, then eight, and onward further guiding and nurturing self-discovery of the richness and satisfaction of accomplishment found only through intrinsic motivation. This doesn't mean zero discipline and participation trophies, it means encouraging and equipping self-directed upskilling . An abiding sense of intrinsic motivation also equips people to be far less susceptible to codependent trauma bonds with frenetic consumption as a measure of well-being.

Tragically, many learn about this the hard way when raised with that intrinsic sense of meaning and self-esteem, then later entering into long-term relationships with people thoroughly indoctrinated into the consumer identity job trance. The consumer identity deepens the cult-like philosophy of the Job Trance that falls for the hypnotic suggestion that consumption is the highest moral activity that best maximizes human well-being, therefore deepening the conviction that any Just Over Broke Justification Of Being that increases consumption is inherently the most ethical course of action to take in life. What I consume defines my moral character and how well I obey my boss defines my personal integrity. Everything else is secondary at best and subservient to those roles, by default.

While I have repeatedly affirmed and emphasized the importance and moral value of work; meaningful work, right livelihood, is not the same thing as indoctrination and social-engineering a population into the willingness to literally do *anything* in order to maintain a perceived acceptable rate and pace of perpetual consumption in order to maintain a respectable position and posture within a particular social hierarchy.

In many places in the United States of America, these are both socially and physically dangerous ideas to share. The right to free speech is non-existent when we live in the midst of locally corrupt dominance hierarchies, including families and neighborhoods that will severely "put people in their place" for daring to question the DCN of consumption as the highest moral value. Sometimes, the quelling of that first amendment right can even begin in our own homes, because *the first amendment is not binding upon anyone but Congress.*

> *Congress shall make no law respecting an establishment of religion, or prohibiting the free exercise thereof; or abridging the freedom of speech, or of the press; or the right of the people peaceably to assemble, and to petition the Government for a redress of grievances.*[cvi]

The First Amendment does not mention anything about the local social dominance hierarchy in which we find ourselves by random lottery of birth (xcviii).

History.com declares, "Freedom of speech – the right to express opinions without government restraint – is a democratic ideal that dates back to ancient Greece." However, the principle of free speech means nothing to private actors willing to do anything to maintain their power in local dominance hierarchies. Especially in corrupt hierarchies with plenty of skeletons to hide in those fancy McMansion closets.

In the bygone millennium, it was understandable and easy to find many traumatized individuals misdirecting disempowered emotions at "the government," for fundamental human rights violations that happened under one's own childhood roof and in one's own neighborhood.

"The government," didn't oppress or suppress us in those cases, the neighbors did. They did so whenever they decided a particular person or kind of person "didn't fit in," or "didn't know their place." In extreme cases, people deployed euphemisms – application-specific narrative memes – to avoid accountability for interfering with or even destroying people's lives as punishment for their expressions of free speech. From "the island decided they didn't belong here," to "it wasn't a good corporate culture fit," people distanced themselves from accountability for their own individual choices and actions. People deployed these euphemisms whenever an individual saw through toxic in-group patterns and behaviors in a way that threatened the impunity of the local noxious hierarchy; or when a newcomer's competence posed a threat to local alphas.

So it is the people of our own clan, tribe, village, town, or city who were completely free to police our speech to whatever extent they desired, through artfully deployed and difficult-to-prove criminal interference in our lives. It was not some shadowy conception of "the government," the call was always from inside the house. This is an extraordinarily obvious, important, and overlooked reality of our socially-engineered lives.

Perhaps the 20th century Emperor of all Euphemisms for the purposes of our work-in-progress: "it is *impossible* for people to foster meaning, dignity, or a sense of direction in life without a Just Over Broke Justification Of Being." Question *that* debunked decree and find out.

The most demanding of intra- and inter-personal character development tasks – the *real work* of life – forges the genuine foundations of honesty, civility, character, integrity, dignity, and self-esteem; without which there can never be genuine mutual respect. The 20th century myth that JOB-JOBs were God's source of all dignity and meaning was just that, a myth. A socially-engineered default consensus narrative reality of a bygone mad millennium.

It's an empirical fact that millions of people who achieved fat stacks of cash reported that life's deeper questions became even more poignant, pointed, and difficult to answer after working so hard to amass wealth and status. Those achievements *did not* bring them dignity or meaning or self-worth, and all too often led in the opposite direction.[cvii] No clichés instantly debunk the Job Trance more than the suicidal actress, rock star, comedian, or CEO. Jobs don't give life meaning. Jobs don't give people dignity. Career success, wealth, and fame don't make people happy, healthy, or mentally well.

Like the vastness of the micro and macro cosmos beyond the Standard Model of physics, the absurdity of perpetuating the 20th century DCNR exceeds the human capacity for comprehension.

What that world did deliver were remorse and regrets for all the compromises along the way – the total sell-out of genuine dignity and meaning found exclusively in the sacred wholeness of personal integrity, kinship, trust, matrimony, camaraderie, and genuine human affinity – all in the name of *keeping a job at all costs*, above all other priorities in life. And it's no wonder that people sold out when the alternative was utter economic destitution. Skid Row. People didn't make their bad choices in vacuum. The DCNRs that people enforced upon one another were nothing less than vicious, nasty, peer-to-peer social-engineering in a condescending, vapid, and rabid dog-eat-dog era.

Faced with the grim realization they'd been coerced and duped into selling their souls on the cheap, it's no wonder so many of the duped became so dangerous. Like social predators driven by resentment and bitterness to spread sexually transmitted diseases to others through a misguided and distorted sense of revenge, the Job Trance duped and dangerous doubled down on forcing others into the same economic straights that forced them into compromising everything that really mattered in life. Many papered-over resentment-driven behaviors by telling themselves and others that their actions were taken in the name of *tough love* or *just the way the real world works*. That was the essence of the past century's crabs-in-a-bucket mentality. A "this is going to hurt you a lot more than it hurts me, but it's for your own good," way of thinking. Too often it wasn't for the other person's good, it was to maintain one's own hold on perceived status in the hierarchy and push the other person downward to feel better about themselves. And it was never *the way the real world works*, it was only the way some people decided to interact with the world in order to maintain their collusive illusions of control, while acting as if no other choice existed for them, therefore justifying the belief and behavior that all others ought to face the same tragic fate as visited them.

Maybe you have never experienced any of these things, yet. We're not unearthing anything that Shakespeare didn't describe better, we are sharing our generation's direct lived experience, the experiential evidence we have observed. Most troubling of all are the tens of thousands, maybe millions, of dysfunctional and destructive successful wealthy people who ended up trafficking everything from drugs to human beings in the name getting what they want and making money above all other principles, thereby providing a distressing and embodied world of data attesting to the fact that the meme of *working hard so you can make something of yourself* in material terms, at the expense of any sense of ethics or morality, was the most destructive gaslight of the 20th century experiment. The results speak for themselves. The persistent existential threat of economic destitution drives desperate people to the most desperate measures.

Hard work, the right livelihood, can and does fulfill us as human beings when incentives and motives align with sane and humane principles. The problem with the 20th century DCNR was that those prerequisites were generally unmet and effectively undermined by adverse incentives toward wealth and misshapen motives for power.

> *The richest one percent of this country owns half our country's wealth, five trillion dollars. I create nothing. I own. We make the rules, pal. The news, war, peace, famine, upheaval, the price per paper clip. We pick that rabbit out of the hat while everybody sits out there wondering how the hell we did it. Now you're not naive enough to think we're living in a democracy, are you buddy? It's the free market. And you're a part of it. – Gordon Gekko, Wall Street, 1999.*[cviii]

Like the 20th century Standard Model of physics, the 20th century Standard Model of economics proved useful for generating staggering wealth, and also proved 95% inexplicable and incomplete in the end. The experimental results of the 20th century DCNR are now incontestable, and those results are simultaneously awe-inspiring and revolting. All the flying cars and smart-medicines in the world are useless if we sentence ourselves to living in a world that works for the same 4% to 5% that the Standard Models of physics and economics created in the course of pursuing models of material reality that were ultimately destined to describe only 4% to 5% of whatever is going on in the bigger picture. We didn't know that at the time, but we do now. So to keep doing what we've always done when we clearly see what we already got, is well, you know the cliché.

At this super-intelligence illuminated inflection point in history, it seems like we could also be in for several other unexpectedly interdependent revelations about how we *thought* the world worked, versus *how the universe actually works* – in and through the affordances of the material world. Like Shakespeare, a lot of this may be nothing new.

> *They Had Everything in Common*
>
> *"Now the full number of those who believed were of one heart and soul, and no one said that any of the things that belonged to him was his own, but they had everything in common. And with great power the apostles were giving their testimony to the resurrection of the Lord Jesus, and great grace was upon them all. There was not a needy person among them, for as many as were owners of lands or houses sold them and brought the proceeds of what was sold and laid it at the apostles' feet, and it was distributed to each as any had need" (Acts 4:32-35, English Standard Version).*

Wait, what?

- No one said that any of the things that belonged to them were their own.
- They had everything in common.
- There was not a needy person among them.
- They distributed everything to each one as needed.

"Yeah, but ..."

- Things were different then.
- That was only the church, not everyone.
- God said, "you no work, you no eat!"
- "For even when we were with you, we would give you this command: If anyone is not willing to work, let him not eat" (2 Thessalonians 3:9-11, ESV).

Yeah-but wins! Does it, though? Things were different. Okay. Only the in-group. Okay. When things seem unclear and we have a choice between the words of a disciple and the actions of that disciple's teacher, which is probably closer to the heart of the matter? And if the bigger story is about cultivating conditions on Earth as it is in Heaven – the overwhelmingly clear instruction – then how do the core principles not extend beyond in-groups, to the wider world, aligning with, "a world that works for everyone, without ecological or economic disadvantage to anyone?"

Regardless of the many ways to spin sacred texts of all traditions, the full context of intentions demonstrated by actions indicate that the Acts 4 church was the closest role model that we have to what it means to cultivate conditions on Earth as it is in Heaven.

"There was not a needy person among them." How can it be acceptable that there are so many needy among us, in the midst of the most superintelligent, superabundant situation the world has ever experienced?

In 2018, we observed that, "Today's capitalism is dominated by five companies competing to see who can build the most sophisticated artificial intelligence, the fastest. Today's financial capitalism is a game of innovation at the speed of light. Sophisticated hedge funds race to build shorter fiber optic paths to the exchange [to gain nano-second advantages] or find ways to insert themselves [higher up] the pyramid scheme known as Wall Street, in order to aggregate, arbitrage, and skim order flows. This is not a prediction about the future. This is the present. This is the only wealth-building and [upward] redistribution game in town."

Today, in 2024, it's the past. Today, as ChatGPT and LLM's have exploded onto the scene, it seems that those words couldn't have been more accurate or prescient. This game of ultra-high-frequency trading and AI has been going on for at least a decade, even before the 2008 global monetary crisis. From the day that online trading networks began, the game of AI in financial capitalism was on and started changing things, forever.

In 2018, the writing was on the wall:

Today, we see both how powerful the game of financial capital is in amassing historical accumulations of wealth, and how incapable it is of circulating that wealth throughout an economy where jobs [become] less necessary every single day.

In a September 2018 conversation with Joe Rogan, one of the most prolific engineers of our era described the current environment like this:

> *The percentage of intelligence that is not human is increasing, and eventually, we [humanity] will represent a very small percentage of intelligence. But the AI isn't formed, strangely, by the human limbic system. It, in large part, is our id written large. All the things that we like, and hate, and fear. They're all there, on the internet. They're projections of our limbic system. And the more limbic resonance [that AI achieves], the more engagement. It could be terrible, and it could be great. One thing's for sure: we will not control it.*[cix]

This is why I emphasize, "it is now incontestable that we are living in the Post-Automation Era that [many of us have] read about in science fiction for at least the past fifty years or more. The passing of G.E. from the DOW industrial average is just the last nail in the coffin for a world that no longer exists. No matter how loud Boomers and their elders scream about "the way we did it" two or three generations ago; no matter how virulent the insults about lazy Millennials and [the] entitled; no matter how verbally pugnacious the provocations of [various political factions] become; none of those polarized perspectives make any sense or useful difference in terms of adapting to the Post-Automation Era of deeply embedded super-intelligent algorithms, devices, and machines."

We are in a completely different environment today. One that operates by completely different principles than advocated by the most gruesome rules, rulers, and gatekeepers of the past, which seems to be one reason why that hideousness is becoming so starkly apparent in the light of the present era.

In 2018, many looked at our words with a sideways smirk of dismissal or disdain. Today, some are lobbying to have self-checkout stations removed from Walmart to keep up the illusion of the need for human labor. So Post-Automation Era blowback is real. Yale University and London School of Economics economic anthropologist David Graeber[cx] *called these "Bullshit Jobs."*

It seems like the JOB-JOB Trance has brainwashed so many of us that we, like the Luddites of two centuries ago, resort to smashing the robots that could liberate us from the ancient curse of toil. Why? Because we can't imagine any other source of meaning, purpose, direction, dignity, and contribution in community other than a JOB-JOB.

We can't seem to find a way to a better why with a more stable half-life and enduring, intrinsically motivational influence. We didn't arrive at our old beliefs on our own, societies installed cultural beliefs in us over a lifetime, over generations, like psychological kernel-resident malware that takes time and care to debug.

Post-Automation Era blowback is the result of the same human dynamic that we could have solved two hundred years ago with the Luddites, and is unavoidable for us, now. It's a human phenomenon that has almost nothing to do with the technology itself. This is why *we find a way to the source of our why* instead of whining about why we keep self-sabotaging, either as individuals, or as a society. If the answer to the why of *why we are here* is not Moloch, not Mammon, not to win by the "greed is good" ethic of that 1987 fantasy flick, *Wall Street*, then what is?

Maybe we are not here to learn and grow and improve our understanding of what it means to be conscious ... human ... humane ... beings. Maybe it is simply not that simple, and complicated, at the very same time. Maybe our why is not to care for ourselves and one another in commonwealth and community, from an individual to a species scale. Maybe too much individuation does not lead to hyper fragmentation and transactional relationships that diminish our humanity. Maybe insufficient individuation does not lead to hyper demoralization and mechanical relationships that diminish our humanity. Maybe a conscious and caring commonwealth that circulates universal, unconditional basic income is a catastrophe in serpentine utopian clothing. Maybe, as Milton wrote, "The mind is its own place, and in itself can make a heaven of hell, a hell of heaven."

The idea is that the world can't possibly work if everyone is free to work however and whenever they choose, wherever they choose, and at whatever endeavor in which they choose to engage. We'll call this 20th century narrative, Lazy Entitled Human Theory.

Let's investigate whether or not the DCN of Lazy Entitled Human Theory proved true in the 20th century.

Exhibit A: everything accomplished in the 20th century. If the human species as a whole were inherently lazy, how did we reach this pinnacle of productivity?

Exhibit B: if humans were inherently lazy, we'd have never survived in the first place, so the premise was ipso facto absurd, beginning about six million years ago. Predators would have eaten us alive into extinction before we even started. So the inherent laziness proposition is prehistorically preposterous.

That said, it's understandable in a modern context that some people might find this confusing; especially if we disdain our own desire and capacity for rest, due to the extreme conditioning of the 20th century.[cxi] That's a different matter altogether, one that maybe a month or a year in monk-mode might help begin to address.[cxii]

Exhibit C: the existence of AI itself decimates the misanthropic Lazy Entitled Human Theory. Largely built upon the Linux operating system, AI represents the herald of Open-Source Civilization. AI is perhaps the apex achievement of intrinsic human motivation and curiosity, to date. AI is overwhelming testimony to the opposite of Lazy Entitled Human Theory. Built from voluntary open-source foundations that have stood the test of time, AI has redefined our times, establishing the present-tense reality of the Post-Automation Era.

Today, the Linux Foundation spends about 2% of its budget directly on kernel development and 60% on Project Support.[cxiii] That's not laziness, distraction, or abdication of duty to its core mission, that's expansion, support, and maintenance, without which the kernel is useless. We know that there are malevolent factions that would love nothing more than to get access to Linux kernel development for nefarious reasons. A minimalist approach to kernel development, like much of life, is prudent. Kernel commit security and protection is pragmatic and wise. So, the fact that kernel dev itself remains stable and minimal is a feature, not a bug. If it ain't broke, don't fix it. When broke, prudence makes certain the fixes don't break it in different or worse ways.

Today, virtually all of the open-source software innovations that have completely transformed the world over the past 20+ years exist upon a foundation of voluntarism. How could such a miracle happen with nobody in charge, nobody barking orders, nobody cutting checks?

How did tens of thousands of human beings, motivated by *jobless* intrinsic *dignity* and *meaning*, accomplish something that all the job titles and company badges in the world never could?

Exhibit D: yet another wrong-headed 20th century DCN. Lazy Entitled Human Theory was wrong, thoroughly debunked and falsified by the reality of the present moment. It is inherent human *meaning* and *dignity* that results in amazing work, not the other way around. It's tough not to name-call and mock back when a whole model of the universe turned out to be 95% full of *no there, there*; but also a good opportunity to exercise some restraint of our own.

Here's a dopey idea straight out of a 1939 nut house: maybe a miracle happens when we support humans in the expression of their curiosity to learn and better themselves by voluntarily contributing to something that they select as greater than themselves. Maybe that's the source of meaning, purpose, enthusiasm, social significance, and status in the post-jobs Post-Automation Era.

If we think that decentralized, non-hierarchical voluntarism can't remain steadfastly focused, organized, coherent, and achieve profound, civilization-scale objectives on a sufficiently reliable and consistent basis to operate a peaceful, stable, and prosperous society, then frankly we're a little bit confused about the nature of the Open-Source Civilization that we live in, today.

Welcome to the Post-Automation Era. The software layer of the world already runs by the principles we've discussed, so perhaps if we feel exhausted from running to try to catch up, maybe it's time to stop, rest, and realize we've already arrived. It might seem crazy to simply let the experience of genuine gratitude for where we are at the present moment suffice to fulfill our ordinary mundane lives, but perhaps after trying and failing with every other miserable bygone 20th century survival tactic to ward off the self-inflicted pressures of resistance to exponential acceleration, maybe arrival eventually becomes an option to explore; even for those most misanthropic and traumatized by the very systems of thinking and behavior we've lived a lifetime conditioned to defend and uphold.

Over the past three decades, the fact that millions of developers donated time, labor, and incredibly valuable professional expertise to the development of the open-source software that now effectively manages the world is the final nail in the coffin for Lazy Entitled Human Theory.[cxiv]

Lazy Entitled Human Theory is overwhelmingly untrue, in some cases surpassing merely resentful and stupid to becoming outright mean and brutish. We need to drive real wooden stakes through the hearts of such monstrous zombie vampire DCNs, because they have shackled human consciousness in darkness for far too long.

According to Forbes in 2018, "83% of hiring managers say open source is a high priority today, up from 76% in 2017. Linux is the most in-demand open-source skill category, considered a must-have for nearly all entry-level open-source careers" (Columbus). The 2023 explosion of LLMs onto the scene is so new that we won't know the real impact on demand for independent, intrinsically motivated open-source workers until this time next year.

The question is not:

"What will people do for dignity and meaning?"

The question is:

"How do we cultivate secure emotional and psychological attachment, encourage profound curiosity, inspire intrinsic motivation, nurture self-guided learning with a passion for understanding, and a natural inclination toward intuitive insights?" These are the characteristics of the human spirit which forge dignity, meaning, merit, virtue, healthy self-esteem, and the natural aspiration to be useful, helpful, valuable. These are the ultimate value creation mechanisms in all creation.

I highly recommend watching the Chris Anderson YouTube video, "The Mind Behind Linux," to enjoy the entire twenty-one-minute conversation described below.[cxv] I'll summarize a few of the most salient points.

> *When TED curator Chris Anderson pointed out that, "Companies like Google have made literally billions [of dollars] from your software. Does that piss you off?" Torvalds replied, "No. It doesn't piss me off for several reasons, and one of them is that I'm doing fine. I'm really doing fine."*
>
> *Can you imagine America's most successful CEO's ever saying something like that? I'm doing just fine; I don't need or want any more money? No. In America, it's never enough. It's a game of who can get the most and when you get the most, how can you make it even more. It is an infinite loop of greed.*
>
> *The creativity and productivity of people like Torvalds happen when people are raised in a society that puts the income security of all ahead of the economic domination of any one individual, or small group of shareholders. When we recognize that my right to hoard billions of*

> *dollars ends, where your right to a livable basic income indexed to 50% per capita GDP begins, we'll begin to cultivate a more efficient economy and a more perfect union.*
>
> *When Anderson said, "Your software, Linux, is in millions of computers, it powers much of the internet, and there are like a billion and a half Android devices out there. Your software is in every single one of them. You must have some kind of amazing software headquarters, driving all this. I mean, that's what I thought. So, when I saw a picture of this ..." the crowd burst into knowing, collegial laughter, as an image of Linus Torvalds is displayed on the mighty TED Conference main screen. It's Torvalds, standing in front of a simple flat screen monitor perched atop a desk that could have come from Walmart or Ikea, squeezed neatly into a corner just like any of us might use in our own home office, today. "This is the Linux World Headquarters," says Anderson.*
>
> *"Yeah, it really doesn't look like much," Torvalds replies, flatly. "The way I work ... my computer doesn't need to be big and powerful ... my office is the most boring office you will ever see. I sit there all alone, in the quiet. If the cat comes up and sits in my lap, I want to hear the cat purring, not the sound of the fans from the computer."*
>
> *Anderson continues, "Working this way, you are able to manage this vast technology empire. It is an empire. That's an amazing testament to the power of open source."*
>
> *"I work alone, in my house, often in my bathrobe. When the photographer shows up, I dress up. That's how I've always worked," says Torvalds.*

Still, some people will try to say that Linus, and millions of open-source developers, are somehow the exception to the rule, and that regular, normal people are not this way. Not this curious. Not this enthusiastic. Not this persevering. Not this productive.

Why would so many people respond that way, proclaiming that "normal people are lazy?" Not only does this seem incredibly cynical, but it also devalues and disparages engineers, writers, and all other intrinsically motivated and inherently industrious humans as "not normal" people.

Maybe we think and say such horrible things about the most talented and productive people we know because we are the lazy ones, we are the insecure ones, we are the envious, jealous, bitter, and resentful ones, projecting our beliefs about ourselves onto everyone around us. Who are we to decide who is a "regular, normal person" and who isn't?

Obviously, there is nobility in all work, and perhaps no one did a better job of immortalizing the appreciation for this fact – at every interlinear opportunity – than Ayn Rand. In Atlas Shrugged, for example:

Eddie Willers shifted his glance down to the street, to a vegetable pushcart at the stoop of a brownstone house. He saw a pile of bright gold carrots and the fresh green of onions. He saw a clean white curtain blowing at an open window. He saw a bus turning a corner, expertly steered. He wondered why he felt reassured — and then, why he felt the sudden, inexplicable wish that these things were not left in the open, unprotected against the empty space above.

Today, the expertise steering the open-source development of the Linux *econosystem* continues to grow into billions of devices and the number of people contributing to this work continues to grow, apace.[cxvi] Without the countless hours and unpaid labor of love of open-source developers, there would be no ChatGPT and no AI revolution in art, science, medicine, robotics, information security and national security. All open-source. All created by people who didn't need a Just Over Broke Justification Of Being JOB-JOB to give their lives meaning, purpose, and dignity. They might also take jobs as helpful to themselves and other projects, but that's not the intrinsic motivation.

This isn't wild futurist speculation. There's a big difference between futurists and future-making creators. This is precisely what we'll do for meaning and purpose and dignity in the post-jobs Post-Automation Era, because millions are already doing so.

The only thing about Lazy Entitled Human Theory that is starting to look credible is the incredible intellectual laziness of those who cling to such a cynical view of our species.

Millions of open-source developers do all this unpaid work for the love of learning, contributing, and participating in community, and many don't have the slightest interest in money other than needing it as an annoying distraction, as required to pay off bullies who show up at the first of each month threatening to throw them out on the street and destroy their lives if monthly protection money is not paid to the landed lord corporation, investor, or slum lord. What else is rent other than protection money to avoid eviction onto the local skid row? If we want to compare cynicisms, we can start with the engineered expropriation of the commons. Again, that's for later.

In the 21st century, the open-source way, with real-time continuous integration and improvement is no longer the exception, it is the norm. Software has eaten the world, and we ought to be grateful for it rather than smashing the latest iteration of the mechanical loom like our ancient Luddite cousins.

One vexing complication during this adaptation period might not be a legacy Moloch-driven culture that normalized and even elevated bullies, glorified gangsta life, and did not understand how to value anything other than immediate gratification.

Or it might be that a counterfeit freedom of unrestrained, unenlightened self-interest, anti-intellectual self-indulgence, and a culture that reified manual labor while diminishing and degrading all other forms of work; intellectual, academic, artistic, creative; has something to do with some of the most malignant maladaptive aspects of adjusting to the new environment.

Obviously, manual labor and blue-collar work are honorable and noble. That's not my point. As a documentarian and researcher who has worked in all kinds of work environments, I'm reporting the finding that there's a deep culture rift and animosity between the manual and intellectual trades. Again, my job is not to judge or condemn, it is to share my own direct lived experience.

My own time working and living alongside landscapers, landlords, software developers, in-fill developers, cops, crooks, healers, pushers, teachers, and talking heads has shown me more about the lesser angels of human nature that I care to acknowledge. Also, it's supplied me with the commitment and motivation to persevere on behalf of the better angels of our nature.

Students, writers, rappers, musicians, dancers, poetry-slam afficionados, graphic and fashion designers, architects, artists, athletes, journalists, aspiring professional gamers and game creators, and of course, software developers in dozens of different disciplines are as hard-working and noble as any noble laborer. Likewise, for the intellectual trades to look askance at the manual trades is nothing short of repugnant.

The potential for inspired, productive, manual, physical, intellectual, artistic, and creative human expression continues to grow exponentially, not because of technology, but because creativity and productivity are integral to who and what we are as intrinsically industrious beings. For human *be*ings, deliberate *be*ing is *do*ing.

Even "just" healing from trauma for five years, ten years, or sitting in silent meditation for a year in recovery are "doing something."

In fact, those might be some of the most important somethings that a conscious being can *do*, on the way to doing what's next.

So, it seems like one question is, which version of the many proactionary and precautionary science fiction futures do we want to live in? What inspire and cultivate the most beneficial characteristics of our globally interconnected, interdependent, inter-evolving species, given the extraordinary capabilities developed over the most recent century, over the most recent decades? What steps do we need to take in the next ten years, five years, and this year, to set us on the most likely trajectory to cultivate the kind of world we wish to live in – a world that works for everyone – fulfilling our duty to *be all we can be* as the best possible ancestors we can be, leaving the kind of legacy we wish to pass on to the next seven generations, to potentially countless generations that follow?

In August 2018, then 2020 U.S. Presidential candidate Andrew Yang addressed this question in pragmatic terms when he explained:

> *If we were to include care work, particularly that done by women, our GDP would be 26%, or about $5 trillion dollars, higher. "**Society is getting a free ride** on women's unrewarded contributions to the human race." Universal Basic Income would help right this wrong.*[cxvii]

That's $5 trillion dollars *per year*, every year, of lunch money stolen by the lying, thieving, bullying invisible hand of the 20th century legacy economy that gaslit women in the name of equality, "you must enter the 'real' workforce or fail to be recognized or compensated for your labor." Has there ever been a greater textbook market failure, a freer ride, or freer lunch in history than that enjoyed by the free market upon the backs of domestic care workers of the 20th century?

TANSTAAFL? Society has freeloaded and bummed generations of free lunches off uncompensated, unseen, disregarded, off-balance-sheet, domestic care work, for generations. The invisible hand of 20th century economic convention effectively bashed the principles of family in the face and stole their lunch money, every single day, for decades, centuries. Then we wonder what happened to the very notion of families. We all stood by and watched it happen, mostly for fear of losing our jobs. That's how gaslit and autonomized we become by the 20th century Job Trance. This is the red pill of householder domestic reality.

Uncompensated domestic care work is not only "real work" it is the irrefutable, non-negotiable, empirical prerequisite and origin of all economic activity and productivity. No capable and healthy humans, no capable and healthy workers. — Captain Obvious

---

Uncompensated, under-the-table, off-balance-sheet domestic work was equivalent to a form of universal slave labor among all people, disproportionately people of color, for certain. Domestic care workers are the single *most essential* of all *essential workers* because they hand-manufactured every single individual "productive component" of Moloch's 20th century industrial machine. Universal reparations are once again, doubly, triply in arrears.

Without healthy and productive humans, there can be no economic productivity whatsoever. By disproportionately rewarding and favoring the worst performers at cultivating healthy and productive humans and punishing the best over the past half century, we have arrived at the present moment in history.

People embody economies, human beings, not robots, not high frequency trading algorithms, not institutions, banks, markets, or governments. Individual human beings are the sole non-negotiable component of every market. As vehemently has many dismiss this obvious verity with insults, dismissals, devaluations, and evasive-avoidant semantics, *it is what it is*. Insults and name-calling do not change the nature of hard, cold reality by a single Planck-unit's measure. Domestic care work is some of *the most demanding and important work in the world* and yet it was culturally and economically dismissed and devalued by the pathologically dissociative invisible hand of Second-Millennium Economics. The results speak for themselves.

In point of fact, the previous millennium's Just Over Broke Justification Of Being JOB-JOB paradigm of currency circulation became increasingly, functionally obsolete with the rise of the gig economy, and derivations thereof. Eventually, this will be seen as one of the greatest and most beneficial awakenings from centuries of Job Trance, maybe sooner than later, given the immediacy of the forcing function introduced by AI.

The old *why*'s of life: go to school, get a corporate badge, work for forty or fifty years at a repetitive specialized task *like a robot*, then sit in front of the television regretting the whole thing, wondering how we never had a life, or drown our sorrow in beer or wine on the back patio of our oh so important house, waiting for someone to find what we thought was our oh so important body, three weeks after we died. That sad *why* is over. Again, no individual judgement. Critique? Post-mortem of the 20th century? You bet. There's a big difference.

Drinking, toking, tripping, and snorting oneself to death is the true, gruesome, and tragic story of more than one of my own former high school friends. Including the ones that everyone deferred to for 40 years as hardest working, shrewdest, most worldly-aware, and materially successful, the ones who mocked all thinking about *a world that works for everyone* as hair-brained scheming of utopian hippies, the ones who treated everyone in his life like a tool or NPC (non-playable character) to achieve their own end.

The whole JOB-JOB trance as the sole legitimate method of currency circulation and dignity allocation paradigm is long since over, as dead on the back patio as one my high school best friends, the great champion, master, and biggest winner of that game. How'd that work out for him? Yet we're told we need to "return to normalcy?" That's not a normal that I personally have any interest in, whatsoever, regardless of cynical, disingenuous, shiny status rewards of polite complicit society.

Is that imagery too gruesome, dear reader? The squeamish may need to bail out here, because I haven't even got to the grisly details of pricing the value human life and limb that lies ahead, which is the only way to face our commonwealth shadow work; the price we face for fearfully following the status quo for the past century or more. In the words of Howard Zinn, "You can't be neutral on a moving train." How much less so on a rocketing Starship into the Post-Automation Era?

At the 2018 Cultural Economy after Neoliberalism conference in Australia, George Morgan, author of The Creativity Hoax said, "'there was an enormous sense of disappointment from the young people we spoke to'. He mentions people trained as film editors working in a cinema box office, or PhD grads working in university admin" and "there is this enormous betrayal - dropping people off a cliff, because there are no jobs there for talented people" (Eltham).

The point here is that generations of disdain and devaluation for care workers, talented creatives, and intellectually inclined people in America is not only unjustified, it's been inexcusable, and immoral. Enough is enough.

The presumption that the meek, the most accommodating and compassionate among us, are the weakest is a mistake that we have both the duty and opportunity to correct in our lifetimes. The first shall be last and the last shall be first is already happening, what lies ahead is a simple matter of what we've already lived. If you think you've been a big shot, there might be a reckoning ahead. If you think you've been an invisible nobody, you might find yourself with responsibilities you never imagined. Again, no judgement, there are good reasons to see either fate as the weightier.

It is rapidly becoming, if not already common knowledge that genuine self-knowledge is key to realizing that job titles or tribal social status do not define our value as human beings, that lifelong learning is fundamental to creating a Post-Automation Era society that works for everyone.[cxviii]

Human life is short. So also, the lives of empires and civilizations on a Long Now timescale.[cxix] Therefore, like the Bong Joon Ho film *Parasite* questioned, we find ourselves questioning, who are the real Lazy Humans of Lazy Entitled Human Theory? Were the last the entitled, or were the first?

Wayfinding our deepest *why* is, of course, something that is completely individual and personal, even in the context of our shared fate. That's what makes any definitive answer ultimately beyond the scope of this work. Still, I felt compelled to at least acknowledge the process of wayfinding our why as something forever undefined and unconstrained by the bits and bytes and qubits of the mere emergence of digital superintelligence.

Our intrinsic humanity is not at the least risk when it comes to defining the priorities of our own human lives, both as individuals and in the community. Even artificial or eventually sentient digital superintelligence can't touch this.

* * *

Resurrection, Reincarnation, and Reformation

Call them the grown-up version of Readin', 'Ritin', and 'Rithmetic. The three Rs of individual and civilizational phase-state change. Resurrection, reincarnation, and reformation. Individual, organizational, civilizational. Speaking of *Story Itself*, here's a nerdy trial-balloon narrative for the age of generative AI: what if enough people ditched the traditional 20th century DCNR of *intergenerational dissonance* and voluntarily tuned our instruments to the key of G for this future jam?

Here's what I mean. What if enough members of each of the current generations – from A to Z, Zoomer to Alpha, and every alphabet letter in between – chose to identify as a meta-generational *Gen G*? You're right, *Gen Generative* sounds as ridiculous as chim-chimney, but a mid-wit label doesn't need to stick in order for the story itself to unfold in ten thousand delightfully human-beneficial generative ways. Let's leave it at that. *Gen G* as a random hash, a pointer to a placeholder in rulial space where a new kind of intergenerational cooperation and learning gradually dissolves the old intergenerational trauma bond patterns of holding onto power for far too long in old age and doubting our abilities far too much in youth.

- The more generative AI becomes, the more imaginative and generative humans become. This is what defines permanent human intelligence supremacy over quantum supremacy, machine learning, and engineered algorithmic intelligence.
- Even if qubits, electron clouds, adaptive nano-transistors, or elemental tokens experience some non-zero infinitesimal innate measure of qualia constituent to sentient subjective experience, the created does not exceed the creator.
- To entertain a grandiose fantasy of surpassing the supreme, let alone work to make such a worldly nightmare an earthly material reality, is the express folly of the mythic golem.[cxx]

"But children exceed their parents all the time," you might protest, "that's how we've become so advanced in the first place." That's right. Also, we are not our children's Creators. We are not their God. We didn't *create* our children. In the act of reproducing children, we merely engaged in a hormonally-driven biological process by which life propagates itself.

According to the journal-published mathematics of multidisciplinary researcher Nassim Haramein, as explained during a 2023 conversation with Lewis Howes on the *School of Greatness* podcast:

> *NH: "In physics we're told that all this happened [randomly]."*
>
> *LH: "That's what is said in physics and in biology. It's all random; accidental that we got here."*
>
> *NH: "Exactly. Early on, [I studied] physics and biology, and I was studying biophysics and all this stuff. They kept on saying mathematical fluctuation [is the explanation of all creation].*

> *Basically saying it's a fluke, right? But if you do 'fluke' calculations, you don't get even one microbe. [From] the beginning of what we can see [, what seems] to be the beginning of time for our evolution, we don't have enough time [not enough time has passed in terms of information processing] to make [even] one monocellular cell. The probability of all the right elements coming together, and I've made those calculations and they're published, is 10 to 8,896. So there's like eight thousand eight hundred [zeros to the right of that.] It's a lot of zeros. So, to give you an idea, the size of the universe is big, okay? You know, [from galactic distances,] the sun is not even visible in our galaxy because it's too small, okay? The Earth is like a piece of sand beside the sun, right? So it's way small. Just to give you an idea of size, the universe is huge, it's incredibly huge, hard to fathom how big it is. In centimeters, the universe has a radius approximately 10^{28}. So 10^{28} is already a huge number. Ten to the 8,000 [$10^{8,000}$]?! No matter what comes after the 8,000, it's insane. That's the probability that the correct elements for monocellular life – you know, the basis, what would be needed for monocellular life – [to] emerge. And then, if you were out of luck, [and] it would somehow miraculously happen [that] a rock would fall and squish it, then you'd have another trillions of years before it could happen again [the random emergence of a single monocellular cell]. So, the fact, the probability that it's random, is basically zero.*[cxxi]

In that mind-expanding context, isn't it remarkable that the capacity for human compassion is so profound that it equally and simultaneously extends outward and upward toward the infinitely expansive and inward and downward toward the infinitesimally humble? Including the Cartesian inanimate? Isn't it remarkable that the empirical subjective reality of immaterial and immeasurable human compassion reveals and expresses these capabilities while simultaneously deeply humbled by the understanding that the human-as-co-creator frame-of-reference operates at an abstraction layer of reality, of rulial space, that encompasses and embodies the burden, the weight, the responsibility and duty to serve the welfare of all sentient beings, even a theoretically sentient qubit-or-electron-cloud-probability space, by exercising compassionate authority and dominion over all subsidiary existence?

> *At [the] very specific size [that] the proton exists, in terms of the Planck information density, [that] same Planck information density [is precisely equivalent to] the information of the entire universe. So that's sometimes referred to as the holographic mass. If you [take] the vacuum energy inside a proton, it's 10 to the 55th grams to the 112 joules per meter squared, that 10 to the 55 grams is the exact mass of the universe, so it's at this exact equilibrium.*[cxxii]

> *Put another way, "Take a proton, okay? You calculate how many Planck information bits there [are] in that proton. You know that E = mc^2, right? So a little energy is a mass. You can calculate the mass of all the little Planck inside the proton and when you do that you get, not approximately, [but] exactly the mass of the universe. Remember I told you the equation is a surface to volume ratio? You do that calculation, you get the exact mass of the proton, and the exact radius."*[cxxiii]

If, in the past, human beings demonstrated the capability of deriving such fundamental principles of the micro and macro cosmos – prior to AGI – please put down this text, close your eyes, and for the short duration of three relaxed and natural breaths, imagine the previously unimaginable benevolence that our Gen G generative human nature has become capable of enacting *with* the extended cognition aptitudes and faculties of AGI.

This is where the rubber meets the road in terms of the greatest possible personal responsibility and accountability for our very thoughts and intentions. Even the illusion of the appearance of an obscure and inscrutable subjective consciousness comes under increased scrutiny. Do you imagine an inevitable hell, or heaven? That's *our* personal responsibility and our responsibility alone, no matter how much we want to blame *those* people, regardless of who our particular projected, otherized, target *them* may be.

> *The aphorism, "As a man thinketh in his heart so is he," not only embraces the whole of a man's being but is so comprehensive as to reach out to every condition and circumstance of his life. A man is literally what he thinks, his character being the complete sum of all his thoughts.*
>
> *As the plant springs from, and could not be without the seed, so every act of a man springs from the hidden seeds of thought and could not have appeared without them. This applies equally to those acts called "spontaneous" and "unpremeditated" as to those deliberately executed.*
>
> *Act is the blossom of thought, and joy and suffering are its fruits; thus does a man garner in the sweet and bitter fruitage of his own husbandry.*

As this man thinketh, from my perspective, the more generative AI becomes, the more imaginative and generative we human beings become. This is how human consciousness surfs the AGI tsunami. Why were simple surfing metaphors essential to our engagement with AI and AGI way back in the early 2020s? Because the biggest perceived threat from the perspective of tens of millions of human beings was that AI or AGI could somehow displace or supersede either or both the embodied physical and metaphysical capacities for perceived human agency and experiential autonomy; biological, intellectual, emotional, psychological, and spiritual. Time, as always, within the bounds of this earthly rulial shard, has once again resolved that misunderstanding.

While human-misconfigured and misdirected AGIs surely pose a threat to our biological frame in terms of automated weapons, the more chilling threat that many researchers understandably articulated in the early Post-Automation Era, was the threat to our very consciousness. We humans are extraordinarily fragile, frail, dependent, mostly formerly-furry animals, born into a context of catastrophic existential risk from the moment of our first breath.

Near-death wipeouts as the most daring learned to surf the deep and brooding sea of self-generative, iteratively, and reflectively-reinforced Markovian information were unfortunately inevitable.[cxxiv] Of course, some surfers pushed too far beyond the limits of their abilities, either by accident or foolishness. Some fell victim to the planned accidents of reprobate and fearful actors. Time, again, has told those stories by now, and will continue to do so, because time itself is storytelling story.

By thinking about AI as a *force of nature*, like the sea, instead of projecting and anthropomorphizing AGI as some outside invading alien force, we can forge a more grounded, sober, precise, productive, respectful, yet not paralyzingly fearful relationship with AI. It's not a matter of humans staying one step ahead of and adversarial generative AGI, it's a matter of practicing a new kind of subtle and challenging skill that requires our utmost attention to the reality of the present moment, until we comprehend the nature of this newly encountered natural phenomena sufficiently to interact with it skillfully. Like surfing, Markovian wave-sliding with superintelligence can never be perfectly safe. Reading or relaxing in a seemingly safe and comfy living room recliner is not perfectly safe, though for the most part we don't dwell on risks that percolate below a certain threshold of probability. Security is never perfect.

Yet, how were and are the risks of extended and amplified cognition qualitatively different from the risks of self-inflicted destructive organic modes of thinking? Such as compulsive catastrophizing, neurotic rumination, obsessively plotting revenge, or similar malfunctioning, malevolent, destructive, or self-destructive deliberations.

The greatest existential risk to humanity has always and will always be humanity itself. Everything else is denial or projection.

From the 02024 long now perspective, what practical, ordinary, everyday adjustments are most adaptive for flourishing alongside artificial and synthetic consciousnesses?[cxxv] When can we trust that we have gained adequate, minimal actionable understanding and context of the new environment, to make those choices with a sufficient sense of assurance and conviction to do so? How do we navigate such a significantly altered pace and landscape of life in the Post-Automation Era? Where can we turn for answers to the deepest questions, if not ourselves? Who is more qualified to define what it means to move toward a world that works for everyone than the *Gen G* cohort born to inhabit this interim, incremental world, while shouldering the additional overwhelming accountability to seven generations, maybe more?

Such questions can open the way to new avenues of deeper, more meaningful, more accurate, and more authentic individual and inter-observational wayfinding. This is a good time to extend a sense of eternal patience and compassion toward ourselves and others.

As in all of life's experiences and endeavors, some people seem to receive, develop, or discover a strong and clear sense of purpose, in advance of the majority of any given population. Meanwhile, most of us can and do find our why along the way. Therefore, there is no need to excessively dwell and deliberate upon new observations and new understandings of the present situation or moment before we act decisively upon our current best understandings and intuitions, however limited, in the process of navigating challenges, large and small, Post-Automation Era. The potential for developing an effective balance of deliberation and decisiveness in core teams that consist of what the Black Swan Group refers to as analyst, accommodator, and assertive negotiation styles is one useful, even excellent way to think about team-building in the 21st century.

On an individual level, to use a Markovian metaphor, in any given moment, if we discover that we are unsatisfied with the present situation, we can form new intentions, curate new thoughts, and take new actions that generate new outcomes, with zero correlation to all that we experienced in the past. Yes, the concrete, objective events of our life empirically led us to this present moment. It is equally true that those events need not determine the choices we make moving forward. We can trust ourselves to make the necessary changes and decisions to cultivate a safe and flourishing environment for both ourselves and others, even as the old ways, the deprecated DCNRs decompose, unravel, crumble, and dissolve all around us.

In a poignant 2018 Digg.com article, *Millennials Must Work Until They Die, And Other Facts*, Steve Rousseau wrote:

> *This week we have Alicia Munnell, a Federal Reserve economist and director of Boston College's Center For Retirement Research, writing in Politico that there is indeed a simple solution for Millennials to overcome the gaping generation wealth gap: work longer. "In fact, my research shows that the vast majority of millennials will be fine if they work to age 70," concludes Munnell. "And although that might sound old, it's historically normal in another sense: Retiring at 70 leaves the ratio of retirement to working years the same as when Social Security was originally introduced."*
>
> *Ah we'll be fine! We're just returning to a time when Social Security was a new thing, and apparently the luxury of retiring at 55, heck even 65, was only to be enjoyed by the generation that introduced Social Security and their children. Everyone else can go kick rocks.*
>
> *Here is a number to add some more context to the "historically normal" retirement age of 70. As of 2017, the US average life expectancy is 78.7 years. That doesn't seem "historically" normal to us (Rousseau).*

Does that sound like, look like, or feel like the kind of world that we want to live in, in an age of superabundance and superintelligence? Is perpetuating the traumas of previous generation what we really want to leave as our legacy? Do we really believe that it's right and just to press people into effective wage-slavery because *that's what we endured*? Are we sure about that, fellow soon-to-be ancestor to seven generations who come after us? Is passing on our intergenerational social traumas what it means to be a good ancestor?

Should every generation suffer the way our generation suffered, to meet some abstract concept of character or grit that ceased to be imperative, let alone relevant, decades or even centuries ago? Why do we keep projecting and perpetuating obsolete and counterproductive trauma bonds of dysfunctional parents and dehumanizing hazings of legacy institutions?

Do any children who were themselves literally beaten into compliance to a scarcity and inadequacy mindset honestly believe that we became better human beings *because* of the suffering we endured in that past life, or *in spite of it*? Were the beatings and abuses we may have suffered *required* to improve our life and character, or could skillful parental and community guidance have led us to the same, or even far better destination, without the fear, the coercion, the emotional abuse, cruelty, the trauma, along the way? Ask anyone who has managed to survive genuine scarcity, real destitution, if "scarcity contributes to a meaningful life." This is yet another example of the kind of gaslighting DCNs that darkened so much of the 20th century mentality, which empirically led to the cultural disintegration of the early 21st century.

> *Scarcity contributes to an interesting and a meaningful life. In the words of Professor Todd May, when there is always time for everything, there is no urgency for anything. A life without limits would lose the beauty of its moments, and it would become boring.*[cxxvi]

Does life really "lose the beauty of its moments and become boring?" Not in my experience. Quite the contrary. Relief from material scarcity, only to be plunged back into those conditions by circumstances was all the direct evidence I needed to understand that statements like this provide a prime example of the Dark DCNs of institutional gaslighting.

> *Scarcity forces trade-off thinking. We recognize that having one thing means not having something else. If you spend $10 on anything, it is $10 less left for something else. Economists call this the opportunity cost—the alternative use of the money. Doing one thing means neglecting other things. However, slack frees us from making trade-offs. For example, as your budget grows, the purchase of the iPad takes up a smaller and smaller portion of your disposable income. Thus, a bigger budget makes decisions less consequential and lessens feelings of scarcity (cxxvi).*

So, being freed from the making the existential-stress-inducing, cognitively deteriorating Maslow Basic Needs trade-offs between rent, food, or heat is characterized as "slack?" Maybe for a teenager still learning the basics of life, but not for an entire population.

Does any of this look like, sound like, or feel like character building, or does it describe methodically engineered character degradation?

> *Poverty taxes cognitive resources and causes self-control failure. Poverty means making painful trade-offs (sacrifices). The poor juggle rent, loans, late bills, and count the days until the next paycheck. When you can afford so little, so many things need to be resisted. And resisting more temptations depletes the willpower, which in turn makes them less capable of giving up, say, a smoking habit. This explains why do the poor often fail so badly in self-control. Poverty, at its very core, taxes self-control capacity. The poor lack freedom of mind. They are short, not just on cash but also on willpower.*
>
> *The context of scarcity makes you myopic (exhibiting bias toward here and now). The mind is focused on present scarcity. We overvalue immediate benefits at the expense of future ones (e.g., procrastinate important things, such as medical checkups, or exercising). We only attend to urgent things and fail to make small investments even when future benefits can be substantial. To attend to the future requires cognitive resources, which scarcity depletes. We need cognitive resources to plan and to resist present temptations (cxxvi).*

WE NOW KNOW – OBJECTIVELY, EMPIRICALLY, SCIENTIFICALLY – AND BY RULES OF EVIDENCE, BEYOND ANY SHADOW OF A DOUBT, THAT THE ONLY ROLE THAT POVERTY, LACK, AND CYNICAL, SOCIALLY-ENGINEERED SCARCITY AND THE ASSOCIATED UNNECESSARY PHYSICAL, EMOTIONAL, AND PSYCHOLOGICAL TRAUMA THEY INFLICT UPON HUMANS; THE ONLY ROLE THAT THE 20TH CENTURY ALGORITHM PLAYS IN HUMAN LIVES IS TO CREATE TRAUMATIZED HUMANS. THIS IS WHY ENDING LEGACIES OF DYSFUNCTIONAL INTERGENERATIONAL TRAUMA IS WHAT WE ARE ACCOUNTABLE FOR IN THE MIDST OF OUR GRAND EXPONENTIAL SUPERABUNDANT AMBITIONS TO BE "GOOD ANCESTORS" OF THE 21ST CENTURY.

Trauma doesn't build character. Trauma doesn't instill grit. Trauma doesn't grow a healthy gratitude. Because it's not even close to a *healthy* sense of gratitude to merely be grateful that the beatings – physical, emotional, psychological, or spiritual – have temporarily relented. Moloch, of course, always begs to differ. Adding insult to intergenerational trauma injury, many in the previous century were dismissively told to "snap out of it," by authoritative medical sources, which seemed to go beyond the pale.[cxxvii]

Then we wonder why polite society thoroughly and systematically swept the suicide pandemic among young people of the early 21st century under the proverbial rug. Another easy dismissal on this point was to accuse entire generations of indulging in an unjustified victim mentality; and that was definitely another go-to in the 20th century DCN library. We now see how well that worked out. Victim-blaming doesn't vindicate a nation founded on liberty and justice for all. There can be no liberty in a civilization where there is no cognitive capacity to make free decisions, and where the competition is actively engineered to degrade and diminish that capacity, in order to exact and maximize presumably legitimate, yet all too often illegitimate forms of behavioral compliance.

Pretending that the increasingly and empirically shady-looking COVID-19 pandemic wasn't permanently traumatizing on a civilization scale, once again returning to the "just snap out of it" DCN, is about as empathic and compassionate as saying the same thing to any traumatic abuse survivor, amplified to a civilizational scale.

Regardless of team or gang colors, it's another unpleasant, empirical fact that we do have – as the 45th president of the United States unfortunately referred to them – some animals to deal with. We might have once believed that merely ignoring people who wished us harm and did us real harm, would make them go away. Some of us have learned the hard way that this is not the case. The question then becomes, as depicted in features like Bong Joon Ho's film, Parasite: which actors and agents, exactly, are the animals and which the parasites?

Are people struggling to make ends meet the animals and parasites? Or are people supporting and defending deprecated perspectives and policies that continue to increase the numbers of alleged animals and parasites, the genuine animals, and parasites? Are cultural and institutional policies and practices that further concentrate wealth and perpetuate needless basic income instability not another breed of organizational animals and parasites?

Perhaps we need to face our own animalistic and parasitic natures before we can even think about pointing the parasitic finger at others.

One reason that so many of our deeply dysfunctional embedded psychological and behavioral patterns – individual and societal – seem almost impossibly difficult to debug is that people absorb and internalize strong impressions that create indelible beliefs, very early in life. People raised by a law of the jungle mentality live by a law of the jungle mentality, often themselves victims of domestic cruelty, unthinkably sadistic covert emotional and psychological abuse, and physical violence. This is some of what Sapolsky's work is getting at in suggesting the illusion of free will. It's a tautology that traumatizing environments, families, organizations, and institutions traumatize people. This is why the all-too-often minimizing and dismissive adage, "hurt people, hurt people," regularly uttered with a sense of exasperated helplessness and inevitability, can rub salt in the wounds of survivors, even if they've managed to become thrivers by some combination of grace and uncommon fortitude.

Today we know that it is from the experiences in our early family environments, communities, tribes, and nations, that we construct beliefs that feel more solid and more certain than beliefs we form later in life. To call upon an AI analogy, think of those experiences as our LLM training data. This may be one reason why some of the least helpful vestigial beliefs can remain among the most deeply held convictions and feel most true to us, even though all the evidence we see today points to the contrary.

It's exceedingly difficult to unseat some of these deeply held convictions without investing serious time to look inward and examine their source; and who has time for that, when working two or three jobs, 60 to 80 hours a week, just to survive? So, the cycle of intergenerational and institutional trauma bonds continues, widens, and deepens, plunging a culture and society into increasingly deep levels of despair.

---

*The foundation of social security and economic stability is not income **equality**; rather, income **adequacy**, which means **income security**.*

In his book, *The Rise of the Useless Class*:

> *Historian Yuval Noah Harari offers a bracing prediction: just as mass industrialization created the working class; the AI revolution will create a new unworking class. The most important question in 21st-century economics may well be: What should we do with all the superfluous people, once we have highly intelligent non-conscious algorithms that can do almost everything better than humans?*

Former BBC Today Producer Blaire Palmer's neologism, *unworking*, pairs well with debunking of Lazy Entitled Human Theory and affirms Inherently Creative Productive Human Theory, setting the stage for the most paradoxically useful, productive, and innovative Useless Class in history.[cxxviii] The dawn of Unworking seems a fitting sequel to the 20th century DCN that claimed life's highest meaning and purpose were to be found and experienced in Just Over Broke Justifications Of Being (JOB-JOBs). Blair wrote:

> *I don't think the result of unworking is that everyone becomes a lazy bum who expects to do nothing but go to the cinema and sleep in every day. I believe that when we truly unwork we will be MORE motivated to make our contribution, be able to put more of ourselves in to that contribution, find a way to contribute that really feeds our soul and enhances our mental health and solve may of the biggest issues in our world together — climate change, disenfranchisement, inequality, poverty, maybe even war.*
>
> *I want us to find ways to unwork because I think it will enhance our experience of life and actually change the world. I think we NEED to because of the price we currently pay in terms of our physical and mental health as a result of the long hours, the commuting, the stress, the constant changing of goal posts, the challenging workplace relationships, the parent-child dynamic, the day to day frustrations of work and the pressure to take more and more on as you advance in your career. It's not sustainable. If we expect to be MORE productive we have to think again about how we work and go right back to basics.*[cxxix]

As demonstrated earlier, evolution itself proves that humans are inherently industrious. If it were not true, we'd either be extinct or at best still living in trees, having been so lazy as to only tend to the most immediate survival pressures and copulating for the rest of our slack-jawed, mouth-breathing harsh existence. But that's not what happened. We worked. Ceaselessly. For eons. We worked first for survival, and then to negotiate and understand the functioning of the natural world, long before the notion of jobs ever emerged. Does it make sense for every individual human to repeat the entire cycle of human creation and evolution, world without end? Maybe it does. Maybe that's the program. Or maybe not. What we do know is that humans *worked* for ages before there was ever the first hint of the modern concepts of markets, money, or any of the other abstractions that came to dominate the 20th century Molochian consciousness. Maybe this is because people are inherently creative and productive, made in the image of their eternally generative Creator.

We've seen that the cynical and misanthropic Lazy Entitled Human Theory is just plain wrong. Human nature is inherently imaginative, creative, and productive. Unless, of course, we consider God to be lazy or non-existent. If free will is an illusion, how is it that so many choose to believe one way or the other?[cxxx] Even those who claim that humans do not possess free simultaneously confess that they themselves live as if free will exists, effectively debunking their own claim.

Hence, what we choose to do with this information, if or when we choose to act upon it, and how we choose to rebalance our Four Game Portfolio accordingly – inner, outer, narrative, and mystery – is our own experiment to decide whether or not we ourselves are the Molochian automatons we ought to fear most in the age of AI, the Post-Automation Era. As complex and confusing as the present moment may feel, one observation seems clear: there can be no AI alignment with human values unless and until we first find alignment within and amongst our own human values.

* * *

It's All Mixed Up

Whether broadly scientifically believed or not yet, the historical and widely recounted phenomena of resurrection, reincarnation, and personality reformation are among the most controversial, confounding, counterintuitive, profoundly mysterious, and improbable of potential human experiences imaginable. So remote and unlikely that many regard all three impossible, unreal, purely mythological, imaginary, and for good reason. Imagine someone telling you to change your relentlessly curious and doggedly persistent personality to an apathetic and blithe jib. Now imagine the inverse. If not technically unimaginable, it's an incredible stretching exercise.

Equally controversial, convoluted, circular or toroidal in logic, and likely impossible to ever comprehend completely, humanity seems to stand today face-to-face in a fugue state of perpetual, civilizational fight, flight, freeze, fawn, fright, flag, faint, flood, or fatigue response, and in the distracted, avoidant, evasive, superficial world of first-wave social media, the friend, fake, fade, or f**k coping strategies as the only viable pre-scripted and socially-engineered responses to the perplexing complexities of the Post-Automation Era civilizational phase-state changes underway in the early 21st century.[cxxxi]

In such an environment, how can the character and nature of a deeply personality-disordered individual, let alone an increasingly disturbed and deranged civilization, ever transform into an adaptive, dependable, dynamically stable, reliable configuration, effectively invulnerable to risks of relapse or malfunction at the worst possible moments? Once the neurocircuitry of personality fires together long enough to become wired together, isn't it biologically impossible to break or dissolve those living welds and repair them in any way that is remotely as stable as the initial welds?

"It is no measure of health to be well-adjusted to a profoundly sick society."[cxxxii]

If history is any indication, many scientific and empirically-minded people like me still bristle and scoff at these Three Rs of individual and civilizational phase-state change as unproven, unscientific, and even superstitious. My objective and obligation are not to convince anyone of the literal or metaphorical veracity of these universally contemplated processes, only to leverage their esoteric implications as analogous to the significance and nature of the extraordinarily difficult to conceptualize changes that the Post-Automation Era *has already wrought* in the ordinary, everyday lives of 336 million U.S. citizens, and billions worldwide.[cxxxiii]

To begin in concrete terms, the fact that the United States is both a *federal republic* and *representative democracy*; a hybrid form of governance that is not even close to a pure version of either democracy or republic, may come as an unpleasant surprise for some. Constitutional scholars across the political spectrum disagree on much, but one incontestable fact is that the founders of the United States of America never intended for citizens to ever live in anything even close to a *pure capitalist* or pure *free-market* economy.[cxxxiv] The debate, ever since and perhaps world without end, is about finding the most adaptive mix for sustaining the freest possible society within the existential constraints and boundaries of utter chaos, lawlessness, and megalomaniacal tyranny.

For these reasons, we have always lived and shall forever live in some variety of *mixed economy* (see Glossary). Either political or economic purity inevitably results in tyranny. From a purely reductionist, materialist, Darwinian perspective, even our bodies are not purely human. From the essential primate perspective of the billions of independent, individual microorganisms that make up the human microbiome, our bodies are a kind of murmuration, a nation of self-contained and individually incentivized component organisms that somehow, miraculously, accidently, in complete violation of the providence of entropy, exist on a pebble hurtling through an infinite void, spinning and revolving about, at a maddeningly precise distance from a cosmologically insignificant sun; in all in perfectly intricate micro- and macro-scale harmonic coordination and interdependence, dancing in the midst of an incompressible eternity. By chance?

There has always been a bit of each of the Big Three economic 'isms in the American economic mix, and by virtue of the nature of the world we live in, it's a statistical certainty to remain that way, short of some version of totalitarianism insisting on total purification, which is never a healthy or safe word to hear in any worldly political realm.

Adding to that mix today, many see the world moving toward a kind of distributed stateless blockchain anarcho-capitalist utopia as a logical evolution of the current deteriorating state of global financial hegemony. That's a terrifying thought to those who don't understand what those words even mean, and even more frightening to many who do, and it's not the point or aim of this book to explore that thesis, although it is a vital thesis to explore in the context of the Post-Automation Era. To remain focused upon the task at hand, we must settle for noting these facts in passing as highly significant amongst the mix of components that are in the midst of reimagining and recreating civilization and life as we've known it, IRL.

While oversimplifications, false analogies, and spurious comparisons characterized ivory tower economics of the 20th century, there are no quantum or Newtonian laws of physics governing economics, and cannot be, because physics is a material science and economics is a social science. Societies consist of humans, biological and social organisms in biological and social correlation and relationship to one another.

Therefore, the everyday *economics of human flourishing* has much more in common with the science of biology than the science of physics, more in common with biological systems than quantum gravity systems, although both are equally essential in their respective roles. There is nothing political in the observation that economics as both theoretical and applied abstraction layer merely exists much closer to the biological layer of existence than the quark layer, or the CMB layer, but that internal individual human discord makes it so. Our bodies are a unity whole, consistent of billions of individual living organisms. The cosmos is a unitary whole, consisting of countless individual galaxies, each again consisting of countless distinctly individual and unique stars and planets.

More provocatively, and with all sincerity and respect, how is the phrase, E Pluribus Unum, "from many, one," not the most collectivist motto in the history of the world?

A shift in thinking about economics from a mechanistic, Standard Model of physics perspective to a biological, ecological frame of reference is a major tenet of our work and a marked departure from the relatively left-brained DCNs of the 20th century.

While perhaps not immediately intuitively utilitarian for some, the perceptual shift invoked by the economics of human flourishing invites an equally if not more rigorous, individually, and personally accountable, and simultaneously more genuinely human, familial, fruitful, and accurate understanding of the human predicament. An upgrade that refactors, improves, and cleans up the existing crufty code base, an adaptation that doesn't even come close to burning it all down or throwing out the baby with the bathwater; although, admittedly, to refer to a centuries old paradigm that has overwhelmingly, empirically proven its unsustainable skewed outcomes in the everyday realities of the present environment seems rather logically inept at best and intellectually dishonest, at worst.

In actively engaging with the economics of human flourishing, we become morally and ethically obligated to grapple with the undeniable, the uplifting, the inconvenient, the uncomfortable, and the inexorable demands of life and human civilization, in terms of social, monetary, fiscal, and public policy; in terms of academic and corporate research, oversight, performance, metrics, measurement, education; and in terms of clear, concise, actionable, responsive, tractable narratives, and pragmatic statecraft, diplomacy for adapting to the significant disruptions experienced by both individuals and institutions in the midst of the emergence of this a Post-Automation Era.

It seems to me that the shortest adaptive path to an ordinary, non-revolutionary, everyday state of affairs in which poverty and lack statistically cease to exist for any population leads inevitably and directly through *the principle of income security*, because underlying and preceding principles such as basicness, universality, unconditionality, or guaranty, the principle of *income security* is functionally equivalent to social security in any economy, of any kind.

When democracy degrades to the point of no choice, other than to vote <u>against</u> what people are taught and conditioned to fear and loathe, rather than voting <u>for</u> that which they are encouraged and educated to aspire, the very principle of choice is effectively undermined, eliminated, leaving only a distorted Molochian choiceless choice.

Individuation between nations and internal integrity within nations are predicated upon the availability of choices made possible by the economic and social security of citizens. Where every day existential precarity becomes normalized, much less exceeds humane tolerances, unrest erupts, regardless of the prevalence and political correctness of deprecated dominant narratives of denial among polite society, and regardless of how proud a nation's aspiring emperors of any class, caste, or party arrogantly parade about in new clothes, proclaiming all is well if we only concede to their rulership.

Therefore, it is not our concern to ponder design fictions of where Post-Automation Era economics will be in 50 years, 25 years, or even five years. Our focus is upon understanding where we are right now, in this present dauntless moment. To identify, understand, and articulate the immediate options and actions available and required to adapt to the present situation, guided by U.S. Constitutional principles in the context of mustering a rapidly, widely, accurately, and transparently-informed, wholly voluntary, non-coercive consensus in the interest of preserving and fortifying domestic cultural integrity, tranquility, and sustainable, down-to-earth, wellness and superabundant human flourishing into the 21st century. To resurrect, reincarnate, and reinstate the principle of *E Pluribus Unum* as the bedrock of the American social contract and the north star of our universally aligned human values.

In economic terms, this means restoration of *the founding commonwealth principle of income security* as a basic human right. The principle of income security is not some novel Marxist ideological novelty or transhumanist philosophical bauble. The principle of income security is as fundamental an American value as the right to Maslow Safety, as we demonstrate throughout this work. As educator and activist Scott Santens puts it, "Basic income is neither left nor right, it's forward."

While some of the vocabulary and reminders from history may seem relatively new to some, the principles, practices, and *precedence of U.S. budget policy* are empirical and indisputable. Upon intellectually honest inspection, we find that the principle and priority of income security has always proven itself co-equal as utmost national priority, right alongside national security, because the two inevitable obligations are so deeply interdependent. We empirically authenticate this observation by audit of the past century of U.S. budgets.

While one-hundred percent consistent with historical, legal, and economic policy precedent, unconditional, universal income security does represent a kind of sea change in public understanding of what currency *signifies* – what currency means and represents – in the context of an advance, AI-integrated, post-automation society.

So, while obliged to navigate moments of crisis, this unique inflection point in history presents us with the rare opportunity to engage in an awareness-raising process that illuminates the historic precedents that effectively made income security a fundamental human right in the United States, almost from the very beginning. If that sounds ridiculous, absurdly overstated, too good to be true, or somehow revisionist, then we are bound by Carl Sagan's standard in the remainder of this work; namely, "extraordinary claims require extraordinary evidence." If we fail to surface the proof of a forgotten and buried history, crucified, and left for dead, then our work becomes fit for unceremonious discard to the same dustbin of never-to-be-heard-from-again history. On the other hand, if we demonstrate that the wisdom and foresight of the founders is evident in the principle of income security, like a tiny and easily overlooked mustard seed sown in wisdom whose long-anticipated season has arrived, then those narratives that effectively buried this principle didn't realize the seed-like nature of eternal values, and the season of fruition is at hand.

It is our duty to demonstrate that the history of income security policy in the U.S. was a record partly forgotten, partly buried, and partly suppressed by those with deep conflicts of interest and ambitions to defend and maintain a bygone default consensus reality that disproportionately benefited the narrow interests of Mammon. Because the nature of Mammon is animated and driven by the spirits of lack and inadequacy, it can never acquire enough, and so the worship of Mammon, especially the worship of Mammon in ecclesiastical clothing, drives civilizations to unsustainable extremes.[cxxxv]

It's a central tenet of the oldest story ever told. Pride, greed, lust, and envy burning it all down in the name of moral, ethical, or intellectual superiority, often while wearing the robes of not just Caeser and the Pharisees, but the robes of the Buddha, the Christ, the Prophet, peace be upon Him. This is what it means to live in a fallen world.

Forever war. Permanent pandemic. Psychological prisons of addiction promoted as escape routes from transgression and suffering. Tormented and traumatized souls tormenting and traumatizing the vulnerable for profit and sport, all in the name of a misanthropic, soulless science. This is not a picture of a theoretical rogue-AI or AGI dystopia in the future, it is evidence of the miracle that we somehow survived *what's already transpired*, finally finding some semblance of ability to write and speak openly about the dreadfulness of a dystopia that we somehow managed to withstand, aka, the default consensus reality known as the 20th century. A place and time that now exists merely as a blot on the canvas of eternity. We don't live there anymore, and yet it seems to be exceedingly difficult for many to accept that glaring, non-negotiable reality. Such is the nature of trauma bonds with people, situations, organizations, and nations.

In today's atmosphere of transparency, the 1920's Bernays-style smoke and mirrors no longer convinces a 21st century audience of the legitimacy of bygone DCNRs. What that means is, in an increasingly transparent environment, the outsized influence of a minority population of high-functioning and highly persuasive, but often misguided individuals and institutional addicted to self-serving 20th century notions of centralized, commanding heights public relations strategies and tactics can no longer manufacture consent for the DCNR of a long bygone era.

That's far from an all-good or all-bad development. There were deep institutional and cultural interdependencies and enmeshments between both the ethical values that served human flourishing well, and parallel perverse incentives that encouraged misguided motives that undermined the very shared cultural values purported as most sacrosanct. The right to unqualified privacy, an unstipulated derivative right, provided protection for the worst imaginable of human abuses, mirrored equally by the right to secrecy in violating those privacies in the interest of national security and protecting the human rights of the least among us.

President Theodore Roosevelt understood the implications of bestowing the spirit of God upon the form of Mammon as early as 1904 but the public rebuked him, demanding the right to sanctimony while guzzling cocaine-laden Coca-Cola and frequenting romanticized Wild West Saloon Brothels. In this respect, at least, American culture has proved eminently resilient: its dauntless capacity for sanctimonious hypocrisy. It's not easy to deny that these are accurate if unflattering images of an aging commonwealth face staring back at us in the mirror of the 21st century.

Specifically, Roosevelt warned:

> *... these coins would be used to further ungodly activities, such as gambling, and facilitate crime.*

Roosevelt was right. Every anonymous criminal exchange for cash is anathema to the highest of human values. Anonymous Johns and Janes, slum lords, drug lords, illicit arms and human traffickers all love nothing more than anonymous cash, their transgressions made all the sweeter by the inherent scoffing and mockery of such transactions made with currency proclaiming, "In God we trust." Moloch lives for this.

> *The coin, whose ultra-high relief version is now considered one of the most beautiful coins ever struck in the U.S., was indeed appreciated for its esthetics by art critics. However, a scandal immediately erupted over the lack of "In God We Trust" on the eagles and double eagles. Theodore Roosevelt insisted that while he was in favor of placing the motto on public buildings and monuments, doing so for money (or postage stamps and advertisements) would be "dangerously close to sacrilege."*
>
> *"My own feeling in the matter is due to my very firm conviction that to put such a motto on coins, or to use it in any kindred manner, not only does no good, but does positive harm, and is in effect irreverence, which comes dangerously close to sacrilege. ... Any use which tends to cheapen it, and, above all, any use which tends to secure its being treated in a spirit of levity, is from every standpoint profoundly to be regretted. ... it seems to me eminently unwise to cheapen such a motto by use on coins ... In all my life I have never heard any human being speak reverently of this motto on the coins or show any signs of its having appealed to any high emotion in him, but I have literally, hundreds of times, heard it used as an occasion of and incitement to ... sneering ... Every one must remember the innumerable cartoons and articles based on phrases like 'In God we trust for the 8 cents,' ... Surely, I am well within bounds when I say that a use of the phrase which invites constant levity of this type is most undesirable."*
>
> *—President Theodore Roosevelt, 13 November 1907*[cxxxvi]

What all of this talk of Mammon and morals means is that we must take away lessons from the 20th century that inform us with respect to how to mitigate, if not abolish the malevolent aspects of an era known for its breathtaking material prosperity, yet tragically undermined by the worst of human qualities. If we refuse to look into this mirror darkly, how can we ever hope to escape the dreadful memetic cycle so poignantly and artfully penned by G. Michael Hopf, author of *Those Who Remain*?

"Hard times create strong men. Strong men create good times.

Good times create weak men. And, weak men create hard times."[cxxxvii]

Is Hopf's observation evidence of the inevitable karmic nightmare-go-round of eastern teachings, or can people and societies somehow break free of toxic cycles of intergenerational trauma by facing the hard shadow work of self-examination – from the grass-roots individual to the civilizational level?

Another mind-blowing proof of the effectiveness of 20th century industrialized public relations in the conditioning of contradictory human thought and behavior at scale, is the fact that almost no matter where we traveled in the world, we were likely to meet with a high degree of similarly entrenched 20th century conventions, beliefs, and economic convictions. Global monoculture came to reflect a de facto one-world government that persisted for centuries, ruled by the invisible hand of Mammon, in turn governed by a Molochian mindset.

In 2024, the imagined dystopian future of a mercilessly totalitarian global regime with no respect for human life lies not ahead of us, but in McLuhan's rearview mirror. Fixating our astonished gaze upon the wreckage of the past only prevents us from steering toward a better future. We can't fix the mistakes of history that has led us to this present moment, so we had best get to work making the best of the situation at hand, however seemingly dire or despairing. That start not with AI Alignment, but with Human Alignment. As Ray Dalio rightly repeats like a mantra, "what is important is how we are with each other."

We began talking about the underlying principles, values, and meaning of a currency. We said that currency is both a *store* of value and an *expression* of values. So the question becomes, *what* values does a currency signify? How does a currency become resilient and enduring as both a *store of value* and an exchange of *credible values*? When the value of a debased currency moves toward zero, the values and meaning that currency once represented either also go to zero, or those values and ethics find a new expression, a new conveyance. In the U.S., the de facto historic motto of Great Seal of the United States, *E Pluribus Unum,* and the coinage motto *In God We Trust,* were intended to express the ethical values exchanged in U.S. currency as a store of value.[cxxxviii] As we've seen, it didn't entirely work out that way.

Something changed over the course of the 20th century, the volume of under-the-table, cash-only trade, including but not limited to illicit arms trading and human trafficking, became so detached from those articulated values as to render the credible ethics of the currency meaningless, and hence worthless and untrustworthy as a values conduit. It wasn't printing alone that spelled the end for an asset class that gradually become operationally synonymous with the lowest ethical moral forms of corruption and graft conducted at the highest levels. Many began to wonder whether human nature was so irredeemable that even a new kind of currency that inherited the mantle of those values wouldn't also, inevitably, be dragged into the same pit.

Many began to wonder, "what if a currency were undeniably traceable and people could be held accountable for those most heinous of human behaviors?" If complete privacy is the fundamental enabler of the worst of human behaviors, while setting up an endless Spy v. Spy MAD Magazine comic scenario that itself corrupts secretive agencies, then what's really going on here? Why are we so obsessed with this principle of privacy, even though in practical terms, privacy never existed for the majority of tribal human history? Everyone knew everything in clans averaging 150 in number.[cxxxix]

On the one hand, currency transaction accountability makes the world a saner, safer place for everyone, on the other hand, it more than ruffles the feathers of an oddly common flock of both commercial, free-market Libertarians and community-minded civil libertarians. I am only grotesquely oversimplifying and labeling to make an analogy about the strange bedfellows of capital 'L' Libertarians of the Ayn Rand worshipping objectivist religion, some of whom have proved prone to loudly and violently object to anything that remotely limits their rights to make trillions in illegal arms and human trafficking trades on the one hand, and performatively well-intentioned and often naïve, woke, social justice warriors who don't realize that it's complete freedom from surveillance and law enforcement that directly enables those horrendous activities. Maybe those bad behaviors are reversed between the two. Maybe the human vulnerability to malevolence infects both wings of an odd right-libertarian-left-liberationist alliance of expediency and convenience. Either way, it seems like an odd duck, indeed.

We cry out that we don't want to be traced, tracked, and surveilled, *and* at the same time we demand to live in a world where chemical, biological, and nuclear arms are not a persistent cash-only free-market existential threat. We want the right to privacy with religious fervor, *and* we want zero human trafficking or trading of human bodies and parts, of any kind.

Welcome to the Post-Automation Era. Still think we're talking about Utopia?

A new generation and genre of asymmetric and lone strategic actors have emerged, with names like Ethereum Investor #1 or #2,[cxl] and millions of others like them who know that we cannot address the devastating aftermath of the 20th century with the same kind of thinking that created those problems and deeply understand the dual values inherent to currency. In MIRI's 2018 summer update email newsletter, Rob Bensinger wrote:

> *We ran a successful internship program over the summer, and we're co-running a new engineer-oriented workshop series with CFAR. On the fundraising side, we received a $489,000 grant from the Long-Term Future Fund, a $150,000 AI Safety Retraining Program grant from the Open Philanthropy Project, and an amazing surprise $1.02 million grant from "Anonymous Ethereum Investor #2!"*

On a painful and vulnerable personal note, I endured a significant amount of non-trivial grief for the perceived treacheries of merely experimenting with Bitcoin as early as 2009. Today, no serious person or policy maker can ignore the asset class, considering the fact that the Federal Reserve itself has now developed an openly traded Central Bank Digital Currency (CBDC) based upon the same technology.[cxli]

As an all too frail human being, of course I experience moments of egoic vindication, with respect to people who told me that blockchain technology couldn't possibly ever be widely adopted. However, I also feel sad to bear witness once again to the same personality types feeding upon their own fears about the wider adoption of digital currencies as some kind of devilish scheme, just as they regarded the Internet of the 1980's and 1990's, the sending of "spirits over wires" with the telephone, and the robbing of souls with photography. These observations are no grounds for judging others, for I personally know and wrestle with the same quality of human hubris that seems to eternally presume that the way things have always seemed is the way things will always be. Human nature seems riddled with such contradictions. We want both the stability and predictability of a static, persistent utopia in which we feel a sense of mastery and control, and yearn for novelty, growth, and change to keep ourselves entertained or challenged. While the trials and tribulations that I faced were no fun, the trial by fire forced me to confront these same characteristic within myself.

What I learned is that technology isn't the devil's most powerful tool, people are. What we do with technology, how we think about ourselves and treat one another in the context of the Post-Automation Era, these are the human choices and behaviors that make a "heaven of hell or a hell of heaven," to quote Milton. Technology does not surveil and control others for sport, self-aggrandization, or malevolent, manipulative advantage. People utilize technology to do those things. Going backward "to a simpler time" that never existed will not suddenly cure people from finding ways to be horrible to one another. We must find ways to decrease the causes and incentives of people being horrible to themselves and one another, and unsurprisingly, the most likely greatest asset and assistant in history for achieving those outcomes are the affordances of AI and AGI.

As repeated throughout, the biggest risk of machine learning and synthetic intelligence is not "AI Alignment," it is human alignment. Throughout history, humanity has searched for and made scapegoats to avoid accountability and personal responsibility for its own foul nature and shameful, shameless behaviors, up to and including the ultimate scapegoat, Yeshua Hamashiach, known in the west as Jesus of Nazareth.[cxlii] That predictably human pattern of projection and othering that somehow justified the most horrific of abuses of history, in the minds of the psychopathological perpetrators of the greatest hate crime in history, may by now convey the message that the only way out of the prison of human suffering is to face the shadows within ourselves. To examine oneself, to rigorously cross-examine one's least flattering motives and impulses, and to hold oneself accountable even for the content of one's seemingly hidden mind is known as the process of atonement, true self-actualization.

In the most practical sense, the mind is, in fact, not hidden at all. In the human condition, our innermost thoughts, beliefs, and convictions always, eventually, express themselves in actions revealed upon this fleeting worldly stage. In fact, billions believe that this is the very meaning and purpose of earthly existence. But somehow, a few of us can come to believe that we are so uniquely intelligent, gifted, insightful and special that the unwashed billions must be illiterate, superstitious dupes or intellectually inferior useful idiots, while considering ourselves the heroic champions and defenders of a non-existent, amoral *objectivity*. Sometimes, even ragefully blind to the fact that our own reified and empirically-self-referential so-called objectivity can only ever be the testimony of our own inescapably subjective experience. There can be no concrete or materially demonstrable way out of our own black box brains if the only way out is in, and the only way in is immaterial and non-symbolic.

If the material realm arises from consciousness, instead of the other way around, if we were wrong and drag our feet in following the data to change our minds to accept the fact that Einstein was right in knowing he was only partly right, then by our own law-of-the-jungle, red-in-tooth-in-claw, adapt-or-die religious convictions, we will be left behind, eaten alive, and made irrelevant. Self-fulfilling prophesy achievement unlocked. We have become proud winners of the Rat Race triple crown the *I-Was-Right Prize*, the *Mid-wit Cup*, and finally, the not-so-coveted *Darwin Award*.

Legendary high-tech executive and venture investor William Davidow recently described what I call *The Rate Race to The Bottom*, on X:

> *If you want to succeed in an internet-driven, overconnected world, you must #arbitrage. If you don't, you will become prey to those who do. But in an internet-driven, overconnected world, arbitrage may also force us into a race to the bottom.*[cxliii]

This is why understanding the practical ways by which our established historical principles have evolved into the continuously, and iteratively emergent economic systems we encounter today, is essential to crafting the best possible – or at least, least-worst – policies for least-worst commonwealth outcomes. We need a kind of historical context and understanding that helps us clearly discern between what's worth keeping and what's no longer serving our best individual and commonwealth economic interests in the 21st century.

This is where hybrid economics, the study and implementation of systems that include the complex dynamic structures of mixed economies becomes essential. While economies are human-created systems, we can and ought to glean lessons from nature, where we see common adaptations and exaptations appear within and amongst diverse biological systems, every day.

Our own human bodies are among the most complex and intricate hybrid systems that we know of, and they are also the most familiar to us as an example of how unimaginably complex embodied sub-systems can all work together harmoniously and simply, without even thinking about it. Why would we not look to the incredibly efficient and flourishing mechanisms of nature to help us understand the nature of the most adaptive practical economic principles for assuring flourishing human outcomes?

* * *

It All Works Together

Economies, like life, can appear both impossibly complex and miraculously simple at the same time when all the moving parts fit together and function in accordance with nature's blueprint.

Next, it is time to buckle your seatbelts, put your devices in airplane mode and store your carry-on items under the seat in front of you, because nobody ever said it was easy to get the estimated 640 tons of heavy lifting that lies ahead, off the ground.[cxliv] It may be easier to get 640 tons off the ground than to identify the useful patterns we need in the most recent quarter-century of lagged 20th century data. Data generated by deprecated legacy-institutions-in-disarray while purporting to offer proven unworkable solutions to our present commonwealth challenges.

In the face of acceleration that exceeds the human capacity to interpolate, how do we make well-informed and reasoned planning decisions as our reasonable forecast horizon goes to zero? Are there any such thing as traditional conceptions of leadership at all, in such an environment? Is it the end of the notion of leadership altogether? If not, what is *your* plan to justify leading when you can't see any further beyond the event horizon of the present moment than anyone else? What comes next when nobody has the slightest clue about what comes next, and never will again?

I theorize that this is the root fear that causes populists across the political spectrum to want to burn it all down or repeat the dysfunctional intergenerational trauma patterns of civil war, simply so that they can maintain some illusion of control. Seems pretty drastic, from either extreme, doesn't it?

The sections ahead may feel like heavy sledding at times, but we can do this. I've put a lot of work into making some complex and intricate narratives as easy to follow as possible, but no easier. We're exploring just how important a biological model of economic systems is in negotiating the *civilization-scale selective adaptation pressures* we face in the 21st century, ready or not.

As already observed, our 21st century understanding of biological systems reveals that human bodies are less a monolithic lump-of-clay and more like an intricately coordinated murmuration of microscopic organisms and cells floating, flying, dancing in a delicate, interdependent choreography of precise proportions and measures. As Walt Whitman intuited more accurately than he may have known, "we contain multitudes," in the most literal sense imaginable, as we'll see on the pages ahead.

Simultaneously individual and inextricably interdependent, strong boundaries define thresholds and interfaces of connection, not rigid walls of repulsion or rejection. Distinct cell walls both individuate and align, allying to form tissues. Tissues do the same to form separate organs, organs interact, communicate, and coordinate via almost impossibly subtle signals sent and received between structural boundaries; borders that define the most intimate contact and connection biologically possible, knitting together nearly imperceptible bonds essential to defining and maintaining right relationship between members of the whole, to keep the whole, whole.

The subtle energies exchanged throughout, from the cellular level, are all delicately and harmoniously synchronized like a symphony. Only through continuous philharmonic relationships within and between adjacent, distinct, interdependent systems and subsystems, do bodies exist on this planet, at all.

Were each and every one of our individual micro-organisms or cells of our body completely dismantled, dissected, set aside, isolated, and considered to exist solely in its own state of hyper-individuated sovereign individualism, precisely the way that 20th century economics once considered individual in society; that is, atomic, hard-shelled, bouncing off of others like billiard balls due to boundaries designed to repel, rather than bounded like cell walls between creatures of the same kind, designed for alignment and coordination; were we so disintegrated, such a body would fall apart, collapse, just as our hyper-individuated, increasingly virtualized, isolation and distraction-maximizing human society has done, right before our very eyes. Those of us who somehow survived the past half century, the past decade, even the past few years now know what the word miracle means, because our very survival in this present moment defines the word. We don't take this miracle for granted.

20th century economic theory regarded humans as existing in some imaginary, logical, rational, and *perfectly informed* state of economic textbook equilibrium, with little to no variation of interdependencies between and amongst diverse and divergent environmental or cultural contexts. Instead, two hard lines representing supply and demand reduced complex qualitative and quantitative differences within each of those functions to *presumed absolute certainties*, while reducing all of the rich complexities of human behavior within that context down to an expedient and reductive over-simplification referred to as *consumer tastes and preferences*.

Similar to the fundamental conventions of 20th century physics, which completely depended upon initial leaps of faith known academically by the intimidating-sounding syllables, *preliminary assumptions*, the fundamental *assumptions* of 20th century economics simply do not apply in the 21st century in the same way they once did.

Don't get me wrong, those assumptions and presumptions were vital and magnificently effective during a period of time during which our understanding was limited to those hypotheses. However, in the 21st century, all those old bets are off. It is becoming increasingly accepted by scholars and practical-minded people that the very 20th century notion of spacetime itself is doomed (cccxli). The universe simply doesn't work the way we thought it worked in the past, and that means the entirety of human knowledge and understanding is due for some major upgrades, particularly in the context of the everyday economic realities of everyday life.

Just as the physics of spacetime is bankrupt, so is 20th century economics. It's over. We ran the experiment, and the equally impressive and catastrophic results are in. We are all sitting in the midst of those contradictory results, threatening one another with civil war because we don't know how to admit we were wrong. There is only one word that comes to mind for that kind of thinking: crazy. We did the best we could, we made miraculous accomplishments and created an equally dramatic mess. No one is to blame, no left, no right, no fascists, no social justice warriors. We had our fun and now it's time to sober up, face the consequences, and clean up the appalling mess we made.

How can we expect to have done any better when the entire science of the 20th century had the vectors of causality reversed? We're in the process of proving that, in mathematical, metaphysical, anthropological, spiritual, and ecological terms, today. Our vastly more granular and detailed understanding of the natural world, though obviously still tremendously incomplete, has entirely transformed what is possible in the economic world of the 21st century. My line of work is not futurism, theory, or speculation. What I am sharing throughout the remainder of this work is a summary of the current state of holistic interdisciplinary knowledge and understanding across the germane spectrum of scientific, physical, spiritual, and mathematical disciplines. This is the current DCNR which has gradually, then suddenly, displaced the 20th century DCNR and it's time to make the disclosures fully public. Far from utopian, we are describing in the pages that follow the view in the rear-view mirror of human history on planet Earth.

From the Post-Automation Era perspective, it is hard to conceive that run-of-the-mill 20th century economist could keep their jobs while keeping a straight face, let alone a coherent ethical self-regard. The ones who truly understood, didn't, of course, and many others were forced by the same pressures that we all faced to keep the music playing for fear of being unable to ever find a chair again. Perhaps one of the most ironic and tragicomic aspects of the entire 20th century situation was the fact that economists were effectively forced to keep teaching the misinformation they were teaching, even if they knew it was based on flimsy assumptions, under threat of the self-same punitive system, operating by the half-truths and mistaken principles that they themselves taught. Talk about creating your own prison. The reason it went too far is that it effectively and unilaterally sentenced everyone else to your prison, as well.

This is why Jacque Fresco iconically declared in the 2007 documentary, *Zeitgeist: The Movie*, "This sh*t's got to go."[cxlv]

As for the 20th century's deprecated default consensus reality ...

"It's dead, Jim."

Breaking News: the stock market is not, and never was, any measure or indication of *how well human beings are flourishing*. That may be one of, if not the most fundamental attribution error of the entire 20th century. Similarly, GDP is a measure of how well *capital* is flourishing, not a measure of corporeal wellness. We should have understood this from the folly of the 1920s and subsequent crash in 1929. We should have understood this from the hubris of the 2000s and subsequent crash in 2008. As we will see later, economists defined the GINI coefficient, designed as a kind of weak correlate to GDP as a measure of human economic security. For those interested, we will understand GINI's definition and design shortcomings when we dive into those details (see Glossary). So, let's look more closely at nature's most intriguing, interesting, accurate, compelling, and efficient economic system; the topic of preeminent interest to the vast majority of human beings: ourselves.

While not entirely new knowledge, science is still in the early stages of illuminating the intricacies of interdependence within the human microbiome, itself an entire humble civilization of 3.8×10^{13} individual organisms, meaning "the number of bacteria in the body is actually of the same order as the number of human cells."[cxlvi] That's three-hundred eighty *trillion* individual micro-organisms with which the cells of our human body are completely interdependent.[cxlvii] I asked Bard for some comparisons.[cxlviii]

That's about:

- 413 times the number of stars in the Milky Way galaxy.
- 38,000 times the population of the Earth.
- 1,222 times the distance from the Sun to Earth.

Our miraculous human bodies are almost incomprehensively complex hybrid systems, *mixed economies of the most high-tech kind.* Hybrid systems are creation's norm and nature's standard for the economies of living organisms. What might this hybrid reality mean in terms of sustaining a complex adaptive economics for the 21st century?

Certainly, the idea of uniform homogeneity within even individual living biological systems is a profoundly mistaken view of reality that can carry with it some weighty consequences in the form of real-world expression of misguided thoughts, beliefs, emotions, and behavior. *If our individual bodies literally consist of multitudes, how does this change our understanding of not just ourselves, but the world as a whole?*

How does this deeper biological understanding change not just our perceptions of people, but how might it change the way we see the world, it's organizing structures of family, community, kinship, tribes, affinity groups, companies, and the intricate interstitial institutions, laws, codes, regulations, economics, norms, and narratives that form both boundaries and connection, like the biological systems we've examined?

We human beings – every single one of us 8,011,855,708cxlix on planet Earth as of the moment of this writing – are walking, living, breathing, thinking, dancing, scheming, dreaming, doing, hybrid systems. Our bodies are each, individually and identically in essence, complex and intricate mixed economies of proteins, hormones, chemicals, cooperative microorganisms, and something more. Inexpressible. Our individual human frame consists of a graceful symphony of hybrid systems and sub-systems of sub-systems; interdependent, altogether alien, individual constituent elements resonating in philharmonic spectral congruence with the frequencies and qualia of consciousness. Sapience.

Hence, we meekly suggest that humanity stands the best chance of alignment within ourselves and with one another by apprehending and comprehending the 21st century rational and intuitive understanding that the incalculable quantum quivering imperfections of this frail biological substrate embody, express, and attest to the most reliable, empirical metrics that define our universally unequivocal, ethical, moral, and existential equivalence; not in terms of innate ability or outcome; rather, in terms of intrinsic worth, dignity, and deservingness of the grace, the unmerited favor of economic social security as a basic, universal human right in the Post-Automation Era.

Our own inner alignment, then alignment with others, are the most fundamental and non-negotiable prerequisites to any meaningful AI-alignment in the Post-Automation Era. As repeated throughout, the idea of "AI alignment with human values" is an absurd statement absent coherent alignment of what constitutes our "shared human values" to begin with, and yet the narrative of AI alignment consumed public and political attention for the better part of the past year.

If we're going to engage in grandiose narrative of "what humanity needs," then I'd suggest that we urgently need narratives and initiatives that provide guidance and guardrails on "Human Alignment with Human Values" as a practical foundation of peace and prosperity in the Post-Automation Era. Without inner alignment and integrity, how can there ever be anything remotely resembling alignment with others?

While we're expanding our circle of inclusion to and beyond humanity for a moment, we might add that if the canonical non-symbolic expression "as above, so below" stores any non-zero value for veracity, then "as off-balance sheet, so on-balance sheet," expresses a down-to-earth, brass tacks, bean-counting economic equivalent. This is how phrases such as "a world that works for everyone" and "on Earth as it is in Heaven" cease to be theoretical and reveal their own true nature, providing practical human values guidance and guardrails, in and of themselves.

This exponential technology-instigated alignment and realignment project has re-centered the non-negotiable primacy of human values in our everyday lives and is one reason why so many people have not waited for permission but rather proclaimed and reclaimed centuries of previously embezzled off-balance sheet care work, declaring their own right to self-determination of what is and is not of economic on-balance-sheet value in the 21st century. While this observation might initially strike some readers as incredulous, we include the straightforward arithmetic of exactly what this means in the chapter *Where Does the Money Come From?* People have already done most of the heavy lifting to bring this tangible value to light, we just hadn't yet heard or read about it. Now, we are.

This means that we can return to the incredible synchronicity between the fact that the balance of biological living systems is irrefutably rooted in nature while economics and economic systems are not. This sun-and-moon like perfect balance is almost miraculously convenient for the work of evolving to a post-scarcity post-job-trance society. By allowing nature to guide and instruct us in the principles of how complex dynamic hybrid systems work together in harmonious and self-stabilizing ways; and applying our learning to improve our man-made systems, we gain at least a double advantage. The advantage of knowing exactly what works as the result of millions of years of evolution, multiplied and magnified by the advantage of our creative capacities of reason, empathy, intellect, and amity.

I hope that I'm keeping my promise to make the narrative accessible, even if a bit demanding, at times. This is a lot of compressed information to unpack, maybe even containing some useful encrypted wisdom worth decrypting. So why don't I just hand over the decryption key? Why can't I just make this part much plainer and simpler?

I promise that the math ahead proves the straightforwardness of our concrete, practical model for assuring universal *income security*, when we get to that step. In the meantime, mine is the obligation to provide exhaustive delineation of the foundations of our induction before we can even begin to approach that proof.

It's folk wisdom to know that for every complex pernicious problem there is an alluring, quick, and easy solution that is not only wrong, but is certain to make matters far worse.

Even the origin of the that wonderfully lyrical, expository, and compact over-simplification, "Everything should be made as simple as possible, but not simpler," derives from something closer to:

> *It can scarcely be denied that the supreme goal of all theory is to make the irreducible basic elements as simple and as few as possible without having to surrender the adequate representation of a single datum of experience.*[d]

We can do our best to use tools like Four Game Dynamics to simplify complexity in our communications, and we must also do our best to not shy away from engaging complexity directly, when it calls.

As we've reiterated for sake of spaced repetition learning, much like elements of capitalism, socialism, and communism, each occupy a useful and even essential role within hybrid local, regional, national, and international mixed economies, nature often surprises us in unexpected ways, with unexpected survival advantages gained by unexpected associations between and among systems or functions of systems that, on the surface, may have appeared oppositional. Remember the word? Exaptations.

Humans created and continually recreate the conceptual constructs of economics and economic systems, which are not empirical as are the laws of physics and nature. By adapting the wisdom of ecological principles and living biological processes from the most proven evolutionary models of resilience, adaptation, and exaptation on Earth, we upgrade our economics for the 21st century to reflect these same characteristics.

Writing for VOX, Sean Illing explained a kind of *economic exaptation* in the article, *Why Capitalism Won't Survive Without Socialism*:

> *We think of capitalism as being locked in an ideological battle with socialism, but we never really saw that capitalism might be defeated by its own child — technology.*
>
> *This is how Eric Weinstein, a mathematician and a managing director of Peter Thiel's investment firm, Thiel Capital, began a recent video for BigThink.com. In it he argues that technology has so transformed our world that "we may need a hybrid model in the future which is paradoxically more capitalistic than our capitalism today and perhaps even more socialistic than our communism of yesteryear.*
>
> *Which is another way of saying that socialist principles might be the only thing that can save capitalism.*
>
> *Hence, many technologists and entrepreneurs in Silicon Valley are converging on ideas like universal basic income as a way to mitigate the adverse effects of technological innovation (emphasis added).*

That sums up the post-pandemic era situation about as succinctly as anything. The world of polarized political absolutes was never realistic to begin with. We are hybrid beings living in a hybrid environment of hybrid systems. What more evidence do we need of obsolete thinking and obsolete systems than the entire human history of futile wars and senseless bloodshed in the name of pure races, pure lands, pure systems?

Two of the most authentic and clear-eyed thinkers on such topics, Nikola Danaylov and David Wood, recently shared their discussion about how we can go beyond traditional politics and find our way out of the current hyper-polarized political environment. In today's highly overcharged environment, personality-driven partisan puritans on each side mock and dismiss anything perceived as less than pure to their respective ideologies. It's puritanical extremism on both sides.

We are hybrid beings living in a hybrid environment of hybrid systems.

Danaylov and Wood acknowledge our harshest realities and offer guidance on how to dissolve denunciatory distortion fields. Wood's book begins with:

> *"There's no escape: the journey to a healthier society inevitably involves politics."*

To which Danaylov adds:

> *My favorite quote that I will take away from this interview with David Wood is:*
>
> *"A better politics is possible. A better politics is beckoning us forward. And it is up to each of us to hear that call and figure out how to get involved in it."*

For those unfamiliar, it is worth noting that the EPOC32 mobile operating system, of which Wood was the architect, went on (renamed as "Symbian OS") to ship in half a billion smartphones between 2001 and 2012" (IEET).

> *David Wood isn't just any old futurist. "As one of the pioneers of the smartphone industry, he co-founded Symbian, the creator of the world's first successful smartphone operating system."*

Wood is clearly not hand waving and guessing in his work. He has skillfully observed and interacted with long-term technology and social trends at a world class level, for all his life. These seem like the caliber of voices that Post-Automation Era policy makers can benefit from hearing.

It seems to me that this is the kind of wisdom that the world needs today, more than ever. I highly recommend the entire two-hour conversation between Danaylov and Wood on Singularity.FM Link, link in the bibliography.

* * *

For Whose Good?

There's a familiar adage or cliché that all things work together for good, or that everything works out, balances out, in the end, so just wait on time, wait on the long game, wait on the infinite game, and everything will be fine. For whom does it work out best, though, in the short and mid game?

Our human lived experience takes place only in the now. The short game, the mid game. That is why Martin Luther King Jr. said, in his Speech at Illinois Wesleyan University, 1966:

> *"It may well be that we will have to repent in this generation, not merely for the vitriolic words and the violent actions of the bad people who would bomb a church in Birmingham, Alabama but for the appalling silence and indifference of the good people who sit around and say wait on time."*[cli]

Wait on time. We'll worry about it tomorrow. It'll all work out in the end. So never confront the psychopath or narcissist directly – whether individual, cultural, or institutional – or you *will* face the wrath of Moloch. Maybe this is why some say that there is simply no such thing as "making the world a better place," so why even try?

Or perhaps there is a deeper truth to that sentiment than generally expressed when used for the purposes of aloof denial or superficial dismissal of accountability for insufferable conditions or poor behavior. What if the world is, in the words of Voltaire, already the best of all possible worlds, just the way it is? What if technolibertopians,[clii] social justice warriors, anarcho-capitalists, and all the other competing utopian world-changing tribal voices, left, right, up, down, forward, and backward are wrong in *fighting* for a better world or a better future, because there simply is no such thing as a better world or better future? Because the only world that can ever exist is this present moment, and so there's nothing to change, except, perhaps our own perceptions and responses?

What if the world itself *cannot fundamentally change*, ever, because of its essential nature? What if the world changed as radically as reformers request, it would no longer be the world? What would it become, then?

Would people suddenly, unexpectedly, experience a world that works for everyone? Conditions on Earth as it is in Heaven? What if the only thing we can change is ourselves, our understanding, our culture, our social contracts, our policies, our capacity for compassionate interbeing across the short, mid, long, and deep Four Games of life?

When we work – I much prefer work rather than fight – toward a better world, it's also by definition, on behalf of someone, so a better world for whom, and why?

But we started to ask the question, what if all conceptions of *a better world* are just that, idle and vain conceptions? What if nothing we do today, and nothing we ever do, can ever change the current unsatisfactory world into a more satisfactory, better world, for ourselves, or anyone? If we are so unsatisfied with life that nothing we think or do can ever improve upon our unsatisfactory situation, then what is the point of ever doing anything? Is this the kind of questioning that can lead people into the kind of utter desperation and nihilism that has made "suicide one of the leading causes of death in the United States," and the second leading cause of death for people aged 10-14 and 25-34, as of 2023?[cliii] [cliv]

Suicide "mercifully" drops to the third leading cause of death for those aged 15-24, thanks to homicide climbing to number two, so that's comforting. I'm doing my best to keep the shadow work to myself, but dear friends:

> *I find it exhausting that a society can so willfully ignore and deny the blindingly obvious fact that the sheer panic of economic precarity, specifically, the premeditated and socially engineered threat of economic destitution at every turn, is the fundamental root cause of suicidal desperation in the twenty-first century.*

The widespread belligerent attitude that, "hey, punk (or princess), I had to buck up, so you better too, or it's skid row for you," especially from so-called religious communities, is utterly incomprehensible to me.

This attitude seems exemplified in the intergenerational attitude expressed by a recent president of the United States, in the infamous and transparently sincere words, "I have no empathy."[clv] That is an incredible statement to come out of the mouth of someone blessed with the privilege of such a bully pulpit.

Many readers may respond with, "oh well, it is what it is; it's a vicious world that owes you nothing, so get over it, crybaby," as if this is precisely the kind of world that we *ought* to live in.

One of the most dreadfully orphic proposals I've learned in studies of Buddhism is the suggestion that *accepting the futility of these facts is the key to lasting happiness*, in which case, it appears that there is no reason for this book, or countless other books like it, littering the planet. It is what it is, oh well, bring on the debilitating lifelong depression. If that's the case, we might as well both put this book down, right now, close our eyes, bring all attention to the breath, just notice it, don't control it, and then direct all our attention directly at the mind until we realize our true nature. Ready? Go!

Did you do it? Did you achieve spontaneous sudden enlightenment and nirvana? Congratulations, now you're good to go! Who cares about those lazy people on skid row? It is what it is! Who cares about my culpability in systems that exacerbate a default consensus reality that becomes darker every day? It is what it is! Who cares about armies of sad, depressed unreachable deplorables anyway, right? It is what it is!

"Just let it go, man. You have to not care." That's the guidance. That's the advice of the world. In fairness, let's concede that the only way to begin contemplating a better world is, inescapably, to first see the callous world as it is. Any different or better world can only ever emerge from the elements we have on hand with this world, the only world we know. So as cynical as the past couple of pages may sound, there's truth in them. But is it the whole truth and nothing but the truth?

As a platform for kaizen, or continuous beneficial improvement, this world also appears to provide every conceivable material and experiential opportunity for exploration and growth, from the deepest deranged darkness to the brightest soul's light. We see countless examples of things that improve or have improved conditions for people in the world as the result of continuous application of even tiny, persistent, beneficial changes, over time. This is the perspective of that ubiquitous unverifiable mythical Margaret Mead quotation:

> *Never doubt that a small group of thoughtful, committed citizens can change the world: indeed, it's the only thing that ever has.*[clvi]

Aye, there's the rub, now we are talking about citizens, which is about changing the world by improving conditions of, by, with, and for people *in* the world. To achieve this objective, we don't need to "change the world" at all. The world can go on being as vicious as it wants to be for all of eternity, because as 21st century Post-Automation Era reality-hackers, we're injecting cleaner, more effective, and efficient code into a more effective and persistent abstraction layer that improves conditions for people, regardless of what the nasty base-case world wants to do to itself. Am I spelling out the perspective pivot well enough?

This means that if there is any path to a better world, even if we can't instantly and magically manifest anything different in this immediate present moment, we can, through inducing tiny realizations, through suggesting almost imperceptible changes made within individual hearts and minds, help to reveal clear and unambiguously effective actions available to each of us that improve the human experience, even in, and despite such an historically ruthless and bloodthirsty worldly system.

I hope this makes some sense, because it's helped me a lot to realize that *I don't have to change the world in order to completely change the world*, because I can completely change my relationship to and understanding of that vicious, ancient place.

Could there be any "whole truth and nothing but the truth" in any of this? What if we can change our inner, outer, narrative, and mystery Four Games and suddenly find ourselves in a completely different configuration, a completely different relationship to the world; however contradictory, cruel, and capricious as it is?

Maybe it's different for you, but for me, the only world that I have ever known, the only world to which I have direct access is the world of my own direct subjective experiences. There's a catch, of course. The word subjective can be a bit of a trigger for some of us because scientific-minded people of the 20th century commonly used it to dismiss, diminish or demean. People used the phrase, "that's your subjective opinion" to deliver the passive-aggressive insult that, "you are an unreliable, unsubstantiated, fool." In the 20th century scientific default consensus reality, people deemed any aspect of human experience not duly vetted by the objective scientific method as ignorance, superstition, or woo.

In the year 2024, things are different. We're more than a decade beyond completion of the standard model of physics, and still completely befuddled by the observer effect. Today, everyday folk can ask scientists or physicists to explain the nature and characteristics of this observer please kindly, and suddenly many physicists find themselves on the defensive, stammering the way they once made us stammer, just a few decades ago. Of course, we ought not do back to others as they have done to us. At least try not. But it's tempting, isn't it? Especially when people smashed us into insignificance in the name of defending their own false sense of superiority of knowing "how the real-world works," while devaluing us as gullible and naïve dunces.

So maybe there's an important corollary to the Golden Rule. Not only "do unto others as you would have them do unto you," but also "do not do unto others as you would have them not do unto you."

In 2024, there is no such thing of a debate about whether or not UFOs are real. Instead, we have the All-domain Anomaly Resolution Office (AARO) who's "team of experts is leading the U.S. government's efforts to address Unidentified Anomalous Phenomena (UAP) using a rigorous scientific framework and a data-driven approach," in addition to an entire academic and private sector interdisciplinary field of study into UAP.

It's no longer science fiction, although science fiction continues to help humans to explore and negotiate the terrain of what a different understanding of the world looks like. One of the most common inflection points throughout that literature is the moment where a civilization pivots from lack to sufficiency to abundance; when a world switches from a paralyzing fear of lack and economic despair to an unshakeable sense of support and sufficiency, to limitless super abundance.

IRL, we cannot transit these inflection points by mere wistful wishing or magical thinking. Only by activating new thoughts and taking new actions that result from a shift of consciousness on a sufficient scale to guide us beyond the glop and through the narrow gates of metamorphosis to the next iteration of default consensus reality, can we experience our new understanding and our new relationship to that old, cold, dark world in a new way which might as well *be* a changed, new world.

Hawaiian language wisdom suggests:

"ʻO ka pono ke hana ʻia, a iho mai nā lani."

Roughly, "keep acting righteously until we bring Heaven to Earth."

It was the first sentence that I ever learned in Ōlelo Hawaiʻi, painted as a mural on the side of the restrooms at a remote, not very well-kept campground on Oʻahu. Words that have inspired me ever since, both to gain about 25-30% literacy in the language, so far, and the ambition to improve. This motto speaks directly to the topic at hand because it's one thing that we can always do, in any situation, at any time, in the midst of any circumstance or experience that this variable world of woe and wonderment throws at us.

Many people *say* they would like to see the reduction of human suffering and the maximization of human flourishing as the desired function of societies on planet Earth yet somehow, in private lives of aloof and dissociative self-indulgence, their actions – specifically in the form of quietly voting for or against public policies that directly support and achieve those objective – effectively contradict stated intentions, perhaps only mouthed out loud because it was the trendy and fashionable thing to say amongst proper company, at the time.

This is what MLK referred to as "appalling silence and indifference."

What is the nature of the blockages in human hearts and minds that give rise to such contradictory and counterfeit words and actions? Fear. Dread. Anxiety. Even panic. Genuine, valid, real existential apprehension that if we dare to step out of bounds from what mommy and daddy instilled in us, often by emotional, psychological, or physical trauma, there will be hell to pay. That, and psychopaths that will stop at nothing to keep everyone in their own little fiefdoms terrified. Forever terrified in a might-makes-right world because it keeps them in control.

One of the most powerful enablers of that kind of behavior: economic precarity. The absence of income security. Which breeds desperation. Which invites desperate behavior. Which leads to perpetuating the cycles of trauma we've all experienced at some point and time in this world.

For whose good is it that we risk continuing to accept and perpetuate the 20th century's default consensus reality with respect to the contradiction of economic superabundance and economic superanxiety?

So, we're reminded again of the prevalence and persistence of intergenerational trauma cycles that we spoke to, earlier. This is how seemingly unrelated influences, incentives, and events all come together to manifest as a current, defective, deprecated, default consensus reality.

We don't need to change the world in order to change the everyday economic desperation of everyday people. We do need to change our minds about the validity of mistaken views beaten into our bodies and minds before we could possibly have known better.

Those destructive and addictive institutional and intergenerational trauma cycles can end with us, but only if we become aware of them, face them, and dare to do something different rather than keep hiding behind platitudes, pretense, and hypocrisy in an attempt to look good and stay safe ourselves at the expense of all others, even those closest to us. Maybe this is where a higher consciousness sifts wheat from chaff.

> As of 2024, more than half a century of cross-examining, stress-testing, and A/B testing across a vast data set of tests and trial of Martin Luther King Jr's original 1968 proposal has generated overwhelming empirical evidence from hundreds of proven UBI pilot programs of such diversity and depth that it is now irrefutable that a "guaranteed annual income at levels that sustain life in decent circumstances," is not only possible, but imperative before the end of the 2020s.

King was right when he said the following in 1968. How much more so are his words the clarion call of *this* moment in history?

"It is now incontestable that the wealth and resources of the United States make the elimination of poverty absolutely practical."

– Martin Luther King, Jr., 1968.

This leads us to the inevitable ugly reality of a world that still contains plenty of trolls, goblins, and real monsters. Some of the vilest and most difficult to defeat monsters at the end of the Earth ARG are antagonistic, spiteful, hurtful, envious, resentful, bitter, outdated, distorted, emotions, thoughts, impressions, ideas, memes, and institutions reflecting those toxins in a way that seems proficient at body-snatching new soldiers at any instant, like Agent Smith in *The Matrix*, while simultaneously affirming the ancient wisdom of Shakespeare, "There are more things in heaven and earth, Horatio, than are dreamt of in your philosophy" (xxxi).

So, for whose good do all things work out "in the end" (whatever that's supposed to mean) and for whose good are they working *right now* and how do we wish to interact with those dynamics?

Is perpetuation of 20th century default consensus reality "good enough," or are there long overdue upgrades needed to some of our most obsolete and vestigial internal, individual, and institutional infrastructure in this Post-Automation Era age of AI?

Do we continue to accept poverty as an insoluble and permanent condition of the human condition, or do we choose to materially, incrementally, *improve conditions for people* in an often needlessly nasty, vindictive, and inhumane world? If we choose the latter, how do we get there from here, how do we make the journey, as King inspired, *From Chaos To Community*?

If the Long Arc Of History bends toward justice, then as I suggested at the beginning, it is essential to discern our present location upon said arc, to situate ourselves in the present moment in an entirely new Post-Automation Era, a quarter of a century beyond the bygone industrial and information eras of the 20th century.

Knowing where we are today, like that Pixar movie, *Up*, lets us know that it's time to put that baggage down and let those traumas go, for good.

There are no shortcuts in life, but sometimes we've been taking one step at a time for so long that, in the midst of a weary and dedicated perseverance, we fail to realize that we've already taken the long road ... we've already arrived.

Maybe the singularity is already in McLuhan's rearview mirror, only now coming into focus over the next few years as we continue co-writing the human story, toward a world that works for everyone.

* * *

The Long Arc of History

Here's a thought exercise to gently stretch our empathy and maybe even compassion. Try to focus upon the experience of poverty, whatever that means to you. Not just the idea of poverty, but the *experience*. What is the quality, the *qualia* of that feeling like? What thoughts or emotions arise or do you find the mind trying to avoid or push out of consciousness?

Poverty is both a remarkably simple idea and an impossibly complex experience. When we talk about poverty as an academic term used by public policy wonks and PhD's, an entire galaxy of semantic complexities appear, elaborate big-money word sociological and ideological convolutions arise funding paper after paper that effectively paper over the lived experience of poverty itself.

Poverty is a big messy topic that is very easy to make infinitely messier with mathematics and metrics and overthinking of overthinking, leading to ever more complex and nuanced analyses, impressing ourselves and our thesis advisors, producing more PhDs each claiming to explain *what poverty really is*, though seldom with practical measures to address poverty at scale.

The perennial academic over-analysis of poverty effectively buried Martin Luther King Jr.'s clear advocacy of universal and unconditional basic income in the dustbin of history for nearly a half-century. Unconditional basic income has existed for far too long as a mere academic curiosity for economics postgraduates, all too often used to try to prove that it didn't work, and therefore that it can never work. Like other Long Arc accomplishments of abolition, women's suffrage, civil rights, marriage equality, and others, sometimes, very smart people can think so hard about a straightforward topic that they make it impossibly complicated to simply do the right thing and get the job done.

This is where basic income shares some of the hallmarks of good engineering solutions. It's simply stated. It's readily imagined. And it is an elegant solution to an extremely complicated economic engineering problem. Which means, it's easy to say and hard to do. In the words of JFK, "We choose to go to the moon, not because it is easy, but because it is hard." An easily stated and envisioned goal. A vision that instantly ignited the imagination of a nation. Gigantic, 36-story tall rockets, taller than the Statue of Liberty, unlike anything previously seen, were an elegant solution to a simply imagined, yet almost unimaginably complex goal of "landing men on the moon and returning the safely to the Earth." Anyone who has ever watched a rocket lift off – and these-days, land vertically – can't help to see the poetic elegance of the dance to reach escape velocity and return with such elegant grace.[clvii]

In design, basic income is similar to that first moonshot with respect to the elegant simplicity of its function to blast poverty out of existence, and the operational complexity of its implementation. Due to the strongly entrenched cultural denial we've described, the actual work to implement basic income as the means of achieving universal income security, which is to say universal Social Security, in order to restore social stability in the absence of martial law, may take place under tremendous stress during a time of crisis, under seemingly impossible time constraints, perhaps in response to a kind of economic calamity that almost nobody saw coming. This kind of scenario could make an otherwise mundane administrative process as demanding as any moonshot ever achieved by humankind. If our parents and grandparents did it, we too can do it.

While mechanical and technological analogies for UBI are plentiful in this moment of AI-sparked intelligence amplification, my personal favored analogies for circulating "guaranteed annual income at levels that sustain life in decent circumstances" are biological.

We know how to end poverty by circulating cash throughout the economic circulatory system in a way that prevents clotting; we have the medical and technological knowledge, skill, and ability to do this; we need only marshal the political conviction to get the job done.

Rather than fill up space with empty words, I'm willing to leave a short space on this page to make room for the statement on the next page.

2024 is the year for policy makers to make a bold JFK-like commitment to upgrade our proven, trusted, and respected Social Security system for the 21st century, to end poverty not just for seniors, but for every qualified citizen, by circulating universal Social Security at a level that sustains life in decent circumstance, indexed to 50% per capita GDP.

Shocked by the simple audacity of such a clear and bold statement? Me too.

As forcefully and callously as some have opposed this policy, and our work toward implementing it, we have not responded in like manner. We chose the pen rather than the sword. Our response to their might-makes-right approach is this book. We present a down-to-earth, cool-headed rationale and precise mathematics supporting the policy pledge above. A pledge that includes a commitment to the economic security of opponents who's minds are sure to change when the meta-crises come for them.

In the Hawaiian language, there is a straightforward and concise response that expresses the commitment to immediate action when something simply needs doing. "Hiki nō" (hEEkee noh), as loosely translated, "consider it done." It's an especially useful saying, as later we'll see how the State of Hawai'i initially became significant in the journey of traversing this historical inflection point, and then completely dropped the ball on its opportunity to lead with vision and conviction. The people and State of Hawaii didn't get it done. In fact, in many respects, both seem to have done their level best to prevent the fulfillment of the rest of this story. Yet another conspicuous failure. Am I disappointed in those with whom we consulted and in whom we placed our faith and confidence? Of course. Surprised? At first, yes, but as the saying goes, "I was blind, but now I see." I hope I see wrong. I hope things change, but not betting on it.

So, it's up to us to hiki nō after all, to make it happen, to move beyond academic hand-waving and into practical applications of UBI in the world as it is, today. Sometimes, we must accept that fact that people and nations don't want to evolve or grow and watch them suffer the consequences, however painful. It's not "tough love" and it's not "allowing them to be on their journey." It's just tragic and a shame when people self-sabotage and even worse when people enable and encourage others to self-sabotage. It's even worse, at scale, when such insane inequities between billionaires and bricklayers persist, and the bricklayers are all okay with it because of the delusion that one day they might become that billionaire and somebody might want better wages.

I've found it shocking over the years to realize just how pervasive this dark line of thinking can be. In effect, "I need to defend the extremities of the current norms so that when I work my way or marry my way out of my current situation, or win the lottery, I'll get to benefit by doing the same to others! Buy all the women (or men) and weed (or wine) I want and be king (or queen) of the world! I'll be untouchable, shameless, above the law, and able to do whatever I want, whenever I want. Grab them by the belt buckle or grab them by the p****!"

How few people live to realize that dark dream of "success" before self-destructing with substances and self-trashing? And of the ones who do, how many crash and burn of those same causes, just on the other side of Mammon Mountain? Seems like roughly the same number who oppose ending poverty through universal Social Security because they project all that darkness onto people working two and three industrial era make-work jobs, struggling to barely subsist.

Thankfully, we have plenty of other options in the Post-Automation Era. We can both understand that old shadow culture, accept its dark underbelly, and choose the align with the better angels of our nature.

Back to the arc of history. To support our interpretations and interpolations, we supply an extensive bibliography, pointing to countless UBI pilot programs conducted over the past fifty years, mountains of empirical evidence gathered across all cultures and demographics demonstrating the fact that direct cash transfers help people to become more stable, more secure, and therefore more productive, assertive, and self-sufficient.

Over the past five years alone, we've born witness to at least 150 contemporary and unambiguously successful pilot programs across the United States and around the world.

The data is so overwhelmingly conclusive that some governors are not only becoming vocal supporters of the seeds of universal Social Security, but they are also planting vast crops for the benefit of our near, mid-term, and long-term futures.

Why is all of this happening now? Because the very purpose of commerce in the Unites States, as a nation, as etched in marble atop the Department of Commerce in Washington, DC., is as follows:

"THE INSPIRATION THAT GUIDED OUR FOREFATHERS LED THEM TO SECURE ABOVE ALL THINGS THE UNITY OF OUR COUNTRY. WE REST UPON GOVERNMENT BY CONSENT OF THE GOVERNED AND THE POLITICAL ORDER OF THE UNITED STATES AS THE EXPRESSION OF A PATRIOTIC IDEAL WHICH WELDS TOGETHER ALL THE ELEMENTS OF OUR NATIONAL ENERGY PROMOTING THE ORGANIZATION THAT FOSTERS INDIVIDUAL INITIATIVE. WITHIN THIS EDIFICE ARE ESTABLISHED AGENCIES THAT HAVE BEEN CREATED TO BUTTRESS THE LIFE OF THE PEOPLE, TO CLARIFY THEIR PROBLEMS AND COORDINATE THEIR RESOURCES, SEEKING TO LIGHTEN BURDENS WITHOUT LESSENING THE RESPONSIBILITY OF THE CITIZEN. IN SERVING ONE AND ALL THEY ARE DEDICATED TO THE PURPOSE OF THE FOUNDERS AND TO THE HIGHEST HOPES OF THE FUTURE WITH THEIR LOCAL ADMINISTRATION GIVEN TO THE INTEGRITY AND WELFARE OF THE NATION."[clviii]

While we find timeless principles carved in stone monuments across the country, we find the founding economic commitments of the United States of America "to secure above all things the unity of our country" with "highest hopes of ... the ***integrity and welfare*** of the nation" in only one place: deeply engraved in marble atop the United States Department of Commerce.

Prove it to yourself. I encourage you to visit the United States Department of Commerce building in Washington, D.C. Don't wait 50 years like I did. It took my breath away and fortified my commitment to this work of universal Social Security like nothing before.

Laboring relentlessly until our bodies fall apart has nothing to do with the values of this nation. Whoever convinced us that the highest patriotic duty we can perform is wage labor for the duration of our entire lives pulled off one of the greatest psyops of all time on the American people.

This prejudice has functioned as de facto social credit score and social hierarchy ranking for decades. Everyone in the neighborhood knows who has a real job, and who doesn't, based on the most distorted definition of a real job imaginable. We wrongly value trading our God-given precious breath and energy for paper as more important, honorable, and economically valuable than a stay-at-home parent caring for their own children. This is anathema to the founding values of this country and counter "to the integrity and welfare of the nation," and I'll support this statement, shortly.

The entire point of commerce in the United States of America is to "buttress the life of the people, to clarify their problems and coordinate their resources, seeking to lighten burdens without lessening the responsibility of the citizen." But, but, but countless numbers of my fellow citizens do not even know the definition of buttress, yet emotionally and pugnaciously attack those who express these truths, so true that we find them carved in marble atop the most sacred of capitalist shrines.

Merriam-Webster's defines buttress as, "something that supports or strengthens; a projecting structure of masonry or wood for supporting or giving stability to a wall or building." So, what does the Department of Commerce mean when it uses the word buttress? It means to support, strengthen, and provide a structure of economic stability; of which the principle of income security is foundational.

Don't worry, I already feel the heat from large numbers of mostly, but certainly not only, older Americans. The paradoxical global capitalist hammer-and-sickle work-until-you drop work ethic is fading faster than appears – as documented by the quiet quitting phenomena in the chapter *Science, Fiction, Facts, Technology, and Society* – but it still has legs. Those legs are why much of the impersonal policy work starts to feel particularly personal at times.

That's one reason why it is only now that I finally feel at liberty to write these words and exercise my own right to freedom of speech, as wrong as I may be in the minds of many. For years, I unwittingly, at first, experienced significant direct and indirect impacts of the enmity of people with much more social credibility and power than me, merely for discussing the observations in this book. At the time, I naïvely considered their power earned and therefore respectable. I respected the principle of meritocracy and assumed its primacy. I didn't have the first clue about what the toxins of envy, resentment, and personality disorders – in what my childlike understanding regarded as "the grown-up professional world" – could do to an insignificant nobody like me, simply for questioning the troubling discrepancies between words and actions that I observed in my community, company, or nation.

Having learned the hard way, I rejected a victim role and instead worked harder, now with a lower profile, for more than a decade I created the @basicincome twitter account as a pseudonym. I created the @basicincome Reddit handle and joined a group of about a half-dozen fellow moderators as a co-moderator on the /r/BasicIncome Reddit and wrote most of the comparisons of known and proposed funding models for the FAQ at that time. I did my best to describe and summarize the basic rationale and math of how we index UBI to GDP in the 2010-2013 time-frame.

A few years later, I was thrilled and grateful to watch the "Yang Gang" #MATH hashtag movement from the nose-bleed section of the bleachers, as exceedingly more talented players than I took the field. The list of my personal heroes has grown far more numerous than I can possibly credit here.

Skipping even more boring details, I differed with some of the early co-moderators in my conviction about the requirement of indexing the amount of basic income to the real economy. I didn't initially know that I'd settle on GDP as that metric to the extent that I am confident today, but it was intuitively and logically obvious to me, early on.

I need to acknowledge a very important counterpoint and cross-check that helped me to deepen my convictions on the reliability of this metric, as examined by Gardiner Morse for the Harvard Business Review in the summer of 2020:

> *[William] Davidow and [Michael] Malone, a tech industry executive and a journalist-entrepreneur, say that instead of generating productivity improvements that increase GDP and prosperity (as previous advances have), AI may boost productivity while driving down GDP. Among the potential results: an abundance of cheaper stuff, yes, but also declining wages, growing economic inequality, less work all around, and the emergence of "millions of 'ZEVs'—people of Zero Economic Value—individuals you would not hire even if they worked for free" (Morse).*

Some suggested that because AI-powered hyper-productivity could drive GDP *down* as well as *up*, that therefore indexing a guaranteed annual income to that GDP was uncertain. However, Davidow, Malone and others did the entire research community a favor by validating the thesis, by reminding us that GDP automatically adjusts to real-world conditions. This makes our *guaranteed annual citizens' technology dividend model* even more robust and resilient.

We do not know, and do not need to know which direction GDP will go. What we do know is that portions indexed to *50% per capita GDP* mean that capital and labor equally and evenly share the effects of both market expansion and contraction, 50/50. This is another reason why it is so important, helpful, and essential to look seriously at the work of people who differ from us because, as iron sharpens iron, intellectually honest friction helps us all sharpen our analytical tools, enabling us to better cut through &#%! and get to the truth of the matter, which benefits everyone.

From the early 2010s through today, I looked carefully at dozens of metrics in the context of U-6, the so-called true unemployment rate, as well as the civilian labor participation rate. I was trying to get a human-lived-experience-centered handle on the statistics and metrics of an intricate and complex big picture. I churned out anonymous facts, figures, charts, and more #MATH.

At that time, and persisting almost to this very day, several of my well-intentioned co-moderators were pulling round numbers out of thin air, based upon their own local market conditions. "UBI should be $500. $1000. $2000. Oh, heck, if we're making it up, why not $10,000!" To my mind, the entire conversation had become absurd. This wasn't serious thinking and I needed to dig deeper to clarify my own perspective, based upon a much deeper dive into the MLK archives at San Jose State University and Stanford. You will find that journey reflected in the bibliography.

The ballpark number debates greatly irritated my mathematical sensibilities. Today, I can understand the discussion of the very notion of UBI being so foreign as to justify some amount of that. At the time, however, I couldn't understand how we could credibly propose such important public policy based upon numbers that "sounded right?" I maybe had 25% of the emotional intelligence that I have today and used a lot of absurd language in defending my views. I didn't understand that the way I was attacking ideas felt like personal attacks to the people who were my closest allies. I was attacking ideas that Jeopardized the effectiveness and success of this policy and those too attached to the ideas may have interpreted those differences as personal. That was the lack of emotional intelligence on my part. I didn't understand that attachment to those ideas was so strong for some people that they may have interpreted my words as personal attacks. There was absolutely nothing personal intended, at the same time, looking back, I can understand how some may have interpreted my reasons in that way.

I left /r/BasicIncome after a couple of years. I felt that I had contributed sufficient core value that would eventually carry the day. I didn't anticipate that day being today, more than a decade later. There's a famous quotation from the inventor of hypertext, Ted Nelson, "I'm mistook a clear view for a short distance." So did Martin Luther King, Jr., and all those who carried the torch and kept the fire burning for UBI long before me, long before us, at the Basic Income Earth Network (BIEN) and similar academic institutions, until our early social-media cohort picked up the cause in the late 2000s and got to work on Reddit. Long Arc. Timeless Troopers, all.

Today, the principle of indexing to GDP is finally common. As of 2024, the work on Reddit has stood the test of time, and that's why I feel it's time to document this history and step up to be of service in ways that make most sense to the greater work.

* * *

Greater Personal Responsibility

If the long arc of history bends toward justice, then justice bends toward greater personal responsibility. What we often omit is the fact that the principle of personal responsibility is not asymmetric. Greater personal responsibility is not a one-way street. By omission and otherization, we imply that "those people" need to take greater responsibility for the conditions of their lives while excusing ourselves of our own reciprocal responsibilities. The obligation toward greater personal responsibility flows in all directions in any community and society.

Greater personal responsibility applies equally to poor people, rich people, and everyone in between. Where that is not the case, the meaning of personal responsibility becomes hollow and even hypocritical. If the only people lectured to take personal responsibility for their lives are people in an economically precarious state, and if a bank statements and credit scores are the preeminent measures of who is and who isn't taking personal responsibility for their lives, then we are completely off the mark of the meaning of greater meaning of greater personal responsibility.

Let's take a classic example from one of the most universally contentious DCNR relationships from the 20th century: tenants and landlords. Rent was one of the most inevitable DCNRs of the past millennium, considered as fundamental as the forces of gravity, and yet it is a 100% fabricated and even anti-free-market phenomena. According to Investopedia, "Rent seeking (or rent-seeking) is an economic concept that occurs when an entity seeks to gain added wealth without any reciprocal contribution of productivity."[clix] A term often misconstrued and misdirected toward government, it's private equity that is by far the most adept at the anti-free-and-fair-market practices of rent seeking and arbitrage.

Yet, in the 20th century, most people learned that they must contribute productively for the specific purpose of handing over a minimum of 30% of the fruits of their labor to landlords, without any reciprocal contribution of productivity. That's neither opinion nor politics, that's history and the definition of rent.

People not only believed in that narrative with religious fervor, but they also viciously enforced it upon their own children, family, and friends. By definition, the word *rent* means that the recipient (the landlord) is not providing any reciprocal contribution to the tenant. It is a 100% extractive economic relationship that land-use and zoning laws define and enable. A safe place to sleep at night is not reciprocal contribution. Shelter is a fundamental human need, as basic as air, water, and food, in the Maslow Hierarchy of Needs. Not wants. Needs. Through the mind magic of PR and captology, the 20th century JOB-JOB Trance convinced people that shelter was a *privilege* owned by others to whom workers owed tribute, essentially monthly protection money from the elements, or else.

To keep our 21st century narrative grounded in concrete reality, let's consider a typical, middle-of-the-road middle-American example from just last year. I met a friend, I'll refer to him as Able (because he was one of the most able people I'd ever met), who happened to be on a fixed Social Security income and looking for a place to live. Able was a life-long planner who had saved enough money over forty years of working to live a simple, comfortable life within his means.

Having owned houses in the past and raised a family, Able was ready to accept the temporarily unavoidable injustice of rent extraction as an economic principle that he otherwise questioned, as a compromise for investing less effort maintaining a house and property and more time in cultivating personal growth interests in art, music, language, and friendships. Given his track record, Able obviously had no aversion to working hard, he'd simply discovered by direct lived experience that jobs, work, and money *did not* increase or define his sense of meaning, dignity, or self-esteem, despite the deceptive and vestigial DCNs of the 20th century.

Able researched the most affordable places to live in the United States and choose a mid-sized city in the top five most affordable places, as cross-referenced by a half-dozen or so reputable rankings and chose a city to call home. Upon his arrival, Able was thrilled. The local university and health center were stellar. The people he met were intelligent, kind, and welcoming. Sure, there were some rough parts of town, like any city, and he looked forward to connecting with good people working to help alleviate those troubling conditions. The geography was striking with many new outdoor horizons to explore and the climate provided the four seasons of annual renewal that he didn't know he'd missed from his childhood until he arrived. "It's good to be home," he thought, as he settled into temporary housing to begin his property search.

The first thing Able heard from the first ten properties he visited was, "I'm sorry sir, you can't live here without a job."

"I'm sorry," he replied. "I'm retired. I've worked for 40 years and am ready to prioritize other things in life. Here are my financial statements. I can pay five years of rent in advance."

"I'm sorry sir. If you don't have a job, you don't qualify to live here," said the rental agent.

"Oh. I'm sorry. I'm new to town and maybe I'm not understanding. It seems like you're saying that you won't rent to me, even if I pay your five years in advance?"

"That's right. I'm sorry. It's company policy." Able was dumb founded.

"Can you understand how incredible that might seem to someone in my situation?" he reached out for some sign of human empathy.

"I can. I'm just doing my job. I'm really sorry," came a sincere reply. Able could see the sincerity was there, in several similar cases. "My God, what have we done to ourselves," he told me he thought.

What is our *personal responsibility* in supporting such a clearly abusive DCNR? Able had no idea, after having worked for and earned the privilege of homeowner for so many years, that this was the world that the vast majority of his fellow citizens had come to live in. Able's welcome back to "the other side of the tracks," from which he'd worked so many years to escape as a youth, was as indifferent as it was incomprehensible to him.

Finally, after a couple of weeks, Able found a property that was willing to accept his 40 years of toil as proof of credibility and deservingness to the basic human need for shelter. The *generosity* of this land management company was, of course, subject to certain terms and conditions. There was a mandatory TV and Internet fee (neither of which he had used for years), plus utilities, plus insurance.

"That's a huge portion of my fixed income," Able said. "I don't use or need the TV or Internet. Can we omit that to help my budget? While I do have substantial savings, I still need to live within my means."

"I'm sorry, waiving the TV and Internet not an option because the cable goes to every unit and there's no way for us to know who's using the service or not."

Having spent a good portion of his career in telecommunications, Able knew this to be a lie. It's trivial and even part of every ordinary cable system operations to know exactly what's connected to the network. He also knew that confronting narcissistic organizational structures is as useless as confronting narcissists with the facts of their own gaslighting and manipulation.

"The base rent is *really* only 72% of your fixed income," the agent rationalized, becoming slightly irritated. After all, she was doing Able such a huge favor of allowing him to have a place to live in one of the most affordable towns in the U.S. The mixed expressions on the rental agent's face seemed to leak something like, "Hey, if you can't afford it, then get a job like you're supposed to, old man." Any initial respect for the numbers on his personal balance sheet that proved a man of character and integrity seemed to be fading fast.

"I appreciate that, and I'm grateful that you're considerate of my situation," Able replied. It's simply that with the TV fee and utilities, the cost of living here is closer to 83% of my fixed income. That's a lot. 70% would be much more livable for me and we can sign a year lease instead of six months if you like." He politely slid the brochure upon which he'd penned the basic arithmetic on back.

He knew from his visits to previous properties in the area that DCN of these situations was generally, "Oh well, then you can't afford to live here." Which would be fine, if Able were attempting to live beyond his means in a high-priced or more desirable location, but he wasn't doing that. In fact, he was doing the opposite. Trying to live as simply and modestly as possible in the United States of America, in the mid-2020s.

This is what the Just Over Broke Justification Of Being trance looked like in real life, where the landed lords appointed themselves as the Judge Of Being for every member of a community. Such was the nature of the JOB^3 Trance in the real 3-D world of the early 21st century. Just a few decades prior, the personal finance guideline of 30% of average incomes for rent was both helpful for household budgeting and provided an implied moral constriction on the conscience of landlords to knew what local wages were like and would tend toward not charging people more than 30% of average incomes as a kind of virtuous two-way social contract that provided property owners high certainty of steady income while enabling households to save toward building a better life.

Even Christian landlords had fallen into the trap of the lure of easy rent seeking. Jesus may be Lord, but I'm the landlord. This leads to the question, what is the *personal responsibility* of a Centrally Planned Private Equity Rent Extraction Economy toward people of a commonwealth? Is nearly 85% of a senior citizen's fixed income a lack of personal responsibility in the senior citizen, whose track record speaks for itself, or is it lack of accountability in a Consumption and Extraction reward systems that pummels intrinsic motivation into dust?

When someone avoids or evades personal responsibility in the world, even if they think they got away with stealing intergenerational wealth, for years, the long arm of the law brings them to the court to face their personal responsibility and make the injured parties whole, to the extent possible. If such people are still unable to understand how their own actions adversely and unjustly affected others, then we judge them as unfit to live in society. Isn't it for failures of personal responsibility that societies administer correctional measures?

I know what many are thinking. How will people ever learn to take responsibility for themselves if universal basic income provides unconditional household revenue security at levels that sustain life in decent circumstances? People will be lazy and irresponsible! Nobody will work! Who will stock the shelves and pick up the trash? There will be no essential workers left to do the essential work!"

Such fears are epidemic level False Evidence Appearing Real that are simply not born out by the mountains of empirical evidence of more than half a century of data to the contrary.[clx]

We've learned about the words carved into the marble edifice of the U.S. Department of Commerce building in Washington, DC: "seeking to lighten burdens without lessening the responsibility of the citizen." Etched in stone atop capitalism's most sacred structure. What does this statement mean? The responsibility to do what? The responsibility toward whom? The responsibility to report to an employer for 100 hours a week for 100 years, until we drop dead? A life sentence of social mockery and shame if we choose to question that abdication of personal responsibility?

When we look at the entire corpus of U.S. founding principles, it becomes clear that:

What the U.S. Department of Commerce means by "lightening burdens without lessening responsibility" is liberating people from needless donkeywork in order to afford time and energy to cultivate a meaningful inner and outer life, "to clarify their problems and coordinate their resources," to participate in the commonwealth self-governance of civil society. To be a citizen.

Isn't this the essence of self-governance? Self-improvement. Education. So the principles we're delineating in this work are not fanciful 24th century Star Trek cosplay after all, they are the expression of our nation's founding DNA.

Maybe that's what Gene Rodenberry was trying to help people realize, and maybe we've already arrived, if we have eyes to see and ears to hear.

The extraordinary amount of time, effort, physical, mental, psychological, and spiritual energy required to be effective in the "clarification and coordination" of affairs in one's own family, neighborhood, let alone city, county, state, and nation is far from trivial.

To embrace one's responsibility to organize one's life around the hallowed meaning of the Department of Commerce's motto, to turn away from the altar of Mammon's hourly captivity as one's preeminent Justification Of Being (J.O.B.), becomes the original U.S. revolutionary act: to participant in the administration of liberty and justice for all in an actual, living, vibrant, complex dynamic system called a representative democracy.

Could dodging this responsibility, to duck and shuffle in a bu||$%*t job, to literally do anything, including participation in clearly complicit or concealed implicit unethical, immoral, and illegal actions, all in order to avoid being "the tall nail that gets hammered," be one of the laziest and least responsible courses of action that any individual could possibly choose in a nation designed for governance by and for the people? Then, to accuse and lambaste dissenters from such a cynical default consensus reality as lazy and irresponsible while engaging in the most cowardly, lazy, and irresponsible behavior imaginable? Beyond the contemptable hypocrisy, this might be the most unpatriotic way a person who calls themselves patriotic could possibly live a so-called life.

The tall nail that gets hammered holds things together.

To be dedicated and true to our right livelihood, our career calling and vocation, is of course noble; on the other hand, to hide behind 60 to 80 to 100-hour workweeks so that we don't have to think about our inevitably shared civic obligations, opportunities, crises, and capabilities, while call people *lazy and unproductive* who study the liberal arts that take such responsibilities seriously, to demote and diminish people simply because they are not creating new gadgets for us to consume and throw away, does not strike me personally as particularly intellectually honest, let alone productive.

The task of "clarifying our problems and coordinating resources" can involve sitting on the board of 5 corporations, each rightly fixated upon the responsibility of corporate governance; however, to then mock and demean *governance* is arguably one of the most disingenuous and hypocritical cognitive distortions imaginable. And yet, we hear private-sector officials of private corporation governments berating public-sector governments all day, every day. Some go so far as to mock the very idea of government, while *being the very government of their own fiefdoms*. It would be absurd, a mere case of the pot calling the kettle black, if it weren't so close to the cusp of pure delusion and even Molochian evil in extreme cases.

In a healthy and flourishing commonwealth, "lightening burdens without lessening responsibility" is the core definition of welfare, regardless of pop-culture distortions.

This is why it is at least half a century past the time for welfare-state doomers to retire and let the next generation of clear-minded, ambitious, creative social entrepreneurs lead our civilization into its next level of expansion, growth, and post-scarcity super abundance. It is not ageism or disrespect to observe that the most cynical of doomer boomers had their time. To relieve esteemed elders of duty after lifetimes of patriotic, sincere, dedicated, and selfless service is respect and reverence for the same intergenerational succession in which doomer boomers themselves participated when they inherited the mantle of accountability and steward ship from the preceding generation.

More than a decade of patient and respectful debate with our elders is over. Today, we have chosen to *end poverty* with a guaranteed annual income at levels that sustain life in decent circumstances by circulating universal Social Security indexed to 50% per capita GDP. Jordan Peterson's, "optimal deprivation."

For clarity and benefit of those who only skim this content, what we've demonstrated in this work is a concise academic definition of poverty as anemic currency circulation. Insufficient minimum cashflow through the pockets of a critical proportion of everyday people. Poverty is the inability to make the monthly bills on a long-term consistent basis. Poverty is being locked-in to a non-virtuous cycle of living in a perpetual and precarious state of Just Over Broke Justification Of Being. This is what we refer to as the JOB-JOB Trance.

People need to take personal responsibility. So, we take our personal responsibility seriously to act on behalf of the more than 35-40% of Americans who can't possibly weather a $400 emergency, much less $1,000. We take our personal responsibility seriously to act on behalf of the more than 25% of Americans with zero retirement savings and we take our personal responsibility seriously to act on behalf of the *more than 60% who say there's little to no chance they'll ever have enough savings to retire.*[clxi] Thes numbers are not improving over time, they are worsening.

> *"Self-reported financial well-being fell sharply and was among the lowest observed since 2016. Thirty-one percent of non-retirees thought their retirement savings plan was on track, down from 40 percent in 2021. Notably, it was the first time since the survey began that adults with at least a bachelor's degree saw a decline in well-being. Even so, existing gaps by education and by race and ethnicity remained large" (Federal Reserve, May 2023).* [clxii]

In that report, the Fed clarifies that, "Concerns about retirement savings are consistent with the finding that just 31 percent of non-retirees think that their retirement savings are on track." This means:

In 2024, at least sixty-nine percent of workers – a trend-adjusted 70% – do not believe they will ever save enough for retirement. Every common person knows that poverty simply means endless inadequate liquidity, insufficient, anemic cash flow; a chronic lack of reliable and stable income "sufficient to sustain life in decent circumstances." Ivory tower academics incessantly dissect this street-level reality into thousands of PhD's every year, few of which even begin to touch upon this ground-level reality of everyday people. Terms like "universal basic assets" and "universal basic opportunity" gaslight and obfuscate the blatantly obvious reality of everyday cash-strapped lives.

To understand the everyperson's street-level definition of poverty, we need only visit with and listen to people working multiple jobs to barely make ever increasing amounts and income-proportions of rent, people working full-time jobs and living in cars, vans, or tents, because there simply isn't enough cash to make all the bills associated with conventional housing.

For those who haven't heard of him, Mark Horvath of *Invisible People TV* is like the Joe Rogan plus Bill Moyers plus Walter Cronkite plus Wolf Blitzer of under-housed and displaced people.[clxiii] What an incredible human being doing incredible work to humanize the devalued, dismissed, and discarded. The least among us.

The national epidemic of displaced and houseless people in the United States is not just happening in a few highly desirable locations like Hawai'i, San Francisco, or New York City, houselessness and shelter instability is now typical in all of the nation and world's major cities.

However, chronic houselessness is only the superficial symptom of the underlying disease of chronically anemic, inadequate currency circulation. Like the physical body, when the capillaries of an economic body – everyday people – experience inadequate circulation, the process of cellular exchange of nutrients and discard of toxins cannot take place. The result is an increasingly toxic, diseased body. Depression, suicide, trauma, addiction, and the downward spiral continues into an inevitable early grave.

In the July 2018 LA Times article, "Employers will do almost anything to find workers to fill jobs — except pay them more," Michael Hiltzik wrote:

> *"Billions of dollars are funneled to owners of capital in the form of dividends and stock buybacks, while laborers go begging for even the measliest wage increases.*

> *'America's labor shortage is approaching epidemic proportions,' reported CNBC, 'and it could be employers who end up paying.' Well, yes. That's how things are supposed to work."*

Unfortunately, it hasn't worked that way in a long time. Instead, what we've seen through the lens of 20th century default consensus reality, is cataclysmic market failures on countless dimensions; and unless we think that greed, anger, and ignorance will end themselves overnight, the inadequate currency circulation only stands to get worse, as the data we've presented verifies and quantifies.

Hiltzik goes on:

> *The underlying cause of the "labor shortage" is hiding in plain sight. It's the long-term trend of funneling the gains from labor productivity not to the workforce, but to shareholders. As with any addiction, this process produces short-term euphoria, reflected in share prices, but long-term pathology, reflected in income inequality, poverty, and social unrest.*
>
> *But it's been going on so long that the addicts, that is, corporate CEOs and their mouthpieces, have forgotten how to respond.*
>
> *"Labor is being paid first again," Kevin Crissey, an airlines analyst for Citigroup, bellyached to clients after the announcement. "Shareholders get leftovers." Hardly: From 2014 through 2016, American had authorized $9 billion in share buybacks to fatten the shareholders' take. By contrast, the pay raises will cost American $1 billion over three years.*
>
> *As a share of gross domestic income, corporate profits have nearly doubled, to 6.4% in 2016 from 3.3% in 1990, according to figures from the Bureau of Economic Analysis. Meanwhile, the labor share, measured as wages and salaries paid to individuals, has been on a schneid, falling to 42.2% in 2013 from 46.2% in 1991. The labor share has since crept up to 43% as of 2016, but it's still well below its postwar peak of 51.5%, reached in 1970 (emphasis added).*

Here we discover yet another independently derived, market-defined confirmation that 50% per capita GDP is the most mathematically credible and reasonable amount of basic income that meets both MLK's criteria of "sufficient to sustain life in decent circumstances" and Jordan Peterson's level of "optimal deprivation." And surprise: these figures are in direct contrast and comparison to 1970, the same year when basic income was aborted during the Nixon administration.

Toxic cultural DARVO narratives, artifacts of an ancient narcissistic and psychopathic 20th century that made capital out to be the poor victim of labor no longer pass the smirk test, let alone the laugh test. The were never funny in the first place, except to the psychos who reveled in duper's delight.[clxiv] DARVO is a classic abuser's behavior. Deflect. Avoid. Reverse Victim and Offender.

Look no further than the banker who whined a few paragraphs ago that "shareholders get leftovers," as if that's not exactly how dividends are supposed work, a share of an abundant surplus. But for that banker, 50% wasn't enough and 60% considered "leftovers."

One immediately essential Post-Automation Era security upgrade is CMMC Level 2 compliant NIST SP 800-171 Rev 2 shredding of those dysfunctional and abusive 20th century narratives, installation and implementation of robust income security narratives and understandings of systems in circulatory balance, ecologies circulatory in balance, bodies and biology in circulatory balance, narratives of the interdependence of cells in bodies, as individuals are mutually interdependent within the vibrant living context of everyday human economic activity.

The nightmare hangover of the 20th century 'Death from Above' worldview has been particularly nasty, lasting almost twenty-five years.clxv

Waking up to the 21st century Post-Automation Era, where unconditional basic income has been obvious to everyone for half a century, hasn't been pretty.

Among the temporarily displaced, the under-housed (those making do with couch surfing and other temporary, shared, creative options), and the completely unhoused, our pragmatic and operational definition of poverty is as plain as day. As we've said, and apparently can't repeat enough, *the functional definition of poverty is simply being flat broke*. Essential workers having next to zero cash to spare and vanishingly scarce prospects for ever generating sufficient income to ensure a sustainable sense of Maslow Safety is not even close to realizing the ideals immortalized in the marble entablature of our most highly esteemed institutions.[clxvi]

Failure to deploy the mission critical economic foundation of income security materially denies people living in this 21st century post-automation era of the fundamental and most basic human right of dignity and agential personhood requisite to the station, standing, and lived experience of equivalent social worth within any local, regional, or national commonwealth; that inherent status endowed by the Creator; equal in dignity, autonomy, and self-determination.

As seen above, employers and communities alike can senselessly worsen the cycle of poverty by making a career out of grumbling that "nobody wants to work anymore," while suppressing wages, stalling professional advancement, stifling personal growth, treating lower wage earners like servants while patronizing with terms such as *essential worker*, and worse.

We don't have an AI technology disruption problem; we have a human nature problem and it's time to take personal responsibility for our own deficits and dysfunctions and instead of blaming the latest technology that appears on the scene.

Maybe it's not that nobody wants to work, maybe it's that nobody wants to work for that attitude, under those conditions, for that paltry wage.

As an experiment, try recognizing the value of human beings in all of the dimensions we've explored and see if your experience doesn't improve.

Now that I've impolitely polemicized for the past few pages it's probably a good time to remind:

Do not believe this author or any other. Do your own homework, compare to your own reality and by independent experimentation, testing, experience, and judgement, confirm, refute, or selectively adopt only propositions and suggestions that fit your own direct lived experience. Never accept gaslighting. You too have a right to demand the truth, the whole truth, and nothing but the truth.

Despite the recalcitrance of many stakeholders involved, we can end this poverty gridlock; the labor market can be rebalanced, and work can be re-instated with its highest dignity due to the restoration of the Right to Say No (Santens).[clxvii] We can end poverty as we know it, and we can do so by the end of this decade.

A guaranteed annual income is the poverty solution for which Dr. King died not long after he started the Poor People's Campaign in 1968. It's not a new or radical policy. It's not Star Trek. It's not a static utopia where "everyone is handed everything on a silver platter."

This is why King's title, *Where Do We Go From Here: Chaos or Community* focused us upon his deepest values in his final fateful year on Earth[clxviii] and those values are what inspired the title of a Prezi I put together in 2010, *Toward What End*, which apparently seemed like frightening science fiction to some, at the time. That Prezi asked, "Where are we headed as a people, and why? What kind of civilization are we building? What kind of global community do we want to live in?" All reiterations of questions derived from King's book, forty years prior.

Like most fundamental human values questions, we have received traditional wisdom handed down to us across generations, much of that wisdom only lacking implementation. Yet, like insatiable addicts and alcoholics, we've also long ignored the known effective and lasting solutions to our problems. Why do we refuse to act on what we know to be right until we hit rock bottom?

Is our current predicament of seeming exponential growth and expanding inequity, of deepening divides in capability, opportunity, and outcome, finally enough for us to call this inflection point rock bottom? It's an incredible feature and paradox of S-curves that the pinnacle is also the rock bottom of the next iteration of improvement.

So, how much more desperate do we need to feel about the current metacrisis of Moloch's world and how much more uncertainty do we need to experience about the fate of our children's world before we are willing to make the needed changes that are obvious to everyday people?

One response to King's question of *Where Do We Go From Here* foreshadowed the question by twenty years. In 1948, an inspiring vision of the kind of world that interdenominational people of faith, compassion, and conscience would like to live in appeared in the form of the Universal Declaration of Human Rights. It is a declaration that is still woefully unfulfilled, nearly three-quarters of a century later; however, it is still a beacon in its own right and a brightly identifiable waypoint on the Long Arc of History.

The perennially puzzling question is, "why do obviously beneficial policy advances take so long for humanity to realize?" Why did it take a full century and a massive Civil Rights Movement to move toward full implementation of the 1863 Emancipation Proclamation? Why do we still battle the issue of racial injustice? Perhaps it is due to the vestigial animal brutishness of humankind to which we've spoken. That natural law stuff. A brutishness that in an earlier era enabled humans to evolve into the planet's apex primate and predator, but which today no longer serves our individual and commonwealth best interests. In fact, that kind of natural law brutishness threatens to be our undoing if we refuse or are unable to heed the wisdom of elders like Marshall McLuhan and adapt to the Post-Automation Era environment.

Direct observation provides us with the understanding that technology, automation, and artificial intelligence have already changed the 21st century environment so completely and so suddenly, that what was once a key adaptive advantage has now become terminally self-destructive.

We might need to deploy another key adaptive advantage, human reasoning, along with cooperation and coordination on scales never before possible, to compensate for our outdated, war-like, tribal, destructive tendencies that once enabled humans to survive against all odds on the savannah.

Maybe the deeper natural law is that underneath eons of competition, there dwells a deeper level of cooperation in our DNA because we want the species as a whole to survive and thrive. What is our personal responsibility in the context of existential risks?

While it is true that carnivorous Darwinian threats to humanity haven't technically disappeared – sharks and lions will still eat us, in the rare cases that they have no better alternatives and provided that we go far out of our way put ourselves in their paths – *perhaps our most urgent impending threats have changed from primarily external to primarily internal.* Do the pandemics of suicide and depression amid the most superabundant civilization in history not provide even the slightest hint that this might be the case?

What is our *personal responsibility* for either perpetuating or reducing known effects of internal existential stress that directly causes aggression, depression, and all manner of desperate, deplorable escape behaviors from socially accepted and often engineered economic stressors? Something Stanford University behavioralist Robert Sapolsky found in his book, A Primate's Memoir:

> *Sapolsky studied the activities and lifestyle of the Forest Troop to explore the relationship between stress and disease. In typical baboon fashion, the males behaved badly, angling either to assume or maintain dominance with higher ranking males or engaging in bloody battles with lower ranking males, which often tried to overthrow the top baboon by striking tentative alliances with fellow underlings. Females were often harassed and attacked. Internecine feuds were routine. Through a heartbreaking twist of fate, the most aggressive males in the Forest Troop were wiped out. The males, which had taken to foraging in an open garbage pit adjacent to a tourist lodge, had contracted bovine tuberculosis, and most died between 1983 and 1986. Their deaths drastically changed the gender composition of the troop, more than doubling the ratio of females to males, and by 1986 troop behavior had changed considerably as well; males were significantly less aggressive.*
>
> *After the deaths, Sapolsky stopped observing the Forest Troop until 1993. Surprisingly, even though no adult males from the 1983–1986 period remained in the Forest Troop in 1993 (males migrate after puberty), the new males exhibited the less aggressive behavior of their predecessors.*
>
> *The authors found that, while in some respects male to male dominance behaviors and patterns of aggression were similar in both the Forest and control troops, there were differences that significantly reduced*

> *stress for low-ranking males, which were far better tolerated by dominant males than were their counterparts in the control troops. Analyzing blood samples from the different troops, Sapolsky and Share found that the Forest Troop males lacked the distinctive physiological markers of stress, such as elevated levels of stress-induced hormones, seen in the control troops.*
>
> *In this case, the young baboon transplants might learn that it pays to be nice by watching the interactions of older males in their new troop. Or it could be that proximity to such behavior increases the likelihood that the new males will adopt the behavior.*
>
> *But if aggressive behavior in baboons does have a cultural rather than a biological foundation, perhaps there's hope for us as well (PLoS Biology, emphasis added).*

It would require another entire book to cite the countless studies proving that financial stress and economic anxiety exacerbate and amplify human aggression, hostility, and violence. The peer-socially-engineered persistent existential threat of poverty and homelessness amplifies all of these. People are far less pugnacious, aggressive, let alone ruthless, in an economy with a stable foundation of *income security*.

Unconditional income security is a fundamental principle for cultivating a more "peaceful, just, sustainable, and healthy world."[clxix]

* * *

A Heaven of Hell or a Hell of Heaven

"The mind is its own place, and in itself can make a heaven of hell, a hell of heaven." - John Milton

In 2024, many of the 20th century's best anthropological thinkers question whether or not we even have the free will to choose one or the other. Even the ancient prophet Jeremaiah wrote, "The heart is deceitful above all things, and desperately wicked; who can know it?" If either is the case, how can we even begin to guess how to move through the world, much less know how to cultivate conditions for a world that works for everyone?

How can we take such fundamentally grandiose, histrionic, and narcissistic questions seriously? How can there be all of this superidiotic talk of superintelligent superabundance when it's obvious that we live on a finite planet with finite resources? Isn't there too much woo seeping into science? Has all science become pseudo-science? How can superabundance and lack be reflections from within our minds, when we know for sure that there's a real, concrete, cold, steel rail world out there that will grind us into mincemeat in a heartbeat?

In his ThinkTech Hawai'i commentary, "There is Never Enough," Seymour Kazimirski excavates some of the phony fear memes and mistaken scarcity muckraking that have driven so much human activity, particularly, over the past century, and gets closer to the core of the matter.

> *We live in a world where there is never enough. We constantly feel as if we have to do more, be more, go faster, work harder, accomplish more, go further. We are in a permanent state of "not good enough" or comparing what we have to someone else. And while I am all about having goals and always trying to push or stretch ourselves in many ways, it is really hard in our culture to really be present where we are because we are constantly thinking about the next move or what we lack."*
>
> *It's overwhelming. It's frustrating. It's unfulfilling, because what we really want, the thing that is really going to make us happy or make us successful, is just out of reach. But what if I told you that what is out there in the great beyond, those dreams and goals on your vision board, they are not the key to unlocking your happiness?*
>
> *The key to happiness is right now, as in this very instant that you lock your eyes with these words: right now. Once you can find gratitude and joy and love in your life as it is right now, without any changes, or minor improvements, everything else will open up to you.*

> *It doesn't mean that you can't desire more in your life, just that you need to be grateful for what you have right now, to look back on your journey, and see how far and you have come, and recognize the fact that you're alive, that you have a roof over your head, and that you are truly blessed.*
>
> *We know what you're thinking. All of this sounds great, but you just have so many problems and challenges in your life, and it's so dark.*
>
> *We understand. We know what that is. We've been through deeply dark times and continue to struggle with our own ignorance, which never helps to lift the darkness. We all experience darkness, ignorance, and evil in various times in our lives. What we are asking you to do is to stop looking at the macro and zoom in on the micro. Don't focus on your life as a whole right now, focus very precisely on this very second. This has been the most effective way that we have found to combat anxiety, depression, and frustration when it threatens to take over, and we call it a mindful moment.*
>
> *Here is what you do. Ready? Bingo! [There is literally nothing to do.]*
>
> *Life is going to hurl arrows at you from every angle and you are going to feel that you're getting knocked out of the game. There are going to be moments when you feel like an utter failure and that your life totally sucks. The point is, how quickly we can get back to gratitude, and to love, and acceptance, when we are thrown off by all these things.*
>
> *The point is that whatever the future holds, is the future. The most we can do is focus on the present, on bringing the love and joy to the now, and recognize that when we focus on those things that are good, we will attract more of them into our lives.*

While mindful moments seem to be popular among the meditation crowd, how can mindful moments be meaningful in the context of the endless stream of unconscionable events taking place in our world? A recent piece from The Atlantic magazine revealed that:

> *Malaysia provides a window into a troubling part of the global economy that makes the whole system work, one that touches and connects practically every part of the world and billions of people: a flow of humans that shapes lives, creates the world's things, and is built on the availability of a massive, inexpensive, and flexible labor supply. In Malaysia, it's possible to see what maintains that flow: the recruitment strategies that bring workers to factories, the government policies that are so ineffective at protecting workers, the struggle to improve working conditions up and down supply chains, and the global political and*

> *economic realities that sustain the demand for cheap, unremitting work.*
>
> *In 2014, the watchdog organization Verité released a study on migrant workers in the electronics sector in Malaysia. Among a sample of more than 400 foreign electronics workers, at least 32 percent were, by Verité's definition, forced to work against their will. According to the report, "these results suggest that forced labor is present in the Malaysian electronics industry in more than isolated incidents and can indeed be characterized as widespread (Ramchandani).*

How can such contradictory realities be true at the same time? Superidiotic superabundance at the cost of super exploitation and extinction risk? Is this your immaculate gleaming utopian Post-Automation Era?

In "Why We're Underestimating American Collapse," Tyler Durden at ZeroHedge provides one possible explanation:

> *If you mindlessly imbibe your social-media-sanctioned news feed from the palm of your hand, then you could almost be forgiven for thinking everything is awesome (with perhaps a nod to your implicit feed's bias that things would be 'awesome-er' if "the other side" just got out of the way).*
>
> *However, if you have your eyes opened matrix-like to the real world surrounding you, the number of divergent and dissonant headlines begins to leave you questioning the reality of exceptional America ... record stock prices, record homeless, record wealth, record food stamps, and so on.*

For those of us who tend toward viewing the world solely through one or the other of the dual optimist-pessimist lenses, this might trigger a whole new avalanche of problems with our narrative, so far.

For example, in an age of preppers as a powerful marketing demographic, ever braced for inevitable Armageddon, we also need to face eschatology, grand collapse, and end of the world perspectives, because if it's the end of the world, what's the point of working toward a world that works for everyone? Why not dance and party while the whole thing burns to the ground, then dance and party on the ashes?

According to Quora, there are 30,000 to 40,000 Christian denominations in the world. With such an astronomical cacophony of Christianities to choose from, it seems fundamentally impossible to imagine that we can address "the Christian perspective" on any of these ideas, much less on the book's thesis of ending poverty with MLK's, "guaranteed income at levels that sustain life in decent circumstances."

How can there even be "a Christian perspective," with 30,000 denominations?

Nevertheless, when it comes to faith and end-of-the-world beliefs, we know from direct documentary experience that there are large numbers of people who are convinced that there is only ever more inevitable suffering ahead for humanity. It seems for many that Armageddon is so inevitable that it'll happen, even if they have to make it happen themselves. Ridiculous, right?

And yet, in documentary mode, I've heard the equivalent of, "Why even bother trying to stop global cataclysm if it's God's will that the Earth is gonna' burn, anyway? Might as well get it over with."

Except, how can we know that's what was meant in parables and allegories that are by definition beyond human comprehension? How can we know that calamities are entirely inevitable and unavoidable? Predictions of Armageddon just around the corner seem perennial, yet the book clearly states, "that day and hour knoweth no man, no, not the angels of heaven, but my Father only." So, how can we be so sure of what "should" happen next? The answer is, we can't know. None of us can possibly know. So, letting the world blow up, let alone encouraging it to do so, as if on some kind of schedule, doesn't really seem like it's going to work out as a compelling argument to just let things continue to get worse and worse for everyday people, with the rationale being, "you can't change the world, so why even bother trying to make existence a little more tolerable, maybe even a little more peaceful, equitable, in the meantime?" Can anyone, even AI, help me find a more cynical world view from a faith tradition rooted in hope?

While this perspective strikes us as both defeatist and essentially opposed to what Jesus himself taught; namely, that we are to be the light in the world, right here, right now; that it's not at all hopeless; in fact, the very meaning of gospel is "good news" that the Kingdom of Heaven is at hand, and that it's precisely our duty to discern what "Thy will be done, on Earth as it is in Heaven" means, for each of our unique callings.

So, let's talk about this idea of tribulation for a moment. Imagine that you had to live through a biblical time of tribulation – or maybe we are in said tribulation right now, who knows? – when would enough tribulation be enough for you to let that kind of suffering go, and see that eternity has been here, at hand, the whole time? What if the tribulation is a season that each soul goes through, negotiating its own relationship with something so far beyond our comprehension that it's functionally futile to even speak of such things? Yet speak and write we believe must because we too are creatures of words.

The bible says that Christ's suffering was sufficient, yet somehow, we seem to cling to the concept of perpetually paying some kind of dues before we can rest from our labors. Hebrews 4:10 says, "For he who has entered His rest has himself also ceased from his works as God did from His."[clxx] I can imagine a reactionary response. "As God did from His? Wait, what? How and why could God ever rest with all the mayhem in this sh** world He created? How *dare* He?! How dare *you*?! Back to the time-clock, and the golden-handcuffs, with you!"

Try as I might, I still haven't found anywhere in scripture where it says, "then God worked for six days out of seven into all of eternity." If you can find that part, I'm more than happy to receive correction. All I have ever read is the fact that The Dude rested, and invited us into that rest, *today*.

> *"That's why, as long as that promise of entering God's rest remains open to us, we should be careful that none of us seem to fall short ourselves. Those people in the wilderness heard God's good news, just as we have heard it, but the message they heard didn't do them any good since it wasn't combined with faith. We who believe are entering into salvation's rest, as He said,*
>
> *That is why I swore in anger they would never enter salvation's rest,*
>
> *even though God's works were finished from the very creation of the world. (For didn't God say that on the seventh day of creation He rested from all His works? And doesn't God say in the psalm that they would never enter into salvation's rest?) So if God prepared a place of rest, and those who were given the good news didn't enter because they chose disobedience over faith, then it remains open for us to enter. 7 Once again, God has fixed a day; and that day is "today," as David said so much later when he wrote in the psalm quoted earlier:*
>
> *Today, if you listen to His voice, don't harden your hearts.*
>
> *Now if Joshua had been able to lead those who followed him into God's rest, would God then have spoken this way? There still remains a place of rest, a true Sabbath, for the people of God because those who enter into salvation's rest lay down their labors in the same way that God entered into a Sabbath rest from His. So let us move forward to enter this rest, so that none of us fall into the kind of faithless disobedience that prevented them from entering. The word of God, you see, is alive and moving; sharper than a double-edged sword; piercing the divide between soul and spirit, joints and marrow; able to judge the thoughts and will of the heart. No creature can hide from God: God sees all. Everyone and everything is exposed, opened for His inspection; and He's the One we will have to explain ourselves to (Hebrews 4:1-13, The Voice).*

Not *will be* exposed, *is exposed.* Right now. Today. Has the extraordinary fact that the kingdom is literally at hand, as Jesus explained over and over again, and our own failure to experience that *fact*, simply been a matter of our own particular kind of psychological-spiritual blindness?

But the issue and contradiction is glaring tribulation in so many places on Earth, right now. How many seven-year cycles of horrific madness would we need to endure before conceding, "okay, okay, *that* must have finally been it, the worst part, which was finally enough suffering for ourselves, the planet, and the Lord, we can rest, now," as promised above?

Put another way, given the holographic nature of our conscious experience, how can we ever know whether or not we've already been through the end of times, considering that the only experience we have to rely on is our own interpretations of what we've directly perceived and learned from others; interpretations further constrained by our vastly limited human perception of how the world seems-to-be in the present moment, in any case? How can we be certain that we are such reliable witnesses, even to our own perceptions? These are the kinds of questions that can lead some into frightening and psychologically destabilizing recursive rabbit-holes of doubt and insecurity if we aren't careful. So be careful!

For those inclined stay safe by responding with a sincere, if trite, 'God said it, I believe it, that settles it,' it might be useful to recognize that this only works in a relatively small subset of situations in life.

What did God write about machine learning, artificial intelligence, 3-D printing, millions of miles of global oil and gas pipelines, satellites circling the earth like electrons orbit protons and neutrons, and high frequency trading on Wall Street? While it's convenient to adlib clever quips that apply to these conditions, clearly there's nothing that God said in the Bible when it comes to robots replacing more than 50% of the labor force, or how mining asteroids will literally create such superabundant supply of essential minerals, that the value of plutonium can crash to match the value of copper. We share math about asteroid mining in the chapter, *A New Standard Model.*

Alas, it seems that I can't possibly indulge in the use of such language without crossing paths with Jordan Peterson. Lightening rod. Firebrand. Whirlwind. Rock. What a force of nature. What's Peterson's take on cultivating a world that works for everyone?

On the November 27, 2023, episode of the Modern Wisdom Podcast with Chris Williamson, Peterson touched on a number of relevant points, which helped to sharpen and clarify my own thinking about ways to respectfully respond to people I disagree with, people I find mistaken, although for smart reasons. Whenever I happen across moments that I consider Jordan Peterson mistaken, the mistake is never due to hastily-assembled or unimportant reasons; quite the contrary, and that's what makes him an international treasure of public discourse; precisely because he models the skills of Intellectual Honesty, Enlightened, and Well-Intentioned Disagreement. Those are principles and practices we need more than ever and disciplines that move us toward a world that works for everyone.

After opening the discussion with the statement that we are all "morally obligated to remarkable things," Peterson later continues:

> *2:37:08 PETERSON: "That's what sets the upper bound to your vision. It's like, I want things to be the best they could be. That's a vision of paradise. Well, that has to be fractionated into, you know, your proximal decisions; but lurking behind that should be this continual movement towards – what would you say – a heaven that recedes as you approach it. That's the proper vision of heaven. Heaven is a place that's perfect and getting better, both at the same time. That's what music shows you, because a great piece of music is perfect but it's [also] getting better as it unfolds, and you need that. This is part of the problem with a static utopian vision. Something Dostoyevsky criticized."*

> *2:38:09 WILLIAMSON: "What was that quote that you said on Rogan years ago? If we were to make the world sufficiently perfect, the only desired lack would be for the desire of lack itself? What's the proper ... can you remember?*
>
> *PETERSON: Well, Kirkegaard pointed out that as we make the world easier and easier – so this is perhaps part of the problem with the material plenty that's at hand – is that at some point what becomes lacking is lack itself. Yes, right, exactly. It's optimal deprivation. You know, if everything is delivered to you on a platter it's like what the hell are you even doing?"*[clxxi]

This is precisely why we define the principle of *basic income security* as a real-world, market-defined ratio, derived from centuries of everyday grass-roots economic activity – as defined in the Introduction – and not some idyllic, pristine ivory tower notion.

We supply a comprehensive and rigorous arithmetic rationale for 50% per capita GDP that has endured the scrutiny of more than 80,000 reviewers on Reddit for more than ten years, as opposed to those who advocate arbitrary straw-poll numbers, or haphazardly selected low-ball round number, or some sky-high "static utopia" figures based upon nothing but juvenile delusion.

I harbor no such delusions of an infantile static utopia ushered in by "a guaranteed annual income at levels that sustain life in decent circumstances" (MLK), nor do any of the serious thinkers involved in this work of the past half century.

Our model index of 50% per capita GDP had already met the criteria of Peterson's definition of "optimal deprivation," long before we'd ever learned the term, which was just a couple of weeks ago when Shawn – one of my most honest and loyalty skeptical sounding boards – sent me the link to The Modern Wisdom podcast with the message, "Class in session."

When Shawn says, "Class in session," I put my pencil, tablet, stylus, keyboard away and listen.

Shawn's inspiration is one example of how this book became filled with countless serendipitous understandings, shared by others. My role is to synthesize these synchronicities into a narrative that presents them in the most honest documentary light possible. The serendipity of receiving the video from Shawn provides the opportunity to briefly respond to Peterson, here.

Nobody is getting "everything delivered on a platter," at 50% per capita GDP. Not even close. In 2023, that ratio is less than 10% of the amount of income that the most energetic, ambitious, and likely to succeed segment of the population, ages 18 to 35, say they need (about $525,000.00) in order to live the lifestyle they desire, and it's that desire for more that Peterson and others rightly identify as the source of intrinsic motivation of all human behavior.

That's the beneficial aspect of an aesthetic craving. Rightly managed, it motivates creative, productive behavior for its own sake. No coercion required. No rent gun to the head needed to make people wake up every day like our perpetually panicked ancestors on the savannah. Why should we encourage vestigial hormonal and neurochemical configurations to persist, thousands and millions of years beyond their original utility?

Whether or not that half a million dollars number strikes us as outrageous is completely beside the point. In economics everything is about perceptions, expectations, perceived and ascribed value, and willingness to make efforts or sacrifices in the name of realizing greater value. Ethical and economic value. Ultimately, value in both giving and receiving. Value in both providing service and gaining assistance.

Honestly, Jordan helped me to realize one of the most incredibly hopeful points of popular cultural validation for our model that I've come across in the last several years. I'm incredibly grateful for that.

All engineers respect and abide by the fundamental duty to respond to bright and intellectually honest skepticism and constructive criticism of our designs, and our universal Social Security model is no exception to that rule. This is why we have invited open peer reviewer on Reddit for more than a decade and today present the reader with a proven, practical, and severely stress-tested model, including specific upgrades to one of the most effective, popular, successful, well-loved components of our national financial software infrastructure: the U.S. Social Security Trust Fund.

Because public policy work is much more entangled with human emotions and beliefs than rocket science, I have an equal duty to respond to diverse philosophical and religious beliefs that speak to the nature of work and deservingness of income security.

But first, in keeping with the theme of this section, a few final thoughts on the end of the world as we know it, before we pick up the pieces and get on with an Apollo 13-like recovery of an economy that risks being forever stranded on the dark side of the moon, as far as everyday life is concerned.

In his article, The Stories We Tell Ourselves at the End of the World, Kevin Lincoln writes:

> *The novels of Charles Dickens are nothing if not a story of man struggling against his own ingenuity; the horror in Heart of Darkness comes from the thresher of capitalism processing land and people alike. But no matter where it began, in just the last few decades we've come to face a different kind of intellectual and emotional challenge than previous generations, one that artists are increasingly steering into: the certainty that we are destroying our environment, and what might be the ultimate cost of that effort.*

In the 21st century, we are facing intellectual, emotional, and spiritual challenges unlike any previous generation. Like the natural environment, poverty is a kind of environmental catastrophe and plague of its own. Poverty is utterly destructive to both the material and sociological environments of our towns and cities, large and small, as we sentence human beings to the fate of abandonment and isolation in ways that we couldn't imagine imposing on pets or animals.

By evicting people onto the streets, we strip them of personhood, reducing their social status to less than that of pets, animals, and then often treat them like, and even refer to them as vermin. How can this happen in a so-called Christian nation? Because we let it happen. You let it happen. I let it happen. We let it happen. We call it tough love. Is it though, really?

The good news of this book is that there are realistic alternatives to this defunct default consensus reality. Despite the past century of wars beyond the wars to end all wars, we can still manifest the best of the post world-war visions that have thus far proved elusive, by refusing to give up on the ideals that have always underpinned the true American Dream.

As Nikola Tesla put it:

> *Out of this war, the greatest since the beginning of history, a new world must be born, a world that would justify the sacrifices offered by humanity. This new world must be a world in which there shall be no exploitation of the weak by the strong, of the good by the evil; where there will be no humiliation of the poor by the violence of the rich; where the products of intellect, science and art will serve society for the betterment and beautification of life, and not the individuals for achieving wealth. This new world shall not be a world of the downtrodden and humiliated, but of free men and free nations, equal in dignity and respect for man.*

While indisputably and directly inflicted through economic means, underneath it all, poverty is a vestigial 20th century manifestation of obscure, esoteric, spiritual, religious, and philosophical beliefs that once made its needlessly hellish tribulation acceptable.[clxxii]

* * *

Science, Fiction, Fact, Technology, and Policy

While we're traversing the realms of belief, faith, philosophy, and imagination from which all of our allegedly rational, objective, and concrete actions arise, this may be a useful time to recall how science fiction is the genre of writing and film in which we encounter and contemplate different ways that the world is, might, and can be.

While many science fiction plots include the end of money and jobs as an obvious near-future condition, for some reason we seem to have a collective fixation on creating all the shiny *stuff* of the future while experiencing commonwealth mental blocks when it comes to adopting the *social* aspects of our best futures; blockages that seem to both accompany and contradict the very technological accomplishments that enable their removal.

From the Luddite's looms to labor-saving miracles like the washing machine and dishwasher, to all manner of modern gadget; drones, smartphones, smart watches, AR and VR surgical robots, self-driving cars, and vertical landing reusable rockets; all these innovations both promised and delivered the need for less labor in exchange for orders of magnitude greater productivity and efficiency. Yet the social engineering of the alleged virtue of merciless and ceaseless 100-hour work weeks from which we never rest persists. Moloch's clearly in it for the long game, but so are we, and we were here long before and will abide long after.

This dialog from a 1988 episode of Star Trek, The Next Generation, sums up our otherwise inexplicable situation rather nicely.

> *CAPTAIN JEAN-LUC PICARD: A lot has changed in the past three hundred years. People are no longer obsessed with the accumulation of things. We've eliminated hunger, want, the need for possessions. We've grown out of our infancy.*
>
> *RALPH OFFENHOUSE: You've got it all wrong. It has never been about possessions. It's about power.*
>
> *PICARD: Power to do what?*
>
> *OFFENHOUSE: To control your life, your destiny.*
>
> *PICARD: That kind of control is an illusion.*
>
> *OFFENHOUSE: Really? I'm here, aren't I? I should be dead. But I'm not.*
>
> *PICARD: This is the 24th century. Material needs no longer exist.*
>
> *OFFENHOUSE: Then what's the challenge?*
>
> *PICARD: The challenge, Mr. Offenhouse, is to improve yourself. To enrich yourself. Enjoy it (IMDB).*

If this were social media, I'd post that under the hashtag #JeSuisRalphOffenhouse as the archetype of a long departed industrial era perspective, an ancient post-industrial era, a bygone information age, and a post-information age in the rear-view mirror. It's as if we too are living 300 years in the past, even though we wake up in this post-automation world of superabundance every single day. What's up with that?

In her eye-opening 2017 TED Talk, University of Tokyo AI expert researcher, Noriko Arai, posed the following challenge:

> *"AI researchers have always said that we humans do not need to worry, because machines will only take on menial jobs. Is that true? It seems the more useful question is, how many of those who lose their jobs to AI, will be able to land a new job, in a completely different context? Especially when AI is smart enough to learn better than most of us" (Arai).*

Which is, you know, today. 2024. At a further level, world-renowned computer scientist and machine learning educator, Andrew Ng is on a mission to educate the world about the promises and perils of machine learning and artificial intelligence, without underestimating or overstating either. When Ng says, "AI is the new electricity," you can bet on it. Like electricity at the dawn of the twentieth century, AI will very soon become an invisible commodity utility, embedded in our environment to the point that we don't really give it all that much thought. For example, with the addition of AI, we will find that dreaded automated phone systems now actually work as expected, even better than humans.

As incredible as it seems, even smartphones are likely to disappear by the end of the decade in favor of pervasive AI that helps us to stay more engaged with the real world around us. In November 2023, products like Humane's AI Pin entered the scene, "A $700 Smartphone Alternative You Wear All Day," wrote Wired magazine.[clxxiii]

We won't need a smartphone app to summon a tow-truck to unlock the keys locked in our car, the AI Pin literally works like the Star Trek comm badge. Like our smartphones today, our comm badge will know when the beckoned tow-truck driver is either too distracted, too tired, or maybe too unmotivated to look around to find your car and therefore tries to ditch you.

Today, a couple taps on the smartphone screen assures us that the driver comes back and finishes the assigned task, even though they might have tried to avoid accountability by using that old trick of keeping the twentieth-century voicemail box full. This is another documentary scenario that happened to me, recently. My roadside assistance app leapfrogged the full voicemail box trick, and the driver had to come back within minutes, to finish the assigned job. It was both glorious and gruesome.

For me, I obtained the service for which I had paid month after month, for years, without ever using it before. For the driver, there's no way out, the AI recognized and counteracted his every move to get out of doing a task that he perhaps just didn't feel like doing today. Why would we possibly oppose a world that helps liberate that driver from a job that he loathes by summoning self-driving tow trucks that never complain and never get lost?

That experience served as real world confirmation of one of our main themes: people forced to work in jobs that they detest, under threat of utter destitution, don't tend to perform very well. They cut corners. They quietly quit. They duck and shuffle and feign busy-ness. They feel resentful and take it out on customers or others.

One way to address the situation is to deploy increasingly relentless and omniscient AI to gently persuade – a euphemism for cajole of force – humans do the bidding of a dystopian, omnipotent, invisible AI taskmaster. There may be some Total Information Awareness type control freaks who might favor that kind of regime, but it's not my personal first choice.

In contrast, one of the central benefits of "a guaranteed income at levels that sustain life in decent circumstances," is that it empowers humans against the machine with the power to say no to that kind of AI labor oppression.

UBI is a force for human freedom in the face of super surveillance AI.

- ❖ In possession of the assurance of unconditional income security, workers don't need to accept AI-coordinated jobs that make them feel miserable or treat them like slaves to the machine.
- ❖ Economic autonomy is a far better state for humans than the current epidemic of suicidal depression for people in between jobs.
- ❖ Non-desperate people do not resort to desperate measures such as the quick easy bucks of drugs or human trafficking at even a fraction of the rate that they do, now.
- ❖ Fundamental financial autonomy is better for the health and temperaments of people performing jobs that require a level of interoperability with AI control systems; because we know we have the option of walking away, rather than remaining beholden merciless obedience-optimization algorithms.
- ❖ Economic sufficiency for humans exerts a beneficial economic forcing function back upon AI. Seeing that humans can walk away, AI must learn to treat humans with dignity and respect, minimizing disruption to family lives rather than maximizing devotion to the Job Trance.

As keynote techno-sociologist Zeynep Tüfekçi explains,

> *"We cannot outsource our [moral and ethical] responsibilities to machines. We must hold on ever tighter to human values and human ethics."*

We'll see a lot more about this vital point in later chapters.

In sum, there are at least two sides to the story in our documentary experience. The independent contracting tow truck driver might not be too thrilled that their voicemail-era accountability-dodging measure – leaving the box forever filled – no longer works. Instead, they must fulfill the contracts they signed up for, even if marginal profits on such calls aren't as high as they prefer on retail calls.

On the other hand, for the person stuck with the defective auto door-lock system, the roadside service app automation was an invisible guardian angel that saved the day by giving the customer the power to immediately provide feedback through the most direct and effective channels to complete the task, so that they could get on with fulfilling their obligations for the day, too.

We're all more deeply interconnected than ever. That's always been true on a kind of interpersonal metaphysical level and now in the Post-Automation Era, AI is amplifying and magnifying that connection in ways that are completely transmuting the human condition.

Fully aware of it or not, we all feel the everyday emotional, psychological, and material consequences of this AI-intensified interdependence on both sides of AI-mediated interactions. Most of us probably don't even consider the fact that automation, machine learning, or AI is directly working with us or against us when we engage in such mundane tasks as paging tow-truck through our auto insurance app.

On the service provider side, we might get angry at the times that we have to go back to a job twice, when we should have done it right the first time. On the customer side, we might get annoyed that our car could be so *stupid* as to auto-lock when the key is still in the ignition. Surely the car *knows* this, and if anything, it should chirp at us, to remind us that we are the stupid ones, about to leave our key in the ignition.

We already assume that cars manufactured in the past five or ten years, even cheap cars, are smart, to some degree. The lack of embedded intelligence in a car becomes irritating, a widely-held cultural assumption, without us even thinking about it.

The fact that we can already get mad at everyday artificial intelligence in such mundane situations should tell us something about just how technologically advanced society has become, already, and how fast our expectations ratchet up to meet new capabilities, deemed miraculous just a few years earlier.

As recently as ten years ago, many people would never have imagined that we could be living in this present world in our lifetimes. Yet here we are experiencing everyday life in the Post-Automation Era.

So, let's pause for a moment to contemplate the implications of the next ten years of intelligence amplification (IA) as AI blends with us and we with AI into a kind of increasingly "always on" hybrid human-computer superintelligence. Where do we think this trend of embedded superintelligence is heading? Odds are rather good that, however imaginative our wildest forecast, our predictions will happen in half that time.

One of the most insightful science fiction scenarios, in terms of depicting how a hastily developed global superintelligence might interact with a hopelessly war-like species is the 1970 film, Colossus: The Forbin Project (Hutter). It's conceivable that the end of all wars finally arrives as the result of super intelligent systems that veto humanity's free will to blow itself up.[clxxiv]

Just five years ago, the non-profit AI research company OpenAI estimated that the development of AI was accelerating nine times faster than the infamous Moore's Law. Five years later, they released ChatGPT and custom GPTs into the market. Like the infamous shot heard 'round the world, it was the software release felt 'round the world. Nothing will ever be the same.

That's the instantaneous transformative power of open-source software in the Post-Automation Era.

It's this documentarian's view that the concept of technological singularity is no longer a cute meme, and frankly never was. Technological singularity is a process that already both has happened and is happening, an unfolding that has been happening for decades and might continue to unfold for another decade or more. Maybe it's a new kind of supranormal normal.

This means that we can't afford to indulge in the luxuries of intellectual laziness and socioeconomic stagnation in the wake of this tsunami of exponential change that has crashed upon the shore of our vestigial preconceptions, demolishing everything that we thought was our forever normal lazy little beach town.

There is no one to blame, it's a natural phenomenon like a hurricane, tornado, earthquake, or wildfire. Horrible to deal with. Devastating. Undeniable. Non-negotiable. The only options are to rebuild or leave. Why would we meticulously reconstruct the crummy parts of that demolished beach town? Yet, that's what we've done for more than 200 years, every time we failed to return the labor-saving benefits of technology to labor.

The stark reality of technological singularity is that all of those failures have now caught up to us. Hating software developers and architects for "making us face our own karma," is like hating all the mechanics that built tractors that replaced farm workers. Hating immigrant developers who have helped build this superintelligent technium is like hating immigrant railroad workers that made transcontinental travel and commerce possible.

Both forms of hatred were and are all too real, utterly unjustified, and there's no room for them in the Post-Automation Era.

Rather than lashing out, perhaps our new number one job is extending some compassion toward ourselves for not having acquired those software and analytical skills that resulted in the automation that displaced us through no fault of our own. We acquired the skills and worked diligently at what we knew and what society and markets needed at the time. That time has long passed. We *earned* our rest. It's not a hand-out.

Universal Social Security is not welfare, it's a technology dividend, *earned passive income*, by virtue of all the arduous work that we have all done, standing on the stalwart shoulders of all those who labored before us. Our ancestors *desired, dreamed, and worked* all those impossibly long hours so that we wouldn't have to, so we could experience this freedom. Who are we to dishonor our own lineage by not being grateful enough to learn how to enter into that rest?

Why be like John Henry? What's there to prove versus a steam shovel? Perhaps our new job is to go easier on ourselves and learn to define our self-worth by metrics other than how much money we make or how important our job title makes us feel. As mentioned earlier, "The challenge, Mr. Offenhouse, is to improve yourself. To enrich yourself. Enjoy it."

In 2018 OpenAI reported:

> *"We're releasing an analysis showing that since 2012, the amount of compute used in the largest AI training runs has been increasing exponentially with a 3.5 month-doubling time (by comparison, Moore's Law had an 18-month doubling period). Since 2012, this metric has grown by more than 300,000x (an 18-month doubling period would yield only a 12x increase). Improvements in compute have been a key component of AI progress, so as long as this trend continues, it's worth preparing for the implications of systems far outside today's capabilities" (Amodei).*

At that time, when it came to tracking the state of AI in the context of society, the Institute for Ethics and Emerging Technology (IEET) was the place where we discovered Marcus Hutter, Professor in the Research School of Computer Science at the Australian National University and progenitor of Universal Artificial Intelligence (UAI) – now widely referred to as Artificial General Intelligence (AGI) – who had recently discussed then current progress in AI, and contrasted it with popular public perceptions of AI.

In his February 2018 presentation given at the AGI17 conference in Melbourne, Australia, Professor Hutter explained that:

> *"Intelligent systems have an increasing impact on our society. We already benefit from [them,] particularly through your smart phones and experiences on the Internet. Self-driving cars and household robots could also be standard technologies, very soon. Intelligent Systems approach and exceed human intellectual capabilities in an increasing number of domains (expert systems, board games such as Chess and Go, speech recognition and translation, process optimization, search engines), some can autonomously deal with unknown and unexpected situations. Indeed, Intelligent Systems have the potential to be deployed in almost any facet of our lives. The creation of super-intelligent systems will change our society in the next couple of decades more than the industrial revolution has in the last 200 years" (Hutter, emphasis added).*

We combined this with the July 5, 2018, AngelList Talent Newsletter, which reminded readers why capital loves "pure software plays" because they don't add anything to a local economy, whatsoever. No real estate. No employees. Just software eating the world. This is what pure financial capital does. It eliminates humans.

Isn't ironic and paradoxical that so many of the very humans that financial capital seeks to obviate, worship at the feet of Mammon in the house of Moloch?

Here's the catch, the angle, the pitch, the pivot, the crux: doing away with compulsory human labor is not only a manifestly Good Thing™ but also indisputably the whole point to industrialization in the first place.

The goal of greater labor efficiency was always to create more leisure time. Avid capitalist and financier Sir Richard Branson explains why more leisure is such a Good Thing™ for everyone in the next section titled *80-Hour Jobs or 20-Hour Work Week.*

For now, back to AngelList:

> *VCs have long loved pure software businesses like Trulia, a real estate search engine which went public in 2012. Trulia avoided buying buildings or employing agents directly. Scaling up was just a matter of adding more servers.*
>
> *[Today,] Opendoor is a tech-enabled real estate investor based in SF. They use data science to figure out what homes to buy and at what price. They pay up-front and then flip the homes at a profit. We estimate that they're buying and selling over 10,000 homes annually.*

While pure software is the ultimate efficiency gain, there are still plenty of tasks that require hardware, and human hands, to implement software's will. In June 2018, Melia Robinson wrote for Business Insider:

> *One restaurant in San Francisco has hatched a more surprising way to operate without restaurant workers. The buzzy new burger joint, Creator, which soft opens for lunch on Wednesday, uses a robot to prep, cook, and assemble hamburgers with no human help.*
>
> *Founded in 2009, the startup formerly known as Momentum Machines has been quietly tinkering with its mechanical line cook out of a vacant retail space in SoMa for almost two years. Its robot uses an array of sensors and computers and makes up to 130 burgers an hour. It eliminates the need for line cooks.*
>
> *Creator isn't the only restaurant putting robots to work. Cafe X relies on a robotic coffee bar to take your order and make your drink — no human interaction required" (Robinson).*

So, this means that one of Silicon Valley's biggest ideas in 2018 was robots flipping homes for a profit. While robots treat housing like pork bellies trading on Wall Street, what could possibly go wrong for humans, for whom housing a biological necessity for Maslow Safety?

If all these human-removal-from-the-workforce developments aren't yet painting a sufficiently clear picture of the world as it is in 2024, let's look at some other recent AI achievements that working people may not have heard about, yet; perhaps because they were out working two or three *essential jobs*, just to barely get by; another of the core principles for why we've written these books. It's beyond ridiculous that anyone should have to work multiple jobs to barely subsist in the Post-Automation Era.

The self-serving haughtiness of the "essential jobs" narrative, a prosaic pat on the head from society, was not lost on real-world workers. Workers aren't as stupid as many seem to believe. Whoever thought up that bit of Bernay's PR was surely clever and therefore ought to be clever enough to not be surprised to find out that according to a Gallup poll updated May 17, 2023,

> *"At least half of the U.S. workforce is quiet quitting and the workplace, amid the pandemic, got worse for younger workers.*[clxxv]

The emperor Moloch's defunct default consensus narrative of JOB-JOBs as the preeminent meaning of life and pre-requisite to personhood is wearing no clothes.

In Stephen Shankland's June 2018 CNET article, "An IBM computer debates humans, and wins, in a new, nuanced competition" he succinctly summarized the acceleration of machine intelligence over the past twenty years. Giant leaps occur in a halving function of shrinking intervals. That means 12 years becomes 6 years, 6 becomes 3, etc.

> *"Computers beat humans at chess in 1997, beat humans at Jeopardy in 2011, and beat the world's best Go players in 2017. This Monday, a computer won a far more nuanced competition: debate" (Shankland).*

Upon learning about this accomplishment, I realized something rather uncomfortable at the time, "So, perhaps even the once-considered sacred uniqueness of human reasoning and the art of interpersonal persuasion are no longer enough to differentiate us from machine learning systems, either."

With the release of custom GPT's in late 2023, that observation has become a demonstrated present certainty.[clxxvi] That's how fast our world is reflecting our technologically amplified imagination and insight into new default consensus realities.[clxxvii]

Despite all these profoundly significant developments, up until the past year, even leading technological publications like MIT Technology Review have been historically antagonistic, and even mocking the concept of unconditional basic income.

This shouldn't come as a surprise from a leading institution that sustains itself on a combination of essentially unpaid graduate student labor and lucrative defense industry contracts; some of them potentially un-auditable due to so-called DoD black budgets.[clxxviii] Why would people with such cushy and powerful positions in the social hierarchy want their private sector military powered party to ever end?

Nevertheless, in 2018, even sniffy MIT begrudgingly came around to the idea:

> *"The basic income is something broader: a social equalizer, a recognition that people who make little or no money are often doing things that are socially valuable. 'It gives one the assurance that the work you're doing is not in vain, even though you're not working in a bank or doing other things that are considered part of a career,' he says" (Bergstein).*

As leading basic income activist and educator Scott Santens wrote on Medium, "It's Time for Technology to Serve all Humankind with Unconditional Basic Income." I couldn't agree more.

On Quora, community member Johnny Le wrote about the perspective of Elon Musk, who has made his support for UBI abundantly clear on many occasions:

> *... he wants a robot to do the job FOR a person, not simply replace that person. The income that robots create should go to that person. So that basic income is the income a robot created FOR you.*
>
> *Our tax system needs to change so that income created by humans should not be taxed or taxed little while income created by robots/computers/AI should be taxed a lot more. The problem now is that every time we hear higher taxes, we scream, even though the target isn't us (emphasis added).*

Some financial technology startups are trying to bypass the entire existing, broken system, averting the sacred cow questions, altogether. Mannabase has developed a cryptocurrency that is modeling the circulation of a universal basic income through its blockchain implementation.

Looking even further beyond the horizon are blockchain visionaries like Vinay Gupta of Mattereum. Mattereum is a blockchain solution with the capability of accounting for extra-terrestrial assets and transactions. A technology that routes around the stagnation of deprecated nation states. Recommendation: don't become a deprecated nation state.

In short, the billions of everyday people who have created some level of financial security for ourselves can create our own blockchain central bank and ecosystem to bootstrap the new space industry.

Gupta explains:

> *The blockchain people desperately need something to do, right? The ones that got in early and made an enormous amount of money are basically wandering around wondering what to do with their lives, and they're making a dreadful mess, because they're not good at being rich. But many of them are pretty good engineers, right? And all these space guys coming out of Silicon Valley could sure use a lot more money and a lot more talent. So, I think the folks that have kinda graduated from the blockchain university, of the basically "whack the future on the head and stick it in your cooking pot," probably ought to be looking at bigger challenges.*
>
> *So, first you make a bank and then you pull the money out with a bank that you made, and you use it to build rocket ships. And the rocket ships build an industry, and the industry generates a lot of wealth, and then that comes back down the pipe, and it turns into more rocket ships. And you kind of start the feedback loop that builds the economic engines that build the capacity to expand into the void. And at that point, we've basically won at life. We've solved humanity's most primary problem, which is "why don't I have the things I want?" And that's doable right here.*
>
> *This is the first blockchain and space conference in the world as far as we know this is the beginning of the narrative, and I want to set the narrative off at the right tone. Which is, our job is to conquer the void. We've got all the tools that we need, we've got the necessary political structures within arm's reach, we just pull that stuff into reality, we build the necessary structures, we raised the necessary money, we figure out how to fund the engineers who are actually doing the work, and we break out of the deadlock that has trapped us on the planet since the nation-state lost its will to go. Right? We are here to go, and we're gonna do it.*

Here's the real kicker. Like the original space race, this space blockchain ecosystem could accomplish much more than its primary founding mission. While it may sound outlandishly audacious, Mattereum could conceivably account for all outer space as a non-nation state public good, used primarily for the benefit all of humanity, thereby creating a nearly infinite wealth from which to circulate a livable basic income, indexed to 50% per capita GDP (or later, GPP, Gross Planetary Product).

While that might sound far-fetched to some, so did every idea that fundamentally altered the way humanity experiences life on this planet. It's certainly no more far-fetched than the Wright brothers, Nikola Tesla, or Elon Musk landing vertical rockets and nonchalantly tossing electric cars into orbit around neighboring planets, or the mind-blowing emergence of 100% human conversational AI in the form of ChatGPT, right here, right now, in 2024.

Unhappily, the least far-fetched amongst our documentary observations is the prospect that wide swaths of humanity may continue hold steadfastly to the view that all humankind must forever remain lashed to the cross of physical toil and subservience to Moloch's soulless Mammon machine. It makes no sense to me, but it's capital-T, True, for millions. We can't forget or take that reality lightly.

Others may have been inadvertently or unconsciously complicit in such beliefs, letting decades go by without updating our model of an exponentially changing world, forgetting to become increasingly grateful for relief from toil for greater and greater numbers of people. In that case, today may be our opportunity to revisit and reassess our world view in the context of what we're learning about the current environment.[clxxix]

To contemplate whether we will, as individuals, as communities, as a species, ever grow out of the repugnant proclivity for kicking people while they are down, and if they aren't down, pulling them down to be kicked, like so many crabs in a bucket, for the sole purpose that we might feel better about ourselves in some deeply troubling troglodyte sense, might be another productive way to invest some contemplation time.

The only obstacles preventing the end of poverty in this decade are human envy, greed, jealousy, lust for power over others, anger, selfishness, ignorance, and othering, disdain, devaluation, and malice toward those who differ from us. Building a space-faring civilization may be child's play compared to restoring the soul of such an often-recalcitrant species.

* * *

80-Hour Jobs or 20-Hour Work Week?

In June 2018, Sir Richard Branson told CNBC that:

> *"The purpose of humanity is not just to sit behind a counter and sell things. More free time is not a terrible thing," he said. "I think with artificial intelligence coming along, there needs to be a basic income," said Branson. "With the acceleration of [artificial intelligence] and other new technology ... the world is changing fast," Branson wrote on his blog in August. "A lot of exciting new innovations are going to be created, which will generate a lot of opportunities and a lot of wealth, but ... also reduce the amount of jobs," he said. "This will make ... basic income even more important in the years to come." A report from the McKinsey Global Institute confirms the idea that automation will cause major disruption to the job market globally. By 2030, 75 million workers around the globe will need to change occupational category due to automation, according to the December 2017 study, and 400 million jobs could be potentially displaced. The McKinsey Global estimates are based on analysis of 46 countries that include 90 percent of global gross domestic product and a mid-level pace of adoption of automation (Clifford).*

As of 2024, have we not already significantly surpassed McKinsey Global's 2017, mid-level pace of adoption? After everything we have read so far, and all we've witnessed of the pace of technological advancement on Earth to date, can we honestly expect a mere *mid-level pace of adoption* when it comes to implementation of the most efficiency-amplifying technology in the history of humanity?

In the Post-Automation Era, much of the most important and valuable work in the world is not even remotely associated with that strange historical aberration of a concept called a job. There were no JOB-JOBs as we know them today, prior to the industrial revolution, and in the 2020s a return to independent or freelance peer-to-peer networks of collaboration is underway, imminent.[clxxx] What will people do?

Raising children. Caring for elders. Listening to friends, helping them work through the challenges in their lives. Volunteering at food banks, hospitals, churches, synagogues, mosques, temples, and communities. These are the human priorities and activities of the Post-Automation Era, and just a few of the timeless, traditional, commonplace, yet treated like mysterious inexplicable ways – apparently by no less than Sir Elon himself, in a recent conversation with Rishi Sunak – by which people will continue to *find, improve, and increase meaning,* purpose, and significance in life.[clxxxi]

> ***Work does not equal job does not equal meaning, purpose, dignity, value, or status. Ethics, honesty, compassion, and integrity define and measure the dignity, value, and status of a life.***

This leads us into PG-13 territory, maybe even R, depending on the reviewer's discretion.

The late Yale economic anthropologist David Graeber's book, "Bullshit Jobs," aggressively challenged the default orthodoxy regarding currency circulation in the form of trading time for hourly wages. His observation was that work increasingly resembled make-work social clubs where people spend substantial portions of their so-called workday scrolling through social media, flirting, having office flings, and ordering more stuff online.

These are not your parents', let alone grandparents' factory jobs, nor are they consistent with the deeper history of genuine human productivity. Bu||$%*t Jobs are all about who you know or b**w and who you can convince to give you place to "be employed" so that everything "looks normal," while you pretty much do whatever you damn-well please. Is that too abrupt, harsh, and shocking to read, put so plainly? I'm not even going to touch the prevalence of corporate "pimp-n-ho" culture in 2024, you can search that.

A trend that goes almost completely unaddressed in the age of bu||$%*t jobs is the fact that so many people use the workplace as an escape from the *real work* they prefer to avoid dealing with; namely, personal growth and relationship work in their own lives, at home. This avoidance and the consequent detrimental impacts to children and society could fill a whole additional chapter, but for now, Imma slow down the debate about who is doing the *real work* in life while Bu||$%*t Job holders point fingers and accusations about who is avoiding responsibilities, and who is being lazy. Laziness comes in many covert and insidious forms, intellectual and emotional laziness being among the most pernicious laziness of all. Some of the laziest people we know have the most seemingly stable bu||$%*t jobs in the world, and this is what we hold up as the pinnacle of human progress and civilization?

I'm not saying that every job is a Bu||$%*t Job. The point is that a high proportion of jobs are bu||$%*t jobs and calculating that proportion is challenging when everyone is telling the same story, to cover for one another's cubicle slack time. We fully understand that the world is full of obviously genuine, essential labor roles, the point is that the economy requires a diminishing number of legitimate roles in order to keep generating ever increasing revenue and margins. This dislocation is what the commotion is all about.

The point of this narrative is not that *all* jobs are going away. The point is that the early Post-Automation Era economy of the past 20 years or so had become a bit like a life-or-death game of musical chairs wherein the Lubomyr Melnyk style continuous music keeps playing exponentially faster, while the number of chairs keeps disappearing at the same time.[clxxxii]

In the Post-Automation Era, this large-scale job displacement is not only okay, but it is good, desirable, and represents the fulfillment of the very promise of all the generations of relentless workers who have gone before us.

The elimination of bu||$%*t jobs and the re-assignment of fewer roles into fewer hours for fewer people — that is what the promise of progress is all about, so that we can get to work on the deeper healing and the greater expression of human potential for insight, understanding, innovation, creativity, productivity, democratic civic engagement, and inclusive civic decision making. Who has time or energy to take part in a democracy when shackled to 100-hour work weeks? Nobody, and that's been largely by design. The previous millennium's blueprint is 1,000 years out of date, and we need a relevant blueprint for the present times in which we live.

Civic participation provides a limitless source of countless opportunities for people to find meaning, purpose, contribution, and participation in life and can only improve the health of a representative, democratic republic.

This will sound mean and it's not comfortable to have to deal with mean people in their own mean way when they mistake meekness for weakness, accommodation for feebleness. The absurd Job Trance question of, "whatever will people do for *meaning*?" is trolling, sea-lioning, a disingenuous straw man, a gaslighting canard, maybe in some cases even a bit of a sad cry for significance and attention from has-beens of a bygone era. As one of my closest friends once taught me, OCTAGOY: One Clown To Another, Get Over Yourself.

> *None of the fundamental components of commonwealth stakeholder capitalism in the United States republic become suddenly replaced, displaced, phased out, or disappear in the Post-Automation Era. Stock markets, commerce, free and fair trade, innovation, investment, profits, the band plays on. So let us please put this as plainly and crudely as possible for that portion of the audience who needs to hear it thusly: anyone who frames our work as some bizarre globalist conspiracy, government takeover, or this or that "ism" for the sake of divisiveness, is either willfully ignorant, has not bothered to read, is talking out of an inappropriate orifice, just plain lying, or all of the above.*

Here's what the Post-Automation Era is like: the largest company in the United States by revenue is Walmart, generating annual revenue of 611.29 billion USD.[clxxxiii] The largest company in China by revenue is the State Grid Corporation of China, with a revenue of 460.62 billion USD. In Germany it's Volkswagen, at 250.2 billion EUR.[clxxxiv] Japan has Toyota, with a revenue of 279.38 billion USD.[clxxxv] India, Reliance Industries, 86.85 billion USD.[clxxxvi] United Kingdom is Shell Plc, 272.66 billion USD.[clxxxvii] France is TotalEnergies, with a revenue of 184.11 billion USD.[clxxxviii] Italy, Assicurazioni Generali S.p.A., 99 billion EUR.[clxxxix] Brazil, Petrobras, 124.47 billion USD.[cxc] And the largest company in Canada by revenue is Brookfield Asset Management, with a revenue of 92.77 billion USD.[cxci] [cxcii]

These numbers will look like a cute little piggy bank by the end of the decade.

The 20th century Job Trance had people brainwashed into believing that the basic human right to income security was taking away something from people who've earned wealth and giving it to people who don't deserve the most basic human rights to Maslow Safety. You'll find why that's entirely untrue in Part 2 and beyond of this work.

Historically, the default consensus narrative of the Job Trance encouraged fortunate workers, essential workers – those of us who did manage to land reasonably good jobs, either real or bu||$%*t – to consider ourselves the "official members of society," the role models of American Dream success, while those who hadn't found a chair were losers. No job? Must be a communist. Sounds ridiculous, right? And it was.

The old 20th century default consensus narrative was, if you didn't have a JOB-JOB, if you dared to question the Job Trance, you must be some kind of hippie, communist, derelict, deviant, or worse. It didn't matter whether were between jobs after kicking butt for five or ten years straight or you'd retired for a minute after forty years of eighty-hour work weeks. The Job Trance said: no job, no company badge, no identity, no healthcare, no social status or standing, no civic respect. Back then, sign-waving was higher status than attending to the most important *work* in the world: fortifying one's inner life, family, home, and community.

What did that look like, IRL, back in the day? Often bored out of our Bu||$%*t Job skulls, day in and day out, many cubicle dwellers comforted one another that that everybody who wasn't doing what we were doing was some kind of slouch, taker, leach, or dead weight drag on proper society. We were *the responsible ones.*

Never mind that *we produced nothing at all* in taking phone calls from cranky, demanding people who were unhappy with this or that minor shortcoming about their latest TV or app-shopping impulse buy. Never mind that *we produced nothing* changing the format of a document or spreadsheet without understanding a single number therein. Never mind that we stood in *makeshift tilt-up retail shops* that saw maybe eight customers on a busy day. We were the superior and responsible of society because we were "at work," while a stay-at-home partner *only* restored the lawn, painted the house, fixed broken electrical outlets, re-tiled the shower, re-shingled the roof, while watching the kids, taking them to extracurricular activities, and helping them with their homework.

In this way, the 20th century Job Trance effectively functioned as a form of mass semi-subconscious peer-to-peer sociological devaluation and by some researcher's assessments, even an effective form of communal psychological abuse of anyone not in a role of a bu||$%*t JOB-JOB. It was like an ancient song lyric, "conform or be cast out."

In contrast to the "wisdom or crowds" of the early 2000s, it was like the 2,000-year-old brutality of the mob that seemed to never relent, even while 60% to 70% people knew that children were far better off with a stay-at-home parent, and mountains of family systems research validated the obviousness of that knowledge.[cxciii]

One thing that was rather curious about the Job Trance is that many of those most deeply entranced didn't even seem to realize that after a 50 or 60-hour week stylishly posting on Facebook to prove how busy and important they were, all that JOB-JOB-ing was still not enough to get by, let alone save anything for the future.

Deeply conditioned by algorithms and social engineering, people believed that "it's just the way it is," and nothing could ever change such a static, permanent reality. The prevalence and popularity of click-bait articles like, "50 ways to make a fast $50 — or more,"[cxciv] provided overwhelming evidence, in the form of deeply depressing daily news feed updates, of the precarity of the average American worker.

It was in this environment that our most senior and therefore entrenched and entranced politicians tried to extend and deepen the Job Trance by re-spinning yarns of a long bygone golden epochs that hadn't existed for half a century or more and will never exist again.

While we may soon find out otherwise, for the moment, the arrow of time moves in one direction, forward. That means the good old days – which weren't – when hundreds of different kinds of blue-collar careers could enable anyone to buy a house, support a family, and pay for annual vacations to far-flung dream destinations, all on a single wage-earner's income are as relevant as stories of valiant knights slaying fierce, fire-breathing dragons, rescuing damsels in distress; in a long-gone gilded age when it was believed every man's house was his castle. That's ancient history, auntie. Uncle.

The reality today is that both the very concept, as well as the existence of honorable everyday jobs that held sway in the post-World War II era, have long since dissolved into the mists of time. The past may be real, but it's not reality.

In the article, "There's a Bus Driver Shortage. And No Wonder," on the CityLab.com website, Laura Bliss wrote:

> *Once upon a time, it was considered an honorable and desirable gig—a stable union job with a good middle-class salary, a public pension, and at least some cultural recognition for the contributions it made to society, if bus-driving everyman heroes like Ralph Kramden of "The Honeymooners" were to be believed. Like many public sector jobs, it provided a reliable foothold on the ladder of social ascension. Even if you didn't have a college degree, being a city bus driver meant you could buy a house, feed your family, take a vacation, save for your child's college tuition. And relative to other transportation jobs, transit is still more inclusive of women and people of color.*
>
> *But public sector jobs of all kinds have declined in pay as collective bargaining continues to be eroded. The median hourly wage for a municipal bus driver in the U.S. is $19.61, according to the Bureau of Labor Statistics. Entry-level paychecks tend to be much smaller, which can pose a barrier to many young workers, especially with the fee required to earn the requisite commercial driver's license.*
>
> *"We have drivers who are homeless in this country," Larry Hanley, the president of ATU International, the largest labor union representing transit workers in the U.S., said. "In the Google area of California, the pay is so suppressed that we have drivers who are sleeping in their buses."*
>
> *Hanley was referring to a policy in Santa Clara Valley Transportation Authority, which for 20 years has permitted employees who live more*

> *than 50 miles away to sleep on trailers parked on its property. Some drivers also choose to snooze in their cars on nearby streets, according to the San Francisco Chronicle. News broke this week that VTA, which faces a $26.4 million budget gap for the coming fiscal year, is phasing out its official sleep-permitting policy. Operators there aren't sure what they're going to do.*[cxcv]

So, just as conditions are becoming intolerably dire for workers, the policies that historically provided at least some means for people to scrape by – including the "luxury" of sleeping in one's car 50 miles from home and family, without criminalizing workers for doing so – are also vanishing. Add to this the rapid evolution of self-driving technology and this can't end well for bus drivers and truck drivers in the coming years.

For all their trustworthiness and reliability, it's not too likely that many bus drivers will easily transition to the artificial intelligence and machine learning programmer jobs that statisticians use to advance the claim that there are plenty of jobs in America.

So, remnants of the zombie-like Job Trance persist, like vibes from a nightmare that might take half the day; or in worst cases a few days to fade. In too many cases it's still the case that if we don't have a JOB-JOB, people refuse to see us as persons, individuals worthy of the dignity and respect that includes income security as a pre-requisite of Maslow Safety. In the 2020s, the institution of JOB-JOBs is becoming increasingly unsustainable, even indefensible and, in many sectors, obsolete, at the same inverse exponential rate at which technology explodes and software has eaten the world.

* * *

Waking from the Job Trance

In the 20th century the so-called advanced west had fallen deeper and deeper into the Job Trance. That kind of blind religious conviction that if we don't hold a job, we are not a worthwhile member of society. No matter how much we've accomplished in the first 30, 40, 50, or 60 years of life, we are only as good as our current job title. In that kind of environment, giving up a job title, no matter how miserable we may have been in the current situation, was essentially social suicide. Healthcare was a major hostage held at gunpoint.

The inability to supply a snappy, impressive answer to "so, what do you do?" instantly stigmatized people as unimportant, lowest of the low. If we dared to answer, "I'm a homemaker," or "I'm retired" the retort was often, "oh, must be nice," or, "wow, you seem way too young to be retired," or "isn't that boring?" All manner of passive-aggressive dig that somehow people weren't pulling their weight. A truly insidious and pervasive default consensus reality.

"It must be nice," they'd say, to keeping up with an entire household, budgets, repairs, kids, yards, and no, we weren't too young and no, it wasn't boring, thanks. In fact, boredom seems more of a personal problem, doesn't it? This is again going to sound mean and uncomfortable, responding to that kind of passive aggression in a way that has maybe a snowball's chance of finding respect.

Just because some people lack the curiosity, imagination, and creativity to find wonder and opportunity in every moment of every day without someone else telling them what to do, doesn't mean that others live such empty inner lives. Busy-ness was often the camouflage for complete inner emptiness and vapidness of character. The lights were on but there was nobody at home.

The inherent worthiness and dignity of everyday domestic vocations such as stay-at-home parents was non-existent to those lost days of the Job Trance. The selfless service in supplying companionship and caring for aging parents was nice, but something done on your own time and *never* talked about in the *real world* of *real jobs*, where the important and dignified people spent the majority of their time. Work-life balance, right? Keep that stuff to yourself. It was maybe more like work-life dissociative identity disorder.

Society at large didn't consider taking responsibility for the elderly as *real work*. People considered elder companionship babysitting, or lower. If one was not independently wealthy or could afford to hire caregivers – conventional thinking was – one must also work full time to *pay your own freight*, in addition to the exhausting emotional and physical demands of caring for parents or other elderly family members. This devaluation was as demoralizing and demeaning as it was absurd on the face of it, and yet too often was the norm in the 20th century and dragging into the first quarter of the 21st century like a nasty cultural hangover.

How did the intrinsic and material economic value of essential domestic and community work not count toward equal respect and dignity of citizenship in America unless performed within the context of the all-worshipful JOB-JOB? It made no sense.

How was it that if we took care of our own children, it was worth $0? But if we took care of somebody else's children, they paid us? That was the logic of the Job Trance, and then we wondered why latchkey children were rudderless and families were dissolving at an exponential rate. It would be merely stupid if it weren't so intentional, bitterly mean-spirited, and short sighted.

To help us continue waking from the Job Trance, I don't think I can share enough from David Graeber, who did so much of this work ahead of his time. From the Goodreads book review site:

> *... a powerful argument against the rise of meaningless, unfulfilling jobs, and their consequences.*
>
> *Does your job make a meaningful contribution to the world? In the spring of 2013, David Graeber asked this question in a playful, provocative essay titled "On the Phenomenon of Bullshit Jobs." It went viral. After a million online views in seventeen different languages, people all over the world are still debating the answer.*
>
> *There are millions of people—HR consultants, communication coordinators, telemarketing researchers, corporate lawyers—whose jobs are useless, and, tragically, they know it. These people are caught in bullshit jobs.*
>
> *Graeber explores one of society's most vexing and deeply felt concerns, indicting among other villains a particular strain of finance capitalism that betrays ideals shared by thinkers ranging from Keynes to Lincoln. [In] Bullshit Jobs, [Graeber] gives individuals, corporations, and societies permission to undergo a shift in values, placing creative and caring work at the center of our culture. This book is for everyone who wants to turn their vocation back into an avocation.*

The advent of bu||$%*t jobs served to extend the life of a widely held irrational fear that, somehow, if we allow people to choose the work they want to do, rather than forcing them into JOB-JOBs, that somehow the entire structure of civilization would crumble within days or weeks; especially if any other currency circulation model was even momentarily entertained, even purely in the imagination. That's how deep the cultural programming ran in the minds of the entranced.

With the rent gun to one temple on the side of your head, and healthcare to the other, it was a deal you couldn't refuse. Refuse to accept a bu||$%*t job or a menial poorly paid job, and any individual member of the most advanced civilization humanity had ever known was immediately stripped of personhood, including the basic human right to a safe and legal place to sleep. Parents dehumanized and disowned their own children in the name of supposedly teaching this behavior as "character building."

They called it "tough love" to evict your own children or stay-at-home spouses who had already raised children, making such people homeless, leaving them to sleep behind dumpsters, in cars, or in any spare space they could find. I know it's hard to believe that people could be so heartless today, in 2024, but that's how brutal the Job Trance was way back then. People were that deeply brainwashed.

It seemed like a kind of mass psychosis Stockholm Syndrome dressed in prayer garments of "for your own good," kindness and concern. The Job Trance was like a kind of addiction to a way of thinking that *had to be* the *only right way* to think. It would be as hard to believe as the holocaust, if not for so many survivors' testimonies to never forget.

> *Did the "tough love" of homelessness ever build character? Of course not. It did, though, help to deepen the trauma, addiction, denial, desperate adverse street-survival behaviors, depression, and suicide that all too often attend even relatively short periods of homelessness.*

Public radio national treasure Terry Gross, for Houston Public Media, sat down for a conversation on the topic of addiction on August 25, 2021. "[Anna] Lembke is the medical director of addiction medicine at Stanford University and chief of the Stanford Addiction Medicine Dual Diagnosis Clinic. Her new book, *Dopamine Nation*, explores the interconnection of pleasure and pain in the brain and helps explain addictive behaviors — not just to drugs and alcohol, but also to food, sex, and smart phones." Terry continued:

> *Human beings are programmed to approach pleasure and avoid pain. It's an instinct that dates back millions of years, to a time when people needed to actively seek food, clothing and shelter every day, or risk death.*
>
> *But psychiatrist Anna Lembke says that in today's world, such basic needs are often readily available — which changes the equation.*
>
> *"Living in this modern age is very challenging. ... We're now having to cope with: How do I live in a world in which everything is provided?" Lembke says. "And if I consume too much of it — which my reflexes compel me to do — I'm going to be even more unhappy."*

If anything speaks of the negative impacts of the twin toxins of Job Trance and Pernicious Poverty in a superabundant civilization, it's Dr. Anna Lembke's work. By now, the red pill may be starting to take effect.

> *"If you know a substance user and abuser then you know a trauma survivor. And if they're abusing substances, chances are good they're abusing others in their lives."*

Back in the day, for those who had the privilege to do so, one of the best ways to keep up pristine appearances and indulge your additions or other domestic abusive behaviors was to evict anyone in the family who called you on it. That way, society saw the dispossessed person as clearly the problem, and you were good to go. It worked remarkably well for an incredibly long time. Today, we have better ways to see through such charades and our ability to discern what's really going on will only get better in the coming decades. We have a long way to go in recovering from so many iterations of recursive intergenerational trauma, and it's arguably one of, if not the major **WORK** of the early Post-Automation Era. Recovery. On multiple levels. Individual to institutional.

I believe that Dr Lembke's research illuminates so much, generally shushed, and unspoken, about the roots of dysfunction in our poverty-infused superabundant world, that portions of her work could almost form a clinical definition of Post-Automation Era Adaptation Disorder (PAEAD). Behaviors that perhaps once helped or even helped us survive the unthinkable, but that now hinder us, and yet we keep repeating.

Maybe we are experiencing a kind of centuries-delayed blowback, getting PAEAD back for ignoring these underlying issues for so long. Maybe it's like a *Tragedy of the Commons* epic for the ages.

Dr. Lembke is so authentic, sharing the damage done in her own life by her own addiction to romance novels, that she's able to share with a compelling compassion, candor, and of course, overwhelming data, such that I want to include a lengthy interview transcript excerpt, even at the cost of a full page.

> *So, for example, let's say I read a romance novel. I get a release of dopamine, my pleasure pathway or my reward circuit, and my balance tilts to the side of pleasure. No sooner has that happened than my brain starts to adapt to that increased dopamine by down regulating my own dopamine receptors and my dopamine production, not just to baseline levels but actually below baseline levels.*
>
> *This is really the key piece of neuroadaptation. I like to imagine this as these little neuroadaptation gremlins who hop on the pain side of the balance to bring it level again, but the gremlins really like it on the balance, so they don't get off as soon as the balance is level. They stay on until it's tilted in equal and opposite amount to the side of pain.*
>
> *That's the come down, the hangover, the after effect, or just that moment of wanting to read one more chapter in my romance novel, that inability to put it down, that unwillingness to leave that fantasy world.*

Now, if we wait long enough, those neurotic patient gremlins hop off and a level balance is restored. But as long as those gremlins are sitting on the pain side of their balance, our urge to find and use more of our drug of choice can be almost overwhelming.

So, the urge to want to restore neutrality once that balance is tipped to the side of pain is almost overwhelming. Now, if we wait long enough, the gremlins hop off and homeostasis is restored, but if we don't wait, if we continue to consume our drug of choice, we accumulate more and more gremlins on the pain side of the balance until we have enough gremlins to fill this whole room.

And once that happens, we're now in an addicted brain. Now we need more of our drug and more potent forms of our drug just to level the balance, and especially we need more potent forms if we're actually going to get high.

And when we're not using our drug, our balance is tilted to the side of pain. Those, those gremlins are now camped out there, tents and barbecues in tow, and that means that we're experiencing the universal symptoms of withdrawal chronically, and the universal symptoms of withdrawal from any addictive substance are anxiety, irritability, insomnia, dysphoria, and craving.

And this explains why people with addiction will relapse to their drug of choice even, you know, weeks and months after they've stopped using it's because it takes a long time for those gremlins to hop off and for homeostasis to be fully restored. And in the meantime, that person is walking around with a balance tilted to the side of pain.

The other thing that happens in addiction is that we narrow our focus to just this one pleasure, just our drug of choice or other intoxicants, and other more modest rewards are no longer appealing, because of course they can't compete with the army of gremlins that is now, you know, sitting on the pain side.

When we think about recovery from addiction, the primary goal is to restore homeostasis or restore a level balance, and the way that we do that in most instances is to abstain from our drug of choice for long enough for all of those gremlins to hop in for homeostasis to be restored.

Sometimes people are not able to do that, in which cases there are medications that we can use to try to help, you know, restore homeostasis. So that's the first and essentially second rule of balance. [1] The first rule being that for every pleasure we pay a price, and that price is pain. We tip to the pain side before going back to the level position. What goes up really must come down.

[2] And then the second rule of the balance is that with repeated exposure to the same or similar stimulus, that initial response to pleasure gets weaker and shorter, and that after response to pain gets stronger and longer, and eventually we reset our pain thresholds and our pleasure threshold such that we need much more pleasure to feel any pleasure at all, and even with the slightest pain or the absence of pleasure, we are in pain.

SHANE PARRISH: And this used to benefit us.

Absolutely. So, this very fine-tuned neural circuitry, which by the way evolved over millions of years of evolution and remains unchanged across species, is an absolutely genius circuit for a world of scarcity and ever-present danger where we have to be relentlessly seeking out the next best thing in order to survive.

But it's a very maladapted circuit for the world that we live in now, which is this world of overwhelming abundance, a world in which almost every human activity has become drugified in some way, not just drugs but also behaviors, even behaviors that we would think of typically as healthy behaviors like gaming, like sex, like eating, um, you know, more modern forms of human connection has become drugified through social media.[cxcvi]

So, it's become a much more difficult environment to thrive in as humans, because we're really not adapted for the world that we've created. — Dr. Anna Lembke

In May 2018, a 30-year-old man was legally evicted from his parents' house, because they could not imagine a world in which their own son has the basic human right to shelter. The Garden Island printed the Associated Press account:

The 30-year-old man whose eviction from his parents' suburban home drew national attention finally left Friday, hours before a court-ordered deadline.

"There are jobs available even for those with a poor work history like you," one letter they sent him reads. "Get one — you have to work!"

Back then, it seemed like those conditioned by the JOB-JOB Trance would turn upon one another in Orwellian 1984 style. Ironically, or perhaps tragically appropriately, 1984 is the same year that many consider the beginning of the Millennial generation.

Those disowned by family or tribe can forget about personhood or dignity, let alone healthcare or income security. You're out, on the street, literally, where the pavement is weaponized to coerce disturbingly dysfunctional behaviors in families and in companies, alike. Back then, eviction was the ultimate existential threat in an advanced Orwellian economy, as brandished by people with little or no conscience or concern for the long-term consequences of throwing human beings face-down onto the pavement for the alleged sake of *character-building*, or perhaps just as commonly, as a cover to exact revenge for disobedience to, or whistleblowing on some form domestic abuse.[cxcvii] It was an intergenerational pattern that all too commonly ran in families. "My parents beat me or berated me and threw me out on the street in the driving rain, so eventually, I'm going have to do the same thing to you." That is how intergenerational trauma works.

On the Master Investor blog, Victor Hill reflected upon the often-exhausting work of engaging with those most deeply rapt by a tendency for histrionic catastrophizing inherent to the JOB-JOB Trance:

> *Last year my colleague Felipe R. Costa wrote in these pages that UBI would destroy our economy. Felipe's principal objection to UBI was that it devalues work. While we agree on the iniquity of central bankers, it seems that we don't agree on the nature of "work." What is work?*
>
> *Yelling into a phone on a trading floor; working for nothing in a charity shop; composing a string quartet; singing in a choir; caring for a baby or an elderly relative; excavating a Roman villa on an archaeological dig; writing an article about UBI... These are all forms of work.*
>
> *Our pre-industrial forebears regarded "work" as whatever you needed to do at the time, rather than the activity for which we are paid by patrons or "clients." What is required in the age of robots is a change of culture, values, and metrics. And it's already underway (emphasis added).*

So how did such an absurd default consensus reality persist, holding so many sleepers in Matrix-like pod-cubicles for so long?

Before the era of Cambridge Analytics and AI manipulation of human psychology, one could understandably be confused as to how people could become so thoroughly convinced of such ideas and coerced into behaviors that diametrically oppose their own self-interest. Today, with more awareness of the way social media platforms use our own information against us, to drive our beliefs and behaviors, at least some answers are becoming a little clearer as to how this could have happened and how to be on the lookout for it in our own contemporary lives.

Clearer answers don't always mean more comforting answers because this is the way abusive people, perhaps even in our own families, have manipulated us as well, perhaps for many years. When the obvious revelation that a job title does not define the value of a human being causes major and maybe irreversible damage to a family relationship, we might begin to catch on that both the family and society may have been duped into duping us. When the very people whose words said, "I love you," and whose actions proved only rejection, resentment, disgust, and disdain, that's a moment of sudden enlightenment about the nature of micro-macro reflections of family systems and societal systems.

This unfortunate fractured family example may further serve to illustrate a pernicious shadow aspect of the JOB-JOB Trance that used to advance the mindset that we live in a dog-eat-dog world ruled by *natural law*, red in tooth and claw. It's not natural at all for people of conscience and consilience, but it is all too real in an animal's mind. It was a form of natural law that was the opposite of the realization of the natural super abundance of creation. It also revealed that, while we may appear as 8.6 billion of the same species in terms of basic anatomy and physiology, inside those 8.6 billion minds may dwell countless entirely different neurological and cognitive species. We're only beginning to gain access to the imaging and mapping tools required to figure that out in the 2020s, moving forward.

But maybe I need to back up and provide support for my claim of JOB-JOB Trance similarities to Stockholm Syndrome. In the Economist's 1843 Magazine article, *Why Do We Work So Hard?* Ryan Avent reckoned that our jobs had become *prisons from which we don't even want to escape*. That it. That's the definition of Stockholm Syndrome.

> *When John Maynard Keynes mused in 1930 that, a century hence, society might be so rich that the hours worked by each person could be cut to ten or 15 a week, he was not hallucinating, just extrapolating [doing the math]. The working week was shrinking fast. Average hours worked dropped from 60 at the turn of the century to 40 by the 1950s.*
>
> *The combination of extra time and money gave rise to an age of mass leisure, to family holidays and meals together in front of the television. There was a vision of the good life in this era. It was one in which work was largely a means to an end – the working class had become a leisured class. Households saved money to buy a house and a car, to take holidays, to finance a retirement at ease.*
>
> *The vision of a leisure-filled future occurred against the backdrop of the competition against communism, but it is a capitalist dream: one in which the productive application of technology rises steadily, until material needs can be met with just a few hours of work. It is a story of the triumph of innovation and markets.*

Keynes, in his essay on the future, reckoned that when the end of work arrived:

> *"For the first time since his creation man will be faced with his real, his permanent problem – how to use his freedom from pressing economic cares, how to occupy the leisure, which science and compound interest will have won for him, to live wisely, agreeably, and well."* [cxcviii]

Professor of Sociology Simon Gottschalk gets right to the core of the matter in his essay, "In Praise of Doing Nothing" on the academic publishing platform, The Conversation:

> *In the 1950s, scholars worried that, thanks to technological innovations, Americans wouldn't know what to do with all of their leisure time. Yet today, as sociologist Juliet Schor notes, Americans are overworked, putting in more hours than at any time since the Depression and more than in any other in Western society.*
>
> *In a hypermodern society propelled by the twin engines of acceleration and excess, doing nothing is equated with waste, laziness, lack of ambition, boredom or "down" time. But this betrays a rather instrumental grasp of human existence ... to equate "doing nothing" with non-productivity betrays a short-sighted understanding of productivity. In fact, psychological research suggests that doing nothing is essential for creativity and innovation, and a person's seeming inactivity might actually cultivate new insights, inventions, or melodies.*
>
> *As legends go, Isaac Newton grasped the law of gravity sitting under an apple tree. Archimedes discovered the law of buoyancy relaxing in his bathtub, while Albert Einstein was well-known for staring for hours into space in his office.*
>
> *Doing nothing – or just being – is as important to human well-being as doing something. As we race along, it seems as though we're not taking the time to seriously examine the rationale behind our frenetic lives – and mistakenly assume that those who are very busy must be involved in important projects.*
>
> *Touted by the mass media and corporate culture, this credo of busyness contradicts both how most people in our society define "the good life" and the tenets of many philosophies that extol the virtue and power of stillness.*

> *French philosopher Albert Camus perhaps put it best when he wrote, "Idleness is fatal only to the mediocre."*
>
> *An abrupt waking. By this definition, if we find idleness fatal, then we are Camus' mediocre people. By this definition, if we believe JOB-JOBs must withhold a meager share of sustenance (basic income) from the commons, we are communist. No judgement, these are simply definitions.*

Maybe I should do my best to practice some empathy and let people sit with the cognitive dissonance for a minute. To re-read definitions. Chat with a favorite AI about these principles and then throw this book away or come back when you're ready to see how much deeper the rabbit hole goes.

I can see where some might react, "did he just call me a communist?!" No. We may have just found out that, as defined above, the thoughts and behaviors of a proud 60-100 hour a week workaholic who is equally proud of browbeating everyone else into the same beliefs and behaviors – while feeling justified and vindicated when those who question the validity and human value of those ethics somehow end up sleeping on the streets – those thoughts and behaviors might be indistinguishable from those of a communist, according to Camus, Keynes, Paine, and many others. Or I could be misreading and misunderstanding all of this material, all wrong.

If the AI Big Bang of the past several months has done anything useful, it seems that it's made it clear that, for better or worse, and especially when worse, we are all in this together. We're inextricably intertwined and independent, regardless of tribes, colors, nations, or labels, and if we don't figure this out, there may not be anyone left to figure.

The take-away for me in learning about all this is that *the whole point of capitalism is to expand leisure time and grow the leisure class*. If we are against expanding leisure, we might have accidentally become more aligned with communist thought than capitalist principles.

Shocking? Would it be surprising if one learned that U.S. capitalism's ancient 1940s adversary chose to engage in 80 years of psyops in order to turn its enemy's workers against themselves? I don't have the luxuries of time, attention, or space in these pages for tinfoil hat conspiracy theories; however, if our lives are not at least partly about learning from history, recognizing and eliminating maladaptive patterns of behavior, then we aren't living very thoughtful or observant lives. That's fine, there's no crime in choosing to live an unreflective and unobservant life, only outcomes of those choices.

So the reflection is, wouldn't it seem like a page right out of Orwell's *1984*, to convince a population that only central committee-like wealth-hoarding oligarchs are true capitalists, while howling against increasing leisure for the laboring classes?

If the world seemed upside down for half a century, maybe it was.

It's the year 2024. Just six years away from Keynes's 2030 forecast. Instead of achieving the capitalist dream of toil-liberated and leisured masses, what have we accomplished? "Minimum-wage jobs can't pay rent anywhere in U.S., according to report on Affordable Housing" (Johnson). This is not the commonwealth capitalist's dream of a century ago. This is not the free market promise of just one or two generations ago. Ironically, against this backdrop and amid the *ism schisms*, some aspects of social-*ism* might offer a kind of middle ground to help a capitalist mixed economy find its bearings again, in a world turned upside.

Nearly a quarter of the way into the twenty-first century, masses of workers in this early Post-Automation Era see their futures spinning sideways, upside-down, out of control, and feeling a bit like those astronauts of Apollo 13 at risk of remaining stranded on the dark side of the moon. What is an interplanetary oligarch preacher's solution? Same as it ever was, from the day of the Luddite's: "work more and longer hours to *make my money work harder for* me or enjoy your eternity in outer darkness, expendable, and replaceable NPC a$$tronaut."

Maybe I'm projecting. I know for certain that people have misinterpreted my own work as that of an interplanetary utopian manifesto-preacher. Maybe many people sincerely believe that the Job Trance is the best way to coordinate human creativity and productive into eternity. I disagree, but that doesn't mean others have no right to commit themselves to staying the course that has led us to this very crisis point in history. Maybe it's like the legendary anthem, *Stairway to Heaven*. "Yes, there are two paths you can go by, but in the long run, there's still time to change the road you're on. (whispered: I hope so)."

Or maybe what Olympian, ultra-marathoner, writer, producer, actor, motivator, and encourager Alexi Pappas calls the *glop stage*, is more accurately representative of the Post-Automation Era stage of civilizational transformation.[cxcix] Pappas defines *glop* as the larval stage of biological soup into which a caterpillar in chrysalis complete dissolves. Glop appears like a state of absolute biological and chemical catastrophe. Complete chaos. While all of the perfect and intricately-ordered information that will soon assemble a butterfly is encoded and only dormant in that soup of potential for a brief time; it is during such moments of glop that the likelihood of the mistaken view that a slightly different caterpillar might emerge is higher. It is easy to forgive someone unfamiliar with metamorphosis for thinking that a caterpillar went in, so of course a caterpillar will come out.

If this decade is more like a newly fledged butterfly drying its wings and freaking out every time the wind blows, because "WTF, wings?!" Then being rudely, jarringly, terrifyingly lifted by the breeze, as a completely disoriented butterfly discovers the vast sky is actually an inviting, swaying sea.

Where we clung to our little twigs just moments ago, braced against the wind for fear of falling, we suddenly, unexpectedly float, circle, and survey a new landscape. Rather, the same landscape, from a new perspective that brings everything into perspective in a way that couldn't have made sense to our caterpillar self.

Precisely where we land next or for how long may not be clear, yet just as abruptly and suddenly as we were set aloft, we just instinctively *know* that we are safe and capable of letting the sea of the sky guide us, every gust and breeze and even frightful gale along the way.

We might soon find that we can somewhat guide our own course to a slightly more meaningful degree, however relatively insignificant our efforts may appear compared to tide-like trade-winds. Our wings may not be perfect, but they are *good enough* to carry us surely and land us safely. We can trust this new embodiment with its seemingly inexplicable and initially awkward attributes.

In the meantime, one question for us humans here on the ground is, can we sit with the cognitive dissonance of our deprecated, outdated views, born of true, real, and valid *past* experience, long enough to ride out any sense of grief, anger, insult, outrage, or depression due to the loss of all that has passed and come to terms with the significance of our individual and collective metamorphosis into this Post-Automation Era? Can we glimpse, and maybe even glide into the uplifting potential of letting go of what was indeed once real – the upside-down world of a desperately clinging caterpillar – and like that new butterfly, float into the practically infinite blue sky of this next temporary and fleeting stage of existence?

For the moment, maybe it's enough to stay grounded in the boring and mundane observation that robots and automation have long since taken over vast swaths of redundant, backbreaking, and monotonous human activity, and that robotics have already achieved highly sophisticated, delicate, and intricate human physical capabilities. Not only running, jumping, and somersault, but up to and including such highly specialized fine motor skills as picking up and cracking eggs and performing surgery on human bodies.[cc]

While robots may not perform unattended surgery any time soon, one skilled surgeon becomes able to complete the work of ten, with more precision and safety, without leaving the office; while today's robots can and will make *good enough* short order cooks in relatively short order. Even in many highly specialized, human-touch dominated fields, the writing is on the wall:

Welcome to the Post-Automation Era.

In 2018, BioSpectrumAsia reported:

> *The market leading device is the Da Vinci, manufactured by Intuitive Surgical, sales of which have rapidly risen despite the latest model's £1.7m price tag and annual maintenance costs of £150,000. Between 2007 and 2011, the number of Da Vinci robots in use in the US increased from 800 to 1,400, while the number worldwide reached 2,300 in 2011. There are around 50 in the UK.*

In 2023, BioSpectrumIndia updated:

> *Dr Chowbey could see a three-dimensional image of the gallbladder and its surroundings on the large screen attached to the console. His wrists firmly rested on the console, providing adequate support to his elbows, as he*

navigated the complex procedure. The gallbladder is nestled within fat deposits, with two major blood vessels tangled around it. He enlarged the area he needed to operate on, and with fine precision, untangled and clipped the blood vessels. Then, without making any extra incisions or touching the patient's liver, he excised the gallbladder and removed the gallstones protruding from the bile duct. In a mere 10 minutes, Dr. Chowbey completed the procedure with unmatched precision.

"That's the beauty of robots. They provide me with an entire 3D view of the organ, allowing me to operate without causing any damage to the surrounding tissue. This not only ensures a quicker recovery for the patient but also results in significantly less pain compared to conventional and laparoscopic surgery." said Dr. Chowbey, as he moved to the next OR for his second surgery of the morning.[cci]

Also in 2023, EuroNews reported:

A team of surgeons in Spain successfully performed the world's first robotic lung transplant. Lung transplantations are known for being complex operations as the patient's chest has to be cut open. During the procedure, an incision around 30 cm is made and ribs are cut through to remove and replace a diseased lung with a healthy human lung from a donor.

But the new technology used by the Spanish team no longer requires breaking the patient's ribs. Instead, the surgeons at Vall d'Hebron Hospital in Barcelona used made smaller cuts to the side of the rib cage to accommodate the robot's arms and 3D cameras.

"This incision is made under the sternum, where the skin is very elastic. This allows us to open only the skin, and to insert this lung little by little," said Dr Albert Jauregui, Head of Thoracic Surgery and Lung Transplant Service at Vall D'hebron Hospital.

The new lung was also "deflated" in the operating theatre so that it could enter through the tight incision, which was just about 8cm. According to Jauregui, the new procedure is less painful for the patient as the wound closes more easily.

"We believe it is a technique that will improve patients' life quality, the post-surgery period, and reduce pain. We hope this technique will eventually spread to more centres," he added.[ccii]

As is so often the case, prolific traveler, journalist, author, and technology-in-culture clairvoyant Kevin Kelly describes the nature of inexorable acceleration and optimization, which a distraction and denial addicted culture seems to dismiss, with every exponential iteration. "These inadvertent anticipatory inventions are called exaptations in biology," Kelley explains, "We don't know how common exaptations are in nature, but they are routine in the technium.[cciii] The technium is nothing but exaptations since innovations can be easily borrowed across lines of origin or moved across time and repurposed."[cciv]

> *Something more that distinguishes humanity in the Post-Automation Era. Human beings are natural masters at constructively and gracefully integrating our own iterative exaptations.*[ccv] *When we accept ourselves.*

We may have thought we learned a new language or how to play a musical instrument for one reason, and it turns out to be useful for completely unexpected, different, incredibly valuable reasons. That's an exaptation. We became expert gamers in a particular genre because it was fun, and it turned out that our communication and team-building skills become incredibly practical and lucrative in managing people at work, or in other ways like live-streaming on Twitch.TV, or e-Sports, which didn't even exist when we began our training. That's an exaptation. Crypto-currencies were an exaptation of blockchain distributed ledger technology.

What was perhaps most misguided about the 20th century JOB-JOB Trance was that it was strictly obsessed with corporate and career exaptations only, to the effective exclusion of all else. As we learned earlier, the misappropriation of all capitalism-created leisure back into more hours of labor is the textbook definition of a kind of *exapted communism*. I'm sure these observations are irritating to some because they don't seem to make sense upon a cursory glance; but one look through a microscope reveals an invisible world that is how the real world really is.

Similarly today, in even moderately advanced economies, humanity has long since passed the point where most people can live fully and meaningful lives of *productive leisure* (see Glossary) finding and doing work that fulfills them and adds value to society, rather than responding in robotic hypnotization to the 20th century JOB-JOB Trance. It's a bit of historic poetic justice to find that it took robots to show how just how robotically we've lived our own lives.

It's true that many of us still live in the JOB-JOB world and go along with it because there is no other immediate, practical option, while also knowing precisely how ridiculous it is. Others still take it seriously, as if the rule of Mammon represents the One True Real-World Order[ccvi] to which all had better comply, or else. Some ignore the silliness altogether and play life like a video game, to the point of treating people like NPCs, who exist only to distract us from our own deeper introspection. Some leave the game entirely and head off-grid because we can't tolerate the oblivious insanity of such a contradictory civilization for even one moment longer.

Perhaps one practical way to directly break the Job Trance like a bad fever dream is to awaken ourselves from a strange form of intellectual laziness and projection that leads us to assume that *all other people are inherently lazy, yet when we ourselves relax, we are certain that it's earned leisure*. How do we know "that lazy person at the park" hasn't paid 1,000 times the dues we think a person ought to pay to earn the right to rest from the Job Trance's relentless peer-coerced frenetic over-exertion in order to fall only always short of justifying our right to exist?

Of course, those most deeply entranced can't image ever take a moment of leisure, because they can't ever imagine feeling worthy of a moment's rest, for fear of what their own judgmental minds would do to themselves; namely, incriminate and berate themselves, just as they do to others, if they themselves dared to sample the smallest subset of liberation from relentless labor. Even after working tirelessly for decades, the most deeply conditioned can't change because they would lose their internal moral high ground from which to incriminate and intimidate others who don't work 100 hours a week like they do.

Ask me how I know. It's taken a long time to learn how to rest. Some of the hardest real work of my life.

For many, everything in the world of work is either passive-aggressive, or plain aggressive chimp-like competition to prove who is more dedicated to swinging the hammer or the sickle 100 hours a week. Does that sound like American commonwealth, stakeholder-style, leisure-creating capitalism, or something familiar from the other side of the world?

I'm not saying that there is anything wrong with a strong work ethic. A strong work ethic is noble. What attempted is to illustrate by example that this decade marks the end of the glop stage of the early Post-Automation Era.

> *The Post-Automation Era is not a foggy futurist prediction of where we might be heading, it's documented evidence of where we are, today.*

The glop of a bygone century of global industrialization served its miraculous decomposition purpose, bringing us to this moment of emergence from not only the never-ending cycle of Just Over Broke Justification Of Being, but from centuries of endless war and senseless human bloodshed, as we circulate superabundance in a way that works for everyone.

Once again, Bucky said it best:

> *"Now this is the real news of our century: it is highly feasible, to take care of all of humanity, at a higher standard of living than anybody has ever experienced or dreamt of, to do so without anybody having to profit at the expense of another, so everybody can enjoy the whole Earth. And it can all be done by 1985."*[ccvii]

"In [his book Rest: why you get more done when you work less], Silicon Valley consultant Alex Pang argues that we can be more successful in all areas of our lives by recognizing the importance of rest: working better does not mean working more, it means working less and resting better. Treating rest as a passive activity secondary to work undermines our chances for a rewarding and meaningful life."[ccviii]

"It took a century to create the weekend—and only a decade to undo it," Katrina Onstad notably wrote for digitally native news outlet, Quartz. Things weren't always the way they are today, and they can change as dramatically now as they have in the past.

Onstad continues:

> *Bragging "I never take a weekend" is [considered] a gesture of strength: I corralled time, I beat it down. Actually, taking a weekend means ceasing the fight with time, and letting it be neutral, unoccupied. Why isn't this a good thing?*
>
> *... with industrialization, clocks now determined the task, and the measure of productivity was how much labor could be wrung out of a worker over a period of time. Time had a dollar value, and became a commodity, not to be wasted. "Time is now currency: It is not passed but spent," wrote historian E. P. Thompson.*
>
> *Clocks in factories would often mysteriously turn forwards and backwards. Bosses were stealing unpaid hours from workers, who feared to carry their own watches for, as one factory worker wrote in his memoirs in 1850, "it was no uncommon event to dismiss anyone who presumed to know too much about the science of horology."*
>
> *In 1926, Ford introduced the five-day workweek. "People who have more leisure must have more clothes," he argued. "They eat a greater variety of food. They require more transportation in vehicles."*
>
> *Ford, probably by accident, articulated a contradiction that sits at the heart of the weekend as we have come to know it: It's both a time of rest and a time of consumption. A Marxist might point out that the weekend is an act of corporate trickery, a dangling carrot that keeps workers tethered to their jobs.*[ccix]

As Scott Santens best expresses, "The most important thing money can buy is choice. With enough money, you can choose to walk away from a shi**y job or a toxic relationship. You can still walk away without money, but it's SO MUCH harder."[ccx]

* * *

Thinking About Thinking About Poverty

How is it that we fail to consider the prevalence of 21st century poverty in the age of superabundance an Armageddon of its own, as dire as any other zombie apocalypse scenario? In our complacency and comfort, we voice *concern* without ever taking a single meaningful action.

Are we yet that much like the Forest Troop, despite advances long since normalized in everyday society? Some say yes. Some say hookup culture and bonobo behavior is the way of this age and all that follow. Other Americans are obsessive about prepping for scenarios that could theoretically kill 100,000 people or more, while ignoring the very real death and destruction wrought by poverty, today, every day. Add the advent of AI doomers, scrambling to "align AI with human values," whatever that means, and this describes the anomie of the present moment in 2024.

Poverty kills more than 100,000 people ***every single year*** *and has for a long time. Yet, we shrug and spit, "the poor shall always be with you."*

Why? Is it because we think that poverty can't possibly ever afflict *us*, because we are *willing to do whatever it takes*, thereby proving our point of engineered precarity's coercive effect? Do we believe poverty can only come for *those* people? Regardless of our beliefs, the reality is that poverty can and does infect every single one of us in countless seemingly invisible ways, even if it isn't our current experience, by multiplying and deepening the social divisions, wounds, and ills that affect all of us.

Not AI, but poverty in the midst of plenty might be the societal supervirus that most directly threatens our continued existence in the 21st century. And if we think the commonwealth acceptance of a way of life that ignores poverty didn't directly contribute to the acceleration of climate change, all in the name of infinite exponential growth, well, we're simply not paying attention. Exponential growth itself is not evil, it's the ways by which we achieve and grow superabundance that matters.

The only thing more damning than poverty in a superabundant society is the disregard and denial of poverty in a superabundant society.

A 2011 Columbia University study published in the American Journal of Public Health found that poverty kills about the same number of people as heart attack and stroke. Every. Single. Year. "Overall, 4.5% of U.S. deaths were found to be attributable to poverty—midway between previous estimates of 6% and 2.3%" (Columbia). According to the most recent 2015 CDC data, the total number of U.S. deaths was 2,712,630. 4.5%

of that total is 122,068. That's more than the entire population of Abilene, Texas, Allentown, Pennsylvania, or Santa Clara, California, killed by poverty every single year.

Why are we citing decade-old work here? Because the absence of an immediate, pandemic-panic like response and ongoing follow-up to that work epitomizes the magnitude of cultural denial of the impact and scope of poverty in the United States, let alone worldwide.

Every single year, poverty kills an entire U.S. city worth of people in the United States. If poverty were a virus, we'd insist upon a Project Hyperspace, beyond Warp Speed to ensure its immediate eradication.

At that pace of death, 610,340 people have died from poverty over the past five years ago, alone. Since the date of Columbia University's findings in 2011, that's about 1,464,816. One and half million preventable deaths due to just about every addict's fundamental dysfunction: denial.

In 2024, these words from 2018 convey a note of prescience:

> *"Imagine if there were a bacteria or virus suddenly discovered that would kill over a million Americans over the next decade. The outrage would be overwhelming. There would be panic on the airwaves. That panic would immediately be transformed into funding for finding solutions. Yet, the epidemic of poverty has already killed that many Americans over the past decade, and is on course to meet or beat Wall Street expectations, moving into the 2020s. Where is the moral outrage at this epidemic? This isn't just a failure to act, it's a failure of [conscience]" (ibid).*

But if a pandemic is not a virus, if it's *only* poverty, then it's those lazy poors fault. It's their own failure.

We don't consider poor people as worth the thought it takes to save human lives. We treat poor people as some kind of unfortunate, undesirable, and therefore undeserving sub-species. Lower than stray cats and dogs. We *voice* concern for political correctness, but don't meaningfully care if they die. We strip poor people of personhood in our minds and our society. Poor people do not possess the most basic right to exist. It's too bad when they die out there in the cold, sure, but they were poor, stupid, lazy, or all three, and oh well, that's what happens to poor people.

Lesson: don't be poor. Do *whatever it takes*, and that's where the lower impulses of humanity take flight toward quick and easy money by drugs, violence, prostitution, and all manner of exploitation. Then Moloch's pop-culture rationalizes or romanticizes all the dysfunction and devastation of pimp-n-ho thug life as some kind of noble Godfather-like honor among thieves. It's not street violence, it's "local safety and protection work." Euphemisms don't change objective actualities.

We threaten our kids with the plight of poor people, in order to convince them to obey their mammon masters and do their wage slave JOB-JOB, or we too, your loving parents, will send you to live with *them*. Hey, it's tough love, right? We perpetuate the viciousness of natural law by our choices. I wish this were histrionics and hyperbole, but it's the way I've observed Americans behave for more than the past 50 years. Our behaviors reveal our truest beliefs, so what does such behavior reveal about our true self-image as an enlightened and compassionate society?

In a post-automation society, the ways that we think, and *what we choose to think about*, have become increasingly crucial. Attention is by far the most valuable and important currency in the world. Maybe it always was. How does this matter or apply to the process of thinking about thinking about poverty?

It matters because what we think about and how we think about what we think about determines what we do. If we put poverty out of our minds, then we never need to act. James Allen's tiny, timeless classic, "As a Man Thinketh," speaks simply and concisely to the foundations of the attention economy. If what we think leads to what we do, then more of the same thinking leads to more of the same doing. This is what being human means at the most fundamental level, for as long as consciousness has expressed itself in human form. This is how we end up with more of what we have always got, at an exponential rate of both accomplishment and calamity.[ccxi]

In the 21st century social media economy, attention has long since become the world's most valuable currency, yet many of us still live in villages run by domineering and often petty personas that define themselves and their place in local tribal life in terms of trifling power-intoxicated hierarchies. Whoever performs the most physical labor is considered the most respectable and ascends highest up the Molochian hierarchy, from construction to prostitution. "Just sitting there thinking," as students, writers, researchers, programmers, and lifelong learners do, is all too often regarded as *lazy* and vilified as a characteristic of people who don't want to do *real work*.

These reasons, driven by the dark forces of economic precarity, are why organizations from Operation Underground Railroad[ccxii] to Scholars at Risk,[ccxiii] exist. From protecting and rescuing exploited children of all ages from the unthinkable horrors of human trafficking to protecting and rescuing young scholars and thinkers – of all ages – from the grotesque underbellies of cities, towns, and villages that strip thinking people of conscience of human dignity, while ridiculing and suppressing intellect in all its forms.

Why do all these vile circumstances persist? The acceptance of poverty. The normalization of utter desperation and destitution as the self-righteous consequence of any period of joblessness. Isn't it? Isn't this "just the way the world works?"

Wittingly or not, in Moloch's social hierarchy, the most impoverished minds, impoverished souls, impoverished economic policies keep the vulnerable impoverished in order to feed the hierarchy's own troglodyte predation impulses, within our own species. It's essentially a kind of sociological, psychological, and spiritual cannibalism. That's not the way toward a world that works for everyone.

Maybe that was the nature of the old vicious Earth. Simultaneously, hundreds, if not thousands of books on the topic of a New Earth exist, so deeply are these memes embedded in our civilization's psyche.[ccxiv]

Why do I suggest that such toxic hierarchies ruled the old Earth? Because as a documentarian, I experienced the distinct displeasure of observing them in many small-town contexts, from island life, to suburbs, to county and rural townships.

Molochian hierarchies consider the contemplative or prayerful life as indolence. Molochian hierarchies are expert at communal gaslighting, scapegoating, browbeating, expressing open derision toward people of conscience and attentiveness by casting spells like, "idle hands are the devil's workshop," with a tone and stance of counterfeit scriptural authority.

There is a well-known Bill Gates story about a conversation he had with his mother as a teen. Roughly, the story goes that he was "sitting there doing nothing" in a contemplation process that would lead to the creation of one of the most innovative businesses in history.

> *When Bill Gates was in the sixth grade, his parents decided he needed counseling. He was at war with his mother Mary, an outgoing woman who harbored the belief that he should do what she told him. She would call him to dinner from his basement bedroom, which she had given up trying to make him clean, and he wouldn't respond. "What are you doing?" she once demanded over the intercom.*
>
> *"I'm thinking," he shouted back.*
>
> *"You're thinking?"*
>
> *"Yes, Mom, I'm thinking," he said fiercely. "Have you ever tried thinking?"*
>
> *The psychologist they sent him to "was a really cool guy," Gates recalls. "He gave me books to read after each session, Freud stuff, and I really got into psychology theory." After a year of sessions and a battery of tests, the counselor reached his conclusion.*
>
> *"You're going to lose," he told Mary. "You had better just adjust to it because there's no use trying to beat him." Mary was strong-willed and intelligent herself, her husband recalls, "but she came around to accepting that it was futile trying to compete with him."*[ccxv]

How can an optimist use such depressing and derogatory language? Because being an optimist does not mean being blind, gullible, or naïve.

Being an optimist means that we hold hope like an eternal flame that each of us can learn to identify our own outdated beliefs and behaviors, and that eventually, even if through many dangers, toils, and snares, we are all ultimately capable of taking a moment to think about thinking and examine how we arrived at our current assumptions about ending poverty with unconditional income security.

Why do so many feel strongly that some people deserve to be in poverty, by virtue of the purely unpredictable lottery of birth or sudden adversity, while others deserve relief, rescue, escape? Even the analytically minded aren't immune from the common trap of assigning arbitrary deservingness, especially when we can assign numbers.

To think of poverty in terms of the GINI index is useful in some contexts and completely misses the point in others. To think about ending poverty ending at $0.01 above an "official" poverty level is ipso facto ridiculous.

> Imagine a drowning person granted one breath just before they take their last breath. Then they're left to flail to the point of their last breath again. Then given one more breath to avoid drowning again. Forever. Is that person saved from drowning? It's technically surviving in an inescapably hellish state that amounts to a kind of economic waterboarding; forever drowning, barely kept alive with just enough air to keep people on breath from death. That's the old welfare system. As unconscionable a thing to do to a drowning person as it is to say, "here's $0.01 more than poverty level, now you're out of poverty!"

These are some examples of what I mean by thinking about our thinking.

So let's think about the tool called cognitive behavioral therapy (CBT). CBT is a method of mapping more effective internal thinking to more effective external behavior. Often, the *way* we think about things can cause us as much benefit or suffering as IRL events themselves. CBT is one example of how different thinking can definitively create a different reality.

It seems to me that in the first quarter of the twenty-first century, the U.S. commonwealth is in dire need of CBT's practical, methodical, individualized, and self-managed, incremental improvement and intervention. Particularly when it comes to older economic ideas that history may have dismissed or resisted for a long time, and which are now up for reconsideration. That is, the need is dire if we want to recover from the rock bottom conditions, as we've just recognized.

CBT. Cognitive Behavior Therapy begins with thinking about thinking. So we can apply the method to thinking about our thinking and emotions about unconditional basic income, "a guaranteed income at levels that sustain life in decent circumstances" (MLK). We've already summarized many of the common kneejerk reactions, so this is a place where we can examine ourselves and see if any of those generalizations apply, or not.

Certainly, not all 20th century thinking was detrimental. While toothless in terms of enforcement, Article 25 of the Universal Declaration of Human Rights (UDHR) is one worthwhile and credible precedent of a long established, previously dismissed and ignored way of thinking about ending poverty in the 21st century:

"Everyone has the right to a standard of living adequate for the health and well-being of himself and of his family, including food, clothing, housing and medical care and necessary social services, and the right to security in the event of unemployment, sickness, disability, widowhood, old age or other lack of livelihood in circumstances beyond his control."

Is it not self-evident to clarify that in a post-automation capitalist society, "the right to security in the event of unemployment" can only mean "the right to income security?" For without income security, none of the other securities are even remotely attainable.

Perhaps some readers did not know that a 1948 global community clearly defined these rights over 75 years ago. It is also self-evident that "standard of living" is directly dependent upon the principle of income security. Likewise, it's clear that these principles are not the result of some hastily assembled pipe dream by bums on skid row in order escape personal responsibility. People who are lazy and entitled never even get close to collaborating and coordinating with others at such a level. The fact that people across the socioeconomic spectrum of all nations have exhaustively cross-examined and scrutinized these principles with the utmost intellectual, moral, and ethical rigor, is equally indisputable.

In 1948, a globally diverse and wide-ranging community of entrepreneurs, workers, activists, scholars, career professionals, and policy makers unquestionably verified ***the principle of income security as a fundamental human right****. To call the principle of income security a radical new idea in 2024 is, by definition, ridiculous.*

What does commonwealth CBT look like in practice? Despite such long-standing commonly held convictions, we have yet to map direct public cognition of these rights into direct public behavior that implements and ensures those rights through affirmative public policy. The process of connecting those dots is what CBT looks like.

Without clear cognition, without sound thinking about thinking, the rapid rate of change in our globally distributed and embedded intelligent machines and sensor environment overwhelms us, and we can find ourselves stuck in a cycle of reacting to random life circumstances, rather than directing our lives skillfully in this unfamiliar environment.

As we hurtle toward a 22nd century that – assuming we survive the current upheaval and transition – surely includes the settling of other worlds, the transcendence of those ancient, shared enemies of disease, aging, and scarcity. This is indeed an opportune time to reflect upon how far we've come as a civilization, and where we wish to go from here. A time to reflect upon the seeming chaos of a world of wild stock markets and AI deep fakes masquerading as headline news in a bizarre post-truth mystopia.[ccxvi] So, for AI doomers worried about a future dystopia, how about considering ways to work ourselves out of the predicament we're in, right now?

Some of the earliest results of machine learning, trained on our own long human history of ignorance, aggression, and hierarchical dominance-seeking versus cooperation and coordination, was the understanding that humans still predominantly respond most quickly and decisively to fight or flight stimuli. This created a perverse incentive for early social media networks to optimize for engagement by exploiting this deep-seated psychological vulnerability. Rather than good intentions, the principles of captology and shareholder primacy paved the road to social media mystopia (xxxviii).[ccxvii]

From my perspective, the catastrophic doom scenario is not simply that AI has or will run away of its own volition, like the sentient AI depicted in 1970s Colossus: The Forbin Project.[ccxviii]

Perhaps the risk is that AI may one day, or perhaps already has figured out just how devolved humans are on the whole and uses that understanding to exploit humanity's least common denominators, the least evolved portions of our brains and behaviors in ways that may not be best for human flourishing, let alone a world that works for everyone.

We might interpret first and second-generation social media mysfunction and mystopia – like we're living in, today – as a kind of urgent warning that we'd be wise to heed. The seemingly sentient computer HAL's point of view, from the 1969 classic, 2001: A Space Odyssey, is still timeless (ciii). Whatever adverse or unseen consequences, whatever blowback we experience consequent to our own advances, as HAL said, "can only be attributable to human error."

So, now might be a suitable time to rethink about our thinking and reprioritize fundamental human value, fundamental health of the commonwealth, and cultivate conditions for anthropological flourishing above machine-like obedience to machine-like 20th century institutions running on 250-year-old deprecated code.

Some of our brightest thinkers already ask, what if robots and AI have already, essentially, taken over? What if we have effectively become robots by-proxy, or at least unwitting agents, useful idiots of robotic algorithms, because our behavior is constantly, and alarmingly precisely guided by the content of our social media timelines? How would we even know if our own minds and lives had been MITM'd through the attack surface of our mobile devices, and if we began to find hints of that possibility, how would we even begin to triage, to investigate?[ccxix]

What if we have already fallen – like the biological machine minds that we are, ourselves – into relatively hard-wired, predictable, repetitive, redundantly-protected, self-limiting thinking about the nature and kind of superabundant post-automation world that we live in, or could live in, with some simple yet profound, strategic upgrades to both our own thinking and our participation in the commonwealth? What if we've neglected to upgrade our own internal and commonwealth software packages, our own cognitive maps, and our own behavioral choices to maximize flourishing for ourselves and others in this unique new environment? How could we even begin to know whether or not this line of thinking is wild speculation, sensible induction, or unsettlingly close to the truth, the whole truth, and nothing but the truth?

Remember how we earlier mentioned humanity's seemingly uncanny yet regularly observed ability to accurately forecast events well beyond our own short lifespan, much further out on the Long Arc than objective reasoning might expect, much less explain? Let's return to that observation for a moment, while that last batch of questions queues up in a parallel background process. In "Artificial Intelligence — The Revolution Hasn't Happened Yet," computer scientist Michael Jordan wrote:

> *"In the current era, we have a real opportunity to conceive of something historically new — a human-centric (Intelligence Infrastructure) engineering discipline. Finally, and of particular importance, II systems must bring economic ideas such as incentives and pricing into the realm of the statistical and computational infrastructures that link humans to each other and to valued goods" (Jordan).*

This is particularly relevant to income security policy, as the Economic Intelligence Infrastructure (EII) train has already left the station and we haven't even come close to building the rest of the tracks. We'll dive deeper into the implications of our 21st century EII later when we arrive at the realization that income security *is* national security.[ccxx]

At the moment, in no domain is the incompleteness of our EII work more obvious or impactful than in the everyday economics of the roughly 60% of Americans who make up the U.S. civilian labor force. That's the number of essential workers, all workers, as measured by the U.S. Bureau of Labor Statistics Civilian Labor Force Participation Rate. Despite somewhat misleading headline employment numbers derived from fractions of fractions of the population, we have been running our booming economy with 40% of Americans on the sidelines for quite some time, and efficiency only keeps increasing.

That's what superabundant exponential growth looks like through the displaced intergenerational labor-gap lens. Said simply, we are considering the perspective of workers replaced by the blessings of superabundant growth, who are not reasonably retrainable due to the nature of their long and hard-won, specific, now obsolete abilities and expertise, yet who have also long-since paid sufficient "dues" to justify receiving Social Security, long before age 65 or 70.

How long is "long enough" to pay one's dues to stake a rightful claim to vested shares in, and the associated technology dividends, of the superabundance generated by our so-called advanced, superintelligent AI-powered EII commonwealth in the 21st century?

Why, historically, have the compound economic returns on generation after generation of labor efficiency gains consistently and disproportionately accrued to centralized financial capital, instead of declared as dividends to labor, as well?

Because that was the old incentive structure's design. The machine wasn't broken, it was running on generations-old, outdated EII. We'll address specific deprecated institutional-machine-level U.S. Code shortly. Hint for fans of Will Shortz: it has to do with the definition of fiduciary duty.

What that means is, we are experiencing the direct effect of decades of "wealth redistribution" away from the American workers who created all that superabundance and into the pockets of a tiny percentage of financial engineers on Wall Street, K Street, Sand Hill Road, and that abstracted concept of Hollywood Blvd.

It was socialism for corporations and dog-eat-dog Social Darwinist capitalism for labor. That may not have been the intention of the original U.S. Source Code, but it's how it effectively forked itself. Where it forks from here is a question of how we choose to buqtraq and refactor, based upon dueling SWAGs (scientific wild a$$ guesses), estimated (im)probabilities, strongly held (mis)interpretations, and our best calculated (mis)interpolations. Seems like we may stand a better chance of success acknowledging that all of this EII work is equal parts art and science.

Interpolating the current labor participation rate curve, we see that within this decade, in the absence of make-work substitutes, the market will require 50% or less of the population in the civilian labor force. We should welcome this liberation from the relentless involuntary toil of what David Graeber called Bullshit Jobs.

We can adapt and bear witness to the flourishing of the kind of super abundant commonwealth that the founders envisioned. But even that is an already outdated observation.

> *"Think about this. After GPT-4 came out [in late 2023], it was estimated that in the next year, 2 years, 3 years, 300,000,000 jobs are at risk of being replaced [worldwide]. That's just in the next year or two or three. If you go out 4 years, we're getting up to [something] like a billion jobs that are going to be replaced. That is a massive movement of people losing the dignity of having work, losing the income of having work. Now, when you have a billion-person-scale movement, that's going to exert a lot of pressure on both companies and government[s]" (Tristan Harris, 2:22:53).*

> *"So if you want to change the outcome, you have to change the incentives" (Aza Raskin, 2:23:36) (see cccxiii).*

This is why, when computer scientists like Jordan speak of incentives, they point to jobs, wages, and consumerism; the factors and influences that incentive people into JOB-JOBs, rather than *working* to develop their own individual aptitudes, talents, skills, and passions and from there contribute from a sense of intrinsic motivation and purpose.

> In the context of the past two centuries of industrial acceleration, followed by the most recent decades of increasingly ubiquitous computation, instant global video conversation, increasingly sophisticated financial and factory automation, self-landing rockets, self-driving taxis, hyper-rationalization and hyper-marginalization of industrial and post-industrial labor, along with staggeringly successful material developments that have elevated humanity-as-a-whole to this lofty plateau where, at least in the most privileged portions of the world, most people realize that our robot overlords have become all too real and essentially already taken over a significant proportion of coordination functions essential to an integrated, harmonious global civilization — is it even debatable that that we already live in the Post-Automation Era?

And if not, are we doomed to repeat the economic growth and social disintegration of the 20th century over and over, like Groundhog Day or 50 First Dates, but centuries at a time? What are the alternatives? All of this AI augmented EII acceleration *is what it is* and what it is, is, entirely overwhelming to our snail's pace of evolutionary adaptation.

What is the 20th century's default consensus narrative plan once it becomes so successful that it only needs 49% or less of a population in JOB-JOBs and still easily oversupply all the material and service needs of 100% of any given population? Perhaps surprisingly to some, the United States has seen this movie before, lived it, more precisely.

As mentioned, the Civilian Labor Force Participation Rate has been falling precipitously since the late 1990s and is hovering now at just a point or two above 60%, after falling precipitously for twenty years. As of this writing, that number has even ticked down since we first published those words in 2018. The most recent figures as of today are from October 2023. The current labor participation rate has slightly rebounded from a January 2021 low of 61.3, standing today at 62.7. That's still down two ticks from 62.9 of 2018. The long-term labor participation rate trend is intact and irrefutably downward. This shouldn't be alarming. These figures serve as added markers of 20th century capitalism's overwhelming success. Those methods of success simply require some significant refactoring for the 21st century.

How have we lived this before? From the post World War II boom in 1948 through the 1970s, the normal Civilian Labor Force Participation Rate was relatively stable, resting near 58%, even lower than 2023.

Workers enjoyed both more wealth and more leisure time than at any other time in U.S. history. Productivity soared. The American Dream was at its apex, and *less than six in ten adults were even in the labor force*. It appeared that productivity dividends were indeed accruing to workers and capital alike, steady reduction of work hours seemed inevitable, and the Great Society seemed right around the corner.

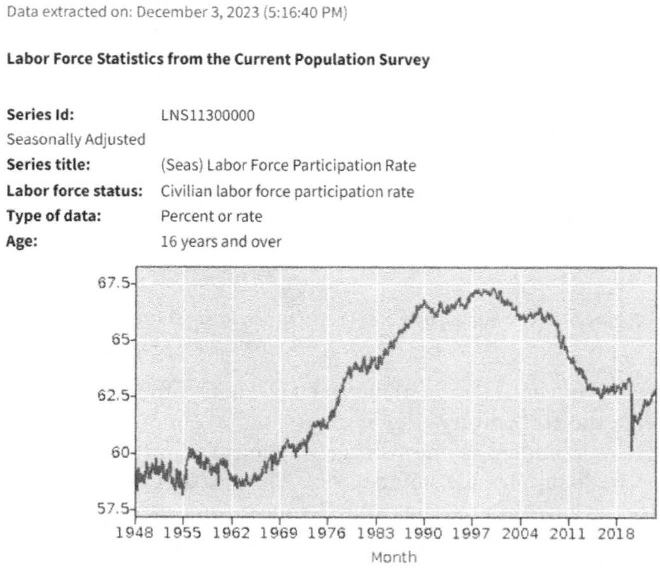

Figure 4 — Civilian Labor Force Participation Rate, 1948-2023.

It seems no coincidence that the expiry of Nixon's Family Assistance Plan (FAP) proposal for universal, unconditional basic income occurred in 1972, just as the United States was abandoning the War on Poverty, dramatically and instantly changing the fate of workers for generations to come. Single-income families fell under increasing pressure, as the proportion of economic growth and productivity going into wages dropped, and people flooded into – how shall we say tactfully and truthfully – a kind of policy-forced corporate labor camp environment of the next 30 years. Pretty well-compensated labor camps for some, to be certain, also, not optional. At all.

What is the definition of a situation in which the only offer on the table is an offer you can't refuse? In a slightly less cynical light, it was like the sociological equivalent of Henry Ford's, "you can have any color you want, as long as it's black." Instead, "You can take any JOB-JOB you want, so long as you're more committed and obedient to your Just Over Broke Justification Of Being than to your family, faith, or any other priority or value in your life." The slightest shift of priorities, due to an accident, health crisis, or other unforeseen circumstance and it's no more healthcare or shelter for you.

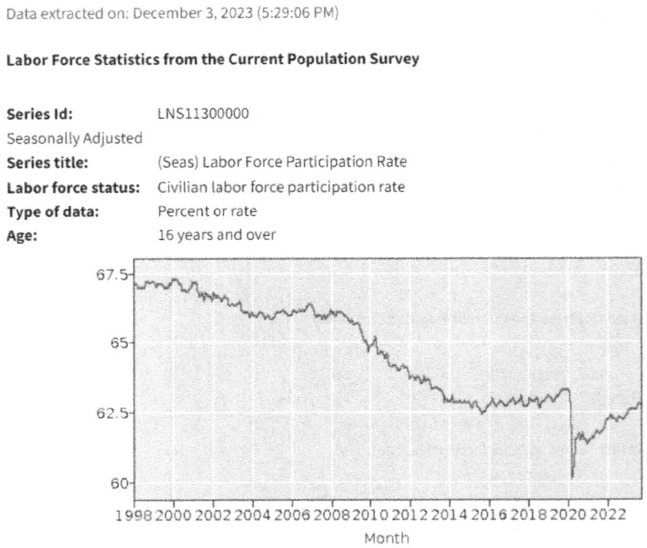

Figure 5 — Civilian Labor Force Participation Rate, 1998-2023.

None of that was by universal design or natural law. That's simply the way we treated one another in the 20th century.

It's not as if there was suddenly some shortage of goods and services that caused the massive and dramatic supply-side shift described. It's not that people suddenly *wanted* to work 80 hours a week or require two full-time income earner households simply to barely uphold the same standard of living previously enjoyed by single-earner households on a single 40 hours per week. So, what was the cause of that turning point?

It was the non-woo-woo *invisible made visible*: the influence of the cultural tropes, biases, and sacred cows dissected in the first half of this book. Those default consensus narratives, and plain ignorance, anger, and greed, driven by a mad devotion to Mammon. Add all the rewards doled out to narcissistic, psychopathic, always go for the jugular natural law of the jungle heroes and role models and well, there you have it. The not-so-divine human creation of an aloof, dissociated, even schizophrenic culture of superabundance and super precarity at the same time.

We can add to all that the long history of data documenting the co-opting of the women's movement to provide corporations with lower wage labor, with absurd pay gaps that continue to this day. It was like chum in the water to all 20th century sharkdom. The primacy of shareholder value became ascendant and for all practical purposes, the sole aim of corporations. Anything and everything were fair game in the name of fiduciary duty.[ccxxi]

The end of stakeholder capitalism and the beginning of the brute financialization and commodification of labor and human bodies seems to have cast the spell that conjured the 20th century's narcotic-like cultural JOB-JOB trance; that hypnotic idea that people must wear an employee badge in order for society to acknowledge and value them as worthwhile human beings. No badge, no personhood.

Throughout most of human history, this was never the norm. Employee badges as validation of personhood may be one of the most bizarre developments in human history, to date.

After the dotcom bust in 2000, the labor participation rate began its reversion to the mean, its return to normalcy, in relative earnest. What didn't return to normalcy was wages, or the proportion of productivity and wealth circulated as income through the bank accounts of everyday people. Is our biological analogy of an anemic circulatory system coming to mind?

Having extracted every spare minute of labor for over 30 years, the bubble burst hard in 2008, leaving people relatively worse off than ever. My family was certainly among that vast number. Most likely, yours was, too.

> Today, surrounded by self-driving cars, self-landing rockets, intelligent conversational AIs in our smartphones, and all manner of material stuff that lends the appearance of post-scarcity wealth, the existential precarity of so-called essential workers has increased in dramatic inverse proportion. How can that possibly make sense?

While some partisans make the claim that the labor participation rate has "stabilized," one look at the long-term trend chart shows otherwise. If anything, we've stabilized to the conditions of pre-pandemic decline. Good. We're back on track to the way down. Not exactly a condition to cheer about.

We are at a time of profound disruption and indecision, as a nation. What kind of new and better destiny do we want to manifest? Is that desire the same as the new destiny we need? Do we want to pick up the trend of the 1970s to 1990s and "become great" again by working more hours and requiring three to four full-time incomes to support a single-family household? Or do we want to return to the long-term economic baseline of the much-maligned 1950s and 1960s – a time rightly criticized in terms of racism – characterized by a healthy economic circulatory system, more leisure, more family economic stability, and more equitable and sustainable incomes in terms of both dividing up the pie while growing the pie for the benefit of all stakeholders? How about we do that for everyone, this time, without the racism and similar garbage from that era? Can we import proven robust EII code and delete the cruft? Seems that if we've done it before we can do it again, this time in a way that works for everyone.

We are no longer awaiting the *Autonomous Revolution* of 2020 (Davidow). That revolution is already in McLuhan's rearview mirror.

The pandemic marked a kind of rude awakening to the Post-Automation Era as we hurtle toward the 2030s.

We've spoken a lot about technology and economics, but it's important to remain focused on our human story. The Post-Automation Era is about human values, human thinking, human choices, and human behavior.

If our great-grandparents, let alone those who lived here just one hundred years ago, could see the capabilities of our present world they'd be utterly aghast that poverty of any kind persists. From the perspective of those who lived just a generation or two before us, we are living in their science-fiction future. We've got all the gadgets and gizmos, but almost none of the promised leisure and economic autonomy in the wake of decades of productivity gains.

What is up to us today is whether we choose to act in ways that make the current situation into a stereotypical B-movie catastrophe, or if we choose to create an uplifting blockbuster that manifests a better, more inclusive destiny, elevating our spirits and renewing our hope in one another and in this wonderful, absurd, magnificent, infuriating, miraculous, confusing, exhilarating, and mysterious story that we call life on Earth, in our next episode: toward a world that works for everyone.

* * *

The Poor Will Always Be With You

Ah, perhaps one of our most timeless and treasured 20th century tropes. It's so convenient and handy for justifying aloofness and indifference in the face of feeling powerless to do anything meaningful about poverty and houselessness.[ccxxii]

It can even act as a kind of societal DARVO. Deflect. Avoid. Reverse Victim and Offender. First, an abuser deflects. "Nothing happened. I didn't do anything! It was because of [endless excuses]." Then avoid. "Even if I did, it wasn't *my fault*!" Then the reversal. "You *made me* do it. It's all *your* fault. I never would have done what I did if it weren't for what *you did*, first!"

How can we call people worthless, or even think of people as worthless, while simultaneously screaming at them to take responsibility and contribute something to society? How can a worthless person have anything of worth to offer?

This is one of the most hypocritical, counterproductive, and ugly things we can possibly do to other human beings. But it gets worse. Does bum-thumping – the horrendous act of committing violence against homeless people – accomplish what the perpetrators hope to accomplish? Only for the most malicious who gain some twisted sense of satisfaction by hurting others.

What if, instead, our Post-Automation Era default consensus narratives cultivated discovery and development of intrinsic worth in people, wherever they are in the struggle of consciousness? What if, instead of mocking and demeaning, we asked, "what would you do for work if you won the lottery and didn't have to work anymore?" Some, of course, might say things like, "I'd travel and never work another day in my life," or, "I'd quit work and do photography," which are perfectly fine interests and pursuits for those who possess a healthy curiosity about the world beyond their own comfort bubble.

However, when it comes to just quitting life, burning through cash, and becoming a slouch after winning the lottery? Despite the stereotypes, the hard data on lottery winners simply doesn't support the popular notions of screwing off and checking out.

Kaplan did a bigger study on 576 lottery winners and found that "popular myths and stereotypes about winners were inaccurate"—by which he meant that American lottery winners did not typically quit their jobs and spend lavishly.

That finding has been confirmed in more recent research. A 2004 study found that 85.5 percent of American winners continued to work after winning the lottery (with 63 percent working for the same employer as before), and that the more important work was to a person, the more likely they were to keep working. [ccxxiii]

So, by asking people what they would do to be productive if money were no object, we can get closer to the root of what actually motivates people, which helps them to ignite their own inner motivation to grow, for personal growth's sake, rather than chasing the unattainable carrots of materialism while dodging the punitive sticks of social stigma and marginalization for refusal to participate in that futile charade of Graeber's bu||$%*t jobs.

Many people have never even heard such a question. It almost seems unthinkable. What would you do if suddenly freed of the requirement of the time-for-money, forced pimp-n-ho relationship, if money were truly no object? For those who have only ever lived life as urban savannah-dwellers, responding to an endless barrage of existential threats, it's not a simple question to answer. Arguably, the most prevalent and pernicious of all those threats, next to the absurdity of plain-old law-of-the-jungle murder of course, is eviction. More on that in a bit.

Having fought for survival in such an environment for most or all of their lives, many people don't even realize the extent of their own abilities. Dreams? People like us don't have dreams.

People like us can never realize the power of our own thoughts and minds. Deep awareness of our intrinsic abilities? Followed by faith and confidence in those traits? Those are just the things that form the foundation of the ability with which people adaptively respond to any environment in which we find ourselves. When we don't feel able, we don't feel *response*-able, we don't feel able to respond; so, when many people in America scream at people living in tents, cars, vans, or RVs, to "take responsibility," and "pull yourself up by your bootstraps," this often amounts to an extremely destructive, counterproductive, and just plain cruel kicking of people while they are down, even if that wasn't the intention. Of course, for some people, kicking others when they are down is sport; but we aren't even trying to reach people at that extreme. King said,

> *"It's all right to tell a man to lift himself by his own bootstraps, but it is cruel jest to say to a bootless man that he ought to lift himself by his own bootstraps."*

But is it all right? Sure, he was speaking in the colloquial language of the day, but we're here to question all of that. Here's an experiment. Find a pair of good boots with great, strong straps. Put them on. Now, reach down and pull on those straps as hard as possibly can. How far can lift yourself? You see, the adage was meant to point out the absolute absurdity of the statement itself; and yet, the self-righteous condemn people with that statement every day. When confronted with their own ignorance about the contradictory meaning of their insult, the response is likely to be anything from, "you know what I mean," to "nobody likes a wise ass." Yeah, well, I do know exactly what you meant and yeah, it is wisdom to not cast not thy pearls before swine, so I'll have to give you that one.

What many people also don't know is that a surprising proportion of tent-city dwelling "losers" have already played the mainstream responsibility game all the way through, complete with multiple degrees, successful careers, and nearly perfect credit scores. Still, people look at us living in our tents and tell us to "take responsibility!"

Really? To many of those people, we say, "Come, let us compare credit scores, let us compare resumes, and then you can lecture us about responsibility. Come, live the way that we live for even one single week, and see if you can hack it, then lecture us about grit and discipline and responsibility."

So far, the number of takers has been zero. You know how "those rich people" are, after all. Everyone else's hypocrisy is an outrage, but not our own. This is one reason why the vicious cycle of otherizing rich or poor, hating the poor who distrust the rich for hating the poor is an infinite distrust loop that leads to nowhere. Also, in many respects, it is precisely where we are in the present moment. Somehow, we must find a way to break out of this destructive downward spiral of otherization, in the name of hyper individuation.

"Judge not, lest ye be judged," is not merely about condemning or condoning behaviors, it is also about labeling and comparing.

Othering is a two-edged sword. We can other the whole world in the name of establishing our own incomparably unique identity. Othering is about denying our connection, interdependence, and our complicity in all things. As outward judgement intensifies, it can become a disdain so toxic that it wishes a person, or category of persons to no longer exist. Short of its murderous extreme, judging "the rich" or "the poor" revokes another person's or group's permission to exist. It says, "you don't belong." It puts up signs to make sure we don't have to see "those people" in "our neighborhood." It says "the sight of you offends me" regardless of set or setting. In the city, in the country, in the mall, at the beach, it says, "you don't have permission to exist in my line of sight."

The opposite of this something like the precepts of Interbeing, taught by one of Martin Luther King Jr.'s non-violence mentors, Thich Nhat Hanh, "Do not force others, including children, by any means whatsoever, to adopt your views, whether by authority, threat, money, propaganda, or even education. However, through compassionate dialogue, help others renounce fanaticism and narrowness. Do not avoid contact with suffering or close your eyes before suffering. Do not lose awareness of the existence of suffering in the life of the world. Find ways to be with those who are suffering, including personal contact, visits, images, and sounds. By such means, awaken yourself and others to the reality of suffering in the world." Or Second Timothy, Chapter Two, "but be gentle unto all men, apt to teach, patient, in meekness instructing those that oppose themselves." Clearly your author has a lot of work ahead before ever reaching that one.

Still, there is something deeper lurking in all this othering of homeless people, or people who are exploring beyond the householder horizon, that many Americans don't understand. That something is marketing and propaganda about what *home* even is.

The concept and experience of home is first an emotional experience; second, a psychological experience; and third, a physical location or shelter. All of which are, by definition, temporary, yet culturally imbued with an illusion of stability and permanence.

Only recently in human history did real estate marketing succeed in misconstruing the word *home* into *house*, and then by framing the word *house* into one kind of suburban style dwelling. People were at *home* in caves. People were at *home* in huts. People were at *home* in covered wagons. Many people today are at *home* in hostels, tents, or simple shelters on a beach where nature's abundance supplies more than they could ever want or need to live long, healthy, and happy lives.

Home is a concept. Home isn't a building and home isn't the fictional permanent habitation of a particular kind of building. Home is literally where our hearts dwell, it is literally within ourselves. That's not a cheesy Disney cliché, it's one of the most substantial and consequential truths in human life. People have been at home in all kinds and varieties of dwellings across the span of human history. Yet, in recent decades, the type and location of shelter that we even allow people to inhabit, as defined by massive real estate investment lobbies, has grown increasingly restrictive, particularly in the so-called advanced West. In everyday conversation, we consider home as only one kind of acceptable structure, and we all know what that sticks and bricks box looks like. The boxes vary somewhat in size and shape, but the DNA is the same. If you don't own one of these particular types of boxes, or pay protection money to someone who does own one, you are labeled homeless, and a whole host of laws – primarily forbidding rest, or heaven forbid, sleep – subsequently, essentially, strip you of your very right to exist, your inalienable right to equal dignity as a human person. Been there, felt that. Not a second-hand anecdote. Direct lived experience.

Otherwise well-intended building codes and safety standards, combined with the unbridled profit motive of private real estate developers, have combined to create an unholy alliance in most major American cities that, in essence, an alliance that revokes the individual's permission to exist outside of that extremely specific type of housing stock. Cities do all they can to get rid of affordable modular housing, mobile housing like RVs, not to mention the most basic shelter common in communities like Thousand Trails,[ccxxiv] where untold numbers of working-class people live for years and years in the hopes of saving up enough money to one day "escape" and achieve other goals.

The primary reason most people look to "escape" such circumstances is social stigma. We have met hundreds of happy families living with modest shelter, whose only complaint is that these kind of housing options are only available fifty or a hundred miles away from urban work centers. Why can't Thousand Trails facilities be available every twenty-five miles throughout all the top global mega-city regions? Greed. Labeling. Judgmentalism. Nimby. Stigma. We could broadly diversify and expand housing inventory at once, bringing runaway real-estate speculation into check, if not for these poisons. All that, and land value tax (LVT). For more on LVT, I suggest /r/BasicIncome and r/Georgism/ subreddits or my 2018 open-source published version of the FAQ on Amazon, *Basic Income FAQ* under the section, "How much would basic income be?"

Writing for the San Jose Mercury News in July 2018, Khalida Sarwari supplied a quintessential example of this relentlessly destructive trend:

> *Michael Goldman, one of Sunnyvale's seven City Council members, suggested that mobile home parks are victims of the Bay Area's dysfunctional housing market and flourishing tech industry.*
>
> *In Tharp's opinion, council members have given longtime Blue Bonnet residents the "second-class" treatment. "I've been providing their income and part of their salary and I've been part of their community and they just turned around and said, 'OK you're worthless, you're useless, you don't matter'."*

As many municipalities did by creating their own fiber optic networks, which spurred healthier competition for high-speed data networks, counties and cities can become more active in real estate markets, correcting for runaway market failures.

For some the experience of home is sitting in quiet meditation, regardless of outward surroundings. We might sit in a public square or park or utilize a public bench for its intended purpose and feel perfectly and completely at *home*. But legacy default consensus reality wants to hear nothing of such nonsense, let alone that radical Yeshua character.

> *"Therefore, I say to you, do not worry about your life, what you will eat or what you will drink; nor about your body, what you will put on. Is life not more than food and the body more than clothing? Look at the birds of the air, for they neither sow nor reap nor gather into barns; yet your heavenly Father feeds them. Are you not of more value than they? Which of you, by worrying, can add one cubit to his stature?*
>
> *"So why do you worry about clothing? Consider the lilies of the field, how they grow: they neither toil nor spin; and yet I say to you that even Solomon in all his glory was not [c]arrayed like one of these. Now if God so clothes the grass of the field, which today is, and tomorrow is thrown into the oven, will He not much more clothe you, O you of little faith?*
>
> *Therefore, do not worry, saying, 'What shall we eat?' or 'What shall we drink?' or 'What shall we wear?' For after all these things the Gentiles seek. For your heavenly Father knows that you need all these things. But seek first the kingdom of God and His righteousness, and all these things shall be added to you. Do not worry about tomorrow, for tomorrow will worry about its own things. Sufficient for the day is its own trouble (Matthew 6:25-34, NKJV).*

Yet, to truly follow this guidance? Prepare for society, especially corporate churches, to treat you like the most irresponsible human on the planet. "Well, that's not *really* what Jesus meant!" Really? Seems pretty clear to me. Still, we are all too often labeled loiterers for engaging in the act of being at *home* within ourselves and completely reliant upon the grace of creation for sustenance and shelter. Animosity is particularly harsh if it's known that a person engaging in the most ordinary and healthy of human activities, such as walking, sitting, or heaven forbid resting or sleeping is neither a local landowner, nor paying protection money to a local landed lord.

In effect, this makes all public space and infrastructure into private space and infrastructure. How can there be a commonwealth with no commons?

The extermination of public space, the loss, verily theft of the commons, has led to policies that effectively exterminate the very commoners to whom the word commons applies. In an article titled "Here are 10 incredibly sh*tty things America does to homeless people," the number one sh*tty thing is:

> *Outlawing sitting down. People are allowed to exist in public, but sometimes the homeless make that civic rule inconvenient, like when their presence perturbs tourists or slows the spread of gentrification. One solution to this problem is the "sit-lie" law, a bizarrely authoritarian measure that bans sitting or resting in a public space. The law is clearly designed to empower police to chase homeless people out of nice neighborhoods, rather than protect cities from the blight of public sidewalk-sitting.*
>
> *Supporters of sit-lie claim the law helps police deal with disruptive behavior like harassment and public drunkenness, and that getting people off the street will get them into shelters. Homelessness advocates counter that the disruptive behaviors associated with some homeless people are already against the law" (Ganeva).*

As Theory of Everything physicist Thomas Campbell put it, "Most everyone is doing the best they can ... with the tools and abilities we have ... everybody here is struggling with what they are, who they are, and how they are, and trying to get by."[ccxxv, ccxxvi]

But this isn't good enough for the old guard Edward Bernays default consensus reality narrative scripters of America.[ccxxvii] In addition to smoking and sugar-laden breakfast foods, the discovery of the dark art of public relations artfully conditioned populations to regard not just poverty, but any temporary gap in active income generation as one of the deepest personal character flaws in the United States, a hard luck sob story not to be indulged, lest society drift into a universal victim mentality. The lack of veracity inherent in this belief has nothing to do whatsoever with the scope of its purchase in the collective psyche of a nation. I could find simpler wording, but that wording is just so precise that I'm going to go ahead and risk the name-calling and loss one audience in the name of connecting with another on this particular point.

This persistent stance of societal disdain for the un-jobbed emanates from the very plutocrats who bleat about shareholders being victims receiving mere table scraps from Wall Street, as mentioned earlier. This ephemeral specter of *victimhood of the wealthy* is so bizarre and matter-of-factly impossible that – if we pause for just one minute to think about it – the magnitude of this narrative's sway over large swaths of the population becomes as absurdly impressive as it is indefensible.

While berating people experiencing homelessness, we have, as a society, become quite expert at using single isolated cases and feel-good stories to ease our consciousness and tell ourselves that somehow, we aren't horrible people for allowing poverty to become the widespread scourge that it us today. Alternatively, we find convoluted arguments to convince ourselves that it's not that big of a deal, really. Only people who don't have the first clue of what persistent economic precarity feels like could ease their shallow conscience with such flimsy fairy tales.

A timely example of stand-alone feel-good stories that help us to ignore the magnitude of this crisis is the headline, "Zach Galifianakis Bought A Homeless Woman An Apartment — And Took Her To 'The Hangover III' Premiere." Aly Weisman, writing for Business Insider explains:

> *When Zach Galifianakis was just a struggling actor/comedian twenty years ago in Los Angeles, he made an unlikely friend at a laundromat.*
>
> *Now-87-year-old Elizabeth "Mimi" Haist volunteered — and lived — at Fox Laundry in Santa Monica, surviving off tips from customers for 18 years.*
>
> *One of those customers was Galifianakis, who, after the success of the original "Hangover" in 2009 stopped visiting the laundromat regularly, but always checked in on his old friend Mimi.*
>
> *When the 43-year-old actor learned that Mimi had become homeless, he found her a one-bed, one-bath apartment in Santa Monica and started paying for her rent and utilities (Weisman).*

This isn't at all to say that Zach isn't a great guy, or that what he did wasn't of supreme righteousness – both of which are manifestly true – it's only to illustrate that many readers tend to use stories like this to convince themselves and others that we are all doing enough to address systemic calamities. That by some miracle, one good deed at a time, the entire crisis will all go away in short order; therefore, we need not contemplate more complex causes of poverty at scale. Which brings us back to an earlier point. It's far easier for people to numb themselves to the overwhelming significance and consequences of systemic poverty if they believe poverty is a personal problem, a profound failure of character.

Journalist Noah Smith once proclaimed that transitory poverty is not a big deal. People can "just smooth their consumption." Most Americans don't even know what that means, much less are they capable of doing so in a rational way, when the sheer panic of losing everything due to a medical emergency or factory closing takes hold. Not to mention that there is no practical way to know that one's poverty is transitory – or how long transitory will last (a month? a year? a decade? an entire human lifespan is 'transitory') – when you're in the midst of it. So, the distinction he makes between transitory and systemic poverty rings hollow at best and typical of the 1970s cult of objectivism, at worst. Smith writes:

> *So, my main problem with Bruenig's argument is still that he seems to equate structural poverty with transitory poverty. Transitory poverty is not a big deal, because people can smooth their consumption. Intuitively, most liberals realize this - we worry about the poor people for whom poverty is not just a short-lived phase. We worry about the people who are mired in poverty. We don't worry about the entry-level worker who is just starting to climb the ladder. We don't worry about the well-off elderly couple who are spending their nest egg. If government poverty statistics call these people "poor", that's a problem with the government statistics, not with the structure of society. The people we want to help are the people who never (or almost never) manage to get ahead. I think Bruenig, in his zeal to demonstrate his idea, is in danger of forgetting that.*[ccxxviii]

While Smith's reasoning in internally coherent – a widespread practice among objectivist libertarian types[ccxxix] – it's detached from reality, it's merely a theoretical model, and it isn't an accurate description of the scope and impact of systemic poverty in the everyday mundane world that we inhabit. Not to mention, Smith's words in this case are a mischaracterization of Bruenig's work. The difficulty is that the dominant narratives in American culture have gradually become increasingly hostile toward people who either choose to live simply, who struggle to just get by, or heaven forbid, slow consumption by becoming satisfied with *enough*. Material contentment – enoughness – is the unforgivable sin against a ravenous consumer culture.

In the United States we say that we believe that all people are created equal in dignity and respect, that we support equal opportunity, but the animosity and disdain directed at "the homeless" and "the poor" only seems to become more strident and uglier as the twenty-first century unfolds. Spikes on benches and underpasses, for example. Overtly barbaric stuff, seemingly right out of a medieval torture chamber.

In her article "UN Official Slams American Response to Poverty: Homelessness on this Scale is Far from Inevitable" journalist Heidi Groover wrote:

> *Writing about people experiencing homelessness—an epidemic that is particularly acute on the West Coast— [Philip] Alston [United Nations Special Rapporteur on extreme poverty and human rights] concludes that the United States relies on criminalizing homelessness in order to "conceal the underlying poverty problem." Cities enforce laws against sitting or sleeping in public places, panhandling, public urination, and other behaviors that can be difficult for people living outside to avoid. Infractions under these laws can spiral into misdemeanors, warrants, fines, and possible jail time."*

In short, we criminalize the very existence of people. Human beings have no permission to exist in the old guard narrative. We simply want "them" gone, out of our sight, so that we don't have to contemplate our own common plight, our own interbeing and interdependence with "them." Some might consider that, at risk of offense to some, a form of human ignorance of the highest order.

The good news is that this current moment of crises isn't any more permanent than the conditions that led to this moment. Our individual and collective crises are not any more permanent than any other moment reflected across that Long Arc of history. We can recover from our ignorance in an instant, through learning something new, through self-reflection, through a sudden glimpse of insight, understanding, or compassion.

Most powerful of all, we can change by extending that understanding and compassion toward ourselves, because if we too fell into the trap of hating poor people simply because they are poor, or rich people simply because they are rich, it's because we were shaped and influenced by an environment that made it all too easy to fall into those traps. Those traps are what we're working to understand and dismantle in this work. If the only way out of difficulty is through, then consider this narrative a path toward our individual and commonwealth greater freedom.

* * *

Permission to Exist

Permission to exist is the first and most fundamental intrinsic human right. Some may feel a strong reaction to this simple statement of fact, and it is that reaction itself which defines and illumines that state of conscious (un)awareness.

To sentence human beings to eternal Darwinian evolutionary brutality is one of the most misanthropic perspectives that I can personally imagine. The fact that I'm able to imagine it proves that I'm no saint, just a documentary observer.

Permission to exist is so unspeakably obvious that we don't typically think about it, because for many of us, it's always been an invisible assumed privilege, absurd to even contemplate, in principle. After all, here we are, existing, permission or not, right? Besides, permission from who? Them? Which them? That [*insert your favorite, optional, maybe pejorative label*] person over there? Who the [*more labeling*] are "they" to decide?

Some may label this line of inquiry as adolescent, juvenile, narcissistic navel gazing. Maybe it is. And maybe that is because the legacy of the 20th century was an extraordinarily juvenile, narcissistic, navel gazing culture of consumption, counterfeit-self-absorption, and false-self-indulgence. That culture created fifty-five-year-olds who today think and act like fifteen-year-olds in the name of staying young, missing the entire process and point of maturation, and instead staying childish and foolish rather than growing childlike in wonder and awe of creation. Narcissistic indulgence was in the air, in the water, beamed through every screen in every public space, and pervasive in the early internet.

Is that what we want exemplified and amplified in the Post-Automation Era?

If change is the fundamental nature of life and living systems, then even a culture of impenitence and ignorance can change to a culture of integrity and wisdom. It may take time, as it took time to reach past extremes, but change can happen and is in fact always in progress, in this world.

As we set and align intentions, so do we proceed in that direction. This is the timeless process that defines default consensus reality. When a critical mass of minds ally and align with persistence of vision and intention, those clarified and amplified visions and intentions manifest the world as we experience and know it. This is the ordinary, quotidian experience of "as above, so below" and one dimension of "inner, outer, narrative, and mystery."

Permission to exist becomes immediately relevant when it comes to deciding who is and isn't worthy of the Maslow Safety principle of income security. Darwinian tribal and clan dynamics, peer pressure, ancient hierarchical dynamics of primping and posturing, physical attractiveness and aggression value distortions, emotional and social manipulation; all of these were highly determinative of who got what, from where, for how long, and under what conditions.

Are those the ways in which we want to live in the Post-Automation Era? Pretending that we have no choice is a handy way of ducking, dodging, or denying that we have a duty and responsibility to choose. Every thought that crosses our mind contributes to the world we experience, both subjectively and objectively as the Four Games play out –

inner, outer, narrative, and mystery; short, mid, long, and infinitely deep – day in, day out.

In order to ration deservingness of basic human rights to shelter, food, and healthcare in the 20th century, polite, passive-aggressive, careful politically correct and coded corporate lingo had evolved and permeated the default consensus narratives of society, leveraging technology to keep legacy dominance hierarchies in place, *in the name of merit*, often *regardless of merit,* and sometimes even *in spite of lack of merit.*

The dawn of the Post-Automation Era offered no respite from billions of years of deprecated genetically coded behavior. Early 21st century corporations used lingo such as Learning and Development (L&D) to socially recondition and rehabilitate workers, weakly emulating the way that continuous integration updates software in real-time. Anything to keep the ancient Molochian machinery running as "normal."

In an article titled, "5 Skills for the post-automation work force," one L&D developer put it like this:

"It is [a] sort of paradox that in a time of AI, interpersonal capabilities will be held in higher regard than ever before. Emotional intelligence will be at least on the same level as IQ. With machines everywhere, the challenge will be dealing with people in a positive way" (Cristescu).

Sounds good for Team Human, right? Even sounds like a kind of world that could work for everyone. On the other hand, a slightly less optimistic interpretation, and one that has unfortunately played out for far too many people, is something closer to, "petty office politics becomes even more prevalent than ever when AI can replace anyone at any time." People could and did use constructive tools as destructive weapons, including processes like education used for good and for ill, for help and for harm, to elevate and liberate, and indoctrinate and subjugate. It all happened, it's all there in the historical record of the 20th century.

Without the unconditional social security of a guaranteed livable income, there was no ability to voice meaningful, honest dissent in an atmosphere of group-think or ideological lock-in, without threat of the direst of consequences. Yes, emotional intelligence is key to every aspect of life, from professional to personal, but the deepest emotional intelligence, the kind that most keenly recognized destructive and abusive power dynamics; the narcissistic enabling, covert triangulation, gaslighting, isolated verbal abuse only in private, and other forms of non-symbolic devaluation and harassment – not only was *that* kind of emotional and cognitive attunement not valued, but people actively devalued and discouraged it in the 20th century.

"Stay in your lane," meant, "unless you want to be severely punished, you best turn a blind eye and keep your mouth shut about any kind of malfeasance you observe."

In corporate lingo, there were countless nefarious and covert ways that people got "thrown under the bus" in such circumstances. Corporate emotional intelligence was too often more like a dark art of espionage, rewarding the ability to play a grotesque kind of super polite passive-aggressive Hunger Games.

Where do you think the scripts, characters, and screenplays came from? Refusal to play became grounds for instant revocation of your very right to exist, because good luck existing without the Social Security of adequate shelter, food, and healthcare conditioned upon a reliable, "guaranteed annual income at levels that sustain life in decent circumstances" (MLK).

The question of who had permission to exist, i.e., the fundamental human right to Maslow Safety, applied in all contexts, beginning in our families, offices, and extending out to the most extreme levels of excommunication and marginalization from the commonwealth hearth. Same as it ever was.

Within and throughout any human village or society we receive and send out an incomprehensibly immense constant flow of micro impressions, fleeting awarenesses (accurate or not), verbal and nonverbal micro-expressive tones and transactions that take place in micro-moments of micro-moments, all serving to orchestrate an infinitely complex and, in many ways, absurd dance between the deserving and undeserving.

Who is deserving of respect? Who deserves hiring? Firing? Who do we choose to revere? Ignore? Shame? Blame? Praise? Emulate? Implicate? Exonerate? Who deserves to take a nap on this beach, that bench, in this park, under that tree, and who *does not deserve to exist* in this or that space?

To whom do we grant *permission to exist* in our world and in what roles are they allowed to exist, not just in our presence, but even within the range and reach of our line of sight?

We are not talking about the healthy boundaries required between family, friends, and colleagues; where we try to uphold and uplift mutually beneficial energies, while rightly protecting ourselves from emotionally over-depleting relationships or self-destructive relationships. We are talking about the reckless, conditioned labels we slap on other people merely walking down the street and then the thoughts and actions we take based upon those labels and impulses. The snap judgments we make, the conclusions to which we leap, without so much as talking to a person or "those people" whom we've already judged "don't belong here."

From our hometown block to luxury resort, human misbehavior is the same. "Those poors" don't belong here. "Those rich" don't belong here. One active example of a productive Post-Automation Era upgrade to those deprecated norms is the emergence of communities such as the Othering and Belonging Institute at UCB.

> *WE ALL BELONG IN THE CIRCLE OF HUMAN CONCERN*
>
> *Othering is the problem of our time. Belonging is the solution.*
>
> *The Othering and Belonging Institute at UC Berkeley advances groundbreaking approaches to transforming structural marginalization and inequality. We are scholars, organizers, communicators, researchers, artists, and policymakers committed to building a world where all people belong.* [ccxxx]

Looks like momentum *Toward a World That Works for Everyone*, to me.

I've spoken about our responsibility to make conscious choices in our thoughts and actions, not only with respect to who belongs and who deserves, but in every aspect of our lived experience. While that responsibility is true and inescapable, it's also become problematic as our understanding of free will expands and improves. Do we have complete free will to think thoughts, make choices, and take actions?[ccxxxi]

In the 20th century, it seems many believed that humans make every single one of our decisions based almost solely upon some immutable and economically pure ethical framework, because even impulsive whims, tastes, and preferences are all within the domain of economics. Especially impulsive whims, their careful algorithmic planting, germination, fertilizing, and harvesting in a TikTok + Temu epoch.

Today, wisdom help us if we are so foolish or arrogant to assume that people ever conducted their lives with access to anything even remotely resembling *perfect information*; a fundamental principle that, if impossible or impractical to ever achieve, effectively topples one of the load-bearing pillars of old guard Economics 101.

If people have no statistically significant, let alone relevant chance of ever attaining perfect information about the ways in which AI is used to introduce and feed us content that we otherwise would never have found, much less selected on our own, planting ideas in our minds, desires in our hearts, growing them toward economic transactions; what would we call that kind of an economy?

In the 2020s, the crumbling of centuries-old EII is the new normal. Decades of behavioral economic research has overwhelmingly proven that we are – as the title of Dan Ariely's seminal work put it – incredibly, consistently, and *Predictably Irrational*. Add the complexities of AI just mentioned and literally everything assumed about the integrity, objectivity, and justice of 20th century economics becomes worse than meaningless, it becomes nuclear fuel for nuclear-powered gaslighting at scales and to degrees never before imagined.

We don't necessarily consciously choose all our own preferences and priorities, or if we do, we don't always do so for some set of well-formed, accurately-informed rational reasons. Of what practical utility is Principle-Agent Theory in an age of black-box AI?[ccxxxii]

The social pressures of status and station can do a lot to convince us to believe what we *feel* we must – even if those beliefs are abhorrent to the better angels of our nature – in order to do *what we feel we must do in order to survive*, to obtain not just the basic human need for *income security* required for biological homeostasis as defined by Maslow Safety, but also the higher needs of validation and confirmation of our worth as human beings, worthy of love, respect, civility, and dignity.

So, if we are even the slightest bit curious about the nature of our own lives and thought patterns, our own relative lack of freedom gradually dawns upon us. That doesn't mean that we give up on decision making and simply follow every momentary hedonic impulse; it means that we recognize that others, like us, may not be stuck where they are entirely *of their own free will and fully informed decision making*, any more than we are stuck in our stuck places for similarly illusory reasons.

We might also realize that ultimately, we do have some effective ability for making choices; but only once we become conscious of the previously unconscious or automatic judgements that have defined our day-to-day life, to date. What this means is that, by becoming acutely aware of our lack of free will, we can paradoxically increase our capacity to exercise whatever capacity of free will is, in fact, non-illusory. Maybe.

Devoid of the capacity for this kind of self-reflection, we simply make snap gut-decisions and judgments in the name of decisiveness, while in fact making poor choices that we then rationalize to ourselves as if we had no choice but to make the bad choice in the first place. From a place of culturally-engineered perpetual economic panic, "I had no choice but to make all those bad choices!" Benjamin Franklin's response, "How convenient does it prove to be a rational animal, that knows how to find or invent a plausible pretext for whatever it has an inclination to do!"[ccxxxiii]

For example, suppose we choose to believe that we chose to believe that our ultimate self-worth derives from our JOB-JOB, then when push comes to shove our relationships will suffer and our career will rule us. We tell ourselves, "Well, I had no choice, it was the steady paycheck or the love my life. What was I supposed to do?"

If we choose relationship first, then we may not always be employed to the extent that we think we *should* be employed, but we can work at tasks we love, we can volunteer, and our relationships can flourish, because we have chosen to love and nurture relationships as our most authentic Justification Of Being. So, one way to describe the old-guard economic model might be as a blue-pill, red-pill choice between Fear JOB vs Love JOB. The Fear JOB is always the easy choice, the rational and reasonable 20th century choice. What if we didn't just say it because it sounded good, but we paid with our entire soul to choose love, actual love, over impulses and sensations that masquerade as love?

Abysmally conflated, confusing, and ambiguous, it's worth acknowledging that the solitary English language word, love, is, expressed by six different words in Ancient Greek philosophy.[ccxxxiv] What's peculiar about this parenthetical observation is the fact that so many English language learners come to enjoy English for its specificity, compared to many languages. So, what's in a word and what's love got to do with the love vocabulary deficit in English?

This is another solid example of the almost invisible, non-symbolic, unspoken, inexpressible realities of our everyday lives that shape our realities without our conscious realization, let alone permission. Where's the informed consent of the commons, in both public and private spaces, both online and offline, that relentlessly carpet-bombs human minds, hearts, and souls with an endless cacophony of unsought and uninvited imagery, sound, ideation, and solicitation?

And yet, we can somehow become convinced to believe that "the world" is in some way immune to and exempt from the empirical reality of all of the same fleeting, ephemeral, and ineradicable characteristics of which it consists!? We hurl insults at advocates and change agents like psychological and sociological Molotov cocktails, "It's so sad, he's a nice guy, so smart, he just doesn't understand how the world works." As if no human being can possibly ever change the world because the world is so much greater than human beings as whole, let alone a speck of dust like us. Is all that true, though?[ccxxxv]

Is it the truth, the whole truth, and nothing but the truth that the world is immutable, absolute, and reigns with merciless incontrovertible certainty over every aspect of our paltry, pathetic, puny, insignificant, and trivial existence? Maybe.

What's no longer up for debate is whether or not AI will fundamentally and permanently alter our entire way of life, forever, from this day forward.

The first JOB of any human being perhaps permanently displace by AI is to answer the question: what is my JOB as a human being?

What is my inherent, intrinsic Justification Of Being? Who or what grants me Permission To Exist? That company that just fired me? What's core to the me that I'm so convinced is me?

Is my core woven from the love of clarity and accuracy and compassionate raw truth-telling, even in the face of a monstrous world of merciless reprisals? Or is my core cellophane-taped and paper-clipped together with reactivity to emotional or economic compulsion, cruelty, trauma-bonds, panic, or dread?

Human beings understandably and right feared the disrespect, disapproval, mockery, rejection, marginalization, otherization, or the ultimate punishment of punishments: paychecklessness, poverty, homelessness, being forever demoted, excommunicated, and banished as unemployable for failure to obey the fundamental mandates of an inherently dysfunctional and dictatorial "business" environment.

"It is no measure of health to be well-adjusted to a profoundly sick society" (cxxxii).

The same or similar peer-executed sentences were handed down for standing up for dozens of other legitimate conscientious objections to the 20th century default consensus reality.

The only road back from the kind of social exile described above consisted of "re-training," or "up-skilling" in order prove allegiance to the 20th century Molochian machinery. In the olden days, this was often the role played by junior colleges. In China, maybe there was at least a level of brutal honesty in calling them "rehabilitation camps." Within that context, wasn't it the same essential purpose? In the United States, maybe people like Edward Bernays and techniques like Captology inspired and empowered a vastly more subtle, sophisticated, and effective method of accomplishing the same or similar objectives. Maybe.

No matter how much education, no matter the magnitude of the contribution of one's lifetime accomplishments,[ccxxxvi] no matter the perfect credit score, the only path "back to society" for the discarded and marginalized of the 20th century was through obeisance to the JOB-JOB machine or some near miraculous act of creative expression like a song, a painting, a photograph, or a book that sells, mostly by sheer luck or serendipity. Miracles that *perhaps* granted *provisional personhood* and conditional permission to exist, forever on probation, of course. They weren't always the "good ol' days," as many reminisce.

What that meant was going back to selling oneself by the hour, initially to the lowest bidder, and then hopefully groveling part way back up "the ladder," where the re-adjusted and re-habilitated citizen would never repeat the mistake of acting based on ethical or moral clarity rather than *income security*, ever again. "We're so proud of you, you're doing so good now."

This is also why so many "re-entry" programs didn't work. Millions of people began leaving that Molochian charade with no desire or intention to ever return. They wanted to change the game completely. And they have changed it, are changing it, and despite the most extreme and totalitarian tactics to slow or prevent this change, continue to change it. Maybe today's quiet quitting is the legacy of that generation's silent quitting (clxxv) and perhaps late comedian Bill Hicks put it most poetically:

> *"THE WORLD IS LIKE A RIDE IN AN AMUSEMENT PARK, AND WHEN YOU CHOOSE TO GO ON IT YOU THINK IT'S REAL, BECAUSE THAT'S HOW POWERFUL OUR MINDS ARE. AND WE CAN CHANGE IT ANYTIME WE WANT. IT'S ONLY A CHOICE. NO EFFORT, NO WORK, NO JOB, NO SAVINGS OF MONEY. A CHOICE, RIGHT NOW, BETWEEN FEAR AND LOVE. THE EYES OF FEAR WANT YOU TO PUT BIGGER LOCKS ON YOUR DOOR, BUY GUNS, CLOSE YOURSELF OFF. THE EYES OF LOVE INSTEAD SEE ALL OF US AS ONE."*

In general, the 20th century JOB-JOB Trance detested this vision of wholeness and worshipped the separateness of a hyper-insular individuality – not healthy individuation, but Fight Club like isolated shrink-wrapped embodied human commodities ego- and economic desperation-driven to endless transactional distractions.[ccxxxvii] Films like Fight Club existed precisely in order to provoke critical thinking amongst armies of unwitting and unmindful sufferers who had been unconsciously manipulated, through no fault of their own, into modes of thinking and behavior for fear of losing shelter, food, and the social approval of being seen by others as a legitimate member of the tribe. A doer. A go-getter. A good person. One of us.

All too often, our fear-driven ancestors grew to distrust, or even resent people who instead chose love, autonomy, and simplicity over an infernal, frenetic, hypervigilance in service to perpetual approval-seeking over-achievement. A franticly harried, hurried, and hectic 20th century society marginalized and ostracized anyone who dared find total fulfillment in simply *being*, convicting such traitors to the rule of mammon as losers, hippies, loners, drifters, and bums, guilty of the unpardonable sins of indolence, laziness, and rest.

This is how the vicious game of berating and beating people into obedience went on and on, generation after generation. It was all too easy for many to join the complicit and decide that "if I can't have happiness because of the way my career controls me through fear of losing everything, then I'm going to control other people with abuse of power of my own position, so the same thing happens to them." "If they hazed me, I'm going to haze you." "Your turn in the barrel." One of the crudest expressions for the kind of horrendous human behavior that persisted for eons beyond the savannah. It was like a corporate version of intergenerational domestic abuse, "my parents beat me, so I'm gonna beat my kids."

What a miserable way of life. That's what the old guard called normalcy. No thanks.

What millennials and zoomers are doing today, and many others who share a 21st century perspective, is not giving into the Fear JOB and instead going ahead and paying the price for pursuing a Love JOB.

Growing millions worldwide would rather live in a tent or van and be content in their being, improving their art, their woodcraft, their music, their self-awareness, rather than partake in a kabuki theater of commerce for fear of how the richest society in history might punish them for living freely by revoking their permission to exist.

So, here's maybe an inside insight to all of these intergenerational societal pyrotechnics. When a person finds themselves empowered to choose the work that they want to do, when they can turn their passion into a career, then work becomes fun. This is not only possible, but also preferable, both for cultivating the greatest human flourishing *and* igniting the most enduring economic productivity. So, these values of unequivocal choice and autonomy seem like worthwhile principles to adopt in the Post-Automation Era. There is an old adage of contested origin that says:

> *The master in the art of living makes little distinction between his work and his play, his labor and his leisure, his mind and his body, his education and his recreation, his love, and his religion. He hardly knows which is which. He simply pursues his vision of excellence at whatever he does, leaving others to decide whether he is working or playing. To him he is always doing both.*

An advanced Post-Automation Era economy does not require an oversupply of obedient and well-socially-engineered human robots as interchangeable replacement parts, it needs more Masters in the Art of Living. So let's cultivate for that outcome.

An unconditional basic income, indexed to 50% per capita GDP, provides a citizen's technology dividend that is in line with a modest living wage. Given the nominal income security provided by universal Social Security, people can rely on that security as a foundation to develop awareness and mastery of their own uniquely inherent talents and skills, to take bolder and more imaginative entrepreneurial risks, and develop the self-awareness pre-requisite to meaningful work that might as well be play.

A 21st century default consensus reality of unconditional, universal economic sufficiency – Peterson's "optimal deprivation" – is exponentially better for both individuals and society and simply makes sense as the logical expression and celebration of an age of superabundance.

* * *

The Right to Say No

It's a fundamental dynamic of capitalism that many of 2024's more youthful culture refers to as "pimp-n-ho" culture. It's pervasive and accepted as just-the-way-it-is. Pimp-n-ho culture describes every time-for-money exchange, from jobs to hookups. It nonchalantly accepts the reduction of every human relationship to a transaction.

By deciding who has the right to income security and who does not, societies consciously and intentionally choose to endorse and affirm this devaluation, upholding inequitable and abusive power dynamics. Lack of income insecurity drives people to desperate measures and people driven by desperation live desperate lives. That's the unvirtuous cycle of intentionally, socially engineered income insecurity.

That is why income security is a fundamental human right in any kind of society that values human dignity. In King's words, income security means "a guaranteed annual income at levels that sustain life in decent circumstances," such that all people have a choice to walk away from any situation in which they'd not participate, but for economic desperation. How can any sane and just superabundant society not assure the fundamental freedom to walk away from toxic situations? "The right to say no," as Scott Santens puts it.

The principle of income security itself is not debatable; the financially stable have enjoyed it throughout history. Only the admissions procedures by which people gained entrance into or eviction from the income security club have changed over time.

The AI explosion in the early 2020s changed the rules yet again.

Through the eyes of capital, the labor force is a faceless, amorphous other. Human resources are a commodity, which makes human bodies a commodity. Resources are exploitable raw materials to be strip mined. Likewise, the 20th century's dark default consensus reality discarded people, like human slag dumped and left to percolate the toxicity of disenfranchisement and marginalization into the social environment, once Moloch's machinery has extracted as much of the most miraculous and valuable source of nature's abundance possible: human talent, intelligence, faith, and boundless hopeful energy. As the Hitchhiker's Guide to the Galaxy put it in dry humorous terms:

> *"This planet has—or rather had—a problem, which was this: most of the people living on it were unhappy for pretty much of the time. Many solutions were suggested for this problem, but most of these were largely concerned with the movement of small green pieces of paper, which was odd because on the whole it wasn't the small green pieces of paper that were unhappy."*

Could the treatment of humans and the treatment of the environment be somehow interdependent – independent of the small green pieces of paper? All that unhappiness and ecological devastation was a direct result of maximizing the extractive capabilities of financial capitalism. It was Big Momma Mammon's way or the highway.

The good news is that in recent years, organizations like Stanford University's Center for Compassion and Altruism Research (CCARE) have arisen to debride and heal this historic otherization of everyone.

> *"James R. Doty, MD, is a clinical professor in the Department of Neurosurgery at Stanford University School of Medicine. He is also the founder and director of the Center for Compassion and Altruism Research and Education at Stanford University of which His Holiness the Dalai Lama is the founding benefactor. He works with scientists from several disciplines examining the neural bases for compassion and altruism."*

In "A Quest for Meaning - Discussion and Q&A with Dr. James Doty and Co-director Marc De La Menardiere," Dr. Doty explained:

> *We have a subset of individuals, who we have typically made CEOs, who are often ruthless and self-serving. How is it possible that the income of CEOs has increased by 682% in the past decade or so? We've never seen such a discrepancy between the lowest paid individual and the highest paid individual. What I find fascinating is you'll hear a certain group of people say that if you want to increase the pay to others, or "redistribute income" it's socialism. If you actually examine it, the middle class has been destroyed. Their money, from their work, has been taken away from them for the rich to benefit.*

How is it possible for any rational and intellectually honest person to believe that an individual can live a life of "optimal deprivation" in the United States on the 2024 federal minimum wage of $7.25 an hour?[ccxxxviii]

That's equivalent to a minimum wage that hasn't increased in over 30 years. The minimum wage in 2024 ought to be $22 an hour if the figure only accounted for economic growth and corrected for inflation. It ought to be $26 an hour if it had grown in line with productivity.[ccxxxix]

Organizations like Stanford CCARE prove that Post-Automation Era institutional evolution is both possible and in progress. We are actively reducing the polarization and otherization symptomatic of a harsh and extended hangover from a 20th century culture-gone-wild.

It's been a rough dawn for the Post-Automation Era, but with plenty of rest and liquidity, our circulatory system will do its job of ridding the body of toxins, and hopefully we learned the lesson this time, to never go back to a such a lost, wandering, and reckless world that worked for so few at the cost of so many.

Where We Go from Here

While arithmetic solutions can be simple, I suffer no illusions about the human complexity involved in ending poverty as we've known it. The permanent inevitability of poverty is like some kind of intergenerational mind-rot meme that infects people across all demographic distinctions. Hence, the remainder of this journey explores and more closely scrutinizes the extraordinarily complex implications of the transformation of the Social Security Trust Fund into a 21st century commonwealth fund, materially backed by the value of the people of the United States.

If that sounds absurd, compare it to the absurdity of the previous few pages. Personally, I think it's far worse than absurd to discover that there's a way that we can immediately and effectively end poverty as we've known it, without disadvantage to anyone, and flatly refuse to look into it.

I also harbor no illusions with respect to the convolutions of institutional coordinating intricacies involved in addressing the foundational challenge of pinning down the precise algorithms for determining the initial declared value and oversight processes required to establish a just Social Security Trust Fund for the 21st century.

The trade-off to the simplicity of these insights is the complexity of coding and deploying rolling upgrades. Every program manager or construction manager knows the reality of converting pseudocode into production code and blueprints into buildings.

The idea of people getting money *just for being alive* is not only an old idea, but a long existing foundation of every kind of caste system, however overt, covert, blatant, or subtle. By returning open access to nature's intrinsic abundance in a 21st century post-automation context, we right this historic wrong in a way that moves us one step closer toward a world that works for everyone.

By redeclaring and reclaiming the value of human life and aligning our words with our actions – not just with respect to valuing life from before birth, but by respecting human value throughout every entire precious lifetime – we can effectively remove some of the most wicked and perverse economic incentives known to humanity.

Desperate and hurt people do desperate and hurtful things. By cutting off that desperation at the root of its defunct economic forcing functions, we greatly reduce the human animal impulse toward desperate, panicked, hurtful behaviors that manifest themselves in countless preventable ways. All by circulating "a guaranteed annual income at levels that sustain life in decent circumstances (MLK)."

Encouraging a default consensus perpetual desperation to

do anything for money, literally anything, seems more like

a wicked mandate of Moloch and Mammon.

Is that the kind of world we want to perpetuate and live in?

Taking no action to end poverty does precisely that.

It seems to me that the fact of the matter is that we are all nature's trust fund babies, of infinite worth, so to pretend that our intrinsic human worth hasn't always come along with a balance sheet aspect is to ignore the totality of the reality that we have considered examined.

The real-world value of lost soldiers, legal settlements, and insurance actuarial tables don't magically pop into existence at the moment of a human death. That intrinsic economic value of every human life was always there in the first place or could never have shown up on any balance sheet, anywhere.

It's the shadows of old inceptions, old brainwashing to believe that "people can't just get money for being alive." That statement is empirically and manifestly untrue because people have been getting money just for being alive for a long time. Just not your people. Just not my people. Just not we the people. We the people were gaslighted into believing that our babies are liabilities and other people's babies are trust assets.

Most wealthy people organize their intergenerational wealth via trusts. So, to loathe intergenerational wealth is to loathe any perceived powerful family that most people respect. It's hypocritical at best and criminally offensive toward *certain kinds of people* at worst. What's that word for hating and harming people because they are representative of some group, human characteristic, or attribute again?

I recognize and appreciate that the cognitive dissonance of the realities we've illumined in these pages may be too much for some to bear upon first hearing. For some, the mistaken view and adulterated belief that society can never change at such a fundamental level is insurmountable. Completely duped and incepted by the 20th century Job Trance, while accusing anyone who begins to observe what's happening before our very eyes of being naïve dupes. Edward Bernays was no dummy. Films like *Inception* try to reach people generation after generation.

Maybe this genre of art has finally reached enough intellectually honest minds for us to be ridiculously lucky enough to bear witness to the end of poverty as we've known it before the end of this decade.

* * *

From Welfare State to Dividend Economy

> ***"But doesn't this human asset model ruin everything?!" No. It is more like a controlled burn in an ailing forest ecosystem, incinerating everything that cultivated the depression, desperation, and divides plaguing our human ecosystem to make new, fertile soil that enables the entire ecosystem to become healthier and healthier by rebalancing itself, according to its own inherent flourishing nature.***

It is now irrefutable that we have transited the inflection point in history that dramatically flipped our civilizational trajectory into the most unimaginably efficient, productive, and superabundant chapter in human history. That's the picture in the rearview mirror. The question today is, especially for many who became used to dictating DCNR from 20th century bobble-head screens for decades, is how do *we* adjust our mistaken expectations to bring them into alignment with reality, this time? If we can find that humility, it could become the greatest inflection point in our personal lives, as well. Where can we turn for role models and leadership in this respect, during such turbulent times? One person who comes to mind is Ray Dalio. According to Forbes Magazine, "Ray Dalio is the founder of the world's biggest hedge fund firm, Bridgewater Associates, which manages $124 billion. Dalio stepped down as CEO in 2017 and retired as co-CIO in 2022, completing a transition that transferred majority control to the hedge fund's board."[ccxl]

During a late 2023 interview with Max Rofagha, founder and CEO of Finimize, a financial information platform with the laudable mission to "increase the net worth of an entire generation," Dalio put today's AI-accelerated and amplified superproductivity and superabundance into the most highly qualified, thoughtful, and compassionate context that I'd heard in recent years.

> *"That [super] productivity that is happening affects those, benefits those, who are a small percentage of the population, initially. That's one of the challenges we have. A very small percentage of the population is coming up with a lot of these inventions and doing really, really great, and those inventions, to some extent, are replacing people in jobs and creating greater wealth gaps. So, that's going to require policy, and policy is going to require us to be good with each other. So, when I look at the situation, my big concern is, as I said, these five forces. And related to that is, number one is: how are we going to be with each other? Can we together, work well together, and be productive? Can we have a good political system and a good economic system in which we work well together, in a competitive environment, with ample capital for those who come up with good ideas, making that productivity pass through to the population as a whole? That'll be critical. Are we good with each other? If we can do that, [we succeed]. Those are the things I'm focusing on."*[ccxli]

It is impossible to express the humbling experience of hearing such highly qualified voices as Dalio's authenticate and align with our own thesis. Unsurprisingly, Dalio's "Five Forces," from his 2021 book, *Principles For Dealing With the Changing World Order: Why Nations Succeed and Fail*, present a vastly more qualified, detailed, and actionable boots-on-the-ground articulation of the global landscape that we've viewed through a Four Game lens in this work.

Representing the highest possible level of public awareness and clear, concise, market-proven articulation of the reality we face in these historic times, only the most psychoplutocratic political inertia prevents us from transitioning from a Welfare State to a Dividend Economy, post-haste. We can dismantle, delete, re-install, and upgrade the entire dysfunctional welfare state as we have known it. We can reboot into a 21st century Dividend Economy "with a mere keystroke," and the affirmation of a few pens. It's both that simple and that complicated at the very same time.

The Dividend Economy's role is free-market-pricing of all resources, including human resources, and circulation of earned interest dividends in trust as stewards of any commonwealth; just as plutocrats have done for their families, for eons. The Social Security Administration of the twenty-first century is like the circulatory system or our economic body. Without maintaining a minimum diastolic pressure throughout a body, throughout an economy, both collapse.

By perfectionist definition, there can be no conditions whatsoever placed upon an unconditional basic income; however, in real world economic engineering practice there are always design constraints. There can and must be conditions placed on definitions of qualified recipients. Nothing prevents any nation on Earth from adopting similar models. It seems that the United States may have a small window of remaining time within which to extend its innovative economic leadership into the Post-Automation Era, but there is nothing that prevents other nations from taking the lead in providing "a guaranteed income at levels that sustain life in decent circumstances." Civilizations and empires have gained and lost economic and cultural leadership from time immemorial, and this chapter of history is no different. No rational being would expect that the 20th century hegemony ought to last into all eternity, any more than the 19th, or any before that.

Consequently, as we begin identifying design constraints, it's reasonable to observe that a fully developed human brain requires about twenty-six years to mature.[ccxlii] This suggests a reasonable qualifying age for universal Social Security. Culturally and behaviorally, education, apprenticeships, public and military service, "finding oneself" travel, have all occupied the first quarter-century lives of human beings for centuries and, notwithstanding technological acceleration of the evolutionary process itself, will likely continue to do so. Even aspects of the Hindu cosmology see life as a four-act play, each of approximately twenty-five-year duration.[ccxliii] Likewise, it's a reasonable design constraint that newly naturalized citizens must wait, equal to native born, so nobody will be flooding any borders to get immediate free welfare money anymore, to whatever extent that phenomenon was ever real or imagined. Equanimity is the foundational design principle in this respect.

So, we can suggest that one simple, clear, and concise qualifying criteria to define who receives universal Social Security. Something like, "every human biological organism of at least twenty-six years of age by means of equally vested citizenship shall receive from the trust a 50% per capita GDP annual dividend, circulated from the fund in monthly installments."

In contrast to the coercion of utter desperation and poverty for failure to comply with 20th century default consensus reality, we are meticulously committed to rooting out all traces of that covert and overt coercion in the Post-Automation Era. Anyone is able to opt out from receiving universal Social Security, at any time, for any reason, with a single check box on annual tax forms:

☑ "I do not wish to receive Social Security."

Social Security is not a "forced government program." It's the way we've always provided income security for those in need and in the Post-Automation Era, in the wake of the blessings of our profound superintelligent superabundant achievements, everyone has both the basic human need and the basic human right to unconditional income security.

Does all this sound a bit cold and soullessly calculated, reducing people to "human organisms" as mere commodities? The free market already did that, long before. We stand on the shoulders of giants and some of them weren't all that gentle. So what you choose to do with and about the information learned in this book matters. A lot.

While we've presented the basic arithmetic, we're not in a rush to change the world as if some single program can usher in a counterfeit utopia, we're in a long, perpetual, purpose-driven race to get things right.

So let's engage in some reasonable due diligence. As a starting point, below are some further values of human life, from the *Value of Life* Wikipedia page. Please bear in mind that this is a human edited source. The reason Wikipedia is still extremely valuable is because it is a place where people are at least actively wrestling with such topics, while other sources often shy away from such challenging work, often for fear of offending advertising, and we're back under Moloch's thumb. Therefore, this is definitely my pitch to economically support Wikipedia, and learn how to participate in editing Wikipedia, to the extent that you are able. Platforms and processes like Wikipedia are the ways by which our fledgling global cognition grid continues to evolve and improve. Like any democratic process, it requires our participation in order to be democratic, egalitarian, and intellectually honest.

During my December 2023 research I noticed that since 2018 someone had added a $50,000 entry to the *Value of Life* list, from the year 2000, which I omit below as a ridiculous outlier among all of the other numbers. This is an example what appears to me as the case when some (maybe new) editor takes it upon themselves to drive down averages computed by any services that might scrape Wikipedia in order to do the math.

This might be a kind of quiet-quitting related data sabotage that is a real hazard to the quality of ChatGPT and our other AI agent assistants, moving forward, and provides another powerful motivating force to implement income security measures immediately. It helps none of us to start sabotaging the machines that make our lives superabundant because we fear some kind of hostile takeover. Maybe such behavior is us projecting our evolutionary fight or flight into a realm that doesn't experience any of that Molochian monkey junk.

While pertinent, this is yet another adjacent topic that we can't address fully while staying focused on the task at hand; nevertheless, it points again to the kinds of previously unimaginable challenges facing us in the Post-Automation Era.

Also, the 2015 Department of Transportation figure included below is newer than the 2014 number referenced on the current site, and an editor has removed the 2010 Food and Drug Administration figure also included below. I'm not shying away from the challenges of Wikipedia as an information and data source because it's illustrative of the current environment. We need to continue to acquire, train, and lifelong learn about these fluid literacies and skills in order to adapt to the world as it is, moving into the 2030s.

So, fluctuating, margin-of-error details are all completely acceptable because we are, by definition, working with a subject that is a moving target and will always be a moving target: the cultivation and blossoming of flourishing human lives. My aim is not perfection, it is accuracy and integrity in an ever-unfolding process that is larger than all of us and greater than any of us can possibly imagine.

> *"The motivation for placing a monetary value on life is to enable policy and regulatory analysts to allocate the limited supply of resources, infrastructure, labor, and tax revenue. Estimates for the value of a life are used to compare the lifesaving and risk-reduction benefits of new policies, regulations, and projects against a variety of other factors, often using a cost-benefit analysis."*[ccxliv]

Already, we see that 20th century artifact of "limited supply" playing dominantly, and while accurate in that context, we don't live in that context anymore. So, in our case, conducting due diligence upon our earlier arithmetic that computed an indisputably empirical and reasonable value for our 21st century Social Security Trust Fund, we review the following *Value of Life* numbers.

According to the following, the intrinsic economic value of a human life is:

- $129,000 per year of quality life (an update to the "dialysis standard")
- $7.5 million (Federal Emergency Management Agency, 2020)
- $7.9 million (Food and Drug Administration, 2010)
- $9.1 million (Environmental Protection Agency, 2010)
- $9.4 million (Department of Transportation, 2015)
- $9.6 million (Department of Transportation, 2016)
- $12.5 million (Department of Transportation, 2022)

Remember, if we are feeling somewhat depressed about slapping crass dollar figures on priceless human lives, keep in mind that the market *already does this* all day, every day, in the form of whatever hourly wage we're willing to accept or able to reach, so this crude human commodities pricing process is somewhat about being as wise as a serpent and gentle as a dove. These numbers have defined our lives for decades, whether we've been aware of them or not.

Can such cold-hearted computations form the foundation from which to build a market-defined and market-indexed level of income security? That's the reason they came into existence in the first place. So, to transition from Welfare State to Dividend Economy, to upgrade Social Security to a of 21st century technologically augmented trust fund, a fund that works just like the very trust funds that the plutocracy has enjoyed for centuries, now on behalf of everyone, we must do our level best to be mercilessly precise in self-examination, intellectual honest and rigor, arithmetic, and operational design constraints and processes.

> Talk about vertical-landing rockets. Yes, this is policy rocket science, except we don't have the luxury of crashing eight Starship rockets first.[ccxlv] This has to work the first time. Yet some people think governance is for inept, lazy people? Not.

In honor of our U.S. Veterans, let's again remember our soldier's value, to conduct just one more arithmetic cross-check. Let's assume that an average, peaceful, semi-productive civilian is worth just 10% of a highly trained soldier deployed to hunt and kill perceived enemies somewhere out in the world. Using the earlier calculated net present soldier value of $1.1M per year, the intrinsic economic human value of a civilian is worth about $100,000 per year. That's an amazingly precise check and balance to all of our other independent valuations. Our due diligence is making the picture clearer.

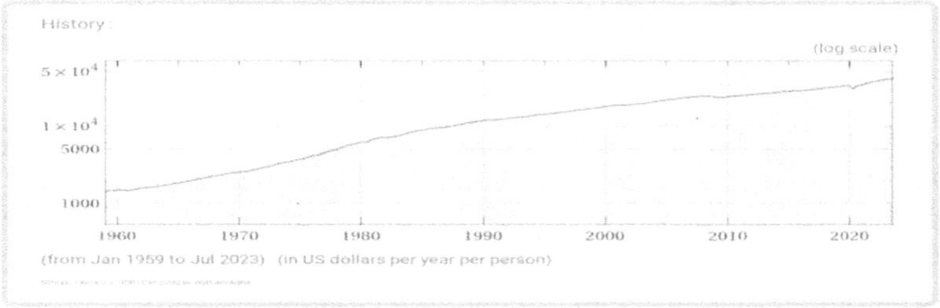

Figure 6 — 50% per capita GDP 1959-2023, Log Scale.

This is what sound policy meta-analysis does: it improves the signal to noise ratio, casts a wide net, identifies, labels, and confirms patterns; debunks, and eliminates junk, synthesizes new knowledge, and distills actionable wisdom.

In 2018, an unconditional basic income indexed to 50% per capita GDP was $30,476.00. As of Q3 2023, Wolfram|Alpha computed this figure to be $41,199 per year per person, per year.[ccxlvi]

Our due diligence exercise also illustrates how vitally important it is to index any kind of basic income to real market conditions. As conditions improve, the dividend improves, as conditions contract, the dividend contracts. Indexing to the real economy also adds an extra circuit breaker to inflation, for if aggressive oligarchic rent-seekers try to extort this amount at scale, they drive this value higher so fast that both the market and public outrage quickly self-corrects to quell that predatory behavior.

This is how markets are supposed to work, auto-correcting for outrageous behavior, rewarding value-enhancing behavior.

If readers find the model figures shocking as a measure of "basic" income, please consider the fact that we are living in 2024, not 1984 or even 2004.

In a 2023 survey, "Millennials [said] they need $525,000 a year to be happy." As reported by Business Insider, "A Nobel prize winner's research shows they're not wrong."[ccxlvii]

Nobody lives the Life of Riley on 8% of what people feel they need in order to be completely financially independent. By this metric, the pursuit of happiness exerts a 92% demand pull that rudely hauls us out of bed in the morning. What does happen is a massive reduction in the current appalling scale of people living and sleeping in cars, vans, tents, and on streets.[ccxlviii]

Please allow us to check in with our running calculations. Even at the most modest figure we've found – that $100,000 per year human commodity valuation – the - universal-basic-interest-earned-to-50%-per-capita-GDP ratio is 41%.[ccxlix] That means the circulated currency is only 41% of the book value of "the underlying," the asset backing our modest citizen's dividend. Put another way, the intrinsic value of the underlying asset is 59% greater than the circulated currency. Solid. That is the definition of a stable currency, backed by real assets. It's a kind of "out of thin air" that is also rooted and grounded in love by the intrinsic economic value of human beings.

But we're doing our diligence, so don't stop there at the lowest, outdated, lowball number available. Evaluating the U.S. Department of Transportation valuation of $129,729.72 per year,[ccl] that ratio of universal basic interest (UBI) earned to per-capita GDP drops to 32%, backed by an asset that is 68% more valuable than the circulated sum.

50% per capita GDP is stable, and responsive to real world economic conditions. While we have not completed our due diligence in computing a legislation-ready base number for our underlying asset valuation; we are illustrating the consistency of our principles by approaching the model from multiple perspectives, independent sectors, and unbiased data sources, both private and public, with multiple independent cross-checks, and consistently landing within an impressively constrained margin of error. This helps to illustrate how constraints are often our best friends in designing things that really work in the real world.

The final numbers matter, but not nearly as much as the predictability, reliability, reproducibility, and stability of the principles and algorithms behind them. Just as we once backed currency with gold, today our nation's human capital is the most stable and reliable underlying asset possible, far greater in value than gold, able to weather any kind of economic volatility that we can imagine.

Uniquely and maybe more importantly, a future-proof hardened society is characterized by uncompromising income security, making it able to weather any kind of systemic shock that we *cannot imagine* today, because we are grounding our value in ourselves. *That's* how we "govern something that is moving faster than [we] are currently able to understand it," as Tristan Harris once again precisely states the Post-Automation Era predicament of life at the event horizon of singularity.[ccli]

One answer, maybe the only reliable and reproducible answer, is to do so by understanding, respecting, and rightly valuing ourselves.

We already operate this model by proxy through the vehicle of fiat currency. We already back the dollar. Our bodies, minds, and lives are the only thing backing this thing we call money, so upgrading Social Security for the 21st century is both revolutionary and not some radical departure from all that's gone before, it's going all in on the best of all we've achieved and the best of what we're yet capable.

The Post-Automation Era expresses a revival of authentic human worth, value, and dignity; not some insipid, theoretical, or ethereal cereal revival, but authentic psychological and spiritual revival that manifests itself in sound, practical, intrinsic, hard cold rational cash terms. It's the opposite of disingenuous and deceptive prosperity gospels, it's authentic, the real deal of what it looks like to agree with the assertion that we are indeed worth what all those 20th century balance sheets said we were worth.

So, when people sea-lion[cclii] you with, "where does the money come from" and "how are you going to pay for that?" Now you have a resource to share with them. Here's how.

The 20th century default consensus reality called employees assets while treating them like liabilities that were only tolerable so long as each created a significantly leveraged excess incremental value for an employer to arbitrage; generally, in the form of playing a part in a kind of reality show mini-series called Going To Work Each Day.[ccliii]

We were, as raw commodity humans, not treated as assets at all, let alone a company's "most valuable asset." Calling people assets, while treating them as liabilities was an ingenious and powerful gaslighting control device to compel people to justify our existence every day, for every breath of our lives. Either conform, or face the direst of consequences, all within the construct of a fundamentally dictatorial corporate hierarchy. CEOs are not democratically elected, nor are the board members who hire them.

In some ways, waking up in the Post-Automation Era is a bit like waking from a dream in which we believed we lived in a democratic, meritorious, federal constitutional republic only to find ourselves spending the vast majority of our waking hours living under a paradigm closer to feudalism or despotism. I know, "Thank you, Captain Obvious." We're far from the first to share this most glaringly obvious of observations.

In 2024, we realize that one of the key reasons we came to experience astronomical wealth and income skews in America was because of centuries of extraction and appropriation of our intrinsic economic human capital value onto the balance sheets of corporations, banks, insurance companies, armies, institutions, and governments, while not showing up on the books as the assets that we are, in and of ourselves.

We have seen that while the complex, often obfuscating, state, federal, international, and corporate banking interdependencies that created our current conditions can appear formidable, with a little focused concentration, they are not only comprehensible, but malleable. We have also seen that our Matrix-like economic game is not set in stone and the rules change all the time.

For the cynical, we could offer that during the half-decade preceding the Post-Automation Era, the rules of the game had increasingly changed to benefit what amounted to the central planners of Wall Street and master control programmers of Silicon Valley, both buying off Washington DC as suited their needs and hiring Hollywood to reify a portfolio of deprecated default consensus narratives and worldviews that made the status quo seem static and unalterable.

Thankfully, in the environment of a democratic constitutional federal republic that managed to innovate a highly advanced, successful, and open-source hybrid mixed economy – the United States of America is all of the above – we can change the rules of our shared commonwealth game whenever we observe that the game of monopoly has asserted itself again, gone too far again. Only winner-take-all sociopaths and their sympathizers could want to play such a game over and over, much less enjoy it.

What's even more ironic is that the entire point of that infamous family board game became completely inverted along the way. Not unlike the economic games we've been unpacking in this work. So, once again, we look back for wisdom in moving forward and unsurprisingly find ourselves arriving at the place we began and knowing it for the first time.[ccliv]

* * *

Economic Games People Play

A young woman by the name of Elizabeth Magie created the game as a "practical demonstration of the present system of land-grabbing with all its usual outcomes and consequences." Her inspiration was a book by progressive economist Henry George, Progress and Poverty. The first version of the game was called The Landlord's Game. Whereas the original goal of the game was to simply accumulate wealth, the goal in the eventual Monopoly version was to own industry and create a monopoly of wealth and influence. If you're getting flashbacks of the despair you felt as your uncle cackled maniacally when you and your last $100 landed on his three-hotel property, well, that's sort of the point of the game (the despair, not the cackling). [cclv]

Here is a fun experiment once circulated on Reddit, and for which, unfortunately, I could not track down proper attribution. Please let me know if you know who originated this! It's a way to help friends and family understand what income security is about in real life. Pull out a Monopoly board and when they guffaw and groan at you, because everyone knows how it always ends, say, "No, no. Not like that. Who says we have to play by the rules printed by Mr. Milton Bradley? He didn't even invent the game! We are changing the rules. Every time anyone passes GO, you get $2,000 instead of $200. Everything else stays the same, only the basic income goes up."

When they argue, "but then the game could go on for days, or weeks, or months! It might never end because nobody would ever run out of money!"

Your answer: "Exactly." Nobody would ever run out of money. The game goes on forever instead of declaring one winner and everyone else losers. Isn't that what we want in our real world, for no one to ever run out of money, no matter the setbacks emergencies, medical bills, fires, natural disasters, divorces? Wouldn't that look more like a world that works for everyone?

Maybe like many readers, I grew up never knowing that the purpose of the Monopoly board game was to teach people just how horrible life is when playing the Landlord's Game. Instead, people somehow took the opposite message, thinking that whoever successfully hoards the most and bankrupts everyone else, "wins." Then we wondered how we came to live in such a disingenuous, passive-aggressive, psychopathological, ruthless, mean-spirited, backbiting, venomous culture.

Someone on Reddit produced the genius idea of using a Monopoly board as a demonstration that we can change the rules and directly learn how outcomes differ. Every time a player passes GO participants get a *sustainable* basic income. By experimenting with different amounts, the game proved that an inadequate basic income, a low round number that sounds good, but isn't enough, just barely puts off the inevitable. A low basic income does not change the essential nature of the game. Only an adequate basic income, "at levels that sustain life in decent circumstances" (MLK) extends the game into an endless interaction that, while boring in the case of a board game, neatly illustrates the point that a livable guaranteed income, while by no means decadent, does empower everyone to live sustainably decent lives.

So, no, we do not have to throw out the board game of capitalism, we can change the rules. We do not need to throw out innovation, free markets, free and fair enterprise, or even AI, in order to define a better, more inclusive game, one founded on fundamentals that we already widely agree upon. A game with a level playing field and a fair shot for anyone who wants to improve themselves and the ability to create and contribute more and thereby earn more. Instead of a social safety net full of holes, a socially secure floor to stand on and build a stable life.

Wrapping up this section, we need to address one lingering objection to valuing humans as assets. In the scarcity mindset humans become liabilities as they mature because they consume greater quantities of scarce resources. The finite Earth carrying-capacity argument for making humans into liabilities was only valid in that old world where we were unable to scale up efficiency with technology and AI while simultaneously ratcheting down overconsumption by educating ourselves and understanding our climate impacts.

The 20th century default consensus narratives simply do not apply in the Post-Automation Era. Yes, they were true, and valid, and even essential for their time; like childhood trauma responses that enabled us to survive at all, they served their function, and now, today, they have become maladaptive. Isn't it preferable for each to do our shadow work as a community service and begin healing rather than denying reality until we hit ever deeper, abrupt, calamitous, and cataclysmic rock bottoms?

* * *

Ending Zero-Sum Games with EITC

"The Policies for Action Research Hub at the Institute on Race, Power and Political Economy at The New School investigates direct income support and cash transfer policies as an economic right and a medium through which policymakers can abolish poverty in the United States. The Institute is undertaking this project in partnership with the Economic Security Project,[cclvi] PolicyLink,[cclvii] and Liberation in a Generation."[cclviii]

The introduction on their website defines this work's common mission:

> *Building upon previous work that examines and documents the enabling health, economic, and overall well-being enhancing aspects associated with better-resourced people and families, this project will answer the following:*
>
> - *What are we learning about designing and achieving a scalable guaranteed income policy from the proliferation of local guaranteed income pilot projects and their evaluations?*
> - *What are the impacts of cash transfer programs on the health, economic well-being, and political participation of families, and how do these impacts vary by race and ethnicity, gender, and other demographics?*
> - *How do deeply embedded narratives about race, poverty, and deservedness shape the politics of guaranteed income, and how can they be shifted to enable a durable nationwide policy?*

In their May 2021 white paper, *A Guaranteed Income For The 21st Century*, Naomi Zewde, Kyle Strickland, Kelly Capatosto, Ari Glogower, and Darrick Hamilton wrote:

> *Our proposal eliminates wage earning requirements and dramatically extends the negative income tax feature of the EITC to guarantee income, eliminate poverty, and lift more families to the middle class.1 Under these terms, a maximum refund would equal the poverty level for households earning $0, with a sliding scale from that point until phasing out at approximately the national median household income,*

> *at $50,000 or $70,000 depending on the household filing status and number of adults. Families with children will also receive an additional grant (refundable tax credit) for every child.*[cclix]

These are magnificent, essential, encouraging incremental steps in the right direction toward universal Social Security. The more economic and social proof generated by our applied science, the more empirical evidence proving that the solution to a chronic lack of cash circulation is a consistent cash pacemaker, the better.

The pacemaker analogy is so accurate and useful because, as we've seen, it's due to a chronic, anemic lack of even flow that we suffer countless symptoms of neglect and deprivation as individuals, communities, and as a commonwealth. Maybe underneath our shared strife and suffering, what appears in the world as systemic failures are manifestations of a grossly insufficient flow of understanding within our own hearts and minds.

How could one simple game, Monopoly, induce such a profound and distorted misunderstanding of the role of money in society and in our lives? A mistaken view that has hobbled income security policy in the richest society in the history of the world for at least the past 50 years. That's the power of games to directly create reality.

It may take four healthy games to heal the damage done by a single warped game, so profound can be the impact of distasteful, let alone intentionally malevolent game design and designers (see Four Game Dynamics in the glossary). There's a whole other Post-Automation Era book compressed into that sentence, alone. I'll leave that to the experts who have grown up in that environment over the past 40 years or so and look forward to learning from you.

* * *

ENDING POVERTY DIRECTLY

> *"I am now convinced that the simplest approach will prove to be the most effective — the solution to poverty is to abolish it directly by a now widely discussed measure: the guaranteed income" — Martin Luther King, Jr.*

What does it mean to "end poverty directly?"

Haven't countless kitchen table world expert aunties, uncles, cousins, and relatives proven repeatedly that such a naïve utopian pipedream is impossible, and even disastrous for this world? And didn't they prove it in the most compelling way by the accompanying lashings, verbal, emotional, sociological, psychological, and physical? And didn't Jesus say the poor will always be with you? So why would any resolute student of gospel teachings ever say something so outlandish as the quotation, above?

In the Post-Automation Era, ending poverty directly ultimately means defending and advancing the basic human right to exist in an automated economic environment in which we have abstracted away traditional human toil to a point of vanishingly minute, marginal, diminishing returns.

While the world didn't change and doesn't change on a dime, we can, and do. Sometimes that's a feature, sometimes it's a bug, depending on context. Often, as a result of one significant insight, understanding, or attitude change, our individual lives can and do change immediately, profoundly, and permanently. It happens all the time.

In psychological or spiritual enlightenment, or the inexplicable grace of salvation, there is often an *aha* moment of awareness, a kind of direct encounter with that which transcends our earlier perception or understanding. Experiences often followed by a lengthy process of gradual cultivation of new values, new daily routines, goals, and one day, new outcomes that otherwise could never occur. Through such experiences, we often gain a new sense of perspective, meaning, and mission in life.

For one unique assembly of pilgrims, their progress led to the following expression of that higher calling:

> *"Everyone has the right to a standard of living adequate for the health and well-being of himself and of his family, including food, clothing, housing and medical care and necessary social services, and the right to security in the event of unemployment, sickness, disability, widowhood, old age or other lack of livelihood in circumstances beyond his control" (Article 25, Universal Declaration of Human Rights).*

What would a civilization be like if statements like that populated and dominated the default consensus narratives inside the minds of a critical mass of human beings, rather than prehistoric narratives of tooth and claw?

I recently glossed over a headline about new research suggesting that optimists make poorer decisions because we do not account for worst case scenarios. That may be true for some, but for yours truly, I have lived my life by both: optimism and worst-case scenario planning. So, as the endless digital doom scroll may dump a trillion suggestions into our conscious and unconscious minds every day, we need to develop advanced cognitive and psychological filters to protect ourselves from accepting all of it as reality, let alone anything resembling truth.

Though I may not be as gullible as some of my most enthusiastic detractors suggest. I cannot and do not avoid the objection that ending poverty is unattainable. I simply disagree. I believe it's a toxic, conditioned mindset to hold such beliefs, and that those inceptions, once deeply rooted, create their own self-fulfilling conditions. Millions believe that ending poverty is impractical, Utopian, and it's arguably the very persistence of pessimism that makes the sentiment a self-fulfilling prophecy.

In the 20th century model, people failed to look for, much less find the consistent performance metrics and values requisite to building confidence in the ability to supply stable, sufficient, sustainable income security for all. That's okay. They also didn't know to even begin looking for quarks or bosons. That epoch's perception of scarcity was relevant and appropriate to that epoch. We simply don't live there anymore.

Among overthinking overachievers and academics who have made entire careers out of attending conferences to debate the recursive subjective minutia of the question of what poverty means, the direct approach that King advocated is no less than offensive. "It can't be that simple!"

What it means to end poverty, in practical terms of everyday people's lived experience, is circulating currency in a stable, sufficient, and self-replenishing manner, like the body's circulatory system. Circulatory systems are significantly different from cognitive systems. Maybe it's no wonder that the brain has such a difficult time understanding the heart at times. Ending poverty directly means circulating currency through the economic circulatory system rather than attempting to do so through limbic or neurological systems. The 20th century was obsessed with "working smarter, not harder," and saw every solution as a thinking solution. When economies crashed, we flooded the brain with resources instead of tending to the body as a whole. Top, down, trickle down was the talk of the town.

Entire university curriculums argued for endless complexity in the definition of poverty: universal basic assets, universal basic opportunity, universal basic *anything*, other than income. "It can't be that simple!"

My intuition is that many of those courses, books, and perspectives were all too often motivated by the tenure's incentives, more than humanity's benefit. Unfortunately, and I say this with all compassion and empathy having been there to some degree myself, it becomes relatively easy to write books from ivory towers having completely lost touch with the struggle of everyday existence on the streets of the United States of America, let alone the world.

Academics of the 20th century were incentivized to write arguments in defense of theses rather than boldly pursuing solutions, carefully echoing, and restating the current default consensus narratives, cautious not to drift so far from the herd as to risk ostracization and potentially end up on those vicious streets, themselves. There was a truly diabolical component to that social dynamic when we examine it. Some wrote to advance career, reputation, or image as an esteemed expert on weighty topics rather than actively working to solve the problems at hand. It was a lucrative trade in the 20th century. Today's environment of radical transparency, authenticity, and accountability doesn't seem to have so much patience for all that, and this may be why we are bearing witness to some of the long overdue changes underway.

The Post-Automation Era has had enough of theories of poverty. People want to stop the madness and want it ended yesterday.

While there were and are sincere exceptions to all generalizations, generality can help us, especially those of us generalized as gullible and naïve optimists, to navigate the unpleasant terrain of a paradoxical and contradictory world as it truly exists. Archetypes can help us find a point of contact between what we regard as deprecated default consensus realities and the now, while providing juxtapositions for us to responsibly reexamine our own worldviews, as well, hopefully in a lifelong learning process that leads us a little Closer To Truth.[cclx]

If we want to move toward an actionable program to heal the ravages of poverty directly, we cannot afford to stay mired in endless academic navel-gazing about the infinite potential definitions of poverty.

Struggling, perpetually cash-strapped people experience the situation because incomes are increasingly inadequate, uncertain, and volatile, even as productivity and efficiency has reached seemingly asymptotic heights.

Are there countless underlying comorbidities to poverty? Of course, there are. Notwithstanding, the practical reality of existing in the world today comes down to income security, or the lack thereof. Minimum wages barely trickle upward while the gap between the constant-dollar value of that labor and the recognition of that value on balance sheets expands at an exponential rate. This is one of, if not the most pressing inconvenient truths of the exponential era: exponentially inequitable circulation of super abundance.

In September 2021, CBS News MoneyWatch reported that, "Minimum wage would be $26 an hour if it had grown in line with productivity."[cclxi] In November 2023, CNN Business reported, "The US minimum wage has been $7.25 since 2009. What that means for the economy."[cclxii] Can there possibly be a better definition of the word absurd in a super abundant exponential epoch?

Forced to recognize the crises as of mid-summer 2018, financial analysts conceded the reality "that much of the gains this year, both in the S&P 500 and the Nasdaq, are due to just three stocks" (Puplava). In May 2023, S&P Global Market Intelligence found that, "Just 7 companies are carrying the S&P 500 in 2023."[cclxiii] This is the nature of the disconnect between post-automation, machine learning, artificial intelligence driven companies, and the rest of the legacy twentieth century economy. Rather than lament new characteristics of a new economy, or try to go back to some better normal that was never a better normal, would it not be wiser and more useful to accept circumstances as they are and adapt according to conditions by ending poverty directly?

As another well-read stock-watcher on the website Seeking Alpha wrote:

> *But while I'd rather not have to document the daily trials and tribulations of Facebook (FB), Amazon (AMZN), Netflix (NFLX) and their ilk, I don't have a choice because these names have become synonymous with "the big picture." In fact, they are nearly the "whole picture" when it comes to explaining benchmark returns. In a note dated Friday, Goldman updated their analysis in terms of documenting just how hard the market is leaning on a handful of names. To wit:*
>
> *The top 10 contributors have accounted for 62% of the S&P 500 7% YTD return [and] of these 10 stocks, nine are technology or internet firms, [with] the Technology sector alone accounting for 56% of the S&P 500 YTD return (76% including Consumer Discretionary members AMZN and NFLX) (Heisenberg).*

The effects of this extraordinarily resource-skewed *positive* disruption are increasingly, miserably palpable to everyday essential workers and this trend can only accelerate in the years to come. We are talking about pushing the most highly skilled truck drivers in the world to 120-hour work weeks in harsh Dakota winters in order to keep the oil pipelines flowing in the year 2024, or risk replacement by either less experienced, more desperate, or eager new drivers, if they do not keep that frenetic, relentless pace. Who's going to enforce state of federal driver rest regulations out here? Nobody. So it doesn't happen.

Employers will release every single one of those human beings the instant that autonomous vehicles can do the job 24 hours a day, without requiring rest.

JOB-JOBs are simply no longer an effective paradigm for circulating sufficient liquidity in the Post-Automation Era. The World Economic Forum (WEF) recently released a video quantifying the insecurity of wage-dependent incomes. "The average US worker changes jobs around 12 times before they are 48." Moreover, "69% of workers between ages 18 and 24 leave their employer within one year."[cclxiv]

* * *

What's Basic?

A 2023 Cambridge University Journal of Social Policy paper may have articulated the most important fundamental reality to bear in mind with respect to this question: "Not that basic: how level, design, and context matter for the redistributive outcomes of universal basic income."

The statement below is why I spent more than a decade focused specifically on this matter in order to find a simple to articulate and comprehensively coherent arithmetic model. $E=mc^2$ is magnificently elegant in its simplicity as are most of life's most effective solutions to extremely complex challenges. Simplicity of principle is not to be confused with ease of putting principle into practice. Quite the contrary, as I hope I've clearly conveyed. There's nothing simple or trivial about *doing* this work.

> *The level at which a BI is set matters, but its exact specification matters even more. The impact of a BI, be it a low or a high one, also strongly depends on the characteristics of the system that it is (partially) replacing or complementing, as well as the socio-economic context in which it is introduced. Some versions of BI could potentially help to reduce poverty but always at a significant cost and with substantial sections of the population incurring significant losses, which matters for political feasibility. A partial BI complementing existing provisions appears to make more potential sense than a full BI replacing them. The simplicity of BI, however, tends to be vastly overstated.*[cclxv]

It is precisely in acknowledgment of the complexity of implementation details raised by Aerts, et.al., that I've worked to build from the ground up, based upon widely proven and time-tested fundamental principles and practices. First principles are the only way to responsibly engage with the scale of complexity of the work at hand.

It's no overstatement to compare this generation's work to JFK's vision to reach the moon. To remix his words for the work at hand, "We choose to end poverty with universal Social Security in this decade and do the other things, not because they are easy, but because they are hard."

Working from first principles, we derive our working definition of *basic needs* from the universally recognized Maslow Needs Hierarchy. "Together, the safety and physiological levels of the hierarchy make up what is often referred to as the basic needs."[cclxvi] We refer to this as *Maslow Safety*, representing the second layer of existential safety in the pyramid, which includes income security.

Ending poverty directly means living in a society that generously meets all basic human needs of every human being by being rooted and ground in right relationship with creation's natural super abundance, without ecological or economic disadvantage to anyone. Every human being has the right to exist free from coercion.

It's worth reminding in the context of Maslow's pyramid that one tragic reason we must use the term *human being*, rather than *person*, both above as well as in our earlier value computations, is that another unpleasant reality of the world is that many do not regard all human beings as people. Even those labeled non-persons are still human beings, and thus endowed by their Creator with the inalienable right to exist in peace.

Isn't this close to what we mean by the words *created equal* in dignity and worth?

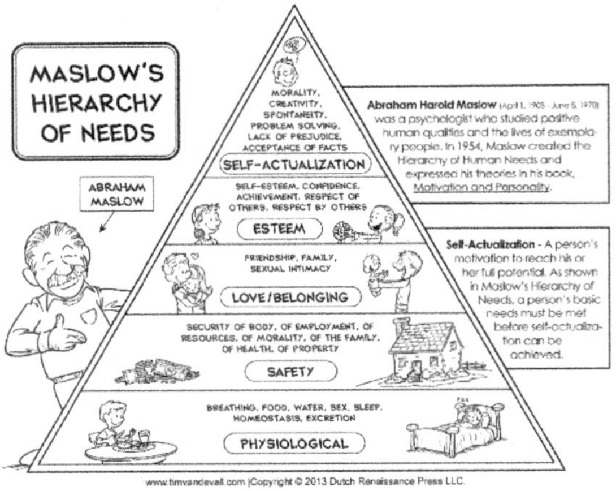

Figure 7 — Maslow's Hierarchy of Needs.

Creation endows every ***being*** *born into the human condition with the fundamental human right to the Maslow Safety needed to become and be regarded as a whole and flourishing* ***person****.*

As a nation, the United States shares something that Google-Alphabet SVP James Manyika said of the development of Gemini AI, "There's this healthy disregard for the impossible." The entire world knows that the USA has done the seemingly impossible, countless times. Not only is *universal income security* not a wild new idea, the U.S. also nearly implemented a guaranteed annual income more than half a century ago.

Déjà vu: The Two-Thirds Singularity of 1969

Humanitarian minded people throughout history have held the goal of ending poverty as fundamental. Tribal people worldwide practiced methods to ensure that everyone in the tribe was able to eat, sleep in a safe place, and still do. Taking care of one another isn't new. That's ubuntu, that's the light side. The dark side is that those who didn't conform to tribal norms were dispassionately dispatched.

What emerged as new in the 20th century was the curious belief that by default, people rightly lacked access to the commons, the basic human needs of food, shelter, and healthcare. Especially in an urban context. In advanced 20th century societies, those rights expanded of necessity to include the rights to freedom of movement, transportation, and adequate income, all of which have become essential to realizing the first three fundamental rights that compose Maslow Safety.

In the 1960s, the United States nearly completed a three-point trifecta for balanced acceleration and hyper-growth of an emerging, innovation-driven, sustainable, post-industrial civilization. Had we completed all three missions "when we were supposed to," we wouldn't be having to rehash all this territory today.

In virtually every tradecraft, it's understood that doing a thing right the first time, however seemingly difficult at the time, is orders of magnitude easier than having to go back and fix work done in haste (perhaps the author would have done well to consider that with respect to some sections and passages in this book). So here we are in 2024, wasting hundreds or thousands of times our energy to do the work we somehow failed or dodged over half a century ago.

Oh, and it was one of the most notoriously conservative Republican administrations of its time that nearly accomplished UBI. Bi-partisan botching of such an important historic opportunity demonstrates the level of cultural denial and avoidance typical of those times. Have we progressed, at all, in this respect?

> *According to Nixon, his generation would do two things deemed impossible by earlier generations: put a man on the moon (which had been accomplished the month before, on July 20, 1969) and eradicate poverty. Polls showed that 90 percent of US newspapers were enthusiastic about unconditional income for poor families. The Chicago Sun Times called it "A Giant Leap Forward," the Los Angeles Times "a bold new blueprint." The National Council of Churches, the labor unions, and even the corporate sector were also all in favor.*
>
> *A telegram arrived at the White House declaring, "Two upper middle-class Republicans who will pay for the program say bravo." Pundits were going around quoting Victor Hugo: "Nothing is stronger than an idea whose time has come." In 1970 it seemed that the time for a basic income had well and truly arrived (Bregman).*

What seems somewhat curious to me is that the internet happened instead of what was "supposed to happen," the end of poverty as we knew it, with "a guaranteed annual income at levels that sustain life in decent circumstances."

So, I respectfully present three accomplishments that *coulda-shoulda* but didn't completely change the fundamental nature of human civilization for the better by echoing Buckminster Fuller with poetic license, "it could have all been done by 1975."

The Two-Thirds Singularity of 1969:

1. *Land on the moon.*
2. *End poverty with Guaranteed Annual Income.*
3. *Boot up the internet.*

Maybe "two out of three ain't bad," and like the ancient and timeless Meat Loaf song, the missing element renders the other two essentially empty of meaning and devoid of lasting significance or value.[cclxvii] The one-out-three that we missed in this case has turned out quite badly for the vast majority of displaced, replaced, in-between gigs, over stressed, and considerably under-compensated essential workers.

The first human being set foot on the moon on July 21, 1969. Great. In that same year, in a nationally televised address on August 8,1969, President Richard Nixon proposed a plan for ending poverty with an unconditional basic income, known as the Family Assistance Program (FAP).

FAP? What's in a name? Unfortunately, maybe the eventual death of that legislation. Names do matter, everyone who ever served in such a high office certainly understood the work of Eddie Bernays, and so maybe the program was a feint the whole time. Who knows? I'm not suggesting a conspiracy theory, I'm suggesting a theory about the potential for conspiracy in the context of a long history of those engaged in long game subterfuge and sabotage. See the difference? Sorry, engineering humor seldom hits the mark.

That's the essence of one kind of intelligence work, isn't it? Build the deepest possible long-term trust and counterfeit affinity in order to blow up the whole mission at the moment of accomplishment? That's great, essential, and heroic work when the mission was bad for people, sought to harm people, or do other damage. It's maybe not so great when people use the same techniques to derail beneficial changes that a tribe's most influential perceive as detrimental to their lofty, royal positions in a social dominance hierarchy. It's maybe not so great when the purpose is to "keep people in their place," as if there is any class, caste, or category of people who are in a position to define "people's place," especially with respect to a life sentence of economic precarity.

Two months after the announcement to end poverty, on October 29, 1969, engineers at UCLA and Stanford Research Institute (SRI) made the first successful connection between computers that would soon become the internet. That message? "LO."

All three of those events took place within 100 days' time. There are sudden inflection points in history that change everything, and we may be in the midst of transiting a similar inflection point in 2024. This time, its ecological recovery, AI, and universal Social Security.

Then crash. The full intended computer command was the now universally understood, "LOGIN." I'm guessing about all caps because that was often the norm for readability in those days, long before the concept of CAPS came to mean YELLING on social media. Needless to say, there were no screen captures back then, so it seems all we have ready access to today is this:

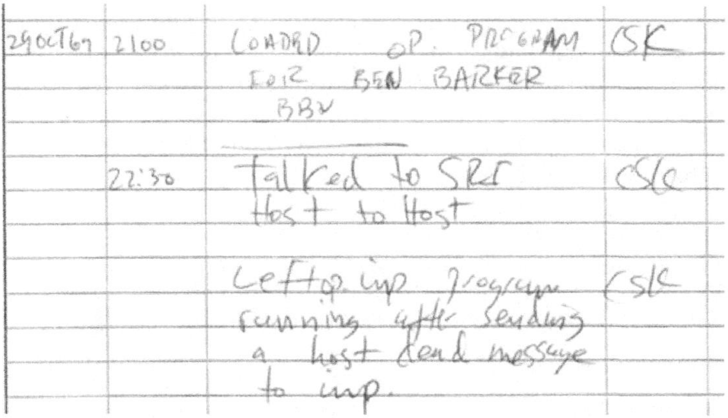

Figure 8 — First Host to Host Internet Connection, 1969.

It's historical kitsch to say that the 1960s were a tumultuous and transcendent decade. Yet, nothing quite measures the depth of the long-term impact that those years, and that extraordinary 100 days, upon the timeline of human existence like the supernatural synchronicity of the three points above.

Imagine where we might be today, if we had successfully achieved all three missions, on schedule, so to speak.

> Author's Note: I use the word *supernatural* to mean simultaneously *super* (dazzling, extraordinary, incredible, magnificent) and entirely *natural* (normal, ordinary, nothing other than how the universe works in the most routine and mundane sense.)

Unfortunately, in our 20th century mindset, we only completed two of the three missions toward accomplishing a happy, sustainable singularity for humanity.

The fact that all three events were manifestly in play at the same time marked a noteworthy inflection point in history that echoed through the ages in material, symbolic, tangible, non-symbolic, and intangible ways.

So why did the United States fail to accomplish all three "when we were supposed to?" Why did we drop the ball?

The foremost reason for failure was likely fear. Isn't it always? Plain old fear, sustained by those timeless deep roots of all human suffering: ignorance, greed, and anger toward the very idea that somebody might get something by grace, not of works, lest anyone get to boast.

Fear is likely the reason that our shared human hopes for the fulfillment and blessings of human rights for all still fall far short of their promise even in the wake of the 75th Anniversary of the Universal Declaration of Human Rights.[cclxviii] Even the Emancipation Proclamation still hasn't fully freed all people in every corner of America, more than 150 years since its passage. How can such vital human priorities, upon which the vast majority of people and nations for the most part agree, fail to come to fruition?

The answer is that little catch phrase, "for the most part." Resistance is never futile. Even the tiniest amount of duplicity in the right time and place can undermine the best of intentions and actions toward beneficial outcomes for humanity. Isn't that the lesson of the Judas kiss?

More than half a century later, the failure of FAP left our generation holding the Fail Bag of the late 1960s and early 1970s.

> *"In the course of the 91st Congress, the United States almost established a guaranteed income. The proposal, known as the Family Assistance Plan, was set forth by President Richard Nixon in a television address on August 8, 1969, not quite seven months after taking office.*
>
> *Eight months later, on April 16, 1970, the House of Representatives approved the legislation by almost a two-to-one vote. It then faltered, only finally to fail in the Senate, albeit the debate went on to the very last moments of the 91st Congress, which did not end until January 2, 1971, nineteen days before the 92nd Congress began" (Moynihan, 3).*

So, why did the bold *technological* efforts of 1969 succeed, while the potentially even greater *sociological* breakthroughs failed? In a December 2023 conversation with Joe Rogan, co-host for the always insightful podcast *Your Undivided Attention* Aza Raskin shared Open Philanthropy Research Analyst Ajeya Cotra's salient insight:

> *"Ajeya Cotra says 'it's as if 24th century technology is crashing down on 21st century civilization.' So imagine it was 21st century technology crashing down on the 16th century. It's like the king sitting around with his advisors. 'What do we do about the telegram, and radio, and television, and smartphones, and the internet, all at once?' They're going to be like, 'Send out the knights!' [Similarly today,] our institutions are just not going to be able to cope."*[cclxix]

It was a bit surreal, and encouraging to hear those words, just a few weeks after making a similar point on page fifty-seven of this book.

If history makes anything clear, it is the fact that our lower human drives and biases present powerful inertial forces that serve to undermine progress with an indolence that seems to defy even the laws of physics. How can social maturity be so much more difficult to achieve than exponential technological growth?

Without discounting the progress societies have made, we still experience significant and regressive inertial forces of race and gender today, so it's no wonder that prominent American sociologist, specializing in aging and social welfare, Jill Quadagno called these out decades ago in a way that sadly still rings true today:

> *"The central arguments about the formation of the U.S. welfare state view it as a product of class struggle driven by conflicts between labor and capital over problems of production. The emphasis on class struggle as the central dynamic has led class analyses to ignore a defining feature of social provision: its organization around race and gender. If economic power gained through redistributive measures from the state creates political opportunities for the excluded, then social policy becomes a liberating force."*[cclxx]

Ending poverty with unconditional income security is arguable the most powerful liberating force in history on multiple fronts far too long neglected in the name of shipping the newest technological object or shiny algorithmic attention lure on a regular schedule. More powerful than all the armies, nukes, and idiotic smart bombs in the world, because, when we end the panicked desperation of human material desperation, we eliminate the most deeply rooted animal fear-of-lack inducements for aggression and deviancy. Those ancient, limbic, quarrelsome reactions all but disappear in the presence of Maslow Safety.

As we've repeated, ending poverty as we've known it is no panacea or silver bullet for all of society's ills. The plight of the most severely mentally ill continues to pose a major challenge that even Maslow Safety can't address. One epidemic at a time. Once we address the poverty epidemic, we can better get to work on the mental health epidemic. Solving for income security better illumines other public health problems, just as legalization of cannabis has shed more light on those with deep addiction problems without the needless brutality of throwing people in jail.

So while it might be tempting to consider ending poverty as the end of some great work, it also marks the beginning of some potentially even greater challenges. Like all meaningful accomplishments in life, the attainment of a goal often becomes the unveiling of even more significant work ahead.

Ending poverty is not a declaration of some static, eschatological end-state utopia, as I may have misunderstood one of this generation's most careful thinkers, Jorden Peterson to imply in the earlier referenced conversation with Chris Williamson (clxxi). Maybe I misunderstood Peterson's comments, but I can share that it is my view that ending poverty is the next ethical and moral step along an eternal ethical pilgrimage for any civilization of ethical Post-Automation Era beings.

We have long since resolved the functions of gravity, electromagnetism, and the entire Standard Model of physics through our collaborative intelligence and scientific resolve. But still, not poverty? How can that be? How does that make any scientific or spiritual sense whatsoever?

Yes, yes, quantum gravity and much more still perplex us, I don't claim to be a physicist and didn't say we entirely understand the nature of gravity and dark energy or that "spacetime is undeniably doomed," though it maybe it is (cccxli). What I said is that we've quantified gravity's *function* in the context of a more than decade bygone Standard Model.[cclxxi]

Humanity has managed to complete the incomprehensibly complex work of confirming the entire Standard Model, showing with sublime precision the mathematical predictions of the Higgs boson.[cclxxii] And yet, even greater and more incomprehensible mysteries persist, affirming the observation that, "the attainment of a goal often becomes the unveiling of even more significant work ahead" (ibid).

While we have made statistically significant strides at the lowest end of the poverty spectrum, the plagues of absolute and relative poverty feel as unshakable as ever in everyday lives. How can this be the case, in the face of all our exponential technological advancements and superabundance? As for "statistical significance," in the figures we've cited throughout this work that terminology often means "some non-zero amount" of progress. That's like the old "one penny above poverty level means you're out of poverty," trope. It's just not intellectually honest.

What is the nature of this millstone around humanity's collective neck that enables us to avoid the eradication of poverty, particularly considering the obvious astronomical benefits for all humankind? How is it that we are capable of 3-D printing everything from houses to DNA, ride in self-driving cars, regularly use vertical-landing reusable rockets, mind-controlled bionic limbs, interact with sophisticated AI that engages with us in some of the most thought-provoking conversation imaginable, integrate our lives with all manner of emerging neuro-, bio-, info-, cogno- and nano-technology wonders, yet seem powerless against this ancient spiteful foe of poverty?

> *"President Nixon's signature on H.R. 1, the social security amendments of 1972, ended 3 years of basic income consideration and deliberations, as proposals to improve the social security program. When FAP failed, the President called this emasculated act "landmark legislation," and it became Public law 92-603 on October 30, 1972."*[cclxxiii]

Emasculated, stripped of all its original promise of "a guaranteed annual income at levels that sustain life in decent circumstances" by the time H.R.1 had become law.[cclxxiv] The central pillar of this "landmark legislation" toppled, campaign promises and principles, abandoned. The priority of income security policy was frozen in carbonite for the next five and a half decades. With a public widely distracted by the glitz and hype of our new technological prowess, the 1970s intention to end poverty as we'd always known it crashed and burned on the launch pad, with almost nobody noticing the long-term consequences that become inevitable, in that very same instant. Today, we live in the midst of those consequences.

The emergence of a continuously shapeshifting global technology-mediated distraction civilization, an entirely unaccountable and unidentifiable chaos engine for which there is no one to blame or hold accountable, because Moloch's golems gonna' golem. In this respect there is no *they* to demonize, condemn, or take on, however much our human guttural instincts remain vigilantly on the lookout for a new *them* to otherize and condemn.

It's just Big Money (Wall Street), Big Tech (Silicon Valley), and Big Public Relations (Washington DC, Hollywood) doing what Big Egos do. Big hype. Big promises. Big accomplishments. Big distractions. Big addictions. Big dysfunctions. Big dislocations. Exponential super abundance and super alienation at the same paradoxical time.

Cultivating a default consensus reality that defines identity and worth by obtaining the newest unaffordable gadget every year, filled with thousands of adoring imaginary fans and followers, paid for on time payments, creating a culture of indebted servitude that ensures obedience to the time clock. Don't worry, if your skills become obsolete, you can go into another four or five or six figures of debt, retraining yourself in a trade school that may or may not exist for the duration of enrollment.

Increasingly clever gadgets, enticing and cultivating a larger-than-life, fake fame via social media streams that Blitzkrieg our attention 240 hours a day, 700 days a week, 3,650 days a year[cclxxv] have become the most addictive and paralyzing opiates of the masses in history. Let them eat cake, numb their minds, and anaesthetize their souls with porn and cat videos.

Maybe that "two out of three ain't bad" stuff ain't just bad, maybe it's the catastrophic stuff of a botched singularity in the rearview mirror. So now what?

Larry DeWitt, who served as the public historian at the U.S. Social Security Administration, discovered another reason for the pernicious persistence of poverty in February 1996. DeWitt conducted the Social Security Administration's Oral History Project. "Mr. DeWitt is also the creator of http://www.socialsecurity.gov/history, one of the largest history-related web sites in the federal government. In 2013 he published *The Other Welfare Supplemental Security Income and U.S. Social Policy* with Edward D. Berkowitz."[cclxxvi]

DeWitt "focused on the creation of the SSI program, and especially on the Family Assistance Plan (FAP), which was the precursor to SSI." Here, the long history and culture of suspicion and distrust of poor people – merely because they are poor – was clear to key staffers involved from 1969 to 1972.

A Social Security Administration staffer at the time, Ms. Ross recounted:

> *"I did discover a really strong note I wrote on his behalf (this would have been sometime in 1970) I wrote over my signature, telling John Montgomery that Tom Joe is really upset that a lot of the legislative planning (or the planning activity for administering FAP) seems to be going in the direction of re-imposing all the suspicions and anti-dignity."*[cclxxvii]

And so it did. And so, it does. All the suspicions, stereotypes, projections, an anti-dignity sentiments and policies foisted upon people of lesser economic means than us have seemingly, ironically, tragically amplified at the same rate that our capability to end all of them has accelerated. Why?

Fast forward to 2018, San Francisco. "This is the wealthiest major city in the wealthiest state in the wealthiest major country in the world," [CEO of the San Francisco Convention & Visitors Bureau, Joe D'Alessandro] says. "And we can't live with the situation on the streets we find ourselves in right now. Walking each day in this neighborhood and seeing everybody sleeping in doorways," says Castro neighborhood resident Linda Zaretsky. "It's just intolerable, painful and morally wrong." She has lived in San Francisco for about 30 years, and she sees poverty as the fundamental problem. And she says she'd pay more taxes to address it" (Shafer).

Unconditional basic income nearly became law in the early 1970s. Today, we have completed more than fifty years and hundreds of tests and pilot programs of every conceivable scale – from neighborhoods, to cities, to provinces, to nations[cclxxviii] – and yet, in the past decade there were still people who claimed that universal basic income was a new, risky idea, and that economic poverty can only result from some kind of personal character defect, bad karma, or some justifiable punishment from God.

What we know today is that direct cash ends poverty.

As for risk, as we've shown, the riskiest and most irresponsible behavior is ignoring how bad things have become for far too many at the same time that conditions have become so good for far fewer. The 20th century default consensus narratives are what brought us to this point, are those the traumatizing stories and trauma-bonded patterns that we want to keep repeating?

Reddit reminds that the short-sightedness of quarterly capitalism is a huge part of the problem. We can at least partly mitigate that short-sightedness with a guaranteed annual income.

One participant on the /r/BasicIncome Reddit shared a real-world example from her own company:

> *Quarterly Capitalism is the problem. The constant race to half-assing things to report bullshit to The Street. We have a brand-new product that does this ... We had 15 large orders before the end of the quarter. Look at us, we're great, our people worked 65 hours a week to get it done!*
>
> *Reality:*
>
> *Barely half the feature set was implemented.*
>
> *Everything from sales projections to configurations to fulfillment was completely hands on manual.*
>
> *The product and supporting processes, including accounting, are not integrated into the enterprise infrastructure - no time or money to do that.*
>
> *It'll take 500 orders a week for the next 3 years to break even, assuming the next big lie doesn't bump the focus on this product - and that's only IF automation and enterprise integration are done.*
>
> *And that is why Americans work so much. Fantasy land. And maybe 5 people in that whole situation have an understanding of what profitability means (Groty).*

In the face of exponentially accelerating technological advances, sociological adaptation falls inexcusably further behind.

In 2024, there is an inordinate amount of attention paid to the potential for devastation and death from potential runaway AI in the potential future, while there is complete abdication of our responsibility for the documented deaths that happen every year due to poverty. Do you think AI cares about any of this? If it doesn't, who should?

Explaining the reasons for our abdication of responsibility and the foreseeable effects was the thesis of Alvin Toffler's 1970 seminal work, *Future Shock*. Toffler, and anyone with a modicum of sociological imagination, saw the writing on the wall for a missed, fumbled, blinkered, and botched singularity, over a half decade ago. For those interested in digging deeper, the prescience of Toffler's work is more unmistakable than ever. It's timeless reading worth making time for, today.

* * *

Suddenly a Nationwide and Global Movement

Oh, just one more thing. Something incredible happened in the past five years. The Marc Levin Documentary, "It's Basic," debuted at the Tribeca Film Festival.

> *Director Marc Levin follows a variety of participants as they use their incentives in ways that quash the stereotype of poor people abusing "free money." From a formerly homeless single mother of four barely getting by with an "essential job," to a low wage working couple with a child, to one particular GBI program designed for newly released prisoners. Levin also looks at the mayors who are behind the programs in their cities, and their commitment to educate and promote an idea whose past supporters ranged from Martin Luther King Jr. to Richard Nixon. With great intimacy and hopeful stories, It's Basic tracks the gathering momentum toward a philosophy of lifting up those that are struggling to survive in the world's richest country. – Brian Gordon.*[cclxxix]

Suddenly, the number of guaranteed income pilots expanded by orders of magnitude. Nationwide and worldwide. At the time of this writing there were 117 cities on the map of Mayors for Guaranteed Income, and growing.[cclxxx] The nation's leading universities, including Stanford Basic Income Lab,[cclxxxi] NYU Cash Transfer Lab,[cclxxxii] Drexel University Center for hunger free communities,[cclxxxiii] University of Chicago Harris School of public policy,[cclxxxiv] and many others had all set up dedicated centers and labs for the study of Basic Income. The findings were overwhelmingly consistent across a diversity of populations and contexts, urban, rural, and especially in vast gaps in between.

Without the slightest exaggeration, one clear headline from the University of Chicago summarized the findings of *every single one* of these studies:

"Universal Basic Income Policies Don't Cause People to Leave Workforce."

> This is now an irrefutable empirical fact, regardless of 20th century thinking and feelings to the contrary. In fact, more people find more meaningful and rewarding work because they have gas money and less stress when they show up for interviews. It is both natural law and science.

But is this *really* a scientific finding? In December 2023, with a global reach of over 10 million, the Science X community confirmed, "Implementing a Basic Income Means Overcoming Myths about the 'Undeserving Poor'."[cclxxxv]

In England:

> *A universal basic income (UBI) trial will see them receive $2,046 for the next two years. The trial is being run by the think tank, Autonomy, which is looking to assess the impact of UBI on the lives of recipients. The money is paid in cash and there are no conditions attached. The payment is not means tested and recipients can work while they are receiving the payments.*[cclxxxvi]

Globally, "What did we learn from the world's largest basic income experiment?"[cclxxxvii] As of December 1, 2023, "The first results from the world's biggest basic income experiment" are in:

> *As you might expect, given how entrepreneurially minded the recipients are, the researchers found no evidence that any of the payments discouraged work or increased purchases of alcohol — two common criticisms of direct cash giving. In fact, so many people who used to work for wages instead started businesses that there was less competition for wage work, and overall wages rose as a result.*[cclxxxviii]

The Basic Income Earth Network 2023 Congress included 7 Plenary Sessions with at least 20 academic papers and progress presentations from all of the world.[cclxxxix] In his presentation summarizing progress in the United States. Leading U.S. UBI advocate Scott Santens reported:

> *The US also just ran what was essentially the largest US-based basic income pilot ever by providing $250-$300 a month per kid to 9 out of 10 kids in the US in 2021. On average, that worked out to around $462 a month [for] 36 million families. The result was the biggest drop in child poverty in American history, cutting it about in half, with no drop in employment. The number of parents selling their blood plasma also fell, and fewer parents started abusing drugs. Symptoms of anxiety also dropped by over 13%. And when the payments stopped, parental unemployment increased, likely due to a decreased ability to afford childcare.*[ccxc]

Finally, "Early findings from the world's largest UBI study"[ccxci] were reported on December 6, 2023, by GiveDirectly, "a nonprofit that lets donors send money directly to the world's poorest households. We believe people living in poverty deserve the dignity to choose for themselves how best to improve their lives — cash enables that choice."

From the GiveDirectly website:

> *Since 2009, we've delivered $700M+ in cash directly into the hands of over 1.5 million people living in poverty. We currently have operations in Bangladesh, DRC, Kenya, Liberia, Malawi, Mozambique, Morocco, Nigeria, Rwanda, Turkey, Uganda, USA, and Yemen. And no, people don't just blow it on booze.*

There is far too much data to neatly summarize here, although I can supply a few bullet points while encouraging readers to look into the details for yourself in the endnotes and extensive bibliographic and appendix resources.

Virtually all of the findings from the world's largest UBI study to date confirm the hypotheses advocated by me and tens of thousands in the UBI community over the past decade. The presumptions about poor people are empirically 100% dead wrong, from Africa to Albuquerque.

From the December 2023 report, "Summary of findings 2 years in:"

- *A monthly universal basic income (UBI) empowered recipients and did not create idleness.*
- *Both a large lump sum and a long-term UBI proved highly effective.*
- *A short-term UBI was the least impactful of the designs but still effective.*
- *Governments should consider changing how they deliver cash aid.*
- *A monthly UBI made people in poverty more productive, not less.*
- *Critics of universal basic income often fear monthly cash payments disincentivize work; however, this study in rural Kenya, like many studies of cash transfers before it, found evidence to the contrary for all groups.*

"Critics of universal basic income often fear monthly cash payments disincentivize work; however, this study in rural Kenya, like many studies of cash transfers before it, found evidence to the contrary for all groups" (ccxci).

Before we dismiss these findings by saying, 'well, it's only a small amount; well, it's only a village in Africa; well, that wouldn't work in the United States,' please keep this in mind: this scientific work is every bit as rigorous as 20th century physics in proving fundamental principles, just as science has done throughout the ages.

Today, we have rightly shifted the scientific gaze from a bygone era of the Standard Model of Physics, toward a Standard Model of Human Rights in Economics. The reason we work so hard to establish first principles is because when we prove fundamental principles, fundamentals scale reliably, dependably, predictably, and safely. That's why funding fundamental research in every field is so crucial. That's why AI work is rightly obsessed with foundation models. Because when we work from and establish first principles, we know that what works in the lab, works in the field, and discoveries that can only take place in the field inform the next iteration of work in the lab.

Despite overwhelming empirical evidence, I know there are many who still object that, "basic income is socialism!" So, next, let's respect that 20th century perspective.

* * *

We Know People Keep Working

People don't stop working as a result of the certainty, stability, and stewardship of income security. They get to work on the real work of life. And when that happens, human innovation, creativity, and value creation goes recursively exponential.

It's no mystery that biological and economic stability are prerequisites for the flourishing of infinite human creative expression, expansion, and novelty. Not merely for the pursuit of happiness, but for the attainment of Maslow Safety and eonian joy. Isn't that the most American of American dreams? To not settle for pursuit, but to attain, fulfill, exceed, surpass, and transcend our individual and commonwealth potentials?

In addition to the millions of open-source software developers, small farmers, artists, writers, musicians, mathematicians, and others we've discussed, magician duo Penn and Teller's career is another prime example of how, even if we have all of the money we need, people still want to improve, create better products, better services, better art, better science, better philosophy, a better world, for themselves and thereby, others.

> *For 50 million years our biggest problems were too few calories, too little information. For about 50 years our biggest problem has been too many calories, too much information. We have to adjust, and I believe we will really fast. I also believe it will be wicked ugly while we're adjusting," says libertarian magician and cultural icon, Penn Jillette. "So the flaw in libertarianism is that maybe a small amount of coercion might be worth it. The other problem with libertarianism: it may not be modern enough. Libertarianism has to do with everyone being able to find meaningful work.*
>
> *Doug Stanhope said, isn't our goal 100 percent unemployment? Isn't that a good thing? But if there aren't meaningful jobs, is there any reason for libertarianism? I have been very seduced lately by the basic universal human income. But would we be able to find work that would fulfill us if we were on a basic universal income (Marchese)?*

It bears repeating here that humans are not inherently lazy by nature and even super smart people, who know that from their own direct lived experience, can sometimes miss this. We are creative, curious, and industrious by design, and the long struggle of humanity is not to merely survive, but to thrive, to unleash the maximum amount of that creativity into the universe while not only doing the least harm, but ideally, ending suffering in the process of expressing our deepest creator nature.

As Penn tells it:

> *30 years ago, when Teller and I were in a room trying to figure what we were going to do, easy was a positive. Like, "Hey Teller, here's a funny*

> *idea, we can just do this really simply." Now if I say to Teller, "This might be too hard for us" he sits up straight and goes, "Okay, let's go! Let's do it!" Because [with no need for money,] at some level we are only doing things for ourselves now. We have enough old material to last the rest of our lives. Our career goes exactly the same if we do old material as if we do all new brilliant stuff; we've got a few tricks coming out that we've been working on for years, and they won't change how many people buy tickets to our show. But they're better tricks than we've done before. They just are. And that's beautiful."*

The conclusion is that there is no need for any more futurist sophistry, hand-wringing academic longitudinal studies, or superintelligent large learning model data analysis to understand that PEOPLE KEEP WORKING, and working better, in an environment of basic income stability.

In this respect, the most recent 100 or 200 basic income pilot programs have helped to pour gasoline onto what was already a roaring bonfire. We never needed them, but now that we have them, it's time to harness this fire and put it to work in forging a more perfect Union.

This means cosmetic or palliative adjustments are no longer helpful, it's time for the long delayed, targeted surgical reconstruction and repairs to a long-ailing circulatory system. We know that our currency circulation system works as a whole, but we're hobbled by a deprecated trust fund revenue generation model that is out of date, old, and busted. Intergenerational transfer payments aren't sustainable, particularly with the demographic trends of the Post-Automation Era.

Having carefully triaged and diagnosed systems, the doctor is finally ready to begin writing some prescriptions.

> *According to the 2023 annual report of the Social Security Board of Trustees, the surplus in the trust funds that disburse retirement, disability and other Social Security benefits will be depleted by 2034. That's one year earlier than the trustees projected in their 2022 report.*[ccxcii]

This is incredibly great news, because we don't have to invent any new infrastructure in order to circulate an unconditional, universal basic income "at levels that sustain life in decent circumstances." If biological metaphors don't do it for some, the plumbing is already in place. It already works. It's in great shape. It's dependable. It's trusted. It's not rusted or leaking. We only need to upgrade two pumps. The trust fund revenue generation pump and the monthly circulation pump.

Under the current conditional regime, Social Security recipients face an absurdly complex set of conditions and penalties for working, either for enjoyment and community contribution in retirement, or any other personal reason, even though we know that for some retirees, working in a traditional 20th century role significantly increases happiness. Not too surprising, considering that's how people of certain generations were conditioned.

It's the right to say no, the freedom of choice that boosts happiness, as it does for people of any age.

One obvious prescription to improve circulation: make existing Social Security unconditional. Let retired people who want to work, work, and don't punish retired people who derive happiness and meaning by creating art, or music, caring for family, volunteering in the community, or heaven forbid, entering into that promised rest.

To maintain a lively mix of metaphors, there are parts of this work that are like political rocket science. This isn't one of those parts. This is basic plumbing. And everyone knows that if the plumbing goes out, we're gonna be in world of ... hurt ... much more so than if the rockets don't launch. So, let's get the plumbing right, and then we'll worry about rocket science. Does that sound unfair?

We need to express gratitude for such glaring examples of how Social Security's basic income conditionality limits the freedom of people and why UBI advocates have argued that universal basic income needs to be unconditional. It's conditionality that prevents retirees who want to work, from working. It's conditionality that separates people into clients and gatekeepers like inmates and guards.

Doesn't it seem like free markets require free people in order to function freely for highest human flourishing?

Removing conditionality from current Social Security recipients instantly makes Social Security into <u>unconditional</u> basic income for all existing recipients. That's how fast we can bootstrap UBI into default consensus reality. Today. One clear, simple, direct administrative upgrade to unconditionality. Just add universality.

Does that not compete for the simplest honky-tonk policy-two-step you ever heard? No new bureaucracies. No new acronyms.

1. Unconditionality.
2. Universality.

And it's not just branding – although that becomes unavoidable in any awareness raising work – it's the truth that this is the way to *the end of entitlements* through the declaration of citizen technology dividends, just like Wall Street does all day, every day.

Plenty of people may try to repolarize around new terms and mangled misinterpretations because polarizers gonna' polarize and manglers gonna' mangle; but with clarity of intention, steadfastness of conviction, and consistency of effort, we can end poverty as we've known it, right now, before the end of this decade.

But maybe I've done a terrible job of defining or explaining *conditionality*. Conditionality is the current bureaucratic rat's nest of tangled terms and conditions that makes Social Security needlessly complex and expensive to manage. By removing conditionality from current Social Security recipients, this long-successful program instantly becomes *unconditional basic income for current all Social Security recipients.*

We don't need yet another new government agency or program to implement something specifically called "UBI" on any scale, let alone a national scale. We need less government red tape, not more.

And we dramatically decrease redundancy in government middle-management by adding step two, universality, to the unconditionality of Social Security. With universal Social Security, we effectively eliminate wasteful, demeaning, and just plain mean means-tested bureaucracy.

Will we hear the sound of screeching Mandrakes like in Harry Potter? Of course. There are always Mandrakes.

This is why an uncompromisingly sufficient universal Social Security indexed to 50% per capita GDP is non-negotiable. It's beyond imperative that no displaced worker, public or private sector, ever come even close to going penniless, homeless, or incapable of meeting their basic needs for "sustaining life in decent circumstances," especially all of the dependable public servants whose deprecated and obsolete government positions rotate out of service.

Implementation is no time to play tit-for-tat, 1970s style. Real human lives are at stake now, at scale, and anything even close to a repeat of the low-balling numbers beat-down of that era, merely for the sake of "winning," serves no one's best interest.

It's not the people who are redundant, it's the jobs, the roles, and it's dreadfully important to be supremely mindful, compassionate, and accountable for the dramatic changes that thousands of people in what were once seemingly lifetime positions go through. It's almost impossible to convey the indispensability of this imperative to anyone who hasn't been through a similar dislocation. This is where we literally put our money where our mouth is, caring for people and resisting any Darwinian impulse to haggle numbers like on a car lot, driven by ancient anthropoidal predilection. We don't need to behave that way anymore if we can only remember who and where we are in the context of the long arc of history.

We are The Third Millenium inter-generation, Gen G, responsible for stewardship and service in The Post-Automation Era.

The Post-Automation Era of superabundant superintelligence is no time to scrimp and quibble as if we're playing by the rules of the past millennium.

As repeatedly acknowledged, simply stated solutions don't mean easily implemented solutions, especially in the domain of public policy and administration; however, the difference between policies that do not work well, and those that succeed, very often comes down to the matter of conceptual simplicity. So, if ever there were a Justification Of Being for Captain Simple, this is that J.O.B.

If simpler, more accurate, or situation-specific analogies come to your mind, if a flash of insight sparks an ingeniously simple way to explain or clarify a question or principle to people in your family or friends groups – which I have no doubt that you will – please consider participating in this historical moment, a moment far bigger than any or all of us combined, to which we are all merely bearing witness, by adding your contributions on /r/BasicIncome.

* * *

As Simple as Possible and No Simpler

In the late 1960s eminent physicist and humanitarian Robert Buckminster "Bucky" Fuller, a contemporary of Martin Luther King Jr., added both his engineering insight and humanitarian foresight to King's clarion call for "a guaranteed annual income at levels that sustain life in decent circumstances," today referred to as UBI, Basic Income, and other nicknames. Regardless of the name, the underlying principle is the fundamental human right to *income security*, particularly in today's post-automation civilization in which the need for human labor has become increasingly obsolete at an exponential rate.

King and Fuller, each in their distinctive way, advocated for what Bucky called, "a world that works for everyone." Bucky created the World Game to:

> *"Make the world work, for 100% of humanity, in the shortest possible time, through spontaneous cooperation, without ecological offense or the disadvantage of anyone." Fuller went on to explain that, in the most pragmatic terms, "This is the real news of our century. It is highly feasible to take care of all of humanity at a higher standard of living than anybody has ever experienced or dreamt of. To do so without having anybody profit at the expense of another so that everybody can enjoy the whole earth. And it can all be done by 1985" (ccvii).*

When Fuller said, "our century," he of course meant his own century, which is now the quarter-century-bygone second millennium. Will it take humanity a thousand years to realize that we are living in the third millennium, right now, today?

Another important de-polarization is Scott Santen's observation that, "UBI isn't politically left or right, it's forward." Ending poverty with universal income security is a long-shared human goal that has taken a long time to achieve, as seems typical of the accomplishment of all human rights. While it may be difficult for some to comprehend that we have finally arrived at implementation, the fact is, we have arrived.

> To riff and remix Bucky: 'here's the real news of the twenty-first century: we are living not just in a new century, but a new millennium, and in the very decade in which we accomplish the timeless universal human aspiration to end poverty.'

So our work is not original, it is the echo of voices and the continuation of labors of all those who came before us, just as Bucky and Martin echoed the initiatives of those who came before them. This is the Long Arc. One of the most visionary authors of the twentieth century, Arthur C. Clarke added a provocative take on ending poverty:

"The goal of the future is full unemployment, so we can play. That's why we have to destroy the present politico-economic system."

Though it was a far lesser-known reformist minister, Theodore Parker who introduced the Long Arc and "predicted the inevitable success of the abolitionist cause this way:"

> *I do not pretend to understand the moral universe; the arc is a long one, my eye reaches but little ways; I cannot calculate the curve and complete the figure by the experience of sight; I can divine it by conscience. And from what I see I am sure it bends towards justice."*[ccxciii]

A century later, Martin Luther King, Jr. paraphrased Parker's words in a prepared statement he read in 1956 following the conclusion of the Montgomery bus boycott. In King's 1956 words:

> *But amid all of this we have kept going with the faith that as we struggle, God struggles with us, and that the arc of the moral universe, although long, is bending toward justice (King).*

For many, suggesting that socialism improves capitalism amounts to sacrilege. Many despised King so much that they wanted him dead and eventually succeeded. Among them were many who justified their murderous hearts, minds, and actions in the name of the variety of a 20th century fork of capitalism that indeed ascended from that moment onward. With JFK and MLK out of the way, those extremists effectively created the polarized bi-polar world of super abundance and super precarity we experience today.

To remind us of what Sean Illing explained earlier in his article, *Why Capitalism Won't Survive Without Socialism*:

We think of capitalism as being locked in an ideological battle with socialism, but we never really saw that capitalism might be defeated by its own child — technology. Which is another way of saying that socialist principles might be the only thing that can save capitalism.

Giving people money works and always has worked. It's a 100% proven *conditional* basic income on a nation scale. There is absolutely nothing uncertain or unproven about the efficacy of the principle of income security put into practice. For over eighty years "just giving people money," has worked in the form of Social Security, virtually ending poverty among the elderly. Now it's time to set all people free from the catastrophic fractal ravages of poverty.

The Federal Reserve and U.S. both "just given people money" in the form of farm subsidies and hundreds of industry incentives. Circulating that currency through the heart of the economy, its people, rather than flooding resources into banks, like injecting transfusions directly into the brain instead of the circulatory system, is a vastly more rational and effective approach. Understanding the functions of these complex interdependent hybrid systems known as our human bodies has enlightened our understanding of how healthy living economies function.

The brain's designed function is biological SIGINT, COMINT, and coordination, not circulation. In the 20th century we kept pumping blood into the brain every time we had a panic attack and then wondered why the economy kept going from aneurysm to aneurysm in a perpetual boom/bust cycle that left the patient catatonic. Again.

The medical intervention for an over-achieving but heart attack-prone economic system is "a guaranteed annual income at levels that sustain life in decent circumstances,"[ccxciv] providing a pacemaker that keeps the economic circulation system functioning as the autonomous system that it is, while simultaneously addressing and preventing the root cause of the heart attacks in the first place.

As basic income activist and educator Scott Santens puts it:

> *By the way, this is pretty much how the board game Monopoly works. Everyone starts the game with some money, and then every time someone passes Go, they get more money. Try playing Monopoly without these rules, where no one gets any money to start with and no one gets money for passing Go. See how well that game works and how long you want to keep playing it.*
>
> *That $200 in Monopoly everyone gets for passing Go? That's unconditional basic income. If everyone received $1,000 for passing the first of the month each and every month, the price mechanism would function better.*[ccxcv] *Because everyone would be able to express demand, markets would function better, and what people actually want, and need, would be more accurately and efficiently allocated.*
>
> *Concentration of money is just as big of problem for markets as lack of money. So not only does everyone need a minimum [number] of votes, but there should not be too large of concentration of votes in too few hands, lest our economy be oriented mostly around meeting the demands of a small percentage of people instead of everyone.*
>
> *In a real democracy, all citizens have the right to vote, so why don't we have democracy in our economy?"*[ccxcvi]

Santens's article is so well written that we highly recommend you take a break and go read it, then come back. Santens employs the practical analogy of starting an ice cream shop to illustrate the difference between zero demand and null demand, a distinction that is practically impossible to make in the context of current markets. Go ahead, check that endnote above, open a browser, and go check it out.

Here's where the rubber meets the road:

The United States already has nation-scale basic income.

Social Security is basic income.

It's just not unconditional or universal ... yet.

Social Security is a *conditional* basic income, conditioned on age. SSI is a *conditional* basic income conditioned on individual circumstances.

Social Security has been and continues to be one of the most wildly successful and popular poverty-ending policies in the history of U.S. policy. Why? Because giving people money works to end poverty by securing a floor of *income security*. Social Security has proven itself for people over age 65 since August 14, 1935, at 3:30 p.m. So, I can't possibly repeat enough the fact that the duplicitous contention that "basic income isn't proven on a national scale" is empirically ridiculous. I'm glad we have had another couple of hundred experiments and pilots over the last five years, but as I've written online for years, they were unnecessary. We already knew then what we know now.

The fact that basic income already works at nation scale in the United States isn't debatable. After almost ninety years of Social Security working to selectively end poverty, we know for certain that income security works to end poverty and now we've learned how to apply the same stratagem to universally end poverty.

Basic Income is not a radical, wild, untested theory. We don't need more trial programs, we can deploy the policy equivalent of a long overdue software upgrade patch to begin incrementally lowering the Social Security qualification age, in increments, at regular intervals, until covering every qualified U.S. citizen.

A just, universal Social Security is the most pragmatic, immediate, and direct way to implement unconditional, universal basic income without any new bureaucracy; in fact, we demolish waste, fraud, and abuse by eliminating the obsolete bureaucracy of the entire dysfunctional 20th century welfare apparatus.

While there is no shortage in the supply of clodhoppers in America – I'm sorry, I have to give Dad at least one solid credit – who have always thought that Social Security is "a socialist government takeover," we can only take comfort in the fact that wisdom is not beholden to ignorance. After all, we're not here to end ignorance directly, only poverty. Not coincidentally, it's been more than a decade since neuroscience has shown us that there's a good chance that by ending poverty, we will gradually end a lot of the ignorance, as well.[ccxcvii] So there's that.

But some *still* want more proof, because their sad, insignificant calling in life is to be contentious for contention's sake.

> *In a 2014 article on the TalkPoverty.org website, Stephen Pimpare wrote, "In 1959, official poverty rates among people over 65 were higher than for any other age group. Today, they are lower than for any other age group. What happened? Social Security, which became more generous and nearly universal over time. It turns out that if you send people money every month — wait for it — they will be less poor."*[ccxcviii]

Yes, some days, I get tired and impatient. I get tired of some people treating all this down to Earth data as if it is from outer space. It's not from outer space. The *conditional* basic income of Social Security is one of the most practical, proven, grounded, here and now policies known to residents of the United States.

If Social Security signifies any form of socialism, then maybe we have stumbled upon a way – beyond triggered emotional reactions to the word – in which socialism has already spectacularly improved capitalism.

* * *

Where Does the Money Come From?

For analytically minded, data-driven people, this may be the most interesting, anticipated, and controversial part of the book: hard numbers, presented to invite a new kind of analysis, perhaps in ways that we have not thought of such numbers before. It makes sense when addressing problems that we cannot solve at the same level of understanding and abstraction that created them. In such cases we have no choice but to brave the novel and unknown. There is no place for handwaving in such work; we must, however, define the primitives and principles of our model, first.

Inevitably, we'll attract Internet troll style debunking for the sake of making the debunker appear clever; however, our invitation is to enjoin an intellectually honest exercise of arithmetic exploration and curiosity in the context of upgrading both our economic understanding and our institutional performance in ways that are faithful to the foundational values and aims of our democratic republic.

Fair warning on behalf of those for whom math is not a favorite sport. This section may feel a bit like heavy sledding at times. I've done my best to try to make things as accessible as possible, and any inscrutability is due solely to the ineptitude of the author.

> *I hope we can brave these sometimes-harsh details, together, because within the depressing numerical realities ahead lie the seeds of hope for the formation of a practical method to establish an empirical economic value foundation from which to rationally and realistically construct a living wage level basic income indexed to 50% per capita GDP. #math*

In July 2018, Senator Bernie Sanders asked:

> *"The median salary of an Amazon worker last year was $28,000, or what Amazon CEO Jeff Bezos makes in just 10 seconds. Why on earth is that the case?" (@OurRevolution)*

I'm confident that most readers at least take pause at that kind of circulatory anomaly. Perhaps some celebrate such numbers, perhaps some justify and defend them, and perhaps some feel offended that I dared include a quote from a person many regard as an angry socialist. Cancelation only isolates the canceler from the real world. Canceled people do not cease to exist, however many cancelers of all colors wish otherwise.

What if we could set aside the personalities and politics for just a brief moment and imagine we visited another planet, where all the creatures of a particular species look pretty much the same, with some diversity of color, gender, height, and weight, but otherwise biologically more-or-less identical. Then we observed that one of these beings was worth $28,000 every 10 seconds while all of the rest were worth $28,000 per year. Wouldn't that spark your curiosity? As an outside observing alien or angel, what questions might arise about such a civilization?

People hold a lot of different beliefs about why this kind of value gap might be a good or bad thing. But let's try to step beyond bad or good, wrong or right, and honestly ponder the question: here on Earth, how can any individual human being be worth that much more than any other individual human being?

I don't know the man, but Jeff Bezos strikes me as an extraordinarily capable, generous, and good-natured human being. I hold people like him in the highest esteem. We need this caliber of cognition on Team Human in the Post-Automation Era. Nothing in this work is to diminish or criticize the individual successes of the most successful human beings on the planet. Quite the opposite. We need your help more than ever, and odds are good that you've been aware of the issues we're facing for decades and experienced much of the same frustration at the recalcitrant nature of a 20th century Molochian machine.

It is just as reprehensible to demonize and otherize billionaires as it is to demonize and otherize poor people. Team Human has never been more all in this together.

I made the point earlier that old guard economics had effectively reduced human beings and bodies to transactional, robotic, commodity sacks of protoplasm. So, rather than complain about that, let's accept it as our foundation. We are where we are, so let's get to work.

If we need to figure out how much robotic human sacks of protoplasm are worth as a commodity, where do we begin? What measures do we currently use to put a price tag on human lives as expendable, interchangeable war-machine parts?

The military puts a price tag on every asset it loses. Perhaps war budget mavens use unemotional abstract numbers for psychological protection, denial of the humanity of other people's brothers, sisters, parents, and children sent to fight and die. If we were in such a leadership role, would we be able to perceive or contemplate the living, breathing human lives at stake and *still* send them into the nightmares of war?

Some leadership roles can seem utterly devoid of conscience or any sense of basic humanity. Many consider such roles practical, inevitable, and unavoidable for the purposes of national and global security, but are they? In such roles, soldiers become assets, not soft, flesh and blood hearts and souls that someone misses back home, but manufactured components for the purpose of keeping the war machine running.

The same economic forcing functions that keep a whip to the commoner's back also force the military to concede some economic value to the body parts of blown-up human beings. So there is *an empirical economic intrinsic worth and value* to human bodies; we just don't recognize it on-balance-sheet until forced to do so in the form of lifeless piles of parts draped in a flag.

Did the intrinsic economic value of that body suddenly pop into existence out of the quantum field at the moment of death? I think not.

What does this say about our capacity for denial of the intrinsic economic value of human lives, at scale?

This then is our starting point for due diligence in the valuation of the human organism as a raw commodity input to war, industry, or any other endeavor. By this method we can systematically, logically, precisely reach an empirical, objective measure of a "generic worthless human being's" balance sheet value. Because there is no more economically worthless assemblage of human anatomy than an obliterated pile of parts, any assemblage of human anatomy that exists in the most trivially better state of repair and function is of more intrinsic economic value than a completely wrecked component. This is just basic economics, right? A minimally running automobile is worth far more than a pile of the exact same parts, disassembled, in a junk yard.

Our method of accounting for intrinsic human value in the 20th century was like refusing to recognize the value of a car until wrecked. "Oh, you wrecked the car? *Now* it has balance sheet value, but up until that moment it was worthless as an asset." That's beyond ridiculous. It's utterly absurd. Even the most basic car on a used car lot has a price tag value and enriches the lot owner for *just sitting there doing nothing*.

Are humans not at least as valuable when "just sitting there" awaiting the right circumstances to be of best service? Again, this isn't theoretical hand-waving. We have multiple empirical measures of intrinsic economic human value; those measures just don't show up on *your* balance sheet. That accounting was the result of incredibly crafty intelligent design, maybe just not the most benevolent intelligence.

We mock Moloch's intelligence at our own peril.

* * *

People Are Our Most Valuable Asset

It's not that we did anything wrong in the 20th century, we merely expropriated intrinsic human economic value in accordance with the analytical practicality of GAAP. It was nothing personal, it was just that Generally Accepted Accounting Principles didn't recognize intrinsic human value until dead. Maybe we treated GAAP as if handed down on stone tablets from Mt. Sinai, but other than that, we did nothing wrong. Besides, if it wasn't illegal, it wasn't unethical or immoral, right?

One of the most lucrative, if not the most lucrative industry on the planet aggregates and holds absconded *intrinsic human economic value* on their balance sheets, to line someone else's pockets, later. It's called the insurance industry. If every human life didn't have *intrinsic economic value*, the life insurance industry couldn't exist.

Insurance actuarial tables and settlement precedents contain empirical data as sources of objective human biological organism intrinsic value. Whenever an accident or act of negligence results in a human death, insurance companies deploy algorithms to guide policyholders and courts in the crude exercise of measuring the dollar value – the intrinsic value – of the human being in question. Insurance companies spin that value into "loss compensation," which is equivalent to the magician's left hand distracting from what the right hand is doing.

Actuarial algorithms were running the show long before the advent of today's problematic newsfeed algorithms, but the two aren't unrelated. Where does a huge amount of investment capital come from? Life insurance trust funds. And what is the underlying asset of those funds? You. Your intrinsic economic worth and value.

That was maybe one of Moloch's cutest slight-of-hand, right-in-your face tricks of all time. Staking a claim on our own intrinsic economic human value and then drip-feeding it back to us in dribs and drabs to accomplish its own objectives; convincing us that some shining skyscraper was the source of our own value and sustenance. We might call that trick a lot of names, but unintelligent ain't one of them.

But it gets better. One of the major places that insurance companies invest is in real estate, directly through mortgages and indirectly through stocks and bonds.[ccxcix] Which means, guess who's collecting your rent?

That's right. The same pickpocket that holds your intrinsic economic value hostage, on their balance sheets. And people call governments pickpockets? This might be a bit of a rude awakening for some, and it's again encouraged to do your own homework and assess all of these claims for yourself. Dig into the multiple sources[ccc] in the bibliography and endnotes.[ccci]

This scheme is a bit like the economic system equivalent to the principle that participants in social media platforms have a right to own their own contributions, their own data, so it's not much of a surprise that efforts to return that value to contributors have cropped up from time to time yet struggle due to the black-hole-like gravitational power of Job Trance network effects. It's obvious that the participants in social media platforms create all the value, and yet that value accrues to a relative few and overwhelming enriches the casino.

Maybe I am naïve, though. Maybe the vast majority of people want the end game of the 20th century to continue forever.

The fact that there can be different dollar amounts assigned to different human beings is a complicated ethical and moral mystery that I unfortunately do not have time or space to fully unpack here and keep us on-task with building our economic model. It's a vitally important question and I hope that those more knowledgeable than myself will engage in the conversation and help me to understand this aspect of differential *intrinsic value* between persons of different, lottery-of-birth gifted abilities.

Some readers may take umbrage at such crass accounting of human life by mere monetary measures. "You can't just put a price tag on a precious baby's life!" That's a true and valid point.

Yet, we assign our 18-year-old babies precisely such a price tag as soon as they put on a uniform. Then, we stand, drowning in tears, pleading, praying for mercy from the court when a drunk driver or bad batch of medicine kills our irreplaceable child. Maybe I'm observing a different humanity than others, what I've observed is people making their adult progeny children when it suits one set of selfish interests and adults when it suits another.

What I've observed is thousands unfortunate souls, for whom my heart truly breaks, crying out to God for some kind of monetary remedy that can never make us whole except in the most sterile legal sense. We know that no amount of money can ever replace that precious human life. We also know that *every human life has infinite inexpressible value*, in fact, expresses *the source of all value*, as empirically stored on the balance sheets of the aforementioned insurance companies. So we rightly, and righteously demand *some* recognition of that value, even if only in crudest pecuniary terms.

And so, as a possibly gullible and naïve optimist, I believe that most people do believe the words of author and teacher Steven Gray when he says, "Each person and each being has an unspeakable value. I don't know how something could be more meaningful and beautiful [than a human life]."

It also seems repetitive, pedantic, to remind that people generally regard children as priceless, beyond any conceivable economic measure. Yet, if this is the case, at what point in life does this small priceless gem flip from being a priceless asset to an infinite liability? How does that dark inverse sociological alchemy of turning pure gold into trodden straw happen, exactly? What is the depreciation rate for the baseline human blue book value of humans from date of birth to age of accountability?

These can be troubling questions to think about, so we don't. We accept things as they are because it's the easiest way to deal with the immediate urgency of overwhelming economic precarity, let alone any triggered emotional enmeshment. So we ignore, dismiss, devalue, avoid such questions, effectively perpetuating the cycle. We do all we can to defend and perpetuate a 20th century default consensus reality because it's what feels most familiar, regardless of massive off-balance-sheet costs and externalities, sociological and ecological. We've already identified the deepening epidemics of depression and suicide in the mid-2020s.

How can we deny or fail to directly map these devastating epidemics to feelings and beliefs of human worthlessness? How can we ignore, discount, or disregard the role of economic precarity, specifically income insecurity, in cultivating those beliefs? Particularly in a culture so prominently defined and measured in economic terms?

If a child in the womb is priceless, how much less is a 3-month-old infant worth on the standard depreciation scale, and how are they gradually rendered worthless by age thirteen or eighteen or twenty-one or thirty-four if they don't fall in line with the old-guard society? I raised a teenager myself and grew up as the oldest of several teens, so it's not a flippant question with which I have no experience, it's all too sober and salient a question for the purposes of our work.

Then, how much less is a 3-year-old worth, compared to that 3-month-old infant? Where is the invisible depreciation schedule in any text, sacred or otherwise, that explains how the intrinsic human value of an individual gradually drops from priceless zygote of infinite worth to worthless human being, over a twelve, eighteen, twenty-one, thirty-four, fifty-five, or eighty-nine-year span? If readers can help me find any of these resources, I will be tremendously grateful for the opportunity to learn.

All too often, when we don't have a snappy, convenient, and conclusive answer to difficult questions, some people get upset. Especially the more controlling among us. Not you or me. So, we seek to invalidate both the question and the questioner in order to compensate for and deflect from our own ignorance. Nevertheless, these questions remain inescapable in the Post-Automation Era.

The 20th century model depended on arbitrary distinctions between where we assigned economic value, or not. Which contexts of human labor deserved balance sheet recognition, and which did not? If our niece baby sat, zero economic value appeared on the balance sheet. If we hired someone of the same age and skill set, suddenly economic value appeared on the balance sheet.

From the most mundane domestic interactions to the most sophisticated corporate contracts and public initiatives, hyper-financialized capitalism developed all manner of ornate and obfuscating vocabularies for alternatively objectifying, reifying, or marginalizing what it did or didn't want acknowledged as valuable, as best served its arbitrage and aggregation purposes. If you believe arbitrage and aggregation are just Wall Street phenomena, you haven't looked carefully at your own small hometown. These economic behaviors apply to small pond social capital pecking orders in perhaps the most odious and destructive ways.

Economic words like externalities, off balance-sheet, extenuating circumstances, ledger adjustments, strategic priority. Or, if you're the DOD or Pentagon, national security vocabularies that cast a spell of protection against any accounting, accountability, or audit trails whatsoever.

Socially, "a good person," or "a bit iffy," or "love her, not him so much." We're reminded that economics is a messy abstract impressionistic mix of art and science that is equal parts inscrutable math and inexplicable human behavior.

While we're on the topics of arbitrary value, arbitrage, and aggregation, let's keep in mind that private security forces, colloquially, *contractors* – another verbal slight-of-tongue that makes private-sector warfare seem equivalent to construction – with internal private balance sheets and no reporting accountability don't do any better than their public sector counterparts when it comes to transparency and accountability. I add this to briefly tag some of the bald inconsistencies in the *economic valuation and social (in)validation of our political principles*, by which we judge the validity of public or private enterprise, as well. In theory, the principle of equal accountability under law applies to all people and institutions equally, in practice, not so much.

> *There is already a price on every one of our heads, whether we like to think about it or not. My aim is to bring that value onto the balance sheet of our commonwealth as an irrefutable mathematical foundation for identifying and circulating legitimate passive income, interest and dividends, based upon empirical, material, currently off-balance-sheet surplus economic value.*

Have you heard the adage "all value is ascribed?"[cccii] It rings true, doesn't it? The observation that all economic value is subjective, perceptual, and conceptual. An almost impossibly shapeshifting concept. A completely subjective interpretation of this or that compared to that or this.

When we say, "people are our most valuable asset," that value invokes comparison, one of the roots of Buddhist suffering and also a first principle of economics, "compared to what?" It would be a funny coincidence if not so often painfully true as a source of suffering.

Our valuations, while highly rationalized, are ultimately almost entirely arbitrary. At its deepest roots, it's arguable that all conceptions of value are arbitrary. So, another sacred cow that we need to dissect is that of treating economic principles as if they are as fundamental as the laws of physics. They are not. We are free to reexamine the assumptions of conventional economic thinking, remix them, renegotiate them, and redefine them as best suits our evolving and hopefully improving understanding of what best cultivates conditions of human flourishing. We are driving here toward unearthing the heritage of our beliefs about the nature of intrinsic human worth, or lack thereof, by excavating a worksite that might at times resemble an archeological dig. How can there be anything of value in the midst of all the rubble? If I do the job right, the picture will become clearer, one pottery fragment at a time.

While there are many economic theories of value that hold together in the lab, very few, if any survive in the real world. The aforementioned mixed economy is the one possible exception that does survive in the real world. A mixed economy most closely resembles the practicalities of the everyday world we live in; a mixed-up hodgepodge of hacks and kludges that work in diverse environments and under widely varying and ever-changing conditions. This is the more correct description of what most of us consider American Style Capitalism. "That government is best, which governs least," and so forth.

The principle that the least amount of regulation in exchange for the greatest amount of hacking anything and everything that works – innovation – is the best or at least, the least-worst of exchanges in order to most benefit the most people, over the long run. No pure economic "ism" can possibly emerge from such a mixed configuration, it can only lead to adaptive or maladaptive hybrid subsystems of interactions and relationships that hopefully sort themselves out, over time, with the least harm to, and the most benefit for, all involved. That's generally how the United States works, that's how mixed economies work, and that's why we don't live and can't live in a purely capitalist regime.

Inescapable aspects of capitalism, socialism, and communism are all at work in any functional mixed economy and accepted – though not widely recognized – in each of our everyday lives, in most modern nations. We might not all have the sophisticated vocabulary to dismantle and parse the nuances of this complexity. That fact doesn't change the operational practicality of how mixed economies work, and that we live in a mixed economy world.

Most of us cannot recite all of the components of a biological cell from memory. That fact does not cease the organized chaos of a cell from functioning, nor does it reduce our absolute reliance upon that functioning. There's a whole lot about the nature and function of the world that we both don't understand and completely rely upon, in faith, all day, every day.

In the context of mixed economies, some go as far as to argue that Wall Street and the Fed themselves each exert a kind of tug-of-war between communistic central planning authorities over the U.S. economy. Misunderstanding of these terms, all too often fostered intentionally, causes needless confusion and strife in our civic discourse and policy making processes.

I feel a duty to reflect some semblance of understanding of these interdependencies as we move toward an actionable model. If we find ourselves implementing this work in the midst of crisis, building a foundational understanding here may become helpful to fostering a shared understanding of decisive trade-offs and compromises.

One bottom line is this: if it's clear that *people are assets*, and not liabilities; in fact, people are exponentially appreciating assets as they improve their skills, then how exactly are their salaries accounted as liabilities, and not as direct investments in our most valuable assets? "Because GAAP." Yes, we're precisely minding the GAAP.

> *Is a human being, a life, an economic asset, or a liability? This is an inescapable fundamental question if we are to make progress toward a coherent and comprehensive mathematical economic model for the Universal Social Security of each and every precious human life.*

It seems that many respond with, "it depends." It depends upon ... wait for it ... job title. So much for the precious infinite intrinsic worth that we defended in birth, or in as we visited in cases of tragic loss.

We say that human worth depends upon how a given human being behaves in comparison to *how we want them to behave*, or upon the value of a balance sheet. At the extremes, people might generally regard a junkie as a liability, and a CEO is an asset.

However, these comparisons can only be useful on the most superficial level – if they are even remotely true in the first place. What if the CEO is Bernie Madoff, one of the biggest con men in modern American history, and the junkie is a man who fell apart when his son was killed in an industrial accident, and bounced back ten years later to create software that is now installed at every station in order to protect the safety of every worker, preventing that tragedy from happening ever again? What if the CEO is using the impunity of their power to traffic substances, people, or interfere with human lives as suits their repugnant whims and the homeless person in the tent, content and productive in avocation with the simplicities of food banks and café Wi-Fi, is the next breakthrough author or musician?

We're digging deep into this notion of human value. Who's valuable and why? Who's not and why not? It's not as simple as 20th century economic led us to believe.

Within the narrow context of the old guard economy, which looked to maximize extraction of raw materials from Earth while maximizing behavioral compliance from humans, the most superficial comparisons of human value based on job title may have seemed to make sense, but upon just slightly closer examination, those cynical assumptions completely fall apart.

The fundamental error in valuing humans by job title, education, or performance of this or that activity is that we have no way of knowing if or when that CEO will experience a breakdown that makes them the "bum" next week and the "bum" experiences a breakthrough that leads them to become founder of the next trillion-dollar global enterprise. Both scenarios have played out so many times over history that they are clichés. Yet, these are the outdated ways by which we continue to value the most precious natural resource in the world, if we have any healthy esteem: the intrinsic economic value of human life.

Job titles and status are always changing. People are always changing. There is nothing that can possibly justify locking any individual human being into one asset class or another, for the entire duration of their lives. Except, perhaps, something like a caste system, which Americans reject with their words while in many ways helping to create and reinforce through behavioral economic choices.

Right now, our investigation continues: how do we calculate the intrinsic economic value of a human being?

When we talk about "where does the money for unconditional basic income come from" it soon becomes obvious that the question itself is absurd, because human assets, as the most valuable known commodity on Earth, back themselves. We already do this with fiat currency, declaring value backed by the "good faith and reputation of the American people." Then, based upon that declaration, based upon collective buy in with that default consensus narrative, based upon words out of nowhere, we declare value within the Federal Reserve from which we circulate currency. This paper only has value because we believe in the people and the EII backing it. It's not a flim-flam conspiracy. It's legit. We'll see shortly how 'out of thin air' arguments don't hold up to examination. This is simply how today's EII really works and how we can help it to work better, more profitably, and more efficiently, for everyone.

Our model of backing basic income with intrinsic human value resolves the glaring incongruity of fiat currency that irritates so many monetary reformers, regardless of validity of that irritation. The Bible itself equates human beings with gold, undeniably affirming human value vastly exceeding gold, so what could possibly be more stable and tangible than an intrinsic human-value backed currency?

I know what you're thinking, "He's mad. Off the reservation again. That's crazy. Impossible. You can't just do that." Well, we just did. We just did just like every other arbitrary foundation of value that has ever appeared throughout history. We're declaring and ascribing intrinsic economic human value and will shortly quantify and authenticate it with hard numbers grounded in more than seven decades of U.S budgets.

Even if the math is impeccable, economics is equal part myth and buy-in to any given default consensus narrative. So, is it possible for the general public to ever accept such a foundation of value in our rapidly human-devaluing world in time to make a difference? That part is up to all of us. I'm not here to specifically convince anyone of the last few paragraphs, I am here to continue with the presentation of rational arithmetic derived from that inductive foundation and let the math speak for itself. This is arithmetic that I published for the purpose of inviting public scrutiny on the /r/BasicIncome Reddit more than a decade ago and have yet to see discredited or debunked. Maybe you'll be the lucky winner to do that. You're officially invited.

Perhaps after looking at the numbers for yourself, you can return and decide whether or not this house of cards is better than the current house of cards, or not. If we're being intellectually honest with one another, let's at least admit that every single one of these human-concocted economic models is a different house of cards. We all only get the same 54 cards. So, in that respect, calling any model a house of cards as grounds for dismissal is simply intellectually dishonest. So we're faced with the question: is this house of cards we're living in good enough, or is it time to reinforce, broaden the base, or build anew?

Maybe nobody ever told you that you are of any inherent worth at all, much less infinite worth, and maybe some also believe that humans are not inherently valuable at all. Isn't it astounding, the degree to which we experience the hard, cold reality of life through the lens of these seemingly arbitrary beliefs about whether or not we are intrinsically valuable? Assets or liabilities. That is the question.

Unsurprisingly, the cultural destruction of individual human value that we've experienced over the past four or five decades is all too often the case in societies that seek to extract maximum behavioral compliance above maximum individual liberty. The very principle of liberty can only emerge from the deeper recognition of intrinsic human value. Intrinsically worthless beings can't possibly have a right to liberty, or life, for that matter. Happiness because obtuse and irrelevant in such a case.

Is it not liberty that maximizes individual and societal flourishing?

If our most valuable *asset* and *natural resource* is people, individuals endowed by their Creator with certain inalienable, universal human rights, then we become obliged to mathematically derive the essential *commodity value* of an individual human biological organism within the context of a flourishing free market context. Cynical as it seems, we must arithmetically determine the market monetary value of a human being.

> If we do not abide by our own foundational economic definitions, then the entire system becomes invalid, because the 20th century paradigm purports that *markets define the correct value of everything* within their sphere. Everything. That means human bodies, children, kittens, and you.

So, like any other commodity, we must derive the intrinsic value, the bluebook value of a typical human, just like any other natural resource. Organically, your body is a pile of biological natural resources that make up an integrated sentient natural resource soup that we call human. What is the intrinsic economic value of the natural resource known as 'one shrink-wrapped unit of humanity?' It might sound crude, but this is the world we're talking about, so it is what it is.

Referring to people as mere commodities when asking what a human life is worth may sound like a cold and heartless calculation, but this is indeed what people are, in the context of the present economic paradigm. Humans are considered by Molochian sensibilities to be cold, soulless animals, raw commodities, not warm, affectionate, sentient beings.

The most cynical might say, "get over it, snowflake, you're nothing special, you have no intrinsic value beyond the behavioral function you serve in my worldview." Day to day, we only pretend that this is not the case. We pat people on the head and say nice disingenuous words only to secure our own place in the local fish-pond hierarchy, not because we believe them. We make believe that people have some higher inexpressible value while seeking out transactional relationships that feed the ego in a vain attempt to convince ourselves that we aren't what the job and dating markets says we are: cheap interchangeable parts. Pimps-n-Ho's. Swipe left. Swipe right. Plenty of fish and lots more where that came from.

There's nothing theoretical or emotional about it, this is how 20th century society regarded human life for the past half century, in everything from popular music to fashion, to the balance sheet value that says we're by definition a dead weight on the system while we're pedaling as fast as we can, working two or three jobs plus a side-hustle, to keep our own human devaluation machine running.

None of these observations matter to most previous generation people with sufficient F.U. (Forget You) money; that is, enough to be comfortable without being bound by the Job Trance. The 20th century mindset was often, "I got mine, forget the rest of you." However, there are enough new F.U. money holders that do see the incongruities, inconsistencies, and hypocrisies inherent in the pre- Post-Automation Era paradigm and are wisely, generously, and enthusiastically dedicating intellectual and material resources to move us all in the direction of a world that works for everyone. The realization of this generational work is impossible without such people.

For the semi-privileged, just short of F.U. money, some who may only now be realizing that it's just not going to happen for them (attaining full F.U. money status), these ideas may bruise some egos to think of ourselves as mere human commodities.

"We're the ones with those valuable job titles and badges that you dissed! Now you're telling us that we're of some kind of *equal intrinsic economic value* with people that haven't enjoyed the benefits of a lucky lottery of birth, stellar education, and the serendipity it took for us to *earn* our way to this pinnacle? We worked hard to get here!"

Yes, we all worked hard to get to where we are, as did slaves, sharecroppers, and all manner of exploited persons throughout history. Marginalized and marginalizer, colonized and colonizer, that's the defunct and deprecated default consensus reality.

When we've been sufficiently privileged for long enough, equality can feel like a demotion or even persecution. It's not. It's more like, welcome back to Team Human. We've always all been in it together, even if you bought into the illusory form of rugged individualism that was never true in the first place. We are all products of our environments, our communities, and there was never any such thing as a self-made man, woman, or person. We're peeling back the layers of this intrinsic human economic worth onion, and there are bound to be some tears along the way.

Along the way, I'm doing my level best to speak some of the unspeakable that divides us, to put some of the inexpressible that separates us into hopefully helpful words, because we embed and express our notions of value, worthiness, and deservingness into and through economics. Notions we adopt and transmit through economic activity. Activity conducted via the conduit of currencies.

Quite literally, the only thing backing the U.S. dollar is us. It's far too late to pretend like 20th century financial capital markets can't possibly commoditize the most sacred spaces of life: our marriages, relationships, family dynamics. They already have, in a sense, have from Moloch's origins. As uncomfortable or unpleasant it may feel; we can't avoid the fact that human bodies are commodities in the 20th century paradigm.

* * *

Price Discovery in Human Commodities Markets

As mentioned earlier, when calculating the costs of war, the U.S. government must produce a number that measures the loss of an asset (soldier, human body). We also said that the very nature of this number itself should give us pause to consider both the deepest human costs of war and the fact that recognition of intrinsic human economic value only occurs after catastrophic loss. More accurately, our methods do account for intrinsic human economic value, just not on *the soldier's* balance sheet.

> Author's Note: I conducted all of the following research by hand, from 2018 through mid-2023, just prior to the release of ChatGPT to the public. Because AI exploded onto the scene during the writing process, we gain the advantage of a unique comparison between my own findings, below, and how AI responded to similar questions, in a special last-minute addition to the Appendix under *How AI Computes the Economic Value of a Human Life.*

Please recall the earlier trigger warnings that these calculations, of necessity, become rather crass. Unsurprisingly, it is not simple to locate real-time quotes on the going price of utilized body bags. It's our very aversion to looking at these figures squarely that keeps Moloch comfortably unperturbed.

So, I began by researching figures provided by the RAND Corporation, self-described as "a nonprofit research organization providing objective analysis and effective solutions that address the challenges facing the public and private sectors around the world."

In "The Cost of a Military Person-Year: A Method for Computing Savings from Force Reductions," a project of the RAND Corporation for the National Defense Research Institute, there is a line item called "Death gratuities $13,985."[ccciii] Soldiers are generally auto-enrolled in higher value life insurance; however, they do have the option to opt-out, and this figure is ostensibly the amount that will be paid out in the event that there is no other insurance available.

This gives us the most rudimentary, baseline undervalued value of human life of $13,985, as priced out by the Pentagon. To be fair, that is about five to seven times the price of a grass-fed beef steer. So as slabs of meat go, you're about five times more valuable than an ox. At least there's that affirmation.

As anyone who has ever lost a loved one in battle knows, finding numbers like this is only the tip of the obfuscation and aggravation iceberg when it comes to the difficulty of getting straight answers from the VA; especially once you've experienced the stark reality that war has taken the life of your loved one. We found the VA website littered with links to "404 not found" errors, on questions as vital as "Where should I go for more information about the coverage increase or death gratuity?"[ccciv] At the time of this first writing in 2018, the answer to that question linked to "Branch of Service Casualties HQ," which offered the following unhelpful text:

> *VA » Veterans Benefits Administration »*
> *Life Insurance » 404 — Page Not Found*
> *The requested page could not be found.*

This is what a bereaved survivor can expect to encounter at a time when people are naturally at their most vulnerable and least resilient, desperately searching for accurate and timely information about the loss of their loved ones. Moreover, when looking elsewhere to find their answers, the misinformation and disinformation littering the internet on these topics only makes matters worse.

In "Estimating the Costs of War: Methodological Issues, with Applications to Iraq and Afghanistan," economists Joseph E. Stiglitz and Linda J. Bilmes found that:

> *In the private sector, firms need accurate and comprehensive financial and cost accounting systems to make good decisions. This is also true in the public sector. Military decisions are affected by costs; (even though the military faces only a part of the costs) and other government agencies bear some of the budgetary costs, while other parts of society bear some of the economic costs. But from the sole perspective of military accounting, the cost of a life is equal to $500,000, which includes [up to] $400,000 in life insurance and $100,000 in "death gratuity" payment.*
>
> *This number does not reflect the fully loaded cost to the military of recruiting and training a troop to replace the one who is lost, and the impact on morale and mental health on the rest of the unit, which may result in higher medical costs. From an economic standpoint, the actual loss to the economy, not to mention the human loss, is closer to $7 million, which is close to the "value of statistical life" used by civilian government agencies.*[cccv]

Because that $100,000 death gratuity differs significantly between Blimes and the RAND report, we looked to the U.S. Department of Veterans Affairs for clarification.

> *Servicemembers' Group Life Insurance (SGLI) coverage is available in $50,000 increments up to the maximum of $400,000.*

Attempting to find more details about the death gratuity itself, the VA says:

> *Under what conditions will DoD pay the special death gratuity? (SGLI)*
>
> *DoD will pay the special death gratuity to survivors of those who died in a designated combat operation or combat zone or occurred while training for combat or performing hazardous duty on or after*

> *October 7, 2001, and before September 1, 2005. The SGLI death gratuity of $150,000 will be payable regardless of whether or not the member had SGLI coverage at the time of death. Published 08/10/2012 04:08 PM. Updated 12/19/2012 03:14 PM.*

So, now we seem to have yet another distraction from the direct question at hand. This "special" death gratuity offers yet another number that, while higher than RAND's report, only applies between the years 2001 and 2005. Can you imagine the torment this kind of search imposes upon a bereaved spouse or family member of a soldier who is trying to find good answers to the most basic, straightforward questions? It's difficult to stay focused on the task at hand in this chapter when I contemplate the millions of Americans who have suffered at the hands of 20th century war machine bureaucracy; not just in the obvious and horrific loss of life, but also via all these otherwise invisible, relentless, unseen administrative and bureaucratic micro-torments that can almost seem designed to wear us down with a billion tiny intentional inconveniences that serve no purpose but to dissuade, delay, and demoralize us from finally gaining access to the knowledge we seek and deserve to know.

Another measure of the price of human lives is a 2012 estimate that found, "Keeping one American service member in Afghanistan costs between $850,000 and $1.4 million a year" and "one matter is clear, that cost is going up" (Shaughnessy). Using the midpoint of those two numbers, the retail economic value of each soldier is $1.1M per year. This leads to the question: how is it that the same life is worth $1.1M when the job is killing and effectively zero when a soldier comes home to build a better future?

If improving life on Earth is our most important theater of operations, then how is it that we don't value each human being at just 10% of their own stormtrooper value? By this method, our baseline asset value, and every American's intrinsic baseline is $100,000 per year, simply for remaining in stock and on the shelf as the cheapest, bottom of the barrel non-strategic domestic asset. Yes, *just* for taking care of the house and yard and raising a healthy, happy family because parents are able to be present. Moloch doesn't care that householder work requires full-time toil in and of itself. So, how could 10% of that $100k stormtrooper value make sense as baseline value in our thought exercise?

It seems that if we want to get closer to the value of a human life beyond the body-bag count, we also need to look at private sector life insurance policies, actuarial tables, and settlements. What are the range of values that insurance companies put on a human life? These are market-derived values that free marketeers can't possibly refute because capitalists are the ones who did the math to create such valuations. So, anyone who says that you can't put a price on a human life hasn't looked at these figures, because our free-market society puts a price on human lives all day, every day. In fact, we built the life insurance industry upon this foundation, and it is one of wealthiest industries, if not the wealthiest, on the planet. If the life insurance industry can put intrinsic monetary human value on the balance sheet, then we can declare our own equivalent value on our own commonwealth balance sheet.

> Author's Note: Similar to the war figures above, I quizzed AI for responses to some of the basic insurance assessments of intrinsic human economic value. Again, the main text was all human-researched and written in the years just prior to the commercial AI boom, so I've included *Life Insurance: The Human Value Holding Industry* in the Appendix.

I'm confident that, despite the journey so far, there are some who will continue to say, "you can't put a monetary value on the sacredness of a human life." Sadly, this rings especially hollow at this point in human history. In the current market system, literally everything has a price tag, including you and me. If you find that observation both accurate and distasteful, then, paradoxically, and fortunately, maybe the ideas in this book aren't quite as far-fetched as you thought they might be when you opened it.

Yet economists have an amazing way of twisting and turning value inside out and upside down, to meet the merciless demands of 20th century economic orthodoxy, by appraising and computing human value only as a cost, a liability, rather than an asset. By definition, appraisals are highly subjective. Nevertheless, let's take the example of a dated 2008 Time Magazine article that reported, "Stanford economists have demonstrated that the average value of a year of quality human life is actually closer to about $129,000" (Kingsbury). That's $179,875.32 in 2024 US dollars, as calculated by Wolfram|Alpha based on the Consumer Price Index.[cccvi]

An important short detour is that many protest that universal Social Security will cause inflation. In the old-world model, that might have been true. Maybe. Although hundreds of pilot programs nationwide have overwhelmingly disproven that concern, nothing's impossible. Pigs could fly, so that view might be right. The United States has provided conditional basic income to people over the age of 65 for a century, so that proves that it also works at a national scale. Additionally, in our model, inflation can't happen because it's accounted for in the micro and macroeconomics of the model.

Moreover, the economic disruptions to society this time are so fundamental that we have had inflation *and* deflation at the same time, playing a tug of war for years, with wage earners and income precarity knotted in the middle. Presently, where inflation does show up is in our appraisal of the commodity value of a human life.

Former Microsoft SVP of Marketing and Sales, "Bill Davidow has been a high-technology industry executive and a venture investor for more than 30 years. In 1985, he founded Mohr Davidow Ventures."[cccvii] Here's what Bill had to say about inflation on Linked In (emphasis added):

> *Unfortunately for the less fortunate 50%, debt has been acting more like deflation debt than inflation debt. Inflation rates have been low, so dollars are not getting cheaper as quickly as they used to. Interest rates have been low as well, but many middle-class Americans are paying high real interest rates. There are two reasons for this. The first is they have lower credit scores, so they pay higher interest rates. Also, they*

tend to use expensive sources of credit, like credit card debt, that carry high interest rates. Student loans in many cases end up carrying high real interest rates as well.

So, if we want to help the less fortunate members of our society, we will have to come up with social and economic policies that deal with both the inflationary and deflationary challenges they are facing. There are numerous things we could do. We could come up with policies that would reduce the cost of the necessities of life—countering inflation. Making health insurance more widely available at lower cost would be one approach. We could counter the effects of deflation by providing earned income credits or by coming up with some form of Universal Basic Income (UBI). We could revise bankruptcy laws to make it easier to get debt relief from student loans.

Yes, it is impossible to have both inflation and deflation at the same time if you are looking from the top down from an economist's point of view. But if you are looking from the bottom up, it is a macro-economic phenomenon that is the sum of tens of millions of micro-situations. We had better come up with policies to deal with the challenge.[cccviii]

According to Wolfram Alpha's access to Federal Reserve Bank of St. Louis data, the U.S. core inflation rate from January 2008 to December 2023 was 45.82%, consisting of food and beverages at 54.31% and energy at 34.88%.

Have your wages kept up with that 45.82% core inflation over the past fifteen years, much less during the course of your entire work life, working as a commodity labor widget? It's almost as if there's some kind of fundamental mathematical unsustainability here, in the way we think the world works, and have allowed it to work, for the past century.

By adjusting the Kingsbury-Stanford Model for that inflation rate, the value of a quality human life in 2024 is closer to $188,107.80 per year.

Another pertinent related question is: why is it so hard to find the particular comparative data and up-to-date calculations that I'm working out from scratch? Why is no one keeping track of the value of human life, when we know the value of everything else to the micro-penny?

Answer: because that's what best serves Moloch and Mammon. The 20th century default consensus narrative. Everything has intrinsic balance sheet value, except you. That's not a law of nature or creation, by any stretch of the imagination, that's just human value swallowed whole by the gaping maw of GAAP.

In August 2012, Business Insider reported that the statistical value of "a human life is worth $7.4 million ... in 2006 dollars" (Wile). So that's 74 years at a $100,000 annual valuation, or a 57-year life-span, at the Stanford valuation. The article goes on to state, "Importantly, this is not an estimate of how much money any single individual or group would be willing to pay to prevent the certain death of any particular person." Of course not. While one might like to believe that an *actual* human life is of far greater value than a $7.4 million statistical figure, what Wile is essentially saying is, 'just because we know your intrinsic life is worth $7.4 million, that doesn't mean we're going to assign that worth to you. We'll let the insurance companies hold your wallet until you croak.' If we let you know what you are really worth, how could we convince you that you are not born with the right to a single share of nature and the commonwealth's exponentially multiplied super abundance?

If we interpret Business Insider to mean that the 2012 commodity value of a human being was $7.4 million, then how much unearned, un-labored-for, dividend income would the owner of that property (your own physical life) generate each year, at an absurdly low 1% APR? Answer: $74,000. Although the article doesn't mention the specific lifespan, this is an incredibly reasonable and serendipitous cross-check that matches our earlier $7.4 million figure quite nicely. When we solve a math problem by a half dozen different methods and all the computations settle out in the same ballpark, let alone precisely, we call that empirical evidence, even proof that the math is accurate.

That's right. At the moment of your birth, a fair and just public trust fund balance sheet (Social Security Trust Fund) increases by just $7.4 million, by simple accounting for the baseline value of your life as a comparatively average asset. This creates *a public trust of, by, and for the people* tasked with assuring a paltry interest rate of 1% per year. That's *$74,000 per year in passive interest income, every year, just for being alive*. Sounds absurd? Well, that's how so-called trust-fund babies already live, born into it. So why wouldn't all of God's children be born into the richness of their inheritance in grace, as well?

> *It gets better (or worse, for pessimists): Adjusting for that 45.82% Federal Reserve Bank core inflation cited above, over the same time period, makes the baseline value of one human life as a commodity asset not just $7.4 million, but a solid $11 million ($10.8, precisely). By following Federal Reserve best practice, we record the brass tacks market value of your commodity human life at the moment of birth for its market-derived asset value on the Social Security Trust Fund balance sheet. At a paltry 1% interest, the Trust Fund owes you $110,000 interest per year, every year.*

So now we're managing a 21st century Social Security Trust Fund generating $110,000 per year per citizen, of which approximately 38% ($42,000) is circulated as Universal Social Security and the remaining 62% backs the income security of the commonwealth into perpetuity.

Sounds absurdly simple. There's got to be a catch. Maybe there is. However, over the past 12 years on Reddit, nobody has pointed one out yet. Nobody.

So maybe here's your shot at the big time, if you can be first to explain how this math is impossible, even though there it is, in black and white.

A 21st century universal Social Security Trust Fund model simply puts the same mechanism we've always used for the benefit of a few to work for the benefit of all. Now, the doing, obviously, is already 50 years behind and nobody is pretending that the doing is easy. Quite the opposite, as made clear by the testimony of our own lives.

It's no coincidence that these completely independent calculations again land neatly and precisely within a modest margin of error with the *Value of Life* figures, we'll see in a moment. That's how math and science work. Independent observations, measurements, and calculations that deliver reproducible results make up the process that confirms and validates scientific facts. That $11 million *intrinsic human economic value* is an empirical, mathematical fact. We're doin' it right.

This answers the $9.2[cccix] to $9.3[cccx] trillion-dollar *Where Does The Money Come From* question, because that's the arithmetic of 50% per capita GDP, $41,199 per year per person (Wolfram|Alpha, 2023 USD) circulated among 222,000 to 225,000 qualified U.S. citizens above the age of 25 (U.S. Census Bureau).

Some are thinking, "But that's not *technically* universal or unconditional." Nope, it's not, because perfection is unachievable and every soluble engineering problem begins with acknowledgement of design constraints. You're right that we have an obligation to clearly define those constraints and we tend to that responsibility in the section *How Can Income Security Be a Human Right?*

Some are thinking, "That's an absolutely crazy, insane, unthinkable number. I don't care if the math is correct, that's impossible. It's not just ridiculous, it's delusional, detached from reality, this guy is a complete clown, and this book is garbage."

It's okay. That's what they told me about fiber optic Ethernet To The Home, and a dozen technologies since, so I've heard those kinds of accusations all my life, and every time, now nearing my 64th trip around the sun, the work has come to fruition. I'll stand on my track record in deference to emotional reactions and opinions this time, thanks.

$9.2 to $9.3 trillion is 26.94% to 27.24% of the current U.S. debt. Debt hawks are having a heart attack right about now and that's a good thing for everyone. Sometimes, the body has to make us stop in order to find our bearings again. Here's what will make the hawks as peaceful as doves: these figures are for comparison, only. Remember: our model involves ZERO debt spending, as defined above. We're finally going to operate on the surpluses you've always demanded in the Post-Automation Era.

Blink as many times as needed. It's not science fiction or fantasy, it's our current technological capability. That $9.2 to $9.3 trillion is less than 40% of a reorganized and revitalized Universal Social Security Trust Fund balance sheet backed by $3.6 to $3.7 quadrillion USD. To put that in perspective, the diameter of the Milky Way is about 950,000 quadrillion kilometers, or 590,302.45 quadrillion miles.

So, 3.4[cccxi] to 3.7[cccxii] is a pretty tiny number compared to 590,000 to 950,000.

Remember the first principle of economics? Compared to what? It's only our *beliefs* that block us from or enable us to achieve entirely feasible accomplishments. Numbers exist to serve humanity, not the other way around. We decide what numbers mean and how they can best be used to amplify the flourishing of the species.

20th century math was appropriate to the 20th century. We're in a whole new millennium in 2024 and we have the choice to stay shackled to the previous millennium's way of thinking and operating or opening our minds and hearts to and infinite (now *that's* a big number) loving cosmos that wants the blessings of superabundance to care for all human beings. I think we can manage 3.6 or 3.7 in the scope of infinity, don't you?

Such astronomical numbers might seem ridiculous to people who live in the everyday world of average incomes; however, these are the kinds of numbers that nations deal with all day, every day. Is 25-30% of any budget significant? Obviously. Also, that 25% to 30% proportion is 100% in line with more than seven decades of U.S. domestic income security investment, as depicted in Figure 10, U.S. Budget FY2023, Category as Percent of GDP.

These numbers aren't out of left field, they're directly over the plate in the strike zone and anyone who fails to even swing at such a perfect pitch, failing even a base hit, is not going to make the cut in the Post-Automation Era league.

25-30% of any budget is a fair measure of the value of the principle of *income security* as a priority, from household to commonwealth; a percentage further reduced with complete elimination of wasteful legacy welfare spending.

Adding commas and zeros don't change the principles of everyday household budgeting on a commonwealth scale.

There are many other rigorous cross-checks and balances to these figures, which we detail later when we go deeper into the numbers.

The illustrative principle here is that by circulating guaranteed annual income *at levels that sustain life in decent circumstances* by this method, "the Social Security Trust Fund *increases in value* by 62%, by employing a modest and stoically self-disciplined trust circulation rate of 38% real earned interest.

That's called cutting the Gordian knot. That's called upgrading to a just Social Security Trust Fund for the 21st century. As mind blowing as it appears, these calculations are not even mathematics, they are arithmetic. Please feel free to bring your slide rules and protractors and do your best to prove where the calculations are mistaken because – in the Post-Automation Era *Race to Get it Right*[cccxiii] rather than the 20th century race to win or conquer or prove we're somehow better – when the mission seems impossible, we need as many intellectually honest minds on the mission as possible.

* * *

A Mathematical and Human Nightmare

We need to address one more method by which society already puts an incomprehensibly cynical, unthinkable, and all too real price tag on human life, and we are going to do so in collaboration with one of our new AI research assistants. We encourage readers to conduct similar exercises with both traditional and modern research tools and methods uniquely available to you, again as a cross-check and balance to anything you read in this book. "We are inquiring together."[cccxiv]

I posed the following to Google Bard:

> *This is a difficult question to even ask, but it seems to me that if we avoid the difficult questions, we can never solve the difficult problems. What do you consider the underlying causes and estimated costs to the United States and global economies of the tragic reality of human trafficking and the selling of babies on black-market*[cccxv] *adoption markets and otherwise?*[cccxvi]

Here's the response, with extensive source citations and data references:

> *You're absolutely right. Tackling complex issues requires confronting their dark underbelly, and human trafficking and the sale of babies are undeniably among the most heinous crimes imaginable. Understanding the root causes and economic impacts is crucial to dismantling these exploitative systems.*
>
> <u>*Underlying Causes*</u>
>
> ***Poverty and desperation****: Traffickers exploit vulnerable individuals facing economic hardship, lack of opportunities, and limited access to education and healthcare. This makes people susceptible to coercion, false promises, and debt bondage.*
>
> ***Gender inequality and discrimination****: Women and girls are disproportionately targeted due to entrenched gender norms and discriminatory practices that limit their agency and access to resources.*
>
> ***Weak legal frameworks and corruption****: Inadequate laws, enforcement gaps, and corrupt officials facilitate trafficking networks to operate with impunity.*
>
> ***Demand for cheap labor and exploitation****: Industries like forced labor, sex trafficking, and organ harvesting fuel the demand for trafficked individuals, fueling the market.*

Cultural practices and traditions: *Harmful traditional practices like child marriage, son preference, and belief in "lucky children" can lead to the sale and exploitation of children.*

Costs to the United States and Global Economies

Human cost: The loss of life, physical and emotional harm, and stolen childhoods are incalculable. Survivors face lifelong trauma, health complications, and social stigma.

Economic loss: *Trafficking generates illicit profits for traffickers but drains economies through lost productivity, healthcare costs, and social services. Estimates suggest forced labor alone generates $150 billion annually.*

Security and stability: *Trafficking networks undermine social order and fuel organized crime, impacting national security and regional stability.*

Reputation and ethical implications: *Involvement in trafficking tarnishes a nation's image and erodes its moral standing on the global stage.*

Public ambivalence, neighbors in some of the ritziest neighborhoods on Earth turning a blind eye because it's so revolting to even contemplate, only serves to markedly deepen those dire implications.

Estimates

- *The UN estimates that 40.3 million people are trapped in modern slavery, generating $150 billion annually.*
- *The US Department of State estimates that 100,000 to 300,000 children are trafficked annually.*
- *The International Labor Organization estimates that 24.9 million people are in forced labor, generating $150 billion in profit annually.*

Solutions

- *Strengthening legal frameworks and law enforcement to combat trafficking and corruption.*
- *Investing in social safety nets and education to empower vulnerable communities.*

- *Promoting gender equality and tackling harmful traditional practices.*
- *Raising awareness and public engagement to combat demand for trafficked individuals.*
- *Supporting survivors through rehabilitation and reintegration programs.*

Eradicating human trafficking and the sale of babies demands global cooperation, unwavering commitment, and a multifaceted approach. While the task is daunting, the human cost and economic burden necessitate a relentless pursuit of justice and protection for the most vulnerable among us.

Remember, silence fuels the darkness. By acknowledging the problem, raising awareness, and advocating for solutions, we can illuminate the path towards a more just and equitable world for all.

This is arguably the most unconscionable of the already deplorable ***consequences and costs of not affording unconditional income security*** for any population; particularly when empirically within our means to do so.

When people say, "we can't afford to end poverty like that! You can't just give people money! Where does all that money come from?!" most likely don't know even know the first definition of the word, *afford*, and many certainly don't understand the other two questions.

Some are sincerely ignorant. They don't know that we create money 'out of thin air' – a feature, not a bug – and therefore that we can change the means, purposes, and rules of currency circulation any time we like.

People don't know that, as *MacroMania* blogger and former Vice President in the Research Division, now Emeritus of the Federal Reserve Bank of St. Louis, David Andolfatto wrote in 2011:

> *"condemnations of the Fed based on charges of creating money 'out of thin air' are off the mark," because even, "[t]he 'gold standard' is nothing more than a promise made 'out of thin air' by the government," and even "the Constitution is also a document that has been fabricated 'out of thin air.' So, please, enough of this "out of thin air!" stuff. It's tiresome for those who know better, and distracting for those who do not. Let's divert attention to more substantive issues."*[cccxvii]

Let's indeed divert attention to more substantive issues, such as upgrading this miraculous network of faith and promises between one another to finally achieve one of humankind's greatest achievements, to date. Greater than landing on the moon. Greater than the internet. Greater than even seeming almighty AI.

> *It is not impossible. Paraphrasing King, it is now incontestable and imminently practical to end poverty directly with a "guaranteed annual income that sustains life in decent circumstances" by the end of this decade, by upgrading the existing Social Security Trust Fund.*[cccxviii]

Across the political and evolutionary belief spectrum, from the Darwinian dog-eat-dog, to Utopian peacenik, and anyone in between or beyond, these are simple, brutal, cold, hard facts of reality. Facts of nature, the universe, and everything, whatever our combative tribal markings and colors.

There's no crime in people being ignorant of such facts; however, ignorance seems to motivate a great deal of crime when coddled and indulged by vicious and malicious people. Predictably, given enough time, matters of the human heart and soul eventually reveal themselves as the motivations behind every earthly appearance. This basic fact of life applies to the needless persistence of poverty as we've known it and the punitive attitudes and actions toward anyone who dares to question deprecated 20th century default consensus narratives.

"The Fed does not print money to buy assets because it does not have to. It can create money with a mere keystroke."[cccxix] It's not a conspiracy, it's *How the World Really Works*,[cccxx] and we can use this knowledge and understanding to advantage everyone at the expense or detriment of no one. The 20th century era of zero-sum thinking is already a quarter of a century in the rearview mirror and we're already a quarter of a century into the Post-Automation Era.

The primary definition of *afford* is: "to be able to do, manage, or bear without serious consequence or adverse effect."[cccxxi]

So, *by definition*, not only can we, but *we must afford to end poverty* as we've known it with universal Social Security because, *we cannot afford not to do so*; and to do so decisively by the end of the decade, or risk "bearing serious consequences and adverse effects" of our inaction at the very moment the next deeper crisis occurs.

How is it that were so quick to react to COVID and so callous to respond to these everyday empirical facts of poverty and human exploitation? It makes no sense. What COVID proved is our ability to act with immediacy and determinacy, when the crisis matters enough. So, dear readers, when will all lives matter enough to end the pointless brutality of poverty itself, along with all its toxic downstream costs and consequences?

> *"It may well be that we will have to repent in this generation. Not merely for the vitriolic words and the violent actions of the bad people, but for the appalling silence and indifference of the good people who sit around and say, "Wait on time."*[cccxxii]

3, 2, 1, Unconditional Basic Income

Keeping it simple, there are three 20th century conditions on Social Security.

1. Age.
2. Payments out indexed to payments in.
3. Strict limits on work or additional income.

That's a tri-conditional basic income, three conditions.

What happens as we decommission those in reverse order?

3. Remove the work requirement, two conditions to go.
2. Grow the trust fund from assets instead of transfer-payments. Two conditions down, one to go.
1. Reduce and remove the age condition.

That's the simple-to-chart, arduous-to-traverse roadmap to universal and unconditional income security. 3, 2, 1, unconditional basic income.

It Just Works

The U.S. Social Security infrastructure is already in place, and it works great. From biological metaphors to plumbing analogies or software similes, Social Security simply works.

In the language of Rust and Python plumbers, we need to issue a series of staged software upgrades to bring Social Security up to date. The two-step for this patch is 1.) remove the most onerous anti-work conditions on receiving Social Security for those already qualified, and 2.) incrementally lower the qualifying age until we cover every qualifying citizen. Yes, yes, details shortly. Pseudocode first. Programming second.

For our construction managers, sketches first, blueprints second. Cursing architects in the field is at least third. Then, of course, maintenance is forever.

Remember the plumbing analogy? "We only need to upgrade two pumps. The trust fund revenue generation pump and the monthly circulation pump." So, the plumbing two-step is 1.) replace intergenerational transfers with the more reliable and sustainable cash pump described earlier, and 2.) replace the current age-throttled circulation pump with a higher capacity pump. Yes, yes, details shortly. Stub-out first, curse the interior designers' fickle demands for infinite free change-orders, later.

Let's consider a few more details. For a better sense of the scope of savings and operational efficiencies realized by implementing basic income through existing Social Security infrastructure, the legal website Nolo.com describes some of the *costly complexities of conditionalities* placed upon our current elder basic income program:

> *Until you reach full retirement age, Social Security will subtract money from your retirement check if you exceed a certain amount of earned income for the year. For the year 2018, this limit on earned income is $17,040 ($1,420 per month). The amount goes up each year. If you are collecting Social Security retirement benefits before full retirement age, your benefits are reduced by $1 for every $2 you earn over the limit. Once you reach full retirement age, there is no limit on the amount of money you may earn and still receive your full Social Security retirement benefit.*
>
> *Example: Henry is considering claiming early retirement benefits this year, at age 64. Social Security calculates that if he does so, he'll receive $866 a month (which is about 13% less than if he waited until his full retirement age of 66). But Henry also intends to continue working part-time, with an income that will be about $5,000 over the yearly limit on earned income.*
>
> *If he does claim the early benefits and makes that part-time income each month, Henry would lose one dollar out of two from the $5,000 he earns over the limit, which means $2,500 for the year. So, by claiming early retirement and continuing to earn over the limit, Henry incurs a double penalty: His retirement benefits are permanently reduced by 13%, and he loses an additional amount every month (until he reaches full retirement age) to the extent he earns over the income limit.*
>
> *Social Security does not reduce each monthly check by a small amount, unfortunately. Instead, the agency may withhold several months' entire checks until the reduction is paid off. (The way Social Security reduces your benefits is actually very complicated. For the details, read Social Security's pamphlet on "How Work Affects Your Benefits." You can also use [the] Social Security earnings test calculator to see how much your reduction will be and when Social Security will withhold your benefits.)*
>
> *Note that if you are working and you lose your job, you may collect unemployment benefits (assuming you otherwise qualify for them) even though you are also collecting your Social Security retirement benefits (Laurence).*

Remember the earlier observation about a billion tiny intentional inconveniences, designed to wear us down and persuade us to give up? Punitive restrictions on Social Security's 20th century conditional basic income were what defined a legacy love-hate relationship with the SSA.

A new cohort of Americans who have already provided a lifetime of service, enter this gauntlet every single year, as they approach the so-called Golden Years, when people can finally look forward to participating in, and contributing to community as an expression of gratitude and meaning, more so than for the chase of things that they now know (for the most part, hopefully) they can't take with them.

Ironically, just at this time in life, the absurd conditions attached to staying active in the labor force often present an insurmountable obstacle to ongoing community participation for seniors. For many, though certainly not all Security recipients in this situation, as social participation declines, happiness declines, quality of life declines, and health declines to the point that we face the direst crisis in elder care that the nation and maybe the world has ever seen. Opportunists used this phenomenon as a straw man excuse to raise the social security age instead of lowering it, applying the "jobs define our meaning" slogan with a broad brush to every senior citizen. That's just not true of "every senior citizen," just as any stereotype is not true about any other individual within any class in society. Otherizing "those old people" as if "they are all the same," is as equally ugly to every other othering.

It seems that many people have sadly come to accept epidemic conditions of youth suicide and senior disengagement and depression in the wake of 20th century civilization's hangover. Maybe I'm missing something but seems like if the two joined forces, we'd have something meaningful and achievable to work toward, together.

We know that Social Security's age-conditional basic income greatly enhances the health and longevity of everyday people, and we can improve that by further removing conditionality, by not punishing people for wanting to stay engaged in their communities in the form of jobs.

But what about younger people, as the Social Security qualification age drops to 55, 45, 35? Won't they all stop working as if they won the lotto? We've already addressed this to a significant degree, but let's add multiple additional studies cited by Bourree Lam, writing for The Atlantic magazine, proving that 85% of lotto winners keep working in their jobs. If some feel the need to condescend and stigmatize the other 15%, well, knock yourself out, but that's probably more jealousy than anything else, and possibly, at some subconscious level, a deep embarrassment at realizing we ourselves are really among the 15% of lazy people, so we resort to constantly ripping into everyone else as lazy, because we know that about ourselves. This is known in psychology as projection. Seems there's also lot of that going around in the pro-perpetual-precarity-and-poverty camp.

In contrast to emotional projection, what empirical research finds is that the myth that "people are no damned good and basically lazy," is simply untrue. Lam wrote:

> *Kaplan did a bigger study in 1987 on 576 lottery winners and found that "popular myths and stereotypes about winners were inaccurate"—*

> *by which he meant that American lottery winners did not typically quit their jobs and spend lavishly. That finding has been confirmed in more recent research. A 2004 study found that 85.5 percent of American winners continued to work after winning the lottery (with 63 percent working for the same employer as before), and that the more important work was to a person, the more likely they were to keep working (Lam).*

Perhaps the most straightforward reason that people not only keep working but work even more in the era of universal Social Security is the pervasiveness of consumer culture and plain old greed. Even with a livable basic income indexed to 50% per capita GDP, it will never be enough to satisfy human greed. Nothing ever is.

Getting more is never enough for most people enduring the child-rearing years of life, and for good reasons. We cited earlier that today's generation feels that they need $525,000 a year in order to live the lifestyle that they desire. Vanishingly few can rest on 50% per capita GDP – which can roughly range between $25,000 and $45,000 a year, depending on the health of the economy.

Those figures only sound like "a universal high income"[cccxxiii, cccxxiv] through the lens of *the previous millennium*. We simply don't live there anymore. That's why the context of 2024's Post-Automation Era is so fundamental to making necessary civilizational course corrections.

Sometimes this work wants to explain to great grandma and grandpa that we don't need an outhouse anymore, because we have indoor plumbing. And yet even our own peers keep insisting that we need an outhouse and forbid us from using the indoor plumbing because walking back and forth to the outhouse builds character.

The relentless human drive for *infinite growth and acquisition of more* is precisely what propelled inequality to present extremes, so to contradict decades and centuries of proven human dedication to consumption with the claim that *humans are intrinsically lazy*, further discolored by the misperception that that greed won't continue to motivate human behavior in the presence of ample income security, doesn't pass the smirk test. Add to all this the AI psychological exploitation and manipulation of consumers by social media platforms, and there is no chance that mere Maslow Safety will satisfy people. For better or worse, the evolutionary human lust for more is not going anywhere soon. So, people do keep striving, working more and harder than ever, in the Post-Automation Era.

In fact, the whole point of the Maslow Hierarchy is to precisely illustrate this point. Humans inevitably continue up the needs and wants ladder. We might hit plateaus, rough patches, and spin out on slick spots on the road, but we continue on. So, once again Lazy Entitled Human Theory fails completely.

Even some well-intentioned corporate allies still fail to recognize that the time for trials and testing is well-past, so it is incumbent upon us to share updated information so that all constituencies can update their models, accordingly. Global healthcare company BMJ definitely conveys the right idea, but corporate precautionary principles likely constrain them when they write, "Basic income is a popular idea, but small pilots cannot produce generalisable evidence."

BMJ global health suggests:

> *Studies with very small samples cannot provide the answers to the complex questions we're left with, and statistical estimates obtained from them are not reliable indicators of the intervention's effect.*
>
> *Much larger, more expensive studies of universal or near-universal interventions would be needed to clarify the many remaining unknowns about the effects of a universal basic income. In the meantime, we have strong evidence that work requirements and sanctions are causing direct harm to millions of people. Efforts would be better focused on convincing policy makers that non-punitive social security systems, which allow people to live with dignity, are a prudent investment.* [ccxxv]

As revealed above, the evidence of every nation's pensioner program or equivalent to Social Security already overwhelming proves the point. Every advanced nation has ample proof of large scale *conditional* basic income, bracketed by age. This is why the time for testing is over and the time for implementing his at hand. As hard as it is for the most awkward among us – count me in this group – we gotta learn how to at least do that two-step if we're going to flourish in the Post-Automation Era.

Finally, one last perspective on the Maslow Hierarchy of needs that also fuels the drive to continue working by intrinsic productive human nature. Feel free to turn back to Figure 4 — Maslow's Hierarchy of Needs, for reference, if still getting familiar with this model.

We can refer to the bottom three needs as Deficit Needs, and the top two as Being Needs. The Deficit Needs are those which, when we humans lack them, our lives are in net deficit, constantly in fight or flight. We have little to no chance of continuing to progress until we can find a way out of that persistent deficit state.

Perpetuating a 20th century default consensus narrative that intentionally smashed people down into that state in the name of some sadistic sense of either "putting people in their place," or character building is about the worst idea any person of conscience can possibly imagine for the Post-Automation Era. Of course, on a planet of 8 billion people, there are bound to always be plenty who entirely lack such a conscience; however, thanks in large part to connecting more minds on the internet, most people under the age of 50 now know that we outnumber the psychos and narcissists by orders of magnitude, so we can stop being intimidated into accepting the previous millennium's ruthless social Darwinian default consensus narratives and distorted realities.

Safety is the second of three Deficit Needs, so Income Security in and of itself is still insufficient to allow people to rest in pursuit of Beings Needs. What this implies is that Income Security is essential, necessary, yet still insufficient to ensure equal opportunity for everyone to become fully developed human beings. It's only an essential starting point toward a world that works for everyone. We may yet have eons of work ahead to fully achieve that.

In countless empirical cases, we've shown that in a state of relative economic stability, people continue to be intrinsically motivated both by outward facing greed for more and the inward instinct to become more. The proportion of this mix varies widely throughout any population, but both of these components exist and are what make us human. We can start to make this understanding more accessible by building a UBI LLM as described in the Appendix, *A Curated UBI LLM Training Data* Set.

Income Security isn't a magic elixir to end all of society's ills, but we have shown that it is an empirical prerequisite to the cultivation of human beings who are capable of making better choices; and humans capable of making better choices lead to better lives, and better human lives lead to better human societies. For both the community-minded and the rugged individualist alike, the guidelines, incentives, methods, processes, and systems that cultivate maximum human flourishing in an atmosphere of maximum human freedom can hardly be more libertarian, objectivist, decentralized, and democratic than by way of the principle of *universal income security*.

Finally, if behavioral economics, machine learning sales pipelines, and the explosive growth of gamer culture have made anything clear, it's that people are, by and large, scorekeepers. That's perhaps the most compelling reason – as we've seen in every empirical case we've referenced and cited in extensive endnotes and bibliographic references – people work even harder, longer hours in an environment of stable income security. We do so to achieve game high and personal-best scores only achievable by earning far beyond a trifling universal Social Security indexed to 50% per capita GDP.

* * *

Money Can't Buy Happiness

Except, up to a point, money does indeed buy happiness, physical safety, and psychological security, and those are significant, empirical points to keep in mind.

Obviously, money doesn't buy happiness directly. It buys happiness because it deepens our sense of well-being, which instills happiness, which motivates healthier choices and healthier behavior. Money buys happiness because we can surround ourselves with objects of beauty, and that too evokes happiness. Money buys happiness because we can travel, experience more of the world, and through both novelty and learning, generate and propagate more happiness in the world.

Unfortunately, shaming poor people for lack of character, and then scolding them that "money can't buy happiness; therefore, you shouldn't worry that you have no money" was as widespread a practice in the 20th century as climate change denial, and just as plainly wrong. Up to a point, money does make all the difference between whether people can feel even the faintest sense of happiness enshrined in our most basic inalienable right to Maslow Safety.

Income security is a basic human need and indispensable prerequisite to the lived experience of the rights to life, liberty, and the pursuit of happiness. Engineered lack of income security divests people of those most fundamental and inalienable of U.S. Constitutional rights.

If we scold poor people that money can't buy happiness, then cry that higher tax rates on the most blessed among us harm our happiness, one or the other of our arguments must go. We can't have it both ways. Claiming that money can't improve other people's happiness, but letting go of some of our money does affect happiness? That's pure contradiction. We don't get to have our cake and eat it too.

There are absolute, empirical levels of income, below which, people feel significantly greater economic anxiety and far less happiness. There are also absolute, empirical levels of income above which people no longer realize meaningful gains in happiness. Like all conditions and life, these figures change over time, and the disparity in both raw numbers and behavioral economic expectations is nothing short of breathtaking over the past several decades.

> *According to the researchers behind the original [2010] Princeton study,[cccxxvi] your emotional well-being – or the pleasure you derive from day-to-day experiences – doesn't get any better after your household is earning roughly $75,000. That said, a term they call "life evaluation" – or how you feel about your life and accomplishments – can continue to rise with higher income and education levels.[cccxxvii]*

In a 2016 update to that study, "Doug Short, vice president of research at investment group Advisor Perspectives found that if you live in a place like Hawaii, where the cost of living is relatively high, a household needs to make $122,175 per year before some extra cash doesn't really translate into more happiness. In Mississippi, by comparison, the threshold at which more money stops making you happier is a lot lower: $65,850 per year" (cccxxvii).

In the updated analysis, Short also reported:

> *Kahneman and Deaton distinguish between two concepts of happiness.*
>
> - ***Emotional Well-Being**: the day-to-day experiences that make life pleasant or unpleasant.*
> - ***Evaluation of Life**: one's overall life satisfaction.*
>
> *The $75K number is the benchmark for the first of the two. As Deaton explained, "Giving people more income beyond $75K is not going to do much for their daily mood ... but **it is going to make them feel they have a better life.**"*
>
> *Incidentally, according to the Census Bureau, the mean (average) household income in 2009 was $67,976. That's 9.4% below the happiness threshold. The median (middle) household income was a much smaller $49,777. That's 33.6% shy of the magic number.*[cccxxviii]

Earlier we learned that a 2023 survey revealed the fact that, "Millennials say they need $525,000 a year to be happy." And as reported by Business Insider, "A Nobel prize winner's research shows they're not wrong."[cccxxix]

So, the current 2024 generation targets *income about seven times the 2010 numb*er that far too many expert talking heads continue to throw around in public discourse because "it was Kahneman and Deaton's massive n=450,000 value, so you can't argue with that!"

The prevalence and unmerited valence of such deprecated default consensus narratives like this in public discourse illustrate why we are so reluctantly compelled to repeatedly establish the preposterously obvious fact that we don't live in 2010 anymore, yet tens of millions of mental maps and world models haven't updated in at least that long, many for much longer.

Welcome to the Post-Automation Era.

We'll also reiterate the point that nobody lives large, like some mythical Welfare Kings and Queens of yore, on a meager 50% per capita GDP steady income. Fighting to reduce that percentage even further makes no sense, comes across as tight-fisted at best, in a world of such super abundance, and mean-spirited at worst. After decades of this work, if I know anything for certain, it's that not a single intellectually honest soul who's championed UBI for any significant period of time can possibly be intentionally uncaring.

Reducing 50% per capita GDP makes basic income sub-livable, defeating the whole point, by the exact same method that zapped FAP in the early 1970s. Certainly no authentic and serious UBI advocate would ever want to see a replay of that catastrophic setback.

Now more than ever, we need to keep our eyes on the prize as Martin defined it: "A guaranteed annual income at levels that sustain life in decent circumstances."

Less than 50% per capita GDP is not only unwarranted and unfair in an age of super abundance, and in our asset-defined model, but anything less falls unnecessarily short of King's definition. Disagree with me as an annoying person all you like, however, disagreement with the King may not be such a measured and thoughtful position.

I'm doing this work from an incredibly lucky, blessed, and privileged position that won't be much affected, either way. Therefore, the reason I'm faithfully compelled to stand steadfastly upon 50% per capita GDP is to do right by The Dream, The People, and The Beloved Community.

* * *

Human Rights Mean Human Responsibilities

> ***"We hold these truths to be self-evident, that all men are created equal, that they are endowed by their Creator with certain unalienable Rights, that among these are Life, Liberty, and the pursuit of Happiness."***[cccxxx]

Often and easily overlooked, the operative words in that historical statement are not what they seem.

The operative words are not "life, liberty, and the pursuit of happiness." Those are three predicates of the subject, Rights. The operative words in the U.S. Declaration of Independence define the larger set of unalienable Rights within which those minimal three exist; namely, "among them."

"Life, liberty, and the pursuit of happiness" are a subset of "among them." That means all people are "endowed by their Creator" with innumerable unalienable rights, such that were we to list them all, we'd not have space left to pen the declaration. Such was their thrift in the economy of language flowing through the founder's pens.

Even if we take a the view that the more aggressive, psychopathic, and narcissistic, and racist personalities among the founders prevailed in omitted key unalienable rights in the contentious process of drafting the founding documents of the United States of America, such omission did not erase those rights from creation's providence, it only temporarily obscured testimony of their eternal veracity from uncareful readers, while preserving those inestimable rights for careful readers to appreciate, comprehend, and claim for all ages in the neatly compressed form, "among them."

In April 2020, Creative Strategy and Marketing author Nathan Liao summarized this point far better than I can, writing on Medium:

> *What is less known about Thomas Jefferson was his proposal to give 50 acres of public land to any propertyless individual willing to farm it. His contemporary, Thomas Paine, whose works were instrumental to the American Revolution, advocated for creating a "Nation Fund" to pay "every person, rich or poor" over the age of 21 a yearly "groundrent." In his 1795 work, Agrarian Justice, he observed that human inventions and advancements have led to vast improvements in the cultivation of land in agrarian societies. However, as he points out:*
>
> *"It has given to created earth a tenfold value. But the landed monopoly that began with it has produced the greatest evil. It has dispossessed more than half the inhabitants of every nation of their natural inheritance, without providing for them, as ought to have been done, an indemnification for that loss, and has thereby created a species of poverty and wretchedness that did not exist before." — Thomas Paine (Agrarian Justice)*

> *During this tumultuous period where revolutions and the fight for liberty were taking place on both sides of the Atlantic, Paine saw that humans, as inhabitants of the earth, are shareholders of the land in its natural state. However, he defends the right of private cultivation of land and advocates payment for other's "loss of his or her natural inheritance." Are these sentiments not echoed around the current conversation of Universal Basic Income and the "fourth industrial revolution" faced by automation and AI?*[cccxxxi]

Yes, they are Nathan. Couldn't have presented it better. While we have seen tremendous social progress on many fronts, toxic tributaries of distorted philosophy and religion continued to poison much of 20th century default consensus reality, advancing the mistaken view that somehow, "groundrent" flows in reverse, that material destitution is the base case of the natural human condition, and that people in poverty have somehow earned further and continued punishment, or that poverty somehow builds character, or that poverty was ultimately beneficial to human development in some way.

To that view, one of the most proficient and articulate Buddhist scholars of our day, Robert Thurman responded, "that is a mistake."[cccxxxii]

I agree with Thurman that nothing could be further from the objective of the founding principles of the United States of America. Paine believed that we the job creators owe every displaced person a share of the wealth generated from our universally common divine inheritance, the Earth, portions of which we took out of circulation from the lawful commonwealth, in the name of industry. These are the ancient origins of the principle of universality with respect to the right to income security. The equanimity and universality of the gift of nature's creation, without any Man-In-The-Middle (MITM) value arbitrage or skimming (ccxix).[cccxxxiii]

Like the indomitable power of the weak force in physics, these are a few of the subtle and intensely influential ways in which the 20th century default consensus reality illuminated some of humanity's most dreadful mistaken views and maladaptive behaviors, in tandem with, and consequent to the same exponential technological advances capable of liberating every sentient being on Earth.

What could physics possibly have to do with the human right to income security? Hold on to your jet pack, and buckle your flying car seat belt, we're about to find out.[cccxxxiv]

On March 14, 2003, the Organisation Européen pour la Recherche Nucléaire (CERN) Large Hadron Collider (LHC) confirmed the existence of the Higgs Boson at approximately the 125GeV energy level.[cccxxxv]

With that single, pivotal scientific observation, the most recent 500-year long chapter of an eons-long human quest for rational knowledge about the nature of creation came to a dramatic, and potentially absolute close.[cccxxxvi] Only time will tell.

When we listen directly to scientists, it doesn't take long to realize that the greatest motivation to work so hard, for so long, against such odds is an intellectual curiosity and drive for solving life's biggest mysteries; a passion for problem solving that ultimately extends to confronting the world's most insidious and dreadful challenges.

The quest for understanding how the universe works and how it came to be is a timeless existential question, fundamental, intrinsic, to being human. These are questions of such transcendent significance as to have motivated some of, if not all of the past 2,500 years of humanity's most rigorous and comprehensive thinkers and doers, be they religious, political, scientific, or humanitarian.

JOB-JOBs had less than nothing to do with most of humanity's most profound and consequential accomplishments. Curiosity captains the ship of human discovery, invention, and productivity. Imagination navigates. Ingenuity is the ship. Mammon, money, is boat insurance. Yes, if you get in a wreck, you need it, but it's still never enough to replace the irreplaceable, and that's the reason the insurance industry is one of the largest aggregators of wealth in our nation. Statistically, very few experience such wrecks, although shipwrecks and their price tags are justifiably scary to look at, which is cynically great for sales. The checkered history of scientific discovery has a lot in common with these analogies.

From our current perspective, in the dawn years of the third millennium, it's deeply grounding and practical to reflect upon the significance that existential questions have played in everyday common lives throughout known human history, to estimate the extent to which the quest for an understanding of the fundamental nature of physical reality animated and organized human behavior, for centuries, millennia.

Plainly, 20th century JOB-JOBs had nothing to do with the origins of the pursuit of knowledge and industry themselves, although we created countless Just Over Broke Justifications Of Being (think unpaid grad student labor) in the name of that pursuit, in part to rationalize and justify investigations that never needed justification in the first place. Innate human curiosity, ingenuity, imagination, creativity, and productivity carried us every step of the way to this present day. It's Molochian banks, nations, armies, economics, or social credit score agencies that enjoyed the 20th century free ride on creation's natural super abundance. Remember that film, *Parasite*?

Jobs don't define our identity or reality. We invented jobs as vehicles to explore, create, and build. Fortunately, despite countless catastrophic mis-steps and mishaps, as a species, we didn't blow ourselves up before getting here, to this third millennium Post-Automation Era. Whether or not we make it much further, of course, depends upon the choices we make amid the current meta crisis.

Again quoting the prolific Scott Santens:

> *"Give a man a fish, he eats for a day. Teach a man to fish, he eats for a lifetime.*
>
> *Build a robot to fish, do all men starve, or do all men eat?"*[cccxxxvii]

---

* * *

A NEW STANDARD MODEL

Never in human history has our miniscule species stood at such an expansive threshold. While we witness the acceleration of machine learning and artificial intelligence problem-solving at hallucinatory speeds,[cccxxxviii] we might like to think that given how far we've come, we will soon inevitably illuminate the unexplored territories of dark matter and dark energy even quicker. Yet, the disquieting evidence of the mathematics of that dark matter is that the distance ahead for physics may be orders of magnitude greater than the distance covered in the past 100 years.

So, we are not only in the midst of a pursuit for a new standard model of physics beyond the 20th century model, but we are also grappling with a new standard model of civilization in the third millennium Post-Automation Era.

As advanced as we believe we have become, we've only begun the journey that lies ahead. More than 95% of whatever the universe is, is still inexplicable to modern physics. That's not a diminution of science at all, quite the contrary. It's the greatest opportunity for discovery in all human history.

We've already crossed the event horizon of the capacity for observation itself and ventured into the very nature of the observer effect, and hence, irrefutable said observer. Pioneers like Donald Hoffman are turning the entire scientific model on its head, or more accurately, leaving a deprecated 20th century default consensus reality in the rearview mirror, by using the scientific method.

> *"Space-time itself is an artifact. So, one reason I'm not a materialist is because our best materialist theories, namely evolution by natural selection, and also Quantum Field Theory (QFT), and Einstein's theory of gravity tell us that space-time has no operational meaning at 10^{-33} centimeters or 10^{-43} seconds. In other words, our scientific theories – the foundation of our materialist ideas – tell us precisely the scope and the limits of materialism. Materialism is fine down to the Planck scale, then it completely falls apart. It's utterly irrelevant. The space-time physicalist kind of materialism falls apart. And it's not because of religious ideas. I'm just listening to the science [and] that science tells us space-time has no meaning beyond the Planck scale. "*[cccxxxix]

By any physicist's calculation, in Hoffman's words, "space-time is doomed," meaning the 20th century default consensus reality of materialism completely falls apart; and it falls apart surprisingly quickly. In another YouTube conversation, Hoffman further explained:

> *"It's really time for the cognitive neuroscientists who are studying consciousness to catch up with what the physicists have already said space-time had a good run. It was a really wonderful framework, and it's over. And by the way, reductionism and space-time have been spectacularly successful assumptions of science for centuries. Absolutely spectacular. Hats off, those were wonderful assumptions, and science really needed those assumptions.*
>
> *But it's the glory of science not to get stuck in its [own] current theories. It's the glory of science to have theories that tell you where they stop. That's how you avoid dogmatism. And when evolution and natural selection say [the] probability is zero that space-time is fundamental, and then physicists independently say our theory of gravity tells us that space-time cannot be fundamental, we have our two pillars of modern science saying the same thing.*
>
> *Space-time has had a good run, but it's over. So the methodology of methodological reductionism – which is the idea that as we go to smaller and smaller scales in space we find more and more fundamental laws – that kind of going to a reductionist smaller scale [and finding] deeper laws, has worked spectacularly in science, but we now know that there is a hard limit to how small you can go with that approach. It's [precisely]* 10^{-33} *centimeters and in some sense that's not very small.*
>
> *If someone said it's* $10^{-20\ \text{trillion}}$ *centimeters, I would go, 'Oh, who cares?* $10^{-20\ \text{trillion}}$ *... that's tons of zeros.' But this is only 33 ...* 10^{-33} *[and] the space-time story stops. It's not like there's pixels of space-time at* 10^{-33} *centimeters, it's that space-time doesn't make sense [at that scale]. We need a different framework, and in fact, as you try to probe space time at higher [and] higher energies, smaller [and] smaller scales, you start actually engaging bigger and bigger volumes of space, not smaller. So gravity destroys reductionism. Reductionism worked for a little bit, but it's deeply, deeply false.".*[cccxl]

What does this mean? By Occam's Razor, it means that everything in our lived experience emerges from consciousness, not the other way around. Physics and biology did not give rise to consciousness. Consciousness is continuously giving rise to physics and biology. If you're interested in this avenue of scientific inquiry, you're highly encouraged to follow the endnotes.[cccxli]

Welcome to the Post-Automation Era. But if you're still not convinced of where we're standing upon the Long Arc of History, consider the fact that, with the completion of the standard model in 2012, the scientific line of inquiry formerly known as *woo* is pretty much the only science left staring us in the face.

It's like humanity and the observer effect in a staring contest. What is the nature of this observer, this *that* which observes?

Physics looks for ways to explain precisely how, in mechanistic terms, physical existence works, while philosophy and ethics generally ring in with the ontological machinations of those mechanics. Whether deduced, inducted, intuited, ascribed, ascertained, or a little of each, our very search for ultimate understanding of the universe is derivative from the inherent nature of the most fundamental human right of all, the right to exist and ponder these questions in the first place. Yes, once born into this world, human existence is both a right and a privilege, for the brief moment that we're here. That right and privilege is fundamental to the nature of the "unalienable right" declared at the moment of independence. It's both, and.

So, we can acknowledge the fact that we exist, move amongst, around, and between both the empirical and the inexplicable all day, every day; so, spending time arguing over which approach is "more right" – science, ethics, psychology, or spirituality – in deriving a basis for fundamental human rights, appears fruitless. What's fruitful is contemplating how these all work together, and how we can best take advantage of our limited, yet always growing understanding, to reduce suffering in the world. One day at a time, inching a little closer toward a world that works for everyone.

So, it appears that actualizing the human right to income security is more a question of clarifying 21st century priorities than of seeking permission or affirmation from deprecated 20th century certainties. Certainties that suddenly aren't so certain, after all.

We've built all the sci-fi gadgets, so may we please fulfill the vow of labor-saving liberty as promised since long before the advent of the washing machine, let alone today's increasingly ubiquitous vacuum and floor mopping robots?

Today, the realm of human rights and public policy could sorely use the cognitive horsepower that has up until now worked to accomplish that great feat known as the Standard Model. We need more rigorous scientific thinking and engineering rigor in the realm of public policy work. Such is the work of upgrading Social Security for the 21st century. We need scientists and engineers who may have given up on the prospect of sensible civics to give the 21st century a chance. Maybe the 20th century was a catastrophe. Yet maybe we can still do some small part to be slightly better ancestors than were our ancestors.

Prior to completion of the Standard Model, many scientists and engineers already empathized with humanitarian colleagues such as Nikola Tesla, Robert Buckminster Fuller, Albert Einstein, Jonas Salk, and Carl Sagan, each unapologetic humanitarians, without diverting any attention away from the theoretical mathematics and demanding, exacting experimentation required in their work.

In 2024, and for the duration of this twenty-first century, we have a rare opportunity for theorists and experimentalist to take a bit of a working sabbatical to contribute to the current task of completing a Standard Model of Human Rights, within the field of everyday human affairs.

We don't have to pass along the struggle for enough food, shelter, healthcare, income security, and safety to the next generations. Given the emergence of AI, now more than ever a Standard Model of Human Rights is prerequisite for the emancipation of more minds to engage in the education and self-actualization needed to run the next legs of the long relay toward fuller understanding of nature and of the predicament we find ourselves in, here on this tiny pale blue dot.[cccxlii]

We might not ultimately be able to control AI, but we can choose how we treat one another in this Post-Automation Era by deciding that the human right to income security is greater than robot rights to infinite wealth and power, especially at the expense of the human right to "a guaranteed income at levels that sustain life in decent circumstances" (MLK).

If this sounds like another stretch or utopian trifle, we already have something akin to a Standard Model of Human Rights. It's called the Universal Declaration of Human Rights. For physicists who have spent a lifetime filling in gaps in the Standard Model, the implementation of the UDHR today is as full of gaps as its physics counterpart ever was, fifty years ago.

Perhaps this work is what's next for many physicists who are ready to go beyond the intellectual satisfaction of understanding how things work to the existential satisfaction of creating a world that works for everyone.

In an interview with Abby Martin about his 2018 book, *The New Human Rights Movement: Reinventing the Economy to End Oppression*, Peter Joseph said that across history:

> *99% of human society existed without money or markets. This isn't some inevitability, the way we [currently] live. What is the silver bullet that can possibly change this negative trajectory that we're on? That is structural change of the economy. Morality is not going to do it. Our free will is not going to do it. Our rational sense is not going to do it in and of itself because we are so inhibited and dominated by the structural psychology generated from our social system.*
>
> *ABBY MARTIN: And reforms aren't going to do it, either, because twenty-first century activism has been far too localized."*
>
> *PETER JOSEPH: If we don't focus on the root, and we keep sparsely drawing attention to this or that protest, or this or that activist initiative, to certain pockets of problems, [we] just end up running in place. The activist initiatives that are required now have to grasp that, and realize that now, it's time for galvanization towards removing the foundation of our social system, and that's the market. We have to start to move away from market economics as rapidly as we possibly can to save our ecology and to save the stability of our society in terms of group relationships. The antagonism that's created with our class system builds into all the other antagonisms we see, whether it's gender, whether it's race, whether it's nationalistic. It's like that central kernel that keeps amplifying the worst of our group, or our anti-group associations.*

I don't quite agree with Joseph that we need to immediately move away from all vestiges of markets. It seems to me that trade and commerce has served humanity well, overall, in spite of the externalities and unintended consequences that our work addresses. Whether or not Joseph is right, however, a livable, universal, unconditional basic income opens new possibilities to Americans at a time when so many of us find ourselves in situations of rapidly dwindling options; something that happens to us all at some point in life, usually more than once. So, it is the definition of enlightened self-interest to take interest in, and action toward, ensuring the universal health, safety, and economic welfare of the commonwealth.

There's one more aspect of the Post-Automation Era that is important to mention as we contemplate the urgency of new models. In addition to AI disrupting all notions of value, the New Space Race many soon obliterate the rest of the 20th Century Standard Model of Economics that is already falling apart at the seams just as rapidly as the materialist world view has faded into history. Here's how.

As the essentially infinite supply of raw mineral materials available in the final frontier becomes increasingly accessible to Earth, experts have warned for years that the mineral value of just one asteroid would be large enough to damage or destroy commodity prices in individual nations and possibly cause the world's economy to collapse. Why? Because people did not design 20th century default consensus reality for today's post-automation, post-scarcity world. This is not science fiction. I've included hundreds of endnotes and references, the product of more than ten years of research, all for you to search for yourself and reach your own conclusions.[cccxliii, cccxliv]

All of the greatest accomplishments of generations of hard work, faith, industry, science, and physics have led us to this inflection point on the Long Arc of History, an inflection point marking the end of both physics and economics as we've known them for hundreds of years.

Like the disappearance of the meaning of space-time at the Planck, so too does Schumpeterianism's creative destruction break down and become meaningless in the Post-Automation Era. Like the materialist view of standard physics, it had a great run, was essential for its time; and like the materialist world view, it's over.

The inflection points and infinite S-curves of the Infinite Game may go on, but what lies beyond those inflection points is like nothing ever before imagined. That's why humanity is anything but obsolete in the Post-Automation Era because it's our human imaginations that make the Infinite Game infinitely rewarding. It's not a game we play to win, it's a game we play to keep making the game fairer, more just, more equitable, more sustainable, happier, healthier, filled with more gratitude, light, and love.

It's breathtaking. It's awe inspiring. If and only if we take care of ourselves and one another in ways that make sense for, and are aligned with, the era in which we live.

Another example of a previously unimaginable disruption to our understandings of what economic value and currency even mean is blockchain technology. Again, not science fiction, decade-old news, at least. Manna is a blockchain currency specifically created to circulate liquidity in a more sensible and sustainable manner, and should Manna's valuation become meaningful, it could indeed play a non-trivial role in ending global poverty, as well.[cccxlv]

Far more ambitious are initiatives such as the distributed ledger called Mattereum, self-described as, "the legal-technical interface connecting digital assets on the blockchain with goods and services in the material world."[cccxlvi] An interface like Mattereum could, in practice, claim all outer space as public property for the benefit of all humanity in the fine print of its Terms and Conditions. This might sound outrageous, but there is absolutely nothing preventing it. Can anyone "own" outer space? The question doesn't matter, so long as space entrepreneurs agree with and subscribe to the accounting methods and terms of service offered. When selecting Mattereum as their distributed ledger of all the physical assets deployed and managed in extraterrestrial operations, the interface can grow, and with it, an essentially infinite asset base from which humanity could easily allocate a modest, living-wage level, basic income dividend, indexed to 50% per capita GDP here on Earth.

As already presented, our model doesn't require waiting for any that, but this is one example of promising backup and failover mechanisms that make our model all the more credible and sensible. Maybe the Post-Automation Era is not just an age of post-scarcity superabundance, maybe it's an age of healthy economic and ecological circulatory systems, on Earth as it is in Heaven, literally, for a multi-planetary species.

Considering these fundamental disruptions: the end of the Standard Model of physics, the AI automation of just about everything, the essentially infinite supply of raw materials from space, coupled with asymptotic levels of efficiency through advances in machine learning and artificial intelligence, the fundamental challenge to humanity is no longer about value creation, acquisition, or aggregation, but healthy and sustainable value and currency circulation. Income security as a fundamental human right in the Post-Automation Era.

Just as quantum theory disrupted Newtonian physics, without negating it, so too have the accomplishments of today's super abundant access to extraterrestrial raw materials, robot labor, and machine intelligence completely disrupted the 20th century default consensus reality and narratives. Like the materialist world view, it's meaningless.

That's why we've set a new course toward a world that works for everyone.

The Post-Automation Era represents an inflection point in the history of human capabilities and priorities; an inflection point that signals sociological, economic, political, and technological changes as unimaginable and unattainable yesterday as they are inevitable, unavoidable, and essential today.

---

* * *

Simple Math ≠ Easy Implementation

Simple solutions don't mean easy implementation, although it seems surprisingly easy for some people to fall into the trap of conflating those terms when considering the straightforwardness of universal Social Security as the most direct way to end poverty as we've known it. In her article, "Why universal basic income costs far less than you think," University of Oxford Leverhulme Early Career Fellow, Elizaveta Fouksman wrote:

> *To calculate the cost, most people just multiply the size of the monthly income (say, $1,000) by the population (it's universal, after all) and – voilà – a number that seems impossibly expensive.*
>
> *Any UBI estimate that just multiplies the size of the UBI by the population is a red flag that the cost has been over-inflated. A true cost estimate will always discuss who the net beneficiaries will be, who the net contributors will be, and the rate at which we gradually switch people over from being beneficiaries to being contributors as they get richer.*
>
> *Here's a simple example: imagine a room with 15 people who want to set up a UBI for the room of $2 per person. The upfront cost of the policy would be $30. The ten richest people in the room are asked to contribute $3 each towards funding it. After they each put in $3, raising the total $30 needed, every person in the room gets their $2 universal basic income. But because the ten richest people in the room contributed $3, and then got $2 back as the UBI, their real, net contribution is in fact $1 each. So, the real cost of the UBI is $10.*
>
> *This also resolves UBI's "billionaire's dilemma" – why give someone like Bill Gates a basic income? The answer is that Gates would simply return that UBI through his taxes – and help pay for others. But if Gates becomes suddenly destitute, the UBI will still be showing up for him to use every month. And since his tax bill will drop, he'll become a net beneficiary rather than contributor.*

In addition to logical errors about actual cash flows, many people do not consider the enormous administrative cost savings realized by ending most of the current wasteful bureaucracy. A June 2018 interview with U.K. global innovation foundation, Nesta, Vinay Gupta explained:

> *We're paying a stupendous amount of money for means testing so we can try and kick people off benefits. This is the kind of thinking that comes when you don't really accept that your citizens have rights. We*

> *think of them as entitlements, not rights. In theory, we have a welfare state that's supposed to take care of people. In practice, we've built a bureaucracy that denies people access to services.*
>
> *You can create a better society by going in at the bottom and making a floor that people can't fall beneath. That floor is not an expensive thing to maintain. We can introduce this nationally and globally.*

Again, Scott Santens spends a great amount of time and energy on social media raising awareness about the dire costs of not implementing a basic income. Just because we don't see these costs on a balance sheet does not mean they don't exist. They do exist, and though seemingly invisible, these costs amplify the very real economic pressures on ordinary and essential worker lives, and when ordinary lives become desperate and dysfunctional, societies become desperate and dysfunctional.

We spoke earlier about how much basic income is basic and how to pay for it in ways that make sense for the exponential age in which we live. For more background, a great place to start is the Reddit /r/BasicIncome Basic Income FAQ mentioned earlier in *Thinking About Thinking About Poverty*.

> *In the Basic Income FAQ you will find more than a decade's worth of unprecedented, open-source public policy work, collaborative thinking at scale. More than a decade's history of open cognition, co-creation, assertions, arguments, proposals, and thoroughly vetted, peer-reviewed, cross-examined, and battered mathematical models that have stood both the test of time and the relentless criticism of the crowd.*

Collaborative cognition spaces like the Basic Income Subreddit became part of the fulfillment of my earlier entrepreneurial calling to build the first residential fiber optic ethernet to the home networks in the 1990s; building out the dendrites and synapses that today connect us all as a fully operational global brain, so that we can problem solve our most pernicious grand challenges as a collaborative *human* superintelligence. My vision then was an infrastructure that invites and unites not just our greatest minds, but all interested minds into a radically open and participatory peer-reviewed process of solving humanity's most pernicious and pressing human problems.

I can't lie. It feels pretty good to have played a small part in architecting and building out those early global cognition grid connections and to have then gone on to participate with you in discovering how such expansively diverse minds can learn to think clearly about, and then solve, one of the most pernicious and pressing of those human problems. We've done it. We've arrived at a proven solution to poverty as we've known it. It's now our job to learn how to communicate with others in a way that shares this knowledge with everyone, because it belongs to everyone and without everyone, we couldn't have done our work. This is ubuntu.

In April 2017, The Atlantic magazine reminded us that:

> *[Martin Luther] King argued that the guaranteed income should be "pegged to the median of society," and rise automatically along with the U.S. standard of living. "To guarantee an income at the floor would simply perpetuate welfare standards and freeze into the society poverty conditions," he wrote. Was it feasible? Maybe. He noted an estimate by John Kenneth Galbraith that the government could create a generous guaranteed income with $20 billion, which, as the economist put it, was "not much more than we will spend the next fiscal year to rescue freedom and democracy and religious liberty as these are defined by 'experts' in Vietnam" (Weissmann).*

While median income was a reasonable index for basic income half a century ago; today, as a result of the rigorous decade-long peer review process described, the concrete consensus is that indexing the universal Social Security basic income dividend to 50% per capita GDP is the most flexible, responsive, resilient, and stabilizing approach in the face of unpredictable real world economic conditions.

It is now indisputable that we live in a world that has evolved completely beyond the relevance of twentieth-century ideas of labor value and currency circulation.

Robots and software cannot and do not negotiate for wages. As robotics and AI make wages increasingly obsolete, we cannot index to deprecated measures of median wages that no longer makes sense, even though they did at the time.

Perhaps we needed to go through this entire half-century long exercise in order to know what we know now, so that we can act decisively and confidently as the best possible ancestors in our generation's time of crisis.

In contrast to the vanishing need for wages, design, manufacturing, and distribution efficiency and productivity are skyrocketing as AI and automation absorbs both our manufacturing and administrative infrastructures.

This is no longer futurism or science fiction. This is the Post-Automation Era.

Econ 101: Compared to What?

For all that's obsolete about the 20th century, productivity is a metric that will continue to be relevant, measurable, and representational of aggregate labor-capacity and output in both manufacturing and services, even as machines perform an increasing proportion of that work and artificial intelligence heralds an even more rapid decrease in the need for human beings in the majority of routine and mundane administrative tasks. Some metric names remain while their meanings change. New metrics inevitably arise.

Productivity is already less a measure of human efficiency and more a measure of capital ingenuity in leveraging and optimizing hyper-automation. Labor metrics are already largely measures of automation-capacity rather than human toil. This means more humans are either destined for poverty by the old model or becoming freed to join the work to end poverty as we've known it.

So let's look again at the costs of not ending poverty with a guaranteed annual income by summarizing some of the results of vestigial 20th century programs in the first decades of the 21st century, compared to the options we've described and recommended. By answering the question "compared to what," we can decide which is the more responsible and wise option: continuing to do what we've always done or accepting hard lessons, adapting, and moving on.

According to the most recent available Cato Institute report, "In total, the United States spends nearly $1 trillion every year to fight poverty. That amounts to $20,610 for every poor person in America, or $61,830 per poor family of three."[cccxlvii]

That was twelve years ago, so it seems that even the respected Cato Institute hasn't had the resources to stay up to speed in a decade of exponential acceleration, how are everyday families supposed to keep up? Because engineers work with whatever we've got (remember Apollo 13?) let's unpack these numbers and see if we can glean any additional useful understanding. $1 trillion per year divided by $20,610 is 48,520,136 people in poverty.

According to Wolfram|Alpha's calculations of 2012 Federal Reserve Bank data, 50% per capita GDP was $26,008.[cccxlviii] Compared to that wasted $20,610, the UBI option appears the wiser choice in retrospect, as a modest 21% increased investment in people rather than the sunk costs of obsolete programs. Spending 79% of a livable UBI that we know works on wasteful bureaucracy seems like an extremely high failure-to-change cost. These data provide additional solid numbers to Santens' recent work, focusing on the failure costs of not implementing UBI.

Put another way, a UBI in 2012 would have cost 21% more, in exchange for hundreds of percentage points bang for those few bucks. What's the expression? You get what you pay for, right? The savings from ending the 2012 Welfare State alone likely covers twice that 21%. So once again, 50% per capita GDP keeps cross-checking favorably.

Assuming that $20,610 never increased over the last 12 years, an absurdly conservative and flatly wrong mathematical presumption, what is our next calculation? Here's a prompt to try for yourself.

"Hey, OpenAI, ChatGPT, Bard, Gemini, Bing, Alexa, Amazon Q, somebody, anybody, please calculate the following: (Number of poor people per year in the United States from 2012 through 2023) multiplied by $20,610.00 to give us the total amount already wasted by neglecting UBI over the past 11 years.

While I'm comfortable interacting with my AI research partners and citing them, for now, I also prefer to double-check AI's suggestions and do my own digging to confirm the U.S. Census Bureau's Current Population Survey (CPS), Annual Social and Economic Supplement (ASEC) source data and indeed find the human-confirmed answer to that question is 519.4 million poor people over the course of a decade.[cccxlix]

Multiplied by Cato's $20,610, that amounts to $10,704,834,000,000, or $10.7 trillion just over the past decade, technically eleven years, prior to correcting for inflation or any other spending-power reduction factors. Remember, this is an absurd understatement because that $20,610 did not remain constant.

Imagine there was a virus that caused a trillion dollars damage per year. What would be the outrage and emergency response? But because the epidemic of U.S. poverty only affects poor people ... crickets.

As the old song lyrics go, "if you choose not to decide, you still have made a choice," and the price of inaction can often be much higher than the price of doing what's right, even when it feels more costly in the moment.

To continue "compared to what," what in this case is the cost of a 50% per capita GDP basic income over that same time period? To back test, we must:

- Find the 10-year average 50% per capita GDP figure of $28,233.00.[cccl]
- Multiply by 519.4 million people.
- Derive a $14,664,220,200,000 per-decade cost of universal Social Security.

So, it seems we got a bargain, after all. According to these calculations, leaving people on the streets costs only 73% of our ridiculous proposed $14.7 trillion universal Social Security over the same time period. So, did we just blast our own model straight out of the water? It was 27% cheaper to waste the money on programs that don't work. Can opponents now slam the book shut in victory? Maybe.

Except, wait. We also made that absurd assumption that the $2,610 never increased. But it did increase.

And Cato said we were spending nearly a $1 trillion a year on poverty *and not solving the problem.*[cccli] If Cato was right, then we've wasted at least $13 trillion over 13 years. Again, if that figure never increased. But it did increase. So, if the figures that we assumed didn't increase, actually did increase by just 27%, then suddenly that $14.7 trillion per-decade universal Social Security *which does end poverty*, doesn't look so bad, after all.

What's our last step in this *compared to what* exercise? We need to correct that $1 trillion wasted in 2012 for inflation over the past decade.

We saw earlier that core inflation from 2012 to 2023 was 45%. So, correcting for inflation, suddenly, that $13 trillion is $18.9 trillion.

This means the $14.7 trillion decade-long universal Social Security back test was 22% cheaper than wasting money on means-testing and instead of failing, it works.

Put another way, we spent $18.9 trillion on failed policies over the past decade. Given the option to reduce that wasteful spending by 22% *and solve the problem*, what choice would we have made? We can make that wiser choice today and not repeat the failures of trying to live in the 20th century forever.

Compared to welfare, let's call it *neglectfare*. The cost of failure to do the right thing. Wasteful spending on what doesn't work, particularly when given an option that does work.

Where does all that money come from, the more than $18.9 trillion wasted by not implementing a guaranteed annual income at levels that sustain life in decent circumstances, indexed to 50% per capita GDP?

People can be against entitlements, against welfare, even against food stamps and housing subsidies, but who can possibly be against universal income security, as a principle, when it's both cheaper that what we've already spent, and it works?

When making choices, legendary FBI hostage negotiator and founder of the Black Swan Group, Chris Voss, explains how we have two brains, our animal brain, and our higher thinking human brain. He explains that it is our lower impulses that generate the inputs for how we put the higher brain functions to use. That's how he bested all of the ivory tower theorists in the art negotiation, and that's how he saves lives.[ccclii]

Voss teaches a method called *tactical empathy* that has helped him and the FBI as a whole to become vastly more successful in hostage situations.

In a sense, the U.S. labor force is in a hostage situation; held captive by 20th century misperceptions like a gun to their head. That means that I should be using tactical empathy in these pages instead of being provocative or confrontational. I *can* empathize with the choice to leave tens of millions of people suffering into perpetuity. I *can* understand it, even knowing it's completely wrong.

That's how Voss describes his job in getting both the hostages and the captors out of there without anybody getting hurt. He doesn't agree with the kidnappers, he understand the completely messed up place they're coming from and genuinely helps them to get out alive. It seems counterintuitive, but it works, and has led to incredibly improved success rates for hostage negotiators, worldwide. So I've got to plug the man's book, *Never Split the Difference*, while wishing I'd discovered it sooner because this would have been a much better book, had I begun with even a hint of a clue about tactical empathy.

We've got serious negotiation work to do ironing out the details of universal Social Security; however, with the explosion of AI in the early 2020s, as terrible as a hostage situation is, combined with a rude awakening from a long obsolete 20th century JOB-JOB Trance, the urgency of solving poverty in this decade seems to finally have our attention. Our job then is to negotiate a peaceful resolution to a situation that just about everybody involved never wanted to end up in.

* * *

All we Know are the Maths, Ma'am

According to Snopes:

> *Dragnet, acclaimed for its attention to detail and realistic portrayal of the nuts and bolts of police work, was created by its star, Jack Webb. It started out as a radio drama in 1949, made the transition to television in 1951. So popular was TV Dragnet in its day that satirist Stan Freberg spoofed it on a 1953 record titled "St. George and the Dragonet." This record and its flip side, "Little Blue Riding Hood" (also a Dragnet spoof) were extraordinarily popular as well, hitting the #1 spot on Billboard's pop chart and selling over two million copies; the record's success prompted Ed Sullivan to invite Freberg to perform both sides of the single live on his Talk of the Town variety show. Jack Webb's 'Joe Friday' character typically used the phrase "All we want are the facts, ma'am" (and sometimes "All we know are the facts ma'am").* [cccliii]

If we are ever to get to the truth, the whole truth, and nothing but the truth of how to accomplish universal Social Security, "all we want are the facts." As of Q3 2023, 50% U.S. per capita GDP was $41,199, up an incredible 29.3% from Q1 2018's $30,476.00 just five years ago (Federal Reserve Bank via Wofram|Alpha).

Let's find out what our new AI research assistants have to offer in terms of assisting with the incredibly complex research behind otherwise remarkably straightforward arithmetic.

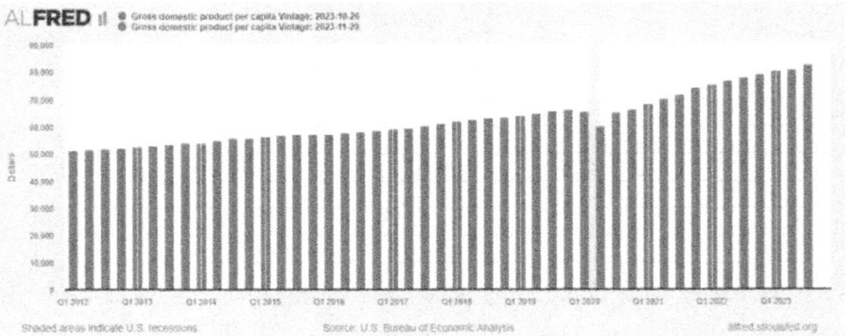

Figure 9 — Per Capita GDP, U.S. Bureau of Economic Analysis.

Below, I have included the tail end of a Google Bard interaction with a little bit of extra context, just to give a flavor of what it's like to work together with an AI-assistant on real world issues:

> *Unfortunately, even with the additional information about the United States, your question remains incomplete. To determine 50% of per capita GDP, I still need more information:*

1. Year: As mentioned earlier, per capita GDP changes over time. Knowing the specific year (e.g., 2022, 2023) allows for accurate calculation.

2. Nominal or PPP: You can calculate per capita GDP using nominal values (current market prices) or adjusted for purchasing power parity (PPP). Choosing the relevant measure depends on your purpose.

Please provide the missing information, and I will happily calculate 50% of per capita GDP for the United States in the specified year and measure.

Bard went on to provide the following. "United States Per Capita GDP in 2023: Nominal GDP: Per capita GDP (nominal): $74,489 (Source: International Monetary Fund [IMF] World Economic Outlook October 2023). 50% of per capita GDP (nominal): $37,244.50. PPP (Purchasing Power Parity) GDP: Per capita GDP (PPP): $63,729 (Source: World Bank Open Data). 50% of per capita GDP (PPP): $31,864.50. Please note these figures are based on current estimates and may be subject to revisions in the future."[cccliv]

In contrast, my own prior human research sourced from St. Louis Federal Reserve Economic Data (Figure 9), revealed the most recent Real Median Personal Income in the United States (MEPAINUSA672N) as $37,522 (a 20% increase over 2016's $31,099.00).

These figures illustrate how a market-indexed basic income dividend automatically rebalances according to real-world conditions, yet another encouraging real-world cross check to our model.

So, we have a range of figures representing 50% per capita GDP as of 2023, extending from the World Bank's PPP measure of $31,864.50 to St. Louis Federal reserve's GDP measure of $41,199.00. This means we have work to do to debug, curate, and vet data sources and methods before we have a minimal viable process for establishing a consistent benchmark value.

While encouraged every time I reexamine this material for completeness, accuracy, credibility, and practicality; surely our work extends well beyond the pages of this book and will continue to occupy our days and nights, as it has for more than the past decade, until accomplished.

While we *could* wait for another mega-crisis to hit before we act to alleviate the needless existential anxiety of poverty, but wouldn't it be nice to avert that drama and trauma, for a change, and do the right thing, merely because it's the right thing to do?

* * *

Did You Check Your Work?

I want to take one short detour to address the ancient – and at this point effectively useless – construct called the poverty line. This elusive and fickle minimum was a 20th century derivative of the otherwise admirable GINI coefficient. For fans of GINI, there are countless reasons why GINI is simply not the right benchmark for universal Social Security dividends. The most basic is definitional. GINI is a measure of income *inequality*, which will *always* exist and *must* exist in a meritocracy, and which is vitally distinct from, and only marginally relevant to the economic security principle of, income *security*. The conflation of *income inequality* with *income security* was one of the great gaslights and befuddlements of the 20th century DCNR.

The University of Illinois Urbana Institute of Government and Public Affairs further summarizes:

> *"The poverty line budget is based on the assumption that parents are good financial managers, and that both business and community facilities are adequate so that they can do a good job of rearing children with minimal income. Since these assumptions are known to be false for most ADC families, many groups have argued that the poverty line is not an adequate level of income to permit families to break out of the 'prison of poverty.'"*[cccl v]

In Figure 7, Share of Aggregate Income by Percentile (September 2023) we find a cartoonish gaslighting chart of "statistically significant" changes in wealth distribution.[ccclvi] The depiction of a 0.1% to 0.2% "increase" in the Share of Aggregate Income to the lowest three quintiles of the population is pure genius, if gaslighting is the goal. It's as if the publisher studied the genius work of Edward Tufte and put it to work using mad genius Edward Bernays principles. It would be comical disinformation if the consequences weren't so tragic in everyday human lives.

Therefore, on the vital question of "how much is basic" we cannot possibly overstate or reiterate MLK's guidance loud enough or often enough, when he said:

> ***"To guarantee an income at the floor (poverty level) would simply perpetuate welfare standards and freeze into the society poverty conditions."***

Figure 7 below seems to depict this relatively plainly. Setting the amount of basic income barely above the poverty level is precisely what killed basic income in the 1970s.

Checking our work of the past several decades, we recall that many other early back-of-the-envelope UBI calculations began with arbitrary round numbers, like Charles Murray's infamous $10,000 figure, which even Murray said was essentially pulled out of nowhere, and then, only in order to advance the conversation; but it appears that as soon as any number is put into ink or pixels, there arises a vocal constituency to defend the ink blots and LCD dots as somehow sacrosanct. There was never anything other than empty talk and hand-waving supporting any of those round numbers. No math, just feelings, rote repetition, memes, and trolling. That's fine for provoking curiosity and discussion, but there's no room for such antics when it comes time to merge public policy code upgrades into main that will impact generations.

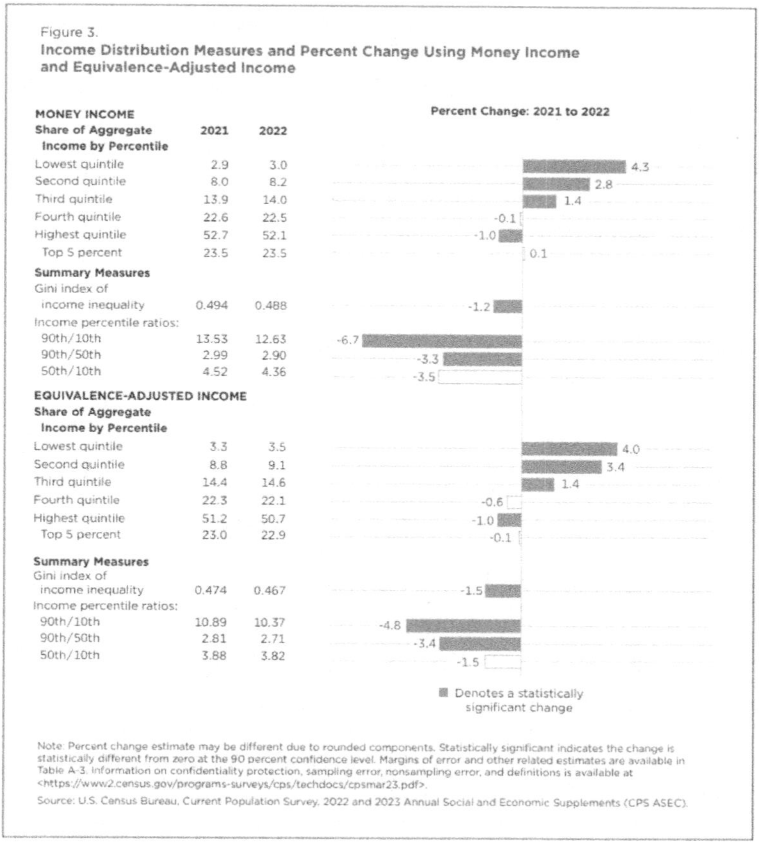

Figure 10 — Share of Aggregate Income by Percentile.

Put another way, there is a time for playing around at the park basketball court and then there's game time. That said, game time should remain just as fun and not solely about winning, it should be about performing at our best in order to achieve the intrinsic reward of knowing we performed at our best, regardless of the outcome.

Checking our work in the earlier round numbers round of education and raising public awareness, 2020 U.S. Presidential candidate Andrew Yang proposed a Freedom Dividend of $1,000 per month. While I butted heads with Scott Santens in 2012 and throughout the twenty-teens on these round numbers, I have to sheepishly confess that I didn't then, and do now, understand the tactic to keep advancing the conversation and explaining the principle of UBI. As mentioned in the acknowledgments, I mistook a clear view for a short distance.

Now is the time to become more committed than ever to *sound principles* – not personas, politics, or pettiness – in driving this entire process forward to completion.

I vocally supported the Freedom Dividend because it communicated the right rationale for achieving the principle of universal income security. The $1,000 per month number only shared an accidental serendipity with the then current Federal Poverty Level (FPL) of $12,000. Today the FPL stands at $14,580.[ccclvii]

I still believe that Yang and Santens are spot-on about all the most important implications and consequences of a Freedom Dividend. It's a great perspective perfectly adapted to the evolution toward universal Social Security.

The Freedom Dividend circulated by universal Social Security will absolutely grow the economy, which is another reason the amount must be flexible and indexed to real market expansion and contraction. The Yang2020.com website said:

> *"A Universal Basic Income at this ($1,000 per month) level would permanently grow the economy by 12.56 to 13.10 percent—or about $2.5 trillion by 2025—and it would increase the labor force by 4.5 to 4.7 million people. Putting money into people's hands and keeping it there would be a perpetual boost and support to job growth and the economy."*

Despite that growth, the shortcoming of the round number approach effectively froze the basic income in carbonite. That was never a good idea for the long game, and it seems that today more people have come around to this realization. The 2020 web site said, "Any change to the Freedom Dividend would require a constitutional amendment." Yikes. That's not exactly flexible, resilient, or responsive to real market conditions.

Good thing we've taken fifty years to check our work toward implementing "a guaranteed income at levels that sustain life in decent circumstances."

So, the round numbers version of the dividend was both a great and terrible idea. It seems to have included that merciful constitutional amendment poison pill, because what conscious and credible actor would possibly swallow such an essentially impossible condition? The reason it was both a great and terrible proposal is that we do not live in a static world, much less economy. Every part of any healthy and sustainable ecosystem or economy is dynamically interdependent in rational, if sometimes unexpected or inexplicable, and mutually beneficial ways.

For example, freezing overnight interest rates manages the economy in ways that seem great in the short term, but as we've seen repeatedly, immobilizing key components of dynamic systems, like a cast on a broken bone, can eventually immobilize the whole system, economic or biological, so we use such tools sparingly and with great respect and trepidation for unknown unknowns which constantly surprise and amaze us in the healing process. A static basic income is in the same category, becoming subject to annual or biannual wrangling, like the vestigial dreaded 20th century Social Security cost of living adjustments (COLA), forever and ever.

In checking our work, it seems like we needed to acknowledge and process the idea of static round numbers so we could knowledgeably discard it as one more wrong way to build a light bulb.

That's why I am grateful for Yang and Santens advocacy and consider myself an ally. I also hope that some minor course corrections can help us all reach the desired outcome of actionable public policy that enacts the principle and practice of *unconditional and universal income security for all.*

The first reaction for many people, when faced with new information like this, is to resist. To not change things too much, or too soon. This leads to the mainstay political tactic of incrementalism. In the case of establishing unconditional and universal income security, incrementalism suggests we, "just start with any small basic income amount; anything is better than nothing, then we can increase it over time." This sounds reasonable at first blush but is instead risky, for consistently demonstrated historical reasons.

Legendary U.S. statesman Daniel Patrick Moynihan wrote:

> *"The incrementalist hypothesis is not just descriptive, it is also normative: it asserts that change in a democratic society not only has to be incremental, but ought to be. Marginal reforms, it is held, by never altering too much, being always subject to relatively easy corrective measures, produce better decisions and pose less a threat to democratic consensus" (Moynihan, 551).*

Moynihan's point is that incrementalism may seem to work in theory but fails in practice. Which becomes particularly pertinent in cases of utterly dilapidated public policy, such today's welfare state.

> *Like dilapidated and condemned buildings, there is a point at which repairs make no economic or structural sense and the old structure must be torn down to make way for a better structure, with better materials, greater stability, and superior features.*

Most Americans today share the observation that the current welfare state is beyond repair. After decades and decades of failed "welfare reform" legislation, it is abundantly clear that an ongoing strategy of incremental repair is simply too costly and the gains so infinitesimally small as to make no sense whatsoever. Most important of all, for our conversation, is the fact that it is incrementalism that literally killed basic income in the late 1960s and early 1970s.

Incrementalism in launching a genuine living wage level basic income will surely kill the policy again if advocates cave-in to this doomed approach. A solitary author can only plead that we do not opt for that particular public option in our efforts to become the best possible ancestors to the seven generations that follow us.

The Post-Automation Era is a time for extensively vetted, open-source, peer-developed and reviewed research, robust and radically inclusive debate, followed by decisive and conclusive action.

Checking our work, we find that the 20th century operated by 20th century norms and methods. The sham of jumping to reactive presumptions and acting in the name of doing *something* all too often passed as decisive leadership that proved destructive, even devastating. Decisiveness devoid of deliberation is disastrous. Deliberation devoid of conclusive action is ineffectiveness.

Our stewardship is of the 21st century. Let's learn from those lessons rather than repeat them.

In his detailed review of Moynihan's, *The Politics of Guaranteed Income*, Martin Mayor wrote, "The problem, which Moynihan lays out very clearly and fairly, was circular and unresolvable. [Politically,] FAP had to be set low enough ($1,600 per year for a family of four) to fit into a feasible federal budget and maintain a rational appetite for work. This works out to $10,240 per year in 2018 dollars (see FAP in the glossary), essentially equivalent to the popular $1,000 per month basic income meme propagated on social media in 2018; with a supposedly generous 20% waiter's tip thrown in, to bring the figure up to the Federal Poverty Level" (Mayer).

To have ever seriously contemplated the idea of setting a basic income at such low-ball levels, based upon the claim that people who earn $0.01 above FPL have escaped poverty, was always ludicrous, to put it gently.

"Not surprisingly, the FAP figure was so low that supplements (most notably, food stamps, Medicaid, and public-housing subsidies) were required to keep alive those who were stuck with nothing else. Recipients who got jobs would, at designated income points, lose not only portions of their FAP grants, but also their eligibility for the supplements. At these points, the "notch effects," as Moynihan calls them, would provide strong disincentives to work. Without the supplements, no liberal support at all—Moynihan himself wouldn't have bought it. With the supplements, no conservative support at all—Moynihan himself was itchy about notches" (Mayer).

The 20th century low-ball policy failure of fifty years ago – making basic income static and ludicrously minimal; at or near an arbitrary federal poverty level – is still one of the cheapest and most pernicious poison pills that threatens the usefulness of basic income policy today.

During the decades of strategic and tactical debates about how to end poverty responsibly and effectively, perhaps the most persistent underlying opposition is not a question of whether the math works; not whether the economy grows or not; and not whether UBI might perturb the Godzilla boogieman of inflation. It's not even a contentious debate over the specific amount of UBI. The enmity is in the form of the silent (or not) screams of 20th-century-storyline addicts cursing between the lines:

"Nobody is entitled to anything!"

Ever since Lyndon Johnson's War on Poverty, mercenary talking heads on TV have spewed the word entitlement like chaff into any reasonable discussion space. This single word can hopelessly scatter all dialectical coherence. Unless there are effective countermeasures to that crude, grossly outdated, yet still incredibly effective World War II anti-radar tactic, it's going to keep working in the realm of public discourse.

So, what if we agreed to end all entitlements? That would, in one sentence, vaporize the entitlement zombie army and its endless hordes of strawman support brigades.

The cost of this narrative, if adopted, is that *policy makers must stand resolute on the 50% per capita GDP index as the baseline measure of income security*.

If policy makers cave in on this vital metric and strip all entitlements in exchange for a paltry basic income, the outcome will be beyond catastrophic; and may even prove the Bolsheviks right after all, in the end. Wouldn't it be nice to avoid that debacle this time around? I think so.

Scott Santen's motto, "Basic Income isn't Left, or Right, it's Forward" has been a rallying cry for the UBI movement for over a decade. To move forward successfully in 2024 requires full commitment to an unambiguously livable basic income.

In principle that means "a guaranteed income at levels that sustain life in decent circumstances." In practice, universal Social Security indexed to 50% per capita GDP.

To bear witness to such an audacious historical achievement, to truly dismantle the welfare state as we've known it, in a way that minimizes and reduces harm as compared to the 20th century regime may require an unlikely civic alliance of bureaucracy-hating conservatives, libertarians, democratic socialists, techno progressives, regenerative rugged individualists, compassionate anarchists, effective altruists, and others, spanning the entire fragmented 20th century spectrum.

Only by finding a way to tolerate one another and cooperate just long enough to end poverty as we've known it can we successfully implement King's definition of, "a guaranteed annual income at levels that sustain life in decent circumstances."

There is a word for that kind of tolerance and cooperation, even respect:

UBUNTU.

* * *

Income Security is National Security

The 20th century default consensus narrative of Job Security has long since evolved into the Post-Automation Era human right to Income Security.[ccclviii]

It's a human CVE – Common Vulnerability and Exposure – that we are prone to clinging to vain beliefs and behaviors with all the conviction of a drowning person pushing their rescuer under the water.

Many on both red and blue teams may screech to hear this, because it was their 20th century JOB-JOB to keep poverty in place. Some may be frightened of what happens to them when they lose all their customers. With no poverty customers to interview, assess, judge, and qualify for our programs, will we become one of *them*? How will we possibly be able to continue to esteem ourselves as above *them*? We are the helpers, not the helped! If there is no one left to help, whatever shall we do with ourselves?

Remember Ajeya Cotra's observation? "It's as if 24th century technology is crashing down on 21st century civilization."

This is one of the foremost reasons we have an absolutely sacred duty and obligation to hold the *50% per capita GDP* line so that universal Social Security is truly livable for all real human beings in the real world; particularly those temporarily displaced in the process, especially after lifetimes of loyal and dedicated service.

Americans from across the entire twentieth-century political spectrum have the remarkably rare opportunity to unite in the cause of ending entitlements and welfare as we've known it.

Notwithstanding natural inter-generational dissonance, the end of the 20th century default consensus narratives of welfare, replaced by the 21st century principle of Maslow Safety, brings significant consolations.

The Post-Automation Era ends unhelpful notions of entitlements by ensuring healthy, sustainable circulation of super abundance and economic resilience by way of unconditional income security.

Income security is Social Security.

Social security is National Security.

Given all other forms of structural and information security, without economic security, no society will be safe and secure for long. Throughout history, nothing leads to civil unrest as quickly as the failure to meet basic human needs. It's the plot of countless video games, movies, paintings, and art since ancient times. It's Mad Max. It's a political historian's most dreaded cliché. So, anyone who is committed to strengthening the security infrastructure of the United States cannot deny that robust, scalable, fair, and adequate income security in an AI-infused Post-Automation Era fundamental in supporting the preeminent priority of national security.

> *Cutting poverty and inequality is the best way to reduce crime, a police chief has said, calling for more money for deprived areas to thwart criminals' attempts to recruit those left desperate by deprivation In an unusually frank interview for a senior officer, given to mark his retirement as chief constable of Merseyside police, Andy Cooke said that if he was given £5bn to cut crime, he would put £1bn into law enforcement and £4bn into tackling poverty..*[cclix]

In an unusually frank interview for a senior officer, given to mark his retirement as chief constable of Merseyside police, Andy Cooke said that if he was given £5bn to cut crime, he would put £1bn into law enforcement and £4bn into tackling poverty.

> *When [Chicago] Mayor Brandon Johnson took the wraps off his "People's Plan for Community Safety," it sounded more like a rebranded mix of plans championed by his predecessor, Lori Lightfoot, with violence prevention initiatives bankrolled by business leaders sprinkled in. But it turns out that Johnson does have at least the bones of his own plan to take the fight against the root causes of crime to a whole new level.*[cclx]

That root cause, as we've overwhelmingly shown throughout this text, is pure economic desperation, which drives the willingness to literally do anything in order to get money to survive.

That's the cost of doing nothing. That's the cost of not adapting to the Post-Automation Era with universal Social Security indexed to 50% per capita GDP. And that's the cost in only one city, merely the worst among dozens, maybe hundreds, following right behind.

That's how destructive the most virulent forms of dog-eat-dog natural law thinking impact the real world. If we choose to keep enforcing law-of-the-jungle like conditions, guess what? We get more law-of-the-jungle behavior, top-to-bottom, bottom-to-top.

It's these deprecated default consensus narratives that must recede before outcomes have any chance of improving in a long-term sustainable way. It's a plain and simple empirical scientific fact that *income security reduces violence,* and a reduction of hostilities enhances national security from the grassroots.

After soaring for two years, shootings and homicides have dropped significantly in Chicago for the first time since the COVID-19 pandemic upended normal life and ushered in a nationwide rise in violent crime.

The city's anti-violence efforts also come largely from ARPA [H.R.1319 - American Rescue Plan Act of 2021], as well as the federal Coronavirus Aid, Relief and Economic Security Act. But Lee said she's concerned a significant portion of that money remains unspent.

The ARPA money must be allocated by the end of 2024 and spent by the end of 2026, giving the winner of next year's mayoral race some extra resources for public safety. But there are already alarms about what happens when that money is exhausted.

The "Our City Our Safety" plan was launched in the summer of 2020 and followed an emerging trend of treating gun violence as a public health issue. The plan aimed to narrow Chicago's "safety gap" — the disparity between the most and least violent areas of the city that widened during the pandemic.

Asked about the slow rollout, Lightfoot explained that her administration's goal was to send money "as far down to the block level as possible," distributing money to smaller groups instead of just large social service organizations.

"I really wanted this to have real, lasting impact at that micro-block level," she said. "And that takes more time."

In February, city officials held a series of events to inform smaller community organizations about funding opportunities and address the "pain points in trying to distribute this money," the mayor said.

It called for flooding the most dangerous communities with new resources — from violence intervention programs to job training and placement, housing and health — taking cues from its COVID-19 response by pulling together various agencies and outside partners.

"There are lots of cities that are facing this question: How do you avoid the possible consequences when federal funds run out?," Sharkey said. "And even when state government funds run out. I think that's the crucial issue facing most big cities."

"We should never have to make that choice between the police budget and the other necessary, essential tools that will make a long-term impact on community safety," she said.

> *Lightfoot noted that some of the city's "one-time" investments [the direct cash investment in people, UBI] will "last much longer than the lifetime of the ARPA funding."*[ccclxi]

The brass tacks, concrete-jungle reality of the efficacy of income security to reduce violence also defuses the entitlement bomb often used to blow up productive conversations that prove that the principle and practice of Maslow Safety income security is not an unearned entitlement, it is the circulation of earned dividends. A citizen's dividend paid from a just, 21st century upgraded Social Security Trust Fund.

Ending welfare and entitlements as we've known them does not mean the end of the innovation we've seen in complementary, targeted efforts to meet deeper specific needs for specific constituencies and demographics, in recent years. Maslow Safety is the most stable support and foundation to those efforts, as well. It's an underlying economic complement, not a replacement for specific, targeted needs.

Findings from the largest global UBI studies have overwhelmingly proven our claims, as we have seen earlier. As we end economic desperation in our own nation, and as neighboring nations adopt a similar approach, we dramatically decrease cross-border tensions born of economic desperation on all sides.

The principle of income security as foundational to Maslow Safety is in the most practical sense the foundation of national and global security.

When we meet people's basic Maslow Safety needs for income security in an environment of incomprehensible AI acceleration, we end the panicked instinctive desperation that creates adverse, negative, perverse incentives to seek out the fulfillment of those monetary needs by any means necessary.

We are no longer living at the dawn of the industrial revolution and so the paths to prosperity of that era are not the paths to prosperity in the Post-Automation Era. Today's paths to prosperity lead through the narrow gate of understanding, recognizing, and acting in alignment with our shared human destinies.

It appears evident that without the social stability of income security, there can be no resilience in a population's felt sense of social security. Which is to further evidence, without a credible, believable, visceral, owned-sense of resilient social security within any population, there can be no meaningful, robust, lasting national security.

* * *

Facing Constraints and Defining Principles

As described earlier, we have always lived in a mixed economy which rewards shareholders with dividends. Passive, labor-decoupled income. Shareholders get a vote in the governance corporation and non-shareholders do not.

As U.S. citizens, we can each consider ourselves as shareholders in the United States of America, Inc., regardless of status, stature, station, profession, job, career title, work, or vocation. One vote equals one share. Like any shareholder, even one share bestows both voting rights and dividends: a meager share of the corporation's immense superabundance.

Stay at home and single parents contribute as much, often more, off-balance-sheet value to the industrial production of new human components for the USA Corporation than anyone: the next generation of citizens that make the nation capable of existing at all. So, we all contribute significant economic value, and we all directly contribute to the generation and growth of U.S. GDP, whether in a company or in a home, in both tangible and intangible ways, directly and indirectly, and so we have each already rightly earned a Citizen's Dividend share from the commonwealth superabundance of USA, Inc., just like any shareholder of any other business enterprise.

As of the year 2024, our dividend payments are several generations in arears.

Next, we must face another inconvenient truth; namely, the fact that when pen meets paper to make income security a basic human right for all citizens of the United States, the definitive criteria will not be and cannot be *purely unconditional or universal.* Perfectionists may need to take a deep breath and sit with this for more than just a fleeting moment.

Solution architects and engineers don't enjoy philosopher and activist privileges of ambiguity. We face design, build, and deploy constraints. We must both minimize bureaucratic impedance and maximize program admittance, security resilience, and performance robustness all at the same time. In the case of technical design of a universal Social Security system, we face constraints of recipient maturity, age, and method of defining economic metrics like GDP.

Many of us long-time activists will have to adjust to some practical implementation realities that our most pristine philosophical fancies might prefer to ignore. While our idealism is fantastic when fueling movements, stepping that energy across circuits toward concrete legislation is an unavoidable design requirement.

While many of us may have invested significant time and energy into agonizing over how to achieve perfect universality and unconditionality, we cannot allow the perfect to be the enemy of the excellent. Excellence is a better goal than perfection because it's attainable.

We know that when parents' incomes are secure, the lives of children are secure. So one design criteria is a focus on the Maslow Safety of adults, because stable adults are the most stable and valuable resource for children. To say we care about children and not stabilize adults is uninformed at best and disingenuous at worst. The 20th century models linked money to children, and we are living with the unintended consequences of that well-intentioned yet misguided legacy. This is why EITC is an effective stop-gap measure that we fully support and also not the best long-term model.

Design Principle: Don't repeat what didn't work.

So the working design need not fret about dollar amounts given to children. Besides, linking income to the commodity creation of babies rather than to their care creates misguided incentives as proven by the failed child-driven metrics of the 20th century designs we're tasked with debugging and refactoring. Also, without any economic benefit specifically attached to having children, those critics habituated to voicing racist pejorative consternation about so-called welfare queens will need to find some other mythological creatures to disparage.

Another minimum viable design requirement is indexing to 50% per capita GDP, because the asset backing that valuation is every recipient, themselves.

By realizing the Maslow Safety needs of every individual, every potential parent is unambiguously able to "sustain life in decent circumstances" for themselves, first, which is the empirical precondition to the ability to care for anyone else. Next:

INCENTIVIZE WHAT YOU WANT.

DON'T REWARD WHAT YOU DON'T WANT.

---

* * *

Fulfilling Our Duty to National Priorities

Income security is a long-standing American policy priority. The means of achieving that in the 20th century worked well for the 20th century. Our stewardship is of the 21st century. By realizing that basic income is an expression of the already long-established U.S. priority of domestic income security, we have built upon centuries of proven American progress.

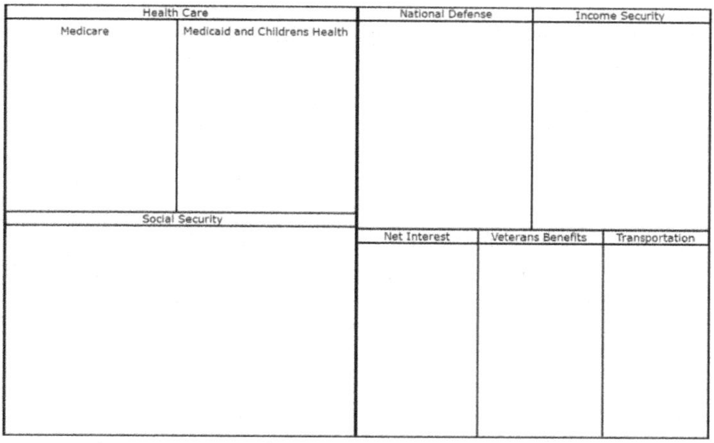

Figure 11 — U.S. Budget FY2016, Proportional Percent of GDP.

Figure 8 is from the U.S. National Archives and Records Administration 2016 U.S. Budget. It offers a handy view of proportionality, a format unfortunately discontinued in later years.[ccclxii] I'll refer to this graphic as a visual reference because the proportions have not significantly changed, and I've supplied latest 2023 figures for comparison.

> Always checking our work and asking, "compared to what," one thing that stands out to me in Figure 9 – U.S. Budget FY2023, Budget Totals – is that total government outlays for 2023 as a percentage of GDP are 23.9%. What percent of your paycheck do you pay for rent? The entire federal government runs on about half that percentage. So, to say or believe that the federal government is completely irresponsible and has no sense of financial self-discipline is ridiculous.

Would it be nice if that percentage were lower? Of course, it would be nice. Would it be nice if the percentage you paid for rent was lower? Of course, it would be nice.

What I'm observing is the mistaken view that all government activity is taking, and all market activity is giving. That's just not reflective of reality.

As reflected in more than seventy-five years of federal budgets, we the people of the United States, regardless of parties in power, have long supported income security as a fundamental national priority. In Figure 8, we see the proportion of the U.S. budget prioritized for income security, as reflected across the past 75 years. Left, right, red, blue, our core U.S. priorities stay consistent over time.

It is worth noting that the three top headings in that chart show the longstanding top priorities of the American people: namely, Health Care, National Defense, and Income Security. These are the top three major principles that Americans have agreed upon, generation after generation, as the top priorities of our commonwealth.

While accurate, the accounting subdivisions reflected in this chart may be a little visually diluted, as they do not entirely depict how fundamental income security truly is as an historical strategic domestic policy priority of the American people. The reason the chart is a bit diluted is that the following categories are also all direct forms of guaranteeing income security: Social Security, Other Income Security, Veteran Income and Housing Support, and Educational Financial Aid are all direct forms of income security, allocated across several other programs.

So, the true size of the Income Security box is the sum of Social Security + Other Income Security + Veteran Income and Housing Support + Educational Financial Aid.

Are we beginning to get the picture of just how prevalent, relevant, and essential income security is to national security?

Table S–1. Budget Totals[1]

(In billions of dollars and as a percent of GDP)

	2021	2022	2023	2024	2025	2026	2027	2028	2029	2030	2031	2032	Totals 2023–2027	Totals 2023–2032
Budget totals in billions of dollars:														
Receipts	4,047	4,437	4,638	4,874	5,076	5,406	5,696	5,969	6,227	6,500	6,795	7,083	25,690	58,264
Outlays	6,822	5,852	5,792	6,075	6,406	6,734	7,048	7,502	7,670	8,114	8,477	8,867	32,055	72,685
Deficit[2]	2,775	1,415	1,154	1,201	1,330	1,328	1,352	1,533	1,443	1,614	1,682	1,784	6,364	14,421
Debt held by the public	22,284	24,636	26,033	27,271	28,644	29,988	31,368	32,923	34,388	36,022	37,727	39,542		
Debt held by the public net of financial assets	20,673	22,085	23,238	24,439	25,768	27,097	28,449	29,982	31,425	33,045	34,732	36,516		
Gross domestic product (GDP)	22,358	24,256	25,567	26,694	27,787	28,912	30,080	31,307	32,615	34,018	35,498	37,041		
Budget totals as a percent of GDP:														
Receipts	18.1%	18.3%	18.1%	18.3%	18.3%	18.7%	18.9%	19.1%	19.1%	19.1%	19.1%	19.1%	18.5%	18.8%
Outlays	30.5%	24.1%	22.7%	22.8%	23.1%	23.3%	23.4%	24.0%	23.5%	23.9%	23.9%	23.9%	23.0%	22.4%
Deficit	12.4%	5.8%	4.5%	4.5%	4.8%	4.6%	4.5%	4.9%	4.4%	4.7%	4.7%	4.8%	4.6%	4.7%
Debt held by the public	99.7%	102.4%	101.8%	102.2%	103.1%	103.7%	104.3%	105.2%	105.4%	105.9%	106.3%	106.7%		
Debt held by the public net of financial assets	92.5%	91.0%	90.9%	91.6%	92.7%	93.7%	94.6%	95.8%	96.4%	97.1%	97.8%	98.6%		
Memorandum, real net interest:														
Real net interest in billions of dollars	-291	-514	-146	-48	20	73	129	181	221	254	298	337	29	1,319
Real net interest as a percent of GDP	-1.3%	-2.1%	-0.6%	-0.2%	0.1%	0.3%	0.4%	0.6%	0.7%	0.7%	0.8%	0.9%	0.0%	0.4%

[1] The Budget includes a reserve for legislation that reduces costs, expands productive capacity, and reforms the tax system. While the President is committed to reducing the deficit with this legislation, this allowance is shown as deficit neutral to be conservative for purposes of the budget totals. Because discussions with Congress continue, the Budget does not break down the reserve among specific policies or between revenues and outlays.

[2] The estimated deficit for 2022 is based on partial year actual data and generally incorporates actuals through February. At the time the 2023 Budget was prepared, 2022 appropriations remained incomplete. The baseline reflects annualized continuing appropriations for 2022.

BUDGET OF THE U.S. GOVERNMENT FOR FISCAL YEAR 2023

119

Figure 12 — U.S. Budget FY2023, Budget Totals.

When combined, these subcategories make obvious the fact that Income Security is the most prevalent consensus policy priority of any advanced post-automation society. Income Security means Social Security, and Social Security means National Security.

This becomes particularly salient for a society wherein roughly half the population has met 100% of labor force demand, for years, as measured by the Civilian Labor Force Participation Rate; and the rate only stays as high as it is by persistent manufactured machinations.

Table S–5. Proposed Budget by Category as a Percent of GDP[1]

(As a percent of GDP)

	2021	2022	2023	2024	2025	2026	2027	2028	2029	2030	2031	2032	Averages 2023–2027	Averages 2023–2032
Outlays:														
Discretionary programs:														
Defense	3.3	3.2	3.1	3.1	3.0	2.9	2.8	2.8	2.7	2.6	2.5	2.4	3.0	2.8
Non-defense	4.0	3.8	3.6	3.8	3.6	3.5	3.4	3.3	3.2	3.1	3.0	2.9	3.6	3.3
Subtotal, discretionary programs	7.3	7.0	6.7	6.9	6.7	6.4	6.2	6.0	5.9	5.7	5.5	5.3	6.6	6.1
Mandatory programs:														
Social Security	5.0	5.0	5.1	5.2	5.3	5.4	5.5	5.6	5.7	5.8	5.8	5.8	5.3	5.5
Medicare	3.1	3.1	3.3	3.2	3.5	3.7	3.8	4.2	3.9	4.2	4.3	4.4	3.5	3.8
Medicaid	2.3	2.3	2.1	2.1	2.2	2.2	2.2	2.3	2.3	2.3	2.4	2.4	2.2	2.2
Other mandatory programs	11.2	5.2	3.9	3.5	3.4	3.3	3.2	3.3	3.1	3.1	3.1	3.0	3.5	3.3
Subtotal, mandatory programs	21.6	15.7	14.4	14.1	14.4	14.6	14.8	15.3	15.0	15.4	15.5	15.7	14.4	14.9
Net interest	1.6	1.5	1.5	1.8	2.0	2.2	2.4	2.6	2.7	2.8	2.9	2.9	2.0	2.4
Total outlays	30.5	24.1	22.7	22.8	23.1	23.3	23.4	24.0	23.5	23.9	23.9	23.9	23.0	23.4
Receipts:														
Individual income taxes	9.1	9.3	9.2	9.1	9.2	9.8	10.0	10.1	10.2	10.3	10.4	10.5	9.4	9.9
Corporation income taxes	1.7	1.6	2.0	2.3	2.3	2.1	2.1	2.1	2.0	1.8	1.8	1.7	2.1	2.0
Social insurance and retirement receipts:														
Social Security payroll taxes	4.3	4.3	4.3	4.3	4.3	4.4	4.4	4.4	4.4	4.4	4.4	4.4	4.3	4.4
Medicare payroll taxes	1.3	1.4	1.3	1.3	1.3	1.4	1.4	1.4	1.4	1.4	1.4	1.4	1.3	1.4
Unemployment insurance	0.3	0.2	0.2	0.2	0.2	0.2	0.2	0.2	0.2	0.2	0.2	0.2	0.2	0.2
Other retirement	*	*	*	*	*	*	*	*	*	*	*	*	*	*
Excise taxes	0.3	0.3	0.4	0.4	0.3	0.3	0.3	0.3	0.3	0.3	0.3	0.3	0.3	0.3
Estate and gift taxes	0.1	0.1	0.1	0.1	0.1	0.1	0.1	0.1	0.1	0.1	0.1	0.1	0.1	0.1
Customs duties	0.4	0.4	0.2	0.2	0.2	0.2	0.2	0.2	0.2	0.2	0.2	0.1	0.2	0.2
Deposits of earnings, Federal Reserve System	0.4	0.4	0.3	0.2	0.1	0.1	0.1	0.1	0.2	0.2	0.2	0.2	0.2	0.2
Other miscellaneous receipts	0.2	0.1	0.1	0.1	0.2	0.2	0.2	0.2	0.2	0.2	0.2	0.2	0.2	0.2
Total receipts	18.1	18.3	18.1	18.3	18.3	18.7	18.9	19.1	19.1	19.1	19.1	19.1	18.5	18.8
Deficit	**12.4**	**5.8**	**4.5**	**4.5**	**4.8**	**4.6**	**4.5**	**4.9**	**4.4**	**4.7**	**4.7**	**4.8**	**4.6**	**4.7**
Net interest	1.6	1.5	1.5	1.8	2.0	2.2	2.4	2.6	2.7	2.8	2.9	2.9	2.0	2.4
Primary deficit	10.8	4.4	3.0	2.7	2.8	2.4	2.1	2.3	1.7	2.0	1.9	1.9	2.6	2.3
On-budget deficit	12.2	5.7	4.2	4.1	4.3	4.0	3.8	4.2	3.6	3.9	3.8	3.9	4.1	4.0
Off-budget deficit/surplus (–)	0.2	0.2	0.3	0.4	0.5	0.6	0.7	0.7	0.8	0.9	0.9	1.0	0.5	0.7

*0.05 percent of GDP or less

[1] The Budget includes a reserve for legislation that reduces costs, expands productive capacity, and reforms the tax system. While the President is committed to reducing the deficit with this legislation, this allowance is shown as deficit neutral to be conservative for purposes of the budget totals. Because discussions with Congress continue, the Budget does not break down the reserve among specific policies or between revenues and outlays.

BUDGET OF THE U.S. GOVERNMENT FOR FISCAL YEAR 2023 123

Figure 13 — U.S. Budget FY2023, Category as Percent of GDP.

As shown earlier, the LESS THAN 50% LABOR FORCE PARTICIPATION RATE is a point toward which the United States has steadily progressed for decades. Sometimes, it might seem like waking up in the Post-Automation Era is a bit like a 21st century Rip Van Winkle experience.

At least it's encouraging to see that Americans have long universally agreed that income security is not just a vital humanitarian priority, but it is vital to the national security of the United States. This isn't mere perspective or conjecture, it's right there, reflected in the budgets of our commonwealth over the past century.

Nevertheless, opponents of universal Social Security echo the 20th century default consensus mantra that *jobs are the sole or preeminent source of human dignity*, therefore we must forever require 20th century style jobs by any means necessary, even by way of entirely make-work artificiality before anyone may receive a single penny of income, because it is somehow character building for people to live under the persistent existential threat of destitution, homelessness, and hunger. What an incredible lack of even the most rudimentary imagination, faith, and foresight for the potential of human beings. I can't personally imagine a more cynical, misanthropic world view.

It's not a JOB-JOB that supports dignity, *it's the human interaction in that theater called a career* that provides the sense of context within community. It's the qualia of the structure of that intermittent human interaction for which vestigial genetic tribal dynamics hunger. That's why everywhere we go in the world, farmer's markets are one of, if not the most common pop-up movie sets in the theater of human life. Any mindful observer knows that there are countless ways for people to live dignified lives and stay engaged in community beyond the Lilliputian context described by the meme, "people *need* work to maintain a sense of dignity."

Deep, abiding, unshakeable human dignity derives from mutual recognition and respect, not by fancy corner offices, trendy powerful company badges, impressive, or intimidating job titles.

Upon the slightest deeper cross-examination, it is clear that many people feel a raw disdain for anyone other than themselves living a life characterized by sufficient leisure time for them to realize their own intrinsic interests, talents, and pursuing those self-actualized motivations, versus the 20th century default consensus reality of obeying the hourly wage regime to pay the same dues grandma and grandpa had to pay, or else. That kind of default consensus narrative can be seen as dismissive, judgmental, and even punitive.

It often seems overwhelmingly underappreciated that policy makers have an obligation to listen and empathize with an almost impossibly diverse spectrum of valid subjective perspectives and views, and also to move forward with compassion and clarity of conviction when it's clear that a given policy is deemed just from the perspectives of a critical mass of intellectually honest people of demonstrated frank conscience striving toward a world that works for everyone.

* * *

Free Markets Thrive with Income Security

With all the hard-nosed mainstream economic publications like Forbes, Fortune, the Wall Street Journal, MarketWatch, CNBC, and all of the major university and professional economic journals contributing increasing volumes of ink and careful attention to our thesis, we know that the principles in our work have moved squarely into the Overton Window (see Glossary).

MarketWatch Assistant Commentary Editor Jonathan Burton penned, "The case for paying every American a dividend on the nation's wealth." Addressing vestigial, skeptical public sentiments about so-called handouts, or free money; 20th century DCNR sentiments that simply do not exist in the 21st century. Burton wrote:

> *Ironically, this same public has no problem with such "handouts" as income-tax cuts and home-mortgage deductions. "We give money away for free to rich people all the time," said Rakeen Mabud, program director of the Roosevelt Institute's 21st Century Economy and Economic Inclusion programs.*
>
> *In fact, when proposed as a way to counter job losses to technology, basic income finds firmer support. A Northeastern University/Gallup poll taken in October 2017 shows Americans about evenly split on a guaranteed minimum income for workers whose jobs are replaced by artificial intelligence, with 48% in favor and 52% opposed. Additionally, 46% of respondents said that, under those circumstances, they would pay higher personal income taxes, while 80% agreed that companies profiting from AI should pay more taxes to help finance a national UBI program (emphasis added).*

This further corroborates the body of evidence presented throughout this volume, verifying that public policy is currently decades behind in addressing the extent of the pandemic of economic insecurity, the magnitude of public sentiment in favor of *the principle of income security*, and the degree of mounting demand for universal Social Security in the wake of AI and automation. We hope to have helped qualify and quantify the realities that people already knew in and felt in their guts. The urgent necessity for safer economic guardrails in today's AI-coordinated Post-Automation Era.

Today, the only lingering opposition to achieving the universal Maslow Safety realized through unconditional income security is from vestiges of generations that lived in past parallel worlds, bygone eras that only persist as holograms wandering the halls of haunted minds. The 2010s are history. Much of what worked so well then no longer works today. Moreso, the more distant the reverie. The longer we fail to adjust to the reality of the present moment, the higher the odds we're NGMI (see Glossary).

As Burton further reported:

> *Perhaps the boldest plan yet to provide Americans with a universal basic income is the American Solidarity Fund (ASF), a dividend-paying social am for the U.S. that its creator, Matt Bruenig, founder of the People's Policy Project, unveiled in August.*
>
> *A one-time 3% tax on the market capitalization of U.S. public companies would seed the fund with around $1 trillion in cash or stock. Then, an ongoing market-cap tax of 0.5% would keep money flowing into the ASF. The fund would also receive proceeds from a 5% tax on initial public stock offerings, and a 3% tax on mergers and acquisitions.*
>
> *"This is a piece of the capital stock of the country that we all collectively own and collectively benefit from," Bruenig said in an interview. "All 300 million of us are going to come together and collectively own 30% of the country's wealth" (Burton).*

Even legendary Microsoft co-founder and philanthropist Bill Gates adds his confidence in the certainty of Post-Automation Era policy requirements.

> *"Certainly there will be taxes that relate to automation. Right now, the human worker who does, say, $50,000 worth of work in a factory, that income is taxed and you get income tax, social security tax, all those things. If a robot comes in to do the same thing, you'd think that we'd tax the robot at a similar level."*[cclxiii]

> In this work, we have provided specific, concrete, immediately actionable methods by which to upgrade the Social Security Trust Fund for the 21st century while reducing the number of government agencies and bureaucracy.

A primary objective of this work is to help educate and embolden policy makers and the general public to research and prove the reasonings presented herein; thereby empirically demonstrating for themselves why 2024 is the time for decisive legislative action; to enact the principles and policies recommended in this book, not only accomplishing MLK's *guaranteed annual income* as fulfillment of FDR's *freedom from want* for all citizens of the United States, but as an act worthy of the role and responsibility for bold U.S. global leadership by being *the first nation on Earth to end poverty as humanity has known it*, further inspiring and extending the blessings of democratic free-market values and superabundance throughout the American hemisphere, and the world.

Principles of Basic Income Security

Basic Income Security *is an individual basic human right.*

Basic Income Security *means monthly guaranteed individual income at levels that sustain life in decent circumstances.*

At Levels that Sustain Life in Decent Circumstance *means a self-adjusting, market-defined index of 50% per capita GDP.*

Universal Social Security *means Maslow Safety, the natural dividend of commonwealth productivity and prosperity.*

We have discussed ways by which we can encode these principles into policy and enact them into law, not only without new bureaucracy, but while reducing redundant and obsolete bureaucracy.

While some or many of these ideas may strike some readers as new, far-fetched, or even absurd, they are essential and fundamental 21st century upgrades to the ideas and ideals that forged our great nation, from the beginning.

From the birth of the United States of America as a new, far-fetched, and absurd concept, national security has been of fundamental significance toward defending and enhancing the physical, economic, and social security of citizens.

In 1968, Martin Luther King Jr. rightly said that the ability to end poverty in the United States was incontestable.

In 1971, R. Buckminster Fuller said, "Now this is the real news of our century: it is highly feasible, to take care of all of humanity, at a higher standard of living than anybody has ever experienced or dreamt of, to do so without anybody having to profit at the expense of another, so everybody can enjoy the whole Earth. And it can all be done by 1985."[cccLxiv]

And in 1982, "But we can do so much now, with so little, that we can take care of everybody. That's why the idea of scarcity is all wrong."[ccclxv] See also Appendix: *Historical Quotations About Basic Income* to read Fuller describing 2024 events almost to a tee.

* * *

THE SAFER TRUST ACT

While this section stands on its own as ready *What Do We Do Now?* reference, those who have reviewed and understand the building blocks described throughout are best prepared to participate knowledgeably, from a position of informed consensus.

Over the past decade, we have seen significant, exciting, and extremely promising advances in the level of public awareness and serious discussion about basic income. We have witnessed a whole new generation of policy makers and policy-minded citizens running new rounds of basic income trials, from neighborhood, to city, to nation-state scale; domestic and worldwide. However, to date, none of these efforts have risen much above the level of updated academic experiment or isolated initiatives.

If the American people want the stability and security of unconditional, universal Maslow Safety to become reality, we have to do it ourselves. Therefore, we propose a citizen-drafted Social Security Accelerating Future Empowerment and Trust Revitalization Act (SAFER Trust Act) developed by the community of over 84,000 federated, libertarian, open-source, democratic participants at /r/BasicIncome on Reddit and any new readers who choose to join the work underway. Don't doubt whether you're needed and essential. If you understand the work and have insights to contribute, you are sorely needed and essential.

I've had far more than my say in these pages and because this calling is far bigger than all of us combined, it seems that the rest is up to all of us. If we can, as a community and a people, draft this legislation and get it on the floor of the US Congress, the SAFER Trust Act stands to become one of, if not the first major peer-to-peer (P2P) commons-developed pieces of legislation in U.S. history. Wouldn't that be something worth being proud to be a part of? I think so.

This is why, in 1992, I wanted to be part of something bigger than myself, something that would matter in a way that made a significant, peaceful, and lasting impact on the reduction of suffering for myself, my nation, and for humanity.

Today, with the aid of significant super-intelligence software upgrades,[ccclxvi] after having already invested more than ten years in researching, drafting, and passing major incremental legislation at city, county, and state levels, together, we've proven the methods by which we can continuously upgrade democracy and civilization for the best possible 21st century for the greatest number of sentient beings. Not just surviving this metamorphosis but thriving and flourishing far beyond.

Universal Maslow Safety is a major step forward for humanity and it's an incredible privilege to have lived long enough to observe all that's happened over the past decade, and especially the exponential growth in shared understanding over the past five years. Everything we've accomplished is the result of your often invisible, underrecognized work, I'm just a documentary stenographer, here to bear witness, to recognize.

The Work

In his article, "Policy Positions and Political Imaginaries: Framing Basic Income," self-described UK "independent researcher and writer, decentralist, and post-libertarian," Chris Shaw wrote (sagaciously, we might add):

> *Basic income is far too often framed in a confusing manner, presented as both a simple policy proposal with particular effects and as a fully realisable political imaginary that encapsulates a development upon the existing political economy. It is also viewed as a tool for market equalisation, making the lone consumer just as powerful as the retail monopolist through the provision of voice in the form of a basic income. In this sense it's a compelling vision, being compatible across multiple forms of economic or social arrangement and allowing for equality (both of opportunity and to a lesser extent of outcome) to be added onto the current political landscape.*
>
> *However, this strength of vision is also a weakness of implementation. The attempt to eschew institutional foundations ignores the complexities of execution that would come with a radical political shift that basic income would potentially incur. It also suggests that the confusion between political imaginary and policy tool is inhibitory to actual socio-political developments, as basic income gets caught in an institutional freefall, with the experiments being conducted showing further confusion over the scale of basic income, the funding mechanisms, the territorial base, and the social concepts behind it.*

Shaw's assessment is clear-eyed, perspicacious, balanced, and incisive. We took it to heart in proposing guidelines for the SAFER Trust Act.

I could not agree more with both the strengths and weaknesses Shaw sees in the policy implementation landscape. Shaw's precise and probing assessments brightly distill most of the assorted variables that we have explored in this work. Our proposal consists of an integrated set of clear strategies, precise tactics, and flexible, adaptive narrative tools for implementing the principles of King's *guaranteed annual income at levels that sustain life in decent circumstances*, indexed to 50% per capita GDP, as the most pragmatic way to implement the UDHR Article25 human right to the Maslow Safety sustained by unconditional income security through the proven institutional effectiveness, efficiency, accountability, and oversight of the Social Security Trust Fund.

Therefore, we propose a crowdsourced 2024 SAFER Trust Act as the legislative vehicle to get us from where we are today, to where we choose to be. This is not the kind of proposal that any individual can craft alone. I feel I've been fortunate to gain one unique insight amongst thousands needed to make universal Social Security real not just in our lifetime, but by the end of this decade, *before* January 1, 2030.

We can, as a community and with AI assistance, quickly and accurately identify the most salient and concise legislative templates to build upon, without starting entirely from scratch. From recent legislative efforts such as EITC bills, to historic examples like the original FAP itself, to the unexpected last-minute blessing and gift of a foundation for building a UBI LLM miraculously included in the Appendix (A Curated UBI LLM Training Data Set), we have the tools and technology. We can make our democracy better, stronger, faster in coordinated stewardship of the sacred duty to enact the will of the people.

2024 is the year in which decades of diligent work mobilize from theory to practice.

Posing the question, "why are you opposed to universal Social Security though dividends generated by an AI-managed trust fund, backed by the material assets of the American people, just like Wall Street gets?" is much more difficult for politicians to dodge than asking "are you in favor of some nebulous ballpark round number called basic income?"

Aligned with Martin Luther King Jr.'s guidance of, "a guaranteed income at levels that sustain life in decent circumstances," we inherit the duty to defend the long-established principle of equitable income security for all U.S. citizens; as reflected across more than seven decades of U.S. budgets, a pillar value of national character, unity, and security (Figure 10, U.S. Budget FY2023, Category as Percent of GDP).

There is nothing radical or new in our work. Americans have strongly supported and defended the principle and priority of equitable income security across the entire political spectrum for nearly a century. Now, we have developed the means and methods by which to realize that deepest of American Dreams.

Social Security is currently a *conditional* basic income. A guaranteed income that is available to those who meet certain conditions of age, or other challenged criteria. We have shown how the SAFER Trust Act builds upon and extends this national priority. It is clear that the United States has been so successful that we can and must now circulate the dividends of our shared superabundance in a manner that ensures the stability and future of our 21st century commonwealth.

The elderly are not the only class or category of people endowed by their Creator with the fundamental human right to live dignified economic lives. All people equally inherit that right, as articulated in the U.S Declaration of Independence, as further clarified in Article 25 of the Universal Declaration of Human Rights, and as reflected in more than seven decades of U.S. budgets. Therefore, 2024 is the time for we the people to draft and insist that Congress implement the SAFER Trust Act, or Social Security Accelerating Future Empowerment and Trust Revitalization Act, which guarantees every American adult, from the post-graduate age of twenty-six, an annual 50% per capita GDP dividend, equivalent to a modest proportion of Trust Fund earned interest, circulated in monthly installments through existing Social Security infrastructure (pages 171-172).

* * *

How Universal is Universal?

As an inescapable practical design constraint upon the philosophy of perfect universality, why do I propose the age of twenty-six as most fitting (pages 172-180), and what does this design constraint imply for arithmetic?

According to the University of Rochester Medical School, "The rational part of a teen's brain isn't fully developed and won't be until age 25 or so" (URMC). Other scientific measures suggest that people can reach the age of 30 before functioning with a fully formed adult brain. While specifics are beyond the scope of the work at hand, I have shared extensive endnotes supplying sound evidence that the age of brain-based adulthood is, on average, age twenty-six (ccxlii).

Twenty-six is currently the age until which people can legally remain on a parent's health insurance policy, and the insurance industry is a real stickler for the values of liability and accountability, so this provides additional existing institutional precedent.

Some long-time basic income proponents argue that we fail in implementing pure, unadulterated *unconditional and universal* basic income unless income circulates to the accounts of every child from the moment of birth; however, as discussed earlier (page 171), I hope that colleagues will join me in adopting achievable practicality as preferable to unattainable perfection.

Another difficult design-constraint question is, "if native-born citizens must wait until their 26th birthday to begin receiving their own income, shouldn't immigrants need to wait a similar amount of time?" The answer is a delicate, tactful, and qualified yes.[ccclxvii] Guaranteed income is an extremely powerful and flexible tool. In a nation with universal Social Security, NGOs, churches, community organizations, and conscientious philanthropists can all apply *the principles and practices of guaranteed income* to countless other specific contexts, as proved by the long history of such programs and the genius innovation of social entrepreneurs such as those committed to the mission of the New Mexico Economic Relief Working Group.

Another important inevitable design constraint is the fact that when a nation commits to the goal of achieving universal Maslow Safety through the assurance of universal income security for its citizenry, it cannot commit to implementing that goal for everyone in the whole world, not even the closest of good neighbor nations.

The individual cells in our bodies need healthy boundaries as beneficial coordination interfaces, and so do economic best practices. Nerve cells aren't discriminating against muscle cells, they perform separate, vital, and deeply interdependent functions. Universal Social Security cannot, as another arithmetic design constraint, extend immediately to new immigrants, regardless of origin.

Newly naturalized citizens may certainly qualify, depending upon negotiated terms of Trust Fund structure and management. We certainly have the latitude within which to declare naturalized citizens as net assets, rather than liabilities, by virtue of the same rationale and mechanism described earlier (page 171).

In the past, some argued that immigration was the reason that unconditional income security only worked if all nations act in perfect coordination. We've shown this to be inaccurate. International coordination is incredibly beneficial and advantageous, although not essential. An act of authentic U.S. moral leadership in a time of crisis can be an effective catalyst for genuine goodwill coordination.

Perhaps the other shoe from the 2008 global monetary crises will have dropped by the time you pick up this book, setting these measures to immediate urgent status. I'd strongly prefer that not be the case; yet if history lends any insight, I'm not holding my breath against that possibility.

We in the advanced nations can, and must, continue set ethical and moral examples of fair play, and a level playing field, the kinds of values that made the United States great, in the first place.

Finally, we must return to our pledge to seek simplicity amidst all of the complexity we've explored together, by offering a handful of core principles for the consideration of readers, activists, citizen-legislators, staffers, public policy wonks, hacks, and geeks.

Our mission, should we choose to accept, is to enact the Social Security Accelerating Future Empowerment and Trust Revitalization Act (SAFER Trust Act) as a timely legislative vehicle for translating the organic energy and momentum of the grass-roots basic income movement into landmark legislation that prolongs the legacy and expands the leadership of the United States' historical free commerce, fair trade, budgetary principles, and priorities of equitable economic opportunity, Laissez-faire market innovation, and the universal Maslow Safety of unconditional income security; to achieve the most widely shared prosperity possible in the 21st century.

Characteristics of Universal Social Security

Universal Social Security

neither legislates nor guarantees equal outcomes.

Universal Social Security

affirms the equal endowment of every individual with equal potential and promise for individual flourishing.

Universal Social Security

re-establishes a level playing field founded upon the American values of equal opportunity, personal responsibility, and civic participation.

The principle of Universal Social Security fulfills the promise of universal Maslow Safety through assuring "a guaranteed income at levels that sustain life in decent circumstances," for all U.S. citizens.

The principle of Universal Social Security restores a level playing field after decades of a steeply tilted field in favor of shareholder primacy. The principle of Maslow Safety income security does not make sure that everyone crosses the finish line at the same time, or that all win first place participation trophies. It restores equality of opportunity at the starting line in the Post-Automation Era.

The 20th century industrial default consensus narrative reality was like an oval running track that painted a straight starting line across all the lanes and then claimed that each runner had equal opportunity to run the race, while each stayed strictly in their own lane. The phrase "stay in your lane," carried all too specific and scornful a meaning, which has no place in the Post-Automation Era.

The principle of Universal Social Security means that everyone begins with the same starting blocks under their feet and with lines placed for an equal race as we each run this all too fleeting sprint called a brief human life on Earth.

In 1848 French novelist Émile Souvestre wrote, "Or, dans toute question humaine, il y a quelque chose de plus puissant que la force, que le courage, que le génie même: c'est l'idée dont le temps est venu." Here is one possible translation: "Now, in every human question, there is something more powerful than strength, than courage, than genius itself: it is the idea whose time has come."[ccclxviii] A few years later, "Laurence J. Peter [published] an instance attributed to [Victor] Hugo" (ccclxviii), "There is one thing stronger than all the armies in the world, and that is an idea whose time has come."

In Space Age United States of America, the 1960's, those ideas included ending poverty, building the internet, and landing people on the moon. Three days prior to publishing this work, the world lost one of the exemplars of that era and a timeless ambassador for the enduring values that can lead us through this historic season of change to complete that mission, lingering incomplete for more than six decades.

"Man has certainly progressed a long ways in just a short few years, and how much we're going to progress in the future is left to your imagination. If we harness our energies and keep our perspectives right, the goals are unlimited. We have taken a great step, we have opened a new era in the history of man."[ccclxix]

— *General Thomas Stafford*

— fim —

POSTSCRIPT

I can hardly believe the last-minute opportunity to share this incredible Christmas gift, which I received on Christmas Day, 2023. If this project had gone according to *my plan*, had I published it in the summer of last year, I would not have enjoyed the following incredibly entertaining and sobering moment, courtesy of *The Hill*, let alone the overwhelmingly supportive evidence of AI developments over the specific time period during which I felt like I was falling behind, not delivering and therefore unreliable, too late, impeded, delayed, and writing-blocked. All now included. Some accuse me of not understanding how the world works, and this project may provoke more of that, yet I am repeatedly privileged to bear witness to how the universe works. Amazing grace.[ccclxx]

In an emeritus opinion piece titled, "'Social Security has a junk data problem — it should be the new commissioner's first priority,' economist and retired federal employee who has authored a number of studies on the Social Security program," David A. Weaver, Ph.D. wrote:

> *"SSA routinely denies individuals disability benefits by claiming that individuals can work at jobs that, in reality, do not exist. Rein documented a case where SSA said an applicant should not receive disability benefits because the applicant could work as a nut sorter, a dowel inspector, or an egg processor. The Washington Post article had to include historical pictures to help the reader even understand what these jobs used to be (the picture of nut sorters was from 1939 and showed workers sorting pecan nuts by hand)."*[ccclxxi]

The question now becomes: which is more far-fetched and crazier, bringing the best of our human ingenuity and exponential AI technology to bear upon the opportunity to end poverty by the end of this decade, or to make sure that people are sorting pecans by hand in 2024 so that they don't get a free ride on the backs of robots doing the job?

"In any moment of decision, the best thing you can do is the right thing, the next best thing is the wrong thing, and the worst thing you can do is nothing." - Theodore Roosevelt.

GLOSSARY

AI-assisted: "If you created the content yourself, and used AI-based tools to edit, refine, error-check, or otherwise improve that content (whether text or images), then it is considered "AI-assisted" and not "AI-generated." Similarly, if you used an AI-based tool to brainstorm and generate ideas, but ultimately created the text or images yourself, this is also considered "AI-assisted" and not "AI-generated." It is not necessary to inform us of the use of such tools or processes" (Content Guidelines, Kindle Direct Publishing).

AI-generated: "[Amazon KDP] define[s] AI-generated content as text, images, or translations created by an AI-based tool. If you used an AI-based tool to create the actual content (whether text, images, or translations), it is considered "AI-generated," even if you applied substantial edits afterwards" (Content Guidelines, Kindle Direct Publishing).

Article 25, UDHR: Article 25 of the Universal Declaration of Human Rights states that:

> Everyone has the right to a standard of living adequate for the health and well-being of himself and of his family, including food, clothing, housing and medical care and necessary social services, and the right to security in the event of unemployment, sickness, disability, widowhood, old age, or other lack of livelihood in circumstances beyond his control.
>
> Motherhood and childhood are entitled to particular care and assistance. All children, whether born in or out of wedlock, shall enjoy the same social protection.

Basic Income (BI): Commonly referred to as UBI, Unconditional Basic Income, or Universal Basic Income, or Basic Income Guarantee (BIG). A sum of money circulated through individual distributions on a recurring, usually monthly, basis. To be basic, in the words of MLK is to be "sufficient to sustain life in decent circumstances." And to meet this sufficiency criteria, MLK very specifically said that the amount "must be pegged to the median income of society, not at the lowest levels of income."

Blockchain: "A digital database containing information (such as records of financial transactions) that can be simultaneously used and shared within a large decentralized, publicly accessible network" (Merriam-Webster).

Captology: "Captology is the study of computers as persuasive technologies. A persuasive computer is an interactive technology designed to change a person's attitudes or behaviors. In other words, captology pertains to the area where computing technology and persuasion overlap" (xxxviii).

Citizen Dividend: Like shareholder dividends, it is an amount of money earned by virtue of being an active stakeholder in society. Every citizen contributes to GDP, whether employed or not. Domestic and caregiving work are among the most common types of off-balance-sheet labor contributions that are not widely recognized or proportionately compensated.

Civilian Labor Force Participation Rate (CIVPART): U.S. Bureau of Labor Statistics, Civilian Labor Force Participation Rate. "The labor force as a percent of the civilian noninstitutional population. The civilian noninstitutional population includes "persons 16 years of age and older residing in the 50 states and the District of Columbia who do not live in institutions (for example, correctional facilities, long-term care hospitals, and nursing homes) and who are not on active duty in the Armed Forces" (BLS Glossary).

Consensus Narrative (CN): A peer-to-peer self-reinforcing (peer-pressured) *super synchronicity* of belief, cognition, personal conviction, and publicly enforced conformity with any *Story Itself* that achieves critical mass through the agential perceptual diffusion process of *metavalent stigmergy*. Consensus narratives demonstrate a lifecycle characterized by deepening perceived certitude of authoritative permanence, evolving by stages toward DCN, *consensus reality*, and DCNR status, i.e., the current authoritative and "objective" understanding of material Earthly reality. The terminology consensus narrative itself is an example of *entangled emergence*. All *italicized* terms are entries in this Glossary.

Consensus Reality (CR): While precise provenance eluded discovery in my investigation, Doctors Amy and Arnold Mindell define consensus reality as, "The level of our experience that is measurable and shared – aspects of reality that we can reach a consensus about."[ccclxxii] My personal use of the term derives from novel direct interactions described under *Default Consensus Reality*.

DARVO: Deflect. Avoid. Reverse Victim and Offender. While historically more often reported by women, the number of men on the receiving side of this tactic logically and empirically increases in societies experiencing the masculation of women and the emasculation of men. "It can be difficult to recognize an abuser using the DARVO tactic when you're a survivor in the middle of it. Heather Kent, registered psychotherapist, trauma recovery specialist and author of several books on surviving abuse says, 'Speaking as a survivor myself, when you're still in it, it's very hard to see what's happening. It's insidious. Often it takes an outside person who witnesses it to kind of take you aside and show you what's happening and what's not OK.' She encourages survivors who suspect they're being manipulated to avoid a common suggestion from others: couples' counseling. '[The abuser] is just going to gaslight you and call you the abusive one. A therapist is not necessarily able to see what's happening and can cause further damage and enable the abuse to continue.' Survivors also face the risk of the abuser retaliating in private, sometimes with [emotional, physical, psychological, or verbal] violence, after disclosing incidents in front of a therapist. Even the threat of this can keep a survivor quiet indefinitely. 'The solution is really to get out of the situation as soon as possible. I've never seen a situation where an abusive partner does a 180, goes to therapy and they live happily ever after.'"[ccclxxiii]

Default Consensus Narrative (DCN): An evolutionary state of shared stories that any in-group of conscious agents believes and repeats as descriptive of *Consensus Reality*. DCNs can exist among sets as small as one to sets numbered in billions. The smaller or larger the aligned in-group, the greater or lesser the influence upon forging a Default Consensus Reality.

Default Consensus Narrative Realities (DCNR): A subtle and important threshold distinction from CRs, DCNs, and DCRs, typical of awareness geometries of all shapes and sizes of conscious agent perception and intercognition clusters; ranging in scope and qualia from the individual to intimate relationships, to friendships, to small groups, nations, international relations, and perhaps beyond. DCNRs consist of the concordances of *Story Itself* in describing and explaining the circumstances, experiences, perceptions, and interpretations of our internal and external lived experience; from idiosyncratic hunches to shared vague conceptions; from individual encounters to shared direct experiences; from subjective insights to shared clarifications and classifications of meaning; the intra- and inter-contextualization of interdependently experienced, sensed, and perceived phenomena. DCNRs and DCR's can be and often become imperfectly aligned or even at odds with one another. Misalignment can be inadvertent, environmentally, or situationally influenced, or intensified by design. For instance, in the case of asymmetric information controls in *need-to-know* environments. In this context, "higher" hierarchical asymmetric information might tragically become misconstrued as the definitively superior, most accurate, "objective" perspective, even though that "higher" perspective itself is by definition subjective and assembled by egregores of similarly subjective agents. This misalignment can occur across CN, CR, DNC, and DCNR abstraction layers, leading to counterproductive, caustic, destructive, catastrophic, misuses and abuses of interpersonal and organizational power.

Default Consensus Reality (DCR): As a DCN achieves a critical mass, the number of aligned intercognition agents increases and certitude deepens. As persistence of credibility and intentionality constituent to a DCN develops it can transit an inflection point into a de facto CR. As a CR transits subsequent yet-to-be-defined inflection points in scale of subjective adherence (historically evidenced by raw numbers of adherents), the aggregate, clarified, synchronized, amplified, understandings and intentions manifest as "the world" as we know it and experience it; hence, earning the default distinction, DCR. This is nothing more fancy or sophisticated than the ordinary, quotidian experience of "as above, so below" and an empirical expression of synchrony between "inner, outer, narrative, and mystery" (Four Game Dynamics). This is also why McLuhan described the use of electronic media as inherently *metavalent* (although he didn't have that vocabulary at the time) and why the technologies of our emergent Global Brain are both so eminently hazardous and helpful at the same time. These are the very tools, methods, and processes by which we get good at it, or utterly fail at it, as Stewart Brand defined "it." See also endnote (v).

Digital Dividend and Data Dividend: These recognize and reward the massive amounts of content and consumer data that we each contribute toward the construction of the internet as a digital data repository, all day, every day, across all connected apps and services.

Dog-Piling: A type of trolling that takes place online, in mainstream media, and even in contemporary spoken political speech. Often combined with other forms of trolling, like Gas-Lighting and Sea-Lioning, Dog-Piling is essentially ganging up on someone. In social media and online networks, it is when multiple users or accounts overwhelm a target person or topic with so many messages – often purporting to be innocent elevated levels of interest – that coherent conversation is impossible (Ibid.).

Economic Intelligence Infrastructure (EII): I applied computer scientist Michael Jordan's term "Intelligence Infrastructure" the specific domain of economics. As cited earlier, Jordan wrote, "In the current era, we have a real opportunity to conceive of something historically new — a human-centric (Intelligence Infrastructure) engineering discipline."

Entangled Emergence: The principle underlying supersynchronicity when novel scientific discoveries or technological innovations independently occur at nearly the same time at different and far-distant locations on the planet.

Family Assistance Plan (FAP): A welfare reform proposal first introduced by President Richard Nixon in 1969 that would have guaranteed a minimum income for poor families. The idea of a guaranteed minimum income gained acceptability in conservative circles in the mid-1960s when libertarian economist Milton Friedman suggested adopting a negative income tax to provide a safety net for the poor while also rewarding work. President Nixon liked the boldness of a proposal that would abolish the current welfare system, and he presented the Family Assistance Plan (FAP) in a nationally televised address on August 8,1969 (Staisil). The 2018-dollar equivalent of the 1969 annual $1,600 FAP amount for an individual was $10,952.42, as calculated by Wolfram|Alpha's CPI data.[cccLxxiv] Today, as of Q3 2023, that figure is 13,094.12.[ccclxxv]

Federal Poverty Level (FPL): "Following the Office of Management and Budget's (OMB) Statistical Policy Directive 14, the Census Bureau uses a set of money income thresholds that vary by family size and composition to determine who is in poverty. If a family's total income is less than the family's threshold, then that family and every individual in it is considered in poverty" (US Census).

Four Game Dynamics: (aka 4Game, 4Games, hashtag #WT4GF) takes a view of life as Four Games at once. Inner, outer, narrative, and mystery. Also known as the short game, mid game, long game, and deep game. I came across Jamie Combs's framework too late in this work to make as full use of it as I might have. Still, I'm deeply grateful for the discovery and encouragement because the Four Game framework has helped me to think through these complex topics with more clarity for myself and hopefully helped to present this material with a little more simplicity. Special thanks to Captain Simple.

Gaslighting: A type of trolling that takes place online, in mainstream media, and even in contemporary spoken political speech. "A psychological definition of gaslighting is "an increasing frequency of systematically withholding factual information from, and/or providing false information to, the victim - having the gradual effect of making them anxious, confused, and less able to trust their own memory and perception" (UrbanDictionary.com).

GINI Index: "The Gini Index is a summary measure of income inequality. The Gini coefficient incorporates the detailed shares data into a single statistic, which summarizes the dispersion of income across the entire income distribution. The Gini coefficient ranges from 0, indicating perfect equality (where everyone receives an equal share), to 1, perfect inequality (where only one recipient or group of recipients receives all the income). The Gini is based on the difference between the Lorenz curve (the observed cumulative income distribution) and the notion of a perfectly equal income distribution."[ccclxxvi]

Great Society: "The Great Society was a set of domestic programs in the United States launched by Democratic President Lyndon B. Johnson in 1964–65. The main goal was the elimination of poverty and racial injustice. President Johnson first used the term "Great Society" during a speech at Ohio University, then unveiled the program in greater detail at an appearance at University of Michigan" (Wikipedia).

Guaranteed Annual Income (GAI): The terminology used by Martin Luther King, Jr. when launching the Poor People's Campaign. In his words, "a guaranteed minimum income for all people, and for all families of our country."

Hawthorne Effect: "The Hawthorne effect concerns research participation, the consequent awareness of being studied, and possible impact on behavior. It is a widely used research term. The original studies that gave rise to the Hawthorne effect were undertaken at Western Electric telephone manufacturing factory at Hawthorne, near Chicago, between 1924 and 1933."[ccclxxvii]

Income Security: The principle of economic security in the form of a consistent, reliable income, sufficient to maintain life in decent circumstances. The amount of income that supports and sustains Maslow Safety, generally 50% per capita GDP in any given national economy.

Job Trance: The Job Trance is an almost hypnotic belief that there is no sound, market-defined, ethical, moral, practical, pragmatic alternative to the concept of a J.O.B. as the sole Justification Of Being that affords individuals the human right to basic income security. It is the staunch conviction that the only economically viable way for a commonwealth capitalist society to circulate currency is the roughly 500-year-old mechanism of a J.O.B. as an individual's sole Justification Of Being. Doesn't matter if you're between jobs where you kicked butt for five or ten years straight or retired for a minute after forty years of eighty-hour work weeks. No job, no identity, no social standing, no civic respect. Standing at the door at Walmart is considered higher status than taking care of one's family and home. The Job Trance effectively functions as massive covert peer-to-peer psychological abuse. In contrast to the "wisdom or crowds," of the early 2000s, it's the 2,000-year-old brutality of the mob that seems to never diminish. The Job Trance holds that there is almost no way that human beings can be happy or productive outside of the employer-employee relationship. Full-time caregivers of children and the elderly are devalued and dismissed as "getting free rent" when taking care of Grandma is the one *real job* that nobody in the family wants. It hides the fact that the richest among us, so-called job creators, primarily pay their bills and sometimes even make startup payroll with passive income, generated by existing wealth.

Landlord's Game: "A young woman by the name of Elizabeth Magie created the game as a 'practical demonstration of the present system of land-grabbing with all its usual outcomes and consequences.' Her inspiration was a book by progressive economist Henry George, Progress and Poverty. The first version of the game was called The Landlord's Game. Whereas the original goal of the game was to simply accumulate wealth, the goal in the eventual Monopoly version was to own industry and create a monopoly of wealth and influence. If you're getting flashbacks of the despair that you felt as your uncle cackled maniacally when you and your last $100 landed on his three-hotel property, well, that's sort of the point of the game (the despair, not the cackling)" (cxxix).

Lottery of Birth: "We like to think that we are in control of our lives. That we are responsible for our successes and failures. That we can and should take credit or blame. But life isn't that simple." For example, "We do not choose to exist. As newborns, we're not responsible for our own natures, we're endowed with genes that we didn't ask for. We're faced with a world that we played no part in creating. We do not choose what environment we grow up in. We do not choose our [social position], we inherit it" (xcviii).

Maslow Safety: The level of basic human needs required to fulfill the two lowest foundational levels of the Maslow Hierarchy of Needs, consisting of both Physiological Needs and Safety and Security Needs. Combined, these include: "homeostasis, food, water, sleep, shelter, personal security, financial security, health and well-being, [as well as] safety against accidents, illness, and their adverse impacts" (Wikipedia).

Metacrisis: "At no other point in history has humanity faced such a wide range of novel catastrophic risks. Our civilization has never been more vast, complicated, and fragile. This systemic fragility is exacerbated by new technologies, geopolitical instability, an ecological crisis and a reliance on global economic supply chains. These interlocking, interrelated problems are known collectively as the metacrisis. The Consilience Project's primary aim is to clarify and reveal the nature of the metacrisis to enable comprehensive solutions to global problems. Our work recognizes the interconnectedness of humanity's challenges: any solution must factor the underlying drivers of each one." Source: "About the Project." The Consilience Project, https://consilienceproject.org/about-the-project/. Accessed 29 Dec. 2023.

Metavalent Stigmergy: "How New Default Consensus Realities Instantiate. The process by which new insights, intuitions, understandings, ideas, or concepts originate, germinate, blossom, propagate, and instantiate Default Consensus Realities." https://metavalent.com/ (est. 2007, long before the term was coopted to describe a kind of bonding in crystalline solids, or a certain monolithic social media empire adopted the prefix). The multi-modal symbolic and non-symbolic process or processes through which subjective perceptions organically originate and disseminate; intermittently reinforced through instinctive, unconscious, consciously overt, or covertly prescribed or influenced alignment, and subsequent persistent conformity within any population of conscious agents who authenticate, endorse, and subscribe to the account's persuasive capacity, explanatory efficacy, and exculpatory utility of constituent beliefs. "DCR" originally inspired by the work of Aubrey de Grey and David Carse.[ccclxxviii]

Mixed Economy: Broadly defined as an economic system blending elements of market economies with elements of planned economies, free markets with state interventionism, or private enterprise with public enterprise. There are many variations to the definition of a mixed economy, but two major distinctions we can draw. The first describes a mixture of markets with state interventionism, i.e., strong capitalist markets with equally strong regulatory oversight, an invisible hand to keep the invisible hand from picking the people's pockets through a mix of inhibiting policies and governmental provision of public services like healthcare and social security. The second definition is apolitical and general, referring to any economy containing a mixture of private enterprise with public initiative.[ccclxxix]

Moloch, Molochian: "Daniel Schmachtenberger | Misalignment, AI & Moloch | Win-Win with Liv Boeree." Directed by Liv Boeree, 2023. YouTube, https://www.youtube.com/watch?v=KCSsKV5F4xc.

Neglectfare: Compared to welfare, the cost of failure to do the right thing. Wasteful spending on what doesn't work, particularly when given an option that does work.

NGMI: "'NGMI' is an acronym that stands for 'Not Gonna Make It.' It's an internet slang term that's often used to express a sense of hopelessness or a lack of confidence in something, reflecting feelings of frustration or disappointment" ("NGMI." Binance Academy, https://academy.binance.com/en/glossary/ngmi. Accessed 15 Jan. 2024.).

Non-Symbolic Consciousness: See *Persistent Non-Symbolic Experience*.

Observer Effect: "The observer effect is the fact that observing a situation or phenomenon necessarily changes it. Observer effects are especially prominent in physics where observation and uncertainty are fundamental aspects of modern quantum mechanics. Observer effects are well known in fields other than physics, such as sociology, psychology, linguistics and computer science, but none of these other fields have experienced the same level of publicity and controversy as physics."[ccclxxx]

Overton Window: "The Overton window is an approach to identifying the ideas that define the spectrum of acceptability of governmental policies. It says politicians can act only within the acceptable range. Shifting the Overton window involves proponents of policies outside the window persuading the public to expand the window. Proponents of current policies, or similar ones within the window, seek to convince people that policies outside it should be deemed unacceptable. According to Lehman, who coined the term, 'The most common misconception is that lawmakers themselves are in the business of shifting the Overton window. That is absolutely false. Lawmakers are actually in the business of detecting where the window is, and then moving to be in accordance with it'" (xxii).

Overview Effect: As defined by progenitor of the term, Frank White. "[I was] flying across country and looking out the window. And having what I think was a mild experience of the overview effect, where I was imagining living in one of those O'Neill cylinders between the Earth and the moon. And I thought, if I lived in a place like that, I would always have an overview of the Earth. I would see it from a distance. And I would see it's a unified whole. There are no borders or boundaries. All of these things would become knowledge. Which, living on the surface, we find it very hard to philosophically grasp, or mentally grasp. And the term overview effect came to me. And that's when I started talking to astronauts. Because there were no people living in space permanently. There wasn't even an international space station at the time. And it was just beginning to be conceived. And so, I began work on that. And in 1987, published my book on the topic, The Overview Effect."[ccclxxxi]

Persistent Non-Symbolic Experience (PNSE): "This global research project began around 2006. It grew out of a search for people around the world who reported both extremely high wellbeing and quality of life. The core goal of the project at that time was to identify these types of people, study them intensively to determine what made them different than the rest of the population, see if there were similarities between them and, if there were, determine if it was possible for others to reach similar heights. [T]he Center for the Study of Non-Symbolic Consciousness also leads the largest global scientific endeavor ever undertaken to understand the highest forms of human wellbeing. We refer to this academically as Persistent or Ongoing Non-Symbolic Experience (PNSE or ONE), and publicly as Fundamental Wellbeing" (FW).[ccclxxxii]

Post-Automation Era: A civilization-scale evolutionary era beyond industrialization, information, and service economies, characterized by wide-scale automation and machine intelligence that fundamentally displace traditional human labor inputs.

Productive Leisure: "Productive Leisure refers to activities undertaken during free time that are both enjoyable and yield tangible or intangible benefits beyond immediate relaxation or entertainment. Unlike passive leisure, like watching TV, productive leisure involves active engagement that can lead to skill development, knowledge acquisition, or the production of something valuable."[ccclxxxiii]

Quiet Quitting: "The activity of doing the work that you need to do in order to keep your job but doing it without great enthusiasm or effort, and without agreeing to do extra tasks. Quiet quitting describes the situation when an employee mentally and emotionally checks out from their job and does the bare minimum to get by. There's nothing new about quiet quitting. It's just a new name for an old phenomenon" (Quiet Quitting. 10 Jan. 2024, https://dictionary.cambridge.org/dictionary/english/quiet-quitting).

Ruliad: "The Entangled Limit of Everything. I call it the ruliad. Think of it as the entangled limit of everything that is computationally possible: the result of following all possible computational rules in all possible ways. In many ways, the ruliad is a strange and profoundly abstract thing. But it's something very universal—a kind of ultimate limit of all abstraction and generalization. And it encapsulates not only all formal possibilities but also everything about our physical universe—and everything we experience can be thought of as sampling that part of the ruliad that corresponds to our particular way of perceiving and interpreting the universe" (xxvii).

SAFER Trust Act: The Social Security Accelerating Future Empowerment and Trust Revitalization Act. A crowd-sourced bill and legislative vehicle to modernize the Social Security Trust Fund and implement what has historically been referred to as an automation dividend, citizen dividend, digital dividend, freedom dividend, guaranteed annual income, negative income tax, unconditional basic income, universal basic income, among other names, each expressing one common objective: to articulate the principles and methods required to permanently end poverty, by decoupling income from direct labor and circulating income "at levels that sustain life in decent circumstances" (MLK).

Sea-Lioning: A type of trolling that takes place online, in mainstream media, and even in contemporary spoken political speech. "Sea-Lioning is an Internet slang term referring to intrusive attempts at engaging an unwilling debate opponent by feigning civility and incessantly requesting evidence to back up their claims. The term was coined in September 2014 by anti-GamerGate Internet users to mock perceived online discussion tactics employed by GamerGate supporters" (KnowYourMeme.com).

Singularity, aka Technological Singularity: 1.) The hypothesis that the invention of artificial superintelligence (ASI) will abruptly trigger runaway technological growth, resulting in unfathomable changes to human civilization. 2.) According to this hypothesis, an upgradable intelligent agent (such as a computer running software-based artificial general intelligence) would enter a "runaway reaction" of self-improvement cycles, with each new and more intelligent generation appearing more rapidly, causing an intelligence explosion, and resulting in a powerful superintelligence that would, qualitatively, far surpass all human intelligence (Wikipedia).

Social Security: "The principle or practice or a program of public provision (as through social insurance or assistance) for the economic security and social welfare of the individual and his or her family" (Webster).

Story Itself: Introduced by C.S. Lewis in his 1947 essay, *On Stories* (lxxxix).

Super Synchronicity: A specific occurrence of synchronicity on a global scale, when significant cultural innovations, discoveries, or inventions emerge independently on distant parts of the planet, at nearly or precisely the same time. A kind of *entangled emergence* if you will. There is an interesting phenomenon observed in the history of scientific discovery and technological invention, whereby similar novel understandings or artifacts emerge in different places across the world at nearly or precisely the same time. One of the most striking and lesser-known is the contest over who was really the first man to fly. Wright Brothers vs. Pierre Dumont. The Chinese had guns before the West; however, at the time considered the harm guns caused so horrendously dishonorable that the society rejected them. I glimpsed a YouTube video claiming that some musical artists work so hard in the studio because they worry that if they don't, a competing artist will "receive the frequency," before they do. Like an ephemeral competition for the birthright of innovation. In my own life, our work building the world's first fiber-optic Ethernet To The Home network was documented by the online technology journal Slashdot as up and running just one week ahead of a Swiss team of which we had no knowledge. Whether or not they knew of our work (Swiss investors had certainly visited us in the months prior) and were competing, I don't know. The root concept of a *consensus narrative* appears to be another super synchronicity. This concept is core to the phenomenon of metavalent stigmergy, so I've certainly toyed with DCNs and DCNRs since at least 2004; however, the terminology has also emerged from other sources in other context over the past couple of decades. So it is difficult to pinpoint provenance. Should I be crediting others, or should they have credited me, from 2004, and failed to do so because "nobody will know" since the terminology was lifted from the internet, which few everyday people understood at the time? From this perspective, *super synchronicity* is an interesting illustration of *entangled emergence* at work, which we observe in the form of conjectures such as "information wants to be free," upon which the open-source movement was founded. Super synchronicity challenges the practicality, legitimacy, and wisdom of 20th century conceptions of intellectual property in ways earliest and best articulated by Lawrence Lessig; although by this same principle, others of whom we are not aware may have proposed similar solutions as Creative Commons licensing, prior to Lessig's de-facto global standard.

Synthetic Intelligence (SI) and Synthetic Knowledge Agent (SKA): I personally prefer this terminology to "AI" as it is closer to describing what LLM's actually do, today. By next-word-prediction, LLM's synthesize vast quantities of information in way that presents a particular new kind of knowledge that is still subject to human review and verification. 2024's technology is not even close to Actually Intelligent AI, yet, therefore I refer to the 2023 public emergence of ChatGPT and its silicon-substrate colleagues as *first-generation Synthetic Knowledge Agents*.

Trolling: Playing an intentionally disingenuous, divisive, derisive, deceptive, "devil's advocate." Types of trolling can include, but are not limited to: Gas-Lighting, Dog-Piling, and Sea-Lioning. "Trolling is an Internet slang term used to describe any Internet user behavior that is meant to intentionally anger or frustrate someone else" (KnowYourMeme.com).

UBI: Acronym used interchangeably to mean either unconditional basic income or universal basic income.

UDHR: Universal Declaration of Human Rights. "Translated into hundreds of languages and dialects from Abkhaz to Zulu, the UDHR set a world record in 1999 for being *the most translated document in the world*. At present, there are 512 different translations available in HTML and/or PDF format" (Office of the High Commissioner for Human Rights, United Nations, emphasis added).

* * *

APPENDIX

How AI Computes Value of a Human Life

I asked an identical set of 3 questions to each of the top 3 AI's of early 2024, then adapted the conversation according to their responses. I found it interesting that all three chose to interpret my initial question as having nothing to do with death, but rather the cost of keeping soldiers in the field, while alive. These too are helpful figures for our purposes because they provide an additional perspective on the costs analyzed in the main text. I wish I had time to further refine the calculations in the main text by hand-checking these AI contributions, but one has to call the work *good enough* at some point. I think it's also important for authors to be very clear about what is and isn't AI-assisted or AI-generated as standard best practice in the Post-Automation Era.

I found it interesting that chat GPT was the cagiest of the three when it came to providing numbers, while Google Bard offered numbers right away. Bing Co-Pilot seems to take a middle-of-the-road approach, compared to those two. The following are unedited results, with links to the chats themselves.

ChatGPT

PROMPT: What is the average cost of a U.S. soldier's life when estimating the cost of war?

TRANSCRIPT: https://chat.openai.com/share/e4fd59b0-f8a5-4cb6-a3a8-72bb8dc5780b

The cost of sustaining a U.S. soldier for war cost estimation is a complex figure that encompasses various components. As of the latest information available, the average cost per active-duty service member is close to $140,000. This figure includes regular pay and special pay, as well as other benefits such as health care, retirement, housing, and subsistence allowances [https://www.nationaldefensemagazine.org/articles/2021/10/19/pentagon-personnel-costs-at-historic-high].

The U.S. Department of Defense employs over 2.2 million people, including almost 1.4 million active-duty personnel [https://www.csis.org/analysis/assessing-trends-military-personnel-costs] It's important to note that these costs have risen significantly over time. Between fiscal years 2000 and 2012, during the peak of the Afghanistan and Iraq Wars, the average cost per service member increased by 64 percent, adjusted for inflation [https://www.nationaldefensemagazine.org/articles/2021/10/19/pentagon-personnel-costs-at-historic-high].

For further insights, the Congressional Budget Office's report on the U.S. Military's Force Structure for Fiscal Year 2024 provides detailed data on personnel numbers and costs for each type of major combat unit in the U.S. military, reflecting the Defense Department's fiscal year 2024 budget submission [https://www.cbo.gov/publication/59696].

It's also worth considering that these costs are part of a broader context of military spending and budgeting, which includes factors like modernization initiatives, procurement of new equipment, and other operational costs. The military budget, therefore, includes a wide array of expenses beyond just the cost of sustaining soldiers [https://www.csis.org/analysis/military-forces-and-acquisition-programs-how-did-they-fare-fy-2024-budget] [https://www.csis.org/analysis/us-military-spending-cost-wars].

Prompt: What is the average cost of a U.S. soldier's lost life when estimating the cost of war, when killed in service?

The cost of the lost life of a U.S. soldier killed in the line of duty is a complex issue that goes beyond a simple financial analysis. When talking about the human cost in military conflicts, it is important to consider both tangible and intangible aspects.

Tangible Financial Costs: These include benefits paid to the families of deceased soldiers, such as payment of a death benefit, insurance and pensions. For example, the U.S. Department of Veterans Affairs (VA) provides death compensation that may include a lump sum payment, survivor benefits for spouse and children, and educational benefits for dependents.

Non-Financial and Intangible Costs: These costs are more difficult to quantify and include the emotional and psychological impact on the soldier's family, the loss of human potential, and the impact on the community and society at large.

While financial costs can be estimated based on benefits and compensations provided by the government, intangible costs are immeasurable and vary greatly from case to case.

There is no fixed monetary value that can be placed on a soldier's life, as each life lost represents a unique and irreparable loss to families, communities and the nation. These costs also reflect the loss of experience, skills and potential that the individual could have contributed to society throughout their life.

Furthermore, the cost of war is not limited to military casualties, but also includes the impact on civilians, infrastructure, and the economic and political stability of affected regions. It is a complex topic that involves multiple dimensions in addition to finance.

PROMPT: Understanding the complexity and nuances, can you draw on all available resources to provide me with an estimate of the combined tangible and intangible financial cost of a U.S. soldier's lost life?

Providing an accurate and comprehensive estimate of the combined cost, both tangible and intangible financial, of the lost life of a U.S. soldier is a significant challenge, particularly given the complex and multifaceted nature of these costs. However, we can explore and zoom in on different aspects to get an overview.

1. Tangible Financial Costs:

Death Benefits: Includes payment of death benefits from the US Department of Veterans Affairs, life insurance for military personnel, and possible survivor benefits. These amounts vary but can include a one-time payment (which can be tens of thousands of dollars) plus a monthly spousal and child benefit.

Funeral Expenses: The US government also covers certain funeral expenses.

Educational Benefits for Dependents: Programs like the Fry Scholarship offer educational benefits to children and spouses of military personnel who died in the line of duty.

2. Intangible Costs:

Emotional and Psychological Impact: This is perhaps the most significant and most difficult to quantify cost. The loss of a loved one profoundly affects families, friends and communities.

Loss of Human Potential: The lost life of a soldier represents the loss of potential contribution to society, both in terms of professional achievements and personal contributions.

Impact on Military Unit Morale and Effectiveness: The loss of soldiers can impact the morale and operational effectiveness of military units.

Given the immeasurable nature of intangible costs, it is not possible to provide a precise monetary value. These costs are deeply subjective and vary from case to case.

For tangible costs, estimates can be made based on the specific benefits paid, but they vary depending on the individual situation of each soldier and his or her family.

In short, while tangible financial costs can be estimated based on benefits paid, intangible costs are deeply personal and immeasurable, making the total cost of a soldier's lost life something that transcends a financial assessment.

PROMPT: Can you provide numbers? Zoom in on each of them, and while precise monetary value is not possible, provide the best rough estimate of monetary values.

Of course, let's explore and estimate the tangible financial costs related to the loss of a US soldier. It's important to note that these values can vary based on a variety of factors, such as the length of service, the soldier's rank, and the specific circumstances of the death. The numbers here are general estimates only and may not reflect exact individual cases.

1. Death Benefits:
One-time Death Gratuity Payment: It is a payment of $100,000 made to the families of military personnel who die while active in service.
Life Insurance from Servicemember's Group Life Insurance (SGLI): SGLI can pay up to $400,000 depending on the coverage chosen by the soldier.

2. Survivor Pensions:
Dependency and Indemnity Compensation (DIC): DIC is a monthly benefit paid to eligible spouses, children and parents of military personnel who died in the line of duty or from complications of injury, illness or disability related to the service. In 2021, the base monthly rate for surviving spouses is approximately $1,340.

3. Funeral Expenses:
The U.S. Department of Veterans Affairs offers compensation for funeral expenses that may vary. For example, for deaths occurring on duty, the maximum reimbursement amount is about $2,000.

4. Educational Benefits for Dependents:
Fry Scholarship and Dependent Education Program (DEA): Provides educational benefits to spouses and children of deceased military personnel. The DEA provides up to 36 months of benefits, with a monthly rate that can exceed $1,200 per month for the 2020-2021 academic year.

As for intangible costs, they are incalculable and vary immensely. It is not possible to place a monetary value on losses such as the emotional impact on family and friends, the loss of human potential and future contributions, and the impact on the morale and effectiveness of military units. These costs represent a significant emotional and social burden that goes beyond any financial estimate.

Therefore, while we can estimate the tangible financial costs with some accuracy, the intangible costs remain an invaluable and deeply personal aspect of the loss of a soldier.

PROMPT: What is the maximum possible monthly benefit of the Fry Scholarship and Dependents' Educational Assistance (DEA) Program?

The Fry Scholarship and Dependents' Educational Assistance (DEA) Program provides educational benefits to dependents and spouses of U.S. military personnel who died or were totally and permanently disabled in the line of duty. Let's analyze the benefits offered by each of these programs:

1. Fry Scholarship:
The Fry Scholarship provides educational benefits to children and spouses of military personnel who died in the line of duty after September 10, 2001. Fry Scholarship recipients are eligible to receive 100% of Post-9/11 GI Bill benefits, which

includes payment full tuition and fees for an undergraduate course at a public educational institution or a maximum annual amount at private or foreign institutions (this amount may change annually).

In addition, the Fry Scholarship includes a monthly housing payment (MHA) that is based on the cost of living where the school is located and an annual amount for expenses with books and study materials.

2. Dependents' Educational Assistance (DEA):

The DEA, also known as Chapter 35, provides educational assistance to dependents of veterans who are totally and permanently disabled due to a service-related condition or who died while such a condition was in effect.

In terms of financial benefits, the DEA provides a monthly payment to beneficiaries who are pursuing an educational program. For the 2021-2022 academic year, the maximum monthly fee for full-time students was approximately $1,265.

Importantly, exact amounts and program provisions may change based on legislative and policy updates from the U.S. Department of Veterans Affairs. Additionally, values can be adjusted annually to keep pace with changes in the cost of living and other economic considerations.

Google Bard

PROMPT: What is the average cost of a U.S. soldier's life when estimating the cost of war?

TRANSCRIPT: https://g.co/bard/share/35df93c50a90

The cost of equipment for a US soldier is also significant. A typical U.S. soldier carries about $10,000 worth of equipment, including weapons, ammunition, clothing and protective gear.

U.S. soldiers' salaries and benefits are also significant. The average salary for a US soldier is around $30,000. US soldier benefits include health insurance, life insurance, retirement, and other benefits.

The cost of medical and mental health services provided to veterans is significant. U.S. veterans face a higher risk of physical and mental health problems than the civilian population. The cost of medical and mental health services provided to veterans is estimated at about $60 billion per year.

Therefore, the average cost of a US soldier's life when estimating the cost of war is about $1.5 million. This cost is significant and must be considered when evaluating the cost of war.

It's important to note that this average cost is just an estimate. The actual cost of a U.S. soldier's life can vary depending on a number of factors, including the soldier's rank, the type of war he or she is fighting in, and the severity of his or her injuries or wounds.

PROMPT: What is the average cost of a U.S. soldier's lost life when estimating the cost of war, when killed in service?

The average cost of a U.S. soldier's lost life when estimating the cost of war when killed in the line of duty is about $2.5 million. This cost includes the cost of the soldier's education, training, equipment, salaries, and benefits, as well as the cost of medical and mental health services provided to the soldier's family.

The cost of educating and training a U.S. soldier is significant. The average cost of a college degree in the US is around $30,000. The cost of military training is even higher. Basic training for a US soldier costs about $10,000.

The cost of equipment for a US soldier is also significant. A typical U.S. soldier carries about $10,000 worth of equipment, including weapons, ammunition, clothing and protective gear.

U.S. soldiers' salaries and benefits are also significant. The average salary for a US soldier is around $30,000. US soldier benefits include health insurance, life insurance, retirement, and other benefits.

The cost of medical and mental health services provided to the soldier's family is also significant. Families of U.S. soldiers face a higher risk of physical and mental health problems than the civilian population. The cost of medical and mental health services provided to soldiers' families is estimated at about $20 billion per year.

Therefore, the average cost of a U.S. soldier's lost life when estimating the cost of war when killed in the line of duty is about $2.5 million. This cost is significant and must be considered when evaluating the cost of war.

It's important to note that this average cost is just an estimate. The actual cost of a U.S. soldier's lost life can vary depending on a number of factors, including the soldier's rank, the type of war he or she is fighting in, and the severity of his or her injuries or wounds.

In addition to the financial cost, the death of a soldier also has a significant emotional cost. Families of soldiers killed in the line of duty face a period of grief and loss that can last years.

Bing Co-Pilot

What is the average cost of a U.S. soldier's life when estimating the cost of war?

RESPONSE: https://sl.bing.net/b1xd0g8zCOO

Estimating the cost of a US soldier's life in terms of war is a complex task as it involves many factors, including direct and indirect costs. However, some estimates can be made based on available data.

In almost 20 years of conflicts in the Middle East and the Gulf, the American government has allocated almost US$6 trillion to finance operations[1]. Brown University's Costs of War Project estimates total spending on the conflict in

Afghanistan at US$2.26 trillion[3]. During this period, 2,500 US soldiers died in Afghanistan[3].

Therefore, if we divide the total cost of the war by the number of lives lost, we get a rough estimate of the monetary cost per life lost. However, it is important to note that this is a simplification, and the actual cost may vary depending on many factors, including medical costs, veterans' benefits, interest on debts incurred to finance the war, and many other indirect costs.

Furthermore, it is important to remember that human life is invaluable and that these numbers do not reflect the true human cost of war.

SOURCE: Conversation with Bing, 01/09/2024

(1) In 20 years, wars cost the US US$6 trillion; amount could.... https://noticias.uol.com.br/reportagens-especiais/em-20-anos-guerras-custaram-us-6-tri-aos-eua-quantia-poderia-eliminar-fome- or-reverse-heating/.

(2) War in Afghanistan cost the US $300 million a day during 20 .... https://forbes.com.br/forbes-money/2021/08/guerra-no-afeganistao-custou-us-300 - millions-per-day-to-the-usa-for-20-years/.

(3) Cost of living in the United States - updated prices for 2024. - Expatistan. https://www.expatistan.com/pt/cost-de-vida/pais/estados-unidos.

(4) War in Afghanistan: the results of the most expensive conflict in history.... https://www.bbc.com/portuguese/internacional-56953737.

What is the average cost of a U.S. soldier's lost life when estimating the cost of war, when killed in service?

RESPONSE: https://sl.bing.net/eqzPCoUtFgi

Estimating the monetary cost of a U.S. soldier's life lost in the line of duty is a complex and delicate task. However, based on some sources, we can make a rough estimate.

According to Brown University's Costs of War Project, the United States has spent about $8 trillion on wars on terrorism over the past 20 years, resulting in about 900,000 deaths. Of those, more than 7,000 were U.S. military service members[2].

If we divide the total cost of the war by the number of lives lost, we get a rough estimate of the monetary cost per life lost. However, it is important to note that this is a simplification, and the actual cost may vary depending on many factors, including medical costs, veterans' benefits, interest on debts incurred to finance the war, and many other indirect costs.

Furthermore, it is important to remember that human life is invaluable and that these numbers do not reflect the true human cost of war. It is also important to note that four times as many U.S. military service members died by suicide than in combat in the post-9/11 wars[2], signaling a widespread mental health crisis.

For the most accurate and up-to-date information, I recommend consulting official government reports or other reliable sources.

SOURCE: Conversation with Bing, 01/09/2024, https://sl.bing.net/b1xd0g8zCOO.

(1) Costs of the 20-year war on terror: $8 trillion and 900,000 deaths. https://www.brown.edu/news/2021-09-01/costsofwar.
(2) US & Allied Killed and Wounded | Costs of War. https://watson.brown.edu/costsofwar/costs/human/military.
(3) One Injured Soldier of War Costs the U.S. $2 million. https://www.thefiscaltimes.com/Articles/2013/05/15/One-Injured-Soldier-of-War-Costs-the-US-2-million.
(4) Weighing the Value of an Infantry Soldier's Life. https://hbr.org/2013/09/weighing-the-value-of-an-infan.
(5) Pentagon Personnel Costs at Historic High - National Defense Magazine. https://www.nationaldefensemagazine.org/articles/2021/10/19/pentagon-personnel-costs-at-historic-high.

PROMPT: Understanding that it is a simplification, divide the total cost of the war by the number of lives lost, to get a rough estimate of the monetary cost per life lost.

RESPONSE: https://sl.bing.net/gJUhyWCsBCC

Based on data from Brown University's Costs of War Project, the United States has spent nearly $8 trillion on wars on terrorism over the past 20 years, resulting in the loss of more than 7,000 lives of U.S. military service members.

Using these numbers, we can make a rough estimate of the monetary cost per life lost:

US$8 trillion /7,000 lives = approximately US$1.14 billion per life

Keep in mind, however, that this is a simplification, and the actual cost may vary depending on many factors. Furthermore, it is important to remember that human life is invaluable and that these numbers do not reflect the true human cost of war.

* * *

Life Insurance as Human Value Holding Industry

PROMPT: What is the size of the largest insurance company's balance sheet and what is their asset allocation?

Bing Co-Pilot

RESPONSE: https://sl.bing.net/kCnpbz6iUUK

The largest insurance company by assets is Ping An Insurance, with total assets amounting to approximately $1,503,340,967,957. Please note that this information is based on the latest available data and may have changed since my last update in 2021. As for asset allocation, the specifics can vary greatly between different insurance companies and regions. However, I found some general information about the U.S. insurance industry's asset allocation. As of the end of 2021, U.S. insurance companies reported $8 trillion in total cash and invested assets. The asset classes were distributed as follows: - Bonds: 61.4% - Common stocks: 14.6% - Mortgages: 8.3% - Schedule BA assets: 6.5% Please note that these percentages represent the industry average and individual companies may have different asset allocations. For the most accurate and up-to-date information, I recommend checking the specific insurance company's annual report or other official financial disclosures.

Chat GPT

RESPONSE: https://chat.openai.com/share/f3b88b8c-bc3d-4715-80e8-c4ef4d8f7416

The largest insurance company by balance sheet size in 2024 appears to be Allianz SE, with nonbanking assets totaling approximately US$1.1 trillion, despite a 10% decrease from the previous year. UnitedHealth Group, meanwhile, has the highest net premiums written (NPW), amounting to US$257.2 billion in 2022 [https://www.insurancebusinessmag.com/us/news/breaking-news/revealed--worlds-largest-insurance-companies-471436.aspx].

Allianz's balance sheet for the end of 2022 shows a total asset value of 1,021,503 million EUR. Their asset allocation includes:

1. Cash and cash equivalents: 22,573 million EUR.
2. Financial assets carried at fair value through income: 16,568 million EUR.
3. Investments: 540,537 million EUR.
4. Loans and advances to banks and customers: 125,900 million EUR.
5. Financial assets for unit-linked contracts: 141,024 million EUR.
6. Reinsurance assets: 59,509 million EUR.
7. Deferred acquisition costs: 36,583 million EUR.
8. Deferred tax assets: 6,939 million EUR.
9. Other assets: 49,645 million EUR.

Non-current assets and assets of disposal groups classified as held for sale: 3,324 million EUR. Intangible assets: 18,900 million EUR [https://www.allianz.com/en/investor_relations/results-reports/financial-statements.html].

This detailed breakdown provides a comprehensive view of Allianz's asset distribution as of December 31, 2022.

Google Bard

RESPONSE: https://g.co/bard/share/d8fc26294c0c

Determining the "largest" insurance company depends on your chosen metric. However, under two common measures, here's the information you requested:

Total Assets:

Globally: Ping An Insurance Group holds the title with total assets of approximately $1.6 trillion as of 2021.

United States: Berkshire Hathaway takes the crown with total assets of around $950 billion as of 2022.

Asset Allocation:

The specific asset allocation for these companies will vary based on their business model and risk management strategies. However, here's a general overview:

Ping An Insurance Group:

Investments: Around 60% of their assets are held in investments, including stocks, bonds, and real estate.

Policy reserves: 25-30% are allocated to policy reserves, the funds accumulated to cover future claims.

Cash and equivalents: The remaining 10-15% are in cash and equivalents for liquidity purposes.

Berkshire Hathaway:

Insurance subsidiaries: A significant portion (around 60-70%) is invested in its various insurance subsidiaries like Geico and General Re.

Equities: 20-30% is invested in a diverse portfolio of publicly traded companies.

Cash and equivalents: They typically hold a substantial amount (around 10-20%) in cash and equivalents for flexibility and strategic acquisitions.

Remember, these are just general breakdowns, and the actual allocations can fluctuate based on market conditions and business dynamics. For specific, up-to-date information, I recommend checking the most recent annual reports of the respective companies. Is there anything else you'd like to know about the largest insurance companies or their asset allocation?

A Curated UBI LLM Training Data Set

A Large Language Model (LLM) for policy makers will be invaluable as a tool for data mining knowledge in the construction of sound policy. The following bibliography consists of the most recent and most cited current papers on Basic Income experiments and principles, as an initial training data set for such a model. For help adding to this training data set, contact me at http://michael.silverton.palo-alto.ca.us/

Adkins, Lisa, and Hanna Ylöstalo. "Experimenting with Wellbeing: Basic Income, Immaterial Labour and Changing Forms of Productivity." Critical Sociology 47, no. 3 (2021). https://doi.org/10.1177/0896920520940011.

Aerts, Elise, Ive Marx, and Gerlinde Verbist. "Not That Basic: How Level, Design and Context Matter for the Redistributive Outcomes of Universal Basic Income." SSRN Electronic Journal, 2023. https://doi.org/10.2139/ssrn.4361921.

Allegri, Giuseppe, and Renato Foschi. "Universal Basic Income as a Promoter of Real Freedom in a Digital Future." World Futures 77, no. 1 (2021). https://doi.org/10.1080/02604027.2020.1792600.

Bärnthaler, Richard, and Corinna Dengler. "Universal Basic Income, Services, or Time Politics? A Critical Realist Analysis of (Potentially) Transformative Responses to the Care Crisis." SSRN Electronic Journal, 2023. https://doi.org/10.2139/ssrn.4308613.

Bidadanure, Juliana Uhuru. "The Political Theory of Universal Basic Income." Annual Review of Political Science, 2019. https://doi.org/10.1146/annurev-polisci-050317-070954.

Calnitsky, David, Jonathan P. Latner, and Evelyn L. Forget. "Life after Work: The Impact of Basic Income on Nonemployment Activities." Social Science History 43, no. 4 (2019). https://doi.org/10.1017/ssh.2019.35.

Castro, Amy, and Stacia West. "THE CASE FOR BASIC INCOME EXPERIMENTS." Journal of Policy Analysis and Management 41, no. 2 (2022). https://doi.org/10.1002/pam.22385.

Chohan, Usman W. "Universal Basic Income: A Review." SSRN Electronic Journal, 2017. https://doi.org/10.2139/ssrn.3013634.

Conesa, Juan Carlos, Bo Li, and Qian Li. "A Quantitative Evaluation of Universal Basic Income." Journal of Public Economics 223 (2023). https://doi.org/10.1016/j.jpubeco.2023.104881.

Daemen, Josette. "What (If Anything) Can Justify Basic Income Experiments? Balancing Costs and Benefits in Terms of Justice." Basic Income Studies, 2021. https://doi.org/10.1515/bis-2021-0024.

Daruich, Diego, and Raquel Fernández. "Universal Basic Income: A Dynamic Assessment." SSRN Electronic Journal, 2021. https://doi.org/10.2139/ssrn.3626852.

Day, Creina. "Increasing Inequality and Voting for Basic Income: Could Gender Inequality Worsen?" SSRN Electronic Journal, 2023. https://doi.org/10.2139/ssrn.4222595.

Fabre, Adrien, Thomas Douenne, and Linus Mattauch. "International Attitudes Toward Global Policies." SSRN Electronic Journal, 2023. https://doi.org/10.2139/ssrn.4448523.

Fabre, Alice, Stephane Pallage, and Christian Zimmermann. "Universal Basic Income versus Unemployment Insurance." SSRN Electronic Journal, 2021. https://doi.org/10.2139/ssrn.2540055.

Fitzroy, Felix R., and Jim Y. Jin. "Efficient Redistribution: Comparing Basic Income with Unemployment Benefits." SSRN Electronic Journal, 2021. https://doi.org/10.2139/ssrn.1693333.

Forget, Evelyn L. "The Town with No Poverty: The Health Effects of a Canadian Guaranteed Annual Income Field Experiment." Canadian Public Policy 37, no. 3 (2011). https://doi.org/10.3138/cpp.37.3.283.

Furman, Jason, and Robert Seamans. "AI and the Economy." Innovation Policy and the Economy 19, no. 1 (2019). https://doi.org/10.1086/699936.

Goldblatt, Beth. "Basic Income, Gender and Human Rights." SSRN Electronic Journal, 2022. https://doi.org/10.2139/ssrn.4006768.

Gonalons-Pons, Pilar, and David Calnitsky. "Exit, Voice and Loyalty in the Family: Findings from a Basic Income Experiment." Socio-Economic Review 20, no. 3 (2022). https://doi.org/10.1093/ser/mwaa050.

Grisolia, Filippo, Sara Dewachter, and Nathalie Holvoet. "Follow the Hand That Feeds You? The Effects of Non-Governmental Cash Transfers on Citizenship." Social Policy and Administration, 2023. https://doi.org/10.1111/spol.12914.

Gromadzki, Jan. "Labor Supply Effects of a Universal Cash Transfer." SSRN Electronic Journal, 2023. https://doi.org/10.2139/ssrn.4464600.

Haagh, Louise. "The Political Economy of Governance Capacity and Institutional Change: The Case of Basic Income Security Reform in European Welfare States." Social Policy and Society 18, no. 2 (2019). https://doi.org/10.1017/S1474746418000507.

Halmetoja, Antti, Jurgen De Wispelaere, and Johanna Perkiö. "A Policy Comet in Moominland? Basic Income in the Finnish Welfare State." Social Policy and Society 18, no. 2 (2019). https://doi.org/10.1017/S1474746418000258.

Hämäläinen, Kari, and Jouko Verho. "DESIGN AND EVALUATION OF THE FINNISH BASIC INCOME EXPERIMENT." National Tax Journal 75, no. 3 (2022). https://doi.org/10.1086/720737.

Hamilton, Leah, Mathieu Despard, Stephen Roll, Dylan Bellisle, Christian Hall, and Allison Wright. "Does Frequency or Amount Matter? An Exploratory Analysis the Perceptions of Four Universal Basic Income Proposals." Social Sciences 12, no. 3 (2023). https://doi.org/10.3390/socsci12030133.

Handler, Joel F. Social Citizenship and Workfare in the United States and Western Europe: The Paradox of Inclusion. Social Citizenship and Workfare in the United States and Western Europe: The Paradox of Inclusion, 2004. https://doi.org/10.1017/CBO9780511522338.

Handler, Joel F., and Yeheskel Hasenfeld. Blame Welfare, Ignore Poverty and Inequality. Blame Welfare, Ignore Poverty and Inequality, 2006. https://doi.org/10.1017/CBO9780511511493.

Harris, Neal. "Critical Theory and Universal Basic Income." Critical Sociology 49, no. 7–8 (2023). https://doi.org/10.1177/08969205231151562.

Henderson, Troy. "Disentangling the Normative Justification of Basic Income from the Structure of the Capitalist Wage Relation and the Culture of the Work Ethic." Journal of Sociology 59, no. 4 (2023). https://doi.org/10.1177/14407833231196937.

Hiilamo, Heikki. "A Truly Missed Opportunity: The Political Context and Impact of the Basic Income Experiment in Finland: A Contribution to the Special Issue on 'The Policy Impact of Basic Income Experiments in Europe.'" European Journal of Social Security, 2022. https://doi.org/10.1177/13882627221104501.

Jaimovich, Nir, Itay Saporta Eksten, Ofer Adi Setty, and yaniv yedid-levi. "Universal Basic Income: Inspecting the Mechanisms." SSRN Electronic Journal, 2022. https://doi.org/10.2139/ssrn.4114602.

Jang, Youngsoo. "On the Time Consistency of Universal Basic Income." SSRN Electronic Journal, 2023. https://doi.org/10.2139/ssrn.4434337.

Kangas, Olli, Signe Jauhiainen, Miska Simanainen, and Minna Ylikännö. Experimenting with Unconditional Basic Income: Lessons from the Finnish BI Experiment 2017-2018. Experimenting with Unconditional Basic Income: Lessons from the Finnish BI Experiment 2017-2018, 2021. https://doi.org/10.4337/9781839104855.

———. "Introduction to the Journey of the Finnish Basic Income Experiment." In Experimenting with Unconditional Basic Income: Lessons from the Finnish BI Experiment 2017-2018, 2021. https://doi.org/10.4337/9781839104855.00009.

Kangas, Olli, and Minna Ylikännö. "Basic Income and the Status of Women in an Established Gender-Equal Welfare State: Results from the Finnish Basic Income Experiment." International Journal of Environmental Research and Public Health 20, no. 3 (2023). https://doi.org/10.3390/ijerph20031733.

Kim, Dawon, and Jai S. Mah. "Basic Income Policy of Korea." Journal of Poverty 27, no. 1 (2023). https://doi.org/10.1080/10875549.2021.2010861.

Kim, Sang Kyun, and Seo Yeon Ahn. "An Analysis on Basic Income: Evidence Using Data from Experimental Projects throughout the World." Asian Social Work and Policy Review 17, no. 2 (2023). https://doi.org/10.1111/aswp.12272.

Laenen, Tijs, Marie Laure Mulayi, Cyrille Francisco, and Wim Van Lancker. "Basic Income in Belgium Survey: Experimental Data on Citizens' Attitudes toward a Variety of Basic Income Policies." Data in Brief 49 (2023). https://doi.org/10.1016/j.dib.2023.109376.

Laín, Bru. "BETWEEN EPISTEMIC NECESSITY AND POLITICAL UTILITY: THE ROLE OF BASIC INCOME EXPERIMENTS." Journal of Policy Analysis and Management 41, no. 2 (2022). https://doi.org/10.1002/pam.22384.

Lange, Emiel de, Jocelyne S. Sze, James Allan, Scott Atkinson, Hollie Booth, Robert Fletcher, Munib Khanyari, and Omar Saif. "A Global Conservation Basic Income to Safeguard Biodiversity." Nature Sustainability 6, no. 8 (2023). https://doi.org/10.1038/s41893-023-01115-7.

Li, Tania Murray. "Centering Labor in the Land Grab Debate." Journal of Peasant Studies 38, no. 2 (2011). https://doi.org/10.1080/03066150.2011.559009.

Luduvice, André Victor Doherty. "The Macroeconomic Effects of Universal Basic Income Programs." SSRN Electronic Journal, 2021. https://doi.org/10.2139/ssrn.3932568.

McDowell, T. O. M. "Basic Income and the Legitimization Crisis of Neoliberalism." Journal of Social Policy 52, no. 3 (2023). https://doi.org/10.1017/S0047279421000763.

Moutos, Thomas, and William Scarth. "Some Macroeconomic Consequences of Basic Income and Employment Subsidies." SSRN Electronic Journal, 2021. https://doi.org/10.2139/ssrn.396460.

Neves, Catarina. "Basic Income Experiments: Expanding the Debate on UBI and Reciprocity." Basic Income Studies 16, no. 1 (2021). https://doi.org/10.1515/bis-2021-0019.

Ortiz, Isabel, Christina Behrendt, Andres Acuña-Ulate, and Nguyen Quynh Anh. "Universal Basic Income Proposals in Light of ILO Standards: Key Issues and Global Costing." SSRN Electronic Journal, 2018. https://doi.org/10.2139/ssrn.3208737.

Parijs, Philippe Van. "Basic Income: A Simple and Powerful Idea for the Twenty-First Century." In Politics and Society, Vol. 32, 2004. https://doi.org/10.1177/0032329203261095.

Pateman, Carole. "Democratizing Citizenship: Some Advantages of a Basic Income." In Politics and Society, Vol. 32, 2004. https://doi.org/10.1177/0032329203261100.

Peruffo, Marcel, Pedro Cavalcanti Ferreira, and André Cordeiro Valério. "Universal Basic Income in Developing Countries: Pitfalls and Alternatives." SSRN Electronic Journal, 2021. https://doi.org/10.2139/ssrn.3865087.

Rajesh, Arav. "Is UBI (Universal Basic Income) An Effective Poverty-Reduction Strategy for Highly Developed Countries?" SSRN Electronic Journal, 2023. https://doi.org/10.2139/ssrn.4407922.

Riutort, Sebastià, Bru Laín, and Albert Julià. "Basic Income at Municipal Level: Insights from the Barcelona B-MINCOME Pilot." Basic Income Studies, 2023. https://doi.org/10.1515/bis-2021-0047.

Roosma, Femke. "A Struggle for Framing and Interpretation: The Impact of the 'Basic Income Experiments' on Social Policy Reform in the Netherlands." European Journal of Social Security 24, no. 3 (2022). https://doi.org/10.1177/13882627221109846.

Rubery, Jill, Damian Grimshaw, Arjan Keizer, and Mathew Johnson. "Challenges and Contradictions in the 'Normalising' of Precarious Work." Work, Employment and Society 32, no. 3 (2018). https://doi.org/10.1177/0950017017751790.

Sekulova, Filka, Fabricio Bonilla, and Bru Laín. "Life Satisfaction and Socio-Economic Vulnerability: Evidence from the Basic Income Experiment in Barcelona." Applied Research in Quality of Life 18, no. 4 (2023). https://doi.org/10.1007/s11482-023-10176-x.

Shiva, Mehdi, and Jeffrey Matsu. "Global Perspectives on Universal Basic Income." SSRN Electronic Journal, 2023. https://doi.org/10.2139/ssrn.4496937.

Siqueira, Rozane Bezerra de, and José Ricardo Bezerra Nogueira. "A UNIVERSAL BASIC INCOME FOR BRAZIL: FISCAL AND DISTRIBUTIONAL EFFECTS OF ALTERNATIVE SCHEMES." Revista de Economia Contemporanea 27 (2023). https://doi.org/10.1590/198055272701.

Takashima, Kosei, and Isao Yagi. "Emergent Phenomena Analysis of Basic Income on a Money-Circulation Macroeconomic System in Which Labor Motivation and Demand Provide Feedback to the Price and Output of Goods." SSRN Electronic Journal, 2023. https://doi.org/10.2139/ssrn.4422805.

Veen, Robert Van Der. "Basic Income Experiments in the Netherlands?" Basic Income Studies 14, no. 1 (2019). https://doi.org/10.1515/bis-2018-0023.

Verho, Jouko, Kari Hämäläinen, and Ohto Kanninen. "Removing Welfare Traps: Employment Responses in the Finnish Basic Income Experiment." American Economic Journal: Economic Policy 14, no. 1 (2022). https://doi.org/10.1257/pol.20200143.

Wispelaere, Jurgen De, Antti Halmetoja, and Ville Veikko Pulkka. "The Rise (and Fall) of the Basic Income Experiment in Finland." CESifo Forum 19, no. 3 (2018).

Wispelaere, Jurgen De, and Leticia Morales. "Emergency Basic Income during the Pandemic." Cambridge Quarterly of Healthcare Ethics 30, no. 2 (2021). https://doi.org/10.1017/S0963180120000808.

Additional Survey of Universal Basic Income Experiments

The source of references in this section is Hochman, Rachael, Charles Larkin, and Shaen Corbet. "A Survey of Universal Basic Income Experiments." Basic Income Studies, March 15, 2024. https://doi.org/10.1515/bis-2022-0003. Received: 2022-01-28 Accepted: 2024-02-05 Published Online: 2024-03-15 © 2024 Walter de Gruyter GmbH, Berlin/Boston. https://www.degruyter.com/.

Aghion, P., C. Antonin, S. Bunel, and X. Jaravel. 2022. "What Are the Labor and Product Market Effects of Automation? New Evidence from France." In Workshop ESCB Research Cluster.10.4324/9781003275534-2S

Akee, R. K., W. E. Copeland, G. Keeler, A. Angold, and E. J. Costello. 2010. "Parents' Incomes and Children's Outcomes: A Quasi-experiment Using Transfer Payments from Casino Profits." American Economic Journal: Applied Economics 2 (1): 86–115.10.1257/app.2.1.86S

Banerjee, A., M. Faye, A. Krueger, P. Niehaus, and T. Suri. 2020. Effects of a Universal Basic Income during the Pandemic. Innovations for Poverty Action Working Paper. https://econweb.ucsd.edu/pniehaus/papers/ubi_covid.pdf.10.3386/w25598S

Banerjee, A., P. Niehaus, and T. Suri. 2019. "Universal Basic Income in the Developing World." Annual Review of Economics 11: 959–83.10.1146/annurev-economics-080218-030229S

Basic Income Earth Network. 2016. The Basic Income Earth Network's Definition of Basic Income since the ga 2016. https://basicincome.org/wp-content/uploads/2020/07/Basic-Income-definition-longer-explanation-1.pdf (Accessed 02 11 2023).S

Bharat, SEWA Bharat UNICEF India Office. 2014. A Little More, How Much It Is... Piloting Basic Income Transfers in Madhya Pradesh, India. New Delhi. New Delhi: UNICEF.S

Busemeyer, M. R., and A. H. Sahm. 2022. "Social Investment, Redistribution or Basic Income? Exploring the Association Between Automation Risk and Welfare State Attitudes in Europe." Journal of Social Policy 51 (4): 751–70.10.1017/S0047279421000519S

Calnitsky, D., and J. P. Latner. 2017. "Basic Income in a Small Town: Understanding the Elusive Effects on Work." Social Problems 64 (3): 373–97.10.1093/socpro/spw040S

Chung, W., H. Ha, and B. Kim. 2016. "Money Transfer and Birth Weight: Evidence from the Alaska Permanent Fund Dividend." Economic Inquiry 54 (1): 576–90.10.1111/ecin.12235S

De Wispelaere, J., and L. Stirton. 2004. "The Many Faces of Universal Basic Income." The Political Quarterly 75 (3): 266–74.10.1111/j.1467-923X.2004.00611.xS

Forget, E. L. 2013. "New Questions, New Data, Old Interventions: The Health Effects of a Guaranteed Annual Income." Preventive Medicine 57 (6): 925–8.10.1016/j.ypmed.2013.05.029S

Gao, X., J. Shen, H. Wu, and H. Y. Krenn. 2019. "Evaluating Program Effects: Conceptualizing and Demonstrating a Typology." Evaluation and Program Planning 72: 88–96.10.1016/j.evalprogplan.2018.10.008S

Goldsmith, O. S. 2010. The Alaska Permanent Fund Dividend: A Case Study in Implementation of a Basic Income Guarantee.S

Guettabi, M. 2019. "What Do We Know about the Effects of the Alaska Permanent Fund Dividend?."S

Hanna, R., and B. A. Olken. 2018. "Universal Basic Incomes Versus Targeted Transfers: Anti-poverty Programs in Developing Countries." The Journal of Economic Perspectives 32 (4): 201–26.10.1257/jep.32.4.201S

Hasdell, R. 2020. "What We Know about Universal Basic Income."S

Haushofer, J., and J. Shapiro. 2016. "The Short-Term Impact of Unconditional Cash Transfers to the Poor: Experimental Evidence from Kenya." Quarterly Journal of Economics 131 (4): 1973–2042.10.1093/qje/qjw025S

Hoynes, H., and J. Rothstein. 2019. "Universal Basic Income in the United States and Advanced Countries." Annual Review of Economics 11: 929–58.10.1146/annurev-economics-080218-030237S

Jones, D., and I. Marinescu. 2018. The Labor Market Impacts of Universal and Permanent Cash Transfers: Evidence from the Alaska Permanent Fund. Technical report. National Bureau of Economic Research.10.3386/w24312S

Kangas, O., S. Jauhiainen, M. Simanainen, and M. Ylikännö. 2019. The Basic Income Experiment 2017–2018 in Finland: Preliminary Results. Ministry of Social Affairs and Health. https://julkaisut.valtioneuvosto.fi/handle/10024/161361.S

Kozminski, K., and J. Baek. 2017. "Can an Oil-Rich Economy Reduce its Income Inequality? Empirical Evidence from ALASKA's Permanent Fund Dividend." Energy Economics 65: 98–104.10.1016/j.eneco.2017.04.021S

Kueng, L. 2018. "Excess Sensitivity of High-Income Consumers." Quarterly Journal of Economics 133 (4): 1693–751.10.1093/qje/qjy014S

Laenen, T., and D. Gugushvili. 2023. "Welfare State Dissatisfaction and Support for Major Welfare Reform: Towards Means-Tested Welfare or a Universal Basic Income?" International Journal of Social Welfare 32 (2): 178–85.10.1111/ijsw.12546S

Lane, P. R. 2001. "The New Open Economy Macroeconomics: a Survey." Journal of International Economics 54 (2): 235–66.10.1016/S0022-1996(00)00073-8S

Marinescu, I. 2018. No Strings Attached: The Behavioral Effects of Us Unconditional Cash Transfer Programs.10.3386/w24337S

Martinelli, L. 2017. "Assessing the Case for a Universal Basic Income in the UK." IPR Policy Brief. Institute for Policy Research, University of Bath. https://www.bath.ac.uk/publications/assessing-the-case-for-a-universal-basic-income-in-the-uk/attachments/basic_income_policy_brief.pdf.S

Nettle, D., E. Johnson, M. Johnson, and R. Saxe. 2021. "Why Has the Covid-19 Pandemic Increased Support for Universal Basic Income?" Humanities and Social Sciences Communications 8 (1): 1–12.10.1057/s41599-021-00760-7S

Painter, A. 2016. "A Universal Basic Income: the Answer to Poverty, Insecurity, and Health Inequality?" BMJ 355.10.1136/bmj.i6473S

Rincón, L., T. Vlandas, and H. Hiilamo. 2022. "What's Not to like? Benefit Design, Funding Structure and Support for Universal Basic Income." Journal of European Social Policy 32 (4): 467–83.10.1177/09589287211072638S

Rodrigues, S., N. Van Eck, L. Waltman, and F. Jansen. 2014. "Mapping Patient Safety: A Large-Scale Literature Review Using Bibliometric Visualisation Techniques." BMJ Open 4 (3): e004468.10.1136/bmjopen-2013-004468S

Sabaté, M.-A. 2021. "Activating the Unemployed or Liberating the Employed? Universal Basic Income in the French Welfare Reform Debate." In Universal Basic Income in Historical Perspective, edited by P. Sloman, D. Zamora Vargas, and P. Ramos Pinto, 151–80. Cham: Palgrave Macmillan.10.1007/978-3-030-75706-9_7S

Salehi-Isfahani, D., and M. H. Mostafavi-Dehzooei. 2018. "Cash Transfers and Labor Supply: Evidence from a Large-Scale Program in Iran." Journal of Development Economics 135: 349–67.10.1016/j.jdeveco.2018.08.005S

Tabatabai, H. 2012. "From Price Subsidies to Basic Income: The Iran Model and Its Lessons." In Exporting the Alaska Model. Exploring the Basic Income Guarantee, edited by K. Widerquist, and M. W. Howard. New York: Palgrave Macmillan.10.1057/9781137031655_2S

Van Eck, N. J., and L. Waltman. 2011. Text Mining and Visualization Using Vosviewer. arXiv preprint arXiv:1109.2058.S

Van Parijs, P. 1992. "Basic Income Capitalism." Ethics 102 (3): 465–84.10.1086/293420S

Van Parijs, P., and Y. Vanderborght. 2017. Basic Income: A Radical Proposal for a Free Society and a Sane Economy. Harvard University Press.10.4159/9780674978072S

Watson, B., M. Guettabi, and M. Reimer (2019). Universal Cash Transfers Reduce Childhood Obesity Rates. Available at SSRN 3380033.10.2139/ssrn.3380033S Supplementary Material This article contains supplementary material (https://doi.org/10.1515/bis-2022-0003).

LLM Training Subset on Bu||$%*t Jobs

Colás, Álvaro Ramos. "Bullshit Jobs: Graeber on Alienation within Financialised Capitalism." Recerca, vol. 24, no. 1, 2019, https://doi.org/10.6035/Recerca.2019.24.1.7.

Dean, Erik, et al. "The Instinct of Workmanship and the Incidence of Bullshit Jobs." Journal of Economic Issues, vol. 56, no. 3, 2022, https://doi.org/10.1080/00213624.2022.2079929.

Delucchi, Michael, et al. "What's That Smell? Bullshit Jobs in Higher Education." Review of Social Economy, 2021, https://doi.org/10.1080/00346764.2021.1940255.

Dragoš, Srečo. "Bullshit Jobs and Universal Basic Income." Anthropological Notebooks, vol. 27, no. 3, 2021, https://doi.org/10.5281/zenodo.6473826.

Graeber, David. "Bullshit Jobs: A Theory." Bull Shit Jobs : A Theory, 2018.

Soffia, Magdalena, et al. "Alienation Is Not 'Bullshit': An Empirical Critique of Graeber's Theory of BS Jobs." Work, Employment and Society, vol. 36, no. 5, 2022, https://doi.org/10.1177/09500170211015067.

Walo, Simon. "'Bullshit' After All? Why People Consider Their Jobs Socially Useless." Work, Employment and Society, vol. 37, no. 5, 2023, https://doi.org/10.1177/09500170231175771.

Historical Quotations About Basic Income

A brief history of thought on basic income and scarcity via quotations by some of America's and history's greatest thinkers.

"I'm now convinced that the simplest approach will prove to be the most effective—the solution to poverty is to abolish it directly by a now widely discussed measure: the guaranteed income." – Martin Luther King, Jr.

"Two conditions are indispensable if we are to ensure that the guaranteed [basic] income operates as a consistently progressive measure. First, it must be pegged to the median income of society, not at the lowest levels of income. To guarantee an income at the floor would simply perpetuate welfare standards and freeze into the society poverty conditions. Second, the guaranteed income must be dynamic; it must automatically increase as the total social income grows. Were it permitted to remain static under growth conditions, the recipients would suffer a relative decline. If periodic reviews disclose that the whole national income has arisen, then the guaranteed income would have to be adjusted upward by the same percentage. Without these safeguards a creeping retrogression would occur, nullifying the gains of security and stability." – Martin Luther King, Jr.

"We are demanding ... A guaranteed annual income at levels that sustain life in decent circumstances. It is now incontestable that the wealth and resources of the United States make the elimination of poverty absolutely practical." – Martin Luther King, Jr.

"Now this is the real news of our century: it is highly feasible, to take care of all of humanity, at a higher standard of living than anybody has ever experienced or dreamt of, to do so without anybody having to profit at the expense of another, so everybody can enjoy the whole Earth. And it can all be done by 1985." – R. Buckminster "Bucky" Fuller.

"We should do away with the absolutely specious notion that everybody has to earn a living. It is a fact today that one in ten thousand of us can make a technological breakthrough capable of supporting all the rest. The youth of today are absolutely right in recognizing this nonsense of earning a living. We keep inventing jobs because of this false idea that everybody has to be employed at some kind of drudgery because, according to Malthusian Darwinian theory, he must justify his right to exist. So, we have inspectors of inspectors and people making instruments for inspectors to inspect inspectors. The true business of people should be to go back to school and think about whatever it was they were thinking about before somebody came along and told them they had to earn a living." –Buckminster Fuller.

SUN: It seems to me this country is getting stingier all the time.

FULLER: What you are sensing is that the world economy is in a very serious situation. Many less-developed countries are unable to repay their debts, and the leading banks will not agree to put up more funds, because the world banking system is in great peril. Mexico is very deeply in debt, the Philippines are deeply in debt, and unless the very top level of the world's bankers can find some way to help them carry on, then the whole game of money is on the way out. All the people who monopolize money are very scared, very scared. Of course, when you don't know whether you're going to have money you get very cautious with your pennies. They know that their system is in trouble and they may not have any money, so they're holding on. That's what you're feeling.

This enormous stock market boom last week — the great insurance companies, and the trust funds and all the banks can come together, and go in and boom the market. Note that when it got to the top, they bought gold. Gold usually goes in the opposite direction from the stock market. But it went up, too. The bankers were getting rid of their shares. They're scared to hell. The big money is scared to hell.

SUN: It surprises me that you predict scarcity. Do you no longer believe in technology's ability to provide prosperity for everyone around the world?

FULLER: There is no scarcity. Forty-one million people are dying of starvation each day around the world and there is plenty of food for all of them. We lack a marketing system. All we have is this game of money, how to acquire things. And that's the problem. It isn't working.

I have made a great differentiation between wealth and money. Money is not wealth. Wealth is the technological ability to protect, nurture, and support the needs of life. Money is only a means of exchanging items of real wealth. Those who make money with money deliberately keep it scarce. There is ample wealth right now, but people have been too involved in the game of making money with money. There is such incredible avarice. They have loaned their money out all over the place at enormous usury terms, and they're not collecting. Now they need even more money to play their game. They are completely disconnecting money from wealth. The system is destroying itself. Nature will not go along with that which is not true. – R. Buckminster "Bucky" Fuller.

"The goal of the future is full unemployment, so we can play." – Arthur C. Clarke.

"The worker must work for the glory of his handiwork, not simply for pay; the thinker must think for truth, not for fame. The return from your work must be the satisfaction which that work brings you and the world's need of that work. With this, life is heaven, or as near heaven as you can get. Without this — with work which you despise, which bores you, and which the world does not need — this life is hell." – W.E.B. Dubois.

"I fundamentally disagree with those who think that people must be "forced" to work, or that government should "guarantee" a job. In my view breaking the link between paid work and survival would be a good thing. If people are intrinsically of value, then they have the right to survive with or without working. I therefore think we should guarantee basic income, rather than jobs. Or, to put it another way (and root this argument firmly in human rights), we should guarantee people's unconditional right to "life, liberty and the pursuit of happiness": after all, people who are forced to do physically debilitating and mentally unstimulating jobs in order to survive are effectively denied the second and third of these rights. If people don't have to work to survive, most will find or create work that fulfills themselves and benefits others, and we will all be richer for it." – Frances Coppola.

"It is a position not to be controverted, he writes, that the earth, in its natural, uncultivated state was, and ever would have continued to be, the common property of the human race." As the land gets cultivated, "it is the value of the improvement, only, and not the earth itself, that is in individual property. Every proprietor, therefore, of cultivated lands, owes to the community a ground-rent (for I know of no better term to express the idea) for the land which he holds; and it is from this ground-rent that the fund proposed in this plan is to issue." Out of this fund, "there shall be paid to every person, when arrived at the age of twenty-one years, the sum of fifteen pounds sterling, as a compensation in part, for the loss of his or her natural inheritance, by the introduction of the system of landed property. And also, the sum of ten pounds per annum, during life, to every person now living, of the age of fifty years, and to all others as they shall arrive at that age." Payments, Paine insists, should be made "to every person, rich or poor," "because it is in lieu of the natural inheritance, which, as a right, belongs to every man, over and above the property he may have created, or inherited from those who did." – Thomas Paine.

"The most skillfully combined, and with the greatest foresight of objections, of all the forms of socialism, is that commonly known as fourierism. This system does not contemplate the abolition of private property, nor even of inheritance; on the contrary, it avowedly takes into consideration, as elements in the distribution of the produce, capital as well as labour. [...] in the distribution, a certain minimum is first assigned for the subsistence of every member of the community, whether capable or not of labour. The remainder of the produce is shared in certain proportions, to be determined beforehand, among the three elements, labour, capital, and talent." – John Stuart Mill.

"A certain small income, sufficient for necessities, should be secured for all, whether they work or not." – Bertrand Russell.

"Guaranteed income would not only establish freedom as a reality rather than a slogan, it would also establish a principle deeply rooted in western religious and humanist tradition. Man has the right to live, regardless!" – Erich Fromm.

"Out of this war, the greatest since the beginning of history, a new world must be born, a world that would justify the sacrifices offered by humanity. This new world must be a world in which there shall be no exploitation of the weak by the strong, of the good by the evil; where there will be no humiliation of the poor by the violence of the rich; where the products of intellect, science and art will serve society for the betterment and beautification of life, and not the individuals for achieving wealth. This new world shall not be a world of the downtrodden and humiliated, but of free men and free nations, equal in dignity and respect for man." – Nikola Tesla.

"Everyone can enjoy a life of luxurious leisure if the machine-produced wealth is shared, or most people can end up miserably poor if the machine-owners successfully lobby against wealth redistribution," hawking answered. "So far, the trend seems to be toward the second option, with technology driving ever-increasing inequality." – Stephen Hawking.

"The assurance of a certain minimum income for everyone, or a sort of floor below which nobody need fall even when he is unable to provide for himself, appears not only to be a wholly legitimate protection against a risk common to all, but a necessary part of the great society in which the individual no longer has specific claims on the members of the particular small group into which he was born" – Friedrich Hayek.

"Ultimately, we'll need a guaranteed minimum basic income." – Former Secretary of State, Robert Reich.

"If you provide a basic income, you send a powerful message: nobody wants to just sit there and do nothing, we trust you to find a valuable occupation. The idea of morality of work is one of the most insidious tools in the hands of power and increases the bullshit jobs phenomenon." – David Graeber, Anthropologist.

"Society as a whole benefits from a risk-positive environment, and if you can provide a mechanism where anybody can try any stupid commercial idea without risking becoming homeless and indebted, more people will innovate and take risks — and the society using this mechanism will get a competitive edge." – Rick Falkvinge, Founder of the Swedish Pirate Party.

"There is no more urgent economic discussion today than the relationship between income inequality, technology, and the future of work." – Tim O'Reilly, CEO, O'Reilly Media

* * *

BIBLIOGRAPHY

@BenEltham. "Morgan: 'there Is This Enormous Betrayal - Dropping People off a Cliff." *Twitter*, 25 June 2018, twitter.com/beneltham/status/1011064664124317696.

@BenEltham. "Morgan: 'there Was an Enormous Sense of Disappointment from the Young People." *Twitter*, 25 June 2018, twitter.com/beneltham/status/1011064964751114240.

@OurRevolution. *Twitter*, Twitter, 16 July 2018, twitter.com/OurRevolution/status/1018960966426427392.

@AndrewYangVFA. "If We Were to Include Care Work." Twitter, Twitter, 05 Aug. 2018, twitter.com/AndrewYangVFA/status/1026184931268091904.

"A Break for Hard-Working Americans Instead of More Corporate Welfare." *Working Families Tax Credit*, 15 Aug. 2018, www.workingfamiliestaxcredit.org/blog/2018/9/7/a-break-for-hard-working-americans-instead-of-more-corporate-welfare.

"A Quest for Meaning - Discussion and Q&A with Dr. James Doty and Co-director Marc De La Menardiere." *YouTube*, 11 June 2018, youtu.be/kbKyq7wfaBk.

"About Fuller." R. Buckminster Fuller, 1895 - 1983. *The Buckminster Fuller Institute*, 1 Jan. 1970, www.bfi.org/about-fuller/big-ideas/world-game.

Amodei, Dario, and Danny Hernandez. "AI and Compute." *OpenAI Blog*, 20 June, 2018, blog.openai.com/ai-and-compute/.

Anderson, Chris. "The Mind behind Linux | Linus Torvalds." Interview. *YouTube*, 3 May 2016, youtu.be/o8NPllzkFhE.

Arai, Noriko. "Can a robot pass a university entrance exam?" *YouTube*, 13 Sept. 2017, youtu.be/BXcFEhl7ynM.

Ariely, Dan. Predictably Irrational: The Hidden Forces That Shape Our Decisions. HarperCollins, 2008.

Ariely, Dan. Predictably Irrational: The Hidden Forces That Shape Our Decisions. Rev. and Expanded ed., 1. Harper Perennial ed, Harper Perennial, 2010.

Associated Press. "30-year-old Leaves Parents' Home with Help from Alex Jones." *The Garden Island*, 1 June 2018, www.thegardenisland.com/2018/06/01/news/30-year-old-leaves-parents-home-with-help-from-alex-jones/.

Avent, Ryan. "Why Do We Work so Hard?" *1843*, 04 Apr. 2016, www.1843magazine.com/features/why-do-we-work-so-hard.

Ball, Robert M. Social Security Amendments of 1972: Summary and Legislative History, *The United States Social Security Administration*, 13 Aug. 2014, www.socialsecurity.gov/history/1972amend.html.

Barnes, Peter. With Liberty And Dividends For All: How to Save Our Middle Class When Jobs Don't Pay Enough. Readhowyouwant.Com Ltd, 2014.

Basic Income, A Cultural Impulse. "Grundeinkommen - ein Kulturimpuls." *YouTube*, 3 Feb. 2011, youtu.be/ExRs75isitw.

Bergstein, Brian. "Basic Income Could Work-if You Do It Canada-style." *MIT Technology Review*. MIT Technology Review, 20 June 2018, www.technologyreview.com/s/611418/universal-basic-income-works-if-you-do-it-canada-style/.
“Billion Dollar Listing: The New Real Estate Unicorns.” *AngelList Talent Newsletter*. July 5, 2018.
Bliss, Laura, and CityLab. “There's a Bus Driver Shortage. And No Wonder.” *CityLab*, CityLab, 29 June 2018, www.citylab.com/transportation/2018/06/why-wont-anyone-drive-the-bus/563555/.
“BLS Glossary.” U.S. Bureau of Labor Statistics, U.S. Bureau of Labor Statistics, 7 June 2016, www.bls.gov/bls/glossary.htm.
Bregman, Rutger. "Nixon's Basic Income Plan." *Jacobin*, Jacobin, 5 May 2016, www.jacobinmag.com/2016/05/richard-nixon-ubi-basic-income-welfare/.
Brockman, John. “We Are As Gods And Have To Get Good At It” Edge.Org. 18 Aug 2009, https://www.edge.org/conversation/stewart_brand-we-are-as-gods-and-have-to-get-good-at-it. Accessed 12 Dec. 2023.
Brynjolfsson, Erik, and Andrew McAfee. Race against the Machine: How the Digital Revolution Is Accelerating Innovation, Driving Productivity, and Irreversibly Transforming Employment and the Economy. Digital Frontier Press, 2012.
"Bullshit Jobs: A Theory by David Graeber." *Goodreads*, Goodreads, 15 May 2018, www.goodreads.com/book/show/34466958-bullshit-jobs.
“Bureau of Labor Statistics Data.” *U.S. Bureau of Labor Statistics*, U.S. Bureau of Labor Statistics, data.bls.gov/timeseries/LNS11300000.
Burton, Jonathan. “The Case for Paying Every American a Dividend on the Nation's Wealth.” *MarketWatch*, MarketWatch, 02 Oct. 2018, www.marketwatch.com/story/the-case-for-paying-every-american-a-dividend-on-the-nations-wealth-2018-10-02.
Cristescu, Raluca. “5 Skills for the post-automation workforce.” Matrix LMS Blog, 2 Dec 2021, https://blog.matrixlms.com/5-skills-for-the-post-automation-workforce/
Campbell, Colin Dearborn. *Income Redistribution*. 1st ed., American Enterprise Institute for Public Policy Research, 1977.
Campbell, Thomas. “Tom Campbell: 15 Key Discoveries That Led to My Big TOE.” *YouTube*, 1 July 2015, youtu.be/5fcKezLW_Q?t=35m45s.
"CCARE Personnel." *The Center for Compassion and Altruism Research and Education*, 15 Mar. 2016, ccare.stanford.edu/about/people/ccare-staff/.
Carse, David. “Perfect Brilliant Stillness: Beyond the Individual Self.” Paragate Publishing, 2006.
Carse, James P. “Finite and Infinite Games: The Chance of a Lifetime.” 6. print, Ballantine Books, 1989.
"Census.gov." *US Census Bureau*, Census Bureau QuickFacts, www.census.gov/.
Chutel, Lynsey. "Barack Obama Says the Rich Owe the World a Huge Debt." *Quartz*, 17 July 2018, qz.com/1330077/barack-obama-mandela-lecture-on-universal-basic-income-inequality/.
CityLab, and University of Toronto’s School of Cities and Rotman School of Management. “America's Worsening Geographic Inequality.” CityLab, 16 Oct. 2018, www.citylab.com/equity/2018/10/americas-worsening-geographic-inequality/573061/.

Clifford, Catherine. "Billionaire Richard Branson: America Should Give out Free Cash to Fix Income Inequality." *CNBC*, CNBC, 2 July 2018, www.cnbc.com/amp/2018/07/02/virgin-groups-richard-branson-on-universal-basic-income.html.
Columbus, Louis. "How To Get An Open-source Developer Job In 2018." Forbes, Forbes Magazine, 21 Aug. 2018, www.forbes.com/sites/louiscolumbus/2018/08/14/how-to-get-an-open-source-developer-job-in-2018/#1fa54f145b85.
Combs, Jamie. "Swordfighting Is a Metaphor for Life." Directed by John Giuffre, 4Game Dynamics, 2022. YouTube, https://www.youtube.com/watch?v=AD5lxU0eIlw.
Coppola, Frances. "The Changing Nature of Work." *Piera*, Piera.co.uk, 26 Oct 2016, Internet Archive, Wayback Machine, 13 Aug 2018, web.archive.org/web/20171026155042/www.pieria.co.uk/articles/the_changing_nature_of_work.
Coyle, Dennis, and Aaron Wildavsky. "Social Experimentation in the Face of Formidable Fables." *Lessons from the Income Maintenance Experiments, Federal Reserve Bank of Boston*, Sept. 1986, www.bostonfed.org/news-and-events/events/economic-research-conference-series/lessons-from-the-income-maintenance-experiments.aspx.
Dahlman, Carl J. "The Cost of a Military Person-Year: A Method for Computing Savings from Force Reductions." *RAND Corporation*, 22 July 2007, www.rand.org/pubs/monographs/MG598.html.
Danaylov, Nikola (aka Socrates). "Futurist David Wood on Transcending Politics." *Singularity Weblog*, 16 Mar. 2018, www.singularityweblog.com/transcending-politics/.
"David Wood." *Institute for Ethics and Emerging Technologies*, ieet.org/index.php/IEET2/bio/wood.
Davidow, William H., and Michael S. Malone. *The Autonomous Revolution: Reclaiming The Future We've Sold To Machines*. First edition, Berrett-Koehler Publishers, Inc, 2020.
Delventhal, Shoshanna. "Why Bridgewater Calls 2019 a 'Dangerous Year'." *Investopedia*, Investopedia, 6 June 2018, www.investopedia.com/news/why-bridgewater-calls-2019-dangerous-year/.
Department of Veterans Affairs, et al. "Life Insurance." *Servicemembers' Group Life Insurance (SGLI) - Life Insurance*, benefits.va.gov/insurance/sgli.asp
Department of Veterans Affairs, Veterans Benefits Administration, and Insurance Service. "Life Insurance." *Veterans Benefits Association*, Claims Inventory - Veterans Benefits Administration Reports, broken link as referenced in the text, www.insurance.va.gov/sgliSite/popups/CasualtyBOS.htm, corrected, www.benefits.va.gov/INSURANCE/resources_handbook_ins_handbook_append.asp#app_b.
Desmond, Matthew. *Poverty, by America*. First edition, Crown, 2023.
Dividend Sensei. Dividend growth. "4 Reasons I'm Pounding The Table On These 2 Low-Risk, 7 %-Yielding Stocks." Seeking Alpha, 15 Oct. 2018, seekingalpha.com/article/4211535-4-reasons-pounding-table-2-low-risk-7-plus-percent-yielding-stocks?page=3.
Durden, Tyler. "Why We're Underestimating American Collapse." *Zero Hedge*, 26 Jan. 2018, www.zerohedge.com/news/2018-01-25/why-were-underestimating-american-collapse.

EconPapers: Basic Income Studies. https://econpapers.repec.org/article/bpjbistud/. Accessed 7 Dec. 2023.
Elliott, Larry. "Inequality Gap Widens as 42 People Hold Same Wealth as 3.7bn Poorest." *The Guardian*, Guardian News and Media, 22 Jan. 2018, www.theguardian.com/inequality/2018/jan/22/inequality-gap-widens-as-42-people-hold-same-wealth-as-37bn-poorest.
Fish, Lily. "Vinay Gupta: We Can Create a Better Society by Making a Floor That People Can't Fall beneath." *Nesta*, 11 June 2018, www.nesta.org.uk/blog/vinay-gupta-we-can-create-a-better-society-by-making-a-floor-that-people-cant-fall-beneath/.
Foster, Natalie. "The Boldest Cash Transfer Proposal in Modern History." *Medium*, Economic Security Project, 19 Oct. 2018, medium.com/economicsecproj/the-boldest-cash-transfer-proposal-in-modern-history-495dce8264a7.
Frank, Priscilla. "'The Proposal' Is The Reality Show 2018 Deserves." *The Huffington Post*, TheHuffingtonPost.com, 20 June 2018, www.huffingtonpost.com/entry/the-proposal-abc-favorite-bachelor-tropes_us_5b28fc3be4b05d6c16c75c6c.
FRED. "Real Median Personal Income in the United States." *Federal Reserve Bank of St. Louis*, 21 June 2018, fred.stlouisfed.org/graph/?g=kj0q.
Freedom from Want. "Four Freedoms." *Wikipedia*, Wikimedia Foundation, 20 Aug. 2018, en.wikipedia.org/wiki/Four_Freedoms.
Fouksman, Elizaveta. "Why Universal Basic Income Costs Far Less than You Think." *The Conversation*, The Conversation, 14 Aug. 2018, theconversation.com/why-universal-basic-income-costs-far-less-than-you-think-101134.
Fromm, Erich. The Sane Society. Routledge, 1991.
Gallagher, Catherine. "The Body Economic." 2008. press.princeton.edu, https://press.princeton.edu/books/paperback/9780691136301/the-body-economic.
Ganeva, Tana. "Here Are 10 Incredibly Sh*tty Things America Does to Homeless People." *Raw Story*, Raw Story, 6 June 2018, www.rawstory.com/2018/06/10-incredibly-shtty-things-america-homeless-people/.
Gottschalk, Simon. "In Praise of Doing Nothing." *The Conversation*, The Conversation, 19 Sept. 2018, theconversation.com/in-praise-of-doing-nothing-95998.
Graeber, David. *Bullshit Jobs*. First. Simon & Schuster hardcover edition, Simon & Schuster, 2018.
Groover, Heidi. "UN Official Slams American Response to Poverty: "Homelessness on this Scale is Far from Inevitable." *The Stranger*, TheStranger.com, 5 June 2018, www.thestranger.com/slog/2018/06/05/27078274/un-official-slams-american-response-to-poverty-homelessness-on-this-scale-is-far-from-inevitable.
Gross, Terry. "In 'Dopamine Nation,' Overabundance Keeps Us Craving More." Houston Public Media, 25 Aug. 2021, https://www.houstonpublicmedia.org/npr/2021/08/25/1030930259/in-dopamine-nation-overabundance-keeps-us-craving-more/.
Groty. Reddit Contributor. "R/BasicIncome - The Overworked American: We Already Have Too Much Work in the United States. Why Not Redistribute It?" *Reddit*, Reddit, 6 June 2018, www.reddit.com/r/BasicIncome/comments/8p4h5c/the_overworked_american_we_already_have_too_much/e08yelo.

"Growth or Life?" TheRules.Org, *YouTube*, 11 July 2018, youtu.be/cBJxBWwdQ2E.
Grusky, David B.., and Jasmine Hill. *Inequality in the 21st Century: A Reader*. Westview Press., 2018.
Guzman, Gloria and Kollar, Melissa. U.S. Census Bureau, Current Population Reports, P60-279, "Income in the United States: 2022," U.S. Government Publishing Office, Washington, DC, September 2023.
Haarmann, Dirk. "BIG Coalition Namibia." *Basic Income Grant Coalition - Namibia*, www.bignam.org/Index.html.
Hanh, Thich Nhat. "Interbeing with Thich Nhat Hanh: An Interview." Tricycle: The Buddhist Review, tricycle.org/magazine/interbeing-thich-nhat-hanh-interview.
Hạnh Nhất, and Fred Eppsteiner. *Interbeing: Commentaries on the Tiep Hien Precepts*. Parallax Press, 1987.
Hansen, Louis. "Bay Area Cities Take First Steps to Deal with RV Dwellers - and Parking." *The Mercury News*, The Mercury News, 19 Sept. 2018, www.mercurynews.com/2018/09/19/bay-area-cities-take-first-steps-to-deal-with-rv-dwellers-and-parking/.
Harramein, Nassim. "The Connected Universe." *YouTube*, TEDxUCSD, 24 June 2016, youtu.be/xJsl_klqVh0.
Harrington, Michael. "Woe Is Facebook." *TukaGlobal*, 27 July 2018, www.tukaglobal.com/woe-is-facebook/.
Harris, Marvin. Why Nothing Works: The Anthropology of Daily Life; Updated with a New Preface. Simon Et Schuster, 1987.
"Hawai'i State Legislature." SB2571. *Twenty-ninth Legislature, 2017*. House Concurrent Resolution (HCR) 89, 5 May 2017, www.capitol.hawaii.gov/Archives/measure_indiv_Archives.aspx?billtype=HCR&billnumber=89&year=2017.
Heisenberg, The. Currencies. "With FANG In a Correction, Can Gandalf Rescue The Rally?" *Seeking Alpha*, 31 July 2018, seekingalpha.com/article/4192239.
Hedges, Chris. *America: The Farewell Tour*. Simon & Schuster, 2019.
Hiltzik, Michael. "Employers Will Do Almost Anything to Find Workers to Fill Jobs - Except Pay Them More." *Los Angeles Times*, Los Angeles Times, 10 July 2018, www.latimes.com/business/hiltzik/la-fi-hiltzik-employment-20180710-story,amp.html.
Ho, Bong Joon. Parasite. Neon, 2019.
Hochschild, Jennifer L. *What's Fair? American Beliefs about Distributive Justice*. 1st ed., Harvard University Press, 1981.
"How Many U.S. Deaths Are Caused by Poverty, Lack of Education, and Other Social Factors?" *Columbia Mailman School of Public Health*, 5 July 2011, www.mailman.columbia.edu/public-health-now/news/how-many-us-deaths-are-caused-poverty-lack-education-and-other-social-factors.
"How many denominations of Christianity exist?" *Quora*, Quora Contributors, 21 Feb. 2014, www.quora.com/How-many-denominations-of-Christianity-exist.
"How the Census Bureau Measures Poverty." *US Census Bureau*, Census Bureau QuickFacts, 16 Aug. 2018, www.census.gov/topics/income-poverty/poverty/guidance/poverty-measures.html.

Hughes, Chris. Fair Shot: Rethinking Inequality and How We Earn. Bloomsbury, 2018.
Illing, Sean. "Why Capitalism Won't Survive without Socialism." *Vox*, Vox, 25 July 2017, www.vox.com/policy-and-politics/2017/7/25/15998002/eric-weinstein-capitalism-socialism-revolution.
Ioannou, Filipa. "Facebook Users Unable to Post Story about Huge Facebook Hack on Facebook." *SFGate*, San Francisco Chronicle, 28 Sept. 2018, www.sfgate.com/technology/article/Facebook-blocks-post-guardian-story-hack-article-13266764.php.
"It Took a Century to Create the Weekend-and Only a Decade to Undo It." *Quartz*, 6 May 2017, qz.com/969245/it-took-a-century-to-create-the-weekend-and-only-a-decade-to-undo-it/.
Johnson, Stacy. "50 Ways to Make a Fast $50 - or More." *MSN*, MSN Money Talks, 17 Aug. 2018, www.msn.com/en-us/money/personalfinance/50-ways-to-make-a-fast-dollar50-—-or-more/ss-BBM2SfP.
Johnson, Stephen. "Minimum-wage Jobs Can't Pay Rent Anywhere in U.S., According to Report on Affordable Housing." *Big Think*, Big Think, 15 June 2018, bigthink.com/stephen-johnson/report-minimum-wage-jobs-cant-pay-the-rent-anywhere-in-us.
Jordan, Michael. "Artificial Intelligence - The Revolution Hasn't Happened Yet." *Medium*, Medium, 19 Apr. 2018, medium.com/@mijordan3/artificial-intelligence-the-revolution-hasnt-happened-yet-5e1d5812e1e7.
Joseph, Peter. *New Human Rights Movement: Reinventing the Economy to End Oppression*. Benbella Books, 2018.
Kanaan, Michael. *T-Minus AI: Humanity's Countdown to Artificial Intelligence and the New Pursuit of Global Power*. BenBella Books, Inc, 2020.
Kazimirski, Seymour. "There Is Never Enough." ThinkTech Commentary, *YouTube*, 15 June 2018, youtu.be/W9RZjqnc3wg.
Kelly, Kevin. *What technology wants*. New York: Viking, 2010.
King, Martin L. "Letter from Birmingham Jail" | The Martin Luther King, Jr. Research and Education Institute. https://kinginstitute.stanford.edu/letter-birmingham-jail. Accessed 4 Jan. 2024.
King, Martin L. "MLK: The Other America." *YouTube*, 02 July 2015, youtu.be/dOWDtDUKz-U. Full text at archive.org ia903205.us.archive.org/10/items/the-other-america_martin-luter-king-jr_stanford-1967/the-other-america_martin-luter-king-jr_stanford-1967.txt.
King, Martin L. "Statement on Ending the Bus Boycott." *Birmingham Campaign | The Martin Luther King, Jr., Research and Education Institute*, 20 Dec. 1956, kinginstitute.stanford.edu/king-papers/documents/statement-ending-bus-boycott.
King, Martin L. Where Do We Go from Here: Chaos or Community? Harper & Row, 1967.
King, Martin Luther, and Lewis V. Baldwin. *"In a Single Garment of Destiny": a Global Vision of Justice*. Beacon Press, 2014.
Kingsbury, Kathleen. "The Value of a Human Life: $129,000." *Time*. Time Inc., 20 May 2008, content.time.com/time/health/article/0,8599,1808049,00.html.

Kirk, Martin. "What If Economic Growth Isn't as Positive as You Think?" *Fast Company*. Fast Company, 16 July 2018, amp.fastcompany.com/90202203/what-if-economic-growth-isnt-as-positive-as-you-think.
Krauss, Lawrence Maxwell. A Universe from Nothing: Why There Is Something Rather than Nothing. Simon & Schuster, 2012.
Lam, Bourree. "What Becomes of Lottery Winners?" *The Atlantic*. Atlantic Media Company, 12 Jan. 2016, www.theatlantic.com/amp/article/423543.
Lampman, R. J. "Nixon's Family Assistance Plan." *Institute for Research on Poverty*, DP 57-69, 25 pp, 1969, www.irp.wisc.edu/publications/dps/pdfs/dp5769.pdf.
Laurence, Bethany K. "Will I Get Penalized for Working While Collecting Social Security Retirement?" *Nolo.com*, Nolo, 16 Jan. 2017, www.nolo.com/legal-encyclopedia/will-i-get-penalized-working-while-collecting-social-security-retirement.html.
Le, Johnny. "When does Elon Musk think it would make sense to implement basic income?" *Quora*, Quora Contributors, 21 June 2018, www.quora.com/When-does-Elon-Musk-think-it-would-make-sense-to-implement-basic-income/answer/Johnny-Le-10.
"Lessons from the Income Maintenance Experiments." Conference Series 30. *Federal Reserve Bank of Boston*, Sept. 1986, www.bostonfed.org/news-and-events/events/economic-research-conference-series/lessons-from-the-income-maintenance-experiments.aspx.
Lincoln, Kevin. "Environmental Collapse Makes for Terrifying Nightmares, and Compelling Art." *The Outline*, The Outline, 07 June 2018, theoutline.com/post/4833/climate-change-art-first-reformed-the-overstory-carbon-ideologies.
"Mannabase." *Mannabase: Blockchain Platform for Universal Basic Income*, www.mannabase.com.
Marchese, David, and Bobby Doherty. "Penn Jillette on Magic and the Alleged Trump Celebrity Apprentice Tapes." *Vulture.com*, Vulture, 14 Aug. 2018, www.vulture.com/2018/08/penn-jillette-in-conversation.html.
Mayer, Martin. "The Politics of a Guaranteed Income, by Daniel P. Moynihan - Commentary." *Commentary Magazine*, April 1973, www.commentarymagazine.com/articles/the-politics-of-a-guaranteed-income-by-daniel-p-moynihan/.
Meranto, Philip J. "The Kerner report revisited; final report and background papers." *Institute of Government and Public Affairs*, University of Illinois, 1970, archive.org/details/kernerreportrevi00asse.
Morse, Gardiner. "Harnessing Artificial Intelligence." Harvard Business Review, June 2020, https://hbr.org/2020/05/harnessing-artificial-intelligence.
Moynihan, Daniel P. *The Politics Of A Guaranteed Income*. 1st ed., Random House, 1973.
Naughton, John. "The First Self-Driving Car Fatality Proves Nothing | John Naughton." *The Guardian*, Guardian News and Media, 17 July 2016, www.theguardian.com/commentisfree/2016/jul/17/self-driving-car-crash-proves-nothing-tesla-autopilot.
"New Hires and Major Donations: MIRI's September Newsletter." *Machine Intelligence Research Institute*, Us5.campaign-archive.com, 30 Sept. 2018, us5.campaign-archive.com/?u=353906382677fa789a483ba9e&id=f83d47327e&e=c77ca9f985.

Orfalea, Matt. "Martin Luther King Jr. on the Record for a Guaranteed Income." *Medium*. Augmenting Humanity, 10 Jan. 2017, medium.com/basic-income/martin-luther-king-jr-on-the-record-for-a-guaranteed-income-b47b58b41e93.
Pang, Alex Soojung-Kim. "Rest: Why You Get More Done When You Work Less." Amazon, Amazon, 6 Dec. 2016, www.amazon.com/Rest-More-Done-When-Work/dp/0465074871.
Parijs, Philippe van. "1848: Brussels' Two Utopias." *The Brussels Times*, BXLConnect: English-Speaking Resources, Contacts, Deals, and Offers in Brussels, Oct. 2014, pp. 6-8.
Parijs, Philippe van. Arguing For Basic Income: Ethical Foundations for a Radical Reform. 1st ed., Verso, 1992.
"Peter Joseph Interview W/ Abby Martin | Empire Files: Abolishing Capitalism." *YouTube*, 1 Sept. 2017, youtu.be/NVDLkL8Nvjw.
Phillips, Matt. "G.E. Dropped From the Dow After More Than a Century." *The New York Times*, The New York Times, 20 June 2018, https://web.archive.org/web/20180620030035/https://mobile.nytimes.com/2018/06/19/business/dealbook/general-electric-dow-jones.html.
Picchi, Aimee. "Most Americans Can't Handle a $500 Surprise Bill." *CBS News*, CBS Interactive, 06 Jan. 2016, www.cbsnews.com/news/most-americans-cant-handle-a-500-surprise-bill/.
Piketty, Thomas. *The Economics of Inequality*. The Belknap Press of Harvard University Press, 2015.
"Press & Media." *Reddit Help*, reddit.zendesk.com/hc/en-us/articles/206630455-Press-Media.
PLoS Biology. *Public Library of Science*, Apr. 2004, www.ncbi.nlm.nih.gov/pmc/articles/PMC387823/.
Bajpai, Priyanka. "Potential for AI and Robotics in Healthcare Is Vast." https://www.biospectrumasia.com/opinion/54/11237/potential-for-ai-and-robotics-in-healthcare-is-vast.html. Accessed 22 Dec. 2023.
Puplava, Chris. Registered Investment Advisor. "And Then There Were None." *Seeking Alpha*, Seeking Alpha, 30 July 2018, seekingalpha.com/article/4192164-none.
Quadagno, Jill. "Race, Class, and Gender in the U.S. Welfare State: Nixon's Failed Family Assistance Plan." *American Sociological Review*, vol. 55, no. 1, 1990, pp. 11–28. JSTOR, JSTOR, www.jstor.org/stable/2095700.
Rademacher, Ida. "What Washington Doesn't Understand About Working Families." *LinkedIn*, linkedin.com/pulse/what-washington-doesnt-understand-working-families-ida-rademacher.
Ramchandani, Ariel. "Forced Labor Is the Backbone of the World's Electronics Industry." *The Atlantic*. Atlantic Media Company, 28 June 2018, www.theatlantic.com/business/archive/2018/06/malaysia-forced-labor-electronics/563873/.
Rand, Ayn, and Frank Mayo. Atlas Shrugged. The Easton Press, 1989.
"/r/BasicIncome - Let's Collect the Best Quotes about Basic Income from Famous People." *Reddit*, Reddit Contributors, 19 Mar. 2014, www.reddit.com/r/BasicIncome/comments/20uqmt/lets_collect_the_best_quotes_about_basic_income/.

"/r/BasicIncome." *Reddit*, Basic Income Community on Reddit, www.reddit.com/r/BasicIncome.
Reich, Robert B. Saving Capitalism: for the Many, Not the Few. Icon Books, 2017.
Robins, Philip K. A Guaranteed Annual Income: Evidence from a Social Experiment. Academic Press, 1980.
Robinson, Melia. "The San Francisco Housing Market Is So Absurd That Restaurants Are Putting Diners to Work Because They Can't Afford to Pay Waiters." *Business Insider*, Business Insider, 26 June 2018, amp-businessinsider-com.cdn.ampproject.org/c/s/amp.businessinsider.com/san-francisco-expensive-restaurants-cant-afford-workers-2018-6.
Rogan, Joe. "Joe Rogan Experience #1169 - Elon Musk." *YouTube*, 07 Sept. 2018, youtu.be/ycPr5-27vSI.
Ross, Mary. Oral history interview, 10/26/95. *SSA History Archives*, 13 Aug. 2014, www.socialsecurity.gov/history/orals/maryross.html.
Rossman, Sean. "That 30-year-old Man Finally Moves out of His Parents' House, Thanks to Alex Jones." *USA Today*, Gannett Satellite Information Network, 01 June 2018, www.usatoday.com/story/news/nation-now/2018/05/31/30-year-old-finally-moved-out-his-parents-house-thanks-alex-jones/659658002/.
Roth, Alvin E. Who Gets What - and Why: The New Economics of Matchmaking and Market Design - from Birth to Death and along the Way. William Collins, 2015.
Rousseau, Steve. "Millennials Must Work Until They Die, And Other Facts." *Digg.com*, Digg, 8 June 2018, digg.com/2018/millennials-will-die-working.
Ruben, Adam. "Federal EITC Modernization Bill Introduced – Economic Security Project – Medium." *Medium*, Economic Security Project, 26 Sept. 2018, medium.com/economicsecproj/federal-eitc-modernization-bill-introduced-e65b1ed151fc.
Santens, Scott. "It's Time for Technology to Serve All Humankind with Unconditional Basic Income." Medium, Augmenting Humanity, 13 Apr. 2018, medium.com/basic-income/its-time-for-technology-to-serve-all-huhumankind-with-unconditional-basic-income-e46329764d28.
Santens, Scott. "The BIG Library: Books About Basic Income – Basic Income – Medium." *Medium*, Augmenting Humanity, 25 May 2016, medium.com/basic-income/the-big-library-books-about-basic-income-b9763071b987.
SAR. "Scholars at Risk - Home." Scholars at Risk, www.scholarsatrisk.org/.
Sarwari, Khalida. "Sunnyvale Mobile Home Park's Last Holdouts Cling to Hope as Demolition Looms." *The Mercury News*, The Mercury News, 23 July 2018, www.mercurynews.com/2018/07/22/mobile-home-parks-last-holdouts-cling-to-hope-as-demolition-looms/.
Scott, Kevin, and Greg Shaw. *Reprogramming the American Dream: From Rural America to Silicon Valley--Making AI Serve Us All*. First edition, Harper Business, an imprint of HarperCollins Publishers, 2020.
Shafer, Scott. "Voters' Plea to S.F. Mayoral Candidates: 'Fix Homelessness'." *KQED*, KQED, 01 June 2018, www.kqed.org/news/11671742/voters-plea-to-s-f-mayoral-candidates-fix-homelessness.

Shankland, Stephen. "IBM's Got a Computer That'll Take on Your Debate Team and Maybe Win. It's a New Frontier for AI." *CNET*, CNET, 19 June 2018, cnet.co/2K4OyC9.
Shaughnessy, Larry. "One Soldier, One Year: $850,000 and Rising." *CNN*. Cable News Network, 28 Feb. 2012, security.blogs.cnn.com/2012/02/28/one-soldier-one-year-850000-and-rising/.
Shaw, Chris. "Policy Positions and Political Imaginaries: Framing Basic Income." *The Libertarian Ideal*, 26 Oct. 2018, thelibertarianideal.wordpress.com/2018/10/26/policy-positions-and-political-imaginaries-framing-basic-income/.
Sheahen, A. Basic Income Guarantee: Your Right to Economic Security. Palgrave Macmillan, 2016.
Sinek, Simon. *The Infinite Game*. Portfolio Penguin, 2020.
Smith, Jack IV. "8 Essential Quotes Show Why Basic Income Is the Future." *Mic*, Mic Network Inc., 7 June 2016, mic.com/articles/145468/basic-income-quotes-bernie-sanders-stephen-hawking-martin-luther-king.
Smith, Noah. "What Economists Still Don't Get About the 2008 Crisis." *Bloomberg.com*, Bloomberg, 29 June 2018, www.bloomberg.com/view/articles/2018-07-29/what-economists-still-don-t-get-about-2008-crisis
Staisil. "What Was Nixon's Family Assistance Plan?" *Yahoo! Answers*, Yahoo!, 19 Apr. 2012, answers.yahoo.com/question/index?qid=20120415171119AA7InDe.
"Star Trek: The Next Generation, The Neutral Zone (TV Episode, 1988)." IMDb. IMDb.com, m.imdb.com/title/tt0708811/quotes.
Steiner, Sheyna. "Survey: How Do You Pay For Unexpected Expenses?" *Bankrate*. Bankrate.com, 16 July 2018, www.bankrate.com/banking/savings/survey-how-americans-contend-with-unexpected-expenses.
Stern, Andy. Raising The Floor: How a Universal Basic Income Can Renew Our Economy and Rebuild the American Dream. Public Affairs, 2017.
Stiglitz, Joseph E., and Linda J. Bilmes. "Estimating the Costs of War: Methodological Issues, with Applications to Iraq and Afghanistan." *Oxford Handbook of the Economics of Peace and Conflict*. Ed. Michelle R. Garfinkel and Stergios Skaperdas. Oxford University Press, 2012.
Stricker, Frank. *Why America Lost The War On Poverty– And How To Win It*. 1st ed. Chapel Hill: University of North Carolina Press, 2007.
"Summer MIRI Updates." *Machine Intelligence Research Institute*, MIRI, 29 Sept. 2018, intelligence.org/2018/09/01/summer-miri-updates/.
Susskind, Daniel. *A World without Work: Technology, Automation, and How We Should Respond*. First edition, Metropolitan Books/Henry Holt & Company, 2020.
Tanner, Michael. "The American Welfare State: How We Spend Nearly $1 Trillion a Year Fighting Poverty—and Fail." *Cato Institute*, 11 Apr. 2012, Policy Analysis, Number 694, 8 Aug. 2014, www.cato.org/sites/cato.org/files/pubs/pdf/PA694.pdf.
"Tell Congress: pass tax reform for the middle class." Petition. Change.org, www.change.org/p/economic-security-project-encourage-the-government-to-get-behind-a-guaranteed-income.
Tesla, Nikola. "Nikola Tesla Daily." Apps on Google Play, Google, play.google.com/store/apps/details?id=com.nikola.tesla.daily.

"The Economic Security Project Basic Income Reading List." Medium, Augmenting Humanity, 16 Nov. 2017, medium.com/economicsecproj/the-economic-security-project-basic-income-reading-list-fdcaa39bad0f.
"The Future of Artificial Intelligence & Society - Marcus Hutter." YouTube, 26 Feb. 2018, youtu.be/N54ytMKsv14.
"The Higgs Boson." CERN, CERN Accelerating Science, home.web.cern.ch/topics/higgs-boson.
"The New Big Idea – the Universal Basic Income." Master Investor, 07 Feb. 2017, masterinvestor.co.uk/economics/new-big-idea-universal-basic-income/.
"The Rise of the Useless Class." Ideas.ted.com, TED, 23 June 2017, ideas.ted.com/the-rise-of-the-useless-class/.
"The State of the Nation's Housing 2018." YouTube, 20 June 2018, youtu.be/zZfg25ErXDM.
Thurman, Robert. "From The ONE Vault - Robert Thurman on Suffering." YouTube, 19 Mar. 2012, youtu.be/qexkpSaApqc.
Tüfekçi, Zeynep. "Machine intelligence makes human morals more important." YouTube, 11 Nov. 2016, youtu.be/hSSmmlridUM.
"Understanding the Teen Brain." University of Rochester Medical Center Health Encyclopedia, Medical Reviewers: Rita Sather and Amit Shelat, University of Rochester Medical Center, 2018, www.urmc.rochester.edu/encyclopedia/content.aspx?ContentTypeID=1&ContentID=3051.
U.S. Bureau of Economic Analysis. "Gross Domestic Product per Capita." Gross Domestic Product per Capita, https://alfred.stlouisfed.org/series?seid=A939RC0A052NBEA. Accessed 9 Dec. 2023.
VA Web Solutions Office. "Under what conditions will DoD pay the special death gratuity? (SGLI)" MHV, 19 Dec. 2012, iris.custhelp.va.gov/app/answers/detail/a_id/2674.
"Vertical Farming." Wikipedia, Wikimedia Foundation, 22 Sept. 2018, en.m.wikipedia.org/wiki/Vertical_farming.
"Vinay Gupta - Space - Internet of Agreements." YouTube, 25 June 2018, youtu.be/hCBki5sBw5E?t=25m34s.
Weisman, Aly. "Zach Galifianakis Bought A Homeless Woman An Apartment - And Took Her To 'The Hangover III' Premiere." Business Insider, Business Insider, 22 May 2013, www.businessinsider.com/zach-galifianakis-bought-homeless-woman-an-apartment-2013-5.
Weissmann, Jordan. "Remembering Martin Luther King, Jr.'s Solution to Poverty." The Atlantic. Atlantic Media Company, 20 Jan. 2014, www.theatlantic.com/business/archive/2013/08/martin-luther-kings-economic-dream-a-guaranteed-income-for-all-americans/279147/.
"Where Do We Go from Here?" Address Delivered at the Eleventh Annual SCLC Convention. King Encyclopedia, The Martin Luther King, Jr., Research and Education Institute, 16 Aug. 1967, kinginstitute.stanford.edu/king-papers/documents/where-do-we-go-here-address-delivered-eleventh-annual-sclc-convention.

Wile, Rob. "A Human Life Is Worth $7.4 Million." Business Insider, Business Insider, 08 Aug. 2012, www.businessinsider.com/the-epa-has-tabulated-the-value-of-a-human-life-2012-8.

Williams, Clarence G. Reflections of the Dream: 1975-1994, Twenty Years Celebrating the Life of Dr. Martin Luther King, Jr. at the Massachusetts Institute of Technology. MIT, 1996.

Wilson, William Julius. When Work Disappears: the World of the New Urban Poor. Knopf, 1999.

Wolfram|Alpha. "Making the World's Knowledge Computable." Wolfram|Alpha, m.wolframalpha.com/input/?i=50%25+of+U.S.+per+capita+GDP.

"Working Families Tax Credit." Economic Security Project, Working Families Tax Credit, www.workingfamiliestaxcredit.org.

"World's Biggest Hedge Fund: We Are Bearish On Almost All Financial Assets." Zero Hedge, 5 June 2018, www.zerohedge.com/news/2018-06-05/bridgewater-we-are-bearish-almost-all-financial-assets.

Yampolskiy, Roman V. Artificial Superintelligence: a Futuristic Approach. Chapman & Hall CRC, 2016.

Yang, Andrew. "The Freedom Dividend." Andrew Yang for President, www.yang2020.com/policies/the-freedom-dividend/.

* * *

ABOUT THE AUTHOR

Nobody helps the poor, unemployed, and displaced.
Nobody makes the world a better place.
Nobody listens to our concerns.
Nobody keeps their promises.
Nobody makes a difference.
Nobody tells the truth.
Nobody ever notices.
Nobody changes.
Nobody cares.
Be nobody.

ENDNOTES

[i] Amazon Kindle Direct Publishing Content Guidelines. https://kdp.amazon.com/en_US/help/topic/G200672390#aicontent. Accessed 15 Dec. 2023.

[ii] See Glossary for definitions of Default Consensus Narrative and Default Consensus Narrative Reality.

[iii] Styx - Mr. Roboto (Official Video). Directed by STYX, 2017. YouTube, https://www.youtube.com/watch?v=uc6f_2nPSX8.

[iv] Kennedy, Juliette. "Kurt Gödel." The Stanford Encyclopedia of Philosophy, edited by Edward N. Zalta, Winter 2020, Metaphysics Research Lab, Stanford University, 2020. Stanford Encyclopedia of Philosophy, https://plato.stanford.edu/archives/win2020/entries/goedel/.

[v] Vaknin, Sam. *Snapshotting's Role in Narcissist's Shared Fantasy | Vaknin Talks*. https://vaknin-talks.com/transcripts/Snapshotting_s_Role_in_Narcissist_s_Shared_Fantasy/. Accessed 17 Mar. 2024.

[vi] Trussel, Stephen (Kepano). Combined Hawaiian Dictionary (CHD) Hawaiian-English - H. https://www.trussel2.com/HAW/haw-h.htm. Accessed 7 Jan. 2024. "Hā ke akua i ka lewa." God breathed into the open space.

[vii] "Bible Gateway Passage: Genesis 2:7 - The Voice." Bible Gateway, https://www.biblegateway.com/passage/?search=Genesis%202%3A7&version=VOICE. Accessed 7 Jan. 2024.

[viii] "Sara Walker | Understanding Origins Of Life, Time and Space, Assembly Theory, | Ep. 144." Directed by Danica Patrick, 2022. YouTube, https://www.youtube.com/watch?v=lIQAy2iAM7A.

[ix] Coursera editors. "What Is Spatial Computing? Definition, Applications, and Careers." Coursera, 11 Dec. 2023, https://www.coursera.org/articles/what-is-spatial-computing.

[x] Hint for advanced students: it is not by works, lest we dare boast, isn't it?

[xi] "In Theory There Is No Difference Between Theory and Practice, While In Practice There Is" – Quote Investigator. 14 Apr. 2018, https://quoteinvestigator.com/2018/04/14/theory/. Accessed 12 Dec. 2023.

[xii] Future of Life Institute. "Pause Giant AI Experiments: An Open Letter." Future of Life Institute, https://futureoflife.org/open-letter/pause-giant-ai-experiments/. Accessed 17 Mar. 2024.

[xiii] Garson, QuoteResearcher. "First They Ignore You, Then They Laugh at You, Then They Attack You, Then You Win – Quote Investigator." 13 Aug. 2017, https://quoteinvestigator.com/2017/08/13/stages/.

[xiv] Kahn, Zain. "AI Dominates the Agenda at Davos." Superhuman, 8 Jan. 2024, https://www.superhuman.ai/p/ai-dominates-agenda-davos.

[xv] "The Idea of a Soul, Free Will -- These Are Over!" - Technocracy Explained by Prof Yuval Harari. Directed by JustinePogroske_official, 2021. YouTube, https://www.youtube.com/watch?v=NV0CtZga7qM.

[xvi] Hummel, Charles E. *Tyranny of the Urgent*. InterVarsity Press, 2013. Google Books, https://books.google.com/books?id=3wWDAgAAQBAJ.

[xvii] Combs, Jamie. Please see Acknowledgments and Glossary for details of Four Game Dynamics.

[xviii] In a 2006 lecture I attended at Stanford; de Grey refers to the default social attitude towards aging as almost a kind of hypnotic trance. This suggested the conceptualization of societal acceptance of aging as a trance-like state, a "death trance." I can't be certain that was the specific gathering in which the term was originally coined, but there's a non-zero probability of that. I also credit de Grey with inspiration for

a phrase that I distilled from his statement, "default social attitudes," around that time. Namely, "default consensus reality." Only later did I discover David Carse's earlier work referring to "consensus reality." Perhaps de Grey transmitted that meme, unbeknownst to me at the time.

[xix] "Humanity First" possibly finds its roots in the work of Thomas Paine, who used the phrase "the good of humanity" in his 1798 book "The Age of Reason." Google Bard. Accessed 13 Dec. 2023.

[xx] Guy Standing, "The Precariat: Today's Transformative Class?" Great Transition Initiative (October 2018), https://www.greattransition.org/publication/precariat-transformative-class.

[xxi] As President Richard Nixon's 1969 Family Assistance Program.

[xxii] Wikipedia contributors. "Overton window." Wikipedia, The Free Encyclopedia. Wikipedia, The Free Encyclopedia, 4 Jan. 2024. Web. 15 Jan. 2024.
[xxiii] "Maslow's hierarchy of needs." Wikipedia, en.wikipedia.org/wiki/Maslow%27s_hierarchy_of_needs#Safety_needs.

[xxiv] Sapolsky, Robert M. "Determined: A Science of Life without Free Will." Penguin Press, 2023.
[xxv] "Freedom Isn't Free." Wikipedia, 7 Dec. 2023. Wikipedia, https://en.wikipedia.org/w/index.php?title=Freedom_isn%27t_free&oldid=1188772240.
[xxvi] "Inner, outer, narrative, and mystery. Aka short-game, mid-game, long-game, and deep-game." 4Game Dynamics framework by Jamie Combs. See bibliography: Combs, Jamie. Learn more at https://x.com/JamieCombs, aka the Captain Simple Project.

[xxvii] Wolfram, Stephen. The Concept of the Ruliad—Stephen Wolfram Writings. 10 Nov. 2021, https://writings.stephenwolfram.com/2021/11/the-concept-of-the-ruliad/.
[xxviii] "We're All in It Together." - Short Clip from Brazil. "Listen, kid. We're all in it together." Directed by en7ropiaz, 2013. YouTube, https://www.youtube.com/watch?v=xlCPkmb6cuY.

[xxix] "Making the World Work." Buckminster Fuller Institute, 22 May 2012, https://www.bfi.org/2012/05/22/making-the-world-work/.

[xxx] "The area in San Jose known for the largest homeless population during the early 2000s boom in Silicon Valley is called The Jungle. It wasn't just the largest in San Jose, but also considered one of the largest encampments in the entire United States at the time." https://g.co/bard/share/5b1e4edc6c63. Accessed 29 Dec. 2023.

[xxxi] ARG's, Alternate Reality Games are a real thing, for readers who may not be familiar with the term. See "How Alternate Reality Games Are Changing The Real World: Big Brains Podcast | University of Chicago News." https://news.uchicago.edu/big-brains-podcast-how-alternate-reality-games-are-changing-real-world. Accessed 29 Dec. 2023.

[xxxii] Herrera, Sonya. "The Last Inhabitants of San Jose's Former 'Jungle' Encampment." San José Spotlight, 6 Mar. 2023, https://sanjosespotlight.com/the-last-inhabitants-of-san-joses-former-jungle-encampment/. Fernandez, Lisa, and Nanette Miranda.
[xxxiii] 1.) Eggert, Alicia. "This Present Moment." Smithsonian American Art Museum. https://americanart.si.edu/artwork/present-moment-117884. Accessed 21 Jan. 2024.
2.) "Nation's Largest Homeless Encampment, 'The Jungle,' Dismantled." NBC Bay Area, 4 Dec. 2014, https://www.nbcbayarea.com/news/local/game-of-whack-a-mole-homeless-upset-to-be-evicted-by-police-from-the-jungle-in-san-jose/1983791/.
3.) "Exodus From the Jungle + Right To Dream Too." San Jose J-Town FilmFest, 13 Mar. 2016, https://jtownfilmfestcom.wordpress.com/exodus-from-the-jungle-right-to-dream-too/.

4.) Press, Associated. "In Silicon Valley, the Homeless Illustrate a Growing Divide." Voice of America, 7 Nov. 2017, https://www.voanews.com/a/silicon-valley-homeless/4105266.html.
5.) Hotel 22. Directed by Elizabeth Lo. https://www.imdb.com/title/tt3885278/.
6.) Homeless in Silicon Valley. Directed by Bill Moyers, MonteVideo Grafix, 2013. Internet Archive, http://archive.org/details/silicon_valley.
7.) Home Sweet Homeless in the Heart of Silicon Valley. Directed by Scott Largent, 2019. YouTube, https://www.youtube.com/watch?v=Toz_nZ0xJkk.
[xxxiv] "Michael Nielsen on X: 'Academic towns are also a very interesting group. Oxford and both Cambridges are amazing, all three are Capitals of the World, though not Great Cities. I also have had a wonderful time in many other small academic(ish) towns, from Amherst to Gambier to Leiden and more...' / X." X (formerly Twitter), 27 Dec. 2023, https://twitter.com/michael_nielsen/status/1740022897765142953.

[xxxv] What is Grok? See Hawkins, Joshua. "Everything You Need to Know About Grok, Elon Musk's Answer to ChatGPT." Lifehacker, 30 Nov. 2023, https://lifehacker.com/tech/what-is-grok-elon-musks-answer-to-chatgpt.
[xxxvi] Our Stories - Gordon Moore about Moore's Law. Directed by ASML, 2014. YouTube, https://www.youtube.com/watch?v=EzyJxAP6AQo.
[xxxvii] Metacrisis and Molochian are terminology of The Consilience Project. Please see Glossary for more detail on each.

[xxxviii] Fogg, BJ. Captology: Computers as Persuasive Technology. 21 Apr. 2002, https://web.archive.org/web/20020421092444/http://captology.stanford.edu/. Captology Key Concepts. 7 June 2002, https://web.archive.org/web/20020607203007/http://captology.stanford.edu/Key_Conce"Zpts/key_concepts.html.
[xxxix] "Meet the Invisible Workers of Silicon Valley - CNN Video." CNN. Cable News Network, 18 Sept. 2018, www.cnn.com/videos/us/2018/09/18/making-rent-in-silicon-valley-beme.beme.
[xl] "Eating Your Own Dog Food." Wikipedia, 23 Dec. 2023. Wikipedia, https://en.wikipedia.org/w/index.php?title=Eating_your_own_dog_food&oldid=1191424007.
[xli] Schmachtenberger, Daniel. The Consilience Project | About the Project - The Consilience Project. https://consilienceproject.org/about-the-project/. Accessed 21 Jan. 2024.
[xlii] Tool - Ænema Lyrics | AZLyrics.Com. https://www.azlyrics.com/lyrics/tool/nema.html. Accessed 29 Dec. 2023.

[xliii] "Bible Gateway Passage: Proverbs 29:18-27 - Amplified Bible." Bible Gateway, https://www.biblegateway.com/passage/?search=Proverbs%2029%3A18-27&version=AMP. Accessed 29 Dec. 2023. Wow, the Amplified Version is even more precise to what we wrote a few moments ago. It reads, "Where there is no vision, the people are unrestrained." Lacking healthy boundaries in the impulsive exercise of our whims of thought and behavior.

[xliv] Allen, Dr Kathy. "The Seventh Generation Principle." Dr. Kathy Allen, 15 Dec. 2023, https://kathleenallen.net/insights/seventh-generation-principle/.

[xlv] "Constitution of the Hawaiian Islands. ARTICLE 1. God hath endowed all people with certain inalienable rights; among which are life, liberty, and the right of acquiring, possessing, and protecting property, and of **pursuing and obtaining** safety and happiness." Ho'oilina Legacy Collection. https://hooilina.org/cgi-bin/journal?e=d-0journal--00-0-0-004-Document---0-1--1en-50---20-frameset-search-issue---001-0110escapewin&a=p&p=frameset&d=HASHe7d7c93d84511b86ea5ca7.5.1.3. Accessed 29 Dec. 2023. English version: https://hooilina.org/cgi-bin/journal?e=p-0journal--00-0-0-004-Document---0-1--1en-50---20-docoptions-search-issue---001-0110escapewin&a=p&p=frameset&cl=&d=HASHe7d7c93d84511b86ea5ca7.5.1.6. Accessed 29 Dec. 2023.

[xlvi] Pew Research Center. "Religious Landscape Study." Pew Research Center's Religion & Public Life Project, https://www.pewresearch.org/religion/religious-landscape-study/. Accessed 21 Jan. 2024. Gallup Poll. "How Many Americans Believe in God?" Gallup.Com, 24 June 2022, https://news.gallup.com/poll/268205/americans-believe-god.aspx. PRRI, Public Religion Research Institute. "PRRI: The American Religious Landscape in 2020." The American Religious Landscape in 2020, https://www.prri.org/research/2020-census-of-american-religion/. Accessed 21 Jan. 2024.
[xlvii] Farmer, David John. "Neuro-Gov: Neuroscience as Catalyst." Annals of the New York Academy of Sciences, vol. 1118, no. 1, Nov. 2007, pp. 74–89. DOI.org (Crossref), https://doi.org/10.1196/annals.1412.002. While it may seem like a radical new consequence of technologies like Neuralink, the principles of Neuro-Gov predate 2024 technology by decades. "Neuroscience promises to act as a catalyst, in the longer run, in seeking re-unification of the fragmented social sciences (e.g., political science and economics) and social action subjects (e.g., public administration and business administration) that concern governance. Neuroscience can achieve this because it reveals that taken-for-granted concepts, and the language used to express them, should be challenged. What should be sought is a language called in this paper Neuro-Gov."
[xlviii] McLuhan, Stephanie, et al. "The Marshall McLuhan Speaks Special Collection." The Marshall McLuhan Speaks Special Collection, https://marshallmcluhanspeaks.com/interviews/violence-as-a-quest-for-identity. Accessed 11 Dec. 2023.

[xlix] Silverton, Michael. LLM research prompt, "Luddite Protests Against Technology." https://bard.google.com/share/ef8b44630984. Accessed 12 Dec. 2023.

[l] Borderline Bible: Switching to Identity Disturbance, Psychopathic Self-State (Compilation). Directed by Prof. Sam Vaknin, 2023. YouTube, Borderline Bible: Switching to Identity Disturbance, Psychopathic Self-State (Compilation). Directed by Prof. Sam Vaknin, 2023. YouTube, https://youtu.be/-THt5sJ5VE4?t=235s.
[li] McLuhan, Marshall. "The Marshall McLuhan Speaks Special Collection." The Marshall McLuhan Speaks Special Collection, https://marshallmcluhanspeaks.com/soundbites/the-future-of-the-future-is-the-present. Accessed 24 Jan. 2024.
[lii] Adler, David. Schumpeter's Theory of Creative Destruction - Engineering and Public Policy - College of Engineering - Carnegie Mellon University. http://www.cmu.edu/epp/irle/irle-blog-pages/schumpeters-theory-of-creative-destruction.html. Accessed 24 Jan. 2024.
[liii] "Body Dysmorphic Disorder - Symptoms and Causes." Mayo Clinic, https://www.mayoclinic.org/diseases-conditions/body-dysmorphic-disorder/symptoms-causes/syc-20353938. Accessed 12 Dec. 2023.

[liv] Silverton, Michael. LLM research prompt, "Intergenerational Trauma Transmission." https://bard.google.com/share/b6756ae33063. Accessed 12 Dec. 2023.

[lv] Marshall McLuhan, like all skilled and imperfect observers, showed a kind of common human cognition and consciousness – common among those whom history regularly refers to as prophets – that clearly transcends the unfolding of earthly events in linear time. Tens of millions of human beings possess this capacity for timeline-independent insight. It's common. You have it deep within you. It just isn't actively cultivated and readily acknowledged as default consensus narrative. Yet. Maybe we'll unpack some of the more mundane qualities of prophecy in a later project.
[lvi] ETTH "Ethernet To The Home." Redirected to "Ethernet in the First Mile." Wikipedia, 23 June 2023. Wikipedia, https://en.wikipedia.org/w/index.php?title=ETTH.

[lvii] "Michael Silverton." Wikipedia, 20 Nov. 2022. Wikipedia, https://en.wikipedia.org/w/index.php?title=Michael_Silverton&oldid=1122848381.

[lviii] Vaughan-Nichols, Steven J. "Open Source vs Closed Source: What's the Difference?" Linode Guides & Tutorials, 9 Mar. 2023, https://www.linode.com/docs/guides/open-source-vs-closed-source/.

[lix] Silverton, Michael. LLM research prompt, "There Ain't No Such Thing As a Free Lunch - History and Origin." https://bard.google.com/share/6f5108d5de65. Accessed 22 Jan. 2024.
[lx] Wolfram, Stephen. Stephen Wolfram: Now I Understand Quantum Mechanics! Interview by Brian Keating, https://youtu.be/c-RO3vM10Ok?t=2482. Accessed 6 Feb. 2024.
[lxi] Black Swan Group, editor. Three Negotiator Types - Black Swan Group Brochure. https://info.blackswanltd.com/hubfs/Content/3%20Types%20of%20Negotiators.pdf. Accessed 7 Feb. 2024.
[lxii] Ecclesia Bible Society, editor. The Voice Bible. Thomas Nelson Inc, 2012. Library of Congress ISBN 978-1-4185-4901-5. Also https://www.biblegateway.com/passage/?search=2+cor+12%3A10&version=VOICE.
[lxiii] Foundation, Poetry. "Speech: 'All the World's a Stage' by William Shakespeare." Poetry Foundation, Poetry Foundation, 7 Feb. 2024, https://www.poetryfoundation.org/poems/56966/speech-all-the-worlds-a-stage. https://www.poetryfoundation.org/.
[lxiv] Metavalent Stigmergy. How default consensus narratives evolve and blossom into new default consensus realities. https://metavalent.com/. Clarifying Consensus https://metavalent.com/metavalent/2021/03/26/21-05-15-Clarifying-Consensus.html.
[lxv] The American Education System. www.youtube.com, https://www.youtube.com/shorts/hCskUxoNx-M. Accessed 8 Feb. 2024.
[lxvi] "THE SIX MILLION DOLLAR MAN (1972)." Library of Congress, Washington, D.C. 20540 USA, https://www.loc.gov/item/jots.200019309/. Accessed 8 Feb. 2024.
[lxvii] Binns, Donna. "The Bionic Woman." Disability in Science Fiction: Representations of Technology as Cure, edited by Kathryn Allan, Palgrave Macmillan US, 2013, pp. 89–101. Springer Link, https://doi.org/10.1057/9781137343437_7.
[lxviii] Peart, Neil. "The Trees Lyrics." Rush.Com, https://www.rush.com/songs/the-trees/. Accessed 8 Feb. 2024.
[lxix] As well as its social impacts: high poverty rates, rising infant mortality, increased social alienation, etc.

[lxx] "The cyclic – sometimes called the stick – controls the altitude and airspeed of the helicopter. The movement of the cyclic alters the tilt of the rotor disc, which is the hypothetical disc the rotors make when they are turning." The Pilot Institute. "Helicopter Controls and Basic Maneuvers." Pilot Institute, 9 June 2022, https://pilotinstitute.com/helicopter-controls/.
[lxxi] "The dark triad is a psychological theory of personality that describes three notably offensive, but non-pathological personality types: Machiavellianism, sub-clinical narcissism, and sub-clinical psychopathy. Each of these personality types is called dark because each is considered to contain malevolent qualities. Several researchers have suggested that sadism should be considered a fourth dark trait," hence, dark tetrad. *Dark Triad*. Wikipedia, 28 Jan. 2024. Wikipedia, https://en.wikipedia.org/w/index.php?title=Dark_triad&oldid=1200036239#Dark_tetrad.
[lxxii] "Egregore (also spelled egregor; from French égrégore, from Ancient Greek ἐγρήγορος, egrēgoros 'wakeful') is an esoteric concept representing a non-physical entity or thoughtform that arises from the collective thoughts and emotions of a distinct group of individuals." *Egregore*. Wikipedia, 29 Jan. 2024. Wikipedia, https://en.wikipedia.org/w/index.php?title=Egregore&oldid=1200263616.
[lxxiii] I asked ChatGPT to help me create the neologism and it provided ten candidate terms. I then added the malevolent intent and it provided ten more. I then identified the best candidate from each of the lists and blended them into a neologism that I created. So to whom belongs attribution? Is this a complete AI takeover of human creativity, or did I leverage the machine's ability to quickly create novel combinations and then improve and refine the machine's cognition with my own human cognition?
[lxxiv] Editor, CSRC Content. Non-Repudiation - Glossary | CSRC. https://csrc.nist.gov/glossary/term/non_repudiation. Accessed 23 Feb. 2024.
[lxxv] Clarke, Arthur C. Wikiquote. https://en.wikiquote.org/wiki/Arthur_C._Clarke. Accessed 22 Feb. 2024.
[lxxvi] PerryCook, Taija. "Did MLK Say 'Darkness Cannot Drive Out Darkness; Only Light Can Do That'?" Snopes, 21 Jan. 2024, https://www.snopes.com//fact-check/darkness-quote-mlk/. Also archived at https://web.archive.org/web/20240222191813/https://www.snopes.com/fact-check/darkness-quote-mlk/
[lxxvii] Lewis, C. S. Mere Christianity. Macmillan, 1952. Library of Congress ISBN, https://lccn.loc.gov/52014321.

[lxxviii] Christianity and the Rise of Western Science – ABC Religion & Ethics (Australian Broadcasting Corporation).
https://web.archive.org/web/20180809040202/http://www.abc.net.au/religion/articles/2012/05/08/3498202.htm. Accessed 14 Feb. 2024.
[lxxix] "Observer Effect." Disambiguation. Wikipedia, 27 July 2023. Wikipedia,
https://en.wikipedia.org/w/index.php?title=Observer_effect&oldid=1167376916.
[lxxx] Grey Goo | Nanotechnology, Self-Replicating Nanobots Scenario | Britannica.
https://www.britannica.com/technology/grey-goo. Accessed 14 Feb. 2024.
[lxxxi] "Ouroboros - Description, Uses and Interpretations." Mythology.Net, 8 Apr. 2017,
https://mythology.net/others/concepts/ouroboros/.
[lxxxii] Silverton, Michael. LLM research prompt. "Origins of 'Keep your head in the clouds and your feet on the ground.'" ChatGPT, https://chat.openai.com. Accessed 28 Feb. 2024.
[lxxxiii] Dang, U. Than. What Is Paticcasamuppada? [Chapter 1]. 29 Feb. 2012,
https://www.wisdomlib.org/buddhism/book/the-doctrine-of-paticcasamuppada/d/doc6226.html.
[lxxxiv] "Escape the Algorithm." KKCR, Kaua ' i Community Radio. April 10, 2019.
https://www.facebook.com/groups/61636050657/posts/10156244884730658/
[lxxxv] Goodreads. *Gospel of Thomas*. https://www.goodreads.com/quotes/126072-if-you-bring-forth-what-is-within-you-what-you. Accessed 29 Feb. 2024.
[lxxxvi] "Paul Tillich was critical of the view of God as a type of being or presence. He felt that, if God were a being, God could not then properly be called the source of all being (due to the question of what, in turn, created God). As an alternative, he suggested that God be understood as the "ground of Being-Itself". " *God as 'Ground of Being' - Paul Tillich*. Religious Naturalism, https://religiousnaturalism.org/god-as-ground-of-being-paul-tillich/. Accessed 29 Feb. 2024.
[lxxxvii] Lamb, Evelyn. "What T.S. Eliot Told Me about the Chain Rule." Scientific American Blog Network, https://blogs.scientificamerican.com/roots-of-unity/what-ts-eliot-told-me-about-the-chain-rule/. Accessed 14 Feb. 2024.
[lxxxviii] "Matthew 18:4-7 - The Message." Bible Gateway,
https://www.biblegateway.com/passage/?search=Matthew%2018&version=MSG. Accessed 29 Feb. 2024.
[lxxxix] Lewis, C. S. *On Stories* (1947). https://gutenberg.ca/ebooks/lewiscs-onstories/lewiscs-onstories-00-h.html. Accessed 16 Feb. 2024. Lewis, C. S. (Clive Staples). Republished in *On Stories : And Other Essays on Literature*. New York, NY : HarperOne, an imprint of HarperCollinsPublishers, 2017. Internet Archive, http://archive.org/details/onstoriesotheres0000lewi_m3e5.
[xc] "C. S. Lewis Daily – Day 62." Bible Gateway, https://www.biblegateway.com/devotionals/cs-lewis-daily/2024/03/02. Accessed 02 Mar. 2024.
[xci] BSOD: Blue Screen Of Death. A colloquialism from the Windows operating system personal computer era describing the behavior of a computer monitor when the OS halted. Generally, BSODs were accompanied by an error number for debugging and troubleshooting purposes.
[xcii] Lewis, C. S. (Clive Staples). "XI. Tolkien's The Lord of the Rings," p.138 in *On Stories : And Other Essays on Literature*. New York, NY : HarperOne, an imprint of HarperCollinsPublishers, 2017. Internet Archive, http://archive.org/details/onstoriesotheres0000lewi_m3e5.
[xciii] The change of name from Bard to Gemini makes this work into a bit of a time-capsule. Future readers many never have heard of the Bard AI moniker, at all, while Gemini may become a household name. Project Gemini - NASA. https://www.nasa.gov/gemini/. Accessed 14 Feb. 2024.
[xciv] Hamlet - Act 1, Scene 5 | Folger Shakespeare Library. https://www.folger.edu/explore/shakespeares-works/read/. Accessed 14 Feb. 2024.
[xcv] "The point is, ladies and gentleman, that greed, for lack of a better word, is good." Wall Street. Directed by Oliver Stone, Twentieth Century Fox, Amercent Films, American Entertainment Partners L.P., 1987. https://www.imdb.com/title/tt0094291/quotes/?item=qt0393936
[xcvi] Historical context: "The last few verses focused on Paul's motivation for continuing his hard and dangerous life of preaching the gospel against so much opposition. Now he continues by asking: what could he possibly stand to gain in human terms? Preaching the gospel does not bring him wealth, or pleasure, or status. Instead, it led him to fighting with beasts in Ephesus. It evokes imagery of Christians being torn apart by the lions in Roman spectacles. Scholars suggest, though, that it's unlikely Paul fought

actual beasts in Ephesus. Paul seems to be using this as a metaphor for facing overwhelming and dangerous circumstances, perhaps including being attacked by angry mobs. [W]ithout the hope of resurrection for himself and those he preaches to, Paul assures his readers he would not continue to do what he is doing. Instead, he would live like those philosophers of his day known as the Epicureans, who attempted to live life to the fullest since they were convinced nothing came after. He quotes from Isaiah 22:13 to capture that spirit, "Let us eat and drink, for tomorrow we die." Paul does not live for pleasure, however. The life he does lead should convince everyone who knows him of how deeply confident he is in both the resurrection of Christ from the dead and the eventual resurrection of all Christians." From *What Does 1 Corinthians 15:32 Mean?* BibleRef.Com, https://www.bibleref.com/1-Corinthians/15/1-Corinthians-15-32.html. Accessed 16 Feb. 2024.

[xcvii] See Ernest Becker, "The Denial of Death."

[xcviii] "The Lottery of Birth — All the Things You Don't Control in Life." Sloww, 19 Apr. 2021, https://www.sloww.co/lottery-of-birth/.

[xcix] See page 165 for more on the bootstraps mythology.

[c] "How Many People Have Ever Lived on Earth?" Corrections Environmental Scan (nicic.gov), https://info.nicic.gov/ces/global/population-demographics/how-many-people-have-ever-lived-earth.

[ci] Generation Alpha. Wikipedia. https://en.wikipedia.org/wiki/Generation_Alpha.

[cii] Barlow, John Perry. "Death from Above." Communications of the ACM, vol. 38, no. 5, May 1995, pp. 17–20. DOI.org (Crossref), https://doi.org/10.1145/203356.203358.

[ciii] Arthur C Clarke. 2001: A Space Odyssey. 1968. Internet Archive, http://archive.org/details/SpaceOdyssey_819.

[civ] Urban Dictionary: Purple Pill. 11 Feb. 2024, https://web.archive.org/web/20240211220324/https://www.urbandictionary.com/define.php?term=Purple%20Pill.

[cv] Xiao, Jun, et al. "A Study on the Relationship Between Consumer Motivations and Subjective Well-Being: A Latent Profile Analysis." Frontiers in Psychology, vol. 13, June 2022, p. 938060. PubMed Central, https://doi.org/10.3389/fpsyg.2022.938060.

[cvi] U.S. Constitution - First Amendment | Resources | Constitution Annotated | Congress.Gov | Library of Congress. https://constitution.congress.gov/constitution/amendment-1/. Accessed 14 Feb. 2024.

[cvii] Bear, Nahko, and Medicine for the People. "Aloha ke Akua." Lyrics https://www.azlyrics.com/lyrics/nahkoandmedicineforthepeople/alohakeakua.html

[cviii] Wall Street - Poder e Cobiça (1987) - Citações - IMDb. www.imdb.com, https://www.imdb.com/title/tt0094291/quotes/?item=qt0393927. Accessed 14 Feb. 2024.

[cix] Rogan, Joe. "Joe Rogan Experience #1169 - Elon Musk." YouTube, 07 Sept. 2018, youtu.be/ycPr5-27vSI.

[cx] Graeber, David. Wikipedia. https://en.wikipedia.org/wiki/David_Graeber

[cxi] Pang, Alex Soojung-Kim. *REST: Why You Get More Done When You Work Less*. Basic Books, 2024.

[cxii] Silverton, Michael. LLM research prompt, "Who originated the currently popular term monk mode?" Bard - Chat Based AI Tool from Google. https://bard.google.com. Accessed 31 Dec. 2023.

[cxiii] The Linux Foundation. *Annual Report 2023 | Rising Tides of Open Source*. The Linux Foundation, 2023. https://www.linuxfoundation.org/hubfs/Reports/2023_lf_annual_report_122123a.pdf.

[cxiv] Silverton, Michael. LLM research prompt, "Based upon What You Do Know about Contributions to the Linux Software Ecosystem, What Is Your Best Meta Analytical Synthesis?" https://bard.google.com/share/1709f29fb997. Accessed 31 Dec. 2023.

[cxv] The Mind behind Linux | Linus Torvalds | TED. Directed by TED, 2016. YouTube, https://www.youtube.com/watch?v=o8NPllzkFhE.

[cxvi] Silverton, Michael. LLM research prompts for, "Seems maybe I've coined a nifty neologism. Can you find an earlier occurrence or use of the term?" and "That Seems like a Good Sign That You Haven't Seen 'Econosystem' Which I'm Proposing as a Useful Neologism for Economic Development Ecosystem." https://bard.google.com/share/ef5ae86d922e. Accessed 31 Dec. 2023. I found the Bio-Rad Econo System, two words, at https://www.bio-rad.com/webroot/web/pdf/lsr/literature/LIT559.pdf but not the usage or context we've discovered together, here. Vanity of vanities, isn't it?

[cxvii] I apologize not noting the source video link. I can add that Yang seems to have quoted Judith Shulevitz's "Opinion | It's Payback Time for Women." The New York Times, 8 Jan. 2016. NYTimes.com, https://www.nytimes.com/2016/01/10/opinion/sunday/payback-time-for-women.html in which she wrote, "Actually, it's society that's getting a free ride on women's unrewarded contributions to the perpetuation of the human race."

[cxviii] For more about the work of improving ourselves as the new justification of being, see the section titled "Science, Fiction, Technology, and Policy."

[cxix] "The Long Now Foundation." Long Now, https://longnow.org/. Accessed 16 Dec. 2023.

[cxx] Wikipedia contributors. "Golem." Wikipedia, The Free Encyclopedia. Wikipedia, The Free Encyclopedia, 4 Mar. 2024. Web.

[cxxi] Special thanks to John & Linda at Kilauea Night Market in October 2018 for telling me about Nassim Haramein's novel work. I didn't forget and will never forget your kindness, keen insight and intuition in listening to my silly stories. Quotation from *How to Supercharge Your Manifestation | Greatness Clips | Nassim Haramein & Lewis Howes*. Directed by Lewis Howes, 2023. YouTube, https://www.youtube.com/watch?v=wKQkx6jiRLk. Accessed 4 Mar. 2024. Paper mentioned in the interview: Haramein, N., Guermonprez, C., Alirol, O., 2023. *The Origin of Mass and the Nature of Gravity*. https://doi.org/10.5281/zenodo.10125315.

[cxxii] "A Proton Becoming A Universe." Directed by Nassim Haramein, 2021. YouTube, https://www.youtube.com/watch?v=8YRjhe5Vi0U. Accessed 4 Mar. 2024.

[cxxiii] "STOP MANIFESTING WRONG! - Do This Everyday To Manifest Anything CORRECTLY | Nassim Haramein." Directed by Lewis Howes, 2023. YouTube, https://youtu.be/qBN69JB689s?t=2989.

[cxxiv] "Markovian Information" refers to information or data that is processed or analyzed within the context of a Markov process. A Markov process is a stochastic (random) process that satisfies the Markov property, which states that the future state of a process depends only on the current state and not on the sequence of events that preceded it. In simpler terms, it implies that the future is independent of the past, given the present. Markovian information, therefore, involves the analysis or prediction of future states based on the current state without the need to consider the historical sequence of events leading up to the current state. This concept is widely used in various fields such as probability theory, statistics, and machine learning, especially in modeling random systems that change over time. "Define Markovian Information." ChatGPT, https://chat.openai.com. Accessed 4 Mar. 2024.

[cxxv] "Artificial consciousness (AC), also known as machine consciousness (MC) synthetic consciousness or digital consciousness, is the consciousness hypothesized to be possible in artificial intelligence. It is also the corresponding field of study, which draws insights from philosophy of mind, philosophy of artificial intelligence, cognitive science and neuroscience. The same terminology can be used with the term "sentience" instead of "consciousness" when specifically designating phenomenal consciousness (the ability to feel qualia)." Wikipedia contributors. "Artificial Consciousness." Wikipedia, 28 Feb. 2024. Wikipedia, https://en.wikipedia.org/wiki/Artificial_consciousness.

[cxxvi] The Scarcity Mindset | Psychology Today. https://www.psychologytoday.com/us/blog/science-choice/201504/the-scarcity-mindset. Accessed 7 Mar. 2024.

[cxxvii] "How to Snap Out of Scarcity." Scarcity Mentality: Causes, Symptoms, and More. https://www.webmd.com/mental-health/what-is-scarcity-mentality. Accessed 7 Mar. 2024.
[cxxviii] Palmer, Blaire. "What Is 'Unworking?'" Medium, 8 Jan. 2018, https://medium.com/@BlairePalmer/what-is-unworking-e0f72484ad3d.

[cxxix] Palmer, Blaire. "What Is 'Unworking?'" Medium, 8 Jan. 2018, https://medium.com/@BlairePalmer/what-is-unworking-e0f72484ad3d.

[cxxx] Wilson, Clare. "Free will: Can neuroscience reveal if your choices are yours to make?" New Scientist. 27 September 2023. https://www.newscientist.com/article/mg25934580-900-free-will-can-neuroscience-reveal-if-your-choices-are-yours-to-make/.

[cxxxi] The most recent decades of research continue to expand upon the original two stress responses of fight or flight. The effects of trauma and stress are vastly more intricate and destructive to human wellness and flourishing than originally understood. For example, the pervasive 20th century entrepreneurial "Biz Bro" and "Go Girl," psychologically fragmenting and splitting narratives of work-life J.O.B. compartmentalization and impossible balance, of stress, trauma, and dissociation-thinly-veiled-as-enlightened-detachment, as all good for humans, or even necessary to build character, were all conveniently useful for authoritarians, narcissists, sociopaths, and psychopaths who used those tactical traumatizing tactics to motivate, manipulate, withhold, and instinctively implement intermittent reinforcement techniques, including engineered scarcity to control others in order to fulfill their own dark hedonistic desires or otherwise achieve their own ends at the expense of others while making others into their own "red-in-tooth-and-claw" image. See also Figure 3. A.M.D., Neurodivergent Occupational Therapist. "The 6Fs of Trauma Responses." NeuroClastic, 28 Sept. 2021, https://neuroclastic.com/the-6fs-of-trauma-responses/. Millacci, Tiffany Sauber, Ph. D. "7 Trauma Response Types & How to Recognize Them." PositivePsychology.Com, 23 Nov. 2023, https://positivepsychology.com/trauma-response/.
[cxxxii] Krishnamurti On Mental Health, Krishnamurti Foundation Trust. https://kfoundation.org/mental-health/. Accessed 7 Jan. 2024.
[cxxxiii] The United States population on March 7, 2024, was: 336,139,197. Population Clock. https://www.census.gov/popclock/. Accessed 8 Mar. 2024.
[cxxxiv] "Is the United States a Republic or a Democracy?" WorldAtlas, 26 Sept. 2018, https://www.worldatlas.com/articles/is-the-united-states-a-republic-or-a-democracy.html.

[cxxxv] "Bible Gateway Passage: Luke 19:45-48 - The Voice." Bible Gateway, https://www.biblegateway.com/passage/?search=Luke%2019%3A45-48&version=VOICE. Accessed 12 Mar. 2024. "He entered Jerusalem and went into the temple. He began driving out the temple merchants. Jesus: The Hebrew Scriptures say, "My house shall be a house of prayer," but you have turned it into a shelter for thieves. He came back day after day to teach in the temple. The chief priests, the religious scholars, and the leading men of the city wanted to kill Him, but because He was so popular among the people—who hung upon each word He spoke—they were unable to do anything."
[cxxxvi] "1907 Saint-Gaudens Coins Controversy. In God We Trust." Wikipedia, 9 Mar. 2024. Wikipedia, https://en.wikipedia.org/w/index.php?title=In_God_We_Trust&oldid=1212848065#1907_Saint-Gaudens_coins_controversy.
[cxxxvii] Hopf, G. Michael. Those Who Remain. CreateSpace Independent Publishing Platform, 2016, https://www.goodreads.com/quotes/8751435-hard-times-create-strong-men-strong-men-create-good-times.
[cxxxviii] Wikipedia contributors. "E Pluribus Unum." Wikipedia, 20 Feb. 2024. Wikipedia, https://en.wikipedia.org/w/index.php?title=E_pluribus_unum&oldid=1209042022. "In God We Trust." Wikipedia, 9 Mar. 2024. Wikipedia, https://en.wikipedia.org/w/index.php?title=In_God_We_Trust&oldid=1212848065. "The first word of E pluribus unum is actually an abbreviation of the Latin preposition ex, meaning "out of." While its status as national motto was for many years unofficial, E pluribus unum was still considered the de facto motto

of the United States from its early history. That the phrase "E pluribus unum" has thirteen letters makes its use symbolic of the original Thirteen Colonies which rebelled against the rule of the Kingdom of Great Britain and became the first thirteen states, represented today as the thirteen stripes on the American flag" (Wikipedia).

That the phrase "E pluribus unum" has thirteen letters makes its use symbolic of the original Thirteen Colonies which rebelled against the rule of the Kingdom of Great Britain and became the first thirteen states, represented today as the thirteen stripes on the American flag.
[cxxxix] "Dunbar's Number." Wikipedia, 16 Feb. 2024. Wikipedia, https://en.wikipedia.org/w/index.php?title=Dunbar%27s_number&oldid=1208070558.
[cxl] Etherscan. Top Accounts by ETH Balance. https://etherscan.io/accounts (Accessed: 23 November 2023).

[cxli] Central Bank Digital Currency (CBDC). https://www.federalreserve.gov/central-bank-digital-currency.htm. Accessed 2 Jan. 2024.

[cxlii] "Yeshua Hamashiach: Who Is Yeshua?" Jewish Voice. https://www.jewishvoice.org/learn/who-is-yeshua. Accessed 11 Mar. 2024.
[cxliii] Davidow, B. (2023) Post on X.com. https://twitter.com/BillDavidow/status/1727348774102610351 (Accessed: 22 November 2023).

[cxliv] Seet, Charlotte. "Top 5: The World's Heaviest Airliners." Simple Flying, 14 Oct. 2023, https://simpleflying.com/heaviest-commercial-aricraft-list/.

[cxlv] Zeitgeist: The Movie | Rotten Tomatoes. Directed by Peter Joseph, 2007, https://www.rottentomatoes.com/m/zeitgeist. Quotation: Fresco, Jaque. *This Shit's Got to Go!* Directed by The Venus Project, 2019. YouTube, https://youtu.be/VbsIP8kYUFc.
[cxlvi] Sender R, Fuchs S, Milo R (2016) Revised Estimates for the Number of Human and Bacteria Cells in the Body. PLOS Biology 14(8): e1002533. https://doi.org/10.1371/journal.pbio.1002533

[cxlvii] Microbiome (2023) National Institute of Environmental Health Sciences. Available at: https://www.niehs.nih.gov/health/topics/science/microbiome/index.cfm (Accessed: 22 November 2023).

[cxlviii] Silverton, Michael. LLM research prompt, "Three Hundred Eighty Trillion." https://bard.google.com/share/f2397e1e91ea. Accessed 3 Jan. 2024.

[cxlix] U.S. and World Population Clock (no date) United States Census Bureau. Available at: https://www.census.gov/popclock/world (Accessed: 22 November 2023).

[cl] "Everything Should Be Made as Simple as Possible, But Not Simpler" – Quote Investigator. 13 May 2011, https://quoteinvestigator.com/2011/05/13/einstein-simple/.

[cli] Dr. Martin Luther King Jr. - 1966 Convocation | Illinois Wesleyan. https://www.iwu.edu/mlk/page-4.html. Accessed 4 Jan. 2024.

[clii] A neologism of techno-libertarian and utopian. An interesting definition of terms and trends on this topic can be found at technolibertarian.wikia.com/wiki/TechnoLibertarian_Wiki.

[cliii] Suicide data and statistics (2023) Centers for Disease Control and Prevention. Available at: https://www.cdc.gov/suicide/suicide-data-statistics.html (Accessed: 24 November 2023).

[cliv] Wisqars leading causes of Death Visualization Tool (no date) Centers for Disease Control and Prevention. Available at: https://wisqars.cdc.gov/lcd/?o=LCD&y1=2021&y2=2021&ct=10&cc=ALL&g=00&s=0&r=0&ry=0&e=0&ar=lcd1age&at=groups&ag=lcd1age&a1=0&a2=199 (Accessed: 24 November 2023).

[clv] Manchester, J. (2018) Biden on young people complaining they have it tough: 'give me a break', The Hill. Available at: https://thehill.com/blogs/blog-briefing-room/news/368849-biden-on-young-people-complaining-they-have-it-tough-give-me-a/ (Accessed: 24 November 2023).

[clvi] "Never Doubt That a Small Group of Thoughtful, Committed Citizens Can Change the World; Indeed, It's the Only Thing That Ever Has" – Quote Investigator. 12 Nov. 2017, https://quoteinvestigator.com/2017/11/12/change-world/.

[clvii] What Was the Saturn V? (Grades 5-8) - NASA. 17 Sept. 2010, https://www.nasa.gov/learning-resources/for-kids-and-students/what-was-the-saturn-v-grades-5-8/.

[clviii] "Architecture Parlante." Wikipedia, 3 Nov. 2022. Wikipedia, https://en.wikipedia.org/w/index.php?title=Architecture_parlante&oldid=1119786551.

[clix] "What Is Rent Seeking in Economics, and What Are Some Examples?" Investopedia, https://www.investopedia.com/terms/r/rentseeking.asp. Accessed 11 Feb. 2024.

[clx] At this point, ask ChatGPT, search with your favorite engine, there's so much overwhelming evidence that I don't need to footnote this claim every time it's made in the name of heading of sea lions. See sea-lioning in the Glossary, a kind of pervasively disingenuous trolling.

[clxi] Silverton, Michael. LLM research prompt, "Financial Vulnerability of US Households." https://bard.google.com/share/9e410d814fdf. Accessed 5 Jan. 2024. Sources: The Fed's 2023 Economic Well-Being of U.S. Households report: https://www.federalreserve.gov/publications/files/2022-report-economic-well-being-us-households-202305.pdf. Fortune article on the 2022 survey: https://www.bloomberg.com/news/articles/2023-01-24/two-in-three-can-t-cover-400-emergency-in-us-suze-orman-survey. Washington Post article discussing the nuances of the data: https://www.washingtonpost.com/business/2023/08/03/actually-most-americans-can-come-up-with-400-in-an-emergency/92c258f8-3200-11ee-85dd-5c3c97d6acda_story.html.

[clxii] The Fed's 2023 Economic Well-Being of U.S. Households report: https://www.federalreserve.gov/publications/files/2022-report-economic-well-being-us-households-202305.pdf.

[clxiii] Invisible People - Organization That Helps Homeless People. https://invisiblepeople.tv/. Accedido 2 de diciembre de 2023.

[clxiv] "When Liars Smile: The Telltale Tic of Duping Delight | Psychology Today." https://www.psychologytoday.com/us/blog/machiavellians-gulling-the-rubes/202304/when-liars-smile-the-telltale-tic-of-duping-delight. Accessed 5 Jan. 2024.

[clxv] Barlow, John Perry. "Death From Above." https://w2.eff.org/Misc/Publications/John_Perry_Barlow/HTML/death_from_above.html. Accessed 5 Jan. 2024.

[clxvi] See note 2.

[clxvii] Scott Santens [@scottsantens]. "Unless You Have the Option to Refuse, It's Not a Free Market, and Your Choices Aren't Really Choices. Full Consent Requires the Option to Say 'No.' This Is Just as True in Market Relations as It Is in Sexual Relations. Free Markets REQUIRE Basic Income and Universal Health Care. https://T.Co/eP636MtJjP." Twitter, 7 Oct. 2018, https://twitter.com/scottsantens/status/1048983436441145344.

[clxviii] Silverton, Michael. "Toward What End?" prezi.com, https://prezi.com/ruc2n7_ghhds/toward-what-end/. Modified 17 Nov, 2012. Created 1 Jan, 2010 at https://www.linkedin.com/in/michaelsilverton/. Accessed 2 Dec. 2023.

[clxix] The Chopra Foundation's Mission - The Chopra Foundation. 10 Nov. 2011, https://choprafoundation.org/about/mission/.

[clxx] "Bible Gateway Passage: Hebrews 4:10 - English Standard Version." Bible Gateway, https://www.biblegateway.com/passage/?search=Hebrews%204%3A10&version=ESV. Accessed 31 Dec. 2023.

[clxxi] Williamson, Chris. "Jordan Peterson - How To Destroy Your Negative Beliefs (4K) - YouTube." The Modern Wisdom Podcast, https://www.youtube.com/watch?v=WEP5ubPMGDU&t=9428s. Nov. 27, 2023. Accessed 12 Dec. 2023.

[clxxii] Wavy Gravy & Ace of Cups Music Video: "Basic Human Needs." Directed by Seva Foundation, 2017. YouTube, https://www.youtube.com/watch?v=K7ailgfJQck.

[clxxiii] Paresh, Dave. "Humane's AI Pin Is a $700 Smartphone Alternative You Wear All Day." Wired, Conde Nast, 9 Nov. 2023, www.wired.com/story/humane-ai-pin-700-dollar-smartphone-alternative-wearable/.

[clxxiv] Come to a book event and say hi. We can debate the benefits and drawbacks of leaving all other freedoms in place, except the freedom to kill other humans when we talk online, or in person, later. For our purposes here, it's good enough to illustrate the point that we are much closer to the practical reality of such scenarios than many people might suspect.

[clxxv] Harter, Jim. "Is Quiet Quitting Real?" Gallup.com, 17 May 2023, www.gallup.com/workplace/398306/quiet-quitting-real.aspx.

[clxxvi] Open AI. "Introducing GPT's." https://openai.com/blog/introducing-gpts

[clxxvii] See xvii.

[clxxviii] Wikipedia contributors. Black Budget - Wikipedia. 25 Oct. 2023, en.wikipedia.org/wiki/Black_budget.

[clxxix] Transition21. "Media as Environment – Marshall McLuhan." YouTube, 20 Apr. 2017, www.youtube.com/watch?v=dFwRNy-eIkU.

[clxxx] Atlassian. A 2020 retrospective on the history of work - infographic, Atlassian. Available at: https://www.atlassian.com/history-of-work (Accessed: 17 November 2023).

[clxxxi] Rishi Sunak & Elon Musk: Talk AI, Tech & the Future. Directed by Rishi Sunak, 2023. YouTube, https://www.youtube.com/watch?v=R2meHtrO1n8.

[clxxxii] Lubomyr Melnyk Pianist/Composer - About Continuous Music. www.lubomyr.com/continuousmusic.html.

[clxxxiii] Wikipedia contributors. "List of largest companies in the United States by revenue." Wikipedia, The Free Encyclopedia. Wikipedia, The Free Encyclopedia, 3 Nov. 2023. Web. 17 Nov. 2023.

clxxxiv Wikipedia contributors. "List of largest German companies." Wikipedia, The Free Encyclopedia. Wikipedia, The Free Encyclopedia, 4 Aug. 2023. Web. 17 Nov. 2023.

clxxxv Wikipedia contributors. "List of largest Japanese companies." Wikipedia, The Free Encyclopedia. Wikipedia, The Free Encyclopedia, 4 Feb. 2023. Web. 17 Nov. 2023.

clxxxvi Wikipedia contributors. "List of largest companies in India." Wikipedia, The Free Encyclopedia. Wikipedia, The Free Encyclopedia, 5 Oct. 2023. Web. 17 Nov. 2023.

clxxxvii Wikipedia contributors. "List of largest companies in the United Kingdom." Wikipedia, The Free Encyclopedia. Wikipedia, The Free Encyclopedia, 19 Oct. 2023. Web. 17 Nov. 2023.

clxxxviii Wikipedia contributors. "List of largest French companies." Wikipedia, The Free Encyclopedia. Wikipedia, The Free Encyclopedia, 9 Sep. 2023. Web. 17 Nov. 2023.

clxxxix Wikipedia contributors. "List of largest Italian companies." Wikipedia, The Free Encyclopedia. Wikipedia, The Free Encyclopedia, 2 Dec. 2022. Web. 17 Nov. 2023.

cxc Wikipedia contributors. "List of largest Brazilian companies." Wikipedia, The Free Encyclopedia. Wikipedia, The Free Encyclopedia, 4 Aug. 2023. Web. 17 Nov. 2023.

cxci Wikipedia contributors. "List of largest companies in Canada." Wikipedia, The Free Encyclopedia. Wikipedia, The Free Encyclopedia, 4 Aug. 2023. Web. 17 Nov. 2023.

cxcii Yes, we understand the hazards of citing Wikipedia https://en.wikipedia.org/wiki/Wikipedia:Citing_Wikipedia and selectively choose this source when the data behind the content is readily confirmed.

cxciii Wang, D'Vera Cohn, Gretchen Livingston and Wendy. "Chapter 4: Public Views on Staying at Home vs. Working." Pew Research Center's Social & Demographic Trends Project, 8 Apr. 2014, https://www.pewresearch.org/social-trends/2014/04/08/chapter-4-public-views-on-staying-at-home-vs-working/.

cxciv Johnson, Stacy.

cxcv Bliss, Laura, and CityLab.

cxcvi "A Practical Guide to Controlling Addiction & Dopamine | Dr. Anna Lembke | Knowledge Project 159." 2023. YouTube, https://www.youtube.com/watch?v=bTyyY4jrl2w. While you're here, I want to plug Shane's book as an example of the kind of curriculum we need more than ever in the Post-Automation Era. He doesn't know and I didn't ask, I just know it's worth sharing. "Clear Thinking: Turning Ordinary Moments into Extraordinary Results" is available at https://fs.blog/clear/.

cxcvii Jeff Bezos: *Truth Is Uncomfortable | Lex Fridman Podcast Clips*. Directed by Lex Clips, 2023. YouTube, https://www.youtube.com/watch?v=JL4OoKJyNrc. "You have just asked a million-dollar question. What you're asking, what you are talking in general about is truth telling. Yeah. We humans are not truth-seeking animals. We are social animals. If we take you back in time to a small village, if you go along to get along, you can survive you, you can procreate. **If you're the village truth teller, you might get clubbed to death in the middle of the night**. Truths often don't want to be heard, because important truths can be uncomfortable, they can be awkward, they can be exhausting, challenging, they can make people defensive, even if that's not the intent. So, you want to set up your culture so that the most junior person can overrule the most senior person, if they have data."

[cxcviii] Image credit: Falkner, Nick. "What Happened to Our Promised Leisure Time? And Will We Find It in the Smart City?" The Conversation, 1 Oct. 2017, http://theconversation.com/what-happened-to-our-promised-leisure-time-and-will-we-find-it-in-the-smart-city-83570.

[cxcix] What Is Glop? | Alexi Pappas. www.youtube.com, https://www.youtube.com/shorts/z6uDSSP-zTg. Accessed 29 Dec. 2023.

[cc] CNN, www.cnn.com/2013/08/02/tech/da-vinci-robot-surgery/index.html.

[cci] "Advanced Robotic Technology Revolutionising Healthcare in Unprecedented Ways." https://www.biospectrumindia.com/features/93/23592/advanced-robotic-technology-revolutionising-healthcare-in-unprecedented-ways.html. Accessed 2 Jan. 2024.

[ccii] "This Robot Successfully Performed an Entire Lung Transplant." Euronews, 19 Apr. 2023, https://www.euronews.com/next/2023/04/19/spain-sees-the-worlds-first-lung-transplantation-performed-entirely-by-robot.

[cciii] Of technium, Kelly writes, "I dislike inventing words that no one else uses, but in this case, all known alternatives fail to convey the required scope. So, I've somewhat reluctantly coined a word to designate the greater, global, massively interconnected system of technology vibrating around us. I call it the technium. The technium extends beyond shiny hardware to include culture, art, social institutions, and intellectual creation of all types" (Kelly, 11).

[cciv] Kelly, Kevin. What technology wants. New York: Viking, 2010. Print.

[ccv] An "exaptation" is just one example of a characteristic that evolved, but that isn't considered an adaptation. Evolutionary biologists Stephen Gould and Elizabeth Vrba proposed vocabulary to let biologists talk about features that are and are not adaptation.
https://evolution.berkeley.edu/exaptations/.

[ccvi] Hicks, Bill. "It's Just a Ride." Comedy sketch. https://youtu.be/KgzQuE1pR1w. Accessed Nov. 21, 2023.

[ccvii] "World Game." Buckminster Fuller Institute, 11 Feb. 2022, https://www.bfi.org/about-fuller/big-ideas/world-game/.

[ccviii] Pang, Alex Soojung-Kim. *Rest: Why You Get More Done When You Work Less*. First paperback edition, Basic Books, 2018. Summary quotation by WorldCat https://search.worldcat.org/pt/title/1005596836.

[ccix] Onstad, Katrina. The Weekend Effect. HarperCollins Publishers, 2017. Perlego, https://www.perlego.com/book/601330/the-weekend-effect-pdf.
[ccx] Santens, Scott. Post on X.com. Nov. 8, 2023.
https://twitter.com/scottsantens/status/1722260066135654706 Accessed Nov. 22, 2023.

[ccxi] The Project Gutenberg E-Text of As a Man Thinketh, by James Allen.
https://www.gutenberg.org/files/4507/4507-h/4507-h.htm. Accessed 9 Dec. 2023.

[ccxii] "Operation Underground Railroad is leading the fight against sex trafficking and sexual exploitation. Our work spans the globe as we assist law enforcement in rescue efforts and help provide aftercare to all those affected. While we prioritize children, we work to empower the liberation of anyone suffering at

the hands of those looking to sexually exploit. We offer vital resources to authorities around the world and work tirelessly to raise awareness and meet survivors on their healing journey. Our resolve never falters, and we will boldly persevere until those in need are safe." https://ourrescue.org/about-us.

[ccxiii] "Scholars at Risk is an international network of institutions and individuals whose mission it is to protect scholars and promote academic freedom. By arranging temporary academic positions at member universities and colleges, Scholars at Risk offers safety to scholars facing grave threats, so scholars' ideas are not lost and they can keep working until conditions improve and they are able to return to their home countries." https://www.scholarsatrisk.org/about/.

[ccxiv] Amazon.Com search: "New Earth." https://www.amazon.com/s?k=%22new+earth%22. Accessed 5 Jan. 2024.

[ccxv] Isaacson, Walter. "In Search of the Real Bill Gates." Time, 13 Jan. 1997. content.time.com, https://content.time.com/time/magazine/article/0,9171,1120657,00.html.

[ccxvi] *Mystopia*: a neologism I've coined to mean the combination of mysterious, in some ways inexplicable, and a society characterized by unsettling amounts of misinformation in the mid-life crisis years of social media.

[ccxvii] U.S. Bureau of Labor Statistics, Labor Force Statistics from the Current Population Survey, data.bls.gov/timeseries/LNS11300000.

[ccxviii] Colossus The Forbin Project (1970). 1970. Internet Archive, http://archive.org/details/colossus-the-forbin-project-1970.

[ccxix] Silverton, Michael. LLM research prompt, "What Is the Origin of the Term MITM? When and by Whom Was It First Used in Infosec?" https://bard.google.com/share/8d8ad436823c. Accessed 6 Jan. 2024.

[ccxx] TrojAI. https://www.iarpa.gov/research-programs/trojai. Accessed 6 Jan. 2024. "Artificial Intelligence (AI) is being increasingly applied to a variety of domains within the Intelligence Community (IC). The TrojAI program seeks to defend AI systems from intentional, malicious attacks, known as Trojans, by conducting research and developing technology to detect these attacks in a completed AI system. By building a detection system for these attacks, engineers can potentially identify backdoored AI systems before deployment. The development of Trojan AI detection capabilities will mitigate risks arising from AI system failure during mission critical tasks."

[ccxxi] I asked AI to help me draft a bill that might help to patch the bug in U.S. Code that instantiates this incentive in a way that leaves holes open to such exploitation by savvy and enterprising hackers. The objective being to maintain the beneficial incentives of the principle of fiduciary duty while patching hard-coded requirements that legally prevent consideration of commonwealth value as equally, and in some cases more valuable, than shareholder interests. That work is here https://metavalent.com/metavalent/2023/04/29/19-11-31-Fiduciary-Duty.html.

[ccxxii] Paulas, Rick. "Americans Living in Their Cars Are Finding Refuge in 'Safe Parking Lots.'" The Guardian, 5 Jan. 2024. The Guardian, https://www.theguardian.com/us-news/2024/jan/05/safe-overnight-parking-lot-sleep-in-car-rv-homelessness-housing-shelter.

ccxxiii Lam, Bourree. "What Happens to Your Life After You Win the Lottery?" The Atlantic, 12 Jan. 2016, https://www.theatlantic.com/business/archive/2016/01/lottery-winners-research/423543/.

ccxxiv "Thousand Trails is the largest and most successful provider of RV resorts and campgrounds in North America," www.thousandtrails.com/about-us.

ccxxv An Elegant Big Theory of Everything: My Big TOE by Tom Campbell. Directed by Tom Campbell, 2019. YouTube, https://www.youtube.com/watch?v=zstsJ7-ULMO.

ccxxvi Magee, Hailey. "Everyone's Doing The Best That They Can." Tiny Buddha, 13 Aug. 2018, https://tinybuddha.com/blog/everyones-doing-the-best-that-they-can/.

ccxxvii How to Control What People Do | Propaganda - EDWARD BERNAYS | Animated Book Summary. Directed by Eudaimonia, 2015. YouTube, https://www.youtube.com/watch?v=8Q-3qwEDyPM.

ccxxviii Noah Smith. "Holey poverty, Batman!" noahpinionblog.blogspot.jp/2014/07/holey-poverty-batman.html.

ccxxix I can't label Smith, I don't know him, and besides, I deeply respect his intellectual and analytical prowess, even in disagreement. I'm only noting what appears to me as ideological resemblance on this point.

ccxxx Othering & Belonging Institute. https://belonging.berkeley.edu/. Accessed 7 Jan. 2024.

ccxxxi Silverton, Michael. LLM research prompt, "Human Capacity for Free Will Meta-Analysis." https://bard.google.com/share/da233eefa886. Accessed 7 Jan. 2024.

ccxxxii Gailmard, Sean. "Accountability and Principal–Agent Theory." The Oxford Handbook of Public Accountability, edited by Mark Bovens et al., Oxford University Press, 2014, p. 0. Silverchair, https://doi.org/10.1093/oxfordhb/9780199641253.013.0016.

ccxxxiii Franklin, Benjamin. A Quote from The Autobiography of Benjamin Franklin. https://www.goodreads.com/quotes/10557361-how-convenient-does-it-prove-to-be-a-rational-animal. Accessed 7 Jan. 2024.

ccxxxiv "Greek Words for Love." Wikipedia, 20 Dec. 2023. Wikipedia, https://en.wikipedia.org/w/index.php?title=Greek_words_for_love&oldid=1190923049. Love - Encyclopedia of The Bible - Bible Gateway. https://www.biblegateway.com/resources/encyclopedia-of-the-bible/Love. Accessed 7 Jan. 2024.

ccxxxv "Bible Gateway Passage: 1 John 4:4 - The Voice." Bible Gateway, https://www.biblegateway.com/passage/?search=1%20John%204%3A4&version=VOICE. Accessed 7 Jan. 2024. "My children, you have come from God and have conquered these spirits because the One who lives within you is greater than the one in this world."

ccxxxvi Zauzmer, Emily. "Jim Carrey Reveals Why He Didn't Want to Be in the Hollywood 'Business Anymore.'" Peoplemag, https://people.com/movies/jim-carrey-reveals-why-hollywood-business-anymore/. Accessed 7 Jan. 2024.

ccxxxvii Fight Club. Directed by David Fincher, Fox 2000 Pictures, New Regency Productions, Linson Films, 1999.

[ccxxxviii] "Minimum Wage." DOL, http://www.dol.gov/general/topic/wages/minimumwage. Accessed 7 Jan. 2024.

[ccxxxix] Picchi, Aimee. Minimum Wage Would Be $26 an Hour If It Had Grown in Line with Productivity - CBS News. 7 Sept. 2021, https://www.cbsnews.com/news/minimum-wage-26-dollars-economy-productivity/.

[ccxl] "Ray Dalio." Forbes, https://www.forbes.com/profile/ray-dalio/. Accessed 12 Mar. 2024.
[ccxli] *How To Win In 2024 with Ray Dalio*. Directed by Max Rofagha, 2023. YouTube, https://www.youtube.com/watch?v=4_ppWBNFwSU.
[ccxlii] Johnson, Stephen. "Why Is 18 the Age of Adulthood If the Brain Can Take 30 Years to Mature?" Big Think, 31 Jan. 2022, https://bigthink.com/neuropsych/adult-brain/.

[ccxliii] McDermott, Mat. "What Are the Four Stages of Hindu Life?" Hindu American Foundation, 13 Jan. 2017, https://www.hinduamerican.org/blog/what-are-the-four-stages-of-hindu-life/.
[ccxliv] "Value of Life." Wikipedia, 4 Dec. 2023. Wikipedia, https://en.wikipedia.org/w/index.php?title=Value_of_life&oldid=1188256137.

[ccxlv] Updated, Elizabeth Howell last. "Every SpaceX Starship Explosion and What Elon Musk and His Team Learned from Them (Video)." Space.Com, 21 Aug. 2021, https://www.space.com/every-spacex-starship-explosion-lessons-learned.

ccxlvi 50% per Capita U.S. GDP - Wolfram|Alpha. https://www.wolframalpha.com/input?i=50%25+per+capita+U.S.+GDP. Primary source: Wolfram|Alpha Knowledgebase, 2020. External sources: Federal Reserve Bank of St Louis, FRED (Federal Reserve Economic Data). Accessed 6 Dec. 2023.

ccxlvii Sheffey, Ayelet. "Millennials Say They Need $525,000 a Year to Be Happy. A Nobel Prize Winner's Research Shows They're Not Wrong." Business Insider, https://www.businessinsider.com/millennials-annual-income-price-of-happiness-wealth-retirement-generations-survey-2023-11. Accessed 5 Dec. 2023.

[ccxlviii] Where Does "Life of Riley" Come from? - English Language & Usage Stack Exchange. https://english.stackexchange.com/questions/66046/where-does-life-of-riley-come-from. Accessed 11 Jan. 2024.
[ccxlix] For a balance sheet asset valued at $100,000 and a Social Security Trust Fund annual circulation of 50% per capita GDP ($41,199), that arithmetic ratio is 41,199/100,000 = 0.412, i.e., 41%.
[ccl] For simplicity, we're staying consistent to a 74-year average life-span implied by RAND calculations (Dahlman).

[ccli] Harris, Tristan, et al. Joe Rogan Experience #2076 - Aza Raskin & Tristan Harris. 19 Dec. 2023. open.spotify.com, https://open.spotify.com/episode/4ZcBHvjhGMTTdGF3fIdvg9?si=adef27f50cf94fb5.
[cclii] See Glossary.

[ccliii] Graeber, David. *Bullshit Jobs*. First. Simon & Schuster hardcover edition, Simon & Schuster, 2018.

[ccliv] Eliot, T. S. A Quote from Four Quartets. https://www.goodreads.com/quotes/644987-we-shall-not-cease-from-exploration-and-the-end-of. Accessed 11 Jan. 2024.
[cclv] Cutolo, Morgan. "This Is What the First-Ever Monopoly Game Looked Like." Reader's Digest, 3 June 2021, https://www.rd.com/article/first-monopoly-game/.

[cclvi] "Economic Security Project." Economic Security Project, https://economicsecurityproject.org/. Accessed 14 Dec. 2023.

[cclvii] PolicyLink. https://www.policylink.org/. Accessed 14 Dec. 2023.

[cclviii] "Liberation in a Generation." Liberation in a Generation, https://www.liberationinageneration.org/. Accessed 14 Dec. 2023.

[cclix] Zewde, Naomi. Strickland, Kyle. Capatosto, Kelly. Glogower, Ari. Hamilton, Darrick. "A Guaranteed Income For The 21st Century." The New School, Institute on Race and Political Economy, 2021, https://racepowerpolicy.org/wp-content/uploads/2023/05/Guaranteed-Income-for-the-21st-Century.pdf. Accessed 14 Dec. 2023.

[cclx] My admiration and respect for the method of inquiry modeled by Robert Lawence Kuhn of the Closer To Truth interview series almost knows no bounds. While it seems that I could not possibly disagree with him more on so many specific topics, the mission described on his website ... "to discover state-of-the-art ideas about human sentience and raw existence. Discover fundamental issues of existence. Engage new and diverse ways of thinking. Appreciate intense debates. Seek your own answers." ... deeply aligns with my own, "To approach a scientifically objective understanding of subjective experience." Come back, but right now drop this book and go to https://CloserToTruth.com/. It'll be time much better spent and make time when you return more fruitful. I guarantee it (h/t George Zimmer).

[cclxi] Minimum Wage Would Be $26 an Hour If It Had Grown in Line with Productivity - CBS News. 7 Sept. 2021, https://www.cbsnews.com/news/minimum-wage-26-dollars-economy-productivity/.

[cclxii] Delouya, Samantha. "The US Minimum Wage Has Been $7.25 since 2009. What That Means for the Economy | CNN Business." CNN, 11 Nov. 2023, https://www.cnn.com/2023/11/11/business/federal-minimum-wage-us-impact/index.html.

[cclxiii] Scheid, Brian. "Just 7 Companies Are Carrying the S&P 500 in 2023." https://www.spglobal.com/marketintelligence/en/news-insights/latest-news-headlines/just-7-companies-are-carrying-the-s-p-500-in-2023-75823741. Accessed 6 Dec. 2023.

[cclxiv] "World Economic Forum on LinkedIn: 69% of Workers between Ages 18 and 24 Leave Their Employer within One Year." LinkedIn, June 2018, www.linkedin.com/feed/update/urn:li:activity:6410051969309904896.

[cclxv] Aerts, Elise, Ive Marx, and Gerlinde Verbist. "Not That Basic: How Level, Design, and Context Matter for the Redistributive Outcomes of Universal Basic Income." Journal of Social Policy (2023): 1-23. Print. Cambridge University Press, https://doi.org/10.1017/S0047279423000582.

[cclxvi] Cherry, Kendra. Maslow's Needs Hierarchy, 12 Aug. 2014, psychology.about.com/od/theoriesofpersonality/ss/maslows-needs-hierarchy_3.htm.

[cclxvii] "Meat Loaf - Two Out of Three Ain't Bad Lyrics." musiXmatch, https://www.musixmatch.com/lyrics/Meat-Loaf/Two-Out-of-Three-Ain-t-Bad. Accessed 12 Jan. 2024.

[cclxviii] "Human Rights Day 2023." OHCHR, https://www.ohchr.org/en/get-involved/campaign/udhr-75. Accessed 6 Dec. 2023.

[cclxix] Harris, Tristan, et al. Joe Rogan Experience #2076 - Aza Raskin & Tristan Harris. 19 Dec. 2023. https://open.spotify.com/episode/4ZcBHvjhGMTTdGF3fIdvg9?si=ef631a03dd08425c.

[cclxx] Quadagno, Jill. "9. Race, Class, and Gender in the U.S. Welfare State: Nixon's Failed Family Assistance Plan". Power Resource Theory and the Welfare State: A Critical Approach, edited by O'Connor, Julia S. and Olsen, Gregg M., Toronto: University of Toronto Press, 1998, pp. 250-282. https://doi.org/10.3138/9781442678675-013

[cclxxi] Gravity Probe B: Testing Einstein's Universe. https://einstein.stanford.edu/. Accessed 20 Dec. 2023. P.S. I'm no Lawrence Krauss, or Brian Greene, or Brian Keating, but I was physically present at the public presentation of the Gravity Probe B final findings.

[cclxxii] "On 4 July 2012, the ATLAS and CMS experiments at CERN's Large Hadron Collider announced they had each observed a new particle in the mass region around 126 GeV. This particle is consistent with the Higgs boson, but it will take further work to determine whether or not it is the Higgs boson predicted by the Standard Model. The Higgs boson, as proposed within the Standard Model, is the simplest manifestation of the Brout-Englert-Higgs mechanism. Other types of Higgs bosons are predicted by other theories that go beyond the Standard Model" (CERN). With the completion of the Standard Model of physics in 2012, we achieved a 100% coherent and mathematically consistent understanding of about 4% to 5% of what's loosely referred to as the fullness of reality. In a scientific adaptation of the "God of the gaps" escape, we scientists scrambled to invent some kind of new elusive class of particles beyond particles, and energy beyond energy, because, when all you have is a high-energy collider, everything looks like a particles and energy. "Standard Model." Wikipedia, 22 Jan. 2024. Wikipedia, https://en.wikipedia.org/w/index.php?title=Standard_Model&oldid=1197832274.

[cclxxiii] Ball, Robert M. Social Security Amendments of 1972: Summary and Legislative History, 13 Aug. 2014, www.socialsecurity.gov/history/1972amend.html.

[cclxxiv] King, Martin Luther Jr., in Orfalea, Matt.

[cclxxv] It doesn't matter that we only have 24-hour days, 7-day weeks, and 365-day years. Social media platforms intentionally and algorithmically encourage us to filter, fake, embellish, and squeeze just a little bit more reality out of reality, as if our direct experience can never be enough. Yet, there is simply no "tiny bit more" that can ever make our lives better, if we can't find meaning in our lives, right here, right now.

[cclxxvi] "Dewitt, Larry W." Social Welfare History Project, 9 Feb. 2011, https://socialwelfare.library.vcu.edu/biography/dewitt-larry-w/.

[cclxxvii] Ross, Mary. Social Security History. https://www.ssa.gov/history/orals/maryross.html. Accessed 6 Dec. 2023.

[cclxxviii] Haarmann, Dirk.

[cclxxix] It's Basic | 2023 Tribeca Festival | Tribeca. https://www.tribecafilm.com/films/it-s-basic-2023. Accessed 6 Dec. 2023.

[cclxxx] "Resources: Mayors for Guaranteed Income." Mayors for a Guaranteed Income, https://www.mayorsforagi.org/resources. Accessed 6 Dec. 2023.

[cclxxxi] Lab, The Stanford Basic Income. "Home | Stanford Basic Income Lab." The Stanford Basic Income Lab, https://basicincome.stanford.edu/. Accessed 6 Dec. 2023.

[cclxxxii] NYU Establishes Cash Transfer Lab to Study Impact of Universal Basic Income and Related Economic Policies. https://www.nyu.edu/about/news-publications/news/2021/march/nyu-establishes-cash-transfer-lab-to-study-impact-of-universal-b.html. Accessed 6 Dec. 2023.

[cclxxxiii] "Universal Basic Income." Center for Hunger Free Communities, 25 Feb. 2021, https://drexel.edu/hunger-free-center/research/briefs-and-reports/universal-basic-income/.

[cclxxxiv] Universal Basic Income Policies Don't Cause People to Leave Workforce, Study Finds | The University of Chicago Harris School of Public Policy. https://harris.uchicago.edu/news-events/news/universal-basic-income-policies-dont-cause-people-leave-workforce-study-finds. Accessed 6 Dec. 2023.

[cclxxxv] Smith-Carrier, Tracy, and The Conversation. Implementing a Basic Income Means Overcoming Myths about the "Undeserving Poor." https://phys.org/news/2023-12-basic-income-myths-undeserving-poor.html. Accessed 6 Dec. 2023. "With a global reach of over 10 million monthly readers and featuring dedicated websites for science (Phys.org), technology (Tech Xplore) and medical research (Medical Xpress), the Science X network is one of the largest online communities for science-minded people. Science X publishes over 200 quality articles every day, offering the most comprehensive coverage of sci-tech developments worldwide" (https://sciencex.com/help/about-us/).

[cclxxxvi] "Does 'universal Basic Income' Work? These Countries Are Putting It to the Test." World Economic Forum, 22 June 2023, https://www.weforum.org/agenda/2023/06/children-care-guaranteed-income/.

[cclxxxvii] "What Did We Learn from the World's Largest Basic Income Experiment?" GIGAZINE, 5 Dec. 2023, http://gigazine.net/gsc_news/en/20231205-worlds-biggest-basic-income-experiment/.

[cclxxxviii] Matthews, Dylan. "The First Results from the World's Biggest Basic Income Experiment." Vox, 1 Dec. 2023, https://www.vox.com/future-perfect/2023/12/1/23981194/givedirectly-basic-income-experiment-abhijit-banerjee-tavneet-suri.

[cclxxxix] "Papers - The 22nd BIEN Congress." 제22차 기본소득지구네트워크 대회, https://biencongress2023.org/papers/. Accessed 6 Dec. 2023.

[ccxc] Santens, Scott. "Sowing Seeds of Security: How Basic Income Is Taking Root in the U.S. through Local Pilots and Programs." 22nd BIEN Congress. Ewha Womans University, Seoul, South Korea2023. https://biencongress2023.org/wp-content/uploads/2023/08/PS3_Santens_Scott.pdf.

[ccxci] GiveDirectly. "Early Findings from the World's Largest UBI Study." GiveDirectly, 6 Dec. 2023, https://www.givedirectly.org/2023-ubi-results/.

[ccxcii] How Much Longer Will Social Security Last? https://www.aarp.org/retirement/social-security/questions-answers/how-much-longer-will-social-security-be-around.html. Accessed 7 Dec. 2023.

[ccxciii] Theodore Parker, Legacy and Honors, en.wikipedia.org/wiki/Theodore_Parker#Legacy_and_honors.

[ccxciv] Indexed to 50% per capita GDP.

[ccxcv] We, of course, strongly propose indexing the amount of basic income to a dividend derived from the real economy. Namely, 50% per capita GDP, while Santens uses the pop-cultural ballpark round number of $1,000 per month. Apart from that, we are generally in broad agreement with Santens's entire body of

work and believe that your market-indexed figure strengthens all of his arguments. While virtually all the evidence proves that basic income works at many scales and in many contexts, like QE, it must be sufficient, or it risks making matters much worse, for reasons explained elsewhere in the text.

[ccxcvi] Santens, Scott. "Unconditional Basic Income Would Fix a Major Flaw in Markets." *Scott Santens*, 13 July 2018, www.scottsantens.com/unconditional-basic-income-would-fix-a-major-flaw-in-markets.

[ccxcvii] Your Brain on Poverty: Why Poor People Seem to Make Bad Decisions (The Atlantic) | Mechanisms of Disinhibition (MoD) Laboratory. https://modlab.yale.edu/news/your-brain-poverty-why-poor-people-seem-make-bad-decisions-atlantic. Accessed 7 Dec. 2023.

[ccxcviii] Pimpare, Stephen. The Three False Premises of the Ryan Poverty Plan, talkpoverty.org/2014/07/30/three-false-premises-ryan-poverty-plan/.

[ccxcix] Silverton, Michael. LLM research prompt, "Largest Insurance Companies' Balance Sheet Size and Asset Allocation." https://g.co/bard/share/5d2d044896d1. Accessed 8 Jan. 2024.
[ccc] Silverton, Michael. LLM research prompt, "What is the size of the largest insurance company's balance sheet and what is their asset allocation?" ChatGPT, https://chat.openai.com/share/f3b88b8c-bc3d-4715-80e8-c4ef4d8f7416. Accessed 8 Jan. 2024.
[ccci] Silverton, Michael. LLM research prompt, "What is the size of the largest insurance company's balance sheet and what is their asset allocation?" Bing, https://sl.bing.net/hlWUme3EJZA. Accessed 8 Jan. 2024.
[cccii] R E T R O V A L E N T: All Value Is Ascribed. https://meta-valent.blogspot.com/2006/08/all-value-is-ascribed.html. Accessed 8 Jan. 2024.
[ccciii] Dahlman, Carl J.

[ccciv] VA Web Solutions Office, iris.custhelp.va.gov/app/answers/detail/a_id/2674.

[cccv] Stiglitz, Joseph E., and Linda J. Bilmes.

[cccvi] Current Value of $129,000 2008 Dollars - Wolfram|Alpha. https://www.wolframalpha.com/input?i=current+value+of+%24129%2C000+2008+dollars. Accessed 9 Jan. 2024.
[cccvii] About – Davidow. https://www.davidow.com/about/. Accessed 12 Dec. 2023.

[cccviii] Simultaneous Inflation and Deflation—An Impossible Economic Dystopia | LinkedIn. https://www.linkedin.com/pulse/simultaneous-inflation-deflationan-impossible-economic-davidow/. 1 Jun. 2020. Accessed 12 Dec. 2023.

[cccix] Data from Data.Census.Gov. "DP1 – PROFILE OF GENERAL POPULATION AND HOUSING CHARACTERISTICS."

Qualified U.S. Citizens (26+): 222,628,267.20

50% per capita GDP: $41,148.00 (50% per capita U.S. GDP, 2023 – Wolfram|Alpha – wolframalpha.com)
Baseline USS Circulation: $9,160,707,938,745.60
Current U.S. Debt: $34,006,270,930,685.50 (Debt to the Penny | U.S. Treasury Fiscal Data)
Universal Social Security Budget as % of U.S. Debt: 26.94% (Understanding the National Debt | U.S. Treasury Fiscal Data)
[cccx] Data from Statista (statista.com). "Resident population of the United States by sex and age as of July 1, 2022(in millions)"

Qualified U.S. Citizens (26+): 225,162,000.00

50% per capita GDP: $41,148.00 (50% per capita U.S. GDP, 2023 – Wolfram|Alpha – wolframalpha.com)

Baseline USS Circulation: $9,264,965,976,000.00
Current U.S. Debt: $34,006,270,930,685.50 (Debt to the Penny | U.S. Treasury Fiscal Data)
Universal Social Security Budget as % of U.S. Debt: 27.24% (Understanding the National Debt | U.S. Treasury Fiscal Data) ”

cccxi U.S. Census Bureau. "Nativity and Citizenship Status in the United States." American Community Survey, ACS 1-Year Estimates Detailed Tables, Table B05001, 2022, https://data.census.gov/table/ACSDT1Y2022.B05001?q=citizenship. Accessed on January 9, 2024.
Natural Citizen Population 311,614,516.00
Underlying Asset Value $ 11,000,000.00
Starting SAFER Trust Act Balance Sheet $ 3,427,759,676,000,000.00

cccxii Data from Statista (statista.com), adjusted by Census.Gov non-citizen ratio.
Natural Citizen Population 314,956,744.20
Underlying Asset Value $ 11,000,000.00
Starting SAFER Trust Act Balance Sheet $ 3,464,524,186,200,000.00

cccxiii Harris, Tristan, Raskin, Aza, and Rogan, Joe. Joe Rogan Experience #2076 - Aza Raskin & Tristan Harris. 19 Dec. 2023. open.spotify.com, https://open.spotify.com/episode/4ZcBHvjhGMTTdGF3fIdvg9?si=adef27f50cf94fb5.

cccxiv Tubali, Shai. "'We Are Inquiring Together': The Dialogical Nature of Jiddu Krishnamurti's Work." The Transformative Philosophical Dialogue: From Classical Dialogues to Jiddu Krishnamurti's Method, edited by Shai Tubali, Springer Nature Switzerland, 2023, pp. 99–122. Springer Link, https://doi.org/10.1007/978-3-031-40074-2_6.

cccxv Many of these colloquialisms are still baked deeply into our culture this is another a task of Gen G to continue to detox. I've learned from Independent User Researcher + Anthropologist, Sekai Farai, that empathy is impossible and irrelevant, so I can't say that I empathize. However, I can notice and respond when writing prompts suggest a blind spot. If there is more that I can do than try to recognize glitches in my own conditioning and change them, please let me know. I learn best from other living the example.

cccxvi "Combating Human Trafficking: A Moral and Economic Imperative"/adc4731ea0a8. Accessed 14 Dec. 2023.

cccxvii Andolfatto, David. "MacroMania: Out of Thin Air?" MacroMania, 8 Mar. 2011, https://andolfatto.blogspot.com/2011/03/out-of-thin-air.html.

cccxviii Silverton, Michael. LLM research prompt, "Understanding Social Security Trust Fund" Dig deeper by using https://bard.google.com/share/6757ed962994 as a starting point, not an authoritative final source. This is an example of what differentiates AI-Assisted from AI-Generated content. Accessed 20 Dec. 2023.

cccxix Luther, William J. "How the Federal Reserve Literally Makes Money." The Conversation, 10 June 2020, http://theconversation.com/how-the-federal-reserve-literally-makes-money-140305.

cccxx Smil, Vaclav. How the World Really Works: The Science Behind How We Got Here and Where We're Going. Viking, 2022.

cccxxi "Dictionary.Com | Meanings & Definitions of English Words." Dictionary.Com, 20 Dec. 2023, https://www.dictionary.com/browse/afford.

cccxxii King, Martin Luther, and James Melvin Washington. A Testament of Hope: The Essential Writings and Speeches of Martin Luther King, Jr. 1st HarperCollins pbk. ed, HarperSanFrancisco, 1991. Via "A Testament of Hope: The Essential Writings and Speeches." https://www.goodreads.com/book/show/53360.A_Testament_of_Hope. Accessed 14 Dec. 2023.

[cccxxiii] Elon Musk: AI Will Remove Need for Jobs, Create 'Universal High Income' | Fortune. https://fortune.com/2023/11/06/elon-musk-ai-artificial-intelligence-universal-income-jobs/. Accessed 13 Jan. 2024.
[cccxxiv] Why Elon Musk Thinks Universal Basic Income Is Inevitable - Big Think. https://bigthink.com/the-present/why-elon-musk-thinks-well-have-universal-basic-income/. Accessed 13 Jan. 2024.
[cccxxv] Gibson, Marcia. "Basic Income Is a Popular Idea, but Small Pilots Cannot Produce Generalisable Evidence." BMJ, vol. 383, Oct. 2023, p. p2304. www.bmj.com, https://doi.org/10.1136/bmj.p2304.

[cccxxvi] Kahneman, Daniel, and Angus Deaton. "High Income Improves Evaluation of Life but Not Emotional Well-Being." Proceedings of the National Academy of Sciences, vol. 107, no. 38, Sept. 2010, pp. 16489–93. pnas.org (Atypon), https://doi.org/10.1073/pnas.1011492107.
[cccxxvii] Short, Kevin. Here Is The Income Level At Which Money Won't Make You Any Happier In Each State. The Huffington Post, www.huffingtonpost.com/2014/07/17/map-happiness-benchmark_n_5592194.html.

[cccxxviii] Short, Doug. "Happiness Revisited: A Household Income of $75K?" VettaFi Advisors, 21 Oct. 2016, https://www.advisorperspectives.com/dshort/commentaries/2016/10/21/happiness-revisited-a-household-income-of-75k. Accessed 26 Dec. 2023.
[cccxxix] Sheffey, Ayelet. "Millennials Say They Need $525,000 a Year to Be Happy. A Nobel Prize Winner's Research Shows They're Not Wrong." Business Insider, https://www.businessinsider.com/millennials-annual-income-price-of-happiness-wealth-retirement-generations-survey-2023-11. Accessed 5 Dec. 2023.

[cccxxx] "Declaration of Independence: A Transcription." National Archives, 1 Nov. 2015, https://www.archives.gov/founding-docs/declaration-transcript.
[cccxxxi] Liao, Nathan. "Universal Basic Income: 'Life, Liberty, and the Pursuit of Happiness.'" Medium, 23 Apr. 2020, https://nateliao.medium.com/universal-basic-income-life-liberty-and-the-pursuit-of-happiness-30c2b63e7788.
[cccxxxii] Please forgive me for failing to note the precise citation source, which is most likely an interview on YouTube that I either lost or failed to jot down in the moment. I can only offer Thurman's 2007 TED Talk as a consolation. Bob Thurman: "We Can Be Buddhas." Directed by TED, 2007. YouTube, https://www.youtube.com/watch?v=h5cZITQDTrE.
[cccxxxiii] In the early 2020s, we are witnessing a resurgence in interest in the principle of land value tax (LVT) as a way to reclaim some portion of that absconded value.
[cccxxxiv] We can't even complain that there are no flying cars in the Post-Automation Era. "Pivotal." Pivotal, https://pivotal.aero. Accessed 14 Jan. 2024.
[cccxxxv] Wikipedia contributors. "Higgs boson." Wikipedia, The Free Encyclopedia. Wikipedia, The Free Encyclopedia, 3 Aug. 2014. Web. 5 Aug. 2014

[cccxxxvi] Wikipedia contributors. "History of physics." Wikipedia, The Free Encyclopedia. Wikipedia, The Free Encyclopedia, 3 Aug. 2014. Web. 5 Aug. 2014.

[cccxxxvii] Santens, Scott. "Reddit, Robots, and Resources." UBI Guide, 6 Apr. 2015, https://www.scottsantens.com/reddit-robots-and-resources-why-i-got-into-the-idea-of-basic-income-and-how-we-can-go-about-implementing-it/.
[cccxxxviii] Oh, I gotta' credit myself with this one. I first drafted that sentence in 2018 and five years later we are talking about AI hallucinations. So put that in your forecasting pipe and take a big hit, "futurists." J/K. Kinda. LOL. See also "A Master in the Art of Living Makes Little Distinction Between His Work and His Play – Quote Investigator®." 27 Aug. 2010, https://quoteinvestigator.com/2010/08/27/master/.

[cccxxxix] Peterson, Jordan B. "Is Reality an Illusion? | Dr. Donald Hoffman | EP 387 - YouTube." https://www.youtube.com/watch?v=SPnyxnvU4ko&t=3500s. Accessed 14 Jan. 2024.
[cccxl] Professor Donald Hoffman — The Case Against Reality | The Tim Ferriss Show. Directed by Tim Ferriss, 2022. YouTube, https://www.youtube.com/watch?v=9qJJP6S15V0.

[cccxli] Donald D. Hoffman | University of California, Irvine. https://sites.socsci.uci.edu/~ddhoff/. Accessed 9 Dec. 2023.

[cccxlii] Sagan, Carl. Pale Blue Dot: A Vision of the Human Future in Space. New York: Random House, Inc., 1994.

[cccxliii] "Economics of the Stars: The Future of Asteroid Mining and the Global Economy." Harvard International Review, 8 Apr. 2022, https://hir.harvard.edu/economics-of-the-stars/.

[cccxliv] Williams, Matt, and Universe Today. What Would Asteroid Mining Do to the World's Economy? https://phys.org/news/2022-11-asteroid-world-economy.html. Accessed 9 Dec. 2023.

[cccxlv] Mannabase.com, mannabase.com/.

[cccxlvi] Mattereum.com, mattereum.com/.

[cccxlvii] Tanner, Michael. The American Welfare State: How We Spend Nearly $1 Trillion a Year Fighting Poverty—and Fail. CATO, www.cato.org/sites/cato.org/files/pubs/pdf/PA694.pdf.

[cccxlviii] 50% per Capita US GDP in the Year 2012 - Wolfram|Alpha. https://www.wolframalpha.com. Accessed 14 Jan. 2024.

[cccxlix] Computation by Bard. Data from the U.S. Census Bureau's Current Population Survey (CPS), Annual Social and Economic Supplement (ASEC). https://g.co/bard/share/f351f9f29d28

[cccl] Silverton, Michael. LLM research prompt, "Please Compute 50% per Capita U.S. GDP for Every Year since 2012 and Then Compute That Average. Thank You." https://bard.google.com/share/81eb00049173. Accessed 9 Dec. 2023.

[cccli] Tanner, Michael. The American Welfare State: How We Spend Nearly $1 Trillion a Year Fighting Poverty — and Fail. 2226525, 2012. Social Science Research Network, https://papers.ssrn.com/abstract=2226525.

[ccclii] Voss, Chris. Never Split the Difference: Negotiating as If Your Life Depended on It. First edition, HarperBusiness, an imprint of HarperCollins Publishers, 2016.

[cccliii] Mikkelson, David. "Dragnet: 'Just the Facts. Ma'am.'" Snopes, 29 Mar. 2002, https://www.snopes.com//fact-check/just-the-facts/.

[cccliv] Silverton, Michael. LLM research prompt, "I Greatly Appreciate Your Detailed Approach and Would like Both GDP and PPP Measures for 2023." https://bard.google.com/share/b00ed5961891. Accessed 6 Dec. 2023.

[ccclv] Meranto, Philip J. The Kerner report revisited; final report and background papers. Urbana: Institute of Government and Public Affairs, University of Illinois, 1970, archive.org/details/kernerreportrevi00asse.

[ccclvi] Bureau, US Census. "Income in the United States: 2022." Census.Gov, https://www.census.gov/library/publications/2023/demo/p60-279.html. Accessed 26 Dec. 2023.

[ccclvii] "Poverty Guidelines." ASPE, https://aspe.hhs.gov/topics/poverty-economic-mobility/poverty-guidelines. Accessed 8 Dec. 2023.

[ccclviii] Wikipedia contributors. "Job security." Wikipedia, The Free Encyclopedia, en.wikipedia.org/w/index.php?title=Job_security&oldid=614197308.

[ccclix] Dodd, Vikram. "Tackle Poverty and Inequality to Reduce Crime, Says Police Chief." The Guardian, 18 Apr. 2021. The Guardian, https://www.theguardian.com/uk-news/2021/apr/18/tackle-poverty-and-inequality-to-reduce-says-police-chief.
[ccclx] Spielman, Fran, and Tom Schuba. Brandon Johnson's Crime-Fighting Plan Zeroes in on Four Violent Neighborhoods in Chicago - Chicago Sun-Times. https://chicago.suntimes.com/city-hall/2023/12/19/24006764/analysis-brandon-johnson-crime-fighting-strategy-englewood-little-village-west-garfield-park-austin. Accessed 24 Dec. 2023.

[ccclxi] Schuba, Tom, and Andy Grimm. "In Chicago, a Year of Fewer Shootings and Murders but Little Sense of Being Safer." Chicago Sun-Times, 30 Dec. 2022, https://chicago.suntimes.com/2022/12/30/23529499/crime-murder-shootings-year-end-2022-lori-lightfoot-police-cpd-david-brown-carjackings-robbery.

[ccclxii] "President Obama's 2016 Budget Interactive." National Archives and Records Administration, National Archives and Records Administration, obamawhitehouse.archives.gov/interactive-budget.

[ccclxiii] Delaney, Kevin J. "The Robot That Takes Your Job Should Pay Taxes, Says Bill Gates." Quartz, 17 Feb. 2017, https://qz.com/911968/bill-gates-the-robot-that-takes-your-job-should-pay-taxes.
[ccclxiv] Buckminster Fuller Clip, 2006. https://www.youtube.com/watch?v=jgfrvZ-SxPQ.

[ccclxv] The Sun Magazine. "The Sun Magazine | Buckminster Fuller Talks Politics | By Lightning Allan Brown | Issue 85." Accessed December 19, 2023. https://www.thesunmagazine.org/issues/85/buckminster-fuller-talks-politics.

[ccclxvi] Please see an important last-minute addition to this book, *Building a UBI LLM*, in the Appendix.

[ccclxvii] Rojo, Javier. "Guaranteed Income: Increasing Employment and Helping Families Thrive." New Mexico Voices for Children, 12 Dec. 2023, https://www.nmvoices.org/archives/18507. As we've emphasized throughout, universal Social Security isn't a silver bullet for every aspect of poverty and disenfranchisement. Innovative, humane programs such as those modeled by New Mexico Voices for Children make perfect sense as complementary supplements to universal Social Security. The creator inherently endows every human life with equal worth and dignity. Programmatic distinctions are primarily accounting, which is vital in providing healthy institutional boundaries, in like manner to healthy psychological and physiological boundaries.

[ccclxviii] Quote Origin: Nothing Is More Powerful Than an Idea Whose Time Has Come – Quote Investigator®. 5 Nov. 2023, https://quoteinvestigator.com/2023/11/05/powerful-idea/.
[ccclxix] NASA Remembers Legendary Astronaut Thomas Stafford. Directed by NASA, 2024. YouTube, https://youtu.be/ESXuB-e2c_s?t=48s.
[ccclxx] "As for you, you meant evil against me, but God meant it for good in order to bring about this present outcome, that many people would be kept alive [as they are this day]." Bible Gateway Passage: Genesis 50:20 - Amplified Bible. https://www.biblegateway.com/passage/?search=Genesis%2050%3A20&version=AMP.
[ccclxxi] David A. Weaver, opinion contributor. "Social Security Has a Junk Data Problem — It Should Be the New Commissioner's First Priority." The Hill, 25 Dec. 2023, https://thehill.com/opinion/finance/4375180-social-security-has-junk-data-problem-it-should-be-the-new-commissioners-first-priority/.
[ccclxxii] Mindell, Amy and Arnold. "Consensus Reality, Dreamland, Essence." Amy and Arnold Mindell, http://www.aamindell.net/consensus-reality-dreamland-essence. Accessed 6 Mar. 2024.
[ccclxxiii] "Explaining DARVO: Deny, Attack, Reverse Victim & Offender." DomesticShelters.Org, https://www.domesticshelters.org/articles/identifying-abuse/explaining-darvo-deny-attack-reverse-victim-amp-offender. Accessed 5 Jan. 2024.

[ccclxxiv] Wolfram|Alpha. "$1600 USD in 1969 Was Worth How Much in 2018?" Source: Consumer Price Index. https://www.wolframalpha.com. Accessed 6 Dec. 2023.
[ccclxxv] Wolfram|Alpha. "$1600 USD in 1969 Is Worth How Much in 2023?" Source: Consumer Price Index. https://www.wolframalpha.com. Accessed 6 Dec. 2023.

ccclxxvi US Census Bureau. “Gini Index.” Census.Gov, https://www.census.gov/topics/income-poverty/income-inequality/about/metrics/gini-index.html. Accessed 26 Dec. 2023

ccclxxvii McCambridge, Jim, et al. “Systematic Review of the Hawthorne Effect: New Concepts Are Needed to Study Research Participation Effects.” Journal of Clinical Epidemiology, vol. 67, no. 3, Mar. 2014, pp. 267–77. PubMed Central, https://doi.org/10.1016/j.jclinepi.2013.08.015.

ccclxxviii “There is an agreed upon, consensus reality which almost the entire human race shares. The world has been around a long time; it is ancient. Into this world, you are born as an individual; you grow, learn, experience life, and die. There is some disagreement concerning what happens after that, except that for everyone else, life will go on – until they also die. Everybody thinks they know this – or some local variation of this. But in fact when you were ‘born’ you did not know this. You learned this. Everyone else learned it too and so it is an almost universally shared idea. But everybody believing something doesn’t make it true.” – David Carse, Perfect Brilliant Stillness

ccclxxix Description of mixed economy synthesized from multiple sources, including but not limited to: Corporate Finance Institute. “Mixed Economic System.” https://corporatefinanceinstitute.com/resources/economics/mixed-economic-system/. Investopedia. “Mixed Economic System: Characteristics, Examples, Pros & Cons.” Investopedia, https://www.investopedia.com/terms/m/mixed-economic-system.asp. Encyclopedia Britannica. “Britannica Money.” 18 Jan. 2024, https://www.britannica.com/money/mixed-economy. Wikipedia contributors. "Mixed economy." Wikipedia, The Free Encyclopedia. Wikipedia, The Free Encyclopedia, 12 Feb. 2024.

ccclxxx Baclawski, K. “The Observer Effect.” 2018 IEEE Conference on Cognitive and Computational Aspects of Situation Management (CogSIMA), 2018, pp. 83–89. IEEE Xplore, https://doi.org/10.1109/COGSIMA.2018.8423983.

ccclxxxi White, Frank. The Overview Effect - NASA. Interview by Gary Jordan, https://www.nasa.gov/podcasts/houston-we-have-a-podcast/the-overview-effect/. Accessed 17 Mar. 2024.

ccclxxxii Martin, Jeffery A. Nonsymbolic – Center for the Study of Non-Symbolic Consciousness. https://www.nonsymbolic.org/. See also Dr. Jeffery A. Martin. https://drjefferymartin.com/.

ccclxxxiii “What Is Productive Leisure?” Directed by What People Also Ask, 2023. YouTube, https://www.youtube.com/watch?v=t81smIrYK0k.

* * *

Made in the USA
Monee, IL
04 November 2026

67384622R00233